ASOKA AND HIS INSCRIPTIONS

ASOKA AND HIS INSCRIPTIONS

PARTS I & II

BY

BENI MADHAB BARUA

GYAN

Published by

Gyan Publishing House
5, Ansari Road
Daryaganj, New Delhi-110002
Phone: 011-47034999, 9811692060
E-mail: books@gyanbooks.com

Distribution Network
gyanbooks.com
India, USA, Canada, UK, Australia

ISBN: 978-93-6280-025-1 (PB)
First Published, 1946

2nd Impression 2024

Printed at: Gyan Press, Delhi.

ASOKA AND HIS INSCRIPTIONS
Author: BENI MADHAB BARUA

ASOKA AND HIS INSCRIPTIONS

PARTS I & II

BARUA

ASOKA AND HIS INSCRIPTIONS

[Written in Commemoration of the Fifty-fifth birth-day of

DR. B. C. LAW, M.A., Ph.D., D.Litt., F.R.A.S.B.,

Buddhagama-Siromani]

BY

BENI MADHAB BARUA, M.A., D.Lit. (Lond)

Professor of Pali and Lecturer in Sanskrit and
Ancient Indian History and Culture,
Calçutta University.

LAURIYA-NANDANGARH
COLUMN

PREFACE

The present work on Aśoka and his Inscriptions is the outcome of a prolonged study of the inscriptions and legends of the great Maurya emperor in their manifold historical bearings. Since I was initiated into the study of Indian inscriptions at first-hand in 1912 by the late Professor R. D. Banerji, then a Superintendent of the Archæological Section of the Indian Museum, Calcutta, my strong conviction was that with a mere knowledge of the palæography indispensable to decipherment and of the dictionary meaning of the words employed was not in itself sufficient for either a correct interpretation of the epigraphs or a thorough grasp of their importance as historical documents. A first-hand knowledge of contemporary literature and its language was as much a *desideratum* as the historical training and intellectual equipment for a proper assessment of their evidentiary values. In other words, the mere epigraphist or the mere linguist was incompetent to fulfil this task. And since I became associated with the Post-Graduate teaching in Arts inaugurated by Sir Asutosh Mookerjee in the premier Indian University of Calcutta I began to press the need of supplementing the teaching of the inscriptians by trained epigraphists with that imparted by capable teachers in the language and literature departments, the epigraphic evidence being inseparable from the collective literary evidence.

The original plan was just to edit the inscriptions including also those subsequently discovered or deciphered since the publication of Hultzsch's work. Failing to publish the edition thus prepared for some reason or other, I had to remain content with the publication of Part II of my first work containing translations and notes. Encouraged by the reception accorded to this publication, I set my heart upon the present work intending it at first to serve as a short historical introduction to the first work. The present extension of its scope was far beyond my original contemplation.

The widening of the historical vision has been partly due to a desire to justify the digression made from the path of the history of Indian Philosophy often regretted by Professor Sir Sarvapalli Radhakrishnan and other sincere friends and well-wishers. and partly due to a desire to vindicate, however imperfectly, the way of studying history from a philosophical and scientific point of view, treating the history of a country primarily as a comprehensive view of its collective life-movement. Here the reader may find the results of an honest endeavour for the realisation of some of the ideas formulated by me in the Presidential Address delivered in the Ancient Indian Section of the Indian History Congress held at Annamalainagar, South India, in December, 1945.

Thus it will be seen that my work on Aśoka and his records has grown up by at least three stages with the result that some of the earlier interpretations have been either completely abandoned or appreciably amended at a later stage ; some of the questions which were left open in the previous publication have been finally decided in the present work. The reader's attention may particularly be drawn to the discussion of the significance of Aśoka's epithets Devānaṃpriya and Priyadasi lājā Māgadhe, the place of Piṭinikas in relation to the Risṭikas and Bhojas, and the precise import of Aśoka's statement silā vigaḍabhī chā kālāpita. The relative values of the Aśokan inscriptions and legends as materials for an authentic history have been carefully discussed. Nothing has been taken for granted. There is no foregone conclusion. The entire position of the history of Aśoka has been critically reviewed in the light of the data derived mainly from a first-hand study of the inscriptions. The official functions of the Aṃta-mahāmātas have been placed on a sure footing. Part I has been devoted to such relevant themes as Aśoka's personal history, empire, state, administration, personal and public life, dharma, dharmavijaya and place in history, while Part II, which is rather of a technical nature and, therefore, of little or no interest to general readers, has been devoted to the important problems that are apt to arise in connection with the study of the inscriptions from a purely linguistic and literary point of view. The appendix to Part I contains an instructive paper written by Dr. Iswarlal Topa of the Osmania University on Aśoka's dhamma-culture.

It will be seen that the legends of Aśoka have been discredited wherever they have been found lacking in corroboration from the inscriptions. I hope, I have not failed to appraise them properly. The historical vision is not confined to India. In dealing with Aśoka, the historian is required to review the whole of the past, contemporary and subsequent history of mankind,— of sava munisā, all men. Accordingly Aśoka's Jambudvīpa in which he sought to commingle gods and men or men and gods, to make, in other words a heaven of earth and an earth of heaven was, in one sense, the sub-continent of India, and, in another, the whole world of men. Concerning Aśoka's own records, that which disappoints us is their incompleteness and the cause of regret is that he had not caused all his dhamma-niyamas to be recorded. This deficiency of his records has been made up with side-lights from as many sources as possible, including the Classical writings.

I am one of those with whom the Arthaśāstra upholding the advanced political views ascribed to one Kauṭilya *i.e.*, the treatise, as we now have it in prose, is the handiwork of a later exponent. There were, nevertheless, an earlier work, probably in verse—a Daṇḍanīti with its prototypes in the pre-Aśokan Mahabhārata and Jātakas. It will be in vain, I think, to father the work in its present form on the political adviser of Chandragupta Maurya. Tables of parallels given in Part II may enable the reader to distinguish, partly at least, between what is pre-Aśokan and what is post-Aśokan in this important treatise on royal polity. I have been concerned to point out the difference and distinction even where at the first sight a verbal resemblance exists between one dictum and another. And I strongly feel that it is as much important to note the points of agreement as to note the points of difference. It is not for me to say how far I have succeeded in returning a correct verdict on the set of facts hitherto known to me. Certain it is that the pronouncement of a verdict on what might have been is not the business of the historian; he is primarily concerned with what it was. The judgements on 'might-have-beens' have gravely prejudiced the part played by Aśoka in the history of India as well as of mankind. I am sorry that I could not help joining an issue with three of the great Indian scholars for whose writings I have otherwise nothing but admiration.

I am painfully aware of the fact that human mind is not free from bias or prejudice either within the four walls of a university or within the bounds of the four oceans. Aśoka who by his Dharmavijaya policy raised India in the estimation of the civilized world for all times to come is held responsible for the political or national decline of the Hindus, forgetting the fact that there was no idea of 'nation' or 'nationality' in India before Aśoka. If Aśoka's grandfather Chandragupta was great, he was great not for being a tool at the hands of an Indian Machiavelli but for his success, as observed by Justin, in making India free, "shaking off from its neck the yoke of slavery." If the Arthaśāstra embodies the political maxims of a

Kauṭilya, this is worked with all its shrewdness and sagacity to strengthen the position of an ambitious monarch aspiring only to be a mighty despot. If Kauṭilya's king believed that he was by his nationality just as much an Indian as his ministers and officers, viceroys and commissioners, there is no reason why he should have been advised not to trust any of them. The Magadhan method of administration, as noticed by Megasthenes, was a method, which evolved through a long line of rulers from the Bṛihadrathas down to the Nandas, and the much idolised Kauṭilya is nothing but a lineal descendant of Varshakāra, the Brāhman minister of Ajātaśatru who proved to be a veteran in the nefarious art of sowing the seeds of dissension in the neighbouring Vrijian confederacy.

It is still uncertain whether Aśoka's Pārindas were the Pulindas of the Purāṇas. The name Pārinda occurs in the Pali Chūlavaṃsa (XXXVIII. 29-30) in which Pārinda and Khuddapārinda are mentioned as two sons of a Pāṇdya King. If is possible, therefore, that the Pārindas were racially connected with the Pāṇḍyas.

The facts are presented as far as these could be gathered from all available sources and ascertained, the findings are given for what they are worth, and the labours of previous scholars are fully utilised. Whether the views and interpretations offered by previous scholars are accepted or rejected, reasons have been given for that. Even if the findings be found untenable, the facts stand as they are, and this alone is my satisfaction that I have honestly tried to facilitate a rational understanding of what is what.

My indebtedness to the whole body of Aśokan scholars headed by Prinsep and Cunningham and led further afield by Buhler and Senart is very great indeed. This does not mean, however, that the data of history should not be re-examined and revalued. If anyone has read or can interpret the Aśokan records and legends better, his or her suggestions and criticisms are always welcome, but mere disparagement is certainly not the better part of valour. Fortunately, I am not altogether alone to take a different view of the history of Aśoka.

When my right to deal with the ancient Indian inscriptions, particularly Aśokan, was challenged by some of the epigraphist colleagues in the University, Mr. P. N. Banerjee, M.A., Barrister-at-Law, then a Fellow and Syndic of the Calcutta University, rendered a most friendly service by asking me to vindicate my position, which in his opinion was unquestionable in this respect. I took up the challenge forthwith and published the paper entitled "Inscriptional

Excursions" in the Indian Historical Quarterly, Vol. II, No. I, 1926, with the kind assitance of its editor, Dr. N. N. Law. I sincerely regret the polemical'rune of my writing, although its worth was openly recognized by Professor D. R. Bhandakar in the revised edition of his Carmichæl Lectures on Aśoka. But the compliment which I then paid to Mr. Banerjee stating that he was "a friend of all earnest scholars" stands justified all the more now when he has assumed his new responsible office of the Vice Chancellor.

Bhandarkar's original lectures on the subject were followed by Hultzsch's masterly edition and translation of the Inscriptions of Aśoka and Professor Radhakumud Mookerji's monograph and Professor Raychaudhuri's Political History of Ancient India. Among the *bonafide* Pali scholars, Mr. Charan Das Chatterji, M.A., now Reader of Indian History at the University of Lucknow, and among my colleagues, Mr. Sailendra Nath Mitra, M A., now Secretary to the Councils of Post-Graduate Teaching in Arts and Science, evinced a keen interest in the study of the Aśokan inscriptions from the Buddhist literary point of view. I particularly wanted Mr. Mitra to prepare a critical edition of these inscriptions with as many close literary parallels as possible. He took up the work in right earnest only to give it up when he was about to reap a good harvest of his arduous labour. Thus I was compelled at last to do the work, with the assurance from Mr. Mitra that he would place at my disposal the new materials he was able to collect from various sources. These have been duly acknowledged wherever I have used them.

I am grateful to Dr. Syamaprasad Mookerjee, President of the Council of Post-graduate Teaching in Arts, Calcutta University, for his genuine interest in the progress of this work and no less to Dr. B. C. Law for his generosity. Among the senior and junior colleagues, I must gratefully mention the name of Professors S. K. Chatterji and Stella Kramerisch, Dr. N. R. Roy, the Bagiswari Professor of Fine Arts, and Messrs D. L Barua, N. N. Dasgupta and Sultan Alam Chowdhury for their helpful suggestions.

Mr. S. N. Mitra, Mr. Amitesh Banerjee, Professor of History, Daulatpur Hindu Academy, and my eldest son Mr. Basubandhu Barua, M.A. have helped me in deciding some of the disputed points. Mr. Anantalal Thakur, M.A., a University Research Scholar attached to me, has kindly prepared the indices, and my sixth daughter, Snehakana, has prepared the maps of Jambudvīpa, Aśoka's empire and five Greek territories.

A critical edition of the Pali counterparts of Buddha's Discourses recommended by Aśoka in his Bhabru Edict, which is prepared by Mm. Professor Vidhusekhara Bhattacharyya' and which is being seen through the press, may be regarded as a useful supplement to this work.

The word tushṭadānam, which is employed in the Arthaśāstra obviously as an equivalent of Aśoka's tuṭhāyatana, does not support Dr. Hetti Arachi's equation of tuṭhāyatana with Pali titthāyatana.

I need not be unduly apologetic as to the quality of printing and paper, there having been little or no choice in the matter under the war conditions. The misprints, however slight, are bound to be when the printing is done in Calcutta where normally the overworked authors are deprived of the service of expert proof-readers.

Dated, Calcutta,
The 20th May, 1946. }

B. M. Barua

Dr. B. C. Law—A Memoir

As one advances in years and begins to feel that the journey of life is nearing its end, nothing is sweeter and more vivid than the reminiscences of early life. It will not, therefore, be out of place to record some of the happy memories of my close scholarly association and comradeship with Dr. B. C. Law, an interesting and instructive account of whose life and career appears in the introduction to Dr. B. C. Law Volume, Part I, written by Professor Radha Kumud Mookerji. It will be seen that in presenting this account Professor Mookerji has mostly depended on the recorded facts of Dr. B. C. Law's life, high academic distinctions, scholarly contributions, and many and various acts of charity and generosity, which eloquently speak of his talents, persevering habits, magnanimity and lasting services to the cause of humanity and of culture. But there is the other side of the picture where we have had chances to watch the man in his day-to day life taking him unawares, so to speak. This is the purely human aspect of his life in which he appears in his daily avocations and manifold relations. Here he appears in his true collours, and what he really is or is not depends on the angle of vision from which his words and actions, gestures and postures, transactions of life and dealings with men and things are viewed and judged. One may say with Shakespeare that unknowingly each man is an actor on the stage. However best the part he plays in his own opinion about himself, both the serious and the humourous elements may be shown to have characterised all the interludes in the drama of life enacted by him through the successive Acts and Scenes. There is, perhaps, no greater truth than this, that every man's life is a novel untold or only partially told. How little we know of another person on whom we pass a peremptory judgment, mistaking him for what he truly is or is not forming our opinion on his dealings or actions in a single meeting or transaction; here we go by our likes and dislikes and the success or failure of our particular mission, personal or public.

It is, therefore, impossible to expect that all will speak in praise of a person and none in dispraise. If we go on collecting information about any person of importance, there is no reason for astonishment that there exists a wide divergence of opinion about him. One of the traditional Buddhavachanas in the Dhammapada warns us, saying :

> Porāṇam etaṃ, Atula ! n'etaṃ ajjatanām iva :
> nindanti tuṇhim āsīnaṃ, nindanti bahubhāṇinaṃ,
> mitabhāṇinam pi nindanti,—n'atthi loke anindito.

"This is an old truth, Atula ! This is not a thing of to-day : They find fault if one sits quiet, they find fault if one talks much, they find fault (even) if one talks moderately,—there is none in the world who is not subject to criticism."

Such is bound to be the lot of all when they are seen with the eye of others who often go by hearsay or, at the most, by momentary impressions.

To judge a man truly is to follow Bergson's way of placing oneself at his point of view and to look at things as he would see them. In other words, the biographer has got to watch how the life-history of a person starts at a certain point and proceeds in a certain direction forming a continuous narrative with its various junctures, how, in other words, a trend of the life-movement emerges out of a biological background and a distinct career of personality is shaped in a domestic, social, political, moral, religious, and cultural environment and it reacts on his own life and the surrounding world. All the noble instincts and impulses, thoughts and aspirations, ideas and imaginations go together to constitute the spiritual life of a human being with its benevolent and effective responses to the stimuli, whether coming from one's study and meditation or arising from contacts and suggestions of others. Without these, a man is spiritually dead, and the task of religion and philosophy and of all true friends and well-wishers is to see that a man does not die spiritually before his physical death which is inevitable.

The Law family of Calcutta, of which Dr. B. C. Law is one of the most notable representatives, stands next to none in respect of its prestige and position, riches and charities. The Bengali surname Lāhā was anglicised as Law when *aw* was pronounced as ā. The Laws belong to the Rārhī section of a mercantile community as distinguished from the Saptagrāmīs. Their original home, as far as it can be traced, was in the district of Burdwan wherefrom they shifted to Chinsurah, the present official headquarters of the district of Hughli, when the Vargis from Mahārāshṭradeśa appeared in the plains of Bengal for the forcible collection of *chauth*. It was at last for the sake of business that they removed their residence to the metropolis of Calcutta where they settled down permanently.

The builder of the fortune of the Law family was Pran Kissen Law. He was formerly an employee of the firm of Motilal Seal, a very distinguished business man of his time, whose bounties are proverbial and whose memory is perpetuated by a free school and a bathing ghat. Thereafter he independently took up the piecegoods business. The first rise of the family to prominence was due partly to the income from this business and partly to a large sum earned from a Port Trust contract. Pran Kissen Law, once an employee of Motilal Seal, proved himself to be the inheritor of all the good qualities of the employer. He has so far been extraordinarily fortunate in having four generations of descendants to maintain his tradition in full vigour and to glorify his line. He left behind him three worthy sons, Maharaja Durga Charan, Syama Charan and Joy Govinda, all of whom figured as noble men with tall stature, manliness with decent mustache, clean shaven chin, full-grown size without bulkiness, fair complexion and a sound mind in a sound body. Among them, Syama Charan is the first in the Law family to gc to England in connection with their common business and Joy Govinda could be easily mistaken in his dress, bodily form and facial expression for Bankim Chandra Chattopadhyay, father of Bengali novels.

The eldest brother was succeeded by his two sons, Raja Kristo Das and Raja Reshee Case, while the second and third brothers were succeeded each by one son, Chandi Charan and Ambika Charan respectively. All of them were gifted with noble personality, fair complexion, amiable disposition, unruffled nature, sound health and fair mind and inherited, more or less, other family characteristics, Chandi Charan and Ambika Charan tending to be comparatively short-statured. Among them, Raja Reshee Case, father of the late Kumar Surendra Nath and Dr. Narendra Nath Law, became most prominent in the public eye, while his two cousins, Chandi Charan, father of Mr. Bhabani Charan Law and his two brothers, and Ambika Charan, father of Dr. Satya Charan and Dr. Bimala Charan Law, were quietly adding to their riches and doing certain works of public utility. In this generation the Laws practically gave up their piecegoods business and were counting almost entirely on the income from their house properties in Calcutta, landed properties outside, bank balances, dividends on shares and interests on Government papers. The company in the name of Pran Kissen Law is being run in name only and rather as a common bond of their old family interests.

From them we pass on to the fourth generation of the Laws of Bengal in which we see them going up for higher education, winning the favour of the Goddess of Learning along with that of the Goddess of Luck, emulating the fame of scholars of international reputation, and being in the róle of the patrons of learning, and some playing the part of industrialists. Among the Laws of this generation, the far-famed are Dr. N. N. Law, Dr. S. C. Law, and Dr. B. C. Law, the third obtaining two Doctorates and being the winner of several prizes, medals and titles from different Universities and academic bodies. Whether all graduates or not, each has a special hobby of his own. If one of them, Kumar G. C. Law, is interested in Botany and producing botanical marvels, another is an artist with a noteworthy art-collection. If one excels others in his knowledge of Hindu polity and study of Mahāyāna Buddhism, another shines forth as an ornithologist and a builder of a big bird-house. They find their powerful rival in Dr. B. C. Law whose researches are mainly directed to Buddhism, Pali Literature, History of Ancient Kṣatriya Tribes, History of India in the 5th century B.C., Geography of Ancient India, Jainism, and the Vaṃsa literature of Ceylon. His publications in the shape of articles, monographs, dissertations, editions of texts and translations are too many to name here. If one has founded a well-equipped press to facilitate the printing of the books and journals on Indology, the other has liberally financed the costly publications of several authors, both in India and Europe.

Certain family traits and virtues are noticeable, more or less, in all the Laws. They are all truthful, honest, intelligent and upright. They do not tell lies, they abhor falsehood. If they give words to any person, they mean to keep them ; they do not make promises in vain. They are frank and outspoken. They do not delude any person with false hopes. If they are approached with any request or business proposal, they will say at once whether they will entertain it or not. If they once say No to anything, it is no use repeating the matter, for they are not men to change their mind under any further persuasion. They do not indulge in gossips and fiivolous talks. They are, as a rule, men of moderate speech.

They are of sober habits. The intoxicants they avoid like poison. Even if they smoke cigars or cigarettes, or chew betel and betel-leaf, they do so moderately and only in fixed hours.

They stand for moral continence. The sexual passions are kept well under control. They do not covet others' wives or riches. They are contented with one wife. Even with her they do not always come in contact. There are fixed hours for their meeting. The widower does not thrust a step-mother on his sons by his deceased wife. They usually marry a girl, handsome and accomplished, from a middle-class family of good moral tradition without the least expectation of dowry or wedding presents. They are mainly concerned with the girl they choose.

They usually keep to Bengal's upper middle-class diet. They are either poor or moderate eaters. But they are particular about the quality of foodstuffs and of cooking. They take their morning meal prepared in the kitchen under the control of the housewife by a Brāhman cook and his assistants attached to the female department. They have their separate cooking arrangements. They generally take their evening meal or dinner, prepared in Indian style by a Brāhman cook and his assistants attached to the male department. If they take fancy to, they may have their dinner prepared in right European style, for which there is altogether a different cooking staff and a different kitchen ; but this they do very seldom. They hate waste and the number of dishes, too, is limited to a few.

They are a very clean people, clean in mind and body, in thoughts, words and actions, in all their worldly transactions. Their residential and garden houses, courtyards and floors, walls and roofs, bed and drawing rooms, book-shelves and writing tables, kitchens, stables, garages and cowsheds are always kept clean and tidy. They are decent in their dress but not fashionable or luxurious.

They are all very particular about the portion of the patrimony which falls to the share of each. This they keep in tact by all means, and they are cautious about their investments. They are neither speculators nor spendthrifts. If they purchase shares or debentures, they do so to hold them. They are not greedy of gains or profiteering by any unfair means. When they enter into any agreement or contract, they mean to fulfil its terms to the very letter of them and insist on their fulfilment also by the other party. Here they spare nobody. So when they do business, they are strictly business-like. As regards their Zemindaries or landed estates, they entrust their management to capable agents who act as intermediaries between them and the tenants. They expect nothing beyond the legitimate dues in the shape of revenues and cesses. They do ungrudgingly what is reasonable and within their means for giving their tenants medical aids and educational and irrigational facilities, but the dues must be duly paid by them. They are good pay-masters. All the officers and employees including household servants and menials are entitled to pensions, annuities and occasional leaves. The hours of work and the nature of their respective duties are fixed beforehand. The dereliction of duty and irregularity in attendance are easily detected and appropriately dealt with. In the matter of accounts they are absolutely clear, and they are intolerant of dishonesty or duplicity of any kind. They scrupulously shun highhandedness and precipitate action.

Although they own house and landed properties all over Calcutta, they prefer to live in the same neighbourhood, and their residential houses are built and maintained on the same pattern. These with their compounds and courtyards, attached gardens and high compound-walls, inner apartments and outer halls and servants' quarters are spacious and commodious. These are typically the residential houses of the landed aristocrats of Bengal. The roof of the rectangular courtyard in the interior is netted to let in rain-water and sunlight and to keep off pigeons and other birds. It has its main entrance towards the gate and Thākur-dālān on the opposite side.

They are Vaishṇavas by their ancestral faith. It is the neo-Vaishṇavism of Bengal which they follow. But they are not bigots. They relegate religious matters to the housewife and female department. They themselves do not make fuss over religion. They stand pre-eminently for the advancement of learning and culture. They have a family idol, which goes round and round, from the custody of one house to that of another according to fixed turns. Just as to other Hindu aristocratic families of Bengal, so to them the Dūrgāpūjā serves as a bond of their unity, and this is performed ceremonially by them, each according to his turn. They scrupulously avoid animal sacrifice; in their case, cucumbers or similar vegetable fruits are sacrified as substitutes for goats.

They try by all means to prevent family hitches and misunderstandings. With this very end in view, the brothers, if they are major and married, usually separate after their father's death, in which case the elder or eldest brother remains in the paternal residence, while the younger brothers shift to the houses newly built by or for them. They do not meddle in each other's affairs: if one Law takes an active interest in any matter, others are generally reluctant to be associated with it. Each member of the family body-politic is aware of his or her limitations and freedom, while conforming to one and the same convention. If the right hand gives, the left hand is not to know or to question the right. When the question of partition of a joint property arises among them, they readily accept the awards made by the elders acting as arbitrators with a fair mind.

They perform funeral rites according to Hindu customs and usages. But they perform the S'rādh once for all and do not think it necessary to offer piṇḍa at Gayā.

They move in a world which is congenial to their nature and life's pursuits. They are interested listeners to all matters of human interest and importance, and they keep accurate information about men and things. They do not forget their friends ; the old register of invitees is maintained and consulted when a new occasion arises for issuing invitations. They gratefully remember the name of Motilal Seal. It is said of Joygovinda Law that if he happened to go past Motilal Seal's house, he used to walk on foot out of his reverence for the employer and helper of his father.

They are constitutionally minded and law abiding. It does not mean, however, that they approve of unfair actions on the part of any government or nation. They traditionally prefer constitutional changes by constitutional methods. They are patriotic in the sense that they do not decry the cultural traditions of their own country. They are capable of meeting good men from all countries on terms of equality and with due courtesy and fellow-feeling. Their conversations are responsive, animated and intelligent, and they do not need secretaries for the purpose. Their legal and business training, sound general education and wide knowledge of men and things enable them to understand who is who and what is what. They studiously shun all active politics.

Dr. B. C. Law is born and brought up in such a family tradition and domestic environment ; he is the inheritor of the riches as well as all the distinctive traits, virtues and limitations of his sires. He is, nevertheless, a distinct type by himself,—a strong personality. That which marks him out from other Law is his great dash within bounds of self-restraint. It seems that he has throughout his life been in the double role of two apparently incompatible characters. Inwardly a humble man and sincere soul, outwardly an aristocrat ; inwardly a willing servant of all, outwardly a strict task-master ; inwardly an ascetic, outwardly a plutocrat ; inwardly attaching no importance to anything worldly, outwardly setting high values on worldly prosperity ; inwardly thinking too little of him, outwardly thinking too much of him ; inwardly always in a resigning mood, outwardly passing with a rapid dash from one attainment to another. He is a healthy middle-sized man, a bit heavy-built and thick-lipped, with as fair and bright a complexion as that of his father. He possesses a strong physique and is capable of bearing the strain of hard work, physical or mental. He is hardly found out of sort, scarcely susceptible to cold ; but his liver is somewhat weak.

The history of our association goes back to the year 1912 when I was a Post-graduate student and he an Under-graduate student of Pali. His father granted his sons the full liberty of appointing their own tutors and of doing what they thought best as regards their education. He was then reading Pali Honours Course in the Presidency College with Professor Nilmani Chakrabarty and Mahāmahopādhyāy Dr. Satis Chandra Vidyabhusan, Principal, Sanskrit College. His principle was to appoint the best of persons to guide him in his studies, not minding the amount demanded as honorarium. His zeal for learning was extraordinary, and he appeared to have a very sharp memory. He would not let off his tutors until he prepared well his lessons or thoroughly understood the subject of study. Thus he combined diligence with intelligence. If he happened to keep any of his tutors beyond his time, he would offer him sweets and fruits. One Ātā was the Oriyā servant appointed to look to his personal comforts. Ātā lived to an old age. He was granted a suitable pension to enjoy his well-earned rest. He proved himself to be a typical old servant of Bengal, always proud of the rise of his young master in life and progress in education. Ātā is no longer in the world of the living, but his memory is evergreen in the mind of Dr. Law.

Nothing was happier to me than to meet again Dr. Law on my return to Calcutta in October, 1917, after an absence of three years, with a Doctorate from London. When we met each other, he was an M.A. Gold Medalist in Pali and a Law graduate. The first thing he expressed to me then was that he had made up his mind to carry on researches in Indology. This was welcome to me as I, too, was eager to continne my own researches in the same field. At this juncture Sir Asutosh Mookerjee's sincere affection and encouragement went a long way. The death of our revered teacher, Principal

Satis Chandra Vidyabhusan, shortly before the publication of his Short History of Indian Logic, snatched from our midst a sire who was then the centre of attraction to the whole Buddhist world.

It occurred to me that Dr. Law was better placed in life with his erudition, diligence and riches to step into Dr. Vidyabhusan's shoes, while, as regards myself, there was an inherent difficulty in aspiring for that place. As researchers, we followed two different paths. He preferred to follow the path of least resistance, while my way was to grope in the dark and to upset the prevalent ideas. He stood for extension, while I cared more for intension. His delight lay in ransacking the sources for data, while my main interest lay in the visualisation of the life-movement beneath the historical facts. Dr. Law went on like a machine. Once he set his heart on a particular work, he would see it finished as quickly as possible, being all the while in intense love with it. But as soon as it was finished and the book was published, he would think it was hopelessly inadequate. The letters of appreciation received from different scholars would keep him satisfied for a short while only, after which he would become restive again for a fresh literary venture. To go from more to more without a feeling of satiety is the trend of his life. This superabundant energy he has kept up till the present.

The life of Mrs. Rhys Davids, who passed as a 'wonderful woman', deeply impressed Dr. Law. She would do everything with her own hand and find time for all her daily duties. She wrote all her letters in her own hand-writing. Her correspondence with Dr. Law, which often found a prompt and warm response, was full of cheering words. I can say that Mrs. Rhys Davids has been worthily rivalled in India by Dr. Law.

He is a kind and watchful father to all in his household ; even if a servant gets sick, he himself would call the family physician over the phone and arrange for his medicine and diet. Whether Mrs. Law, or his son, or an officer, or even an ordinary servant is sent out of Calcutta, he will find that everything has been kept ready for him. If any of the bearers carries letters or papers, he would see that these are properly put on his table or handed to him, but if any of them falls perchance on the ground through his fault, he should himself pick it up. Thus he tries to be fair to himself as to others.

Though he is a good shot, he is not naturally fond of hunting as a diversion. He keeps in his service an expert music master who comes and goes, but he has not much fondness for music either.

There is even a physical instructor, but his body is sufficiently strong and does not need any further building-up. To the cinemas and theatres he is not easily persuaded to go unless the best of shows or plays is going on. All outdoor games and sports have no fascination for him. Among the indoor games, playing at cards he does not like ; he prefers one which is of a somewhat exciting nature and he generally plays to win. The radio set which he keeps is too talkative to interest him. But he would have a taste of everything, of giving a radio talk, of having a gramophone record of his speech, of playing a game at badminton ; all these are but of ephemeral interest. At midday he prefers to be alone musing or to be prattling with an intimate friend in a drawing room with all its doors and windows closed until 4 P. M. This is his *siesta,* the life of solitude and detachment.

Dr. Law is a man of limited commitments in money-matters. "Thus far and no farther" seems to be his motto. He is temperamentally incapable of large risks. A considerable portion of his yearly budget is set apart for various charities. Here he stands for an equitable distribution. If an author or writer, a society or institution approaches him with a request to finance a publication and he be convinced of its worth, he would press for having a complete manuscript and a total estimate of the cost of printing, binding and paper from the press. In the case of permanent endowments in the shape of free studentships or prizes, he would see that the amount is just sufficient for the purpose. He is keenly interested to watch what results his donations are producing year after year. He follows with interest the subsequent career of his free-students and prize-men.

He usually shuns appearance in public. If he agrees to preside over a meeting, his address is generally short, effective and to the point. If he is anywhere for a discussion, he is a hearty participator in it. He is a believer more in action than in words, more in literary productions than in empty talks about them.

Dr. Law has seen several places worth seeing in India in company with his father in his younger days and afterwards with Mrs. Law, children and friends. These are so far confined to Bengal, Behar, Orissa, U. P., C. P., Bombay, Madras, South India and Rājputānā. Although going out of Calcutta was primarily intended for a change of air and sight-seeing, each occasion was availed of for a first-hand knowledge of the places of historical, religious, industrial, commercial and cultural importance. He made it a point to publish accounts of his visits drawing attention to all things of interest and importance. Dr. Law has never dared to be out of touch with dry land; he has carefully avoided a trip covering a journey by steamer.

One may call him a 'lucky man' reminding us of the Thera Sivali of old. His books have a speedy sale. He has been lucky in his investments. He has won prizes on lottery tickets; once the first prize. He was exceptionally lucky in getting Miss Kamal Kumari Seal, the only sister of three elder brothers, to be his most devoted wife with her steady youth, charming personality, motherly heart, and moral virtue. He was lucky in having Gopal Chandra for his only son, bright, promising, social, polite, full of vigour and aspiring to emulate his father's name and fame. He was lucky in being constantly amused with the sweet prattle and sprite-like movement of his only daughter Radharani with her wistful looks, graceful nature, lovely appearance and innocent soul. He was lucky in finding in Aditya Nath Chakrabarty a bosom friend who was always prepared to lay down his life for him and his family and whose heart leapt with joy at all happy news concerning him.

Aditya Nath is no longer in his mortal frame to make his daily enquiries or to express his joyous feelings. Death entered the well-guarded mansion, disguised in typhoid, to snatch away Radharani. Gopal Chandra followed suit after a short period of nine years as a victim to the same fell disease, as if to reunite with his beloved sister and old playmate. The lawrels won, the books written and published, and the donations made are the many children to keep alive the name and memory of Dr. Law to posterity.

Since the death of his daughter he lost all faith in medicine and its prescribers. They sadly failed to bring back her consciousness, although she died after a struggle for fortyfour days. "Physicians who cannot save themselves pose as saviours of others!" is the remark often ironically made.

He found in me a person who is an interested listener to all that he cared to read out to me. I found in him a noble friend who could read my difficulties in the face and well studied my inner feelings. We have either agreed to differ or differed to agree.

It may be that the ascetic view of life is the internal characteristic of the Laws, but this appeares to be a dominant trait of Dr. Law's nature. When we in our early days read Pali together, he became so fond of the Dhammapada that he could recite all its verses The following stanzas were uppermost in his lips :

Ko nu hāso, kim ānando, nichchaṃ pajjalite sati,
andhakārena onaddhā padīpaṃ na gavesatha ?
Passa chittakataṃ bimbaṃ arukāyaṃ samussayaṃ
āturaṃ bahusaṅkappaṃ yassa n'atthi dhuvaṃ ṭhiti.
Parjiṇṇaṃ idaṃ rūpaṃ roganiḍḍaṃ pabhaṅguraṃ,
bhijjati pūtisandeho, māraṇantaṃ hi jīvitaṃ !
Yathā daṇḍena gopālo gāvo pācheti gocharaṃ
evaṃ jarā ca maccu cha āyūṃ pācenti pāṇinaṃ.

Aśvaghoṣa as a poet and exponent of Buddhism made a deep and lasting appeal to his heart. He has never been tired of reciting the following stanzas from the Saundarananda Kāvya since he translated the poem into Bengali :

bādhātmakaṃ duḥkham idaṃ prasaktaṃ
duḥkhasya hetuh prabhavātmako 'yaṃ
duhkhakshayo niḥsaraṇātmako 'yaṃ
trāṇātmako 'yaṃ praśamāya mārgah.
Dīpo yathā nirvṛitim abhyupeto
naivāvaniṃ gachchhati nāntarīkshaṃ
diśaṃ na kāñchit vidiśaṃ na kāñchit
snehakṣhayāt kevalam eti śāntim.

Since the death of his son he sought to find his consolation in the following stanza from the Garuḍa Purāṇa :

Sukhasya duḥkhasya na ko 'pi dātā,
paro dādtātīti kubuddhir eshā,
svayaṃkṛitaṃ svena phalena yujyate
śarīram me nistara yat tvayā kṛitam.

B. M. Barua

PART I

ASOKA

CONTENTS

CHAPTER I

Pages

INTRODUCTORY 1-4

1. Sources of information 1-2
2. Their relative values 2-4

CHAPTER II

PERSONAL HISTORY 5-62

1. Consecration 13-19
2. Conversion 19-32
3. Accession 32-34
4. Viceroyalty 34-35
5. Early life, parentage, brothers and sisters ... 35-38
6. Predecessors and pedigree 38-47
   (a) Social status 47-51
7. Wives and children 51-54
8. Successors 54-58
9. Length of reign and last days 58-62
10. Reign proper 62-62

CHAPTER III

EMPIRE 63-120

1. Extent of domain proper 64-69
2. Extent of empire 69-106
3. Sphere of influence 106-118
4. Pāṭaliputra, the capital 118-120

CHAPTER IV

STATE 121-165

1. Population 124-125
2. Territory 125-131
3. Sovereignty 131-145
4. Government 145-146
5. Constitution 146-154
6. Method and policy 154-162
7. Military strength and war policy ... 162-164
8. Sources of revenue 164-165

CHAPTER V

ADMINISTRATION 166-201

1. Imperial administration 166-188
2. Provincial administration 188-201

CHAPTER VI

PERSONAL AND PUBLIC LIFE 207-224

1. Asoka the man 207-217
2. Asoka the king 217-224

CHAPTER VII

DHARMA 225-282

1. As rājadharma 226-266
2. As upāsaka-dharma 266-270
3. As universal religion 271-282

CHAPTER VIII

DHARMA-VIJAYA 283-328

1. Definition of Dharma-vijaya 283-287
2. Dharma-vijaya of Great Epic 287-299
3. Trailokya-vijaya of the Kāraṇḍavyūha ... 299 302
4. Digvijaya of Agni 303-318
5. Dharma-vijaya of Aśoka 318-328

CHAPTER IX

PLACE IN HISTORY 329-355

1. Services to Buddhism 329-337
2. Role as nation-builder 337-347
3. Political reaction of Dharma-vijaya ... 347-355

APPENDIX

ASOKA AND HIS DHAMMA CULTURE 356-366
By Dr. Ishwarlal Topa

INDEX

SELECT BIBLIOGRAPHY

Aiyangar, Rangaswamy—Rājadharma (Dewan Bahadur K. Krishnaswami Row Lectures).
Aiyangar, S. K.—Beginnings of South Indian History.
Aung, Shwe Zan—Points of Controversy.
Banerjea, Gouranganath—Hellenism in Ancient India.
Banerjea, J. N.—Development of Hindu Iconography.
Barua, B. M.—Inscriptions of Asoka, Part II.
Ceylon Lectures.
The Ājīvikas.
Beal, Samuel—Buddhist Records of the Western World.
Bhandarkar, D. R.—Aśoka (Carmichæl Lectures).
Political History of Ancient India (Carmichæl Lectures).
Chatterji, S. K.—Origin and Development of the Bengali Language.
Chirnock.—Arrian.
Cunningham, General—Ancient Geography.
Dikshitar, Ramchandra—Mauryan Polity.
Dutt, N.—Early History of the Spread of Buddhism and the Buddhist Schools.
Fausboll—Jātaka Aṭṭhakathā.
Fleet, J. F.—Gupta Inscriptions.
Geigar, Wilhelm—Dīpavaṃsa and Mahāvaṃsa (English Translation).
Mahāvaṃsa, Text and Translation.
Griffith, C. L. T.—The Story of Letters and Numbers.
Herzfeld—Archælogical History of Iran.
Hultzsch—Inscriptions of Asoka, Texts & Translations.
South Indian Inscriptions.
Jayaswal, K. P.—An Imperial History of India.
Hindu Polity.
Law, B. C.—India as described in the Early Texts of Buddhism and Jainism.
Debates Commentary.
Tribes in Ancient India.
Law, N. N.—Ancient Indian Polity.
Inter-state relations in Ancient India.
Legge—Fa Hien.
Levi, Sylvain—Pre-Aryan et Pre-Dravidian dans l' Inde.
Majumdar, G. P.—Some Aspects of Indian Civilization.

Mahendae, M. A.—A Comparative Grammar of Asokan Inscriptions.
Malalasekera, G. P.—Dictionary of Pali Proper Names.
Marshall, Sir John—A Guide to Sānchī.
Mohenjodaro.
Masuda, J.—Early Indian Buddhist Schools.
Mookerji, Radha Kumud—Asoka.
Fundamental Unity of India.
Nationalism in Hindu Culture.
McCrindle—Ancient India.
The Invasion of India by Alexander.
Motichandra—Geographical and Economical Studies in the Mahābhārata.
Oldenberg—Dīpavaṃsa, Text and Translation.
Vinayapiṭaka, Text.
Pargiter—The Purāna Text of the Dynasties of the Kali Age.
Plutarch—Life of Alexander.
Raychaudhuri, H. C.—Political History of Ancient India, 4th edition.
Ray, Nihar Ranjan—Maurya and Sunga Art.
Rhys Davids, Mrs.—Buddhism (Home Univeosity series), also its revised editition.
Rhy Davids, T. W.—Buddhist India.
Sastri, Nilkanta—Dharmavijaya and Dhammavijaya.
Sastri, Shama—Arthaśāstra of Kauṭilya, Text and Translation.
Schūbring, W.—Ācharānga Sūtra.
Senart, E.—Inscriptions de Piyadasi and its English translation.
Sircar, D. C.—Select Inscriptions of India, Vol. I.
Smith, Vincent A.—Early Hiftory of India, 4th Edition.
Asoka, Revised Edition.
Oxford History of India.
Stein, Otto—Yavanas in Early Indian Inscriptions.
On India between the Cultures.
Watters—On Yuan Chwang.
Winternitz—History of Indian Literature (English translation).
Cambridge History of India, Vol. I.

The Pali works, if not mentioned otherwise, are those published by the Pali Text Society.

Asokan Messages

1. Kalāṇaṃ dukaraṃ. Yo ādikaro kalāṇasa so dukaraṃ karoti.

"Doing good work is difficult. He who does it first, does a difficult thing."

2. Nāsti hi kaṃmataraṃ sarvalokahitatpā.

"There is no greater duty than doing good to the whole world."

3. Vipule tu pi dāne yasa nāsti sayame bhāvasudhitā va kataṃñatā va daḍhabhatitā cha nīchā bāḍhaṃ.

"Notwithstanding his extensive charity, he who hath not self-control, purity of sentiment, gratitude, and strong devotion, is very low."

4. Nāsti etārisaṃ dānaṃ yārisaṃ dhaṃmadānaṃ dhaṃma-saṃstavo cha dhaṃmasaṃvibhāgo vā dhaṃma-saṃbaṃdho vā.

"There is no such gift as that of the Dharma,—no such association as that through the Dharma, no such distribution as that of the Dharma, and no such connection as that through the Dharma."

5. Sāravaḍhī asa savapāsaṃḍānaṃ. Savapāsaṃḍā bahusrutā cha asu kalāṇāgamā cha asu.

"May there be the growth of all sects in matters essential.

May all sects be well informed and inheritors of noble traditions."

6. Iyaṃ chu mokhyamute vijaye e dhaṃmavijaye.

"That indeed is to be considered the best of conquests which is a conquest by piety."

Eulogies on Asoka

"The fragrance of his fame has travelled afar ;
He lived in wonderful perception of the Truth."

Chiang Hsia-pias

"Amidst tens of thousands of names of Monarchs that crowd the columns of history, their Majesties and graciousness and serenities and royal highness and the like, the name of Asoka shines, and shines alone, a star."

H. G. Wells

Errata

P. 13, l. 37—Read 'Bindusārassa' for 'Bindusūrassa'; P. 13 l. 38—'khattiyo' for 'hhattiyo'; P. 21, l. 15—'Sthavira' for 'Shavira'; P. 31, l. 21—'Were' for 'Vere'; P. 37, l. 13—'Āryaputra' for 'Arypaputra'; P. 39, l. 1—'dynasties' for 'dynastfes'; P. 63, l 8—'clearly defines' for 'clearly efines'; P. 70, l. 4—'regards' for 'regaards'; P. 72, l. 1—'division' for 'civision'; P. 77, l. 16—'sea-coast' for 'seat-coast'; P. 85, l. 1 'Bhojas' for 'Bho)as'; P. 85, l. 14—'eighteen' for 'elghteen'; P. 85, l. 21—'enjoying for 'enoying'; P. 85, l. 39, 'parent' for 'pareut'; P. 93, l. 33—'capital' for 'eapital'; P. 104, l. 17—'India' for 'Iudia'; R. 108, l. 9—'further' for 'fnrther'; P. 108, l. 15—'between' 'for bstween'; P. 110, l. 14—'conqueror' for 'conqneror'; P. 110, l. 24—'modern' for 'moders'; P. 123, l. 21—'must' for 'wust'; P. 123, l. 24—'the Jātakas' for 'one of the Jātakas'; P. 124, l. 7—'sarva' for 'sarav'; P. 148, l. 31—'anusvāra' for 'anasvāra'; P. 149, l. 7—'autonomous' for 'antonomous'; P. 149, l. 16—'autonomy' for 'antonomy'; P 155, l. 11—'has arisen' for 'has not arisen'; P. 157 l. 30—'humanitarian' for 'hnmatarian'; P. 163, l. 1—'with' for 'we'; P. 165, l. 9—'rāshṭra' for 'rāsṭra'; P. 168. l. 29—'councillors' for 'counciilors'; P. 179, l. 3—'Suvaṃṇagiri' for 'Suvaṃṇagirl'; P. 191, l. 3—'accordingly' for 'acoordingly'; P. 193, l. 21—'in' for 'ln'; P. J95, l. 21—'justice' for 'justfce'; P. 196, l. 36, 'in the midst' for 'in fthe midst'; P. 197, l. 2—'procedure' for 'proceedure'; P. 200. l. 32—'maintenance' for 'maintanance'; P. 200, l. 38—'Amarokosha' for 'Amarorkosha'; P. 288 l. 27—'countries' for 'conntries'; P. 301, l. 33—'in several' for 'inseveral'; P. 307, l. 5—'sovereignty' for severeignty'; P. 351, l. 11—'Dhruva' for 'Dhurva' P. 321, l. 17—'Anaxarchus' for 'Anaxarchns'; P. 338, l. 14—'occurred' for accurred'; P. 342, l. 33—'siya' for 'sitya'; P. 341, l. 29—'one man' for 'one man's'; P. 368, l. 1—'the' for 'tha'.

Abbreviations

I. A. = Indian Antiquary.
I. C. = Indian Culture.
I. H. Q. = Indian Historical Quarterly.
J. R. A. S. = Journal of the Royal Asiatic Society.
J. B. O. R.S. = Journal of the Behar and Orissa Research Society.
Epi. Zeyl. = Epigraphia Zeylanica.
The rest are self-evident.

Illustrations

1. Lauriyā-Nandangarh Column (Frontispiece)
2. The Empire of Asoka (Pl. I)
3. The Map of Jambudvīpa (Pl. II)
4. Five Greek Territories (Pl. III)
5. Herzfeld's Map of the Achæmenian Empire (Pl. IV)

CHAPTER I

INTRODUCTORY

1. **Sources of information :** There are two sources from which materials for a comprehensive history of Aśoka can be gathered, *viz.*, literary and archæological. The literary source consists in (1) the various legends of Aśoka and other Mauryas in Pali, Sanskrit, and other languages ; (2) the texts and commentaries throwing lights, direct or otherwise, on divers points of Aśokan thoughts, records, dominions, and system of administration ; (3) the Greek accounts having bearings upon the Mauryas, their foreign relations and administration, as well as the geography and general history of India ; (4) the dynastic lists in the Divyāvadāna, the Mañjuśrī Mūlakalpa, and the Purāṇas setting forth the chronology of the successive rulers of Magadha, including the Mauryas ; (5) the Samanta-pāsādikā and the Pali Chronicles offering us the chronology of the rulers and ruling dynasties of Magadha ; and (6) the itineraries of such Chinese pilgrims as Fa-Hien, Hwen Thsang, and I-tsing in respect of the facts recorded by them as eye-witnesses and the current legends that have been narrated by them.

The archæological source consists primarily in Aśoka's own inscriptions and monuments, and secondarily only in the inscriptions and monuments left behind by others. An elaborate account of Aśoka's inscriptions constituting as they do the main direct source of his history is given in Part II of this work. Among the inscriptions of others, those standing nearest to Aśoka's time are the three Nāgārjunī Hill-cave inscriptions of Daśaratha. The right half of an Aramaic inscription, which is discovered at Taxila and believed to have been a record of the time of Aśoka and something concerning him (Herzfeld, E. I. XIX, p. 251), still awaits satisfactory decipherment and convincing interpretation. Other inscriptions and coin-lengends that belong to the post-Mauryan period are important as indicating the palæographic, linguistic, literary, political, social, economic, religious, and artistic changes that took place subsequently. Some of them show the continuance of the official designation of the Mahāmātras and Rajjukas, while one of them, namely, the Junāgarh Rock inscription of Rudradāman I, mentions Chandragupta Maurya and Aśoka and an official agent of the former in connection with the history of excavation and subsequent enlargement and repair of the Sudarśana Lake. The hymn of praise composed in honour of the Trikāya and set up at Bodhgayā by a later Chinese pilgrim, named Chiang Hsia pias, wrongly describes the great temple of Bodhgayā as a memorable erection of Aśoka. The Bodhgayā and Gayā inscriptions of Aśokavalla and Daśaratha of Sapadālaksha (Sivalik) are interesting as showing how the name of Aśoka and his successor Daśaratha were kept up in the personal names of even much later Buddhist rulers of a place in India. Similarly the early Brāhmī inscriptions of Ceylon are important in that they prefix the epithet of Devanapriya to the ancient kings of the island. Attention may be drawn also to the Hāthigumphā inscription in which Khāravela is represented as the most powerful king of Kalinga who emulated obviously the fame of Aśoka in respect of honouring all sects, all denominations. The numerous short inscriptions in the seals from Mohenjo-daro and Harappa may be utilised in accounting, partly at least, for the origin and development of the Brāhmī characters, and their animal figures, plant representations, as well as symbols may be carefully studied for their legacies to Aśokan art. Nearer home are the inscriptions of the Achæmenian king Darius of Persia and the architectural designs of Persepolis that must be taken into account in effectively dealing with Aśoka's inscriptions and his monuments in general and monoliths in particular. The later Indian monuments, sculptures and symbols, Buddhist or otherwise, deserve to be studied for a first-hand knowledge of the legacy of Aśokan art traceable in them.

2. **Their relative values :** The persistent undervaluation of the Buddhist traditions and legends of Aśoka as preserved in the Pali Chronicles, Buddhaghosa's Commentaries, particularly the Samanta-pāsādikā, the Si-yu-ki of Hwen Thsang, and the Aśokāvadāna in the Divyāvadāna on the part of a powerful section of Aśokan scholars raised an issue of far-reaching importance on which we have decisive findings of the French savant M. Senart and the late lamented Professor Rhys Davids.

Senart believes that "the Chronicles have in certain details, under the name of Aśoka, preserved of our Piyadasi recollections sufficiently exact, not only to allow a substantial agreement (*une concordance sensible*) to appear but even to contribute usefully to the intelligence of obscure passages in our monuments" (Inscriptions de Piyadasi, II, p. 231, Buddhist India, p. 276).

To call the Chronicles "the mendacious fictions of unscrupulous monks" is in the considered opinion of Rhys Davids to "show a grave want of appreciation." In arguing in favour of the Pali Chronicles, he observes : "Just as in the case of Megasthenes, of the early English Chroniclers it would be unreasonable to expect that sort of historical training which is of quite recent growth in Europe. . . . . The opinion of scholars as to the attitude to be adopted towards such works is quite unanimous. The hypothesis of deliberate lying, of conscious forgery, is generally discredited. What we find in such Chronicles is not, indeed, sober history, ... but neither is it pure fiction. It is good evidence of opinion as held at the time when it was written. And from the fact that such an opinion was then held we can argue back, according to the circumstances of each case, to what was probably the opinion held at some earlier date. No hard words are needed : and we may be unfeignedly grateful to these old students and writers for having preserved as much as we can gather from their imperfect records" (Buddhist India, p. 274f., Geiger's Dīpavaṃsa und Mahāvaṃsa in Erlangen, 1902).

And in arguing against Aśoka's own records, he characteristically points out : "The inscriptions are scanty . . . . They give only a limited view of the set of circumstances they deal with. Royal proclamations, and official statements, are not usually regarded as telling the truth, the whole truth, and nothing but the truth. To put it mildly, there is an economy of candour in these documents, intensely interesting though they are. And they are enigmatic. It is not possible to understand them without the light thrown upon them by the later accounts" (Buddhist India, p. 275).

The traditional episodes of Aśoka and those of his predecessors and successors in the Maurya line as coming down to us from the Buddhist, Jaina and Brāhman writers of later ages are certainly not without their intrinsic value. Their main importance as sources of information lies in certain reliable data of the chronology and personal history of Aśoka and other Maurya rulers. But for them and for the contemporary and later Greek accounts, we could have known nothing of Aśoka's grandfather Chandragupta and his father Bindusāra. Aśoka's inscriptions completely ignore them. One might argue that Chandragupta Maurya is mentioned in the Junāgaṛh Rock inscription of Rudradāman I. But considering the late age of this inscription, the facts recorded in it in connection with Chandragupta and Aśoka might be more a legendary than sober history. The same remark holds true of the inscribed hymn of the Chinese pilgrim Chiang

Hsia-pias wherein Aśoka's wide fame is said to have rested on his pious erection of the great Bodhgayā temple.

The traditional stories are entitled to serious consideration not only for the additional historical data by which these supplement inscriptions constituting the main direct source of information but also for their suggestiveness. It is not only at the beginning of the Aśokan researches that these were of most service, but even now the narratives are of no less service as means of suggesting various interesting problems for solution to the critical students of the Aśokan inscriptions and monuments. As helps to the clarification of certain knotty and obscure points in the inscriptions and the correct interpretation of the historical bearings of certain statements in them, these have already been appraised for what they are worth.

However connected the narratives may be, particularly those related in the two Ceylon Chronicles in Pali, the introduction to Buddhaghosa's Samanta-pāsādikā, and Aśokāvadāna, they, when considered *per se*, are equally incomplete and one-sided, having been written exclusively from the Buddhist theological point of view. They not only stand in need of supplementation from the inscriptions but also in that of checking and rectification where they are of a conflicting character.

The study of the inscriptions has at last gained an independent foothold of its own. Among the recent writers, Professor D.R. Bhandarkar deserves great credit for vigorously having taken his stand on the inscriptions and convincingly shown how they serve as real landmarks of Indian history, and his treatment of the subject is analytical throughout. Professor Radhakumud Mookerji's is more a synthetic spirit and his attention is equally divided between the inscriptions and literary traditions[1]. Though not a partisan either by training or temperament, by conviction I fall in line with Professor Bhandarkar rather than with Professor Mookerji. To me also the traditional episodes, however interesting and instructive they are for other reasons, are of secondary importance only. To properly evaluate the inscriptions is not only to trace through them the successive stages of the workings and outpourings of Aśoka's active mind but also to consider them cautiously and critically in their manifold bearings on the contemporary, earlier and later Indian as well as world civilization.

---

[1] Theoretically Mookerji too admits the greater evidentiary value of the inscriptions, See his *Asoka* p, 2.

CHAPTER II

PERSONAL HISTORY

Nothing is more striking and more disappointing to the students of Aśoka's inscriptions than that nowhere in them he has either mentioned or referred to his father and grandfather, his mother and maternal relations, as well as relations of his queens. He has not even cared anywhere to introduce himself as a scion of the Maurya family. His allusions to the former kings who had reigned in the long past and during several centuries (R.E. IV, P.E. VII) are too vague and indefinite and of too general a character to be construed as an allusion to his immediate predecessors. One may argue at best to establish the fact that they are not necessarily precluded from his mental view. His main concerns in the inscriptions are to render an easily intelligible and illustrative account of his notable acts of piety, to clearly set forth the circumstances and the nature of reflections that caused a change of heart and brought about a turning point in his life and kingly career, and to inculcate and promulgate the principles of piety or duty with a view to seeing that these were widely appreciated and acted upon. Persons, peoples, kings, princes, officers, places, countries, rocks, pillars, caves, means, methods, and the rest come in just by the way.

Chronology is the backbone of history. The inscriptions of Aśoka as well as the Pali Chronicles and Buddhaghosa's narrative in his Samanta-pāsādikā give us a chronological setting of certain relevant incidents in the life and career of Aśoka. The Avadāna story narrates the life of Aśoka following some sort of a chronological order without assigning the facts to definite dates. The chronological scheme followed in the inscriptions is serviceable as a means of filling in gaps and testing the accuracy of some of the dates within admittedly the wider outline of Aśoka's personal history in the Pali Chronicles and the Samanta-pāsādikā. The Hāthigumphā inscription of Khāravela excels both in punctiliousness when it presents a year by year account of the activities of Khāravela all through his reign within a biographical scheme.

Just as in the life of Buddha the attainment of Buddhahood marks the beginning of the history of his great career worth knowing, so does the *abhisheka* or consecration in the life of a sovereign. Unless one's business be to excel in the art of Boswellising, precisely as it is in a Prakrit piece of panegyric like Khāravela's inscription, the pedigree, boyish idiosyncrasies, education, practical training, conscious pursuits, and such other details of the early life of a high personage are unnecessary and out of place. So these are safely left out of account in the earlier Vinaya life of the Buddha which is in Pali, and so also in Aśoka's sober account of his own mind and activities.

Thus the basic date of Aśoka's personal history is the date of his consecration. This has so far been tentatively fixed at 270 or 269 B.C. on a twofold basis : (1) the traditional, and (2) the epigraphic.

As regards the t·aditional basis, the Pali Chronicles definitely state that Aśoka's consecration took place 218 years after the demise of the Buddha.[1] The Buddhist traditions of the later age differ from one another regarding the date of the Buddha's demise. The date which gained currency in Ceylon from a late period of its history and is now adhered to in Siam and Burma as well is equivalent to 544 or 543 B.C., which, according to Professor Raychaudhuri's hypothesis, was really the date of Bimbisāra's accession to the throne of Magadha (Political history, p. 186). The date of the Buddha's demise, as may be fixed by adding 218 years to the date of Aśoka's consecration, is 488 or 487 B. C.[2]

---

[1] Confounding evidently Dharmās'oka with Kālās'oka of the Pali Chronicles, the Divyāvadāna (p. 402) places As'oka's coronation just one hundred years after the Buddha's demise : Bhagavatā nirdishṭo varshas'ata-parinirvṛitasya mama Pāṭaliputre nagare 's'oko nāma rājā bhavishyati.

[2] This date agrees very nearly with that which has been fixed by Takakusu, *viz.* 486 B.C., on the strength of the Chinese 'dotted record' kept up at Canton up to the end of the year A.D, 489 (975-489) J.R.A.S., 1905, p. 51, and differs from the date fixed by Wilhelm Geiger, J. F. Fleet, and D. M. de Z, Wickramasinghe, *viz.*, 483 B.C., on the strength of the available chronological data afforded by the ecclesiastical history of Buddhism in Magadha and Ceylon up to the end of the 6th century A D. (Mahāvamsa, Transl. by Geiger, Introd. p. XXII f. . Fleet, J. R. A. S., 1906, p. 984 f. ; Wickramasinghe, Epig. Zeyl., iii, p. 4 f. ; John N. Senerveatne (J. R. A. S., Ceylon Br., XXIII, No. 67, p. 141 f.) has sought to prove that the Buddha era of 483 B.C. was in use in Ceylon up to the close of the 15th century when a reform of the calendar was effected, 544 B.C. being adopted as the year of the Buddha's demise. Fleet goes so far as to suggest October 12, 483 B. C. as the actual date on which the Buddha passed away, while Mr. C. D. Chatterjee (Acharyya Pushpanjali D. R. Bhandarkar, p. 329 f.) shifts it back to April 26. The suggested date is inclusive and not exclusive of the year of consecration. For reasons, see Mookerji's Asoka, p. 184, f. n. 6.

The epigraphic data enable us to test the accuracy and workability of the above date. From Aśoka's statements, it is clear that the five Greek contemporaries of Aśoka were all reigning monarchs when he promulgated his second Rock Edict not later than the 12th year and his Thirteenth Rock Edict not later than the 13th or 14th year of his *abhisheka*. The first four of them, namely, Aṃtiyoka, Tulamaya, Aṃtikini, and Maga, have been satisfactorily identified with Antiochus II Theos, king of Syria and Western Asia (261-46 B. C.), Ptolemy II Philadelphus, king of Egypt (285-47 B. C.), Antigonas Gonatas, king of Macedonia (276-46, 276-39, or 278-30 B. C.) and Magas, king of Cyrene (300-258 or 300-250 B. C.) respectively. The fifth Greek contemporary of Aśoka should be preferably identified with Alexander, king of Epirus (272-255 B. C.). To be contemporaries of Aśoka in the 13th or 14th year of his reign, the corresponding year of the reign of the five Greek rulers must not be earlier than 256 or 255 B.C., may be later. And this test of the reliability of the date of Aśoka's consceration fixed on the traditional basis is satisfied by lengths of the reign of his five Greek contemporaries determined on the strength of Greek writings.

The workable date of Aśoka's *abhisheka* having thus been settled, it has been easy to prepare from his inscriptions a chronological table of events and achievements like one offered below for discussion :

Consecration	c. 270 or 269 B.C.
Conquest of Kalinga	263 or 262 B.C.
Pilgrimage to Sambodhi implying Aśoka's conversion to Buddhism.	261 or 260 B.C.
Dedication to the Ājīvikas of the first two caves in the Khalatika (Barābar) hill. ...	259 or 258 B.C.
Promulgation and engraving of R.E. I-IV.	259 or 258 B.C.
Creation of the office of the Dharma-mahāmātras.	258 or 257 B.C.
Promulgation and engraving of R.E. V-XIII.	258 or 256 B.C.
Promulgation and engraving of R.E. XIV.	257 or 256 B.C.
Enlargement of the stūpa of Buddha Koṇāgamana.	257 or 256 B.C.

Dedication of two more caves in the Khalatika hill to the Ājīvikas.	252 or 251 B.C.
Pilgrimage to the village of Lumbinī and the erection of a commemorative monolith with an appropriate emblem thereon.	251 or 250 B.C.
Pilgrimage to the enlarged stūpa of Buddha Koṇāgamana and erection of a commemorative monolith.	251 or 250 B.C.
Erection of similar commemorative monoliths at such places as Pāṭaliputra, Lauriya-Ararāj, Lauriya-Nandangaṛh, Rāmpūrvā, Benares City, Sārnāth, Mīrāṭh, Siwalik, Saṃkāśya, Kauśāmbī, Sāñchī and Bhuvaneśwar (Tosali), probably in ...	251 or 49 B.C.
Promulgation of a special ordinance to suppress schisms in the Sangha at such places as Pāṭaliputra, Sārnāth, Kauśāmbī, and Sāñchī, probably in ...	251 - 49 B.C.
Engraving of the Queen's Edict on the monolith at Kauśāmbī, probably in ...	250 - 49 B.C.
Twenty-five general jail-deliveries effected evidently once a year prior to the promulgation and engraving of P. E. V. in the 26th year of *abhisheka* corresponding to ...	245 or 244 B.C.
Engraving of the first six Pillar Edicts at such places as Pāṭaliputra, Lauriya-Ararāj, Lauriya-Nandangaṛh, Rāmpūrvā, Mīrāṭh, Siwalik, and Kauśāmbī.	245 or 244 B.C.
Engraving of the Minor Rock Edict at such places as Sahasrām, Bairāt, Rūpnāth, Gavīmaṭh, Pālkiguṇḍu, Maski, Yerraguḍi, and Isila (Brahmagiri, Siddāpura and Jatinga-Rāmeswara) probably in. ...	245 - 44 B.C.
Engraving of the Seventh Pillar Edict at Siwalik, better, Toprā.	244 or 243 B.C.
Promulgation and engraving of the two separate Rock Edicts at Dhauli and Jaugaḍa probably during the closing period of Aśoka's reign.	

The chronological table of events of the life and reign of Aśoka which may be prepared from the narratives of Aśoka in the Pali Chronicles and Samanta-pāsādikā is as set forth below :

Conquest of Ujjayinī[1]	c. 285 or 284 B.C.
Viceroyalty of Ujjayinī, *i.e.*, of Avantī.[2]	285-74 or 284-73 B.C
Married Devī at Vidiśā.[3]	285 or 284 B.C.
Birth of Aśoka's son Mahendra by his Vaiśya wife Devī at Vidiśā.[4]	284 or 283 B.C.
Birth of his daughter Sanghamitrā by his wife Devī.	282 or 281 B.C.
Death of Bindusāra, victory in a fratricidal war, and accession to the imperial throne of Magadha when Mahendra was ten years of age.[5]	274 or 273 B.C.
Consecration under the title of Aśoka (Asokam abhisiñchayi) when Mahendra was of 14 years of age.[6])	270 or 269 B.C.

Adherence to religious sects and schools of thought other than Buddhist (ito bahiddhā pāsaṇḍā), 96 in number[7], for the first three

---

[1] Samanta-pāsādikā, I, p. 45 : Asoka-kumāro attanā laddhaṃ Ujjenirajjaṃ pahāya.

[2-4] Mahāvaṃsa, VIII. 8 : Avanti-raṭṭham bhuñjanto pitarā dinnam attano, also ibid, V. 39 : pitarā dinnam rajjam Ujjeniyam. As'oka's viceroyalty broadly covered a period of 10 years, from the advent of his son Mahendra in his mother's womb to the completion of his 9th year. The first event took place in the first year of As'oka's viceroyalty, Cf. Samanta-pāsādikā, I, p. 70 : Asoko kira kumārakāle janapadaṃ labhitvā Ujjenim gachchhanto Vedisanagaram patvā Vedisa-seṭṭhissa dhītaram aggahesi. Sā tam divasam eva gabbhaṃ gahetvā Ujjeniyam Mahinda-kumāraṃ vijāyi.

[5] Dīpavamsa, VI. 2.

[6] Ibid, vi. 22, which agrees with the traditions recorded by Buddhaghosa, first, in his Samanta-pāsādikā, I, p. 70, stating (Mahinda-) kumārassa chuddasavassakāle rājā abhisekam pāpuṇi, and secondly, in his Sumangala-vilāsinī, II, p. 613, stating Piyadāso nāma kumāro chhattam ussāpetvā Asoko nāma Dhammarājā hutvā. According to the second tradition, Prince Piyadāsa (Piyadassa, and not piyadassi as wrongly suggested by me in Inscriptions of Asoka, pt. II, p. 221) assumed the title of As'oka at the time of his consecration.

[7] Dīpavaṃsa, VI. 24-27 ; Samanta-pā , I, p. 44 ; Mahāvamsa, V. 34-36. Dīpavamsa alone gives the total number of existing sects and schools as 96 (chhan-navutika),—a traditional figure given also by Fa Hien, cf. Beal's Buddlist Records, I, p. xlvii.

years of his reign, daily feeding 60,000 Brāhmans and Brahmanical ascetics, and occasionally giving gifts to the Paṇḍaranga parivrājakas, the Ājīvikas, the Nirgranthas, and others[1]	c. 270-68 or 269-67 B.C.
Conversion to Buddhism and contact with the Buddhist Sangha in the fourth year of abhisheka[2]	268-67 or 267-66 B.C.
Conceived the idea of erecting 84,000 ārāmas or vihāras in 84,000 towns of Jambudvīpa, one at each town, including the famous Aśokārāma at the city of Pāṭaliputra, while seated in the midst of a congregation of 60,000 Buddhist monks[3] ...	267 or 266 B.C.
Aśoka's younger uterine brother Tishya, then a crown prince, and his nephew and son-in-law prince Agnibrahmā joined the Buddhist Order in the fourth year of abhisheka[4]	267 or 266 B.C.
Completed at the cost of 96 crores and in three years' time (anto tīṇi vassāni, tīhi vassehi) the erection of 84,000 ārāmas or vihāras which was started in the 4th year of abhisheka[5]	265 or 264 B.C.
Aśoka's son Mahendra, then of 20 years of age, and daughter Sanghamitrā, then 18 years old, both by his Vaiśya wife Devī of Vidiśā, were ordained as monk and nun respectively, whereby he became the dāyāda ("Inheritor") of Buddha's śāsana (Buddhist Order") in the 6th year of abhisheka[6] ...	265 or 264 B.C.

[1] Samanta-pā., I, p. 44. Dīpavaṃsa, VI. 26 introduces them as—

Nigaṇṭhāchelakā ch'eva itarā Paribbājakā
itarā Brāhmaṇā ti cha aññe cha puthuladdhikā.

Cf. also Dīpavaṃsa, VII. 35 ;

Paṇḍarangā Jaṭilā cha Nigaṇṭhāchelakādikā
aññaladdhikā nānā dūsenti sāsanam.

Ibid, VII. 38 ; Ajīvakā.

[2] Dīpavaṃsa, VI. 18, 30f. ; Samanta-pā., I, p. 44f. ; Mahāvamsa, V. 68f.

[3] Dīpavaṃsa, VI. 96 98 ; Samanta-pā., I, p. 48f. ; Mahāvaṃsa, V. 78-30.

[4] Samanta.pā., I, p. 55 ; Mahāvamsa, VI. 154-71.

[5] Dīpavaṃsa, VI. 99 ; Samanta-pā., I, p. 49.

[6] Dīpavaṃsa, VI. 20f. ; Samanta-pā., I, p. 51, Mahāvaṃsa, V. 203-4.

Consecrated under the title of Priyadarśin when Mahendra was 20 years old[1] ... 265 or 264 B.C.

Sad death of the Venerable Kauntīputra Tishya without treatment for want of drugs, which caused much regret to Aśoka and suggested the idea of founding stores in Pāṭaliputra for free supply of drugs[2] ... 265 or 264 B.C.

Mahendra figured foremost amongst the resident pupils of his preceptor by his proficiency in the knowledge of the Piṭakas and Commentaries[3] ... ... 264 or 263 B.C.

Internal dissension in the Sangha and suspension of the uposatha and other Buddhist ecclesiastical duties in the Aśokārāma in Pāṭaliputra for seven years[4] ... 260-54 B.C.

The samāgama (general conference) of 60,000 monks held at Pāṭaliputra at which the inmates of the Aśokārāma were examined, batch by batch, and Aśoka compelled those (60,000 outsiders in a Buddhist garb) whose views did not tally with the Theravāda doctrine, i.e., Vibhājyavāda, to revert to their old orders, giving them white robes to put on and thereby made the Sangha united (samaggo sangho)[5] ... ... 254 or 253 B.C.

Compilation of the Kathāvatthu by Maudgalīputra Tishya (Moggaliputta Tissa) who conducted the examination of the monks as to their respective views at the above conference[6] ... ... 254 or 253 B.C.

The Council (Sangīti) of 1,000 representative Sthaviras was in session under the leadership of Maudgalīputra Tishya for the rehearsal of the Piṭakas as then fixed[7] ... 254 or 253 B.C.

---

[1] Dīpavaṃsa, VI. 24 : Piyadassābhisiñchayum.

[2] Samanta-pā., I, p. 52 : Rañño pana aṭṭhavassābhiseka-kāle yeva Kontiputta—Tissatthero··· ; Mahāvamsa, V. 212 f.

[3] Samanta-pā., I, p. 52 : Tadā Asoko Dhammarājā navavassābhiseko hoti.

[4] Ibid, I, p. 53f : anekarūpam sāsanassa abbudañ cha malañ cha kaṇṭkañ cha samuṭṭhāpesuṃ...Asokārāme sattavassāni uposatho upachchhijji. Cf. alsa Dīpavaṃsa, VII. 33-36 ; Mahāvaṃsa, V. 228f.

[5-6] Dīpavaṃsa, VII. 38-41, Samanta-pā., I, p. 61, Mahāvamsa, V. 266-74.

[7] Dīpavaṃsa, VII. 51-3 ; Samanta-pā., I, p. 61, Mahāvaṃsa, V. 275-79.

Despatch of Buddhist missions to different parts of India and to Suvarṇa-bhūmi[1]	254 or 253 B.C.
Death of king Muṭasiva and consecration of his son and successor Devānampiya Tissa[2]	254 or 253 B.C.
Erection of the Vedisagiri mahāvihāra for Mahendra by his mother Devī[3] ...	254 or 253 B.C.
Mission to the island of Tambapaṇṇī (Ceylon)[4]	253 or 252 B.C.
Arrival of the Buddhist mission under the leadership of Mahendra in the month of Jyaishṭha and propagation of Buddhism in Ceylon[5]	253 or 252 B.C.
Aśoka started with great eclat for Mahābodhi (Bodhgaya) in the company of a fraternity of advanced Theras (ariyasangham ādāya) and returned to Pāṭaliputra with a graft from the Bo-tree in the month of Kārttika[6]	253 or 252 B.C.
Despatch of Sanghamitrā to Ceylon together with the graft from the Bo-tree, in the month of Mārgaśīrsha, the king himself seeing them off at the port of Tāmralipti[7]	253 or 252 B.C.
Death of Aśoka's first queen consort Āsandimitrā which took place 30 years from his accession and 26 years from his consecration[8]	245 or 244 B.C.
Tishyarakshā (same as Tishyarakshitā) was placed in the position of his queen consort[9]	243 or 242 B.C.
Destruction of the Bo-tree due to an	

1 Dīpavaṃsa. VIII. 1f., Samanta-pā., I, p. 63f., Mahāvamsa, XII. 1f.

2 Dīpavaṃsa, XI. 11-10 ; Samanta-pā., I, p. 71-3.

3 Samanta pā , I, p. 70, Mahāvamsa, XIII. 7.

4, 5 Dīpavamsa, XII. 16f. ; Samanta-pā, I, p. 69f ; Mahāvaṃsa, XII f.

6 Samanta-pā, I, p. 92f. ; Dīpavaṃsa, XVI. Mahāvamsa, XIII. 18-21.

7 Samanta-pā , I, p. 96f. ; Dīpavaṃsa, XVI. 1f. ; Mahāvaṃsa, XVIII. 26foll.

8 Ibid, XX. 2, 9 Ibid, XX. 3.

inimical action on the part of Tishya-rakshā[1] ... ... 240 or 239 B.C.

Death of Aśoka and end of his reign[2] 234 or 233 B.C.

The inscriptions and Buddhist traditional narratives of Aśoka rightly attach much importance to these two events in his life and career : (1) Consecration to the throne of Magadha, (2) Conversion to Buddhism.

Indeed, the main interest of his personal history centres round them. But for the first, there could not have been the formal recognition of his earthly power, and but for the second, even as he tells us in his M. R. E., there would not perhaps have been any vigorous action on his part towards the promotion of the cause of piety, far and wide. Before, therefore, discussing other points of interest, I will take up these for consideration and throw the light on each of them which may be obtained from his inscriptions as well as other sources.

1. **Consecration** : Abhisheka is primarily a ritualistic term implying as it did the ceremonial consecration of the person to be anointed as king or king overlord. A warrior who underwent the ceremony of consecration is described in the Pali Nikāyas and Amarakosha (Kshatriyavarga) as a (mūrddhābhishikta kshatriya, *i.e.*, "a warrior whose head is besprinkled with holy waters." The abhisheka is the time honoured and age old Indo-Aryan custom which involved an elaborate ritual, 'described in several Brāhmaṇas' and provided with appropriate formulas (mantras) from the Vedas.[3] It was performed in one or another of the four approved forms of the Vedic 'sacrifice of royal inauguration,' called Vājapeya, Rājasūya, Punar-abhisheka, and Aindra mahābhisheka respectively.[4]

In the Vājapeya form, the sacrificer (*i.e.*, the person to be installed on the throne) was to come out as the winner in a race of seventeen chariots. This was to be followed by the mounting of a chariot wheel, placed on the top of a long pole, by the sacrificer and his wife, and paying homage therefrom to the Mother Earth. According to the

---

[1] Ibid, XX. 5.

[2] Dīpavaṃsa, V. 100, 101 ;

Chandagutto rajjam kāresi vassāni chatuvīsati.
Bindusūrassa yo putto Asokadhammo mahāyaso
Vassāni sattatimsam pi rajjaṃ kāresi hhattiyo.

Cf. Mahāvaṃsa, XX. 6 ; V. 18-9.

[3], [4] Raychaudhuri, Political Histroy of Ancient India, 4th Ed., p. 138.

Satapatha Brāhmaṇa V. 2, I. 25, the royal sacrificer was to be offered thereafter a throne-seat with a goat-skin spread over it and installed thereon by the Adhvaryu (Vedic priest) in the set form of words declaring him to be the ruler, the ruling lord (yantrin, yamana), firm and steadfast, seated on the seat "for the tilling, for peaceful dwelling (kshema), for wealth (rayi), for prosperity, i.e., for the welfare of the people, the common weal."[1]

The Śatapatha Brāhmaṇa, V. 2. 3f., offers us an elaborate account of the Rājasūya form which consisted in a long succession of sacrificial performances commencing on the first day of Phālguna and ranging over a period of upwards of two years.[2] Its popular features, as enumerated by Professor Raychaudhuri,[3] chiefly consisted in (1) the distribution of the sacrificial honours among their worthy recipients, the Ratnins, namely, the chief queen and ten different court officials, (2) the abhishechana or besprinkling, (3) the dig-vyāsthāpana or the king-elect's walking towards the various quarters by way of symbolising his world-wide campaigns and conquests ; (4) treading on a tiger-skin by way of symbolising the gaining in strength and pre-eminence ; (5) the narration by the Hotṛi priest of the story of Śunaḥśepa ; (6) a mimic cow-raid against a relative or a mock fight with a rājanya ; (7) enthronement, and (8) a game of dice in which the king designate is made to be the victor. The abhishechana or besprinkling was to begin with offerings to such Vedic divinities as Savitā Satyaprasava, Agni Gṛihapati, Soma Vanaspati, Bṛihaspati Vāk, Indra Jyeshṭha, Rudra Paśupati, Mitra Satya, and Varuṇa Dharmapati, and it was to be performed by a Brāhman priest, a kinsman or brother of the king-elect, a friendly Rājanya and a Vaiśya.

The Punarabhisheka or 'Renewed anointment' was intended for a ruler who conquered other monarchs. In this form, the king-elect was to ascend the throne made of udumbara (fig) wood, a ceremony which was to be followed by the besprinkling. The officiating priest formally installed him on the throne in these words : Rājñāṃ tvaṃ adhirājo bhaveha, mahantaṃ tvaṃ mahīnāṃ samrājaṃ charshaṇīnām. "Do thou be here the overking among kings, the greatest amongst the great, the supreme ruler of fellow men." The king-elect was thereafter required to descend from the throne to make obeisance to the

1 Ibid, p. 139f. ; Radhakumud Mookerji, The Fundamental Unity of India, p. 80

2 S.B.E., Vol. XLI, Introd., p. xxvi.

3 Political History, p. 140f.

Brāhmans present. As opined in the Aitareya Brāhmaṇa, VIII, which contains an interesting account of the whole ceremony, "Verily thus the lordly power (kshatra) falls under the influence of the holy power (brāhman). When the lordly power falls under the influence of the holy power, that kingdom is prosperous, rich in heroes, in it a hero or heir (vīra) is born".[1]

The Aitareya Brāhmaṇa, VIII. 11, contains a description of the Aindra Mahābhisheka form, according to which the king-elect was to go through these five main ceremonies : (1) the taking of an oath to the officiating priest, (2) ārohaṇa or ascending the throne, (3) utkrośana or proclamation, (4) abhimantraṇa or the repitition of certain special formulas, and (5) abhishechana or anointing.[2]

Over and above these, the powerful rulers performed from time to time the Aśvamedha or 'Horse sacrifice' which, in the oft-quoted opinion of Bhavabhūti, was "the super-eminent touchstone to test the might of warriors conquering the world and an indication of the conquest of all the warriors."[3] In performing it, a steed was set at liberty to roam about for a year under the guardianship of a hundred princes, a hundred nobles, a hundred sons of heralds and charioteers, and a hundred sons of attendants, the features of the rite including the eulogy of the king by a Kshatriya and a Brāhman luteplayer, and the narration of a circle of tales of exploits.[4]

The besprinkling which was the essential part of the function of abhisheka was to be followed by the investiture of the king-elect with five insignia of royalty (Pali pañchakakudhabhaṇḍāni) by the king-makers (rājakṛits, rajakattāro), the pronouncement of blessings by the priests and elders, the panegyrics by the Sūta-Māgadhas and Vaitālikas, the receiving of presents, the shouts of joy by the crowd, the processions, and the feasts and festivals.[5]

In accordiance with the opinion then held in the Satapatha Brāhmaṇa, V. 1.1.12-13 and the Kātyāyana Śrauta Sūtra, XV. 1.1.2, the Rājasūya form entitled the king-elect only to the office of a Rājā,

---

[1] Raychaudhuri, op. cit. p. 142f.

[2] Ibid, p. 143.

[3] Uttararāmacharita, Act IV : As'vamedha iti vis'vavijayināṃ kshatriyānāṃ ūrjasvalaḥ sarva-kshatriya-paribhavī mahān utkarsha-nishkarshaḥ, cited by Raychaudhuri.

[4] Raychaudhuri, op. cit., p. 144.

[5] Cf. S'abdakalpadruma, sub voce abhisheka; account of Kūṇika-Ajātas'atru's consecration in Aupapātika Sūtra, Sec. 40 et seq ; description of Devānampiya-Tissa's consecration in Dīpāvaṃsa, XI-XII.

while by the Vājapeya form he might aspire to the office of a Samrāj, the office of Rājā having been inferior to that of a Samrāj or Samrāṭ.[1]

Devānampriya (Ardhamāgadhī Devāṇuppiya) employed whether as a substitute for the word rājā (R. E. VIII) or as a prefix to the name Aśoka (M.R.E., Maski) or Priyadasi, was nothing but an honorific pūjāvachana) or auspicious mode of address like Tatra Bhavān, Dīrghāyus, and Āyushmat. Considered, however, from the ceremony of consecration undergone by a king-elect, it meant no more than one who was divinely favoured, divinely gifted. We have seen that at the time of consecration such Vedic divinities as Savitar the true progenitor, Agni the Lord of the household, Soma the Lord of plants, Bṛihaspati the Logos, Indra the Supreme, Rudra the Lord of cattle, Mitra the True bond of friendship, and Varuṇa the Lord of righteousness were invoked by the officiating priest to bestow their special favours on the king-elect in order to see him fully endowed or gifted with majesty, suzerainty, power, glory, health, wealth, beauty, prosperity, safety, security, increase in family, name and fame, friendship, culture, truth, piety and righteousness.[2]

Asoka, Priyadasi, and Rājā are the three names, titles or epithets which seem to have special significance of their own in connexion with Aśoka's consecration.

According to the Dīpavaṃsa tradition, when prince Priyadarśana, son of king Bindusāra, was consecrated for the first time in 219 B.E. (Dīpava., VI. 1), just four years after his accession to power (ib., VI. 21), he was consecrated under the name or title of Aśoka (Asokam abhisiñchayuṃ, ib., VI. 22). This accords, as we saw, with the tradition independently recorded by Buddhaghosa (Sumangala-vilāsinī, II, p. 613), but conflicts with the Sarvāstivāda, better Mūlasarvāstivāda account in the Divyāvadāna (p. 370), according to which Aśoka was the name given to the prince by his father at the instance of his mother. The probability of truth, however, seems to be more in the Theravāda tradition.

Whatever the actual date and however late was the date of the engraving of M. R. E., the dhamma-sāvaṇa ("proclamation of piety") contained in it must indeed be assigned to the earlier part of Aśoka's reign. And what is particularly important to note in this connexion is that in none of the various versions of

---

[1] Raychaudhuri, op. cit , p. 135.

[2] Note that the Pali significance of the epithet Devānaṃpr'iya is different. See Ch. III.

M. R. E. the epithet Priyadasi Rājā or Piyadasi Lājā is employed. In one of the versions, namely, that of Maski, we have quite unexpectedly the use of the name or epithet of Aśoka, after the colourless general honorific prefix Devānaṃpiya : Devānaṃpiyasa Asokasa. As regards the remaining versions of M.R.E., the free employment of Devānaṃpiya as a substitute for Rājā or Lājā has no special significance at all.

The full royal or imperial epithet which is employed in the Rock and Pillar Edicts, engraved from the 12th and the 26th year of abhisheka respectively, is Devānaṃpiye Piyadasi Lājā. Without the honorific prefix Devānaṃpiya, the epithet stands as Piyadasi Lājā or Lājā Piyadasi, which latter is met with in the Third Barābar Hill-Cave inscription, engraved in the 19th year of abhisheka. The passive form Lājinā Piyadasinā occurs in the first two Barābar Hill-cave inscriptions, which were engraved in the 12th year of abhisheka. Thus it may be established beyond a doubt that the important epithet Piyadasi Lājā or Lājā Piyadasi came to be systematically employed in the inscriptions dating from the 12th year of abhisheka. A longer form of this epithet is happily met with in the Bhābru Edict, namely, Priyadasi Lājā Māgadhe, which cannot but remind us of the earlier Pali conventional phrases, Rājā Māgadho Seniyo Bimbisāro and Rājā Māgadho Ajātasattu Vedehiputto. It certainly indicates that by the epithet Lājā or Rājā was meant Lājā Māgadhe, "the Magadhan king" or "the king of Magadha." In the verdict of the Śatapatha Brāhmaṇa and Kātyāyana Śrauta Sūtra, as we noticed, the epithet Rājā indicated the status of a ruler which was inferior to that of a Samrāṭ and to which a ruler was entitled by the Rājasūya form of consecration. Going by the Dīpavaṃsa account, it may not be improbable to think that by the first consecration which was celebrated according to the Rājasūya form, Prince Priyadarśana (Buddhaghosa's Piyadāsa, Piyadassa) was really anointed as Rājā Māgadho Asoko, "The Magadhan king Aśoka" or "Aśoka the king of Magadha."

Now, what about the title or epithet Piyadasi or Priyadarśin, used as a personal name ? The Dīpavaṃsa definitely states that king Aśoka was anointed again as Piyadassi[1], six years after the first consecration.

Mahinda-chuddasame vasse Asokam abhisiñchayuṃ (ib., VI. 22).
Paripuṇṇa-vīsavassamhi Piyadass' abhisiñchayuṃ (ib., VI. 24).

---

1 This was probably a title conferred on As'oka by the Buddhist Fraternity of Pāṭaliputra after his conversion to Buddhism.

3

If this tradition of the second consecration be true to fact, as would seem likely, it must be that of Punar-abhisheka or 'Renewed anointment.' As a traditional instance of renewed anointment, Professor Raychaudhuri cites the case of Devānampiya Tissa from the Pali Chronicles[1]. But the example cited is inapt, inasmuch as the second consecration of king Devānampiya Tissā of Ceylon was not performed after the conquest of other monarchs or territories. The second consecration (dutiyābhiseko, Dīpava., X. 39) was celebrated in the month of Vaiśākha, five months after the first (Dīpava., XI.14), just to oblige his great Indian contemporary and friend Asokadhamma whose abhisheka presents arrived untimely[2]. According to the Brāhmaṇa definition of Punar-abhisheka, a reigning king was justified in performing it only after subduing other monarchs and thereby establishing him in the position of an overking among other kings (rājñām adhirājah). The second consecration of Aśoka under the title of Piyadassī was a different case altogether, and it might be cited as a typical instance of renewed anointment. Aśoka assumed the title of Piyadasi or Priyadarśin in his inscriptions dating from the 12th year of abhisheka, which is to say, from the 5th year after the conquest of Kalinga and annexation of the conquered territory to his own dominions (R.E. XIII). By the Punar-abhisheka form of consecration alone, a ruler might be declared to be mahantaṃ mahīnām. And most probably on the strength of this Aśoka was able to claim his domain or empire to have been mahaṃte hi vijaye (R. E. XIV).

It was no exaggeration on the part of the Pali chronicler to say that by the consecration prince Priyadarśana gained in the true royal dignity and imperial majesty, that, in other words, he came to be formally declared and publicly acknowledged as the supreme ruler whose imperial command prevailed in the whole of Jambudvīpa, extending southwards from Mt. Kailāsa in the Himalayan range at the foot of which was situated the Anotatta Lake or Mānas Sarovar[3],

---

[1] Dīpavamsa, XI. 39-9, Mahāvamsa, XI. 41 : puno pi abhisiñchimsu Lankāhitasukhe rataṃ ; Geiger, Mahāvaṃsa, English Transl., p. xxxii ; Raychaudhuri, op. cit., p. 143.

[2] Paranavitāna, in J.R. A. S., 1936, p. 445 f., seeks to establish that the so-called second coronation was the proper form of coronation by which Devānaṃpiya Tissa was installed as the first king of Ceylon, and that before him, the rulers of Ceylon, were not kings but leaders of the community deriving their authority from popular sanction.

[3] B-C-Law, India as described in the early texts of Buddhism and Jainism, p. 12,

in the aerial region above to a depth of one yojana, and in the nether region beneath to the same depth. In the language of the Divyāvadāna (p. 432), Aśoka became the Lord of Jambudvīpa (Jumbudvīpeśvara). The Pali Chronicles and the Samanta-pāsādikā give us but a legendary account of Jambudvīpa, as we shall see more of it in the next chapter, describing it as a subcontinent consisting of 84,000 towns, large and small, and ruled over by one thousand crowned subkings under Aśoka.

In the language of Aśoka's inscriptions, by his consecration king Priyadarśin gained unquestioned supremacy over an extensive domain (mahaṃte vijaye, mahālake vijite, R. E. XIV), and wielded moral and cultural influence over the whole of India (M.R.E.) as well as the territories of his five Greek contemporaries and allies ranging over a distance of 600 yojanas (R. E. XIII). Even in Aśoka's phraseology, the word sava-puthaviyaṃ (R. E. V, Dh) occurs as a variant of savata vijitasi, the whole of Aśoka's vijita together with the independent but friendly territories of the southern frontagers being commensurate with Jambudvīpa.

The Pali Chronicles and the Samanta-pāsādikā tell us nothing but the truth when they state that Aśoka's consecration took place in the city of Pāṭaliputra[1], otherwise called Pushpapura[2] or Kusumapura[3]. Aśoka himself in his R. E. V., speaks of Pāṭaliputra and outer towns, thereby corroborating the truth in Buddhist literary traditions.

Thus on the strength of all these data, gathered from Aśoka's own records as well as the Buddhist traditional accounts, particularly those in Pali, it is not difficult to establish that by the full epithet Piyadasi Lajā Māgadhe was meant that Aśoka was popularly known as 'the King of Magadha and Emperor of Jambudvīpa'.

2. **Conversion** : This word implies a change of faith, which is preceded by a change of heart. According to Buddhist literary traditions[2], the full effect of conversion did not take place until the complete transformation of Chaṇḍāśoka (Aśoka the Wicked) into

---

[1] Dīpavaṃsa, VI. 18, XI. 28, Samantn-pā., I, P. 93, Mahāvaṃsa, V. 39, V. 120, 212, et seq.

[2] Mahāvaṃsa, V. 189 :

Chaṇḍāsoko ti ñāyittha pure pāpena kammunā
Dhammāsoko 'ti ñāyittha pachchhā puññena kammunā.
Divyāvadāna. p. 382 ;
Chaṇḍāsokatvaṃ prāpya pūrvaṃ prithivyām
Dharmās'okatvaṃ karmaṇā tena lebhe.

Dharmāśoka (Aśoka the Pious). Such a transformation as this was the ripe result of an ideological change, of a strong mental resolve to lead a reformed life. It also implies the transfer of allegiance and moral and earthly support from one religious denomination or sect to another, and of adherence from one set of opinions to another. From the Buddhist point of view, it meant a triumph on the part of the Buddhist Sangha or Church of Pāṭaliputra in that its members succeeded in winning Aśoka over to their faith. In its technical sense, it meant no more than that Aśoka accepted the Upāsakatva ("Upāsakahood"), which is to say, the position of a Buddhist lay worshipper with the formal and open declaration on his part to the effect that he became a firm believer in the Triad consisting of the Master, the Doctrine, and the Order :

Ahaṃ Buddhañ cha Dhammañ cha Saṃghañ cha saraṇaṃgato
Upāsakattaṃ desemi Sakyaputtassa sāsane.

The Buddhist narratives in Pali and Sanskrit show an agreement in so far as these relate that Aśoka's first connection was not with the Sangha as a whole but only with an individual representative of it, whom he accidentally met and through whose instrumentality was effected his conversion. This individual representative, according to the Pali account, was a gifted novice called Nyagrodha, and the Venerable Samudra, according to the Divyāvadāna legend. Thus in the language of the Divyāvadāna (p. 380), the first profession of faith by Aśoka was expressed thus :

Daśabalasuta kshantum arhasi māṃ
kukṛitam idaṃ cha tavādya deśayāmi
śaraṇaṃ ṛishim upaimi, taṃ cha Buddhaṃ
guṇavaram āryaniveditaṃ cha dharmam.

Addressing Samudra, Aśoka said :

"I take refuge in (thee), the sage, and also in Buddha, the supreme embodiment of qualities as well as the Doctrine taught by the elect."

And in the language of the Dīpavaṃsa, VI. 55 :

Ajj'eva tumhe saraṇam upemi, Buddhañ cha
Dhammañ cha saraññañ cha Sanghaṃ
saputtadāro sahanāṭakajjano upāsakattaṃ
pativedayāmi taṃ.

Addressing the wise Nyagrodha, Aśoka said :

"This very day I accept as my refuge thee and the Buddha and the Doctrine and the Order, together with my wives and children, with my kith and kin. I declare to thee the fact of my having become a lay worshipper."

The general agreement between the two accounts may be shown to lie in the following points :

I) Predictions regarding Aśoka's great service to Buddhism.

2) Conversion of Aśoka to the Buddhist faith through the agency of an individual representative of the Sangha.

3) Aśoka's visit to the local monastery.

4) Collection of Buddha's relics from the pre-existing stūpas.

5) Erection of 84,000 vihāras with the dharmarājikās, one in each of the 84,000 towns in Jambudvīpa.

6) Transformation of Aśoka the Wicked into Aśoka the Pious.

7) Final acceptance by Aśoka of the guidance of the leading man of a Buddhist Fraternity or Church in religious matters.

The agent of Aśoka's conversion, as we noted, was the young but wise novice Nyagrodha, according to the Pali Chronicles, and the saintly Shavira Samudra, according to the Divyāvadāna.

The name of the existing local monastery of Pāṭaliputra was Kukkuṭārāma according to the Mahāvaṃsa,[1] and Kurkuṭārāma, according to the Divyāvadāna.[2] This earlier name of the monastery which was reconstructed afterwards by Aśoka is not met with in the Dīpavaṃsa and the Samanta-pāsādikā.

According to the Pali Chronicles[3] and Samanta-pāsādikā[4], Nyagrodha was instrumental in having replaced by 60,000 Buddhist monks the sixty thousand Brāhmans and Brahmanical ascetics who were daily fed from the royal kitchen prior to Aśoka's visit to the local monastery. According to the Divyāvadāna story, on the other hand, Sthavira Samudra mysteriously disappeared from the scene immediately after the king's profession of faith[5], and thereafter Aśoka visited the local monastery[6].

According to the Pali Chronicles[7] and Samanta-pāsādikā[8], Aśoka had not conceived the idea of erecting the 84,000 ārāmas or vihāras with the chaityas before he visited the local monastery, while, according to the Divyāvadāna story[9], he had made up his mind to erect

---

1 Mahāvaṃsa, V. 122.

2 Divyāvadāna, pp, 381, 384.

3 Dīpavaṃsa, VI. 56 ; Mahāvaṃsa, V. 73-4.

4 Samanta-pā., I, p. 48.

5 Divyāvadāna, p. 380 . sa bhikshu tad eva riddhyā prakrāntaḥ.

6 Ibid., p. 381.

7 Dīpavaṃsa, VI. 93-8, Mahāvaṃsa, V. 73 f.

8 Samanta-pā. I, p. 48.

9 Divyāvadāna, p. 381.

84,000 dharmarājikās even before that. According to both the traditions, however, he undertook to construct the edifices after his visit to the local monastery.

According to the Mahāvaṃsa Comentary,[1] Aśoka became notorious as Chaṇḍāsoka for having killed his ninety-nine half-brothers for the sake of the throne, while, according to the Divyāvadāna, for the beheading of 500 councillors by Aśoka with his own sword and the burning of 500 court ladies alive to death in his pleasance.[2] According to both the traditions, he came to be honoured as Dharmāśoka on account of his meritorious deeds, particularly the construction of 84,000 Buddhist chaityas or dharmarājikās.[3]

The greatest known personage of the Orthodox Church of the age was Māudgalīputra Tishya, according to the Pali tradition[4], and Upagupta, according to the Divyāvadāna story.[5] The guidance of the latter was badly needed for the restoration of the normal life of the Fraternity of the local monastery by turning out the disturbing elements who were really outsiders in a Buddhist garb,[6] and the latter was needed to act as the pilgrim's guide.[7]

The predictions mentioned in the Pali Chronicles, Commentaries, and Milindapañha regarding Aśoka and the expansion of Buddhism during his reign are four, and those mentioned in the Divyāvadāna are two. The four predictions in Pali are as follows :

1) That prince Piyadāsa (Priyadarśa, Priyadarśana) will be anointed as Aśoka 218 years after the Buddha's demise.[8]

2) That king Aśoka will in time collect the relics of the Buddha, deposited in one stūpa by Ajātaśatru, and spread them far and wide.[9]

3) That when 118 years after the session of the Second Buddhist Council the righteous king Aśoka will reign in Pāṭaliputra with his sovereignty established over the whole of Jambudvīpa and will, as a strong believer in Buddhism, greatly increase the gain and fame of the Buddhist Fraternity, the heretics, greedy of gain and fame, will

---

1 Vaṃsatthappakāsinī, I, p. 228 : abhisekato pubbekatena ekūnasatabhātughātakena lāmakakammunā Chaṇḍāsoko ti ñāyitthā..

2 Divyāvadāna. p. 373 f.

3 Ibid, p. 381 ; Mahāvaṃsa, V. 189.

4 Dīpavaṃsa, V. 55 f. ; Samanta-pā., I, p. 55 ; Mahāvaṃsa, VI. 100-2.

5 Divyāvadāna, p. 350.

6 Dīpavaṃsa, VII-VIII, Samanta-pā , I, p. 56f., Mahāvaṃsa, V. 246 et seq.

7 Divyāvadāna, p. 389.

8, 9 Sumangala-vilāsinī, II, p. 613 f.

surreptitiously enter into the Buddhist Order and raise commotion in it, propounding their own views, and to cope with it will appear the powerful leader Maudgalīputra Tishya and he will compile the Kathāvatthu.[1]

4) That in time to come, more accurately 236 years after the demise of the Buddha, Sthavira Mahendra will propagate the Buddhist faith in the island of Lankā.[2]

These are easily reducible to two, viz., one regarding Aśoka's reign and his rôle in the expansion of Buddhism, and the other about Maudgalīputra Tishya's advent and his part in the reformation of the Orthodox Church and the propagation of Buddhism. And these two predictions may be shown to correspond with the two mentioned in the Divyāvadāna, one regarding Aśoka, the other regarding Upagupta :

1) That when one hundred years after the Buddha's demise will the righteous king Aśoka reign in Pāṭaliputra as overlord of the earth extending as far as to the four seas, he will spread the bodily remains of the Buddha far and wide, and erect 84,000 dharmarājikās.[3]

2) That one hundred years after the Buddha's demise will Upagupta, son of Gandhika of Mathurā, do the work of Buddha (Buddha-kāryaṃ karishyati).[4]

In spite of the fact that the two narratives have several points in common between them, and that both allow miracle and poetic exaggeration and dramatic skill to have their full play in them, and both are vitiated by what Vincent Smith aptly calls *odium theologicum,* when tested by the data afforded by Aśoka's own inscriptions, the narrative in Pali cannot but appear to be comparatively more realistic and reliable, chronologically sounder and nearer the truth. The Sanskrit narrative oversteps the limit of truth and good sense when it speaks of the ugly appearance and fierce nature of Aśoka and presents a grotesque and gruesome episode of how Aśoka converted his royal pleasance into a place of terror, horror, oppression and tragic death of the unwary visitors and passers by through his agent Chaṇḍagirika. It has hopelessly erred on the matter of chronology when it places the reign of Aśoka and the advent of Upagupta as the accredited Buddhist leader of the time just a century after the Buddha's demise and represents the Venerable Yaśa as a contem-

---

[1] Dīpavaṃsa, V. 55 et seq. ; Samanta-pā., I, p. 55, Mahāvaṃsa, V. 100-2.

[2] Dīpavaṃsa, XII. 9f. ; Samanta-pā., I, pp. 71, 72.

[3] Divyavadāna, pp. 379, 385.

[4] Ibid, p. 350.

porary of Aśoka, evidently confounding Aśoka with Kālāśoka and distorting the Pali tradition about the Second Buddhist Council held at Vaiśālī under the presidentship of Revata and mainly through the instrumentality of Kākaṇḍakaputta Yasa.

A legend of Aśoka, such as one incorporated in the Divyāvadāna and still more exaggerated in the later poetical version of the Aśokāvadāna, found its place in the somewhat sober itinerary, Fo-kwo-ki, of Fa Hien who did not, however, commit himself to dates and names.[1] The full-fledged Divyāvadāna and similar other legends misled Hwen Thsang so far that while placing the reign of Aśoka in the hundredth year after the Nirvāṇa of the Tathāgata[2] he came to glibly represent Aśoka as the great-grandson of king Bimbisāra, evidently confounding Aśoka with Udāyibhadda of the Sāmaññaphala Sutta, Udaya of the Dīpavaṃsa, Udayabhaddaka of the Mahāvaṃsa, and Udayāśvā of the Vāyu Purāṇa, the son of Ajātaśatru and the grandson of Bimbisāra, who transferred his capital from Rājagṛiha to Pāṭaliputra.[3] The confusion of Mahendra, represented in the Pali tradition as the son of Aśoka by his Vaiśya wife Devī, with Aśoka's uterine brother Tishya or Vītaśoka is just another glaring instance of Hwen Thsang's misrepresentation and inaccuracy.[4]

Neither the earthly existence of Upagupta, a great Arhat, who is eulogised in high terms in the Divyāvadāna and Hwen Thsang's Si-yu-ki, nor that of Rādhasvāmī, a powerful Brāhman adherent and exponent of the Great Vehicle, who is extolled in Fa Hien's Fo-kwo-ki, is proved by any of the inscriptions of the Maurya age; that of Moggaliputta Tissa is proved, as will be shown further on.

It behoves us, therefore, to examine how far the Pali account of Aśoka's conversion and its sequel is consistent with the evidence of Aśoka's own records.

According to the Theravāda tradition, Aśoka's father Bindusāra was a votary of the Brāhmaṇs, and as such, he daily fed the Brāhmans and Brahmanical sects, the Paṇḍaranga Parivrājakas (Ash-bodied Wanderers) and the like, 60,000 in number. Aśoka, too, was doing the same by way of giving in his household the alms set up by his father. In doing so he, standing one day at the lion-gate of his palace, watched them while they were taking their meal, and disappointed by their

---

1 Beal, Buddhist Records, Vol. I, pp. lv-lviii, lxiii-lxvi.

2 Ibid, Vol. II, p. 85.

3 According to Oldenberg (Vinaya Piṭaka, Vol, I, Introd., p. xxxii), the king referred to is not Dharmās'oka.

4 Beal, Buddhist Records, Vol. II, pp. 91f.

ugly manners and gluttonous habits, thought to himself, "Such alms should be given in a proper place (to deserving persons), on due examination." Thereupon he asked his courtiers to bring in the religionists, namely, the S'ramaṇas and the Brāhmaṇas, whom they held in their high esteem, so that he might make gifts to them. The courtiers brought in severally the Paṇḍaranga Parivrājakas, the Ājīvikas, the Nirgranthas, and the rest, informing the king that they were their arahants (worthy saints). Thereupon the king had arranged for different kinds of seats for them, and as they came in, requested them to take the seats befitting them. Some of them sat on gentle seats, some on seats made of pieces of wood. Having noticed this, he came to understand that they had no substance in them (n'atthi tesaṃ antosāro) and let them off after having given them hard and soft food to eat. Thus the king for the first three years of his abhisheka adhered to other religious orders and sects who were out of the fold of Buddhism (abhisekaṃ pāpuṇitvā tīṇi saṃvachchharāni bāhirakapāsaṇḍaṃ parigaṇhi).[1]

It was in the fourth year of his abhisheka that Aśoka professed his faith in Buddha's system (chatutthe saṃvachchhare Buddhasāsane pasīdi). Nyagrodha established the king together with his people and courtiers in the Three Refuges and Five Precepts, established him indeed in the firm faith of a common believer in Buddha's system (Buddhasāsane pothujjanikena pasādena achalappasādaṃ katvā patiṭṭhāpesi).[2]

Thereafter the king having made one day a large gift at the local monastery, was seated in the midst of 60,000 monks, and providing the Fraternity with the four requisites, enquired of them, saying, "How much is the Doctrine propounded by the Master ?" "From the point of view of types, O great king ! it comprises nine types (navangaṃ), and from the point of view of sections (khandhas), it consists of 84,000 sections." Pleased to get this information about the Doctrine, the king made up his mind to erect a vihāra in honour of each section of it, and ordered his officers to erect a vihāra at each of the 84,000 towns of Jambudvīpa, himself undertaking to erect at Pāṭaliputra the great monastery named Aśokārāma after him. The Fraternity appointed the capable Thera Indragupta to guide and supervise the construction work of those vihāras which was started on one and the same day and completed in three years' time, costing him ninety-six

[1] Samanta-pā., I, p. 44.

[2] Ibid., I, p. 45f.

crores. Each monastery was provided with a chaitya (shrine) for the purpose of worship (chaturasīti-vihāra-sahassāni kārāpesi chaturasīti-sahassa-chetiya-patimaṇḍitāni).[1] The chaityas then built up along with the vihāras were no other than dhātu-chaityas or what the Divyāvadāna calls dharmarājikās [2] and Hwen Thsang stūpas[3].

The Dīpavaṃsa account of Aśoka's conversion, which is presupposed by the Samanta-pāsādikā, the Mahāvaṃsa, and the Divyāvadāna is not only the earliest known but the very best for comparison with Aśoka's own records concerning the subject.

According to the Dīpavaṃsa, as we noted, the conversion of Aśoka meant just the acceptance on his part of the position of an upāsaka (upāsakatta) with an open declaration of his faith in the Triad.[4] Buddhaghosa is right in suggesting that thereby Aśoka was not only established in the Three Refuges but also in the Five Precepts of conduct (tīsu saraṇesu pañchasu cha sīlesu),[5] which is to say that he became a firm believer in Buddha's sāsana[6] or Saddhamma (the Good Faith).

Aśoka's position as an upāsaka is corroborated by his own statement in the M. R. E., particularly in its three Mysore copies: Ya hakaṃ upāsake. It is borne out also by the evidence of the Bhābru Edict in which Aśoka has addressed the Sangha in the capacity of "Priyadarśin the King of Magadha" and which is to say, as a lay worshipper. In this edict Aśoka has declared his sincere faith in and deep veneration for the Triad: "It is known to you, Venerable Sirs, how far (goes) my veneration for and sincere faith in the Buddha, the Doctrine and the Order."

The tradition stating that he was established also in the precepts of moral conduct (sīlesu) is borne out by his own exhortation: dhaṃmamhi sīlamhi tisṭaṃto, "taking stand on piety and morality" (R. E. IV). His strong faith in Buddha's Doctrine is equally borne out by his pronouncement: "All that is said by Buddha the Blessed One is well said" (Bhābru).

According to the Dīpavaṃsa account, when Nyagrodha was asked

---

1 Ibid., I, p. 48f.

2 Divyāvadāna, p. 381.

3 Beal, Buddhist Records, II, p. 89,

4 Dīpavaṃsa, VI. 55, XII. 5.

5,6 Samanta-pā.. I, p. 48.

by the king to acquaint him with the fundamental tenet of Buddhism as he knew it, he based his reply on the under-quoted verse :

Appamādo amatapadaṃ, pamādo machchuno padaṃ ।
appamattā na mīyanti, ye pamattā yathā matā ॥[1]

"Earnestness is the way to immortality, lethargy the way to death. The earnest do not die, the indolent are like the dead".

The Dīpavaṃsa does not name the text from which the above verse was cited ; the Samanta-pāsādikā does.[2] But it was a very faithful and correct representation of Buddha's Doctrine when the king was told that apramāda was the root principle or basic idea of Buddha's teachings.[3]

As employed in the Dhammapada and other Canonical texts, appamāda is just another word for uṭṭhāna, viriya, purisa-kāra, purisa-parakkama, all signifying a life of exertion or strenuous effort.

There is nothing to be astonished at that the reply of Nyagrodha made an immediate and lasting appeal to Aśoka who has laid so much stress in his inscriptions on the self-same principle of action, his own words for it being usṭāna (R. E. VI), uyāma (R. E. XIII), usāha (P. F. I), pakama (M. R. E.), and parākrama (R. E. X).

Hultzsch and Bhandarkar rightly maintain that in all the three Mysore versions of M. R. E., Aśoka has given but an account of his religious career as an upāsaka during a short period of upwards of two years and a half and discriminated within it two successive stages, the earlier one characterised by less activity and the later one by vigorous activity. But in its remaining versions, the account given is one of a period of upwards of three years and a half, discriminating two stages, the earlier one of less activity covering upwards of two years and a half (sātirekāni aḍhatiyāni vasāni), and the later one of greater activity covering upwards of one year (saṃvachhare sātireke). As regards the second stage, all the versions show a complete agreement.

According to the remaining versions, in the first stage he remained a mere upāsaka, and in the second, by inplication, he became an upāsaka who went to meet, approach, or wait upon the Sangha, in

[1] Dīpavaṃsa, VI. 52-3.

[2] Samanta-pā,, I, p. 47, cf. Mahāvṃsa, V. 68.

[3] Dīpavaṃsa, VI. 54 : ye kechi sabbaññubuddha-desitā sabbesaṃ dhammānaṃ imassa mūlakā. Cf. Aṅguttara-N.. I, p. 17 : Nāhaṃ. bhikkhave, aññaṃ ekadhammaṃ samanupassāmi yo evàṃ saddhammassa ṭhitiyā ...... saṃvattati ; also, ibid, p. 16 yam evaṃ mahato atthāya saṃvattati. Here appamāda stands for viriyārambha or energetic action.

a literal rendering of his expression—saṃghe upayīte. Having failed to ascertain what Aśoka had precisely meant by this expression, some of the scholars have been inclined to suggest that he assumed, for the time being at least, the vows of a monk ; partly placing their reliance on the testimony of the Chinese pilgrim I-tsing who witnessed an image of Aśoka dressed in the garb of a monk[1] ; some, that he came to stay for the time being in a monastery, taking up the position of a bhikkhugatika (bhikshu-like religieux), though not exactly that of a bhikkhu.

As for I-tsing's testimony, it deserves no credence, first, because it is of a much later age, and secondly, because it is of a doubtful nature. Happily for us, the Dīpavaṃsa employs Aśoka's expression as well as tells us in clear terms what it actually signified. Sabbe saṃghaṃ upayantu, "All of you go to the Sangha." By this he wanted all of his household and capital to go to meet or wait upon the Śangha (gachchhantu saṃghadassanaṃ. ib , VI. 68). It is clear then that by his statement, yaṃ mayā saṃghe upayīte, Aśoka just wanted to say, "when the Saṅgha was met or waited upon by him".

Prior to this, the king said to Thera Nyagrodha,

.........ichchhāmi saṃgharatanassa dassanaṃ
samāgamaṃ sannipatanti yāvatā abhivādayāmi,
suṇāmi dhammaṃ. [2]

"I desire to see the revered Sangha. I will pay homage to as many (bhikshus) as they meet together in an assembly, (and) hear (from them all about) the Doctrine."

The Dīpavaṃsa in detail[3] and the later Pali accounts in substance set forth the significance of Aśoka's phrase—saṃghe upayīte. It is to be noted that they nowhere suggest that Aśoka either assumed the vows of a monk or resided in a monastery as a bhikshu-like religieux.

We should also note that the mode of meeting the Sangha as described in the Dīpavaṃsa is almost literally the same as expressed in the Bhābru Edict : Priyadasi lājā Māgadhe saṃghe abhivādetūnaṃ āha : apābadhataṃ cha phāsuvihālataṃ cha.

"The Magadhan king Priyadarśin having saluted the Order, said : (I wish you) health and welfare."

---

1. On this point, see J. R. A. S., 1908, p. 496f.
2. Dīpavaṃsa, VI. 58.
3. Ibid, VI. 60-96.

The tradition of Aśoka's intimate acquaintance with Buddha's Doctrine is also borne out by the evidence of the Bhābru Edict and textual quotation in R. E. IX—asti pi ti vutaṃ.

We have still to discuss and settle what precisely Aśoka meant when he said, "while I was an upāsaka", whether during a period of nearly three years or during a period of nearly four years.

In Buddhist literature in general, and in the Pali Canon in particular, the word upāsaka denotes a lay disciple or worshipper of Buddha. By upāsakatva the Dīpavaṃsa definitely means Aśoka's position as a Buddhist layman. The same is undoubtedly the case with the Bhābru Edict in which the word upāsaka and its feminine form upāsikā apply exclusively to the lay worshippers of Buddha, male and female respectively. The Rūpnāth and Maski variants, pakāsa sake (Hultzsch's prakāsa sake) and budhaśake, taken uncritically and at their face values, are evidently in support of this Buddhist technical sense of the word upāsaka. But seen critically, in writing vasāni pāsake in the Rūpnāth text, the scribe has written va pākāsa sake ; in the Maski copy, he has by mistake written budhaśake for upāsake.

The Pali tradition leads us to explain Aśoka's statement in his M. R. E. either as meaning that he has sought to distinguish between the two stages of his career as a lay worshipper of Buddha, the first stage when he was a devotee of an individual member of the Sangha under whose personal influence he accepted the position of a Buddhist layman, and the second stage when he met the local sangha as a whole; or as meaning that he has just intended to distinguish between these two stages, the first, when he remained a lay adherent of the religious sects outside the Buddhist fold (bāhirakapāsaṇḍaṃ pariganhi, itobahiddhā pāsaṇḍā), and the second, when he took the Sangha to be his guide in religious matters, which is to say, when he was fully converted to the Buddhist faith, having transferred his allegiance from other religious Orders to the Buddhist Church.

The cogency of the second interpretation depends on the soundness of the following arguments :

(1) That though in the Pali Canon the word upāsaka has a restricted use and the word sāvaka is used instead to denote a Jaina layman, in the Jaina Āgama itself the word is freely amployed to mean a Jaina or an Ājīvika layman.

(2) That this interpretation is in accord with the Pali tradition stating that in the first stage of his religious career Aśoka remained a lay adherent of other religious sects.

(3) That the Dīpavaṃsa introduces other religionists and religious sects almost in the same way as that in which Aśoka has done :

Dīpavaṃsa, VI. 26 :

Nigaṇṭhāchelaka ch'eva itarā Paribbājakā ı
itarā Brāhmaṇā 'ti cha aññe cha puthuladdhikā ıı

Ibid, VII. 35, 38.

Pabhinnalābhasakkārā titthiyā puthuladdhikā ı
Paṇḍaranga Jaṭilā cha Nigaṇthāchelākādikā ıı
Ājīvakā aññaladdhikā nānā ... ... ı

R. E. XIII :

Bramaṇa va śramaṇa va aṃñe va prashaṃḍa grahatha va.

P. E. VII :

Pavajitānaṃ cheva gihithānaṃ cha sava-(pāsaṃ)ḍesu...
Bābhanesu Ājīvikesu pi...Nigaṇṭhesu pi.

(4) That the Dipavaṃsa account stating that Aśoka not only made a great gift to them but discussed with them the question of higher religious experience may be substantiated by Aśoka's own statements in R. E. XII.

The point which really goes against this interpretation is that Aśoka nowhere in his inscriptions gives us to understand that his Buddhist faith stood in the way of honouring other sects, whether of ascetics or of householders, with gifts and various other modes of honouring. discussing the problems of religion with them, as well as listening to their doctrines and views from time to time. On the other hand, he tells us in his R. E. XII that he continued to honour them with gifts and various other modes of honouring (sava-pāsaṃḍāni pūjayati dānena cha vividhāya cha pūjāya).

As for the first interpretation, I may observe that Rhys Davids has wrongly accused Aśoka of the economy of candour, since it is not true that Aśoka has not given credit to others for his conversion to the Buddhist faith and its sequel. Otherwise his statement, "when the Sangha was met by me", would be altogether meaningless. We cannot deny the reasonableness of the tradition stating that previous to his introduction to and meeting with the congregation of monks of the local monastery he accidentally met an individual member of it, whose saintliness and profoundness deeply impressed him, and, as a matter of fact, it was his personal charm that first attracted the king and induced him to embrace the Buddhist faith, no matter whether that individual was Nyagrodha or Samudra.

But to say with the Pali chronicler that a novice of seven years of natural age like Nyagrodha was the person to convert Aśoka is certainly to go too far to bank on the reader's credulity. Bhandarkar rightly poohpoohs this puerile suggestion. One must not for that reason deny the truth of the story in its substance. The Nyagrodha story, as met with in the Dīpavaṃsa, is not of so miraculous a character as in its Samanta-pāsādikā or Mahāvaṃsa version. And strangely enough, in the Samanta-pāsādikā Nyagrodha has been represented in the same breath as a novice (sāmaṇera) as well as an elder (thera). In the Dīpavaṃsa, however, he has been systemtically represented as a full-fledged recluse (samaṇa) or an elder (thera) who, though young (taruṇa, kumāraka), was an Arhat, full of wisdom and virtue, and fully conversant with the then known Buddhist Canon.[1] Over and above this, Nyagrodha is nowhere connected with the elder step-brother of Aśoka who was killed by him. The Dīpavaṃsa speaks indeed of a Nyagrodha who was initiated in the third year of Aśoka's abhisheka (tīṇi-vassamhi).[2] But he might have been altogether a different personality.

As regards the periods of time during which the two stages of Aśoka's religious life leading to his conversion to the Buddhist faith vere gone through, an agreement may be shown to exist between the traditional account and Aśoka's own. The difficulty lies in harmonizing the traditional chronology with that which is suggested in the inscriptions.

The main drawback of the traditional narratives is that they have nothing to say about the Kalinga war which was waged in the 8th year of abhisheka and marked the real turning point in Aśoka's life and career (R. E. XIII). Neither coercion nor temptation was a a factor in Aśoka's conversion. Nor was it again an ordinary kind of conversion. If we can take him at his own word, as we should, the profound reflections on the after-effects of the aggressive war waged against Kalinga served to produce in him an ardent desire or intense longing for piety (tivre dhaṃmavāye dhaṃmakāmatā) and imparting instructions in piety (dhaṃmānusathi). He felt remorse for the violence, death, separation, and sufferings caused to the

---

[1] Dīpavaṃsa, VI. 34-57.

[2] Ibid, VI. 18 : abhisitto tīṇi vassāni pasanno Buddhasāsane.

population of Kalinga. But that which was a matter of deeper regret was that the cause of culture greatly suffered thereby. By those reflections he perceived the truth and came to certain definite conclusion as to what ahould be the principle of action and what the ideal of conduct and of duty. It dawned on his consciousness that the conquest by piety far outweighs the conquest by force in its sffect and importance and that the lower instincts and brutal passions should be controlled and the higher principles of ethics and piety should be followed.

Thus his mind was in readiness to grasp at once the meaning and appreciate the significance of Buddha's Doctrine which he readily accepted as he found that it wholly tallied with his own inner perception and vision. His own account of his conversion must therefore be connected with the instructive account of his change of heart and outlook. In other words, we have to assume that his conversion to the Buddhist faith did not take place before but sometime after the conclusion of the Kalinga war and the annexation of Kalinga to his dominions. The question is how long after that ?

The pilgrimage to Sambodhi (the sacred spot of the Bo-tree) which was undertaken by Aśoka in the tenth year of his abhisheka (R. E. VIII) may be construed as an immediate result of his conversion to Buddhism. The interval of time which elapsed between this pilgrimage and the annexation of Kalinga in the eighth year of abhisheka which is apparently two years, might be really upwards of two years and a half. The Pali tradition gives us a graphic description of Aśoka's pilgrimage to Mahābodhi, which goes to indicate that it was as grand an affair as his first visit to the local congregation of monks. It assigns this, however, to a later year of Aśoka's reign, and its purpose, too, differs from that of Aśoka's pilgrimage to Sambodhi as stated in R. E. VIII.

3. **Accession** : The Pali Chronicles definitely state that Aśoka's consecration was preceded by his accession to the throne of Magadha through a fratricidal war in which he came out as the victor. The Samantapāsādikā tells us the same story of his coming to power. It is said that he killed all of his ninety-nine half-brothers but spared the life of his uterine brother Tissa-Vītsoka, according to the Pali legend. Sumana (Susīma, according to the Divyāvadāna story) was not only the eldest of Aśoka's step-brothers but eldest

also among all the sons of Bindusāra,[1] one hundred and one in number, and entitled accordingly to succeed his father. As an unanointed ruler, Prince Priyadarśana reigned for four years, after which he was anointed as Aśoka. It was on account of the sin committed through fratricide indeed that he had passed as Chaṇḍāśoka (Aśoka the Wicked), according to the Mahāvaṃsa and its Commentary, before his soul was regenerated through his conversion to Buddhism and meritorious deeds. The Samanta-pāsādikā and the Mahāvāṃsa have, moreover, used the earlier tradition of the fratricide on the part of Aśoka as the peg for connecting with it the episode of the novice Nyagrodha, represented as a posthumous son of Sumana.

The Divyāvadāna story, too, speaks of Aśoka's coming into power through a fratricidal war ending in the defeat and death of his elder step-brother Susīma who was by his seniority as well as his father's choice entitled to the throne, but does not specify any period of time which elapsed between his accession and consecration. Thus according to both the traditions, Aśoka was no better than a usurper of his father's throne. The two traditions show an agreement when they state that he seized the opportunity created by his father's old age and illness.

For the story of Aśoka's accession we have to depend entirely on the Buddhist traditional accounts. There is not the slightest hint in Aśoka's inscriptions as to the fratricidal war and its results save and except that they insist throughout on the practice of respectful attention to parents but nowhere expressly on that of respectful attention to elder brothers. But this is just an *argumentum ex silentio*, which is inconclusive. Whilst giving the chronological succession of the Maurya rulers, the Purāṇas do not suggest any interim period during which Aśoka reigned as an unanointed ruler between the termination of the reign of Bindusāra and his consecration.[2]

If the Buddhist traditions be true, none but his uterine brother of Aśoka, Tishya or Vītaśoka, was alive after his accession and during

[1] Mahāvaṃsa, V. 38 :
Bindusārassa puttānaṃ sabbesaṃ jeṭṭhabhātuno ।
Sumanssa kumārassa ॥
The Dīpavaṃsa, however, does not mention the name of Sumana, nor does it represent Nyagrodha as his posthumous son.

[2] Pargiter, The Purāṇa Text of the Dynasties of the Kali Age, pp. 27, 70.

his reign, all of his step-brothers having been previously killed by him. Vincent Smith has challenged their truth by the evidence of R. E. V, in which Aśoka speaks of the households of his brothers (bhātinaṃ cha me), and not of that of a single brother whose life was spared by him.

There is much to be said, no doubt, in favour of this contention, but, strictly speaking, Aśoka's statement concerning his brothers constitutes at the most a presumptive evidence. As I have sought to maintain, "The households of Aśoka and those of his brothers, sisters and other kith and kin, situated in Pāṭaliputra and outlying towns, are mentioned in R. E. V in connection with the distribution of charities, and the same as to his sons and other princes of the blood royal mentioned in P. E. VII. Unless his brothers were then alive, at least some of them, and held important positions, it would be difficult to account for the prominence accorded to them···It is, of course, quite possible to speak of the households of one's brothers even when they are all dead and gone. What is more probable in the circumstances is that at the time of promulgation of R. E. V his brothers were still the recognised heads of their households, not their sons."[1]

4. **Viceroyalty :** The Pali Chronicles speak not only of Aśoka's accession preceding his consecration but also of his viceroyalty preceding his accession. The Pali tradition connects his viceroyalty with Ujjeni. The Divyāvadāna does not precisely speak of the system of viceroyalty. All that it has got to say is that Aśoka was deputed once by his father to Takshaśilā to suppress a revolt of the people of the frontier province, which was really directed against the highhanded officers, and not against the king himself.[2] Subsequently on receiving the news of popular risings in the same frontier province his father desired him to proceed again to Takshaśilā, but Bindusāra's ministers who were displeased with his elder step-brother, Susīma, and wanted to keep him away from the capital, made a contrivance to depute him instead of Aśoka.[3] It was rather a military expedition directed to Takshaśilā or province of Gandhāra than viceroyalty.

---

[1] Inscriptions of Asoka, II, p. 281. Mookerji (Asoka, p. 5) pertinently observes : "Strictly speaking, we cannot positively state from this passage which refers to the existence of the harems of his brothers and sisters that the brothers were living at this time. But the fact of Asoka's affection for his brothers and sisters and their families...can be positively asserted from this passage".

[2],[3] Divyāvadāna, p. 371 f.

According to the Dīpavaṃsa, Bindusāra appointed his son, Prince Priyadarśana, to rule Ujjeni or the province of Avantī, "charged with the collection of revenue" (Ujjeni-kara molī).[1] The designation, Karamolī, may be taken also to mean "one entitled to enjoy the revenue of the province." In the language of the Mahāvaṃsa, he was offered by his father the kingdom of Avantī to enjoy almost as an independent ruler :

> Avanti-raṭṭhaṃ bhuñjanto pitarā dinnam attano ।
> so Asoka-kumāro hi Ujjeni-nagaraṃ purā ॥[2]

The Samantapāsādikā has a slightly differet story to tell us, namely, that the kingdom of Ujjeni was annexed by him (attanā laddhaṃ Ujjeni-rajjaṃ). If so, the case would seem analogous to that of Prince Bimbisāra who was appointed the viceroy of Anga by his father when he had conquered and annexed it permanently to the kingdom of his father. The story of conquest of Avantī by Prince Priyadarśana is not, however, supported by the Pali Chronicles.

All the Pali accounts agree in so far as they relate that he ruled over Avantī as a viceroy for eleven years, and that while still the viceroy of Avanti, he hurried back to Pāṭaliputra to seize the throne as soon as he received the news of his father's serious illness.

The possibility of his having been appointed by his father the viceroy of Ujjeni or deputed as a royal military leader to Takshaśilā is evident from Aśoka's S. R. E. I, which speaks of three Kumāra Viceroys, one stationed at Ujeni, one at Takasilā, and one at Tosali.

5. **Early Life, parentage, brothers and sisters :** The inscriptions of Aśoka throw no light on his early life and parentage. His brothers and sisters along with other kith and kin find mention in R. E. V in connection with the distribution of charities from their households by the Dharmamahāmātras. Aśoka introduces them in such a manner as to suggest that they were persons who ranked with him in family relationship, and that they had their family establishments in Pāṭaliputra and outlying towns.

The Pali tradition speaks of just one sister of Aśoka to whose son, Prince Agnibrahmā, was married his daughter Sanghamitrā and to whom she bore a son called Sumana.

The Pali Chronicles expressly tell us that king Bindusāra married sixteen wives by whom he had one hundred and one sons. Amongst

---

[1] Dīpavaṃsa, VI. 15.

[2] Mahāvaṃsa, XIII. 8.

them, Aśoka was second to none but Sumana, the eldest of all. The Divyāvadāna names the eldest son of Bindusāra as Susīma.

Aśoka's only uterine brother was Tishya who is called Vigataśoka or Vītaśoka in the Divyāvadāna,[1] and Sudatta or Sugātra in some Chinese works.[2] The Theragāthā contains two psalms, one attributed to the Thera Ekavihāriya and the other to another Thera named Vītasoka.[3] The scholiast Dhammapāla identifies Ekavihāriya with Aśoka's brother Tishya and the second Thera with Aśoka's another brother Vītasoka, and represents them as two different individuals.[4] This identification is not at all borne out by the earlier Canonical legends in the book of Apadāna,[5] and may therefore be dismissed as pure invention.

According to the Pali narrative, when Aśoka seized the throne of Magadha, taking advantage of his father's old age and illness, his ninety-nine step-brothers made a common cause with Sumana-Susīma who was the rightful heir to the throne and were all slain with him. The Tibetan historian Tāranātha "makes Asoka kill only six brothers" while in the Divyāvadāna the fratricidal battle is described as one fought only between Susīma-Sumana and Aśoka. Susīma's defeat was mainly due to the lack of support from the ministers of his father who were all up against him. The substance of truth in these legends seems to be that Aśoka's succession was a disputed one,[6] which, however, has no corroboration from his records.

The evidence of Aśoka's inscriptions may be construed in a sense to run counter to the trend of the Buddhist stories. In R. E. V, engraved not later than the 13th or 14th year of abhisheka, Aśoka mentions their brothers as having their family establishments in Pāṭaliputra and outlying towns. On the other hand, in P. E. VII, engraved in the 27th year of abhisheka, he replaces his brothers by other princes of the blood royal (devikumālānaṃ) ranking with his sons in family relationship. The inference which may reasonably be drawn from this is that in the course of thirteen years his brothers either died or retired from the world.

According to Pali legends, Aśoka appointed his uterine brother

---

[1] Divyāvadāna, pp. 370, 309, Mookerji, Asoka, p. 3.

[2] Mookerji, op. cit., p. 5.

[3] Mrs. Rhys Davids, Psalms of the Early Buddhists, p. 133.

[4] Mookerji, op. cit., p. 8

[5] Apadāna, XI, p. 390, No. XLIV. It knows of no thera by the name of Vītasoka

[6] Mookerji, op. cit., p. 4.

Tishya-Vītaśoka as uparājā or vice-regent. After Tishya had joined the Buddhist Order, the offer went to Aśoka's nephew and son-in-law Agnibrahmā, and when he too joined forthwith the Buddhist Order in the fourth year of Aśoka's abhisheka, the office of the vice-regent went abegging.

If reliance be placed upon the Pali accouut, there was no brother of Aśoka left after the 4th year of his abhisheka to function as his viceroy. But the preamble or forwarding note of the three Isila or Northern Mysore versions of M. R. E., probably engraved not earlier than the 26th year of abhisheka, seems to suggest that the fact was otherwise. The Isila copy of the edict in question was to be forwarded to the Mahāmātras of the place under the authority of the Ārypaputra and the Mahāmātras stationed at Suvarṇagiri, which was evidently the head-quarters of the southern viceroy. If the forwarding note of the Isila versions were despatched by Aśoka, as seems more probable, by Āryaputra (Ayaputa) Aśoka could not but have meant a brother of his. If locally drafted at Suvarṇagiri, as would seem less likely, by Āryaputra one must understand just a son of Aśoka.

As for Aśoka's early life, the Buddhist story as narrated in the Dīpavaṃsa has nothiug to say beyond the fact that he was the second son of Bindusāra and a grandson of Chandragupta of the Maurya family, or that his personal name was Priyadarśana, meaning "one of amiable mien", "one whose handsome appearance was comparable to that of the moon". According to the same authority, Aśoka and Priyadarśin were the names or titles assumed by Priyadarśana at the time of his two consecrations. The Divyāvadāna story, on the contrary, says that Aśoka was the name of the prince given him by his father at the instance of his mother. Furthermore, the Sanskrit legend goes to represent him as a person of ugly appearance and fierce nature evidently to build thereupon the grotesque and repulsive story of how he came to pass as Aśoka the Wicked.

The earlier Pali account, met with whether in the Dīpavaṃsa or in the Samanta-pāsādikā and Mahāvaṃsa, is silent on Aśoka's mother. The Mahāvaṃsa-ṭīkā introduces us for the first time to his mother Dharmā (Pali Dhammā) who was a princess from the Maurya clan of Kshatriyas (Moriyavaṃsajā) and whose family preceptor was an Ājīvika named Janasāna, Jarasāna or Jarasona. She is represented as the chief queen of Bindusāra. She is called Subhadrāngī

[1] Barua, Inscriptions, ii, p. 221.

in the Avadānamālā. The Divyāvadāna story does not name her but certainly represents her as "the beautiful daughter of a Brāhman of Champā." Jealous of her excessive beauty. the queens of Bindusāra made her do the work of a female barber. Highly pleased with her work, the king granted her a boon, which she availed of by asking him to marry her. Satisfied with her social position which she disclosed, the king made her his chief queen. The Divyāvadāna legend, too, associates an Ājīvaka named Pingalavatsa with Aśoka's mother. Precisely as in the Pali story, Aśoka received him with due honour when his prediction about his succession came true.

In the Mahāvaṃsa-ṭikā, Bindusāra's mother is said to have been Chandragupta's eldest maternal uncle's daughter whom he married.

The tradition is a late one and of a very doubtful character. It is very strange indeed that none of the Indian legends says anything of the daughter of Seleukos Nikator who gave her in marriage to Chandragupta to make a matrimonial alliance with him. It would have been a more interesting fact, if Bindusāra were represented as a son of Chandragupta by his Greek wife.

6. **Predecessors and pedigree** : Aśoka, in his P. E. VII, speaks of the former kings who had reigned in the long past and during several centuries, who too were the sincere well-wishers of their subjects, and by whom too various public works of a philanthropic nature were done. He introduces them, however, just to throw into bold relief the ineffectiveness of the means and methods adopted by them, the insufficiency of the results obtained, and the lesser value of the works done as compared and contrasted with those adopted, obtained and done by him. Similar deficiencies are pointed out also in his R. E. IV-VI.

Whom did he mean by these predecessors ? Such expressions of his as atikaṃtaṃ (in the long past), bhutapuve (formerly) and bahuni vāsa-satāni (during many hundred years) correspond to such introductory Jātaka phrases as atīte (in the past) and bhūtapubbaṃ (bhūtapūrvam, "formerly"). Going by this correspondence, one cannot but take it that Aśoka had within his mental purview rather the legendary monarchs noted for their righteous rule and noble deeds, such as those extolled in the Brāhmaṇas, Āraṇyakas and Upanishads, the Sanskrit Epics, and the Canonical texts of the Jainas and Buddhists.

Aśoka's predecessors in the Magadha line of kings belonged to five royal dynastfes, to wit, (1) the Bārhadratha or Bṛihādratha,[1] (2) the Haryanka,[2] (3) the Śaiśunāga or Śiśunāga,[3] (4) the Nanda, and (5) the Maurya (Pali Moriya).

The Bārhadratha dynasty founded by Bṛihadratha, son of Vasu Uparichara of the Chedi race and father of Jarāsandha of the Great Epic fame, came to an end in the 6th century B. C.,[4] prior to the rise of Buddhism. The founding of the hill-girt city of Girivraja or Rājagṛiha is the notable work of this dynasty.[5]

The Bārhadratha dynasty was followed at about the rise of Buddhism by the Haryanka, which latter is said to have come to an end seventytwo years after the Buddha's demise (c. 416 or 415 B.C.). Bimbisāra,[6] Ajātaśatru[7] and Udaya[8] are the three successive rulers of this dynasty who are noted in history. Amongst them, Bimbisāra deserves to be honoured not only as the real founder of the Haryanka dynasty but also as that of the imperial power of Magadha. The Pali Nikāyas credit him with the creation of some permanent land-endowments and royal fiefs (rājadeyyaṃ brahmadeyyaṃ) in favour of certain Vedic colleges[9] in his dominions[10]. He is also known as the builder and donor of the Veṇuvana monastery at Rājagṛiha dedicated to the Buddha and his followers which was the first Buddhist monastery in India. He lent the service of his court-physician, Jīvaka, to the Sangha and befriended the Buddha and his followers in various ways. He allowed his talented queen Kshemā to become a bhishuṇī. It was indeed during his reign and in his dominions that many new movements of religious thought were

---

[1] Mahābhārata, I. 63-30 ; Pargiter, Purāṇa Text, p. 14.

[2] In As'vaghosha's Buddhacharita (XI. 2) indeed Bimbisāra is described as a scion of the Haryanka-kula, Raychaudhuri, op. cit, p. 18.

[3] Purāṇas wrongly apply the name of S'ais'unāgas or S'is'unāgas to the kings of the Haryanka family, while the Pali Chronicles definitely state that Sisunāga was the first king of the dynasty by which the Haryanka was the replaced by the people.

[4],[5] Raychaudhuri, op. cit., p. I 66.

[6] The alternative spelling of the name, as met with in the Lalitavistara, is Bimbasāra, The Jaina spelling is Bhimbasāra.

[7] He is called Kūṇiya or Koṇiya in the Jaina Agama texts.

[8] Also known by the name of Udāyibhadra, Udaya, Udayabhadra, and Udayās'va ; Udadhi in the Garga Saṃhitā.

[9] Mahāsālā, better Nahātaka-sālā (Snātaka-s'ālā) as they are called in the Mahāgovinda Suttanta, Dīgha, II.

[10] e.g., one under Kūṭadanta at Khānumata near Rājagaha, and the other under Sonadaṇḍa at Champā.

started and fostered.[1] In these respects, the name of his great contemporary, Prasenajit of Kośala, is equally noteworthy.

Ajātaśatru paved really the way for a further extension of the supremacy of Magadha in Northern India.[2] It is evident from the Sāmaññaphala Sutta that he occassionally met the well-known religious teachers and leading thinkers of the time to discuss the problem of importance. Later Buddhist traditions credit him with the extension of patronage to the Buddhist Theras when they met at Rājagṛiha to hold the First Buddhist Council,[3] as well as with the erection of a memorable stūpa at a suburb of Rājagṛiha for the preservation of the bodily remains of the Buddha collected from the stūpas erected by others. The Jainas claim that he greatly honoured Mahāvīra and his doctrine.[4]

Ajātaśatru's son and successor,[5] Udāyi, is said to have transferred his capital from Rājagṛiha to Pāṭaliputra, [6] definitely in the fourth year of his reign, according to the Purāṇas.[7]

The Mañjuśrī-mūlakalpa would in vain have us believe that he committed the Words of Buddha to writing,[8] though it may be true, as suggested, that he was able to effect a further extension of the supremacy of Magadha.[9]

Even as regards Udāyi's grandson, Muṇḍa, it is stated in the Anguttara Nikāya[10] and its Commentary that deeply grieved at the death of his beloved queen, Bhadrā, he sought solace through

---

1 For details see Barua's A History of pre-Buddhistic Indian Philosophy, Secs. III & IV.

2 Mañjus'rī-mūlakalpa, V. 322 (Text edited by K. P. Jayaswal), restricts Ajātas'atru's suzerainty to Anga-Magadha :

> Yāvādad-Anga-paryantaṃ Vārāṇasyām-atatparam ।
> uttareṇa tu Vais'ālyāṃ rājā so 'tha mahābalaḥ ॥

3 Dīgha-N., II, p. 86f., Vinaya-Piṭaka, I, p. 226-30.

4 The Vinaya account of the First Council assigns no part to Ajātas'atru. Aupapātika Sūtra, Sec. 20 *passim*.

5 Grandson, according to the Purāṇas.

6 The Pali tradition is silent on this point. But from the fact that Udāyi's grandson, Muṇḍa, was residing at Pāṭaliputra which is stated in the Anguttara Nikāya, it may be safely inferred that the capital was removed earlier.

7 Pargiter, op. cit., p. 22.

8, 9 Mañjus'sī-Mūlakalpa, v. 825 :

> Tad etat pravachanaṃ s'astu likhāpayishyati vistaram ।
> pūjāṃs' cha mahatīṃ kṛitvā dik-samantān nayishyati ॥

10 Anguttara-N., III, p. 57f.

instructions from the Buddhist Thera, Nārada,[1] a fact which goes to indicate that in the matter of meeting holy persons of wisdom he followed in the footsteps of his forefathers.

Ajātaśatru and his successors earned, according to the Pali Chronicles, the notoriety of being patricides, and sick of it, the citizens deposed the last king of their line and replaced him by his popular minister Śiśunāga. Thus the Haryanka dynasty was supplanted by the Śaiśunāga (S'aiśunāka).

The S'aiśunāgas ceased to rule one hundred and forty years after the Buddha's demise (c. 348 or 347 B.C.). The only king of this family, worthy of mention, is Kālāśoka (Aśoka the Blackie), apparently the same person as Bāṇa's Kākavarṇa S'aiśunāgī.[2] The Pali Chronicles relate that during his reign, just a century after the Buddha's demise, and under his royal patronage was held the Second Buddhist Council at Vaiśālī, which is not improbable[3]. It may be noted here that the confusion made between Dharmāśoka (Aśokamukhya of the Mūlakalpa) and the crow-black Kālāśoka was accountable for the Divyāvadāna description of the former as a man of ugly appearance.

Even the Mahābodhivaṃsa records nothing noteworthy of the reign of Kālāśoka's ten sons and successors whom it names. According to this later Pali Chronicle, his eldest son and immediate successor was Bhadrasena.[4] His ninth son, Nandivardhana, may be identified with his namesake in the Purāṇas, in which case his tenth or last son, Pañchamaka, will figure as the same person as Mahānandi, the last king of the S'aiśunāga dynasty, according to the Purāṇas.

The Mūlakalpa praises Viśoka (same as Kālāśoka?) as a good king who worshipped Buddha's relics for 76 years, and his successor, S'ūrasena, who reigned for 17 years as a monarch who "caused stūpas to be put up to the confines of the sea,"[5] which is evidently a baseless exaggeration.

The S'aiśunāga dynasty came to an end with the rise of the Nandas into power one hundred and forty years after the Buddha's

---

1 Malalasekera, Dictionary of Pali Proper Names, II, p. 641.

2 Raychaudhuri, op. cit., p. 187.

3 The Vinaya account of the Second Council in the Chullavagga, Ch. XII, has nothing to say of the part played by Kālāsoka.

4 Acc. to Jayaswal, An Imperial History of India, p. 14., the same person as S'ūrasena of the Mālakalpa, which is farfetched.

5 Mañjus'rī Mūlakalpa, 416-21, Jayaswal, op. cit., pp. 12, 14.

demise (c. 348 or 347 B.C.). Both the Pali Chronicles and the Purāṇas speak of nine Nandas, but they differ when the former represent them as nine brothers with a short reign of 22 years and the latter represent them as father and eight sons with a much longer reign of 40 (28 + 12) or 100 (88 + 12) years.[1] The first king of this dynasty is Ugrasenananda according to the Mahābodhivaṃsa, and the last king Dhanananda.[2] The Purāṇas name the first king as Mahāpadmananda but leave his sons unnamed.[3] The Greek writer Curtius speaks only of two Nandas, namely, Agrammes[4] who was a contemporary of Alexander the Great, and whose father was a usurper of the throne[5], while the Mūlakalpa speaks only of one Nanda who is said to have died at the age of 66.[6]

The traditional accounts differ as to how the Nandas came to replace the Śiśunāgas. According to the Mahāvaṃsa-ṭīkā, the founder king of this dynasty accidently fell into the hands of a gang of thieves and freebooters (chorā) who used Malaya[7] as their hiding place. He was a warrior-like man (yodhasadiso puriso). After the death of their leader he managed to secure their leadership and went on as theretofore to plunder villages and kingdoms. Pricked by conscience that such a life as this did not behove a warrior like him, he made up his mind to take a kingdom. He declared himself under the name of Nanda, and getting his brothers and people to side with him, beseized a frontier town, the citizens whereof made an alliance with him instead of accepting his ultimatum. In this very manner he gained the support of a large number of the inhabitants of Jambudvīpa, and ultimately marched into Pāṭaliputra. Thus he seized the kingdom of Magadha. But he was destined to die shortly after that.[8]

---

1 Pargiter, op. cit., p. 25 ; Raychaudhuri, op. cit., p. 180. Tāranātha assigns a reign of 29 years to Nanda.

2 Mahābodhivaṃsa, p. 98.

3 Pargiter, op. cit., pp. 25, 69.

4 Raychaudhuri, op. cit., pp. 188, 190, equates the Greek name with the Sk. Augrasainya, a patronymic from Ugrasena (Pali Uggasena).

5 Quoted by McCrindle, see The Invasion of Alexander, p. 222 ; Raychaudhuri, op. cit., p. 187.

6 Mañjus'rī-mūlakalpa, vv. 422-37.

7 Probably the name of a mountain beyond Pāṭaliputra.

8 Vaṃsatthappakāsinī, P, p. 178f. Iminā va nayena so yebhuyyena Jambudīpavāsino manusse hatthagate katvā tato Pāṭaliputtaṃ gantvā tattha rajjaṃ gahetvā raṭṭhaṃ anusāsamāno na chirass eva kālam akāsi.

According to the Mūlakalpa story, on the other hand, Nanda rose into power and gained the throne from a position of the prime minister, as though by a magical process. He was surrounded in his capital by the Brāhman controversialists with false pride and big claims. Though pious and a man of judgement, the king gave them riches and did not deny them his patronage. But he had a Buddhist saint for his good spiritual guide under whose influence he became a believer in Buddha, honoured his sacred relics, and built 24 vihāras. Vararuchi is represented as his prime minister, and Pāṇini as his friend, a tradition to which Jayaswal attaches undue importance. The Purāṇas extol Mahāpadmananda as an "extirpator of all kshatriyas" (sarva-kshatrāntakaḥ) and as a "sole monarch bringing all under his sway" (ekarāṭ, ekachchhatraḥ)[1]. The historical justification of this praise has been fully discussed by Raychaudhuri. It may suffice here to add that the epithet Mahāpadma is a numerical term, which is expressive of the enormous wealth of the founder of the Nanda dynasty. The signification of the Pali name, Dhanananda, of the last king of the family is the same. Raychaudhuri rightly observes indeed when he says, "The first Nanda left to his sons not only a big empire but a large army and a full exchequer as well."[2] None need be surprised, therefore, that Indian literature preserves the tradition of fabulous riches of a Nanda king.

As for the last king, we read in the Mahāvaṃsa-ṭīkā, "The youngest brother was called Dhanananda for his passion for hoarding wealth. He collected riches to the amount of eighty crores... Levying taxes even on skins, gums, trees and stones, he amassed further treasures which he disposed of similarly."[3] The same authority also relates that Dhanananda built a dānasālā at Pāṭaliputra, from which he gave away abundant riches to the Brāhmans according to their seniority and ranks,[4] a fact which finds mention also in the Mūlakalpa account of king Nanda. The Mūlakalpa has evidently mixed up the two accounts, namely, that of the first Nanda and that of the last.

With regard to the fall of the last Nanda king 140 years after the Buddha's demise, c. 326 or 325 B. C., the Mahāvaṃsa[5] and its ṭīkā[6]

---

[1] Raychaudhuri, op. cit., p. 188 f.

[2] Ibid, p. 190 f.

[3] Vaṃsatthappakāsinī, I, p. 179 f. ; Turner, Mahāvaṃsa, p. xxxix.

[4] Ibid, I, p. 181 f.

[5] Mahāvaṃsa, V. 17-7.

[6] Vaṃsatthappakāsinī, I, p. 181 f.

on the one hand, and the Purāṇas[1] on the other show a complete agreement in so far as they attribute it to the machination of the Brāhman named Kauṭilya-Chāṇakya. The Mūlakalpa alone suggests that the fall of the Nanda king was due to the alienation of the feeling of the whole body of ministers inadvertently caused by him.[2]

The tradition of extermination of the Nanda dynasty by Vishṇugupta-Kauṭilya is met with in the concluding verse of the Kauṭilīya Arthaśāstra, the opening verses of the Kāmandakīya Nītisāra, as well as Viśākhadatta's Mudrā-rākshasa and the Mūlakalpa.

In the Mahāvaṃsa and the Mūlakalpa, Chāṇakya, the prime minister of Chandragupta Maurya, is described as "full of fierce wrath" (chaṇḍakkodhavā), "successful in wrath, who was Death (Yamāntaka) when angry." The Mahāvaṃsa-ṭīkā and the Mudrārākshasa give us slightly different stories of how Chāṇakya avenged the humiliation suffered by him at the hands of the last Nanda by using Chandragupta as a tool and established the latter in the throne of Magadha in c. 326 or 325 B. C. .

In the Mahāvaṃsa-ṭīkā Chāṇakya is described as an erudite, resourceful and tricky Brāhman of Takshaśilā who was well versed in the Vedic lore, and an expert in the principles of polity. But his teeth being all broken, his face became ugly to look at. As a controversialist he came to Pāṭaliputra, and as a Brāhman leader he took his seat when king Dhanananda was distributing large gifts among the Brāhmans. Disgusted with his uncomely sight, the king ordered his men to turn him out. Enraged by this, Chāṇakya pronounced his curse, saying, "In this earth bounded by the four seas let there no longer be the prosperity of the Nandas." This being reported, the king became very angry and ordered his men to arrest him forthwith. Whilst trying to escape in the disguise of an Ājīvika, he cleverly managed to evade the detection, though still inside the inner court of the royal residence. In the meantime he got hold of prince Parvata whom he tempted with sovereignty, made good his escape together with the prince and went to the Vindhya mountain. On looking out for a person who was worthy of sovereignty he chanced to see prince Chandragupta of the Maurya family who was then being brought up in the family of a cowherd unaware of his royal origin. He took Chandragupta to his retreat in the Vindhya mountain and trained him

---

1 Pargiter, op. cit., pp. 26, 69.

2 Manjus'rī-mūlakalpa, vv. 455-6 ;
Jayaswal, An Imperial History, p. 16 f.

up. First he employed him to behead prince Parvata and subsequently to collect treasures by plundering villages and towns. When he was thus able to prove his ability and to raise an army Chāṇakya set him to march to Pāṭaliputra and seize the throne by putting Dhanananda to death.

The connection of Chāṇakya with Takshaśilā is interesting. The explanation for the introduction of Parvatakumāra in the story lies really in the Mudrārākshasa in which the machinations of Chāṇakya against Nanda were directed to conciliating Rākshasa, a minister of Nanda, and getting Malayaketu of Parvata as an ally. I am inclined to identify Parvata with Hwen Thsang's Po-fa-to, a country which was situated 700 li (about 116 miles) south-east of Multān. Viśākhadatta's Parvata is the same country as that which Pāṇini IV. 2.143 mentions as the name of a country under the group Takshaśilādi iv. 3.93.[1] In other words, for the early career of Chandragupta it is necessary to watch in the light of the available Greek accounts his activities and position in the Punjab and North-western Frontier Provinces at the time of and immediately after Alexander the Great's invasion. And for the same the reader may be referred for the present to Raychaudhuri's critical summary.[1]

As for the most notable events of the life and career of Chandragupta mention may be made of the following six :

(i) The unification of all the states and fighting forces of North-western India beyond the Middle Country under his leadership.

(ii) The liberation of India from foreign yoke.

(iii) The overthrow of the Nanda power.

(iv) The defeat of Seleukos Nikator ending in a treaty by which the Greek general and successor of Alexander the Great ceded certain territories to Chandragupta and which was consummated by a matrimonial alliance.

(v) The foundation of a mighty Indian empire.

(vi) The coming of Megasthenes as an ambassador of Seleukos Nikator to Chandragupta's court and capital.

The account of India left by Megasthenes in his Indika is invaluable as presenting to us a contemporary picture of Chandragupta's palace, capital, kingdom, country, administrative system, etc.

Chandragupta who is otherwise praised in the Mūlākalpa as 'a very prosperous lord of the earth', 'true to his word', and 'a man of

---

[1] Raychaudhuri, op. cit., p. 214 f.

pious soul' (mahābhogī satyasandhaś cha dharmātmā sa mahīpatiḥ), is said to have killed many living beings on the advice of a bad spiritual guide (akalyāṇamitra.)[1]

He died[2] after a successful reign of 24 years and was succeeded by his son Bindusāra. According to the Mūlakalpa legend, Bindusāra was a minor when he was placed on the throne by his father. It is said that 'while a minor he obtained great comfort ; when of full manhood he turned out to be bold, eloquent and sweet-tongued.[3] He reigned for 28 years,—25 years according to the Purāṇas, and 70 years according to the Mūlakalpa,[4] which is improbable. Strangely enough, the Mūlakalpa represents the wicked Chāṇakya as his prime minister.[5] The royal family in which he was born is called Nandarājakula instead of Maurya[6].

One may just be amused by the ingenuity of the Mahāvaṃsa-ṭīkā in the invention of stories to account for the etymological significance of the names, Chandragupta ("one who was guarded by a bull called Chandra") and Bindusāra[7] (one on whose body flowed the blood of she-goats"), both of which are far-fetched. The son and successor of Sandrokottos (Chandragupta) is known to the Greek historian Strabo (XV, p. 702) by the name of Amitrochades, Allitrochades, and to Athenaios by that of Amitrachates equated by Fleet, and subsequently also by Jarl Charpentier, with Amitrakhāda[8] ("Devourer of enemies") which is traceable in literature as an epithet of Indra[9]. Raychaudhuri still sticks to his equation with Amitraghāta, a term which is met with in Patañjali's Mahābhāshya

---

[1] Mañjus'rī-mūlakalpa, V. 441 : akalyāṇamitram āgamya kṛitaṃ prāṇivadhaṃ bahu.

[2] 'Fainted with boils at his death', according to the Mūlakalpa, V. 441.

[3] *Ibid*, V. 449 : Prauḍho dhṛishṭas' cha saṃvṛitaḥ pragalbhas'chāpi priyavādinaḥ.

[4] *Ibid*, V. 449.

[5] Tāranātha, quoted by Raychaudhuri, op. cit., p. 243, says, "Chanaka, one of his ('Bindusāra's) great lords, procured the destruction of the nobles and kings of sixteen towns and as king he made himself the master of all the territories between the eastern and western seas."

[6] Mūlakalpa V. 448 : Jāto (Nanda-) rājakule Chandraguptasya dhīmataḥ.

[7] Called Nandasāra in the Vāyu Purāṇa, Bhadrasāra in the Brahmāṇḍa as well as the Vāyu, and Siṃhasena in the Sinhalese Rājāvalikathe.

In the Mudrārākshasa, Chandragupta is called Mauryaputra (Act II) as well as Nandanvaya ("one of Nanda descent", Act. IV). McCrindle, Ancient India, pp. 12, 19.

[8] See, for references and discussion, Raychaudhuri, op. cit., p. 243.

[9] J. R. A. S., 1909, p. 24.

and corresponds to Amitrāṇām hantā in the Aitareya Brāhmaṇa. I may prefer to equate the name with Amitrasvātī ("Terror to enemies"). or Amṛitakhāda ("Eater of ambrosia").

The following two facts are really important to be noted :

(i) That Ptolemy Philadelphos, king of Egypt, sent Deimachos as his ambassador to Bindusāra ;

and (ii) That, according to the Dīpavaṃsa and Samantapāsādikā, Bindusāra was a votary of the Brāhmans and a staunch supporter of the Brahmanical sects.

6. **Social Status** : The barber story is almost proverbial in the ancient royal tradition of India. When a reigning monarch was found stingy in the payment of rewards or in making gifts, he was taken to be a barber's son.[1] There must have been some such reason at the back of the Brahmanical tradition regarding the Śūdra origin of the Nandas and Mauryas. The Purāṇās predict, "As son of Mahānandin (the last Śaiśunāga) by a Śūdra woman will be born a king, Mahāpadma (Nanda) who will exterminate all kshatriyas. Thereafter kings will be of S'ūdra origin."

The founder of the Nanda family is called 'the leading vile man' (nīchamukhyaḥ) in the Mūlakalpa (verse 424).[2] In the Mahāvaṃsa-ṭīkā the first Nanda, who was a warrior-like man, figures, as we saw, as the powerful leader of a gang of thieves and a band of freebooters. He is not, however, connected by the Pali tradition with the last Śaiśunāga through blood-relationship. The Mūlakalpa legend says that originally he was the prime minister of the last king of Viśoka's family.

Curtius narrates a story from an Indian source, which is devised to account for the S'ūdra origin of Agrammes (Augrasainya Nanda). According to this story, father of Agrammes was a wretched barber, who could be in love-intrigue with the queen of the reigning king because of his prepossessing appearance. By her influence he gained so much confidence of the king as to figure ultimately as a trusted adviser. Taking advantage of this privileged position, he treacherously murdered the king, and 'under the pretence of acting as guardian to the royal children, usurped the supreme authority, and having put the royal young princes to death begot Agrammes. The suggestion is that the Nanda contemporary of Alexander was a barber's son by the queen dowager of the last S'aiśunāga. Hemachandra in his

---

1 Pargiter, op. cit., pp. 25, 69.

2 Jayaswal, An Ancient History, p. 14.

Pariśishṭaparvan (VI. 231-32), however, represents the first Nanda 'as the son of a courtezan by a bárber', while, according to the Purāṇas, he was 'a son of the last S'aiśunāga by a S'ūdra woman.[1]

The process of myth-making did not stop short there ; the Śūdra or barber story continued. Despite the fact that neither the Pali Chronicles nor the Purāṇas suggest any blood-connection between the Nandas and the Mauryas, Viśākhadatta in his Mudrārākshasa (Acts IV, VI), describes Chandragupta not only as Mauryasuta but also as Nandanvaya (one belonging to the Nanda dynasty). "Kshemendra and Somadeva refer to him as Pūrvananda-suta. The commentator on the Vishṇu Purāṇa (IV. 24, Wilson, IX, 187) says that Chandragupta was the son of Nanda by a wife called Murā, whence he and his descendants were called Mauryas. Dhuṇḍirāja, the commentator on the Mudrārākshasa, informs us on the other hand that Chandragupta was the eldest son of Maurya who was the son of the Nanda king Sarvārthasiddha by Murā, daughter of a Vṛishala Śūdra."[2] In the Mudrārākshasa itself Chāṇakya addresses Chandragupta as a Vṛishala or Śūdra.

Mr. C. D. Chatterjee rightly points out to me that the derivation of the dynastic name Maurya as a matronymic from Murā is grammatically incorrect ; it may be treated as a patronymic from Mura. It is untenable also on the ground that according to the Vishṇu Purāṇa (IV. 10. 12) and the Arthaśāstra (III. 7), the child takes the càste of its father, whether born of conjugal wedlock or not.[3]

The force of the story of the barber mother or grandmother of Chandragupta may be counteracted by the Divyāvadāṇa story of the barber-mother of Aśoka himself. His mother was not a woman of the barber caste but a very handsome and accomplished Brāhman girl from Champā whom other queens of Bindusāra, jealous of her, employed her in the palace to attend on the king as a female hair-dresser. When she disclosed the real fact to the king, she said, "Lord, I am not a barber girl but a daughter of a Brahman by whom I am offered to be your wife."[4]

Hemchandra in his Pariśishtaparvan, derives the name Maurya

---

[1] Raychaudhuri, op. cit., p. 187f. The Avas'yaka, too, describes the first Nanda 'as the son of a courtezan by a barber." In the Jaina Vividha-Tīrthakalpa, p. 6, Nanda is described as nāpita-gaṇikā-sutaḥ.

[2] Raychaudhuri, op. cit., p. 216.

[3] This has been upheld by R. K. Mookerji in his Chandragupta.

[4] Divyāvadāna, p. 370 : Deva, nāhaṃ nāpinī ; brāhmaṇasyāhaṃ duhitā tena devasya patnyarthaṃ dattā.

from mayūra ("peacock") and suggests that Chandragupta came to be styled Maurya from the circumstance that he was "the son of a daughter of the chief of a village of peacock-tamers (mayūraposhakāḥ)[1]. If the Greek writer Justin describes Sandrocottus as a man "of mean origin", it does not mean much, since he must have based his account on an Indian tradition.

The Pali Chronicles, on the other hand, and Buddhist legends[2] generally represent Chandragupta as a scion of the Moriya clan of kshatriyas, the Moriyas of Pipphalivana[3]. Led, however, by a Śākya-phobia, the Buddhist legends describe the Moriyas as descendants of the S'ākyas who fled away from their own territory when it was overrun by the army of Viḍuḍabha-Virūḍhaka, the usurper king of Kośala, and founded a new territory.[4] The story is guilty of anachronism because, as borne out by the Mahāparinibbāna Suttanta, the Moriyas of Pipphalivana were, precisely like the Śākyas of Kapilavastu, one of the eight rival claimants for the bodily remains of the Buddha.

As for the connection of the Mauryas of Pāṭaliputra with the Moriyas, the Mahāvaṃsa-ṭīkā tells us that Chandragupta's mother who was the chief queen of the then reigning Moriya king fled in disguise from the Moriya capital to Pushpapura (Pāṭaliputra) during her advanced pregnancy, and gave birth to her son there when the Moriya territory was seized by a powerful neighbour (sāmantaraññā). The story built up in this connection reads somehow as a later replica of the earlier legend of the birth of Aśoka's elder step-brother's son Nyagrodha, and at the root of the ingenuity of the one, precisely as at that of the other, is a fantastic philological justification of the personal name.

Chandragupta does not appear to have been known to Megasthenes, and, for the matter of that, to most of the Greek writers, as a scion of the Maurya family. None need be surprised at all if the connection of the Mauryas with the Moriyas was due to an after-thought on the part of the Buddhists when they wanted to especially honour their Dharmāśoka and claim him as their own man. The Buddhist legends

---

1 Raychaudhuri, op. cit. p. 216.

2 Beal, Buddhist Records, i. p. 128.

3 Acc. to Raychaudhuri, Pipphalivana "probably lay between Rummindei in the Nepalase Tarai and Kāsiā in the Gorakhpur district".

4 Hwen Thsang narrates a legend (Beal, Buddhist Records, I. p. 126), which connects the S'ākya-Mauryas with the country of Udyāna.

concerning the S'ākya lineage of the Moriyas or Mauryas would seem accountable also for the representation of the Mauryas in certain late mediaeval Mysore inscriptions as Kshatriyas who sprang from Mandhātṛi of the solar race.[1]

Hemchandra, as we noted, accounts for the dynastic name Maurya by the tradition that Chandragupta was a son of the daughter of the headman of a village of mayūraposhakas ("peacock-tamers"). The Mahāvaṃsa-ṭīkā which connects Chandragupta with the Moriyas, accounts for their name also by a tradition averring that they built in their capital 'peacock palaces that were filled and resounded with cries of peacocks.[2]

In support of the connection of the Mauryas with peacocks, Raychaudhuri notices the following two facts[3] which create but a presumptive evidence :

(i) That Aelian speaks of tame peacocks that were kept in the parks attached to the Maurya palace at Pāṭaliputra ;

and (ii) That figures of peacocks were employed to decorate some of the projecting ends of the architraves of the east gateway as Sāñchī.[4]

If any light is thrown on this point by Aśoka's R. E. I, it is rather this, namely, that the Mauryas of Pāṭaliputra were inordinately fond of peacock's flesh. All the animals could be dispensed with and exempted from daily slaughter in the royal kitchen for the purpose of curry but not two peafowls (dvo morā). In other words, the Mauryas were rather mayūrakhādakas than mayūraposhakas. The figure of a peacock carved on the lower part of Aśoka's pillar at Rāmpurva does not necessarily indicate that the peacock was the emblem of the Mauryas. It may at the most be interpreted as a cognizance of Pipphalivana, which was the fatherland of the Moriya race of kshatriyas.

---

1 Epigraphia Indica, II, p. 222 ; Raychaudhuri, op. cit., p. 216.

2 Vaṃsatthappakāsinī, I, p. 180 : mayūra-gīva-sankāsa-chhadaniṭṭhaka-pāsāda-paṇtikaṃ......mayūrakekanādehi pūritaṃ ugghositaṃ. It records another theory according to which the Moriyas "were so called because they rejoiced in the prosperity of their city (attānaṃ nagarasiriyā modāpīti,......dakārassa rakāraṃ katvā Moriyā ti laddhavohārā)", which is forced and far-fetched.

3 Raychaudhuri, op. cit., p. 216.

4 Sir John Marshall, A Guide to Sanchi, pp. 44, 62. Attention might be drawn to the representation of a 'peacock-palace' as a decorative device on the outer railing of the Stūpa of Bharhut.

There is no conclusive evidence as yet to establish Chandragupta's lineal descent from the S'ākya-Moriyas or Nandas. Plutarch's remark that "Androkottus himself, who was then a lad, saw Alexander himself and afterwards used to declare that Alexander might easily have occupied the whole country, as the then king was hated by his subjects on account of his mean and wicked disposition"[1] must be taken with a grain of salt. There was nothing in Chandragupta's conversation to enrage Alexander who, according to Justin, 'did not scruple to give orders to kill the intrepid Indian lad for his boldness of speech'. It was quite against the youthful spirit of Chandragupta who in Justin's opinion was the brave hero and military leader to make India free, shaking off 'from its neck the yoke of slavery' since Alexander's death.[2]

To me Chandragupta was a man of the Uttarāpatha or Gandhāra, if not exactly of Takshaśilā. His early education, military training, and alliances were all in that part of India. He added the whole of the province of Gandhāra and the surrounding tribal states (in the Punjab and N. W. Frontier Provinces) to the growing Magadha empire together with the territories ceded to him by Seleukos Nikator. The love was never lost between this aparānta and the Mauryas. Some at least of Aśoka's scribes were all persons whose habitual script was Kharoshṭhī, and a few of his artists were those who were still carrying on the tradition of the architecture of Persepolis. Chandragupta and Aśoka of the Maurya dynasty who could create a glorious history for themselves and their country did not need credentials based upon royal lineage. The Greek writers speak only of one matrimonial alliance by which Seleukos ratified his treaty with Chandragupta.

7. **Wives and Children**: The Pali Chronicles and Samantapāsādikā tell us that while a prince Aśoka married Devī, daughter of a banker, at Vidiśā on his way to Ujjayinī to join the office of the Viceroy (Uparājā) of Avantī. The Mahāvaṃsa-ṭīkā describes her as a very handsome and accomplished lady and names her father Deva.[3] It is quite possible that, like Pushyagupta of the Junāgaṛh rock inscription, Deva was a Rāshṭriya or Rāshṭrapāla. In the Mahābodhi vaṃsa (pp. 98, 110), she is honoured as Vedisa-mahādevī, and

[1] Life of Alexander, LXII.

[2] McCrindle, Ancient India, p. 7.

[3] Vaṃsatthappakāsinī, I, p. 324.

represented as a S'ākya princess. It is said that after her marriage, she was taken to Ujjayinī, where she bore him immediately a son called Mahendra, and two years later a daughter named Sanghamitrā. She is said to have built a vihāra at Vidiśā for her son when he came to see her back *en route* to the island of Tāmraparṇī. Devī stayed back at Vidiśā but her children accompanied their father when he came back to Paṭaliputra and seized the throne. Sanghamitrā was given in marriage to Prince Agnibrahmā, a nephew of Aśoka, to whom she bore a son named Sumana. Agnibrahmā, Sumana, Mahendra and Sanghamitrā joined all the Buddhist Order. The above authorities offer us a systematic chronology of certain important events of Aśoka's reign in terms of the age of Mahendra. The Buddhist mission to Ceylon was led by Mahendra, and his sister, too, went over to the island when her services were needed for the founding of an order of nuns there.

The story of Devī and her children is conspicuous by its absence from the Sanskrit legends. The inscriptions of Aśoka are lacking in confirmation of its truth. In the edicts promulgated up till the 14th year of Aśoka's abhisheka we have no mention of his sons, his daughters being altogether out of the question. In his R. E. V, promulgated not earlier than the 13th year of abhisheka, he speaks of charities from the households of his brothers, sisters and others ranking with him in family relationship. He speaks indeed also of his different family establishments at Pāṭaliputra and outlying towns. On the other hand, in his P. E. VII, engraved in the 27th year of abhisheka, his brothers, sisters and other kinsmen ranking with him go out of the picture, and his own sons (dālakā) and other princes of the blood ranking with them are expressly introduced instead. The way in which they are mentioned leave no room for doubt that his sons were then grown up enough to make charities out of their own funds, though not exactly from their own family establishments (orodhas).

His statement in P. E. VII is sufficiently explicit so as to make the meaning of that in R. E. V clear as to his own households. It goes to show that by his households or family establishments (to avoid the word harems) he chiefly meant his queens (devis). The Queen's Edict contains his direction to the Mahāmātras concerned as to how the donations and benefactions of his second queen (dutiyāye deviye) Kāluvāki (Chāruvāki or Kalavinkā), mother of Tīvala (Tivara), should be recorded or labelled with inscriptions.

Thus the Queen's Edict clearly proves that Aśoka had at least two queens at the time of its promulgation. Although the king's orders were issued to the Mahāmatras everywhere (savata mahāmatā), it was engraved only on the pillar at Kauśāmbī, a fact which may lead us to think that her residence was at Kauśāmbī, an outlying town. But Aśoka speaks of outlying towns, and not of one town only. Are we to understand from this that his queens were not kept in one place, say, in his palace at Pāṭaliputra, but at different towns, each having her separate establishment ?

The Pali tradition about the Vidiśā residence of Devī favours the idea of there being separate family establishments for individual wives at different towns. But from Aśoka's statement, it does not necessarily follow that each establishment was allotted to one queen.

If Kāluvāki was his second queen, who was his first or chief queen ? According to the Pali tradition, his beloved first queen consort (piyā aggamahisī) was Asandhimittā, a name, better title, which I am inclined to equate with Sk. Āsandimitrā ("consort at the time of ascending the throne"). She died in the 26th year of Aśoka's abhisheka, and four years later Tishyarakshā (Tishyarakshitā of the Divyāvadāna) was made his queen consort. The Mahāvaṃsa and Divyāvadāna legends make her jealous of the Bo-tree on account of the king's fond attachment to it. The Divyāvadāna legend which is unaware of her predecessor Āsandimitrā goes further to build up a most scandalous story of Tishyarakshitā and her wrathful vengeance on Aśoka's favourite son, Kuṇāla, when he was deputed to Takshaśilā to quell a revolt.[1] The story of Tishyarakshā has no place in the Dīpavaṃsa, nor even in the writings of Buddhaghosa. It must have grown up at a later period. Aśoka, as he appears in his inscriptions, could not have lost his sanity so much as to behave as a religious maniac with regard to the worship of the Bo tree as he has been represented to be.

It is more reasonable to think and say that his wife by his side at the time of his coronation was the wife who accompanied him from Ujjayinī, and she may be no other than the Vedisa-mahādevī.[2]

The Divyāvadāna legend represents Aśoka's queen Padmāvatī as mother of Kuṇāla who was also known by the name of Dharmavardhana or Dharmavivardhana ('the promoter of the cause of piety').

---

[1] Divyāvadāna, p. 407. [2] F. W. Thomas in Camb. Hist. I.

Mookerji (Asoka, p. 9) catalogues Devī, Kāruvāki, Asandhimittā, Padmāvatī, and Tishayarakshitā as five wives of Aśoka, without the least attempt to understand their real identities.

To my mind, Tishayarakshitā is a faic ; Padmāvatī of the Sanskrit legend and Kāluvāki of the Queen's Edict are one and the same second queen ; and the Vaidiśa-mahādevī and Āsandimitrā are the identical person.[1]

The identity of Padmāvatī and Kāluvaki rests on the identity of their sons, Kuṇāla and Tīvala. Both Kuṇāla and Tīvala (Tīvara) were nicknames. As for the first, Mookerji (Asoka, p. 8,) rightly remarks that Aśoka first gave to Padmāvatī's new-born babe the name of Dharmavivardhana but on seeing the beauty of his eyes, as his amātyas, or ministers in attendance, pointed out were like those of the Himalayan bird Kuṇāla[2] (=Chitra-kokila), Aśoka nicknamed him as Kuṇāla. He was called Dharmavivardhana because he was born when Aśoka had been reigning prosperously with righteousness.[3] According to the Divyāvadāna legend, he was born as soon as the 84,000 dharmarājikās were built,[4] the 7th year of Aśoka's abhisheka being mentioned in the Pali Chronicles as the date of completion of the construction of the 84,000 vihāras with chaityas. The name Tīvala or Tīvara, which is met with in a much later Indian inscription as the name of a king of Kośala,[5] signifies a 'keen-eyed' hunter.[6] Prince Tīvala, too, was born when Aśoka had been prosperously reigning with righteousness.

8. **Successors** : The Pali Chronicles and Samanta-pāsādikā do not carry the Maurya history beyond Aśoka. They create rather the impression that the whole glory of the dynasty vanished with him. His uterine brother Tishya-Vītaśoka, son and daughter Mahendra and Sanghamitrā, son-in-law Agnibrahmā, and daughter's son Sumana joined the Buddhist Order. Nothing but the Buddhist religious

---

1 This is to discard my earlier suggestion (Indian Culture, I, p. 123) about the identity of Kāluvāki and Asandhimittā. See Raychaudhuri's criticism on the point in his Political history, p. 284, n.

2 Divyāvadāna, p. 406,

3 *Ibid*, p. 405 : dharmeṇa rājyaṃ kurvato hi jātaḥ suto Dharmavivardhano 'stu.

4 *Ibid*, p. 405.

5 Fleet, Gupta Inscription, p. 293 ; E.I, Vol. VII, p. 103.

6 In the Saṃyutta, II, p. 19, the primitive dwellers of Mt. Vaipulya are rightly called Tivaras.

edifices which he had built and the memory of other pious deeds performed by him remained to keep his name alive to posterity.[1]

According to the Divyāvadāna legend, Aśoka was succeeded by his grandson Sampadi, son of Kuṇāla who was found unfit for the throne. Sampadi's lineal successors were Bṛihaspati, Vṛishasena, Pushyadharma and Pushyamitra.[2] The last king of the family who began his career as a reactionary in favour of Brahmanism brought an end to himself and the Maurya dynasty by his ruthless act of vandalism directed to the destruction of the Buddhist vihāras and stūpas built and the killing of the Buddhist monks and nuns entertained by Aśoka.

Jayaswal suggests that the Buddhist tradition of Pushyamitra is preserved also in the Mūlakalpa account of the hostile action of Gomin who is said to have destroyed "monasteries with relics" and killed "monks of good conduct."[3]

The Buddhist traditon is misleading and inconclusive. Pushyamitra who, according to the Purāṇas, was the founder of the next dynasty, is represented as the last Maurya king and the lengths of the reign of Aśoka's successors are not given.

Raychaudhuri's critical summary of the history of Aśoka's Maurya successors seeks to build up a cosmos out of a chaos. The Matsya Purāṇa speaks of ten Mauryas whom it enumerates so clumsily as to make it uncertain whether by the number ten it meant ten or seven successors of Aśoka. Some versions of the Vāyu Purāṇa definitely stand for nine successors, and try to reduce ten to the traditional number of nine Mauryas (nava Mauryāḥ) by combining Bandhupālita and his son Indrapālita into one reign. The Vāyu and Brahmāṇḍa Purāṇas speak of six successors who, together with the three first Mauryas, make up the traditional total of nine. The Pūrāṇas, moreover, mention 137 years (sapta-triṃśach-chhatam) as the total length of the reign of the Mauryas, of all the nine Mauryas including the first three, according to the Vāyu and Brahmāṇḍa Purāṇas, and

---

[1] Divyāvadāna, p. 433 As'oka nāma rājā babhūveti, tena chaturas'ītidharmarājikā-sahasraṃ pratishṭhāpitaṃ yāvad Bhagavachchhāsanaṃ prāpyate tāvat tasya yas'aḥ sthāsyati.

[2] *Ibid*, p. 434: Yadā Pushyamitra rājā praghātitas tadā Mauryavaṃs'as samuchchhinnaḥ.

[3] Jayaswal, An Ancient History, p. 18.

of the nine successors of Aśoka, according to some MSS. of the Vāyu, the position of the Matsya being uncertain in this respect[1].

In the circumstances one may reasonably question the accuracy of Raychaudhuri's statement when he says, "The Matsya Purāṇa gives the following list of Aśoka's successors : Daśaratha, Samprati, Śatadhanvan and Bṛihadratha", inasmuch as their number, even together with that of the first three Mauryas, does not come up to the given total of ten (daśa Mauryāḥ). The lengths of reigns suggested in the Matsya Purāṇa as well as in some versions of the Vāyu do not, when joined together, fit in with the traditional total length of 137 years. Better in this respect is the position of the Brahmāṇḍa Purāṇa as also of the Vāyu, both of which give only 48 years as the total length of the reign of Aśoka's six successors.

The Vishṇu Purāṇa list of six successors, viz., Suyaśas[2], Daśaratha, Sangata, S'āliśūka, Somaśarman S'atadhanvan and Bṛihadratha[3] may be reconciled to a great extent, as suggested by Raychaudhuri, with that in the Matsya, if Suyaśas and Sangata of the one be identified with Kuṇāla and Samprati respectively of the other. Other names do not call for comment as these are mere passing shadows without any historical importance so far.

The immediate successors of Aśoka was, according to the Divyāvadāna legend, his grandson Sampadi (Samprati), and not his son Kuṇāla, Kuṇāla-Tīvala or Kuṇāla-Dharmavardhana whom Fa Hian distinctly mentions as the Viceroy of Gandhāra. According to the Divyāvadāna narrative, too, Kuṇāla was deputed as his father's Vice-regent to Takshaśilā, the headquarters of the province of Gandhāra. The Jaina author, Jinaprabhasūri claims Samprati, son of Kuṇāla, as a great king who reigned in Pātaliputra as an emperor of India and founded vihāras for the Jaina S'ramaṇas 'even in non-Aryan countries.'

Regarding Kuṇāla and his immediate successor or successors, Raychaudhuri observes : "Tradition is not unanimous regarding the accession of Kuṇāla to the imperial throne. He is reputed to have been blind. His position was, therefore, probably like that of Dhṛitarāshṭra of the Great Epic and, though nominally regarded as

---

1 Pargiter, op. cit., p. 27f.

2 Mentioned also in the Bhāgavata Purāṇa. Raychaudhuri, op. cit., p. 290.

3 See, for the comments on the tradition of Sālisūka, S'atadhanvan, and Bṛihadratha, Raychaudhuri, op. cit., p. 292.

the sovereign, he was physically unfit to carry on the work of government which was presumably entrusted to his favourite son Samprati, who is described by Jaina and Buddhist writers as the immediate successor of Aśoka. Kuṇāla's son was Bandhupālita according to the Vāyu Purāṇa, Sampadi (Samprati) according to the Divyāvadāna and the Pāṭaliputra-kalpa of Jinaprabhasūri, and Vigataśoka according to Tāranātha. Either these princes were identical or they were brothers."[1]

In the Gārgī Saṃhitā Śālisūka is represented as a wicked king who had to abdicate the throne in favour of his virtuous elder brother, Vijaya[2].

In deciding on the question of Aśoka's successors, the flashes of light that may be obtained from the ancient Indian inscriptions are as follows :

(i) The Queen's Edict which was probably engraved during the second period of Aśoka's vigorous activity, 19th-21st year of abhisheka, mentions Tīvala as his young son by his second queen Kāluvāki.

(ii) In P. E. VII engraved in the 27th year of abhiṣheka, Aśoka speaks of the charities of his sons.

(iii) M. R. E. (Mysore copies), engraved probably in the 26th year of abhisheka, speaks of the Āryaputra Viceroy of Suvarṇagiri.

(iv) S. R. E. I, engraved probably in the 32nd year of abhisheka, speaks of three Kumāra Viceroys stationed at Tosali, Ujeni and Takasilā respectively.

(v) The Nāgārjunī Hill-cave inscriptions record the three cave-dedications made by Daśaratha to the Ājīvikas immediately after his consecration (anaṃtaliyaṃ abhishitena).

(vi) The form of Brāhmī letters employed in Daśaratha's inscriptions indicates certain changes to account for which one must allow an interval of time, however short, between Aśoka and Daśaratha.

The question arises—what was the course of action followed by the four Viceroys immediately after Aśoka's death, if they had survived him as would seem most likely ?

---

[1] Raychaudhuri, op. cit , p. 290f.

[2] Barua, The Yuga Purāṇa Legend of Sālis'ūka, Calcutta Review, Apr., 1945.

The conflicting traditions, Buddhist, Jaina and Brahmanical, serve to make confusion worse confounded instead of returning a satisfactory answer to this question.

According to the Nāgārjunī Hill-cave inscriptions, Daśaratha was a duly anointed king. From the situation of the caves dedicated by him, it is easy to infer that he was the sovereign of Magadha, better of Anga-Magadha.

Vincent Smith had strong reasons to believe that Samprati's dominions 'included Avantī and Western India.'[1] But, as Raychaudhuri points out, the Jaina writers represent him 'as ruling over Pāṭaliputra as well as Ujjayinī'[2]. The tradition recorded by Jinaprabhasūri, however, describes Samprati as an emperor of India whose capital, like that of Aśoka, was Pāṭaliputra. The hypothesis that Aśoka was succeeded by his two grandsons, Daśaratha and Samprati, by the first in respect of his eastern and by the second in that of his western dominions is 'little more than a guess' even on Vincent Smith's frank admission.[3]

If at a future date the veil be properly lifted from the history of Aśoka's successors, it will most probably be seen that no sooner had Aśoka passed away, no sooner had his strong hand been withdrawn than his four Viceroys asserted their independence, parcelling out his empire into as many as four, if not more, separate principalities.

9. **Length of reign and last days** :—The length of Aśoka's reign since his abhisheka, which is evident from his dated inscriptions, consists of 27 years, while the same consists of 37 years according to the Pali Chronicles, and of 36 years according to the Purāṇas. Adding to the later 37 the ealier four years during which he reigned as an unanointed king since his accession acrording to the Pali tradition, we get the total length of his reign as comprising 41 years.

It may be noted here that the Pali Chronicles and the Purāṇas give the same length of reign, namely, 24 years, to Chandragupta but slightly differ as regards the length of reign of Bindusāra which, according to the former, is 28, and, according to the latter, 25 years. Correcting the Purāṇa figure 25 to 28 and adding up the lengths of the three first reigns we get the total of 89. This total being added

---

1 Early History of India, 3rd. Ed., p. 70.

2 Raychaudhuri, op. cit. p. 291.

3 Ibid, p. 292.

to the total length of 48 years of the reign of Aśoka's six successors, yields the traditional Purāṇa figure of 137 years representing the duration of the Maurya dynasty of Magadha. If so, one has to discard the tradition of Aśoka's reign of four years as an unanointed king since his accession. This tradition may be maintained if the duration of Bindusāra's reign be accepted as 25 years and that of Aśoka's reign since coronation as 36 years, as suggested in the Purāṇas, in which case the required figure of 89 years may be obtained by adding up 24, 25, 4 and 36 years.

The S.R.E. I and S.R.E. II represent the set of Aśoka's edicts which may be supposed to have been promulgated and engraved in the closing period of his reign. If he had followed the quinquennial system, the date of their promulgation cannot be earlier than the 32nd year of his abhisheka.

S.R.E. I is addressed to the City-judiciaries of Tosali and Samāpā. In it, they are taken to task for their failure in fully grasping the meaning and spirit of his instructions to them. They are urged not to cause oppression to his subjects by sudden arrest and coercion as well as summary trial. In it, he proposes to send forth every five years the Mahāmātras under him on tours of inspection so as to check the miscarriage of justice. Here he modifies his quinquennial system and insists that the Kumāra Viceroys at Tosali, Ujeni and Takasilā should send forth on tours within every three years similar officials under them for the very same purpose.

Thus this edict goes to suggest that highhandedness and arbitrary action of the City-judiciaries, particularly in the outlying provinces, served to cause annoyance to the people.

Similarly S.R.E. II, which is addressed to the Viceroy-in-Council at Tosali and the Mahāmātras who were Royal Commissioners at Samāpā, presupposes hostile attitude and action of some of the 'frontagers' in violation of the terms of treaty or alliance. Whilst he wanted to assure them of his best intentions and friendliness, he did not omit to mention that he would tolerate them as long as their hostilities had not exceeded the limit of his patience.

The state of things as portrayed in these two edicts is faithfully represented in the Divyāvadāna legend which, while giving an account of the last days of Aśoka, relates that the highhandedness and arbitrary action on the part of the officers in charge caused the citizens of the Uttarāpatha to revolt (viruddha). On the arrival of the Kumāra Viceroy, Kuṇāla, at Takshaśilā, the citizens said, "We have revolted neither against the Kumārá nor against king Aśoka, but the wicked ministers indeed come (here) and humiliate us."[1]

The Mahāvaṃsa describes the last days of Aśoka as unhappy, and the Divyāvadāna as both unhappy and tragic. The causes of his unhappiness were, according to the Pali Chronicle, the death of his beloved queen consort Āsandimitrā in the 26th year and the destruction of the Bo-tree out of jealousy by Tishyarakshā (rakshitā) whom he appointed as queen consort four years later.[2] Over and above her attempt at the destruction of the Bo-tree, Tishyarakshitā caused, according to the Divyāvadāna legend, deep remorse to the king by her machination in getting the eyes of his beloved son Kuṇāla plucked out after he had been deputed to Takshaśilā to quell a revolt in Uttarāpatha. She is painted in the exaggerated Sanskrit story in the blackest of colours as a wily, passionate and revengeful woman of vilest character. Her story, which has happily no place in the earlier Pali Chronicle, Dīpavaṃsa, was evidently developed, to heighten the glory of the Bo-tree as the living symbol of Buddha's enlightenment and Buddhism and the importance of its worship, as also to throw into bold relief the purity and magnanimity of the character of Kuṇāla by a contrast with the vileness of the character of his step-mother.

The Sanskrit legend on the strength of which Jayaswal placed much reliance goes a step further and introduces a pathetic episode of the virtual abdication of the throne by Aśoka.

It is said that when Aśoka was about to exhaust the royal treasury by his over-extravagant subsidies to the Āryasangha or Sthavira Church, his Amātyas determined to put a stop to it approached Sampadi, the heir-apparent, and said, "King Aśoka, O Prince ! who will live for a very short time is sending on this wealth to the Kurkuṭārāma, but the treasury is the real strength to the kings, so this (wreckless ruinous action of the king) must be stopped." Thereupon the Crown-prince prevented the Steward (Bhāṇḍāgārikaḥ) from letting out any money from the treasury on the king's demand and instructed him to exercise a gradually restraining authority on all goods of value, even including metal plates, that might be given

---

[1] Divyāvadāna, p. 408.

[2] Mahāvaṃsa, XX. 3-6.

away as gifts to the Sangha. Thus the king was reduced to the position of a nominal ruler, although the administration was being carried on in his name until his death. Neither the amātyas nor the citizens, when asked by him, denied that he was all the time the supreme lord of the earth (pṛithivyām īśvaraḥ).[1]

Obviously this episode, too, was added to stress the significance of giving away everything, treasures, world-wide kingdom, wives and households, officers of the State, self and beloved son, by a powerful and benevolent monarch like Aśoka to the Buddhist Church for the sake of religion (koshaṃ sthāpayitvā mahāpṛithivīṃ antaḥpurāmatya-gaṇam ātmānaṃ Kuṇālaṃ chāryasaṃghe niryātayitvā).[2] But Aśoka was not so foolishly extravagant in his charities as to behave like that.

Aśoka, however, speaks of his sons who were sufficiently grown up in the 27th year of his abhisheka to be able to distribute charities on their own account. From all the traditional sources, namely, the Pali Chronicles, the Divyāvadāna, Kalhaṇa's Rājataranginī and Tāranātha's Tibetan history, one can collect names of just four sons of Aśoka, to wit, Mahendra who became a Buddhist monk, Kuṇāla-Tīvala who was deputed as a Viceroy to Takshaśilā,[3] Jalauka who, as suggested in the Rājataranginī, was appointed the Viceroy or Governor of Kāśmīra,[4] and Vīrasena who, according to Tāranātha, "apparently wrested Gandhāra from the hands of the feeble successor of the great Maurya at Pāṭaliputra."[5]

The inscriptions of Aśoka themselves corroborate none of the three traditions regarding Mahendra, Jalauka, and Vīrasena. The truth of the tradition about Kuṇāla being his father's Viceroy at Takshaśilā is borne out by the eivdence of S. R. E. I, which expressly refers to three Kumāras functioning then as Viceroys at Tosali, Ujeni, and Takasilā. As long as any strong evidence is not forthcoming to prove the contrary, these Kumāras must be taken to represent Aśoka's three sons. Probably Tīvala-Kuṇāla was one of them.

---

1 Divyāvadāna, p. 430f.

2 *Ibid*, p. 429.

3 Divyāvadāna, p. 407f. Referring to Gandhāra, Fa Hian says (Beal, Buddhist Records, I, p. xxxi), "This is the place which Dharmavardhana, the son of As'oka, governed." Mookerji, op. cit., p. 8.

4 Raychaudhuri, op. cit., p. 300.

5 *Ibid*, p. 300. Note that Jayaswal, identifies Vīrasena of Tāranātha with S'ūrasena, son and successor of Vis'oka-Kālās'oka mentioned in the Mūlakalpa.

The problem of identification of the Kumāra Viceroy of Gandhāra may thus be solved by the legend of Kuṇāla-Dharmavardhana. As regards the remaining two, we have still to grope in the dark, no light coming from traditions. And to add to the difficulty, the forwarding note of the Mysore copies of M. R. E. introduces us to an Āryaputra who was obviously functioning at the time as Viceroy at Suvarṇagiri. He was certainly a brother or son of Aśoka. This is also a problem on which no further light can be thrown from any source.

The giving away of the whole of the vast earth (kingdom, empire) extending as far as to the seas and oceans with all its treasures by Aśoka in the name of religion and culture and their propounders and promulgators was but a formal affair with several ancient kings of India who aspired to gain renown and popularity in this world.

All that is possible to believe is that Aśoka virtually retired from active work of administration at his ripe old age, handing over its charge to the heir-apparent and ministers who might in the meantime have formed a conspiracy to upset the methods and policies initiated and followed by him.

10. **Reign proper :** The most vigorous period of Aśoka's reign commenced with the conquest of Kalinga in the 8th year of his abhisheka and ended with the promulgation of the two Separate Rock Edicts probably in the 32nd year. The notable incidents of his reign, as far as these may be gathered from the inscriptions and legends, have been separately tabulated. They give rise to several problems which have been dealt with by previous scholars. A few select problems are left to be discussed in the following chapters in connection with Aśoka and his inscriptions.

CHAPTER III

EMPIRE

By his full title, Priyadasi Lājā Māgadhe, Aśoka passed, as we saw, as the "King of Magadha and Emperor of Jambudvīpa." The word by which he himself denoted the whole of his royal domain is vijita (R. E. II, R. E. III, R. E. XIV), vijaya (R. E. XIV), rāja-vishaya (R. E. XIII), or puthavī (R. E. V). The word vijita or vijaya [1] implies that the royal realm which he held was held as though by the right of conquest. In R. E. XIV, his vijita is described as a vast or extensive one (mahālake, mahaṃte). The large extension of his empire may be deduced from the very word puthavī (pṛithivī, earth) which is etymologically defined as 'that which extends.'[2] The expressions, mahāpaṭhavī (Dīgha, II, p. 234), pṛithivī (Arthaśāstra IX) chaturantā mahī (Arthaśāstra, I·6) ; mahāpṛithivī, āsamudrā pṛithivī, samudraparyantā mahāpṛithivī (Divy.), and āsamudrā kshiti (Raghuvaṃśa) are all meant to signify Jambudvīpa. The Buddhist legends extol Aśoka as the sole monarch or supreme lord of Jambudvīpa. Aśoka himself in his M. R. E., records with pride that he was able to commingle the gods and men in Jambudvīpa.

In R. E. II, on the other hand, his own vijita is distinguished from the pratyantas or contiguously situated bordering territories of 'the Frontagers' (Āntas). In S. R. E. II, the Āntas are characterised as 'unconquered borderers' or 'independent frontagers' (Aṃtānaṃ avijitānaṃ). The pratyantas represented, nevertheless, the territories of the Āntas to which his Dūtas ('envoys' or 'emissaries') had their access and where they were sent on certain definite missions. There were countries or territories even beyond them, which were not visited by his Dūtas (Yatra duta Devanapriyasa na yaṃti—R. E. XIII). It is, then, evident from Aśoka's own statements that his vijita was circumscribed by the bordering territories of the independent but friendly 'Frontagers'.

Even within his own empire, we are to discriminate the portion which was at first entirely under his direct rule and subsequently under the direct rule of himself and his Viceroys, from that which

---

[1] Cf. supavata-vijaya-chaka (supravarta-vijaya-chakra) in the Hāthigunphā inscr., and vijaya-rājya in the inscription of Lalāṭendu Kes'arī.

[2] "Prathate vistāraṃ yāti." "Pattharatī-ti paṭhavi."

was occupied by the semi-independent tribal territories or states (R.E. XIII). Thus his domain proper was further circumscribed by the surrounding semi-independent tribal territories of which two typical lists are supplied in R.E. V and R.E. XIII.

1. **Extent of Domain proper :** It cannot be strictly maintained that Aśoka's Rock inscriptions indicate the broad outline of his empire ; these together with some of his Minor Rock and Pillar inscriptions give us but a broad outline of his domain proper. In other words, his empire was far wider than his vijita in the restricted sense of the term, and if we take into our consideration the independent but friendly territories of the Frontagers[1], the sphere of his moral and cultural influence was not only as wide as Jambudvīpa but wider even than it to include in it certain parts of the three other Continents then known to the Indians, nay, gradually all of them in their entirety, as was expected by him when he viewed the world from the angle of a visionary (R.E. XIII). Aśoka's grandson and successor Samprati came to be claimed in the Jaina tradition to have been the 'Lord of Bhārata with its three divisions (trikhaṇḍa-Bhāratādhipati).

Thinking, more or less, on the lines suggested by Professor D.R. Bhandarkar, one may take it that by the Rock inscriptions was indicated the outline of his domain proper, by the Minor Rock inscriptions was demarcated his domain proper from the semi-independent tribal States situate within it, and by the Pillar inscriptions the places personally visited by him in course of his pilgrimage.

The extent of Aśoka's domain proper, as outlined by his inscriptions,[2] may be defined as follows :

In the south east it included the newly created province of Kalinga (i.e., Orissa), and extended as far as the western shore of the Bay of Bengal. In the south, it extended below the Krishṇā and the Tungabhadrā to include the southernmost province with its headquarters at Suvarṇagiri. In the west it included the countries of Sūnāparānta and Surāshṭra as well as the Western province of Avantī, and extended as far as the eastern shore of the Arabian sea. In the north-west, it included the province of Uttarāpatha or Gandhāra, and extended at least as far north as Peshāwar and Abbotabad,

1 Vividhatīrthakalpa of Jinaprabhasūri, Visvabhārartī ed., p. 69.

2 See location in part II.

Pl. I

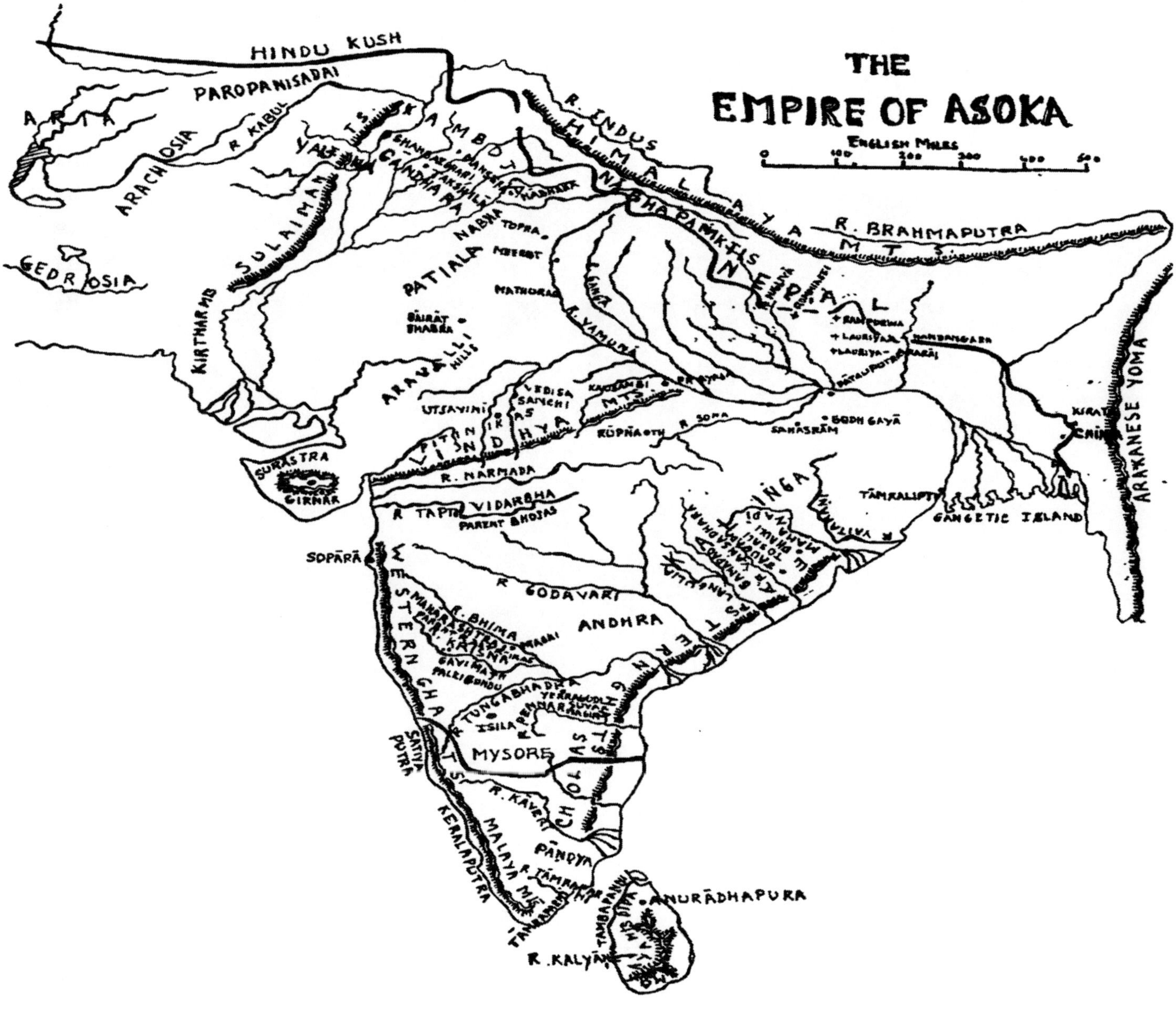
THE EMPIRE OF ASOKA
ENGLISH MILES
0 100 200 300 400 500
HINDU KUSH
PAROPANISADAI
ARIA
ARACHOSIA
R. KABUL
GEDROSIA
SULAIMAN
KIRTHAR MTS
GANDHARA
TAKSHILA
R. INDUS
HIMALAYA
R. BRAHMAPUTRA
NEPAL
TOPRA
MEERUT
MATHURA
PATIALA
BAIRAT
BHABRA
ARAVALLI HILLS
R. YAMUNA
KAUSAMBI
PATALIPUTRA
BODH GAYA
SAHASRAM
R. SOMA
UTSAYINI
SANCHI
R. NARMADA
SURASTRA
GIRNAR
R. TAPTI
VIDARBHA
SOPARA
WESTERN GHATS
R. GODAVARI
ANDHRA
R. BHIMA
R. KRISHNA
TUNGABHADRA
ISILA
MYSORE
SATIYAPUTRA
KERALAPUTRA
R. KAVERI
CHOLAS
PANDYA
MALAYA MTS
ANURADHAPURA
R. KALYANI
TAMRALIPTI
GANGETIC ISLAND
ARAKANESE YOMA
EASTERN GHATS

on two sides of the Indus, west and east. In the north, it extended as far as the Nepalese Tarai and the districts of Dehra Dun and Champāran.

As regards its extension in Bengal and Assam, the Pali Chronicles and Samanta-pāsādikā include in Aśoka's domain proper the port of Tāmralipti. In the Pali Chronicles and Fa Hian's Fo-kwo-ki, Tāmralipti is correctly described as the sea-port (in Lower Bengal) which was reachable from Pāṭaliputra by a boat 'following down the river Ganges in an easterly direction', and from which the sea-going vessels carried their passengers to Ceylon',[1] and by implication, to other sea-ports. The Pali tradition speaks also of a land-route by which Aśoka arrived in one week's time at Tāmralipti from Pāṭaliputra across the Vindhya forest (Viñjhāṭaviṃ atichcha).[2]

Raychaudhuri bases his argument in favour of the inclusion of Bengal in and the exclusion of Assam from Aśoka's domain on the authority of certain Greek writers headed by Curtius, the Divyāvadāna and Hwen Thsang's Si-yu-ki. "We learn from the Classical writers", says he, "that the country of Gangaridæ, *i e.*, Bengal, formed a part of the dominions of the king of the Prasii, *i.e.*, Magadha, as early as the time of Agrammes, *i.e.*, the last Nanda king. A passage of Pliny clearly suggests that the 'Palibothri', *i.e.*, the rulers of Pāṭaliputra, dominated the whole tract along the Ganges. That the Magadhan kings retained their hold on Bengal as late as the time of Aśoka is proved by the testimony of the Divyāvadāna, and of Hiouen Tsang who saw stūpas of that monarch near Tāmralipti and Karṇasuvarṇa (in West Bengal), in Samataṭa (in East Bengal) as well as in Puṇḍravardhana (in North Bengal). Kāmarūpa (Assam) seems to have lain outside the empire. The Chinese pilgrim saw no monument of Aśoka in that country."[3]

The extension of Aśoka's empire in Bengal thus made out may be true to fact. But in the absence of any inscription of Aśoka throwing light on the point the evidences cited and relied upon must be treated all as presumptive in nature and inconclusive in effect. Hwen Thsang was an eye-witness to the existence of four stūpas built by Aśoka near the chief town of each of the four divisions of Bengal. Fa Hian, too, stayed for a long time at Tāmralipti but he had to say nothing

[1] Mahāvaṃsa, XIX. 4 ; Beal, Buddhist Records, I, p. lxxi.

[2] Ibid. XIX. 6,

[3] Raychaudhuri, op.cit., p, 256.

about any monument of Aśoka to be seen there. Thus the testimony of the later Chinese pilgrim lacks corroboration from the itinerary of the earlier visitor.

The Divyāvadāna mentions Puṇḍravardhana in connection with an impossible episode of a ruthless persecution of the Nirgranthas (confounded with the Ājīvikas) by Aśoka's order, which was issued forthwith to avenge an insult meted out by them to an image of Buddha. The existence or worship of a Buddha image in Aśoka's time is yet to be proved. The cruel persecution of the Nirgranthas and Ājīvikas attributed to Aśoka[1] was against the spirit of the Maurya emperor and the general trend of his edicts and inscriptions. The only relic of the Maurya time hitherto discovered at Puṇḍranagara is the small Brāhmī inscription from Mahāsthān in the district of Bogrā serving as it did to carry from the town of Puṇḍra paddy and small coins to the settlement of the Shaḍvargikas. An additional support to the theory of inclusion of Puṇḍravardhana might be sought from the Divyāvadāna definition of the Middle Country.

As defined in the Pali Vinaya Piṭaka (I, p. 197), "it extended in the east to the town of Kajangala, beyond which was Mahāsālā ; on the south-east, to the river Salalavatī."[2] The Divyāvadāna (p. 21 f.) on the other hand, "extends the eastern boundary to include Puṇḍravardhana, roughly identical with North Bengal."[3] Puṇḍravardhana was inded the first division of Bengal which lay contiguous to Kajangala as borne out by the itinerary of Hwen Thsang[4] and the Mahābhārata description of Bhīma's digvijaya in Eastern India.[5]

Curtius and other Greek writers describe indeed Agrammes the Magadhan contemporary of Alexander as "king of the Gangaridæ and the Prasii".[6] What did the Greek writers themselves understand by the two terms, Prasii and Gangaridai ?

---

1 Divyāvadāna, p. 427.

2 Also Jātaka, I, pp. 49, 80, Malalasekera, Dictionary, II, p. 419. As I maintain, the eastern boundary of the Buddhist Midland as defined in Pali was to all intents and purposes identical with that of the modern province of Behār.

3 Malalasekera, op.cit., II, p. 419 ; B. C. Law, India as Described, p. 21.

4 Beal, Buddhist Records, II, p. 194 ; "Going from this country (of Kajangala) eastward, and crossing the Ganges, after about 600 li (100 miles) we come to the kingdom of···Puṇḍravardhana."

5 Mahābhārata, Sabhā-Digvijayaparva, 30.21.

6 McCrindle, Invasion of India by Alexander, pp. 221, 281.

According to Schawnbeck, the Greek word Prasii "bears a very close resemblance to the Indian word Prāchyas (*i e.*, 'dwellers in the East')." In the Indika of Megasthenes the Prasii are described as "an Indian people," the most distinguished people in all India in whose country is situated the city called Palibothra (*i.e.*, Pāṭaliputra)[1]. To the same effect it is stated in Fragment XXVII, "the greatest city in India is that which is called Palimbothra, in the dominions of the Prasians."

The Aitareya Brāhmaṇa distinguishes the Prāchyas from the Dākshiṇātyas, Pratīchyas, Udīchyas, and Madhyamas, and defines them as the Eastern peoples who were 'anointed for overlordship'. It suggests that they were the ruling peoples who lived to the east of the territories of the Kurus, the Pañchālas, the Vasas and the Uśīnaras. The Kurus and the rest were the typical Midlanders (Madhyamas)[2].

If we take the name Prāchyas in the Aitareya Brāhmaṇa and Great Epic sense, the Prasii of the Greek writers must be treated as the Eastern peoples of India identical with the Gangaridai or Gangaridæ. But this equation is not maintainable in view of the fact that Megasthenes definitely represents the Prasians as the ruling people of Palibothra, *i.e.*, the capital of Magadha, from which circumstance they were also known by the name of Palibothris, *i.e.*, Pāṭaliputrians.[3]

Megasthenes introduces the Gangaridai in connection with the Ganges system of rivers and the Ganges' course, both of which he correctly described. In one passage he says, "Now this river, which at its source is 30 stadia broad, flows from north to south, and empties its waters into the ocean forming the eastern boundary of the

---

1 McCrindle, Ancient India, pp. 55f. 66, 67.

2 Aitareya Br.. VIII. 14 ; Etasyām prāchyam dis'i ye kecha Prāchyānām rājānaḥ sāmrājyāyaiva te abhishichyante. According to the Mahābhārata, too (Sabhā-Digvijayaparvā, 29. 1. ff.), the Eastern countries were those which lay to the east of Kuru-Pañchāla.

Raychaudhuri, op.cit , p. 134.

3 McCrindle, Ancient India, Fragm. LVI. B of Megasthenes, p. 161. This led General Cunningham (Ancient Geography.) to suggest that Prasii 'is only the Greek form of Palās'a or Parās'a, which is an actual and well-known name of Magadha, of which Palibothra was the capital. It obtained this name from the Palās'a or *Butea frondosa*, which still grows as luxuriantly in the province as in the time of Hiwen Thsang......Curtius......calls the people Pharrasii, which is an almost exact transcript of the Indian name Pārāsiya. The Praxiakos of Aelian is only the derivative from Palāsaka'.

Gangaridai, a nation which possesses a vast force of the largest sized animals."[1]

In another passage, he observes : "...it flows out with a gentle current, being at the narrowest eight miles and on the average a hundred stadia, in breadth, and never of less depth than twenty paces (one hundred feet) in the final part of its course, which is through the country of the Gangarides."[2]

He clearlyd efines the Gangarides as a people who lived 'in the farthest off part' and whose king possessed '1000 horse, 700 elephants, and 60,000 foot in apparatus of war.' They are distinguished from a very powerful nation who occupied an extremely populous island in the Ganges, and whose king kept 'under arms 50,000 foot and 4000 horse.'[3]

From Pliny's account of the Palibothri, it appears that the Gangaridai represented all peoples who lived along the whole extent of the Ganges' course, while, in one context at any rate, Megasthenes seems to make 'the Gangarides a branch of Kalingae : *Gangaridum Calingarum Regia*.[4] Pliny, too, 'mentions the Macco-Calingae and *Gangarides-Calingae* as separate peoples from the Calingae."[5] "The tribes called Calingae", says Megasthenes, "are nearest the sea, and higher up are the Nandei, and the Malli in whose country is Mount Mallus, the boundary of all that district being the Ganges." From this McCrindle concludes that 'the Gangaridae or Gangarides occupied the region corresponding roughly with that now called Lower Bengal and consisted of various indigenous tribes, which in course of time became more or less Aryanised."[6]

The Allahabad stone-pillar inscription of Samudragupta leads us to think that probably the task of subduing such eastern frontier countries as Samataṭa (East Bengal), Ḍavāka and Kāmarūpa (Assam) was left to him to accomplish. The Great Epic account of Bhīma's military expedition in the eastern region envisages the conquest of the whole of Bengal and Assam and agrees in all important respects with Hwen Thsang's travels. The Mahābhārata account may not, therefore, speak of an earlier state of things. But from this account

---

1 *Ibid*, p. 32, Fragm. 1.
2 Ibid, p. 160, Fragm. LVI. B.
3 Ibid, p. 160, Fragm. LVI. B.
4 Ibid, p. 137.
5 Cunningham, Ancient Geography, p. 518 f.
6 McCrindle, op. cit., p. 136.

and Hwen Thsang's itinerary, it may be inferred that the Gangaridae as a people allied to the Calingae were no other than the dwellers of Tamralipta and Suhma, in short, of the modern district of Midnapore. The inclusion of this part of Bengal in Aśoka's domain proper is suggested, as we saw, by the Pali tradition. As for other parts of Bengal, including the district of Purnea on the river Kauśikī, now included in the province of Behār, it is not impossible that those adjoining the Middle Country came within Aśoka's domain proper, although we must wait for a more positive evidence to establish it.

2. **Extent of Empire** :—Aśoka's earthly empire consisted of his domain proper and the semi-independent tribal territories (R.E. V, R.E. XIII). On the north, it was bounded by the Himalayān range. On the south, it abutted on the independent but friendly territories of the Cholas, the Pāṇḍyas, the Satiyaputras, the Keralaputras, and the Tāmraparṇyas (R.E. II, R.E. XIII). On the east, it extended as far as to the Bay of Bengal, at least after the annexation of Kalinga. On the west, it extended as far as to the Arabian sea. And on the north-west, it bordered on the independent but friendly Asiatic territory of Antiyoka (Antiochus II Theos, king of Western Asia and Syria).

"Alexander indeed," says Arrian, "came and overthrew all in war, all whom he attacked, and would even have conquered the whole world had his army been willing to follow him. On the other hand, a sense of justice, they say, prevented any Indian king from attempting conquest beyond the limits of India."[1] According to Megasthenes, the western side of India was bounded by the river Indus.[2] But since the treaty following the Seleukidan war with Chandragupta the Maurya empire extended not only beyond the Indus but also beyond the Sulaiman and Kirthar ranges to include in it the four former Greek satrapies of "the Paropanisadai, Aria, and Arachosia, the capitals of which were respectively Kabul, Herāt, and Kāndāhār, and also Gedrosia, the modern Belochistan," in short, the whole of Belochistan and Eastern Afghanistan.

Pliny rightly observes : "Many writers, however, do not give the river Indus as the western boundary of India, but include within it four satrapies······making the river Cophes[3] its furthest limit, though others prefer to consider all these belonging to the Arii. Many

---

[1] Ibid p. 209.

[2] Ibid, pp. 29, 47 f.

[3] *i.e.*, Kābul, cf. I.A., V. pp. 329, 330 ; McCrindle, Ancient India, p. 156.

writers further include in India even the city of Nysa and Mount Merus....... They include also the Astakani[1] in whose country the vine grows abundantly."[2]

As regaads the geographical extension of Bhāratavarsha or India proper, there is hardly any material difference to be noticed between the foreign and native accounts.

According to Eratosthenes and Megasthenes, for instance, "India is bounded on the eastern side, right towards the south, by the great ocean ; --its northern frontier is formed by the Kaukasos (Himalayan) range as far as the junction of that range with Taurus ; and the boundary towards the west and the north-west, as far as the great ocean, is formed by the river Indus."[3]

To the same effect is the description of Diodorus, according to whom "India, which is in shape quadrilateral,[4] has its eastern as well as western side bounded by the great sea, but on the northern side it is divided by Mount Hemodos (Himādri) from that part of Skythia which is inhabited by those Skythians who are called the Sakai, while the fourth or western side is bounded by the river called the Indus."[5]

As described by Hwen Thsang, "The countries embraced under the term of India (In-tu, anciently called Shin-tu, Hien-tau) are generally spoken of as the five Indies. In circuit this country is about 90,000 li (15,000 miles) ; on three sides it is bordered by the great sea ; on the north, it is backed by the Snowy Mountains. The north part is broad, the southern part is narrow."[6]

The Mārkaṇḍeya Purāṇa describes India as a typical peninsula with the great sea on the south, west and east, and the Himālaya on

---

1 Same as Assakanae, Assakeni, Assakanoi, Aspagani, Aspagonae, Sk. As'vagaṇāḥ, As'vakāḥ, from which the modern name Afgan may be derived.

2 McCrindle, Ancient India, p. 160.

3 *Ibid*, p. 43.

4 The idea of the quadrilateral shape is derived from the Indian word chaturantā. This need not, however, trouble us. In the Great Epic the topographical shape of India is likened to that of 'a bended bow of which the string being pulled by the hand forms an apex at Dhanushkoṭi.' Hwen Thsang represents it figuratively by the shape of a half-moon. In the Pali Mahāgovinda Suttanta, the topographical outline of India is represented by the shape of a bullock-cart with its face towards the south (uttareṇa āyataṃ, dakkhiṇena sakaṭamukhaṃ). B. C. Law, op.cit., p. 13.

5 McCrindle, Ancient India, p. 29.

6 Beal, Buddhist Records, I, p. 70.

the north,[1] and gives it a length of 1,000 yojanas from south to north.[2]

The name Bhāratavarsha is not employed by the Buddhists to denote India ; their familiar term is Jambudvīpa. This Jambudvīpa may, for all practical purposes, be treated as India proper plus the inhabited tracts in the Himalayan region extending as far north as the Altyn range, if not still further up, as far west as the Hindukush range, and as far east as the Namklu mountains. Jambudvīpa, as defined in Buddhist literature, is the southern subcontinent of the mainland of Asia, situated to the south of Mount Sumeru and between the two subcontinents of Aparagoyāna and Pūrvavideha, situated respectively to the west and east of the same mount. It excludes the eight upadvīpas or adjoining islands of Bhāratavarsha, Tāmraparṇa (Ceylon) included.

Aśoka's empire was not co-extensive with either Bhāratavarsha or Buddhist Jambudvīpa in so far as it excluded from it the independent territories of the Āntas in the south ; it was wider than both in so far as it included within it the four Greek satrapies in Afghanistan and Beluchistan. As regards its extension towards the north beyond the Himalayas, it is still a disputed question, and it largely depends, as we shall see further on, on the determination of the territories of the Nābha-lines of ruling tribes.

Jules Bloch is said so have once casually remarked that the inscriptions of Aśoka afford data for the first linguistic survey of India. But one may go even further and say that they afford data also for the first geographical survey of India. Accordingly, in connection with Aśoka's empire, we may examine with profit the nature of the light these records throw on the traditional divisions of India.

Though the definition varies with diffeaent authorities, the geograpnical divisions of India are generally enumerated as five, *viz.*, the Eastern (Prāchya, Pūrvānta, Pūrvadeśa) ; the Southern (Dakshiṇa, Dakshiṇāpatha, Dākshiṇātya) ; the Western (Pratīchya, Aparānta, Paśchāddeśa) ; the Northern, better the North-Western (Ūrddhva, Udīchya, Uttarāpatha) ; and the Middle (Madhyama, Madhyadeśa,

---

1 Mārkaṇḍeya Purāṇa, Ch. 57 : Dakshiṇāparato asya pūrveṇa cha mahodadhiḥ Himavat uttareṇāsya.

2 Cf. Vishṇu Purāṇa, II, Ch. 3. Yojanānāṃ sahasran tu dvīpe 'yaṃ dakshiṇottarāt.

Antarvedī). The Mārkaṇḍeya Purāṇa adds two more eivisions to the usual list of five, namely, the Vindhyan (Vindhyapṛishṭha) and the Mountainous (Parvatāśrayī). Pali literature, too, speaks of a sixth division but terms it the Himalayan (Hemavata, Himavanta-padesa).

The Eastern division was represented, according to the Aitareya Brāhmaṇa, VIII. 14, by the rulers who were anointed for overlordship (sāmrājyāya) and passed accordingly as Overlords (Samrāṭ) ; the southern division by those of the Satvat race who were anointed for military regime (bhaujyāya) and passed accordingly as Military Chiefs (Bhojas) ; the Western division by those of the southern and western peoples (nīchyānām, apāchyānām) who were anointed for self-rule (svārājyāya) and passed as Self-rulers (Svarāṭ) ; the Northern division by the ruling peoples like the Trans-Himalayan Kurus and Madras who were anointed for sovereignty (vairājyāya) and passed accordingly as Sovereigns (Virāt) ; and the Middle division by the ruling peoples like the Kurus, the Pañchālas, the Vaśas and the Uśīnaras who were anointed for kingship (rājyāya) and passed accordingly as Kings (Rājā).[1]

(a) As to Middle division : The scope of the Middle division was gradually widened. Bodhāyana placed it between the place of disappearance of the Sarasvatī (*i.e.*, Vinaśana) on the west and the Black Forest (Kālakavana) on the east, and between the Himalayas on the north and the Pāripātra (Pāriyātra) mountains on the south.[2] Manu's Middle Country is placed between the Himalayas and the Vindhya range and taken to extend from Vinaśana as far east as Prayāga (Allahabad).[3] Rājaśekhara extends it further east to include Benares.[4] The Gopatha Brāhmaṇa includes in it not only Kāśī and Kośala but also Anga and Magadha.[5] The Pali definition extends it still further east to include the country of Kajangala which is the modern district of Santal Parganas,[6] while ultimately in the Divyāvadāna definition it includes even Puṇḍravardhana or North Bengal.[7]

---

1 Aitareya Brāhmaṇa, VIII. 14 ; Raychaudhuri, op. cit., p. 133 f.

2 Bodhāyana, Dharmasūtra, I. 1. 22.

3 Manu, II. 21.

4 Kāvyamīmāṃsā, p. 93 ; B. C. Law, India As Described p. 16.

5 Gopatha Br. II. 9 ; Raychaudhuri, op. cit., p. 55.

6, 7 Malalasekera, Dictionary, II, p. 418 f., B.C. Law, India As Described, p. 19 f.

As defined in Pali, the eastern frontier of the Middle Country lay to the east of Mahāśālā beyond the township of Kajangala. It was bounded on the south-east by the river called Salalavatī, on the south by the town of Śatakarṇikā[1] which was probably the place of origin of the Śātakarṇis, on the west by the Brāhman village of Sthūṇa, and on the north by the Usīradhvaja mountain near Kankhal.[2]

The countries of Kuru and Pañchāḷa, Anga and Magadha, Kāśī Kośala, Sālva and Matsya, Vasa and Uśīnara were contained in the Middle Country, according to the Gopatha Brāhmaṇa. The Pali list includes also the countries of Vṛiji and Malla, Chedi and Vatsa, and associates Śūrasena with Matsya instead of Sālva.

It may, upon the whole, be premised that the Middle Country as known to the early Buddhists[3] covered that middle part of Northern India which was watered by the entire Ganges system of rivers[3] to the exclusion of those which now flow through Bengal.

This division is outlined on the north by Aśoka's Rock Edicts at Kalsi (Dehra Dun), Minor Pillar inscriptions at Lumbinī and Niglīva (Nepalese Tarai) and pillars and Pillar Edicts at Lauriya Nandangarh and Rāmpurva (Champāran district), on the east by his Pillar inscription and palace at Kumrāhār, Patna, on the south by his Minor Rock inscription at Sahasrām (Shāhbād district, Behār), and on the south-west and west by his pillar at Saṃkāśya, Schism pillar inscriptions at Sāñchī and Kosām, Minor Rock inscripion at Bairāt, Pillar inscriptions at Mīrāth and Toprā, and Rock Edicts at Kalsi. It was wholly included in his domain proper and empire.

(b) **As to Vindhyan division :** The northern boundary of the Southern division was gradually pushed further and further south from the Ganges to the Pāriyātra and Vindhya mountains, to the Narmadā and the upper Godāvarī. Rājaśekhara places it to the south of Māhīshmatī, once the capital of Avantī and now identified with Mandhātā on the Narmadā. While commenting on Hwen Thsang's five Indies, Cunningham takes Southern India to denote

---

1 Malalasekera is the first scholar to correct the name from Setakaṇṇikā to Satakaṇṇikā. See Dictionary, II, p. 419.

2 Raychaudhuri, op. cit., p. 55.

3 In commenting on Hwen Thsang's five Indies, Cunningham (Ancient Geography of India) takes Central India to comprise the whole of the Gangetic provinces from Thāneswar to the head of the Delta, and from the Himalayas to the banks of the Narmadā.

'the whole of the peninsula from Nāsik on the west and Ganjam on the east, including the modern districts of Berār and Telingana.'

As I have sought to maintain,[1] Dakshiṇāpatha was at first the name of ā trade-route, the Southern High Road, which extended from Rājagṛiha, the old capital of Magádha, to Pratishṭhāna (modern Paithān) opposite Nāsik on the right bank of the upper Godāvarī, not far from its source. Its extension may be divided into two stages, as pointed out by Rhys Davids, *viz.*, (i) North to South-west, from Śrāvastî to Pratishṭhāna ; and (ii) North to South-east, from Śrāvastī to Rājagṛiha. The main stopping places between Śrāvastī and Pratishṭhāna, beginning from the north, were Sāketa, Kauśāmbī, Vanasa (otherwise called Tumbavana or Vana-S'rāvastī), Vidiśā, Gonarda (afterwards called Godhāpura), Ujjayinī (the later capital of Avantī), and Māhīshmatī (the earlier capital of Avantī). And the principal stopping places between Rājagṛiha and S'rāvastī, beginning from south-east, were Nālandā, Pāṭaliputra, Vaiśālī, Bhāṇḍagrāma, Hastigrāma, Pāvā, Kusīnārā, Kapilavastu, and S'vetavyā.[2] By the expressions, Pāṭaliputraḥ Dakshiṇāpathe and Avantī-Dakkhiṇāpathe, one should understand either 'Pāṭaliputra and Avantī on the Southern Road' or 'Pāṭaliputra and Avantī in Dakshiṇāpatha.' In the latter case, we may presume that Dakshiṇāpatha as the Southern Road lent its name to the countries below the Ganges and above the Godāvarī across which it lay.[3] When the name Dakshiṇāpatha or Dākshiṇātya came to be applied to Southern India below the Pāriyātra and Vindhya mountains or below the Narmadā and Mahānadī, it simply meant the Deccan peninsula to which the Southern, better South-western, Road ultimately led.

The Mārkaṇḍeya Purāṇa characteristically suggests a Vindhya-pṛishṭha or Vindhyan division in between the Middle aud Eastern divisions on the north and the Southern division on the south, and locates it to the east of the Western division. Its southern boundary is roughly the Narmadā on the west, the Mahānadī on the east, and the Vindhya range in the middle. The Purāṇa locates in it such typical peoples with their territories as the Uttamarṇas,[4] Daśārṇas, Bhojas,

---

1 Old Brāhmī Inscriptions in the Udayagiri and Khandagiri Caves, Notes.

2 Buddhist India, p. 105.

3 Even now a portion of Central India to the north of the Vindhya range is known as Deccan.

4 Evidently the same people as the Uttamas in the Mahābhārata, VI. 9. 41. Cf. the name Utamabhadra in the Nāsik Cave inscription of Usavadāta.

Kishkindhyas, Anūpas, Avantis,[1] Vīrahotras,[2] Karūshas, Malajas (Malayas),[3] Mekalas[4] and Utkalas.

The northern boundary of this division which really formed the southern fringe of the Middle and Eastern divisions may easily be taken to be indicated by the Rupnāth and Sahasrām copies of M.R.E. Its western boundary may similarly be taken to be indicated by the Schism Pillar inscription at Sāñchī.

(c) **As to Western division :** The Western division of India is outlined by Aśoka's Rock inscriptions at Sopārā and Girnār in the west, and the Sāñchī copy of the Schism Pillar Edict and the Bairāt copy of M.R.E. in the east. This division contained his westernmost province of Avantī with its viceregal headquarters at Ujjayinī. Kauśāmbi, Sāñchī, *i.e.*, Vidiśā, and Ujjayini were situated on the Southern Road. Bairāt (Virāṭanagara) in the modern state of Jaipur was the capital of the Matsya country which, according to Bhandarkar, comprised parts of Alwar, Jaipur and Bharatpur.[5] Eastern Matsya itself, like Vatsa with Kauśāmbī as its capital, was included in the Midland or Middle Country.

The Sopārā set of Aśoka's Rock Edicts was incised at S'ūrpāraka, which was known in the Buddha's time as a famous sea-port in Sūnāparānta, simply called Aparānta in the Pali Chronicles and the Samanta-pāsādikā. But it would seem that the Pali Sūnāparānta is the same territorial name as Kukkurāparānta.[6] The name Kukkurāparānta occurs in the Nāsik Cave inscription of Vāsishṭhīputra Pulumāyi along with Surāshṭra, Anūpa, Vidarbha, and Ākarāvantī, and in the Junāgarh Rock inscription of Rudradāman I along with Ākarāvantī, Anūpa, Ānarta, Surāshṭra, S'vabhra, Marukachchha, Sindhu-Sauvīra, Nishāda tracts, and the like, the dominions mentioned in Rudradā-

---

[1] Their territory must have been the Vindhyan Avantī or what is called Pūrvāvantī in the Junāgarh Rock inscription of Rudradāman I.

[2] Their territory may be best identified with Barhut of which the more correct form is Berhut.

[3] Obviously the same as the people called Malayas in the Nāsik Cave inscription of Usavadāta.

[4] Their name is still preserved in the name of the Maikal range, a part of the Ṛiksha mountains, to which the source of the two rivers, Narmadā and Sōn, may be traced.

[5] Carmichael Lectures, 1918, p, 53.

[6] In the Pali Nemi-Jātaka, the word sonā (sk. s'vānaḥ) stands for sunakhā, meaning 'dogs', i.e., kukura or kukkura.

man's inscriptions being the typical countries of the Western division. The Kāvya-mīmāṃsā list of such countries contains, among others, the name of Surāshṭra, Bhṛigukachchha (Pali Bharukachchha), Kachchha, Ānarta and Arvuda (Ābu). The Mārkaṇḍeya Purāṇa, which contains a longer list, mentions, *inter alia*, the name of Nāsika, Surāshṭra, Kachchha, Avantī, Arvuda, Tripura and Vidiśā, while, according to Hwen Thsang, the Western division appears to have comprised 'Sindh, Western Rājputānā, Cutch, Gujarāt, and a portion of the adjoining coast on the lower course of the Narmadā.'[1] The countries from the Mahābhārata lists, which may be located in the same division, include Aparamatsya, Kantāra, Avantī, Arvuda, Apara Kuntibhoja, Surāshṭra, S'ūrpāraka, Nishāda, Kālamukha (a cannibal tract), Kachchha Kukkura, Kundāparānta, and the like.[2]

In the opinion of Bhagawanlal Indraji Aparānta denoted the whole western sea-board of Western India. But in the case of Sūnaparānta or Kukurāparānta, as distinguished from Aparānta as the name of the Western division, Aparānta had presumably a limited territorial extension, which is represented now by Northern Konkan. Probably the whole of Konkan, north of Karṇāṭa, was sought to be denoted by the compound name Sūnaparānta or Kukurāparānta, which was the south-western destination of a caravan route extended from the Southern Road[3]. The Mahābhārata mentions two Kukura countries, one of which, namely, that which is not connected with Aparānta, might perhaps be located in North Kaṭhiāwār near Ānarta[4].

I cannot agree with Dr. Sircar that Marukachchha, distinguished in the Mārkaṇḍeya Purāṇa from Kachchha (Cutch), is a compound of two territorial names, namely, Maru denoting Western Rājputānā and Kachchha denoting Cutch.[5] It is evidently a variant of Bharukachchha or Bhṛigukachchha (modern Broach, Barygaza of the Periplus). Marukachchha, as its name implies, was indeed a Desert Cutch, but the desert was not the Kantāra or Marukantāra of Western Rajputānā; it was the desert adjoining Surāshṭra or Gujarāt.

---

[1] Cunningham, Ancient Geography, p. 690 ; B.C. Law, India As Described, p. 73f.

[2] Mahābhārata, II. 31, VI. 9.

[3] From Sūnaparānta Puṇṇa Thera 'went with a caravan to Sāvatthi.' Theragāthā-Commentary, I, p. 158 ; Malalasekera, Dictionary, ii, p. 1210.

[4] Mahābhārata associates the Kukkuras with the Das'ārṇas (VI. 9. 42), and with the Konkaṇas and others in *ibid*, VI, 9, 60.

[5] Select Inscriptions, Vol. I, p. 172.

The Girnār version of Aśoka's Rock Edicts was incised at Girinagara, the capital of Surāshṭra, now identified with South Kaṭhiāwār. It is not improbable that in Aśoka's time the whole of Gujarāt, including Ānarta, was within the jurisdiction of Surāshṭra.

(d) **As to Southern division :** Aśoka's empire excluded the independent but friendly territories of the Cholas, the Pāṇḍyas, the Satiyaputras, the Keralaputras and the Tāmraparṇyas but included those of the Andhras, the Pārinda-Pāradas and other Aparāntas. It included also the entire territory of the Kalingas. We have two sets of Aśoka's Rock and Separate Rock Edicts within the newly created province of Kalinga, *viz.*, one set in the Puri district and the other in the district of Ganjam. Both of these districts are included in the modern province of Orissa.

According to the Great Epic tradition, the territory of the Kalingas, which was reachable by a route along the seat-coast from the Ganges' mouth[1] and lay beyond Tāmralipti, Karvaṭa and Suhma[2], included the river Vaitaraṇī, if it was not exactly its northern boundary.[3] Its southern limit along the sea-coast may be guessed from the position of Aśoka's Rock inscriptions at Jaugaḍa in the district of Ganjam as well as from the fact that Dantapura near Chicacole[4] (Dantakura of the Great Epic, V. 48. 76, and Pālura of the Nāgārjunikonda inscriptions) is mentioned in the Pali Mahāgovinda Suttanta as the ancient capital of Kalinga. Raychaudhuri may be right in suggesting that probably the name of Dantapura is still preserved in that of the fort of Dantavaktra in Ganjam.[5] It is evident from the Hāthigumphā inscription that the kingdom of Kalinga included Pṛithudaka or Pithuṇḍa on the sea-coast, which was situated near the river Lāngala (Lānguliyā)[6]. Hence it may be safely presumed that Kalinga comprised the whole

---

[1] Mahābhārata, Vanaparva, 114, 4.

[2] *Ibid*, Sabhāparva, 30, 24-25.

[3] *Ibid*, 114. 4 : ete Kalingāḥ yatra Vaitaraṇī nadī. Raychaudhuri, op. cit., p. 75.

[4] Cf. Sylvain Le'vi, Pre-Aryan et Pre-Dravidian dans 1 Inde, J. A., Julli et Septembre, 1923 ; also I. A., 1926 (May), p. 94 f.

[5] Pliny says, "From the mouth of the Ganges to Cape Calingae and the town of Dandagula 625 miles." Yule identifies Cape Calingaon as Point Godāvarī. McCrindle, Ancient India, p. 144.

[6] Acc. to Pliny, the Calingae were nearest the sea. Cf. I. A., 1877, McCrindle, Ancient India, p. 62.

of the sea-coast from at least the river Vaitaraṇī to the Lānguliyā and abutted on the borders of the Andhra territory[1].

The river Salalavatī (Saraṇavatī, Svarṇavatī), which formed the south-eastern limit of the Buddhist Midland, may indeed be identified with the modern Svarṇarekhā[2] which divides the state of Mayurbhanj and the district of Bāleswar from that of Midnapore. Some of the hill-tribes and a branch of the Kalingas (say, the Madrakalingas of the Great Epic, VI. 9. 42, the Modogalingae of Pliny)[3] may be placed in the region between the Suvarṇarekhā and the Vaitaraṇī.

The independent territories in the south lay, according to the specification suggested by Aśoka himself, below the province of Kalinga on the east, the southernmost province in the middle, and the province of Avantī on the west. It lay also below the Andhra and Pārinda-Pārada territories on the east, and the territories of the Rāshṭrikas and Bhojakas and their offshoots in the middle and on the west. And so far as Aśoka's inscriptions are concerned, the most eastern point of the dividing line is represented by the Rock inscriptions at Jaugaḍa, the central part by those at Yerraguḍi, Brahmagiri and Gavīmath, and the most western point by those at Sopārā. On the east, the southern limit of Aśoka's empire can indeed be pushed as far south as the upper Pennār, the region between this river on the south and the Kṛishṇā on the north being included in it. On the west the same may be pushed as far south as the tract about Karṇāṭaka. In the middle, Aśoka's empire may be easily taken to have comprised the northern part of Mysore which is watered by the Tungabhadrā and its southern tributaries. Whether or not the most southern limit of the same can be pushed further below depends largely on the location of Suvarṇagiri, which was the viceregal headquarters of the Southern province.

As for Suvarṇagiri, Mookerji (Asoka, p. 107 f.) inclines to think that "from its name, the 'gold mount', the place might be in the ancient gold-mining areas, and this edict (M.R.E.) has been found at Maski near Raichur, which shows numerous traces of ancient gold workings, a shaft of which is the deepest in the world known so far (Hyderabad Arch. Series, No. 1)." This is identified by Hultzsch with Kanakagiri, south of Maski.

---

1 Raychaudhuri, op. cit., pp. 75, 251.

2 B. C. Law, India as Described, p. 26.

3 McCrindle, Ancient India, p. 134.

The proposed identification of Suvarṇagiri with Kanakagiri, 'south of Maski and north of the ruins of Vijayanagara', is unconvincing for the simple reason that the Maski copy of M.R.E. differs materially from the Isila version in Northern Mysore. In the neighbourhood of Suvarṇagiri one must expect not only a text of M.R.E. which is similar to that of the Isila version but also a set of Rock Edicts.[1] The Yerraguḍi rock in the Karnool district, bearing as it does a complete set of Rock Edicts besides a version of M.R.E., which is substantially the same as that of Prahmagiri, Siddāpura and Jatinga Rāmeswara, satisfies, no doubt, this twofold test. But this rock, as appears from the M.R E. incised on it, was situated rather within the jurisdiction of a Rajjuka than within that of a Viceroy-in-Council.

One must search for Suvarṇagiri farther south in Mysore and in the upper valleys of the Kāverī. The Rāmāyaṇa refers to a great mountain by the name of Ayomukha, which abounded in metallic ores and which lay in the centre of territories of the Andhras, the Puṇḍras, the Cholas, the Pāṇḍyas and the Keralas and in a sandal district near the valleys of the Kāverī.[2]

The territories around Aśoka's southernmost province below the Vindhya, below the Narmadā and the Godāvarī, were, according to Aśoka's own showing (R.E. II, V, XIII), those of the Andhras and Pārinda-Pāladas and the countries of the Cholas, Pāṇḍyas, Satiyaputras, Keralaputras and Tāmraparṇyas. These are obviously the territories mentioned in the Rāmāyaṇa (IV. 41.8-20, in which, however, we have the Puṇḍras instead of Aśoka's Pārindas, and the Keralas in place of of Aśoka's Satiyaputras and Keralaputras.

(e) **As to North-western division :** Uttarāpatha and Dakshiṇāpatha, as I am inclined to think, are two relative terms and both denoted at first two high roads or caravan routes, the former the Northern, better North-Western Road, and the latter the Southern, better South-Western Road, each with its various

---

[1] One may reject on the same ground Raychaudhuri's tentative suggestion as to the site of Suvarṇagiri being in the neighbourhood of Wāghli in Khāndesh. (Political Hstory, p. 257.) Cf. the city of Suvarṇa-parvata in the Hitopades'a.

[2] Rāmāyaṇa, IV. 41. 12-14 :

Tathaiv-Andhrāṃs' cha Puṇḍrāṃs' cha Cholāṃ Pāṇḍyāṃs' cha Keralān ।
Ayomukhañ cha gantavyaḥ parvato dhātumaṇḍitaḥ ॥
Vichitras'ikharaḥ s'rīmān chitra-pushpita-kānanaḥ ।
sachandanavanades'o mārgitavyo mahāgiriḥ ॥

branches and extensions. Several roads having started from the main halting places on the South-Western Road, such as Śrāvastī Sāketa, Kauśāmbī and Mathurā on the right bank of the Yamunā, merged in the North-Western Road (Uttarāpathenāhṛitāḥ, to use the phrase of Pāṇini, V. 1. 77), and several roads having branched off from the North-Western, led to different destinations, such as Śrughna, *i.e.*, Dehra Dun, Kekaya, and Sindhu-Sauvīra. The well-known destination of the main road was Takshaśilā (Pali Takkasilā, modern Taxila). The Rāmāyaṇa speaks of two routes, longer and shorter, by which one might travel from Ayodhyā (Oudh) to the Kekaya capital in Uttarāpatha and back.[1] The Kekaya territory itself "lay between the Vipāśā or Beas and abutted on the Gandharva or Gandhāra Vishaya."[2]

Some of the roads that branched off from the South-Western Road passed through the Maru-kantāra or great desert of Rājputānā. The Mahāniddesa, the Serissaka story in the Peta and Vimâna Vatthus, as well as some of the Jātakas mention the names of different parts of the North-Western Road which, like the main road, lent their names to the places in the Uttarāpatha division across which they lay.[3] Pāṇini's aphorism, too, suggests that all these went together into the make-up of the Uttarāpatha or North-Western Road.[4]

Thus from the point of view of the Buddhist Midland the Uttarāpatha was rather the Western North-Western than the Northern division of India. With Manu the river Dṛishadvatī was the dividing line between the Midland and the North-Western region, while Rājaśekhara takes the latter to have extended westward from Pṛithudaka (modern Pehoā) near modern Thāneswar.

Broadly speaking, the North-Western division comprised that portion of India which was and is watered by the entire Indus system of rivers, and was and is placed between the river Dṛishadvatī

---

1 Rāmāyaṇa, II. 67. 7, et seqq., VII. 113-14.

2 Raychaudhuri, op.cit., p. 52f.

3 Barua, Old Brāhmī Inscriptions, Notes ; B. C. Law, India As Described, p. 69f. Note that the same set of names, as convincingly shewn by Sylvain Le'vi in his *Etudes Asiatique*, ii, p. 45f. (cf. also R. C. Majumdar's Survarṇadvīpa, i, p. 56f.), was applied subsequently to denote the different parts or stages of an Eastern or North-eastern trade-route connecting Eastern India with China and Java through Further India.

4 B. C. Law, India As Described, p. 71.

on the south-east and the Kubhā or Kābul on the north-west. For Hwen Thsang, as made out by Cunningham, this division 'comprises the Panjāb proper including Kāshmir and the adjoining Hill States with the whole of Eastern Afghanistan beyond the Indus and the present Cis-Sutlej States to the west of Sarasvatī river.'

The North-Western division of Aśoka's time may be supposed to have comprised not only the whole of the Punjab, Sind and North-Western Frontier provinces but also Beluchistan and Eastern Afghanistan. So far as the inscriptions of Aśoka along the banks of the Yamunā go, the Midland would seem to have included in it the region between this river and the Dṛishadvatī.

In Pali literature Kāśmīra and Gandhāra are excluded from the Haimavata division or the Himalayan region (Himavantappadesa),[1] and Vajirā is distinguished from Uttarāpatha.[2] The Dīpavaṃsa uses the name Apararājagiri[3] as a substitute for Vajirā,[4] which may be identified with the modern Bajauri in the North-West Frontier province.

The Uttarāpatha division of India including the modern state of Kāshmīr and Jammu as well as the four Greek satrapies ceded by Seleukos Nikator to Chandragupta Maurya is represented by Aśoka's North-Western Province and the semi-independent tribal states of the Yaunas, Kāmbojas, Gāndhāras and other Aparāntas. The southern boundary of these tribal states is indicated by the Shahbaz-garhi and Mansehra sets of Aśoka's Rock inscriptions.

(f) **As to Himalayan division :** The Himalayan region (Himavanta-padesa) of Jambudvīpa extended northward, according to Pali legends, as far as the south side of Mount Sumeru (Pali Sineru). The Gandhamādana range with its two branches called Nārada and Parvata is located in it. This range was penetrated by the ancient hermits. It contained seven great lakes, the two of which, *viz.*, the

---

1 Dīpavaṃsa, XXI ; Mahāvaṃsa, XXI. 25, 41.

2 This is inferred from the name of the Buddhist sects called Hemavata, Uttarāpathaka and Vājirīya in the Kathāvatthu—Commentary, p. 3. The Mahāvaṃsa, V. 12, 13, omits the Uttarāpathakas from the list.

3 Mahāvaṃsa, V. 12, speaks of such Buddhist sects of India as the Rājagiriya, Siddhatthika, Pubbaseliya and Aparaseliya, all of whom are represented by Buddhaghosa in his Kathāvatthu-Commentary as offshoots of the Andhaka (Andhra) sect.

4 Buddhavaṃsa, XXVIII. 8 ; Dīpavaṃsa, III. 20 ; Malalasekera, Dictionary, II, p. 810.

Anotatta (Anavatapta) and the Chhaddanta (Shaḍdanta) are frequently mentioned in the Jātakas and several Buddhist legends including those of Aśoka.[1] These lakes may even be seen today situated between the Great Himalayan range on the south and the Altyn range on the north. Anotatta Lake which is identified by Dr. Law with Mānas Sarovar[2] is said to have been surrounded by five mountain peaks.

A more or less clear idea of this part of Jambudvīpa may be formed from the Great Epic description of Arjuna's northern military expedition[3], and Hwen Thsang's travels, as we shall see anon in connection with the Haimavata division of India and the Central Himalayan extension of Aśoka's empire.

The southern boundary of this division of India and Aśoka's empire is indicated by the Kalsi set of Rock Edicts, the Aśokan monoliths at Niglīva, Lumbinī and those in the district of Champāran. Aśoka evidently locates in it the semi-independent tribal states of the Nābhakas and Nābha-lines.

(g) As to Eastern division : The Prāchya or Eastern division may be defined as consisting of the easternmost portion of Northern India extending as far north-east as the Patkai, Nāgā and Chin Hills. In Aśoka's time it must have comprised the province of Assam and the state of Manipur, as well as that portion of Bengal which lay beyond his domain proper and outside the Buddhist Midland as defined in the Divyāvadāna.

The western limit of this division is roughly indicated by the Pillars and Pillar inscriptions of Aśoka in the district of Champāran and the southern limit by the Dhauli set of Rock Edicts. The eastern extension of his empire through Nepāl and Assam depends on that of the semi-independent territories of the Nābha-lines of the ruling tribes.

A. Aparāntas and Aṭavis as determinants : The position of Aśoka's empire thus made out may be further tested by Aśoka's statements concerning certain semi-independent ruling peoples within his empire, all of whom are broadly termed Aparāntas. The Yaunas,

---

1 Dīpavaṃsa, VI ; Mahāvaṃsa, V. 24, 27.

2 B. C. Law, India As Described, p. 10f.

3 Read Dr. Moti Chandra's suggestive article—Geographical and Economic Studies in the Mahābhārata : Upāyana Parva, in the Journal of the U. P. Historical Society, Vol. XVI, Pt. II.

Kāmbojas and Gāndhāras are mentioned in R.E.V. as the most typical of such Aparāntas belonging to the Uttarāpatha and Haimavata divisions, while the Risṭika-Peteṇikas typify these Aparāntas belonging to the Vindhya, Aparānta and Dakshiṇāpatha divisions. The list supplied in R.E. XIII omits from it the name of the Gāndhāras but adds those of the Nābhakas and Nābhapaṃktis, and replaces the Risṭika-Peteṇikas by the Bhoja-Pitinikas adding to them the name of the Andhra-Pārindas or Andhra-Pāradas. We are introduced in this very edict also to the Aṭavis (Āṭavikas or Āṭavyas) who lived within Aśoka's empire. It is equally necessary to ascertain who they were and what tracts were inhabited by them in order to form a correct idea of the extent of Aśoka's empire.

(i) **Risṭika-Peteṇikas, Bhoja-Pitinikas** : It may be reasonably presumed that Aśoka spoke of the Risṭika-Peteṇikas (R.E.V.) and Bhoja-Pitinikas (R,E. XIII) and other Aparāntas with reference to Vindhya region in the broadest sense of the term. There exists a sharp difference of opinion on the signification of the two compound names. Jayaswal takes each of them to be a combination of two names, the Risṭikas and the Bhojas representing the non-hereditary Risṭikas and Bhojas, and the Petenikas the hereditary Risṭikas and the hereditary Bhojas, while Bhandarkar treats peteṇika as an adjective to the Risṭikas and the Bhojas, and takes the two names to mean the hereditary Risṭikas and the hereditary Bhojas respectively. There are two Pali passages in the Anguttara Nikāya, in which Raṭṭhika, Pettanika and Gāmagāmaṇika (*i.e.*, Bhojaka) are met with as official designations implying the enjoyment of varying degrees of sovereignty. In one passage Raṭṭhika and Pettanika seem to go together, and in the other, they appear as two different designations. Arguing from Buddhaghosa's explanations of the terms, I could not help accepting Bhandarkar's interpretation as the more convincing of the two. There is even a third interpretation, according to which, the Peteṇikas were the ruling people of Pratishṭhāna (modern Paithān). Here the matter needs further orientation.

Peteṇika as a territorial patronymic from Patiṭṭhāna is improbable. Its Pali equivalent is Pettanika beyond doubt. Michelson rightly Sanskritises it as Paitrayaṇika, which is a patronymic from pitrayana. The Aitareya Brāhmaṇa broadly distinguishes between the Bhojapitaras and the Bhojas. In Jayaswal's opinion the intended distinction is between the hereditary and non-hereditary Bhojas. The distinction, as I am now inclined to think, is between the Bhojapitaras and the Bhojaputras, which is to say, between the parent or senior Bhojas and the offshoot or junior Bhojas. Jayaswal has obviously missed the force of the term Bhojapitaraḥ which is a word like the Pali gopitaro,[1] meaning the bulls who make seniors or elders among the cattle.[2] Thus the distinction is betwaen the Ṛishṭika-Rāshṭrikas and Bhojas of the parent stock on the one hand, and their offshoots on the other, and not between the hereditary and non-hereditary Ṛishṭika-Rashṭrikas and Bhojas. The Ṛishṭika-Rāshṭrikas and the Bhojas represented the parent tribal States and the Paitrayaṇikas their offshoots,—the branch States.

Let us now see how far this interpretation tallies with the epigraphic and literary representation of the Ṛishṭika-Rāshṭrikas, the Bhojas and the Paitrayaṇikas. In R.E V, the Ṛishṭika-Rāshṭrikas and the corresponding Paitrayaṇikas typify the Aparāntas. In R.E. XIII, the Paitrayaṇikas are grouped together with the Bhojas instead of with the Ṛishṭika-Rāshṭrikas. From a comparison of the two statements, it cannot but appear that the Ṛishṭika-Rāshṭrikas and the Bhojas were two allied peoples, while the Paitrayaṇikas were just their offshoots or branches.

There must have been some definite reason for specifically mentioning the Ṛishṭika-Rāshṭrikas and the Bhojas with their offshoots as the typical Aparāntas and adding to the list the name of the Andhras and the Pārinda-Pāradas. According to the later traditional definition in the Purāṇas and the Kāvyamīmāṃsā, the Aparāntas were the peoples within the Western division of India. Buddhaghosa records a tradition, according to which the Aparāntas were the Indian, peoples that were originally immigrants from the Western subcontinent called Aparagoyāna. "Some of the inhabitants came with Mandhātā (*i.e.*, in pre-historic time) from Aparagoyāna to Jambudīpa and settled down there. The country they colonised was called Aparānta.'[3]

In Aśokan phraseology, however, the Aparāntas should rather be taken to stand for the semi-independent ruling races and their territories, situated near about the lower end of the Southern or South-western Road, in which case it becomes easy to understand why they are typified in the edicts of Aśoka by the Ṛishṭikas, the

[1] Mahāgopālaka Sutta, Majjhima, I.

[2] Guṇṇaṃ pituṭṭhānaṃ karonti gopitaro (Buddhaghosa).

[3] Papañchasūdanī, I, p. 484 ; Sumangala-vilāsinī, II, p, 482 ; Malalasekera, Dictionary, I, p, 417 ; B. C. Law, India As Described, p. 2.

Bho)as, the Paitrayaṇikas, the Andhras and Pārinda-Pāradas, and no less to connect them also with Aṭavis mentioned in R.E. XIII.

The Khoh Copper-plate inscription of Saṃkshobha connects with the kingdom of Dabhālā (Bundelkhand) the eighteen Forest kingdoms (ashṭādaśāṭavi-rājya) 'the tiny kingdoms that must have extended (according to Bhandarkar) from Baghelkhand right up almost to the sea-coast of Orissa'.[1] In other words, going by this opinion, we are to locate these Forest kingdoms in the Vindhya division of India which is said to have been inhabited and ruled, according to the Mārkaṇḍeya Purāṇa, by such peoples as the Uttamarṇas, the Daśārṇas, the Bhojas, the Kishkindhyas,[2] the Anūpas, the Tuṇḍikeras, the Vindhyan Avantis, the Vīrahotras, the Karūshas. the Malajas (Malayas), the Mekalas and the Utkalas. But to be more precise, the elghteen Forest kingdoms may be taken to correspond to the eighteen Vidyādhara settlements with their sixty towns, associated in the Jaina Jambudīva-paṇṇatti with the Vaitāḍhya or Vindhya range. It was undoubtedly with reference to this very region that the Jātaka tradition speaks of the sixteen Bhoja rulers (Bhojaputtā)[3] and the Hāthigumphā inscription of Khāravela of the Vidyādhara settlements (Vijādharādhivāsaṃ) ruled by the Raṭhikas and the Bhojakas enoying varying degrees of sovereignty. Many at least of the Forest kingdoms, mentioned in Sumudragupta's Allahabad Stone-pillar inscription, if not all of them, may be confidently referred to this very region. If so, the total of eighteen Forest kingdoms or Vidyādhara settlements, ruled by the Rāshṭrikas and the Bhojakas, may easily be supposed to have been made up of the sixteen territories ruled by the sixteen Bhojaputras, *i.e.*, by the Paitrayaṇikas and the two parent states of the Ṛishṭika Rāshṭrikas and the Bhojas, which is to say, of the Bhojapitaras. The pareut state of the Ṛishṭika-Rāshṭrikas was Ṛishṭika (Pali Aṭṭhaka), and that of the Bhojas Vidarbha, both of these territories being placed in the Rāmāyaṇa (iv. 41. 9-11) within the belt of the Vindhya, the Narmadā, the Godāvarī and the Kṛishṇā (Kṛishṇaveṇā), along with Avravantī, Avantī, Mahishika, Matsya and Kalinga. Once king Bhīmaratha of Vidarbha, king Ārshṭaka of Rishṭaka (Aṭṭhaka) and king Kālinga of Kalinga

---

[1] As'oka, p. 47.

[2] In the Mahābhārata, II. 31. 17 as well as Samudragupta's Allahabad Stone-pillar inscription, Kishkindhyā is placed in the Southern division of India.

[3] Jātaka, i, p. 45 ; Saṃyutta, i, p. 61f. ; B. C. Law, Geography of Early Buddhism, p. 62.

acknowledged the suzerainty of king Dāṇḍakya of Daṇḍaki, known as Dāṇḍakya Bhoja in the Arthaśāstra (1. 6). The capital of Daṇḍaka was Kumbhavatī according to the Sarabhanga Jātaka, Madhumanta according to the Rāmāyaṇa, and Nasika according to the Mahāvastu. The tradition in the Sarabhanga Jātaka and the Arthaśāstra aver that king Dāṇḍakya perished with his kingdom for a heinous sin committed by him. It is also important to note that the Mārkaṇḍeya Purāṇa, the Sarabhanga Jātaka and both the Sanskrit Epics speak of two Avantis, the Purāṇa of the Vindhyan Avantī and the Aparānta Avantī, the Rāmāyaṇa of Āvravantī and Avantī, the Jātaka of the kingdom of Caṇḍa Pradyota and Avantī, and the Great Epic of the Vinda Avantī and the Anuvinda (Upavinda) Avantī. The Purāṇa distinction between the Vindhyan and Aparānta Avantis is evidently the same as that made in the Junāgarh Rock inscription of Rudradāman I between the Pūrvākara and Aparākara Avantis. The Great Epic places the two kingdoms of Avantī in the Narmadā region.[1]

These facts go to locate the parent states of the Ṛishṭika-Rāshṭrikas and the Bhojas to the south of the two kingdoms of Avantī, and, for the matter of that, to the south of the river Ṭāpī or Tāptī. Modern Berār preserves the reduced identity of the ancient territory of Vidarbha, the parent state of the Bhojas. The Hathigumphā inscription refers to the territory of a S'ātakarṇī which lay on the west side (pachhimadisaṃ) of Kalinga. It alludes also to the Vidyādhara tracts, no doubt, in the Vindhya region, which were being ruled by the Rāshṭrikas and the Bhojakas. It is clearly suggested that S'ātakarṇi's dominions included the town of Asika (Ṛishika) on the river Kaṇhapeṃṇā (Kṛishṇaveṇā, i.e., Kṛishṇā).[2] This river appears to be no other than the Karaveṇā mentioned in the Nāsik cave inscription of the time of Nahapāna and what is wrongly called Kṛishṇavarṇā in the Mārkaṇḍeya Purāṇa, having its origin in the Sahya mountains or Western Ghats.[3] According to the Sankhapāla Jātaka (No. 524), the river Kaṇṇapeṇṇā (variant Kaṇṇavaṇṇā) flowed through the Mahiṃsakaraṭṭha (Mahishaka of the Rāmāyaṇa, IV. 41. 8-11, Mahishika of the Mārkaṇḍeya Purāṇa).

---

[1] Mahābhārata, II. 31. 10.
Tatas tenaiva sahito Narmadām abhito yayau |
Vindānuvindāvantau sainyena mahatā vṛitau ||

[2] *Ibid*, VI. 9. 16.

[3] This fact precludes the possibility of identification of Kaṇṇapeṇṇā with the Pennār.

In the Mahābhāṛata, VI. 9.59, the Mahishakas are associated with the Vanavāsikas, the Karṇāṭakas, the Vikalpas and the Mūshakas. In both the Mahābhārata and the Rāmāyaṇa Ṛishika[1] (Ṛishṭika)[2] is associated with Vidarbha (Berār) and distinguished from Mahishaka. In the Mārkaṇḍeya Purāṇa, on the other hand, Ṛishika-Ṛishṭika is replaced by Mahārāshṭra, while in the Pali Chronicles Mahiṃsaka (Mahisaka) appears just as another name of Mahisamaṇḍala, which may be identified with the whole or northern portion of the state of Mysore.

The relative geographical positions of Ṛishika-Ṛishṭika, Vidarbha and Avantī may be inferred from the list of places included in the dominions of Gautamīputra S'ātakarṇī, as well as from the Pali list of halting places on the Southern Road. In the Nāsik Cave inscription of Vāsishṭhīputra Pulumāyi, Ṛishika (Asika, Patañjali's Ārshika), Aśvaka, Mūlaka, Surāshṭra and Kukkurāparānta (Pali Sunāparanta) are evidently mentioned as countries that lay to the south-west and west of Vidarbha, which is grouped with Anūpa and Ākarāvantī. A similar territorial environment of Ākarāvantī is suggested also in the Junāgarh Rock inscription of Rudradāman I, though to the exclusion of Ṛishika, Aśvaka, Mūlaka and Vidarbha. Aśvaka and Mūlaka were the two territories situated, according to Pali Canonical tradition, opposite each other, on two sides of the Godāvarī, while Pratishṭhâna (modern Paithân), the capital of Mūlaka, was the south-western terminus of the Southern Road. Mūlaka on the left bank and Aśvaka on the right bank of the Godāvarī were evidently situated immediately to the east of Pañchavaṭī and Nâsika, both of which were presumably included in the kingdom of Daṇḍaka. This māy enable us to locate Ṛishṭika-Rāshṭrika or Maharāshṭra to the west of Aśvaka, to the south of Daṇḍaka and to the east of Sūnaparānta, and broadly in the region between the Godāvarî and the Kṛishnâ. Below Sūnaparânta containing the Sopārā set of Aśoka's Rock Edicts lay the coastal territory of Karṇâṭa to the east of which and to the south of Ṛishṭika was the territory of the Mahishakas who are grouped together with the Vanavāsikas and the Mūshakas. It may be supposed that Vanavasī lay in between Maharāshṭra in the north and Mahishaka in the south and extended from North Kānârâ as far east as to include in it the south-western corner of Hyderabad containing two copies of Aśoka's M.R.E. at the

[1] Ibid, VI. 9. 64.

[2] Rāmāyaṇa, IV. 41. 8-11.

town of Kopbal, while Mūshaka, the territory of the Mūshakas grouped in the Epics and the Purâṇas with the Vanavâsikas, may be identified with Maski (Mosage) in the district of Raichur, Hyderabad, within the angle formed by the Kṛishṇâ and its lower tributary called Tungabhadrā.

From the above location of the parent states of the Ṛishṭikas and the Bhojas, it is clear that they were situated near about the south-western end of the Southern Road. But the Ṛishtika-Rāshṭrikas and the Bhojas may be regarded as aparāntas also in Buddhaghosa's sense, inasmuch as the Great Epic places them as peoples also in Uttarāpatha or Punjab proper.[1] The way in which Aśoka introduces them in his edicts leaves no room for doubt that they were not only neighbours as rulling peoples but also offshoots of one and the same people. According to the Aitareya Brāhmaṇa (VII. 14), the Bhojas as a people were all Satvats who anointed their rulers from amongst them. In the Purāṇas, they are described as offshoots of the Yādavas (*i.e.*, Sātvatas) of Mathurā, and to the same scions of the Yadu family is attributed the foundation of Mahīshmatī, Avantī and Vidarbha. We learn from both literature and inscriptions that the scions of the ruling races like the Matsyas and the Chedis, too, founded kingdoms in the Vindhya region, even as far east as Oḍra, Utkala and Kalinga.

The Risṭika-Rathikas and Bhojas of R. E. V and R. E. XIII were evidently the predecessors of the Raṭhikas and Bhojakas of the Hāthigumphā inscription as well as of the Mahāraṭhis and Mahābhojas of the S'ātavâhana period. The S'ātavâhana inscriptions go to connect the Mahârathis with Chitaldrug, Nānāghāt, Kārle and Kanheri (in North Konkan), the Mahābhojas with the Chutu rulers of Kanheri and Vanavâsī, and the Mahāsenāpatis with Nāsik and Bellary.[2]

In the Yerraguḍi copy of M.R.E. we have mention of the Raṭhikas in addition to the Janapadas, to all of whom the Rajjuka in charge of the administrative area was to proclaim Aśoka's message of piety. These Raṭhikas were not probably to be mistaken for the semi-independent Ṛisṭika-Raṭhikas of R.E. V, their position being similar to, if not the same as, that of the Rāshṭriya Vaiśya in Surashṭra of Chandragupta Maurya's time.

1 Raychaudhuri, op. cit., p. 108ff.

2 Ibid, p. 420f.

(ii) **Andhras and Pārindas :** In view of the fact that the Andhras are associated with the Pārinda-Pāradas and other Westerns in R. E. XIII, it must be presumed that their territories lay near about the south-western terminus of the Southern Road, *i.e.*, Ujjayinī, Māhīshmatī on the Narmadā, or Pratishṭhāna on the Upper Godāvarī. According to the Sutta-nipāta, close to Pratishṭhāna were the territories of the Assakas and the Mūlakas,[1] and according to its commentary, both Aśmaka (Aśvaka) and Mūlaka were Andhra territories.[2] Mūlaka lay to the north of Aśmaka, which is to say, on the left bank of the Godāvarī. Hence it is easy to think with Bhandarkar that Mūlaka abutted on the territory of Avantī.[3] It is quite possible that the Aśmakas or Aśvakas had their settlement, as Raychaudhuri suggests, also in the Uttarāpatha or North-Western division and were no other people than those who were known to the Greek writers as the Assakenoi,[4] and this may be taken to corroborate the truth in the tradition recorded by Buddhaghosa that the Aparāntas were the peoples or races who had originally migrated into India from the Aparagoyāna or Western sub-continent of Asia.

The Mahābhārata, however, speaks of several Andhra peoples (Andhraś cha bahavaḥ).[5] With Vincent Smith the Andhras were 'a Dravidian people now represented by the large population speaking the Telugu language, who occupied the deltas of the Godāvarī and the Kṛishṇā. But Srinivas Iyengar would seem to be more in the right in suggesting that 'the Andhras were originally a Vindhyan tribe and that the extension of Andhra power was from the west to the east down the Godāvarī and Kṛishṇā valleys.'[6] 'The Serivāṇija Jātaka locates Andhrapura, *i.e.*, the capital of the Andhras, on the river Telavāha which Bhandarkar identifies with the modern Tel or Telingiri[7] and Raychaudhuri inclines to treat as another name of the Tungabhadrā-Kṛishṇā. Raychaudhuri construes the evidence of the Mayiḍavolu plates of the early Pallava ruler Śivaskandavarman as

---

[1] Sutta-nipāta, verse 977.

[2] Paramatthajotikā, II, p. 581.

[3] Carmichael Lectures, 1918, p. 53f.

[4] Raychaudhuri, op. cit., p. 121.

[5] Mahābhārata, VI. 9. 49.

[6] I.A., 1913, p. 276f. The opinion receives an additional support from the fact that the Pali Canon places the town of S'ātakarṇikā, which was evidently the place of origin of the S'ātakarṇi rulers of the Andhra race (Andhrajātīyaḥ), to the south of the Buddhist Midland.

[7] I.A., 1918, p. 71.

implying that 'the Andhra country (Andhrāpatha) embraced the Kṛishṇā district and had its centre at Dhaññakaḍa or Bezvāda.'[1]

In Aśoka's own record (R. E. XIII), the Pārinda-Pāladas are associated with the Andhras. The Kalsi Pālada is phonetically the same name as Pārada, as pointed out by Raychaudhuri. The Mārkaṇḍeya Purāṇa places the Pāradas as a barbarous tribe in the Udīchya-Uttarāpatha or North-Western division along with the Aparāntas, Gāndhāras, Yavanas, Kāmbojas and the rest. The Harivaṃśa and the Vāyu Purāṇa, too, mention them in a list of barbarous tribes (Mlechchhajātayaḥ) along with the Śakas, Yavanas, Kāmbojas, Pahlavas, Khaśas, Mahishikas, Cholas, Keralas, etc., some of whom belonged to Uttarāpatha and some to the Deccan. On the other hand, the Puṇḍras or Pauṇḍras and Pulindas are the two tribes who are associated in the Purāṇas with the Andhras and whose names approached those of Aśoka's Pārinda[2]-Pāladas. The Mārkaṇḍeya Purāṇa places the Pulindas in the Madhyadeśa, the Aparānta as well as the Dakshiṇātya division. They are distinguished in the Matsya Purāṇa from the Pauṇḍra (Puṇḍras of the Rāmāyaṇa, IV. 41. 12). In this Purāṇa the Pauṇḍras are associated with the Vaidiśas, Mekalas and Gaunardas, and the Pulindas (Kulindas) with the Andhras, Śakas, Chulikas and Yavanas.[3]

It need not worry us that the Pāradas as a tribe who are placed in the North-Western division should be associated in Aśoka's R. E. XIII with the Andhras who were a Vindhyan as well as a Deccan people. Like the Chulikas, Mūshikas and others, the Pārinda-Pāradas had their original settlement in Uttarāpatha.

As I now find, the Mahābhārata (VI, 9. 62, 63) speaks of the Pulindas,[4] Kulindas and Kāladas and places them all in South India, the Pulindas in association with the Vindhya Chulikas, and the Kulindas with the Kāladas. Here the Kulindas and the Kāladas are the same peoples as the Pulindas and the Pāladas respectively, cf. Sindhu-Pulindakāh (Mbh. VI. 9. 40) and Sindhu-Kulindakāh (Padma Purāṇa, Bhūgolavarṇanam), Kakudha Kātyāyana, Pali Pakudha Kachchāyana. One may be tempted to connect the Pāradas

---

1 Raychaudhuri, op. cit., p. 78f.

2 The name of As'oka's Pāriṃda is still preserved in that of Pārenda, which is situated due east of Poona.

3 Pargiter, The Purāṇa Text, pp. 2, 52, 65. Barua, Inscriptions, ii, p. 267f.

4 Acc. to D. C. Sircar, Select Inscriptions, I, p. 87, Pālada=Paulinda. Cf. Pali gāravo=gauravaḥ.

with the river Pāradā[1] mentioned in the Nāsik cave inscription of the time of Nahapāna.

From these facts, it may be inferred that Aśoka's Pārinda-Pāradas were no other ruling tribes than Pauṇḍra-Pulindas and Kulinda-Kāladas who were closely allied and had territories spread over a large area near about the territories of the Ṛishṭika-Rāshṭrikas, the Bhojas and their offshoots.

(iii) **Other Aparāntas**: The significant expression, 'other Aparāntas', which occurs in R.E. V as an appendage to Aśoka's statement concerning the Risṭika-Peteṇikas has, I think, been sufficiently explained in the foregoing account of the Risṭika-Peteṇikas, the Bhoja-Peteṇikas and the Aṃdhra-Pārimdas. The Ṛishṭikas and the Bhojas with their offshoots, the Paitrayaṇikas, have been taken to represent the eighteen Forest-kingdoms in the Vindhyan region, and in Aśoka's time the semi-independent states near about the south-western extension of the Southern Road between the Yamunā and the Godāvarī, and within the mountain belt of the Vindhya, the Ṛiksha, the Pāriyātra and the Sahya. The various peoples that are placed in this region in the Epics and the Purāṇas to the exclusion of those included in the dominions under Aśoka's direct rule came within the definition of other Aparāntas.

(iv) **Aṭavis**: The position of the Aṭavis in relation to these Aparāntas needs further orientation. In R.E. XIII the Aṭavis are mentioned apart from the peoples that are introduced in R.E.V as Aparāntas, while we have been inclined so far to identify the Ṛishṭikas, the Bhojakas, and the Paitrayaṇikas with the ruling peoples of the eighteen forest territories or Vidyādhara settlements in the Vindhya region. Bhandarkar, too, inclines to identify the Aṭavis mentioned in R.E. XIII with the semi-independent Āṭavikas or Āṭavyas of the inscription of Saṃkshobha from Central India. How far is it correct to do so?

The Mārkaṇḍeya Purāṇa mentions the territory of the Āṭavyas side by side with those of the Śabaras, the Pulindas, the Vindhya-mūliyas, the Daṇḍakas, the Vaidarbhas, the Paurikas, the Maulikas, the Aśmakas (Aśvakas), the Bhogavardhanas and the Andhras, and places all of them in Dakshiṇāpatha. The Great Epic, II. 31. 2-15, seems to have counted the rulers of Matsya, Aparamatsya, Adhirāja, Nishāda-land, Gośṛinga hill, Tarasa, Śreṇimanta, Narāṛāshṭra,

[1] Modern Vāradā, which is a northern tributary of the upper Tuṅgabhadrā.

Kuntibhoja, Charmaṇvatī-kula, Seka, Paraseka, Vindāvantī, Anuvindāvantī, Bhojakaṭa, Veṇvātaṭa, Kantāraka, Nāṭakeya, Herambaka, Marudha, Ramyagrāma, Nāchīna, Vāta and Pulinda among the Āṭavikas of the Vindhya region, including, no doubt, the region covered by the Pāriyātra branch of the Vindhya range of hills. The Great Epic expression, Āṭavikān sarvān (II. 31. 15), is paralleled by sarvāṭavikarājyasya in Samudragupta's Allahabad Stone-pillar inscription. The Nāsik Cave inscription of Vāsishṭhīputra Pulumāyi, too, speaks of the rulers of the hill tracts of the Vindhya, the Ṛikshavat, the Pāriyātra, the Sahya (Western Ghats), the Kṛishṇagiri (Kanheri), the Mahendra (Eastern Ghats), the Malaya and other ranges in the Western, Central and South India. But by the Aṭavis of R.E. XIII we may not, I think, understand, the rulers or ruling races of the hill tracts or forest kingdoms of the Vindhya region only. "The Aṭavis in the sense of jungle tracts, inhabited by semi-independent aboriginal tribes or used as hiding places by the gangs of thieves, were not confined to any particular place. The Jātakas clearly show that Āṭavis in this sense existed in each kingdom, and that the ruler of each kingdom had to reckon with the permanent or temporary dwellers of these areas."[1] The Arthaśāstra speaks of a special class of officers called Aṭavīpālas, and the Jātakas of the Aṭavīrakkhikas.[2]

(v) **Yaunas, Kāmbojas and Gāndhāras** :—As for the Yaunas, the Kāmbojas and the Gāndhāras, they are mentioned in R.E. V as typical Aparāntas, whose semi-independent tribal states were within Aśoka's empire. R. E. XIII adds to this list the name of the Nābhakas (Sk. Nābhagas) and the Nābhapaṃktis who were obviously the representative ruling races of the Haimavata region.

It must be also with reference to the western or north-western end of the Uttarāpatha or North-western Road that Aśoka represented the Yaunas, Kāmbojas, Gāndhāras, Nābhakas, Nābhapaṃktis and others as Aparāntas or Westerns, inasmuch as their territories were situated near about it.[3]

As regards the Yaunas, the Kāmbojas and the Gāndhāras, their emi-independent territories in Aśoka's time were situated in the Uttarāpatha proper which is now covered by the North-Western Frontier Province.

---

1 Barua, Inscriptions, ii, p. 319.

2 Jātaka, VI, p. 335.

3 Barua, Inscriptions, ii, p. 258.

The Pali texts mention Kaśmīra with Gandhāra, otherwise called Gandharva-vishaya in the Rāmāyaṇa.[1] In one of the Jātakas, the Jātaka No. 406, as pointed out by Raychaudhuri, Kāśmīra is included in the kingdom of Gandhāra.[2] Some of the Jātakas represent Kāśmīra and Gandhāra as two countries ruled by one king.[3] Hekaitos of Miletos (549-486 B.C.) "refers to Kaspapyros (Kaśyapapura, *i.e.*, Kāsmīr) as a Gandaric (Gandhāra) city."[4] We have got to see if the same was the state of things also in Aśoka's time.

The Gāndhāras or Gandharvas of Uttarāpatha founded their territories on both sides of the Indus (Sindhur ubhayataḥ pārśve).[5] The principal city of their trans-Indus territories was Pushkarāvatī[6] or Utpalāvatī,[7] which is now "represented by the modern Prang and Charsadda, 17 miles N. E. of Peshāwar, on the Swāt river."[8] Takshaśilā (Pali Takkasilā, modern Taxila), which is now situated in the Rāwālpindi district of the province of the Punjab, was the main city of the hinter-Indus territory of the Gāndhāras.[9] Hwen Thsang locates the kingdom of Gandhāra, with Purushapura (Peshāwar) as its capital, between the Sulaiman range and the Indus, the latter being mentioned as its eastern boundary.

In Aśoka's time, however, the major portion, if not the whole, of the trans-Indus territory of the Gāndhāras and the southern portion of their hinter-Indus territory were under his direct rule, and only the northern portion of both above Shahbazgarhi and Mansehra formed the semi-independent tribal state of the Gāndhāras.

In the Great Epic, the Yaunas, Kāmbojas and Gāndhāras are counted among the typical peoples of Uttarāpatha,[10] precisely as in

---

1 II. 68. 19-22, VII. 113-14.

2 Raychaudhuri, op. cit., p. 124.

3 Jātaka, III, pp. 346, 378 ; Malalasekera, Dictionary, I, p. 548.

4 Raychaudhuri, op. cit., p. 124.

5 Rāmāyaṇa, VIII. 113. 11, VII. 114. 11. Raychaudhuri, op. cit., p. 50.

6 Variant Pushkalāvatī, Pali Pokkharāvatī, Prakrit Pukkalāotī, Arrian's Peucelaotis.

7 Divyāvadāna, pp. 407, 474, 476, where Utpalāvatī is described as the capital of Uttarāpatha.

8 Raychaudhuri, op. cit., p. 51.

9 Rāmāyaṇa, VII. 114. 11. Vāyu Purāṇa, 88. 189-90, quoted by Raychaudhuri, op. cit., p. 50.

10 Mahābhārata, XII. 207. 43.

Uttarāpatha-janmānaḥ kīrtayishyāmi tān api ।
Yauna-Kāmboja-Gāndhārāḥ Kirāta-Barbaraiḥ saha ॥

Cited by Raychaudhuri, op. cit., p. 50. In the Achaemenian inscriptions, too, the name of the Ionians is spelt as Yaunas.

Aśoka's R.E. V they figure as the typical Aparāntas. In the Pali Assalāyana Sutta, the Yonas and Kāmbojas are represented as typical peoples of the North-West frontier countries (pachchantimā janapadā). Yona, Yauna or Yavana is the only name whereby all Greeks, whether Macedonian, pre-Macedonian or post-Macedonian, were known to the Indians. But this name was obviously derived from Ionia, and the first Greeks known to the Persians and Indians were all, *ex hypothesi*, Ionians.[1] It is, therefore, most probable, as opined by Jayaswal and others, that there was a pre-Alexandrian Ionian Greek settlement on the banks of the river Kābul, notably at Nysa.

As regards the Kāmbojas or Kāmbhojas, the Arthaśāstra classes them with the Saurāshṭras in so far as they lived by agriculture, trade and professional fighting.[2] The Great Epic speaks of the Kāmbojas and Paramakāmbojas, just as the Mahāniddesa does of Yona and Paramayona. The Kāmbojas are grouped together with the Daradas (Dards)[3] and the Paramakāmbojas with the Lohas and Northern Ṛishikas.[4] From these facts, it cannot but be inferred that there were two distinct settlements or territories of both the Yaunas[5] and the Kāmbojas.[6]

The country of the Daradas (Dards) was situated in a valley of the Dari on the right bank of the Upper Indus, watered by the river Darin or Daril[7] and hence may be taken to have extended from Chitral to the Indus.[8] Ptolemy "locates them east

---

[1] There were four chief divisions of the Greek people, *viz.*, the Dorians, Aeolians, Achaeans and Ionians. Of these, the Achæans were the first to sail across the Aegean and to occupy Thessaly. They were the most important people in Homer's time. * * It was the Ionians and Dorians who played the most important part in the history of Greece.

[2] Vārtās'astropajīvinaḥ, Arthas'āstra, XI. 1.

[3] Mahābhārata, II. 27. 23 : Daradān saha Kāmbojaiḥ.

[4] *Ibid*, II, 27. 25 : Lohān Paramakāmbojān Ṛishikān uttarān api.

[5] In the Naqsh-i-Rustam inscription (*a*) of Darius, the Yaunas grouped with the people of Sparda (Sardis) and the sea-coast dweller S'akas are distinguished from the Yaunas takabharas grouped with the Skudras and the Puntrāyas (Puntians). In the Persepolis inscription (*h*) of Xerxes, the Yaunas, too, are described as a people who lived on the sea-coast as well as on the further sea-shore. Herzfeld (Archaeological History of Iran, Pl. I) locates the two Yona territories in Asia Minor.

[6] The Divyāvadāna distinguishes the Kāmbojas associated with the Yaunas.

[7] Fa Hian's Ta-hi, Cf. Daripatha in the Mahāniddesa, pp. 155, 415.

[8] Hwen Thsang's Ta-hi-la.

[9] Yule, Marco Polo, i, p. 173 ; Lassen, I.A., i, p. 505, iii, p. 138 ; Cunningham, Ancient Geography, p. 81f.

of the Lambatai (= Lampāka, Langhan) and of Soustane (basin of the Swāt river) and to the north of the uppermost course of the Indus." The modern Dardistan still preserves the name of the Dards.[1] The Kāmboja territory may thus be located somewhere in this very region between the Darada country on the north and the Yona territory on the south, on the west side of the Indus.

In connexion with the Pāṇḍavas' digvijaya, the Great Epic relates that after conquering the Daradas together with the Kāmbojas, Arjuna in his march towards the north proceeded north-east to conquer the robber tribes (dasyavaḥ)[2] and also the tribes who dwelt in the forest, and thereafter 'the allied forces (sahitān) of the Lohas, Paramakāmbojas and the Ṛishikas of the north' (*i. e.*, Paramaṛishikas).[3]

Professor Jayachandra Vidyālankāra identifies the Paramakāmbojas 'with the Galcha speaking Yāghnobis in the valley of Yaghnob at the head water of the Larafshān river, a tract of country considerably to the north of the Pāmīrs and separated from them by the hill states subordinate to Bokhārā.' He identifies the Ṛishikas of the north with the Yūe-chis and the Kāmboja country with Badakshān and the Pāmīrs.[4] From the fact that the Kāmbojas and Vāhlikas are often associated together in the Great Epic, he is led to think that their countries were conterminous.'

Arguing more forcibly the case made out by Vidyālaṃkāra, Dr. Moti Chandra seeks to establish that the Lohas, Paramakāmbojas, Northern Ṛishikas and robber tribes must have been settled in the country which is now represented by the Tadzhik Soviet Social Republic which till recently was divided in the Russian Wakhān, Shignān, Roshān and Darwānz. It is clear even from Kalhaṇa's description of Muktapīḍa's northern campaign that the Kāmbojas, Tukhāras, Bhauṭṭas and Daradas were neighbours. If the Bhauṭṭas be rightly relegated to Baltistān and Bolor and the Darads to Dardistān, the Kāmbojas can only be placed in Kāfiristān, Balkh-Badakshān and the Pāmīrs. Dvārakā mentioned as the capital

---

1 B. C. Law, Tribes in Ancient India, p. 86.

2 Acc. to Moti Chandra, op. cit., p. 19 ; they were "the descendants of the Eastern Iranian speaking ancestors of the Wakhānis, Shighnis, Roshānis, and the Sarīkolis of the Pāmīr plateau."

3 Mahābhārata, II. 27. 23-26.

4 Bhāratbhūmi aur uske nivās, pp. 297-305, 313 ; Moti Chandra, op. cit., pp. 18-19, 43.

of the Kāmbojas in the Petavattu-Commentary[1] need not create any prejudice against their being a people in the north-west of India,[2] here Dvārakā being no other place than what is known in Persian as Daṛwāz in the north of Badakshān. The place which Ptolemy locates to the south of the Oxus under the name of Tambyzoi is identified by Sylvain Lévi with Kamboja on the ground that Tambyzoi is only a Greek transliteration of the Austro-Asiatic spelling of Kamboja.[3] In the time of the Muslim geographer Idrisi Badakshān bordered on Qanauj (*i.e.*, Kamboja), then a dependancy of India.[4] Apollodorus mentions the Asii, Pasiani, Tochari and Sacarauli as the four nomad tribes who conquered Bactria. The Torogus source attributes the conquest to two peoples called Asiani and Saraucae. Here the Asii or Asiani correspond with Chang Kien's Yue-chī, and Asiani and Pasiani are but Iranian forms of the Indo-Aryan Asika-Ṛishika and Paramarshika.[5]

I have no definite suggestion as yet to make about the location of Paramayona as distinguished from Yona.[6] There being nothing until now to show that there was any pre-Alexandrian Yona territory on the east side of the Indus, it is conceivable that the distinction aimed at was one between the trans-Kabul Yona territory and that between the Kābul river and the Upper Indus. It is quite possible that by the name Paramayona were meant the Yona territories in Asia Minor which find mention in the Achaemenian inscriptions. Alexander's invasion of India was followed, however, by 'the establishment of a number of Yavana settlements in the Uttarāpatha', *e.g.*, the city of Alexandria (modern Charikar or Opian) in Paropanisadae *i.e.*, the Kabul region, Boukhepala on the spot where Alexander began to cross the Jhelam, Nikaia, where the battle with Poros took place, Alexandria at the confluence of the Chinab and the Indus, and the Sogdian Alexandria below the confluence of the Punjab rivers.[7]

---

1 Paramatthadīpanī, p. 43, to which attention is first drawn by T. W. Rhys Davids, Buddhist India, p. 184.

2 This is not certainly the Dvārakā in Kāṭhiāwār.

3 I. A., 1923, p. 54.

4 La Geographic de al-Edresi, transl. by Jaubert, Vol. I, p. 478f.

5 Moti Chandra, op. cit., p. 22f.

6 Mahāniddesa, pp. 155, 415.

7 Raychaudhuri, op. cit., p. 212f. The Mahāniddesa mentions one Alasanda as an emporium of trade, but it is difficult to say which Alexandria is actually meant. The Alasandadīpa mentioned in the Milindapañha must be either Alexandria at the confluence of the Chinab and the Indus or the Sogdian Alexandria, preferably the latter.

It is difficult, however, to say that by the Yonas in Aśoka's edicts were meant the Yonas other than the pre-Alexandrian Ionian colonists or 'Perso Greeks' who were associated with the Kāmbojas and Gāndhāras and other semi-independent peoples of the Uttarāpatha within Aśoka's empire.

The close association of the Yaunas or Yavanas with such other peoples of North-Western India as the Kāmbojas, Gāndhāras, Śakas, Madras, Kaikeyas, Sindhus and Sauvīras is certain. The fact is well attested by the Epics and Purāṇas as well as the edicts of Aśoka.[1] They passed as most esteemed of foreigners, though according to some authorities they were regarded as born of Śūdra females by Kshatriya males. In Pāṇini's time Yavanānī was the only feminine form of Yavana,[2] while Katyāyana, Patañjali and other later grammarians found it necessary to recognize Yavanī as another form, and to restrict the use of Pāṇini's form to the writing of the Greeks. It will be unhistorical to father this difference between the two forms on Pāṇini when evidently he was acquainted with only one form. The Mahāvastu (I, p. 171) rightly represents the Yaunas as a ruling people with a republican form of government. The existence of a pre-Alexandrian Ionian colony somewhere on the bank of the river Kophen, Kubhā or Kābul may be taken for granted. The pre-Macedonian Greek settlers in the border-land of Uttarāpatha were known to Megasthenes and other Greek writers as Nysaioi (Nyseans) evidently for the reason that they planted their colony in the district of Nysaia named after Mount Nysa with Nysa as its principal city. The location given of this city goes to show that it lay close to and was built on the lower slopes of the mountain which is called Méros (Meru, Pali Neru) and which, according to the legend in the Great Epic and the Purāṇas, was one of the four mountains that surrounded Mt. Sumeru, say Pāmīr Knot. Identifying Mt. Meros (the name meaning 'thigh' to the Greeks) with the Sulaiman range, and Mt. Nysa with a spur of the same, one may get very near to the site of the hill-state formed by these earliest known Greek colonists on the north-western confines of India. Holdich is inclined to locate the site of Nysa in the lower spurs and valleys of Kohi-i-Mor, while Bhandarkar would have us place it somewhere between the river

---

1 B. C. Law, Tribes in Ancient India, p. 153ff.

2 Gautama Dharmas'āstra, IV. 21 ; Cambridge History of India, I, p. 290f. n.

3 Pāṇini, IV. 1. 49.

Kophen (Kābul) and the Indus.[1] According to M. de St. Martin, the existing village of Nysatta 'near the northern bank of the river of Kābul at less than two leagues below Hashtnagar' preserves the traces of the name of Nysa, the place which 'ought to be of Median or Persian foundation, since the nomenclature is Iranian, the name of Nysa or Nisaya which figures in the cosmographic geography of the Zendavesta being one which is far-spread in the countries of Irān.'[2] Ivy and the vine were known to have grown on Mt. Méros or Méron, whence Nysaia became known as a vine-growing country.

In support of his view that the Yonas of R. E. XIII 'settled in large numbers in some outlying province of India long before Alexander' 'outside the kingdom of Antiochus Theos' and 'in Aśoka's empire in a territory adjoining Gandhāra but outside India,' Bhandarkar cites the evidence of the coins resembling those of the earliest type of Athens which are known to have been collected from the north-west frontiers of India.[3]

The Nysians were known to have dressed themselves in muslin, worn the turban, and arrayed themselves in garments dyed of bright colours. They marched to battle with drums and cymbals.[4] In them were found by the Macedonians certain customs and traits of their own. Three hundred of them joined the army of Alexander on their mountain horses and followed him to battle in the plains of the Punjab.[5]

There is no wonder that the territory of the takabhara (cap-wearer ?) Yaunas is mentioned immediately after Skudra in the Achæmenian inscriptions or that, according to the legend recorded by Strabo, the Nysians recognized the Oxydrakai (Kshudrakas) who were evidently their neighbours as equally being the descendants of Dionysos.[6] The admixture of blood through intermarriage between these two peoples may have been the fact behind the Brahmanical castigation of the Yavanas as born of the S'ūdra mothers by the warrior fathers.

The name of Kamboja or Kambhoja is older in Indian literature than that of Yauna or Yavana. The Vaṃśa Brāhmaṇa list includes

---

[1] Carmichael Lectures, 1921, p. 82.

[2] McCrindle, Ancient India, p. 183, f.n.

[3] Carmichael Lectures. 1921, p. 26. Cf. Numismatic Chronicles, XX, 191 ; B.C. Law, Tribes in Ancient India, p. 155.

[4] McCrindle, Ancient India, pp. 36, 97, 201.

[5] Cambridge History of India, I, p. 354.

[6] McCrindle, Ancient India, p. 111.

the name of a Vedic teacher called Kāmboja Aupamanyava. According to Yāska's Nirukta (II. 8), the Kāmbojas spoke a dialect in which the original sense of an ancient verb, śavati, was retained while it was lost among other sections of the Indian people. Yāska's remarks have led Grierson to think that 'they either spoke Sanskrit with an infusion of Iranian words to which they gave Indian inflexions, or else spoke a language partly Indo-Aryan and partly Iranian'. The verb śavati is in Grierson's opinion an Iranian and not a Sanskrit word.[1]

Yāska indulged only in a folk-etymology when he sought to account for the name of Kamboja or Kambhoja by taking *kam* to be an abbreviation of *kambala,* meaning 'blanket', which is to say, of kamanīya, meaning 'a lovable thing'. Thus the Kāmbojas were Kambala Bhojas or Kamanīya Bhojas, the blanket being treated as a lovable thing. Their country was noted undoubtedly for 'many of the best kinds of skins, wollen blankets, blankets made of the fur of animals'[2], but that does not mean that for this very reason the people became known as Kāmbojas or Kambhojas and their country as Kamboja or Kambhoja.

The Gaṇapāṭha on Pāṇini's rule, II. 1.72—Mayūravyaṃśakādi, speaks of persons who were shaven-headed like the Kāmbojas and Yavanas (Kāmboja-muṇḍaḥ, Yavana-muṇḍaḥ). This was evidently based upon a legend like one in the Harivaṃśa (XIII. 763-64, 775-83) purporting to say that king Sagara who was bent upon annihilating the Śakas, Yavanas, Kāmbojas, Pāradas and Pahlavas relented and so he released the first after having half of their head shaved, the second and third after having the whole of their head shaved, the fourth after compelling them to keep their hair dishevelled, and the fifth after compelling them to keep their beards.[3] The tradition gained ground in later Indian literature that these were the distinctive habits of these five peoples.[4]

According to the Pali Assalāyana Sutta, the Yonas, Kāmbojas and other frontier peoples of the Uttarāpatha region had altogether a different social organisation of their own, admitting only of two social grades of masters and slaves, with no impassable barrier placed between them. The Bhūridatta Jātaka expressly states that the

---

[1] J.R.A,S., 1911, p. 801f. ; B. C. Law, op. cit., p. 1f.

[2] B. C. Law, op. cit., p. 2.

[3] The same legend is met with also in the Vāyu Purāṇa.

[4] Max Müller, History of Ancient Sanskrit Literature, p. 28.

Kāmbojas followed a crude religion of their own, contrary to the accepted Ahiṃsā cult of the Indo-Aryans. Manu (X. 43-44) classes them as Kshatriyas who became degraded for the disregard of the purificatory rites.

In the Great Epic, XV. 207. 42-44, the Andhrakas, Guhas, Pulindas, S'abaras, Chuchukas of South India, together with the Madrakas, are all described as inferior types of men, while the Yaunas, Kāmbojas, Gāndhāras and Kirātas of the Uttarāpatha, together with the Barbaras, are castigated as peoples who lived as criminal tribes with predatory habits like those of hunters and vultures.[1] And from Aśoka's R. E. XIII, it is clear that the Yonas were the last people to welcome the Indo-Aryan faiths propagated by the different sects of the Brāhmaṇas and the S'ramaṇas. In Buddhaghosa's opinion the Yonas, Kāmbojas and other frontier peoples of the Uttarāpatha region were Pārasakavaṇṇā, Persian or Persianised in their general habits, customs and usages.[2] The Divyāvadāna speaks of a popular revolt in the Svaśa-rāshṭra of Uttarāpatha during the closing period of the reign of Bindusāra.[3] Raychaudhuri inclines to think that probably the Svaśas were the same people as the Khaśas of Indian Literature.[4]

As for the Achæmenian or Persian influence in this part of India, Raychaudhuri rightly points out that Kurush or Cyrus (558 30-B. C.), the founder of the Persian empire, led in vain an expedition against India through Gedrosia (Beluchistan). According to Pliny, however, he was able to destroy the famous city of Kapiśa. Arrian tells us that the Astacenians (Ārshṭakas) and the Assacenian (Aśvakas), the two Indian tribes who inhabited the district west of the river Indus as far as the river Cophen (Kābul) and who may be identified with the Kāmbojas, 'were in ancient times subject to the Assyrians, afterwards to the Medes, and finally they submitted to the Persians, and paid tribute to Cyrus, the son of Cambyses, as ruler of their land.'

During the reign of Darius I (c. 522-486 B. C.), the people of Gandhāra (Gadara) appear among the subject peoples of the Persian empire. "Kshayarsha or Xerxes (486-65 B.C.), the son and successor of Darius I, maintained his hold on the Indian provinces. In the

---

[1] Ete pāpakritās tāta charanti prithivīm imām I s'vapāka-balagṛidhrāṇāṃ sadharmāṇo narādhipa.

[2] Barua, Inscriptions, II, p. 259.

[3] Divyāvadāna, p. 371.

[4] Raychaudhuri, op. cit., p. 250.

great army which he led against Hellas both Gandhāra and 'India' were represented."

On one occasion, as Strabo tells us, the Hydraces (Kshudrakas) from 'India' (*i. e.*, the Punjab) were summoned by the Persians to serve them as mercenaries. None need be surprised, therefore, that the army of Darius III Codomannus (335-30 B.C.) included the Indians when he fought a battle with Alexander.[1]

The Yonas, Kāmbojas and Gāndhāras were Aparāntas even in Buddhaghosa's sense, *i.e.*, they were peoples who immigrated into India from the trans-Sulaiman and trans-Kābul regions.

(vi) Other Aparāntas, Nābhakas and Nābha-lines :—Who were Aśoka's other Aparāntas who held semi-independent territories in the Uttarāpatha? In one context the Great Epic broadly divides the peoples of Uttarāpatha into five ruling races, *viz.*, the Yaunas, Kāmbojas, Gāndhāras, Kirātas and Barbaras,[2] and in another mentions and locates them in three different orders, *viz*, those who dwelt in the northern portion of the Punjab proper including the North-Western Frontier Province and the whole of the State of Kashmīr and Jammu, those who dwelt in the southern portion of the Punjab proper including the modern province of Sind, and those who dwelt in the Central and Eastern Himalayan regions extending up to Assam and Manipur.[3] The last-mentioned region roughly constitutes the Haimavata division of Jambudvīpa in respect of which Aśoka introduced the Nābhakas and Nābhapaṃktis in his R. E. XIII.

In the northern part of the Uttarāpatha are placed the hill-tribes and rulers of the Antargiri, Bahirgiri and Upagiri, the Bṛihantas of Ulūka, the towns of Senābindu, Modāpura and Vāmadeva, Susaskula, the principal town of the Sudāmas, the Ulūkas of the north, the country of the Pañchagaṇas, Devaprastha, the Pārvatīyas, the capital of the Pauravas, the robber tribes, the Saptagaṇas, the Kāśmīrakas, the Lohitas, the Daśamaṇḍalas, the Trigartas, Dārvas and Kokanadas, the Abhisāras, the people of Uraga (Urasa ?), Siṃhapura, the Suhmas and Cholas, the Vāhlīkas, the Daradas and Kāmbojas, the robber tribes who dwelt in the north-east, the Lohas, Paramakāmbojas and Ṛishikas of the north and the Ṛishikas proper. Beyond the S'vetaparvata (White range) are placed the Kiṃpurushas or Kinnaras, Guhyakas or Hāṭakas adjoining the Mānas Sarovar, and

---

[1] Raychaudhuri, op. cit., p. 198f. Chinock, Arrian's Anabasis, p. 142f.

[2] Mahābhārata, XII. 207. 43.

[3] Ibid, II. 27-28, 32.

war-like peoples of Harivarsha beyond which lay the land of Uttarakuru.[1] And in the southern part of the Uttarāpatha division, which lay to the west of the Midland (Khāṇḍavaprasthāt pratīchīṃ diśam), are located, among others, the S'ūdras and Ābhīras who dwelt on the banks of the Sarasvatī, Rohitakas, war-like and frenzied Mayūrakas, S'airīshikas (Pali Serissakas), Mahehas, S'ivis, Trigartas, Ambashṭhas, Mālavas, Pañchakarpaṭas, Madhyamakeyas, Vāṭadhānas, dwellers of Pushkarāraṇya and other republican tribes who dwelt along the banks of the Lower Indus, Rāmaṭhas (lit., the asafœtida-growers), Hārahūṇas, Madras of S'ākala, Pahlavas, Barbaras, Kirātas, Yavanas and S'akas.[2]

Over and above the Gāndhāras, Yavanas and Kāmbojas, the Mārkaṇḍeya Purāṇa refers the following peoples to the Udīchya-Uttarāpatha division : the Vāhlīkas, Vāṭadhānas, Ābhīras, Kālatoyakas, Aparāntas, S'ūdras, Pahṇavas (Pahlavas), Charmakhaṇḍikas, Sindhu-Sauvīras, Madrakas, S'atahradas, Lalitthas, Pāradas, Mūshikas, Rāmaṭhas, Rakshāhantakas, Kaikeyas, Daśamāṇikas, Barbaras, Angalaukikas,[3] Nīchas, Tushāras, pot-bellied Pahlavas, Ātreyas, Bharadvājas, Prasthalas, Daśerakas, such Kirātas as the Lampākas, Sūnakāras, Chūlikas, Jāhṇavas, Āpadhas and Alimadras, Tāmasas, Haṃsamārgas, Kāśmīras, Tangaṇas,[4] Chūlikas, Huḍukas, Ūrṇas and Darvas. The Nirhāras, Haṃsamārgas, Kūpathas, Tangaṇas, Khaśas, Kutsas, Pravaraṇas, Ūrṇas, Darvas, Huḍukas, Trigartas, Kirātas and Tāmasas are specified as Parvatāśrayis (Mountaineers).

The eastern Punjab States of Nābhā and Patiālā (Paṃktipālāḥ) still preserve the name of Aśoka's Nābhakas (Sk. Nābhāgas) and Nābhapaṃktis. The Nābhā and Pātiālā were originally and are even now the Haimavata or Central Himalayan States above Kalsi and below Kāśmīra. In the Purāṇas, Nābhi figures as a mythical king of the Central Himalayan kingdom, the name Nābhi denoting the meeting place of the Greater or Eastern and the Lesser or Western extensions of the Himālayas. Raychaudhuri inclines to think that the town of Na-pei-kia located by Fa Hien to the south-east of

---

1 Ibid, II. 27, 28.

2 Ibid, II. 32, Read Moti Chandra, op. cit., and also his Hindi article in the Vikramānka number of the Nāgarī Prachārlnī Patrikā.

3 Cf. Angaloka (variant Anganeka) in the mahāniddesa, p. 155.

4 In the Mahāniddesa, p. 155, we have mention of Tangana and Paramatangana, and also of Gangana which may be identified with Hwen Thsang's Ki-kiang-na situated to the south of Saukūṭa.

S'rāvastī and to the west of Kapilavastu[1] is perhaps reminiscent of the Nābhaka territory[2]. The Central Himalayan States, too, pass as Northern in respect of the Midland.

The Great Epic locates in the eastern extension of the Himalayan range such peoples as the Ānartas, Kālukūṭas, Kulindas and Sumaṇḍalas in the Kulinda territory, the dwellers of the island of S'ākala, Prāgjyotishapura,[3] *i.e.*, the kingdom of Kāmarūpa under the descendants of Naraka, the tribes who had their settlements in the valleys of the Lauhitya[4] (Brahmaputra), *i. e.*, in the whole of Assam, and the Kirātas and Chīnas[5] who lived in the eastern and north-eastern confines of Assam, say, in the Chin Hills, Manipur. Bhutān, Sikkim and Nepāl as Himalayan territories to the west of Assam and to the north of the Buddhist Midland do not find mention in the Mahābhārata. The present inhabitants of Bhutān and Sikkim are, in respect of their dialects and racial traits, Tibetans. The Tarai portion of Nepāl, included in the Buddhist Midland and Aśoka's domain proper, was occupied by the S'ākyas and Kaulīya territories.

As attested by the Classical writers, the Uttarāpatha was at the time of Alexander's invision of India parcelled into innumerable small kingdoms and republics. "The Nandas of Magadha," says Raychaudhuri, "do not appear to have made any attempt to subjugate these states of the Uttarāpatha (North-West India). The task of reducing them was reserved for a foreign conqueror, viz., Alexander of Macedon...... he obtāined assistance from many important chiefs like Āmbhi of Taxila, Sangaeus (Sanjaya ?) of Pushkarāvatī, Kophaios or Cophæus (of the Kābul region ?), Assagetes (Aśvajit ?), and Sisikottos (S'aśīgupta) who got as his reward the satrapy of the Assakenians. The only princes or peoples who thought of combining against the invader were Poros and Abisares, and the Mālavas (Malloi), Kshudrakas (Oxydrakai) and the neighbouring autonomous tribes. Even in the latter case personal jealousies prevented any effective results. Alexander met with stubborn resistance from individual chiefs and clans, notably from Astes (Hasti or Ashṭaka ?), the Aspacians, the Assakenians, the elder Poros, the Kathians, the Malloi, the Oxydrakai, and the Brāhmaṇas of the kingdom of Mousikanos............But all

---

1 Beal, Buddhist Records, I, p. XLXIII ; Legge, Fa Hien, p. 64.

2 Raychaudhuri, op. cit., p. 254.

3 Mahābhārata, II. 26.9.

4 Allahabad Stone-pillar inscription of Samudragupta.

5 Mahābhārata, II. 30. 26.

this was of no avail. A disunited people could not long resist the united forces of the Hellenic world led by the greatest captain of ancient Europe. Alexander succeeded in conquering the old Persian provinces of Gandhāra and 'India', but was unable to try conclusions with Agrammes, king of the Gangaridæ and the Prasii."[1]

In connection with Seleukos Nikator and Chandragupta, Justinus (XV. 4) observes : "He (Seleukos Nikator) carried on many wars in the East after the division of the Makedonian kingdom between himself and the other successors of Alexander, first seizing Babylonia, and then reducing Baktriane, his power being increased by his first success. Thereafter he passed into India, which had, since Alexander's death, killed its governors, thinking thereby to shake off from its neck the yoke of slavery. Sandrokottos had made it free : but when victory was gained he changed the name of freedom to that of bondage for he himself oppressed with servitude the very people which he had rescued from foreign dominion.........Sandrokottos, having thus gained the crown, held Iudia at the time when Seleukos was laying the foundations of his future greatness."[2]

Here we are not concerned, however, with all the tribes of the Uttarāpatha and Haimavata divisions of Jambadvīpa who were reduced to subjection by Chandragupta but with only those who held semi-independent territories within Aśoka's empire. As far as Aśoka's Rock inscriptions at Shahbazgarhi, Mansehra and Kalsi, his Minor Pillar inscriptions at Niglīva and Lumbinī and Pillar inscriptions in the Champārān district indicate, these tribal states were situated in the northern part of the North-West Frontier Province, the State of Kāshmīr and Jammu, the kingdom of Nepāl, Bhutān and Sikkim, and the hilly portion of Assam. The ruling races who dwelt in these regions were typified by the Yonas, Kāmbojas, Gāndhāras, Nābhakas and Nābha-lines in the language of Aśoka, and the Yonas, Kāmbojas, Gāndhāras, Kirātas and Barbaras in the language of the Great Epic.

B. Extent of empire in the light of Hwen Thsang's testimony : Hwen Thsang was a personal witness to the stūpas, saṅghārāmas and stone-pillars, in short, monuments in several places in India of his time that were popularly known as pious and memorable erections of Aśoka. If his testimony can be relied upon, which I think is of a doubtful certainty, one may presume indeed that the places

---

1 Raychaudhuri, op. cit., p. 210 f.

2 McCrindle, Ancient India, p. 7.

MAP OF JAMBUDVIPA

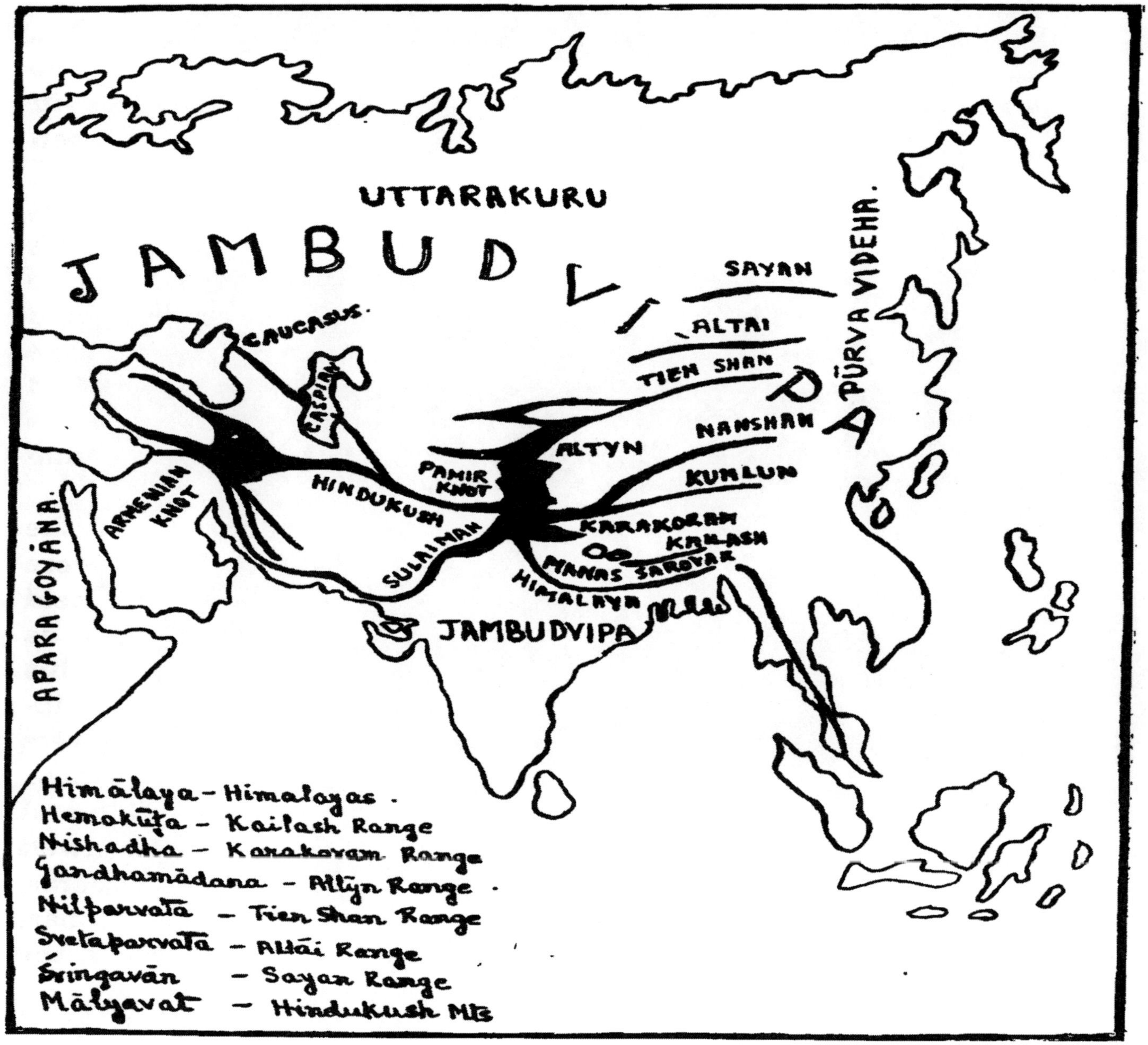

where these monuments were found *in situ* were all included in Aśoka's empire.

The Chinese pilgrim saw one stūpa known to have been built by Aśoka on Mt. Pi-lo-sa-lo (Pilusāra) near the capital of the country of Kapiśa, and two stūpas near the city of Nagarahāra. The country of Kapiśa abutted on the north on the Snowy mountains and on the remaining three sides it bordered on the Black ridge (Kālakūṭa ?) which is identified with the Hindu Kush. It lay at a distance of about 120 miles west from Lan-po (Lampāka, modern, Langhan, a small country lying along the northern bank of the Kābul river). Kapiśa was included in the Persian empire, as we noted, during the reign of the first Achæmenian king Cyrus. The site of the town of Nagarahāra, the old capital of the Jalālābād district, may be placed 'in the angle formed by the junction of the Sukhar and Kābul rivers, on their right banks.' The fact of inclusion of Kapiśa and Nagarahāra in Aśoka's empire is rendered probable by the unambiguous testimony of the Classical writers regarding the inclusion of Paropanasidai, Aria and Arachosia in the Maurya empire. The same remark holds equally true of the country of Saukūṭa (Taukūṭa, modern Sewistān) with Ho-si-na and Ho-sa-la as its two chief towns in which the pilgrim noticed 10 stūpas attributed to Aśoka. If Pītaśilā and Avanda were places beyond the Sulaiman and Kirthar ranges and somewhere in Beluchistān, their inclusion in Aśoka's empire is completely in accord with the testimony of the Classical writers vouchsafing for the inclusion of Gedrosia in the Maurya empire.

The city of Po-lu-sha (Purushapura, modern Peshāwar), near which the pilgrim saw three stūpas of Aśoka, and the city of Takshaśilā, near which stood four stūpas, were evidently places in the trans-Indus and hinter-Indus Gandhāra territories within Aśoka's domain proper. Similarly Udyāna or Oḍḍiyāna, the city of Siṃhapura, the town of Sākala, Chīnapati, Kuluta, Śatadru and Parvata, which were honoured with the stūpas of Aśoka, were all places in the Uttarāpatha division within Aśoka's empire.

As for the country of Kāśmīra where Aśoka was reputed as a builder of 500 sanghārāmas and a stūpa, its inclusion in Aśoka's empire is vouchsafed for by the testimony of Kalhaṇa's Rājataranginī crediting Aśoka with the building of the town of S'rīnagara and speaking of Aśoka's son Jalauka as having been appointed the governor of Kāśmīra. So far as Aśoka's own records are concerned, the ruling races of Kāśmīra may come in either as some of the semi-independent Himalayan tribes representing the Nābha-lines or as representing some of the unnamed Aparāntas connected with the Yonas, Kāmbojas and Gāndhāras, and there is no other way.

Mathurā, Thāneswar, S'rughna, Govishāṇa, Ahikshetra (Ahichchhatra), Kanauj, Ayodhyā, Hayamukha, Prayāga, S'rāvastī, Kapilavastu, Rāmagrāma, Kuśīnagara, Benares, Sārnāth, Mahāśāla, S'vetapura, Vaiśālī, Vṛiji country, Pāṭaliputra, Rājagṛiha, Nāḷandā, Gayā, Bodhgayā, Oḍra, Kalinga, South Kośala, Andhra, Ajaṇṭā, Valabhī and Ujjayinī, the places where the pilgrim came across monuments of Aśoka, need no comment as these were all included in Aśoka's empire, and many of them even in his domain proper.

As regards Bengal, he saw a stūpa of Aśoka near the town of Tāmralipti, one near the town of Karṇasuvarṇa, one near the town of Puṇḍravardhana, and one near the capital of Samataṭa. The pilgrim's itinerary goes to exclude Assam and Nepāl proper from Aśoka's empire.

Chola and Drāviḍa, where, too, the pilgrim saw the stūpas of Aśoka, cannot be included in Aśoka's empire. The pilgrim's Chola and Drāviḍa constituted together the territory of the Cholas, better, the Cholas and Pāṇḍyas, which lay, according to R. E. II and R. E. XIII, outside Aśoka's empire.

3. **Sphere of influence** : Aśoka in his M. R. E., claims that the sphere of his moral and cultural influence was as wide as Jambudvīpa. In Jambudvīpa he was able to create that noble and unprecendented atmosphere of piety which enabled him to commingle the gods and men or men and the gods and entitled all to the attainment of the grand heaven (vipule svage ārādhetave). This was indeed, according to the Pali Apadāna and Buddhaghosa's Manorathapūraṇī, the true signification of the honorific Devatānaṃpiyo[1] (Dear to the gods) applicable to a righteous king overlord :

> Imasmiṃ Bhaddake kappe eko āsi janādhipo ।
> mahānubhāvo rājā 'si chakkavatti mahābalo ॥
> so'haṃ pañchasu sīlesu ṭhapetvā janataṃ bahuṃ ।
> pāpetvā sugatiṃ yeva Devatānaṃpiyo ahuṃ[2] ॥

---

[1] Anguttara N., I, p. 24. To the same effect says Buddhaghosa in his Manorathapūraṇī, I, p. 154 ; "Certain devas who had been born in the deva-world as a result of Pilinda's guidance in a former birth, out of gratitude, waited on him morning and evening. He thus became famous as being dear to the devas". Malalasekera. Dictionary, II, p. 209.

[2] Apadaāna, I, p. 60.

"In this Gentle Era", said Thera Pilindavachchha, "there was a lord of men ; of great personality was he, a mighty king overlord. In his identity I became 'dear unto the gods' by establishing the multitude in the moral precepts of conduct and enabling them to get a happy destiny (in heaven, after death)".

Buddhist literature mentions Jambudvīpa as one of the four Mahādvīpas ("Great Islands") of the earth as known to the Indians, the other three islands being Pūrvavideha, Aparagoyāna,[1] and Uttarakuru. Pūrvavideha is the Eastern sub-continent of Asia which is located to the east of Mount Sumeru, Jambudvīpa is the Southern sub-continent which is located to the south, Aparagoyāna is the Western sub continent located to the west, and Uttarakuru is the Northern sub-continent which is located to the north of the same mountain.[2] The Mahābhārata, too, speaks of the four Mahādvīpas and locates them in the same way. It names, however, Pūrvavideha as Bhadrāśva, and Aparagoyāna as Ketumāla.[3]

In many respects the Great Epic account anticipates the description of Jambudvīpa in the Mārkaṇḍeya Purāṇa and other later works, according to which Jambudvīpa is just one of the seven islands or continents, the remaining six of them being situated to the south of Jambudvīpa and one on the south side of the ocean forming its southern boundary.

Furthermore, Jambudvīpa is said to have consisted of nine varshas or countries,—of seven, according to the Great Epic.[4] Mount Sumeru is placed in the middle of the Ilāvṛitavarsha and between the Gandhamādana range (towards the east), and the Mālyavat (towards the west). It is also spoken of as the highest mountain of the earth which is surrounded by the four lesser mountains called Mandara, Merumandara, Supārśva, and Kumuda, and situated on four sides viewed from east to north.

From the east side of the Ilāvṛitavārsha extends the mountain range of Gandhamādana to the east of which lies the country called Bhadrāśvavarsha with the ocean as its eastern boundary.

---

1 Variant Aparagodāna.

2 B. C. Law, India as Described, p. 2f. ; Malalasekera, Dictionary, I, pp. 117, 355, 941 ; II, pp. 286, 1136 ; Beal, Buddhist Records, I, p. 11.

3 Mahābhārata, Bhīshmaparva, 6.12, 13 ; 7.13, 44 ; B. C. Law, op. cit., p. 8f.

4 Ibid, 6.53 : ityetāni sapta-varshāṇi.

From the west side of the same country extends north and south (east to west, according to the Great Epic) the Mālyavat range to join with the Nīla and Nishadha ranges. To the west of this range lies the Ketumālavarsha with the ocean as its western limit.

To the north of the Ilāvṛitavarsha extends east and west the Nīla or Blue range to the north of which is situated the country called Ramyakvarsha. On the north side of the Ramyak country extends east and west the Śveta or White range beyond which lies the Hiraṇmayavarsha. Further north extends east and west the Śringavān range decked with peaks and beyond it is the country called Kuruvarsha (i. e., Uttarakuru) with the ocean as its northern boundary.[1]

On the south side of the Ilāvritavarsha extends east and west the Nishadha range[2] to the south of which is Harivarsha. To the south of this country extends east and west the Hemakūṭa range bstween which and the Himalayan range lies the country called Kiṃpurusha-varsha. The last-mentioned range forms the northern boundary of Bhāratavarsha or India proper with its eight upadvīpas or minor islands, which include Tāmraparṇa[1], i.e., the island of Ceylon.

Thus the Jambudvīpa, as described in the Purāṇas, as also in the Great Epic, may be treated as co-extensive at least with the main-land of Asia. The mountain system of Central Asia from the Himalayan range on the south to the Śrinagavān (Tienshan) on the north may be rendered intelligible if we assume that the Ilāvritavarsha is the highest plateau of the world which covered the whole of Pāmīr and western part of the tableland of Tibet, and that Mount Sumeru with the four surrounding mountains was situated in the midst of what is now called the Pāmīr Knot.

The Jaina work Jambudīva-paṇṇatti divides the Himalayas into two ranges, namely the Greater (Mahāhimavanta) and the Lesser (Chullahimavanta). The Greater range extends eastward down to to sea (i. e., the Bay of Bengal) below the varshadhara mountain, say the Arrakanese Yoma. Similarly the Lesser range extends westward down to the sea (i. e., the Arabian sea) below the varshadhara

---

[1] Mahābhārata, VI. 6. 56.

[2] Lassen (Ind. Alt. I, p. 22) identifies the Nishadha with 'the mountains belonging to the range which lies to the north of the Kābul river' and inclines to think that it was the same range which the Greek writers called Paropanisidae (Parvata Nishadha).

mountain, say the Sulāiman and Kirthar ranges.[1] Just at the junction of these two ranges it locates the Lotus Lake (Padmahrada) or Mānas Sarovar consisting of two juxtaposed lakes, one on the side of the Eastern and the other on that of the Western range.[2]

Eratosthenes and Megasthenes, too, speak of four parts, the largest of which was India. The parts were not, however, of the whole of Asia but those into which Southern Asia was divided. The smallest part was the region which was situated between the Euphrates and the Mediterranean sea. The two remaining parts were separated from the others by the Euphrates and the Indus, and lay, therefore, between these two rivers.[3]

The main point of difference between the Purāṇic and Buddhist accounts of Jambudvīpa lies in the fact that the former includes in Jambudvīpa the Bhadrāśvavarsha corresponding to the sub continent of Pūrvavideha, the Ketumālavarsha corresponding to Aparagoyāna, and the Kuruvarsha corresponding to Uttarakuru, while the latter exclndes them.

Aśoka's sphere of influence coincided rather with the Jambudvīpa as described in the Great Epic and the Purāṇas than with the Jambudvīpa of Pali literature. It comprised the five Mediterranean countries in the west, the territories of the Cholas, Pāṇḍyas, Satiyaputras, Keralaputras and Tāmraparṇyas in the south, and Southern Asia around India.

In his R.E. XIII, Aśoka mentions 600 yojanas as the extent of the regions outside his empire where he was able to achieve an effective conquest by piety. In this outermost zone of the sphere of piety he was able to create are located the territories of the five Greek rulers called Aṃtiyoka, Tulamaya, Aṃtekini, Maga and Alikasudara, and in the south, those of the Cholas, Pāṇḍyas, Satiyaputras, Keralaputras and Tāmraparṇyas.

Among his Greek contemporaries and allies, Aṃtiyoka is to be identified with Antiochus II Theos, king of Syria and Western Asia,

---

[1] The Jaina Mahāhimavanta seems to correspond with the Emodos or Hemodes (Pali Hemavata, Sk. Haimavavata, Lassen) of the Classical writers which represents that part of the Himalayan range which extended along Nepāl and Bhutān and onward toward the ocean.' McCrindle, Ancient India, pp. 182, 186. Note that the terms 'the Great Himalayas' and 'the Lesser Himalayas or Pir Panjan Range' are employed in a different sense to denote two parallel ranges, the higher and the lower. See The World by L. Dudley Stamp, p. 254.

[2] B. C. Law, India As Described, p. 4f.

[3] McCrindle, Ancient India, p. 48.

and not with his father Antiochus I Soter, son and successor of Seleukos Nikator. Thus he was the nearest Greek 'frontager' of Aśoka. The nearest southern Greek 'frontager' of Antiochus I and Antiochus II was Tulamaya identified with Ptolemy II Philadelphus, king of Egypt. The nearest western Greek 'frontager' of Antiochus II was Aṃtikini, i. e., Antigonas Gonatas, king of Macedonia. The nearest western Greek 'frontager' of Ptolemy II Philadelphus was Magas, half-brother of Ptolemy and king of Cyrene in North Africa. The nearest western Greek 'frontager' of Antigonas Gonatas was Alikasudara better identified with Alexander of Epirus. 'Evidently the five Greek potentates were the direct descendants and successors of Alexander the Great's generals and successors and their territories were but once component parts of the Greek empire left behind by the great Macedonian conqueror.'[1] Upon the whole, all of them represented but the contemporary Mediterranean States and Powers. As regards the Asiatic dominion of Antiochus II Theos, it abutted on the north-west frontier of Aśoka's empire.

The Chola territory lay between that of the Andhras on the north and that of the Pāṇḍyas on the south, and extended along the entire sea-coast of Kolapaṭṭana or Coromondel, say roughly between the river northern Pennār and Kāverī.[2] Buddhadatta's description leaves no room for doubt that in the south the Chola kingdom comprised the lower Kāverī valley, with Uragapura (modern Uraiūr in Trichinopoly) as its capital and Kāveripaṭṭana (moder Pugar) as its inland river-port. Kāñchīpura (modern Conjeeveram) was once its capital as attested by the Skanda Purāṇa and Hwen Thsang. The journey of Buddhaghosa from Kāñchīpura to Anurādhapura lay obviously via Madhurā (Madoura). The inhabitants of the Chola country are known in the Chronicles of Ceylon as Damilas (Drāviḍas).[3] According to Raychaudhuri, the Chola country "was drained by the river Kāverī and comprised the districts of Trichinopoly and Tanjore"[4], which, howevər, leaves the question of its northern limit open.

The Pāṇḍya territory in South India corresponded, according to Raychaudhuri, "to the Madurā, Rāmnad and Tinnevelly districts and perhaps the southern portion of the Travancore State, and had its

---

[1] Inscriptions, ii, p. 324.

[2] Cf. Hultzsch., South Indian Inscriptions, Vol, I, p. 34; Raychaudhuri, op. cit., p. 271.

[3] Barua, Inscriptions, ii, p. 230f.

[4] Raychaudhuri. op, cit. p. 271,

capitals at Kalkāi and Madurā."[1] But it would seem that there was a separate Tāmraparṇya territory in the southernmost part of the Deccan below those of the Pāṇḍyas on the east and the Keralaputras on the west,—a fact which is well attested by Hwen Thsang[2]. In the days of Ptolemy there were in the southern part of South India the kingdom of Karoura ruled by Kerobothros (Keralaputras), the kingdom of the Aioi (capital Kottiara) in South Travancore, the kingdom of Madoura (Madurā) ruled by Pandion (Pāṇḍyas) and above that the kingdom of the Batoi (capital Nikāma), that of Orthoura ruled by Sornagas (Chola-Nāgas ?) and that of Sora (Chola) ruled by Arkatos.

Evidently the territories of the Satiyaputras and the Keralaputras, who are mentioned as peoples in the Mansehra version of R. E. II, lay to the west of those of the Cholas and the Pāṇḍyas and extended along the western sea-coast of South India. The name of Satiyaputra or Satiyaputras is nowhere met with in Indian literature. The geographical name approaching Satiyaputra is Seriyāputa, which finds mention in one of the Barhut inscriptions. There still exists a difference of opinion as to the relative positions of the Satiyaputra and Keralaputra territories. From the manner in which Aśoka has mentioned them, it follows that the Satiyaputras had their territory above that of the Keralaputras. "Satiyaputra must have stood north of Keralaputra on the western side of the far south of South India, to the south of (Aśoka's) own vijita......From the location of Aśoka's Rock and Minor Rock Edicts, it may be inferred that the country of Satiyaputra or Sātiyaputra lay along the western coast of South India to the south of Sopārā (ancient Suppāraka, S'ūrpāraka) and the Chitaldrug district of Mysore, to the west of Mysore and to the north of Keralaputra."[3] "Still the best suggestion on this point is one from R. G. Bhandarkar, drawing attention to the fact that along the westernmost portion of the Deccan tableland we have Marāṭhā, Kāyastha and Brāhman families, bearing the surname 'Sātpute' which cannot but be treated as a modern transformation of Aśoka's Satiyaputa."[4]

---

[1] Ibid, p. 271.

[2] Beal, Buddhist Records, ii, p. 230, where the country of Malayakūṭa, i.e., the South Indian Tambapaṇṇi, is placed opposite to Siṃhala and below Drāviḍa or Southern Chola, and associated also with the mission of Mahendra.

[3],[4] Barua, Inscriptions, ii, p. 233f. Note that in the Mahābhārata, II. 31. 69, 71 the Kerala (*i.e.*, northern Kerala) associated with Vanavāsī has been distinguished from the Choṇḍrakerala (*i.e.*, southern Kerala) mentioned after Pāṇḍya and Drāviḍa.

The Girnār variant Ketala for Kerala of other versions and the absence of the variant Sacha for Satiya render dubious the equation of Satiya with Satya and all the identifications of Satiyaputra on that basis.[1]

"The edicts of Aśoka enable us to locate Keralaputra, Kerala or Chera as a country west of Pāṇḍya,[2] south of Satiyaputra; it must have been situated along the western coast of South India. According to Dr. Bhandarkar (Aśoka, p. 45), this country must have once 'included South Canara, Coorg, Malabar, and north-west part of Mysore with perhaps the northernmost portion of Travancore', while Dr. S. K. Aiyangar would prefer to locate it in the region including Cochin and extending southwards therefrom. At the time when the Periplus was written Mouziris (Mujirikudu) or modern Kranganur was the seat of government of Cerobothra (Keralaputra) which when Ptolemy wrote was in the interior at Karoura, that is, Karur on the Amarāvatī in the Coimbatore district (I. A., VIII, p. 145, XIII, p. 367f, Bhandarkar, Aśoka, p. 45f.). Raychaudhuri upholds the view according to which Keralaputra or Chera is the country south of Kūpaka (or Satya), extending down to Kanneti in Central Travancore.

The question arises—what did Aśoka mean by Tambapaṃṇī (R. E. II, G) and Taṃbapaṃṇiyā (R. E. XIII, K)? Vincent Smith takes Tambapaṃṇī to stand for the river Tāmraparṇī in Tinnevelly, while others take it to denote the island of Ceylon.

The Taṃbapaṃṇī of R. E. II may indeed be taken to stand both for the river Tāmraparṇī and for the Tāmraparṇis as a people and their territory. But the Taṃbapaṃṇiyā of R. E. XIII stand certainly for the Tāmraparṇyas as a people and their territory. And all that R. E. XIII contains is nothing but a restatement of what Aśoka has said in R. E. II. The question still is—where to place the Tāmraparṇyas and their territory?

There are apparently these three arguments that may be put forward in favour of the second view :

1. That the Pali Chronicles and the Samanta-pāsādikā speak of the friendly relationship which existed between Aśoka and his con-

[1] Ibid, ii, p. 233. Proposed identification of As'oka's Satiyaputra, *e. g.*, with (1) Kāñchīpura described as Satyavratakshetra ; (2) the Tuluva country or the region round about Satyamangalam Taluk of Coimbatore ; (3) Satyabhūmi of the Kerolalpatti including a portion of Kasergode Taluk, south Kānārā ; (4) Konganādū ruled by the Kosar people noted for their truthfulness.

[2] This fact is well attested by Cūlavaṃsa, iii, 7-9.

FIVE GREEK TERRITORIES

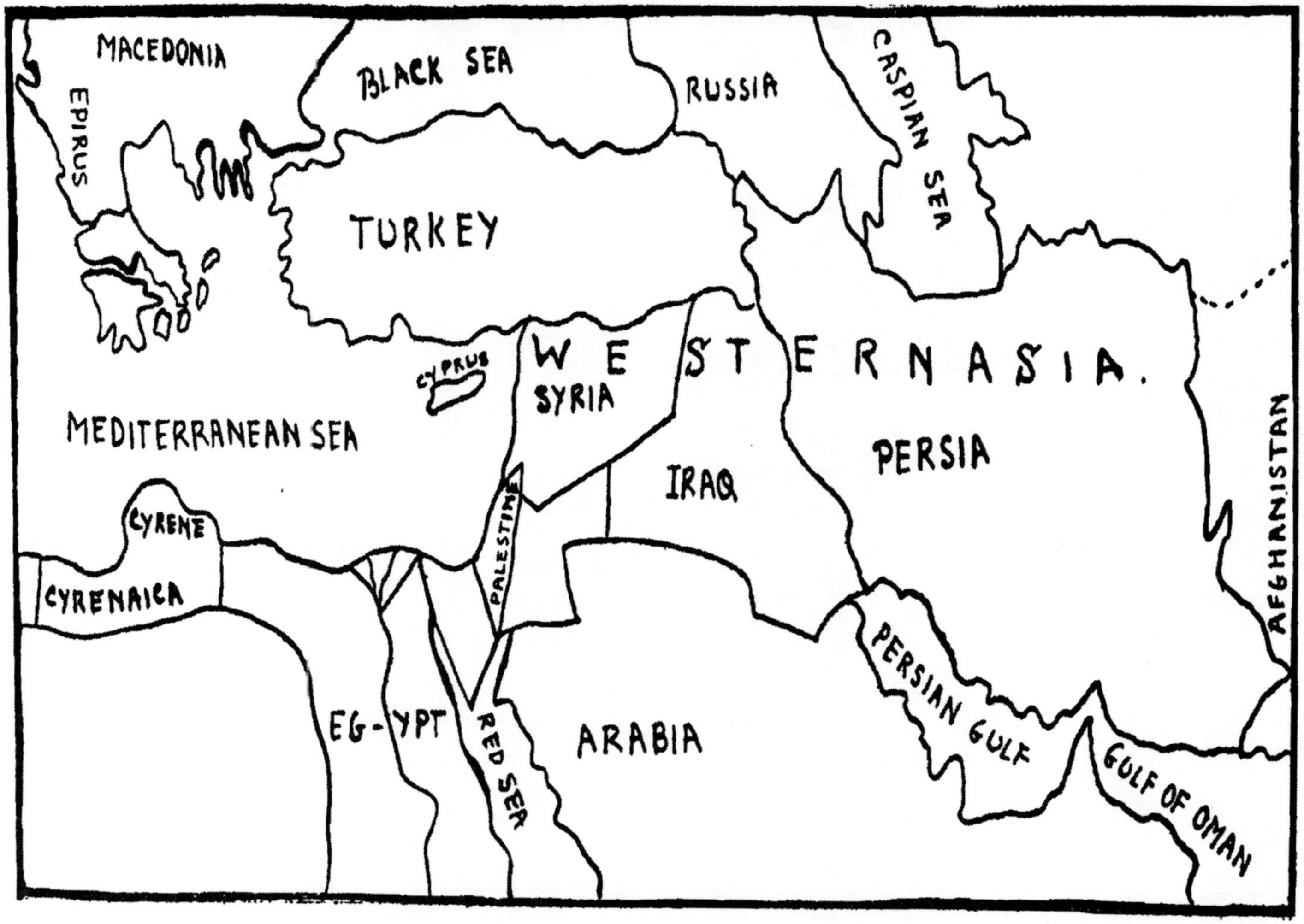

temporary, king Devānampiya Tissa of Ceylon, and give a graphic account of the conversion of Ceylon to Buddhism by the mission despatched during the reign of Aśoka.

2. That Indian literature generally speaks neither of an Indian country called Tāmraparṇī nor of a people known by the name of Tāmraparṇyas.

3. That Ceylon was really known to Megasthenes and other Greek writers as Taprobané.

The fact which goes against it is that wherever by Taṃbapaṃṇī or Tāmraparṇī is meant Ceylon, the word dīpa (dvīpa) or 'island' is associated with it[1]. Megasthenes and other Classical writers speak of the sea-girt island of Taprobané.

Ceylon is called the island of Tāmraparṇa or Tāmravarṇa in the Great Epic and the Purāṇas. But as regards the Rāmāyaṇa, Ceylon is known by the name of Pārasamudra.[2] The name Pārasamudra (Greek, Palaesimundu)[3] is met with also in the Arthaśāstra (II. 11). In both the Rāmāyaṇa and the Arthaśāstra, as we saw, Pāṇḍyakapāṭa (-kavāṭa) is associated with Tāmraparṇī. In both, Tāmraparṇī denotes obviously a South Indian river and by implication only, a riverine region. This region is represented now-a-days by Tinnevelly.

In R. E. XIII the Tāmraparṇyas are placed below the territories of the Cholas and the Pāṇḍyas, and in R. E. II, below those of the Cholas, the Pāṇḍyas, the Satiyaputras and the Keralaputras.

The Mārkaṇḍeya Purāṇa names four rivers, the Kṛitamālā, the Tāmraparṇī, the Pushyajā and Utpalavatī that rise from the Malaya mountain. The Kṛitamālā, which flows past Madoura, is identified with the Vaigai[4] and the Tāmraparṇī with "what is locally called Tāmbravarī or with the combined stream of the latter and Chittar."[5] The Tāmraparṇī is described in the Rāmāyaṇa as a great river, which goes to meet and dive into the sea (samudram avagāhate), containing the row of islands covered with the beautiful sandal woods.[6] It is connected, precisely as in the Arthaśāstra (II. 11), with Pāṇḍyakapāṭa noted for its gems and pearls.[7] The Malaya mountain to which

---

1 Barua, Inscriptions, ii, p. 236.

2 Rāmāyaṇa, VI. 3. 21 : sthita pāre samudrasya.

3 Raychaudhuri, op. cit., p. 273.

4-5 B. C. Law, Geographical Essays, p. 101f.

6 Rāmāyaṇa, IV. 41. 16-17.

7 *Ibid*, IV. 41. 18 : muktāmaṇi-vibhūshitaṃ yuktaṃ kapāṭaṃ Pāṇḍyānām.

the Mārkaṇḍeya Purāṇa traces the source of the Kṛitamālā, Tāmraparṇī and other rivers, is singled out in the Rāmāyaṇa as the rocky landmark of the Tāmraparṇī region,[1] precisely as in the Mahābhārata the mountain finds mention as the rocky landmark of Tāmraparṇa.[2] Malaya was the name of a mountainous district in South India,[3] and also that of a mountainous part of Ceylon.[4]

The Pali Chronicles apply the names Lankā, Sīhala and Tambapaṇṇī to one and the same country and island of Ceylon.[5] At the same time the Mahāvaṃsa refers to Tambapaṇṇī as a district in Lankā,[6] with a town of the same name as its capital,[7] which is distinguished from Anurādhapura.[8] The Sirīsavatthu (Srīśavastu), evidently a sea-port, described as a Yaksha capital, is located in Ceylon.[9] Vijaya, the eponymous Indian coloniser of this island, is said to have returned therefrom to Tambapaṇṇi[10] and entered into a matrimonial alliance with the Paṇḍu (Paṇḍya) king of South India whose capital was South Madhurā, i.e., Madoura.[11] The Damila (Drāviḍa) hordes under Elāra who conquered Ceylon for the time being at least, are said to have come across from the Chola country.[12]

As Megasthenes heard, Tāprobané was a large island in the great sea, which was 'separated from the mainland by a river' and was 'more productive of gold and large pearls than India.' Its inhabitants were called Pelesimundu (Pārasamudra).[13]

In the Arthaśāstra, on the other hand, the Pārasamudraka is distinguished from the Tāmraparṇika and Pāṇḍyakavāṭaka regions, which are associated together in the Rāmāyaṇa. It is also important to note that the Rāmāyaṇa tradition speaks of dvīpa (island or islands) in the river Tāmraparṇī, covered by beautiful sandal woods (chandanavanaśchitraiḥ prachchhanna-dvīpa dhāriṇī). Thus there was at least one Tāmraparṇī-dvīpa in South India below the Pāṇḍya country,

---

1 *Ibid*, IV. 41. 15.

2 Mahābhārata, VI. 6. 56 : Tamraparṇa-s'ılā rājan s'rīmān Malaya-parvatah.

3 Jātaka, IV, p. 327.

4 Mahāvaṃsa, VII. 68.

5 Ibid, VII. 7, 41, 42.

6 Ibid, VI. 47 : Lankāyaṃ.........Tambapaṇṇī dese.

7-8 Ibid, VII. 39, 43.

9-10 Ibid, VII, 43. The Valāhassa Jātaka (No : 196) places Sirīsavatthu in Tambapaṇṇidīpa.

11 Ibid, VII. 38, 49, 50.

12 Ibid, XXI. 13 : Cholaraṭṭhā idhāgamma.

13 McCrindle, Ancient India, pp. 60, 61, 178f.

as there was one in Lankā on the other side of the sea. And it is not unlikely that the Pāṇḍyakapāṭa is the modern Aruppakottai in the Rāmnad district on the right bank of the river Vaigai. From these facts, one cannot but be led to think that Tāmraparṇī (better Tāmravarṇī from having copper coloured sand-beaches), which was originally a riverine region in the southernmost part of South India below the Pāṇḍya territory, came to denote afterwards, probably in about the Maurya time, also the north-western sea-coast region of Ceylon between the Nāgadīpa and the river Kalyāṇī, and ultimately the island of Ceylon. This riverine region of South India must have the river valleys and deltas and entire sea-coast areas below Pāṇḍya and included also the entire area occupied by the Tinnevelly district[1].

The location suggested above of Aśoka's Tāmraparṇī as the land of the Tāmraparṇyas may now be placed on a solid foundation. In the Nāgārjunīkoṇḍa inscription, marked F by Dr. Vogel, Taṃbapaṃṇa (Tāmraparṇa) is clearly distinguished from Taṃbapaṃṇi-dīpa.[2] The Great Epic distinctly speaks of Tāmraparṇī as a country south of Pāṇḍya, which in some contexts is included in Drāviḍa, and locates in it the Gokarṇatīrtha and the hermitages of Agastya and his disciple.[3] This Tāmraparṇī with Mt. Vaidūrya as its rocky landmark corresponds with Hwen Thsang's country of Mo-lo kiu-ch'a (Malayakūṭa), with Mt. Po-ta-la-kia (Vaidūryaka) as its rocky landmark and placed south of Drāviḍa.[4]

The extension of Aśoka's sphere of influence, south of the Kṛishṇā-Tungabhadrā, even south of Sopārā and the river Pennār, thus made out, would seem to be substantially in agreement with the tradition recorded by Mamulanar, an ancient Tamil author, and other Tamil writers like Paranar and Kallil Attiraiyanar, regarding the 'Vimba Moriyar' ('Maurya upstarts') and their invasion of South India. "The invaders advanced from the Konkan, passing the hills Elilmalai, about sixteen miles north of Cannanore, and entered the Kongu

---

[1] Barua, Inscriptions, ii, p. 235.

[2] E. I., XX, p. 22 :......Taṃbapaṃṇidīpa-pasādakānaṃ theriyānaṃ Taṃbapaṃṇakānaṃ suparigahe ; which must be translated by "dedicated to the Theriyas who were converters of the Island of Tāmraparṇī (and other countries named) (and those who were) Tāmraparṇyas".

[3] Mahābhārata, III. 88. 13-18 : Kumāryaḥ kathitāḥ puṇyāḥ Pāṇḍyeshveva nararshabha, Tāmraparṇīn tu Kaunteya kīrtayishyāmi tach chhṛiṇu. Cf. ibid, III. 118. 3, 4, 8.

[4] Beal, Buddhist Records, II, p. 230ff.

(Colmbatore) district, ultimately going as far as the Podiyil Hill (in the Tinnevelly District)."[1]

The only point needing further orientation is whether or no, the list of Antas or Pratyantas given by Aśoka in his R. E. II and R. E. XIII is exhaustive or typical only. From his mode of enumeration of the Antas or Pratyantas in R.E. II, it cannot but appear that the list produced was intended to be typical only, and not an exhaustive one.

In Pali literature the word pachchanta (pratyanta) is employed in a twofold sense : (1) to denote the outermost region of a principality, the frontier of a dominion forming nevertheless the hinterland,[2] and (2) to denote the outlying districts or territories (pachchantima-janapadas), *i.e.*, the places outside the territorial limit of the Buddhist Midland.[3] In the Allahabad Stone-pillar inscription of Samudragupta, on the other hand, the term pratyanta occurs in the sense of border-lands, bordering territories instanced by Samataṭa,[4] *D*avāka,[5] Kāmarūpa,[6] Nepala and Karttṛipura.[7] Strictly speaking, the term was applied to the erstwhile independent principalities outside the territorial limit of the Āryāvarta or Aryandom.

So far as Aśoka is concerned, he has distinguished in R. E. XIII the Antas or Pratyantas listed in R. E. II from the semi-independent States and Aṭavis (Āṭavyas, Āṭavikas) within his empire, the semi-independent States of which the ruling races are broadly termed Aparāntas or Westerns in R.E. V. And in M.R.E., too, particularly in its Yerraguḍi copy, the Antas have been sharply distinguished from the populace under his direct rule, namely, the Jānapadas and Raṭhikas. It should be noted that in Samudragupta's praśasti the Pratyanta principalities are distinguished not only from those included in the Āryāvarta but from those forming the Āṭavika States.

---

1 S. K. Aiyangar, Beginnings of South Indian History, p. 89. Summary by Raychaudhuri, op. cit., p. 219.

2 Cf. Rājovāda Jātaka, No. 151.

3 Kathāvatthu, I. 3.

4 The Mehār Copper-plate inscription of Dāmodaradeva goes to prove that Samataṭa included in it the whole or part of the district of Tippera.

5 Identified by Dr. Bhattasali with Modern Dabok in Naogong district, Assam.

6 *i.e.*, the Gauhāti region of Assam.

7 It "seems to have comprised Katarpur in Jalandhar district and the Katuria (Katyur) of Kumaun, Garhwal and Rohilkhand."

As for the connotation of the term Antas or Pratyantas, Aśoka does not keep us at all in the dark. In his S. R. E. II, the Āntas are expressly characterised as avijitas (Aṃtānaṃ avijitānaṃ), 'the unconquered ones', 'those who did not territorially belong to his domain or empire', which amounted to saying, 'the independent borderers', 'the independent frontagers', 'the independent rulers or peoples around.' If so, it is difficult for me to agree with Bhandarkar in thinking that by the Āntas in S.R.E. II Aśoka must have meant but the Āṭavis in R.E. XIII on the ground that to both of them he held out threats, both of them he wished to pacify precisely in same terms, or that both of them were mischief-makers and creators of troubles from time to time.

In my opinion, Aśoka has placed the Āntas, Aparāntas and Āṭavis in three separate categories. The Aparāntas and Āṭavis cannot be treated as Āntas or Pratyantas unless we can show that Aśoka employed the term pratyanta also in the Buddhist sense to mean either the people of a frontier region or the territories outside the Buddhist Midland.[1] By the expression pratyanta janapadas or frontier districts the author of the Divyāvadāna has evidently meant those located in Uttarāpatha, such as the Svaśa-rāshṭra and the city of Takshaśilā where popular revolts took place on account of misrule or high-handed tyranny on the part of the Maurya high officials. Aśoka's S.R.E.I bears evidence to such tyrannical action on the part of the City-judiciaries in the province of Kalinga, and by implication also in those of Gandhāra and Avantī.

Kauṭilya's Arthaśāstra, too, contemplates a clear distinction between the Āṭavis and the Āntas, the former being placed in charge of the Aṭavīpālas and the latter in that of the Antapālas.

Here one might pertinently ask with Bhandarkar who were the independent borderers within the reach of the Viceroy-in-Council stationed at Tosali and the Lājavachanika mahāmātras at Samāpā, if they were not the Āṭavis? The nearest such borderers in the south were the Cholas and Pāṇḍyas. As for those towards the north-east, some light may be obtained from Pliny who speaks of a very large island in the Ganges which was inhabited by a single tribe called Modo-galingae. Beyond them were the Modubae answering to the non-Aryan people called Muṭibas in the Aitareya Brāhmaṇa who occupied the country north of the Ganges, the Molindae identified

---

[1] Cf. Divyāvadāna, p. 871.

with the Maladas whom the Mārkaṇḍeya Purāṇa places in the Prāchya division, the Uberae who are 'referred to the Bhars, a numerous race spread over the central districts of the region spoken of, and extending as far as to Assam', the Galmodroesi, Preti, Calissae, Sasuri, Passalae, Colubae, Oxexulae, Abali and Taluctae. The king of these is said to have kept under arms '50,000 foot-soldiers, 4,000 cavalry and 400 elephants.'[1]

4. **Pāṭaliputra, the Capital** : Whether of Aśoka's domain proper, or of his empire, or of his sphere of influence, the centre was his capital called Pāṭaliputra (R.E.V.). It was known to Megasthenes and other Classical writers as Palibothra. It is known in Pali also by the name of Pupphapura (Pushpapura), a synonym of Kusumapura, by which the city is not infrequently designated in Indian literature. The evidence of the Pali Mahāparinibbāna Suttanta and the Suttanipāta is conclusive as to its earlier name Pāṭaligāma implying as it does that it was at first but a mere village, from which humble position it rose afterwards into the eminence of the greatest city in India under the Mauryas. The Pali evidence is important also for the reason that it supplies us with an authentic account of the circumstances that led to the fortification of Pāṭaligāma by king Ajātaśatru of Magadha as a timely measure against the advance of his powerful rival, the Vṛijis of Vaiśālī. From the same realistic account, it is clear that Pāṭaligāma situated on the southern bank of the Ganges, stood as an important halting place on a high road, known as the Southern Road in the Buddha's time. Just opposite to Pāṭaligāma and on the side of the rival territory of the Vṛijis was the halting place called Koṭigāma.

The first step to the building of the city of Pāṭaliputra lay in the fortification of Pāṭaligāma. The work was in full swing when the Buddha passed through this place in course of his last journey, and that under the personal supervision of the two able Brāhman ministers of Ajātaśatru, Sunīdha and Varshakāra by name, who must have been well-versed in the science and art of town-planning and fort-building, of which a comprehensive idea may be formed from the rules stated in detail in the Arthaśāstra (II. 3, II. 4), and no less from the Pali description of a well-fortified city in the Mahāparinibbāna Suttanta, Ch. I. "The Buddha prophesied the future greatness of Pāṭaligāma (Pāṭaliputta ?) and also mentioned the danger of its destruction by

[1] McCrindle, Ancient India, pp. 139 f., 160 f.

fire or water, or internal discord."[1] This prophecy about Pāṭaliputra, put into the Buddha's mouth, was prospective in its purpose but retrospective in fact.

The origin of the name of Pāṭaligāma had mnch to do with the Pāṭali tree. The village was called Pāṭaligāma either because a Pāṭali tree was its cognizance, or because it abounded in Pāṭali trees, or because, as suggested by the Pali scholiasts, "on the day of its foundation several[2] Pāṭali-shoots sprouted forth from the ground."[3] Who changed the name of Pāṭaligāma after its fortification into Pāṭaliputra is not known. But the traditions are unanimous that the capital of Magadha was for the first time transferred from Rājagṛiha to Pāṭaliputra by Udāyī, son and successor of Ajātaśatru. The city as the capital of Magadha was definitely known by the name of Pāṭatiputra in the time of the next king Muṇḍa, gransdon of Ajātaśatru. As Hwen Thsang, the great Chinese pilgrim, came to know, the city which became afterwards known by the name of Pāṭaliputra was at first called Kusumapura, 'because the palace of the king had many flowers," which, however, is doubtful. Whatever the origin and significance of the other name, Pushpapura or Kusumpura, the collective literary and epigraphic evidence goes to show that this poetic name was acquired later. This is not, however, to deny that the Maurya capital outgrew its humbler beginning. With these reservations we may readily accept the following comment of Vincent Smith on the position of Pāṭaliputra :

"Pāṭaliputra, Chandragupta's Capital, was a great and noble city extending along the northern bank of the Son[4] for about nine miles, with a depth of less than two miles. Much of the area is now covered by Patna, Bankipore, and sundry neighbouring villages. Kusumapura, the more ancient city, stood on the Ganges, and evidently became merged in Pāṭaliputra, for the two names are often used as synonyms. The Maurya city was built in the tongue of land formed by the junction of the Son with the Ganges, a defensible position recommended by the writers of text-books, and frequently adopted by the ancient Indian in practice....The old river beds and even the ancient embankments of quay may still be traced. The city was

---

[1] Malalasekera, Dictionary, ii, p. 178.

[2] 'Three' according to Dhammapāla : tayo Pāṭalankurā. Commentary to Udāna, VIII. 6.

[3] Malalasekera, Dictonary, ii, p. 179.

[4] Cf. anu-S'oṇaṃ Pāṭaliputram, Patañjali's Mahābhāshya, II. 1. 2.

defended by a massive timber palisade, of which the remains have been found at several places. The gates were sixty-four, and the towers five hundred and seventy in number. The palisade was protected by a deep moat."[1]

The main advantageous position required in the Arthaśāstra of a city deserving to be used as a capital (sthānīya) is that it must be centrally located and possess all the easy communication facilities. Its position was in this respect really enviable. It was situated at the junction of the two great highways of commerce, namely, the Southern Road extending from Rājagṛiha to Pratishṭhāna and the Ganges system of rivers connected with the coastal trade of India and the oversea trade of Eastern India. The connection of the Southern Road with the Northern with its various branches afforded facilities also for land communication with such distant places in Uttarāpatha as Takshaśilā and Pushkalāvatī. The internal arrangement and life of the city, with the imperial palace as the cynosure, may be easily inferred from the inscriptions, as also from the foreign accounts, the Arthaśāstra, II. 4, and the typical description of the city of Sāgala in the Pali work called Milindapañha.

---

[1] Oxford History of India, p. 77. According to Arrian, "The greatest city in India is that which is called Palimbothra in the dominions of the Prasians, where the streams of the Erannoboas (Son) and the Ganges unite......Megasthenes informs us that this city stretched in the inhabited quarters to an extreme length on each side of eighty stadia, and that its breadth was fifteen stadia, and that a ditch encompassed it all round, which was six hundred feet in breadth and thirty cubits in depth, and that the wall was crowned with 570 towers and had four-and-sixty gates." McCrindle, Ancient India, p. 67f.

CHAPTER IV

STATE

The historico-critical study of the Maurya State under Aśoka involves at every step the dispassionate consideration of these three points, each of importance : (1) the earlier Indian administration, particularly Mauryan, (2) the innovations introduced by Aśoka, and (3) the combined effect of both on the later systems, particularly one which is embodied in the Arthaśāstra as a prose treatise, ascribed to Kauṭilya Vishṇugupta.

To put the matter in this fashion is to modify considerably the debatable assumption of Mookerji, Jayaswal, Jacobi, Shama Sastri, N. N. Law, Bandyopadhyay and other writers that the Arthaśāstra in its extant prose form is a treatise written by Kauṭilya[1] or Vishṇugupta Chāṇakya, the uprooter of the Nanda dynasty, political adviser of Chandragupta Maurya and Chancellor of Magadha.

Such gifted writers, on the other hand, as Vincent Smith, Jolly, Hillebrandt, Winternitz and Otto Stein, who have doubted or challenged the above position, have erred on the wrong side by putting their implicit faith in the testimony of the Classical writers whose accredited authority was the Indika of Megasthenes. Even to the Classical writers like Arrian, much of what the Indika of the Greek ambassador to Chandragupta's court contained was fabulous and, therefore, incredible. It survives, moreover, only in a few fragments preserved or reproduced by some later historians and geographers. This fact alone goes to lessen the value of the work otherwise lost and render it into a work of questionable authority.

Avoiding at all events these two extreme positions, the scientific historical method will be not so much to interpret and appraise the matters concerning Aśoka's state in the light of either the Indika or the Arthaśāstra as to see and show what actual light is shed on the subject by Aśoka's own records and the collective literary tradition of the age.

Whatever the actual date of its composition or compilation, the Arthaśāstra has certainly this advantage over both the fragmentary Indika of Megasthenes and the inscriptions of Aśoka that it presents a complete system of the Indian royal polity. The inscriptions of Aśoka keep us, on the other hand, entirely in the dark as to the

[1] Kauṭalya, acc. to Ganapati Shastri.

military side of his administration. They give us but a few glimpses, here and there, into the guiding principles of administration, its type and basic character, its aims and methods, its machineries, the administrative divisions, the feudatory states, the foreign relations and policies, the personal epithets or titles of the king, the position and function of the king, the private life of the king, the position of the queens, the king's near relations, his personal staff and agents, the princes of the blood, the position, function and constitution of the council of ministers, the king's power of legislation, the judicial system, the means of communication, the conveyances and means of transport, the king's prerogatives and proclamations, the nature of despatches, the method of supervision and inspection, the public works, the philanthropic deeds, the sources of revenue or state-income, the remission of taxes and duties, the decentralisation of power, the position and function of the Viceroys and Mahāmātras, the rules of conduct for public servants, the war and peace, the suppression of revolts and internal troubles, and the like.

The oldest known stock-passages in the Pali and Ardhamāgadhī canons bear ample testimony to the development of the science of of royal polity in the country and in the interest evinced and active part played by certain S'ramaṇas and Brāhmaṇas in the matter. The Arthaśāstra itself quotes by name and criticises the views of different teachers and schools of political thought, and sets itself the task of defending and expounding the views of Kauṭilya.

(1) Individual teachers :—

Dīrghaśchārāyaṇa, ghoṭamukha, Vātavyādhi, Viśālāksha, Piśuna, Piśunaputra, Kauṇapadanta (all nicknames), Bhāradvāja, Kaṇinka Bhāradvāja, Kiñjalka, Parāśara and Kātyāyana.[1]

(2) Schools :—

The Mānavas, Pārāśaras, Auśanasas, Bārhaspatyas and Āmbhīyas.

The agreed opinion of the individuals and schools other than those who held dissentient views is obviously referred to the body of Āchāryas (accredited teachers).

Among the individual teachers, Dīrghaśchārāyaṇa (Pali Dīgha Kārāyana) was the Commander-in-Chief of Kośala and a younger contemporary of the Buddha.[2] Ghoṭamukha (Pali Ghoṭakamukha)

[1] In the Mahābhārata, XV, Rājadharma and Apaddharma sections, we have mention of Vis'ālāksha, Sahasrāksha, Mahendra (Indra), Purandara, Us'ana, Nārada, Bhāradvāja, Kaṇika Bhāradvāja, Gauras'ira, Svāyambhuva Manu, Pracetas Manu, S'ukra (Kāvya), Kārtsnya, Nāḍījangha Vakarāja.

[2] Majjhima, ii, p. 118.

was a Brāhman contemporary of the Buddha.[1] Parāśara may be regarded as the putative author of the Mahābhārata, and Kātyāyana as a Smṛiti-writer.

Among the schools, the Mānavas and Pārāśaras were exponents of of the rules of polity embodied in the Smṛiti texts ascribed to them. The Bārhaspatyas and Auśanasas represented the Smṛiti schools of law as well as the schools of politics. The Āmbhīyas who are connected by Professor F. W. Thomas with Taxila,[2] derived their name from Āmbhi, king of Takshaśilā at the time of Alexander's invasion of India.[3]

Vishṇugupta's prose treatise preserves certain maxims of Kauṭilya in verse and reproduces many in prose, which must somehow or other be discriminated from their later elucidations in order to understand what was precisely in the immediate background of Aśoka's administration. The principles of royal polity and good government as well as the duties and responsibilities of kings as inculcated by various sages in the Great Epic, particularly those embodied in the Rājadharma section of the Śāntiparva, deserve careful consideration. The earlier Magadhan system of administration as may be envisaged from incidental references in the Pali and Ardhamāgadhī texts is of an invaluable aid to the study of the same. Above all, the light must be constantly sought from the duties and ideals of the king overlord adumbrated and repeatedly emphasized in the Pali Nikāyas including one of the Jātakas, and, to some extent, also from such Vedic texts as the Brāhmaṇas, earlier Sūtras and Upanishads.

Admittedly there is no ancient Indian term corresponding to the modern State, the nearest approximation being Rājya, nor is there any conception or definition exactly fitting in with the modern theory of State. But Aśoka certainly gives us a fairly clear idea of all the four elements of the Maurya State as it shaped in his hands, namely, the population, territory, sovereignty and government. He indicates and, in some respects, sets forth also the functions and aims, methods and contrivances, foreign relations and policies of the State, the constitution and machineries of his government, and his achievements through it.

---

1 Ibid, ii, p. 157.

2 Bārhaspatya Arthas'āstra, introd,, p. 15.

3 Raychaudhuri, op. cit., pp. 199, 210.

1. **Population** :—The Indian technical terms denoting the population of a territory, *i.e.*, the ruled or subjects, are prakṛitayaḥ[1] (same as pakatiyo of the Hāthigumphā inscription), Paurāh (Mbh. XII. 68.29), paura-jānapadāḥ (Arthaśāstra, II. 1), prajāḥ (Mbh., XII. 28.51), and sarva-prajāḥ (Buddha-charita, II. 35). As defined by Amarasiṃha, the prakṛitis denote the collective body of citizens.[2]

Corresponding to Aśvaghośha's sarav-prajāḥ we have the Aśokan expression sava-munisā, "all men" (S.R.E. I, S.R.E. II), jana-jānapadā (R.E. VIII), or simply janā (R.E. IV, VI, etc.). In the wider sense of the term, the population consisted of pasu-munisā, "men and animals" (R.E. II, P.E. VII), *i.e.*, both citizens and denizens, further distinguished as bipeds and quadrupeds, birds and aquatic beings (dupada-chatupadā, pakhi-vālichalā, P.E. II). In terms of religion, all men are represented by the term sava pāsaṃḍā, "all sects", "all denominations", "all communities" (R.E. VII, R.E. XII, P.E. VII).

The population, in the political sense of the term, is spoken of as placed in three categories : (1) that within the territory under his direct government, and subsequently, within the territory under the direct rule of himself and his Viceroys, (2) that within the semi-independent tribal or feudatory States, and (3) that within the independent but allied territories, denoted respectively by the terms, janapadā, aparantā-aṭaviyo-raṭhikā, and aṃtā (M.R.E., Ye, R.E.V, R.E. XIII). The population of the earth living outside the territorial limit of the unconquered āntas or pratyantas is broadly distinguished as peoples whose countries were not frequented by Aśoka's Dūtas (Envoys or Emissaries), *i.e.*, the territories to which they had no access (yata dūtā Devānaṃpiyasa no yaṃti).

The Āntas were not Aśoka's subjects since they territorially belonged to principalities or dominions of which the sovereignty was vested in other rulers or ruling races ; politically they were extra-territorial. They might, if at all, be regarded as intra-territorial only in a non-technical sense, on the strength of the good will cherished by Aśoka towards them as towards his own subjects (S.R.E. II), by virtue of the works of public utility and philanthropic nature Aśoka was able to accomplish in their lands (R.E. II), on the ground of acceptance of Aśoka's principles of piety or duty by them (R.E. XIII), in short, as Aśoka himself put it, by the

---

[1] Arthas'āstra, vii. 4 : utsāhayuktā me prakṛitayaḥ.

[2] Amarakosha, Kshatriyavarga : Prakṛitayaḥ paurāṇām s'renayo'pi cha (87).

right of cultural conquest (dhamma-vijaya) he was able to achieve (R.E. XIII). Thus they came indeed within the sphere of Aśoka's moral influence and became dwellers of the Greater India Aśoka aspired to found on the basis of good will and mutual understanding, particularly through appreciation by the outsiders of the goodness of human heart and the nobleness of human spirit and their tangible expressions in word and deed.

The Aparāntas formed the population of certain tribal States within Aśoka's empire that were internally free and externally only acknowledged the suzerainty of Aśoka, however real or nominal their allegiance to the imperial state might be.

The position of the Jānapadas as the population proper, broadly divided into two classes, *viz.*, urban and rural, is self-evident. Even as representatives and supporters of different religious communities, their position is easily understandable.

The denizens consisting of beasts and birds and fishes, of the beasts of burden, live-stocks and games, formed in a sense the population under the name of pāṇā, "life", "living beings", of a civilized state like the Aśokan.

2. **Territory** : The Indian technical terms to denote territory are Janapada[1] and Rāshṭra[2] (Pali Raṭṭha). The Kāmandakīya term svarāshṭra stands for one's own territory as distinguished from Pararāshṭra, the territory of others. Aśoka's own words for territory, such as Vijita, Vijaya, (R.E. XIV), Rāja-visaya (R.E. XIII), Desa (S.R.E. I) and Puthavī (R.E. V) are met with in the contemporary, earlier as well as later Indian literature, particularly in Pali. The later Indian inscriptional term for territory is Vijaya-chakra[3] or Vijaya-rājya instead of Aśoka's Vijaya. The literary as well as the inscriptional word Rājya[4] (Pali Rajja) for territory is nowhere employed in Aśoka's inscriptions. Deśa and Pṛithivî are treated as synonymous terms in the Arthaśāstra, IX. 1 : deśaḥ prithivī.

An ideal territory including population is defined thus in the Arthaśāstra, VI. 1 :

---

[1] Arthas'āstra, VI. 1 : Svāmātya-janapada-durga-kosha-daṇḍa mitrāṇi Prakṛitayaḥ. Amarakosha, Kshatriyavarga, 36 : Svāmātya-suhṛit-kosha-rāshṭra-durga-balāni cha Rājyāngāni.

[2] Cf. supavata-vijaya-chake in the Hāthigumphā inscription.

[3] Cf. Gupta inscriptions.

[4] Cf. Suganaṃ raje (S'ungānāṃ rājye) in the Barhut Gateway inscription.

"Has favourably situated cities and towns, with means to maintain its own population and others in times of calamity, well-guarded, with easy means of livelihood, averse to the enemy, can cope with neighbouring rulers, free from miry, rocky, marshy, uneven and thorny tracts, as well as from tigers, wild beasts and wild tracts, attractive, containing plenty of good cultivable lands, mines, timber, elephant forests and pasture grounds, excels in arts and crafts, has hidden passages, rich in cattle (livestocks), not dependent on rain-water only, provided with land and waterways, has an extensive trade in various kinds of merchandise, can bear the burden of a vast army and heavy taxation, has a good and active peasantry, full of intelligent masters and servants, with a population noted for its loyalty and moral purity —these are the characteristics of a good territory."

Aśoka refers to his territory as a vast domain (R.E. XIV), with the city of Pāṭaliputra as its capital (R.E. V). He alludes also to the outer towns containing his family establishments or residences, and to residences also of his brothers, sisters and other kith and kin (R.E. V, P.E. VII). Among outer towns, we have mention of such important cities as Takshaśilā (S.R.E. I), Kauśāmbī (Queen's Edict), Ujjayinī (S.R.E. I), Tosali and Samāpā (S.R.E. I & II), Suvarṇgiri and Ṛishila (M.R.E.). The existence of other towns may be inferred from the location of other inscriptions, *e.g.*, the city of Kapilavastu from the Lumbinī Pillar inscription, that of Śrughna from the Kalsi set of Rock Edicts, those of Rājapura and Abhisāra from the Mansehra set, that of Pushkarāvatī from the Śhahbazgarhi, that of Girinagara (Jaina Girināra) from the Girnār, that of Sūrpāraka from the Sopārā, that of Virāṭanagara from the Bairāt copy of M.R.E., that of Vidiśā from the Sānchī Pillar inscription, and that of Gayā from the Barābar Hill-cave inscriptions.

It is only in respect of his conquest by piety, *i.e.*, the sphere of his moral influence, that Aśoka's domain was or might be claimed to have been as wide as Jambudvīpa (M.R.E.), which traditionally contained in Aśoka's time as many as 84,000 towns, large and small. His earthly empire, as we saw, was less extended than Bhāratavarsha.

As king of Magadha or Magadhan king (lājā Māgadhe, Bhābru), his territory in the sense of his narrow royal domain, confined within the four corners of Magadha, or, at the most, of Anga Magadha. To put it in the language of the Classical writers, he was just a king of the Prasii or Palibotris (Pāṭaliputriyans). His imperial domain proper, *i.e.*, the major portion of his empire which was under his direct government excluded the semi-independent territories of such oligarchical tribes as the Yaunas, Kāmbojas, Gāndhāras, Nābhāgas and Nābha-lines on the north and north-west, and the senior Rāshṭrikas and Bhojas and their offshoots, as well as the Andhras and Pārinda-Pāradas in the south. His earthly empire as a whole included in it also these territories as well as the wild forests occupied by the Āṭavyas (Aṭaviyo, R.E. XIII) of more or less nomadic habits and predatory propensities, but it certainly precluded from it the pratyantas or unconquered territories of the Āntas ("Frontagers", "Borderers") who might otherwise be called Sāmantas ("Neighbours", R.E. II). Even these territories were sought to be distinguished from those beyond them by the fact of their having entered into some sort of an alliance, having some common bonds of friendship. Aśoka gives us to understand that these territories were favoured than against favouring by way of remaining quiet and pacified (R.E. II, R.E. XIII, S.R.E. II). The territories without lay beyond the range of his Dūtas.

From his mode of enumeration and placing of the Āntas or Sāmantas, it is easy to infer that Aśoka had before him a clear mental picture of the inter-state circles (Sāmanta-maṇḍalam) forming an intricate subject of lengthy academic discussion in the Arthaśātra[1].

According to the general terminology of the Indian science of polity, the Sāmanta or 'Frontager' whose territory stood immediately contiguous (on any one side) to the territory of a king in the role of a conqueror was to be termed śatru ("the enemy") ; the Sāmanta whose territory lay just beyond that of the śatru was to be termed mitra ("the conqueror's friend") ; the Sāmanta who stood next to the mitra was to pass as udāsina ("the neutral") ; and the Sāmanta who stood just in the rear of the conqueror to help the latter's enemy was to go by the name of pārshṇigrāha ("the rearward enemy.")[2]

In the frontal order the Arthaśātra places the Sāmantas, each in front of the man behind, and carries their relative positions beyond the fourth degree. The nearest Frontager is termed ari ("the conqueror's enemy"), the next man, mitra (the conqueror's friend"),

---

[1] For a clear idea of Kautilya-Vishṇugupta's treatment of the subject, the reader is referred to N. N. Law's excellent monograph.—Inter-state Relations in Ancient India, Calcutta Oriental Series, No. 4, E. 1, Part I.

[2] Amarakosha, Kshatriyavarga, 20 :

Vishayānantaro rājā s'atrur mitram ataḥparam ।
udāsīnaḥ parataraḥ, pārshṇigrāhas tu pṛishṭhataḥ ॥

the third man, arimitra ("the enemy's friend"), the fourth man mitra-mitra ("the friend's friend"), and the fifth man, ari-mitra-mitra ("the enemy's friend's friend")[1].

"In the rear of the conqueror, there happen to be situated a rearward enemy (pārshṇigrāha), a rearward friend (ākranda), an ally of the rearward enemy (pārshnigrāhasāra) and an ally of the rearward friend (ākrandasāra)[2].

A rival whose territory lies contiguous to that of the conqueror is a natural enemy. He who is antagonistic or creates enemies to the conqueror is a factitious (kṛitrima) enemy. An ally whose friendship is based upon family relationship and whose territory is next to that of the enemy is a natural friend. He whose friendship is courted for self-maintenance is an acquired friend. The Sāmanta whose territory lies close to those of both the conqueror and his enemy and who is capable of helping both is a mediatory ruler (madhyama).[3] He whose territory lies beyond those of all of the above and who is capable of helping or resisting any of them individually is a 'superior' ruler (udāsīna).[4]

The canqueror, his friend and his friend's friend constitute together a circle of states on one side. Thus one is to think in respect of all the four sides of the conqueror's territory of altogether four inter-state circles.

The inter state relations which are carried to the highest degree of nicety in the prose treatise of the Arthaśāstra are far beyond the scope of the Maurya State under Aśoka.

On the western side of Aśoka's territory, the nearest frontager was Antiochus II Theos. The next man whose territory lay contiguous on the south to that of Antiochus was Ptolemy II Philadelphos. The frontager whose territory lay contiguous on the west to that of Antiochus was Antigonas Gonatas. The third frontager whose territory lay contiguous on the west to that of Ptolemy was Magas, and the third Frontager whose territory lay contiguous on the west to that of Antigonas was Alexander of Epirus. The territories beyond

---

1 Arthas'āstra, VI. 2.

2 Ibid, Shama Sastri's transl., p. 312.

3 I fully agree with Dr. N. N. Law when he maintains that here the term madhyama stands for a ruler or state of medium power.

4 As Dr. N. N. Law aptly points out, the udāsīna in the terminology of the Arthas'āstra does not mean 'neutral' but one who is placed higher (ut āsīnah).

those of Magas and Alexander lay outside the range of Aśoka's foreign relations, diplomatic or otherwise.

On the southern side of his territory, the nearest frontagers were the Cholas and below them the Pāṇḍyas along the eastern sea-coast. The nearest frontagers along the western coast were the Satiyaputras and below them the Keralaputras. Below all of them were the Tāmraparṇyas. The peoples whose countries lay on two sides of the Indian Ocean were all situated beyond the range of Aśoka's foreign relations.

The existence of some Āntas or Sāmantas on the eastern and north-eastern sides of his territory in Northern India may be inferred from Aśoka's S.R.E. II. The Pali tradition speaks of a Buddhist mission sent to Suvarṇabhūmi during Aśoka's reign, but it lacks as yet corroboration from Aśoka's inscriptions and reliable foreign accounts.

The independent peoples whose territories lay immediately beyond those of the Yaunas, Kāmbojas and Gāndhāras in Uttarāpatha proper, and on the north beyond those of the Nābhakas and Nābha-lines are not expressly mentioned. It is vaguely stated that all the peoples in Jambudvīpa, which in its northernmost reach extended up to the southern side of Mt. Sumeru, came under his moral influence, if not precisely under his rule.

The semi-independent peoples who were hinter-landers may be shown to have formed territorial gradations of buffers : the Yaunas and Kāmbojas above the Gāndhāras, and probably the Barbaras and Kirātas not only above the Yaunas and Kāmbojas of Uttarāpatha but also above the Nābhakas and Nābha-lines of Central Himalayan region. Similarly in the south were the Andhras and Pārindas below the Rashṭrikas, Bhojakas and their offshoots in the Vindhyan and Narmadā regions.

The poet Bhāsa, two of whose verses may be shown to have been cited in the prose treatise of the Arthaśāstra (X. 3), restricted the territory of a paramount sovereign of Rājasiṃha's type to Northern India situated between the Himalayas and the Vindhya hills and extending (east to west) from sea to sea :

> Imāṃ sāgaraparyantāṃ Himavad-Vindhya-kuṇḍalam ।
> mahīm ekātapatrānkaṃ Rājasiṃhaḥ praśāstu naḥ ॥ [1]

[1] Bharatavākya in Bhāsa's Svapnavāsavadattā and Bālacharitam.

Though the words chāturanta (I. 6) and chaturantā mahī (III. 1) occur in the Arthaśāstra, from Shama Sastri's rendering of the actual definition of the domain of a king overlord in the same considered as a developed prose treatise, it appears that it was similarly limited to Northern India :

Deśaḥ pṛithivī ; tasyāṃ Himavat-samudrāntaram udīchīnaṃ yojana-sahasra-parimāṇam atiryak chakravarti-kshetram (IX. 1).[1]

This might be made to tally with the Purāṇic definition of Bhāratavarsha[2] only by the following rendering of the passage from the Arthaśāstra :

"Country is the earth, thereof the portion between the Himalayas and the ocean in extent one thousand Udīchī[3] yojanas (*i.e.*, judged by the Udīchī or North Indian standard), measured lengthwise (*lit.*, not crosswise),[4] forms the domain of an overlord."

"In it", precisely as according to the description of Jambudvīpa in the Jaina Jambudīvapaṇṇatti, "there are such varieties of land as forests, villages, waterfalls, level plains, and uneven grounds.... Time consists of cold, hot and rainy periods. The divisions of time are the night, the day, the fortnight, the month, the season, solstices, the year, and the yuga cycle of five years."

As appears from his inscriptions, Aśoka's domain, which in a sense was co-extensive with Jambudvīpa, contained mountains and hills (pavata), hill-caves (kubhā), forests (aṭaviyo), and watery regions suitable for the purpose of fishery (kevaṭabhoga). The year, too, was divided into three seasons (tīsu chātuṃmāsīsu), the lunar months into fortnights (better, half months as in the Arthaśāstra), and days and the

---

1 "Country (space) means the earth, in it the thousand yojanas of the northern portion of the country which stretches from the Himalayas and the ocean form the dominion of no insignificant emperor."

2 Vishṇu Purāṇa, II. 3 :

Uttaraṃ yat samudrasya, Himādres'chaiva dakshiṇam ।
varshaṃ tad Bhāratam nāma Bhāratī yatra santatih ॥
Yojanānāṃ sahasras tu dvīpo 'yaṃ dakshiṇottarāt ।
pūrve Kirātā yasyānte, pas'chime Yavanāh sthitāh ॥

3 Cf. Mārkaṇḍeya Purāṇa-Dakshiṇe' parato tasya
pūrveṇa cha mahodadhiḥ......।
Himavān uttareṇāsya.........॥

4 In Pali the word tiriyaṃ (Sk. tiryak), as distinguished from uddha and adha, means 'across' ; elswhere 'slantingly, transversely, horizontally' Cf. Pali—English Dict., sub vooe tiriyaṃ.

populace was familiar with the cycle of five years (paṃchasu vasesu,[1] R.E. III, S.R.E. I) yielding an additional month (adhimāsa) at the end of every half cycle[2] within the third year (S.R.E. I).

Aśoka evidently placed the five Sāmanta territories in the west, as well as the five in the south, within an extension of six hundred yojanas from his empire (ā shashu yojanashateshu, R.E. XIII).

3. **Sovereignty** :—The Maurya State under Aśoka, precisely as under his father and grandfather, was apparently an absolute monarchy in its form, 'in the legal and political sense of the term' (in the words of Mookerji), and as such, its sovereignty or supreme power might be taken to have belonged to him, vested in his person. In his inscriptions, Aśoka has been variously represented, e g., as Devānaṃpiya Asoka (M.R.E., Ma), Devānaṃpiyo Piyadasi Rājā (R.E. III, G), Priyadasi Lājā Māgadhe (Bhābru), and not infrequently, as Devānaṃpiye (M.R.E., S.R.E., P.E. VII). He has referred to former kings either as rājāno (plural of rājā) or as Devanaṃpiyā (plural of Devānaṃpiyo, R.E. VIII). He himself has been referred to in the same set of edicts under the two titles of Rājā and Devānaṃpiye (S. R. E. II). One can say indeed on the authority of the commentary on the Harshacharita that Devānāṃpriya was no more than a pūjāvachana or honorific, which, according to Patañjali, was on a par with such other honorifics as Bhavān (Sa Bhavān, Tato Bhavān, Tatra Bhavān), Dīrghāyus and Āyushmān (under Pāṇini, V. 4. 14). But this, as applied to Aśoka, had, as will be shown anon, had a deeper signification of its own.

No ruler passed as a Rājā until he went through the ceremony of coronation, anointment or consecration (abhisheka), in other words, of formal installation on the throne. To be a king a warrior had to be crowned and consecrated.[3] Aśoka was duly anointed as king, his regnal years are all stated in terms of his abhisheka.[4]

---

[1] Arthas'āstra, II. 20 :

Pañcha-saṃvatsaro yugam iti.
Evam ardha-tritīyānām abdānām adhimāsakam ।
grīshme janayataḥ pūrvaṃ pañchābdante cha pas'chimam ॥

[2] Implied in the direction :

no atikāmayisati tiṃṇi vasāni.

[3] Amarakosha, Kshatriyavarga :

mūrdhābhishikto . . . kshatriyah, Pali
muddhābhisitto Khattiyo.

[4] Cf. Hāthigumphā inscription of Khāravela :

abhisitamato cha padhame vase.

According to the tradition in the Dīpavaṃsa, as we saw, he was anointed twice, the first time as Aśoka, and subsequently as Priyadarśin, which was in accordance with the prescription in the Brāhmaṇas. As Rājā, he passed as the king of Magadha or Magadhan king, and as Priyadarśin, he was to be considered the emperor of Jambudvīpa (India).

Two lunar constellations, *viz.*, Tishya or Tishyā and Punarvasu, find repeated mention in Aśoka's inscriptions (P.E. V, S.R.E. I). The two constellations to which the Arthaśāstra (XIII. 5) attaches importance are called rāja-nakshatra (i.e., the birth-star of the king in the rōle of a conqueror, the jāta-nakshatra as it is otherwise termed (ibid, II. 36), and deśa-nakshatra (the national star, i.e., the coronation star). The scholars are divided in their opinion on the question of which is which. With Būhler Punarvasu was the birth-star of Aśoka, while with Bhandarkar it was Tishya or Tishyā. The Tishya constellation which enjoys precedence over the Punarvasu was probably the birth-star, and the latter the coronation.[1]

In connection with the Aśokan state the question may pertinently be asked—who was the legal sovereign and who the political? Under the British constitution in which the king is only a figurehead of the state and which, therefore, entertains the idea of a limited monarchy, the legal sovereign is the king-in-the-Parliament. Under the Maurya constitution as it shaped in Aśoka's hands the legal sovereign was the king and the Council of Ministers (Parisā, R.E. VI, the Mantri-parishad of the Arthaśāstra, I. 15). The two points of difference between the two constitutions are these: (1) in the former, the ministers who are appointed in name by the king, are chosen out of the people's representatives and as such, are subject ultimately to the control of the electorate, while in the latter, the ministers were all chosen and appointed by the king independently of any reference to the popular will; and (2) in the former, the initiative in all matters of national well-being and policy lies with Cabinet as the executive body of the Parliament, and the power of legislation belongs entirely to its two houses and the Crown, while in the latter, the real initiative in all matters of national well-being and policy as well as the power of enforcing the laws, even if not exactly of enacting them, rested with the king himself. Minus the elective factor, the king-in-Council might be taken to be the legal

---

[1] Barua, Inscriptions, ii, pp. 332, 373.

sovereign of the Aśokan State. The relative positions of the king and the Council of Ministers changed with times and became, for all practical purposes, reversed.[1] The general opinion is that the Aśokan constitution is neither a limited monarchy of the English type nor an undiluted despotism of the Czarist type ; it is something between the two.

R. E. VI goes to show that whenever king Aśoka gave verbal orders concerning any donation, announcement or proclamation to be made, or entrusted any urgent matters of state-business to the Mahāmātras, these were, as a matter of course, referred to the Council of Ministers which met to consider them independently of the king. It was only the reporters (Prativedakas) who were present to watch its proceedings that were to be immediately reported to the king. There is nothing to indicate that the Council's decision was binding on Aśoka. According to some versions of R. E. III, it was the duty of the Council of Ministers to instruct the Yuktas (subordinate officers in the Imperial Secretariat) in the matter of codifying the king's orders. One cannot be sure on this point inasmuch as other versions appear to have assigned this duty to the Purushas instead of to the Parishad. In Bhandarkar's opinion "the Parishad was like a modern Executive Council which was an intermediate body between the king and the Mahāmātras, and it appears that whereas, on the one hand, it saw that the written orders of the king were carried out by the different officials, it had, on the other, the power to scrutinise his oral orders before they were executed and to suggest what course of action would meet what pressing contingencies of the Mahāmātras for the information and approval of the king, who was, of course, the final arbiter."[2]

It is emphatically asserted by Mookerji that the king in India "was not the source of Law but rather its support."[3] By way of an argument in support of this, he adds, "Sacred Law, according to Manu and other legal authorities, is derived from four sources, viz., (1) the Vedas, (2) the Smṛitis, (3) the practices of the pious (śishṭāchāra), and (4) the opinions of the pious on doubtful points, while the sources of secular law were the manifold groups and communities which legislated for themselves, so that 'whatever may have been practised by the virtuous, and by such twice-born men as are devoted to the

---

1 Barua, Inscriptions, ii, p. 292 ff.

2 Asoka, p. 67.

3 Ibid, p. 47.

law, that only he shall establish as law if it be not opposed to the laws of castes, communities (jānapada), guilds and families' (Manu, viii. 41, 46)...'it is the quasi-instinctive postulates and conventions of group-life which came to be formulated as law, and not the mandate, command, or decree of a single, central authority in the state.' 'Law, under these conditions is not an artefact, but a natural growth of consensus and communal life.'[1]

Mookerji's opinion, which is admittedly based upon Manu and other post-Aśokan Smṛiti writers, cannot decide the point at issue. It is besides too categorical in its assertion to bear scrutiny. We have a more thoroughgoing discussion of the question in the informative notes appended to Professor Rangaswami Aiyangar's Dewan Bahadur K. Krishnaswami Row Lectures on Rājadharma, University of Madras. But, even Rangaswami Aiyangar, whose conclusion ultimately tallies with Mookerji's opinion, would seem to have proceeded on a doubtful interpretation of the data relied on.

In the Kauṭilya-vachana in verse (Arthaśāstra, III.), it is opined that the adjudication of cases should be guided by these four things: dharma, vyavahāra, chāritra, and rājaśāsana,[2] which find mention alike in the Law-books of Yājñavalkya and Nārada. Kauṭilya allows to each that follows to have precedence over each that precedes (paśchimaḥ pūrvabādhakaḥ) while, according to Aiyangar, Nārada, (I. 10) reverses this order in maintaining that what precedes is to be given precedence over what follows (uttaraḥ pūrvabādhakaḥ). In Aiyangar's words, with Kauṭilya "each following overrides the preceding" and with Nārada "what precedes overrides what follow."[3] Here he has sadly missed, I regret to observe, the meaning of the word uttaraḥ which is just a synonym of paśchimaḥ. So, in point of fact, Nārada simply reiterated the opinion of Kauṭilya.

Immediately after this, Professor Aiyangar argues his case in the following manner to establish that it was beyond the province of the Indian king to make a new law:

"Śukra, who is also an Arthaśāstra authority, gives the king power to declare the law, but it must be in accordance with dharma and usage. He cannot make a new law. The royal edict is merely

---

[1] Mookerji, Nationalism in Hindu Culture, p. 99.

[2] Dharmas' cha vyavahāras cha chāritraṃ rājas'āsanam |
vivādārthas' chatuspādaḥ . . . . ||

[3] Rājadharma, p. 132 ff.

declaratory, and not innovative. This is specially indicated by Kātyāyana (verse 38).

Nyāyaśāstra-avirodhena deśa-dṛishṭes tathaiva cha ।
yad dharmaṃ sthāpayet rājā nyāyyaṃ tat rājaśāsanam ॥

The edict has to conform to dharma, nyāya and deśachāra if it is to be operative. Yājñavalkya refers to the edict as 'dharma as declared by the king' (dharmo rājakṛitasya tat).[1]

Without going into the question of the relative authority of the Dharmaśāstra and the Arthaśāstra as such, I find that Aiyangar's interpretation of the four terms, dharma, vyavahāra, chāritra, and rājaśāsana, as "smriti law, secular law, custom and edicts of the king"[2] respectively is arbitrary, and he appears to have owed it to Jayaswal.[3] Kauṭilya himself defines, though enigmatically, the four things of which one stands superior to the other previously named, or the four terms employed by him in the following verse :

Atra satyasthito dharmo, vyavahāras tu sākshīshu ।
chāritraṃ samgrahe puṃśāṃ, rājñamājñā tu śāsanam ॥

"Here dharma (the fundamental principles of human action, the basic rules for the righteous and judicious discharge of man's duties in a socio-moral, politico economic and religio-cultural order) is established on truth (the order or nature of reality as revealed, ascertained and affirmed), vyavahāra (the procedure or operational feature of law) is concerned with the reliable evidence from witnesses called chāritra, (the tradition or approved usage) is to be gathered from the people concerned, (and) śāsana (the edict or the law as proclaimed or promulgated, the law in force) is in its essence the king's command (mandate or decree)".

The same is differently expressed thus :

Anuśāsaddhi dharmeṇa vyavahāreṇa saṃsthayā ।
nyāyena cha chaturthena, chaturantāṃ mahīṃ jayet ॥

"If a ruler administers justice in accordance with the general law of piety or duty, the accepted moral principles of the cultured society (in short, righteously and judiciously), in accordance with the prescribed or definite law of procedure, the approved usage of a social group or locality, and the principle of equity as the fourth, he can conquer the earth extending as far as to the four seas."

---

1 *Ibid*, p. 133.
2 *Ibid*, p. 133.
3 Manu and Yājñavalkya, p. 13 ff..

And in the very first verse, Kauṭilya says :

Chaturvarṇāśramasyāya lokasyāchārarakshaṇāt ।
naśyatāṃ sarvadharmāṇāṃ rāja dharma-pravartakaḥ ॥

"By virtue of guarding the observance of respective duties of the four castes (lit., colours, social grades), and the four stages of life, maintaining the approved manners and customs of the populace and guarding against the deterioration of all good things and noble qualities, the king passes as the founder of a socio-moral, politico-economic and religio-cultural order". The dharma-pravartakah is "the fountain of justice", according to Shama Sastri's rendering, which, to my mind, is too narrow to cover the meaning of the expression.

Even conceding to Professor Aiyangar that, so far as Brahmanism was concerned, the nature of the sacerdotal or sacred law (dharma) formed the fit subject of discussion in the Dharmaśāstra and the nature of the profane rājadharma or secular law was the fit subject of discussion in the Arthaśāstra as such, I do not see any reason for his inference from the evidence before us that the king in India was debarred from the power of legislating for the people, from being the supreme authority for making secular laws. According to modern jurists' finding, there is nothing of law as we now understand it in the Vedas or Śruti proper, and there is hardly anything of law in the older Dharmasūtras, and, for the matter of that, in the earlier Sūtra literature of the Brāhmans. And on his own showing even such later Smṛiti texts as those of Manu, Yājñavalkya, Vishṇu, and Parāśara, devote but small spaces to the enunciation of the principles of rājadharma and secular law.[1]

Neither Aśoka nor any other sane man of India claimed that he was the maker of the dharma, whether in the sense of the law of piety or duty which underlay the socio-moral, politico-economic and religio-cultural order of men, or in the metaphysical sense of dharmatā or the cosmic law, the order of reality.

The Buddha, for instance, stated his own position thus : "in so far as dharma in the sense of ancient or eternally abiding reality (paurāṇa dharmasthititā) is concerned, it is a self-regulating order of cosmic life (dharma-niyāmatā), the suchness, realness and actuality of things (tathatā, bhūtatā, satyatā) which exists by its own right, independently of all truth-finders and path-finders, which is to say, of all thinkers and teachers, divines and philosophers ; only

[1] Rājadharma, p. 70.

in so far as it signifies the pratyātma-dharmasthititā, its nature is accessible to an individual contemplative through intuition at a supreme moment of experience or realisation. As thinker and teacher, he simply declared the truth with regard to the nature of reality as intuited by him *per se*, affirmed it, and pointed out the way of reaching or apprehending it, each individually by his or her own efforts. On the basis of that intuition or enlightenment was formed the basic concept of his thought which, in the sphere of religion and ethics, was interpreted, propounded and promulgated as a moral law. The path or the road which he discovered was not claimed to be new; it was the one trodden by the Enlightened Ones of the past milleniums.[1] The *summum bonum* of human life and the ideal of human conduct and character which he set forth was shown to be in complete accord with the noble experience and life of all great contemplatives and saintly personages of the past.

Thus, like other great men of history, the Buddha said, "My work is to indicate rather than to originate." He, too, came not to destroy the Law but to fulfil it.

In reality, nevertheless, he came to set the wheel of the Law in motion, to occupy the proud position of the founder of a new kingdom of righteousness, of a great religion as we now say, inculcating, on the one hand, the fundamental principles of dharma in the sense of a psycho-ethical religion, and framing and enforcing the laws and disciplinary rules for his followers in the light of circumstances, amending, repealing or modifying them, on the other, as the circumstances changed. Thus *pari passu* developed two classes of Buddhist canonical texts, viz., the Dhamma or Sutta and the Vinaya or Āṇatti, the latter together with a system of judicial administration. The inner circle of his great disciples served the purpose of a Council of Ministers. The felt necessity for the framing of laws and rules, not to say, legislation, arose from varying circumstances. Great care was taken by the framer of the laws and rules of civic, criminal and ecclesiastical import that they were consistent with the psycho-ethical principles of Dharma and conducive to the growth of the kingdom of righteousness from within.

---

[1] Lankāvatāra Sūtra, ed. by Bunio Nanjio, pp. 143-4; D. T. Suzuki's Transl., pp. 125-6; Saṃyutta N., ii. p. 28; ii, p. 104 ff.; Kathāvatthu, vi. 1; Points of Controversy, vi. 1; Mrs. Rhys Davids, Buddhism (Home University Library), p. 33 ff.

It should also be noted that the Buddha while he spoke of and laid down the fundamentals of human conduct, put himself in the double role of a king overlord (rāja-chakravartin), which he would have assumed had he remained in the world, and of a Dharmarāja, which he had to play well as a Perfect type of Buddha.

Here the question arises—Whatever his mental attitude towards the Dharma as the eternal order of reality existing by its own right and the path which he discovered, was he not historically the founder of Buddhism and the framer of the laws and rules in the Vinaya Piṭaka ?

Aśoka's position, *mutatis mutandis*, was the same. Just as, on the one hand, the Buddha said, "Because of birth comes decay and death : whether Tathāgatas arise or not, this element stands as the establishing of things as effects"[1] and described the path which he discovered was an 'ancient path (purāṇaṃ maggaṃ) trodden by the Buddhas of the past ages', so, on the other, said Aśoka the Beloved of the gods : "Respectful attention must be paid to mother and father, likewise to seniors ; tender regard for living beings be strengthened, truth must be spoken, these very attributes of piety must be propounded : likewise the teachers must be honoured by pupils with submissiveness and it must be fittingly propounded to the teacher's relatives. This is the ancient tradition, and a thing of long standing is this, thus should it be practised" (esā porāṇā pakiti dighāvuse cha esā hevaṃ esa kaṭaviye).[2] He, too, expressly stated that all that he did or wanted to do was directed to this single end, namely, the promotion of the cause of piety (dhamma-vaḍhi) throughout the length and breadth of his empire. He, too, nowhere claimed that he was the originator of the Dhamma in the sense of the principles of piety or duty. With regard to the sufficient promotion of the cause of piety among his subjects, which was the real business of his as a ruler precisely as it was of the former kings (P. E. VII), he said that he tried to effect it by this twofold means, viz., the regulations of piety and the inculcation of the principles of piety (duvehi yeva ākālehi-dhaṃmaniyamena cha nijhatiyā cha), of which the second in his opinion was more effective than the first (lahu se dhaṃmaniyame, nijhatiyā va bhuye).[3]

---

[1] Saṃyutta., ii, p. 25 : Jātippachchayā jarāmaraṇaṃ uppādā vā tathāgatānaṃ anuppādā vā tathāgatānaṃ ṭhitā va sā dhātu.

[2] M. R. E.

[3] P. E. VII.

Now, what were the many and sundry 'regulations of piety' that had been promulgated by him (bahukāni dhaṃmaniyamāni yāni me kaṭāni, P. E. VII) and out of which just one was placed on record, namely, the game-laws embodied in P. E. V? From the general tenor of Aiyangar's argument, one may deduce that these regulations were not pieces of legislation or enactments, they having been merely declaratory of existing laws, rather customary laws, codified in the Brahmanist Law-books. The vulnerable point in his argument is that the authorities cited, such as Manu, Yājñavalkya, Vishṇu, and Medhātithi, are all post-Aśokan, the majority post-Christian in date.

With regard to the regulation of piety in P. E. V, it may be observed that, though Aśoka was a strong advocate of the principle of non-injury to life (anāraṃbho prāṇānaṃ, R. E. IV), having taken human nature as it then was, having taken into his consideration the social habits of his subjects in general, as a wise ruler he could not reasonably expect to enact any such law as meaning total prohibition for all men and for all times, if he would like it to be really operative and effective. So minimisation of the slaughter of life was the express aim of this particular regulation carrying legal force, to avoid calling it technically a piece of legislation for want of a legislature elected by the people having voting rights. There is nothing of the kind to be seen in the older Dharmasūtras, such as those of Gautama, Āpastamba, Bodhāyana and Vasishṭha. In this regulation a few species of birds, fishes and quadrupeds were declared inviolable on this twofold ground : (1) that they were neither eaten by men, nor (2) did they come into man's use.

From the first of the two grounds stated by Aśoka, it is evident that the creatures included in the list of inviolables passed as uneatables. Behind it were the authoritative views of the Buddha and the older Smṛiti writers as to what animals should be eaten as food and what animals should not be eaten. Upon the whole, Aśoka's list of inviolables may be shown to be specially in agreement with those of uneatables in the Law-books of Bodhāyana and Vasishṭha with whom the āchāra (custom) of the Midland was the standard. But the question which interested the earlier Brāhman Law-givers was of eating and not eating certain creatures as food, and in this respect their interest was the same as that of the Israel Law giver Moses.[1] The standpoint of the Mosaic law as well as the

---

[1] Barua, Inscriptions, ii, p. 360 ff. Note that the Mbh. list of uneatables (XV. 36. 21) includes kshudra-pipīlikāḥ corresponding to As'oka's aṃbā-kapilikā and obviously meaning "small ants".

socio-demestic law of the earlier Smṛiti writers was hygienic and aesthetic, while that of Aśoka's regulation was humanitarian. The remark which applies to Moses and earlier Smṛiti writers, applies equally to the Buddha's prohibitive injunction. Further, Moses meant his domestic rules of eating for the Israels, the Buddha for his followers, and the Smṛiti writers for those of the twice-born classes, while Aśoka's regulation was meant for all his subjects as it should be in order to pass as a law of the land. Equity, custom, progressive moral idea of the society and expediency guide modern legislation as they must have guided Aśoka's regulations, and, for the matter of that, all rājaśāsanas. If the later Smṛiti writers insisted on this point, as I find they did, they were very sensible and prudent. But that was not to say that Aśoka or any Indian king of the past was debarred from the right to legislate for the people, specially that Aśoka's regulations were not pieces of legislation.

The question of political sovereignty is not so easy to answer as that of legal in the case of the Aśokan State. In a constitution such as the British, political sovereignty may be said to belong to the electorate in the sense that 'the legal sovereign is bound in the end to carry out its wishes'. It must have been in view of the absence of any elective system in the Maurya State that Professor Mookerji characterised it as an absolute monarchy in the legal as well as political sense of the term. The upshot of his remark is that under the Maurya constitution the king was responsible to none but himself, his God or conscience. But to understand and appreciate the real situation we need not attach undue importance to the elective system which exists in the limited monarchy of England or the modern democracy of any other country of Europe or America. To speak of the British constitution in particular, it cannot be said that its political sovereignty belongs to the British people as a whole for the obvious reason that it has not extended the franchise to all as, for instance, was done by the Greek City States. Instead of looking at the narrow technical aspect of the matter, let us better look to the essential point in the definition of political sovereignty. The political sovereign, according to its accepted definition, is 'that power in the State whose will prevails.' As distinguished from the legal sovereign, the political sovereign is unable to enact and enforce the laws directly.

In all the monarchical States of Ancient India but those in which the reigning monarch happened to be a reckless, ruthless and incorrigible tyrant, political sovereignty theoretically inhered in the impersonal authority of Dharma and actually belonged to the ruled, the subjects, or the people at large, who were the real beneficiaries of the State.

When only the Police type of State prevailed in India, occupied with the business of maintaining law and order within the territory, the Upanishad teacher proclaimed : "Dharma is the king of kings (kshatrasya kshatraḥ), there being nothing mightier than it. It is by (the power of) Dharma that the weaker person controls the stronger as it were by (the might of) a ruler. Dharma is satya, therefore, when one affirms the satya, he affirms the dharma, or when one affirms the dharma, he affirms the satya. Thus verily it becomes an affirmation of both."[1]

The Buddha expanded this Upanishad idea of Dharma when he, too, came to declare : "Dharma is the king of king overlords (dhammo rañño chakkavattissa rājā). Here a king overlord who is virtuous and a righteous monarch, depending on the dharma, honouring the dharma, respecting it, submitting thereto, acting as the standard-bearer of the dharma, having the dharma for the banner of his imperium, and acknowledging the sovereignty of the dharma, provides the lawful protection and safeguard among his own people, and alike among the subordinate rulers, the army, the Brāhmans and rich householders, the townfolks and country people, the Śramaṇas and Brāhmaṇas as religious teachers, (nay, even) among the beasts and birds. Thus verily by dharma he sets the wheel in motion (i.e. founds paramount sovereignty) of which the course cannot be resisted by any inimical human being whosoever."[2]

Aśoka himself, who sought to fulfil the chakravartī or imperial

---

[1] Bṛihad Āraṇyaka Up., I. 4. 14 : Tad etat kshatrasya kshatram yad dharmas tasmād dharmāt paraṃ nāsty-ato abalīyān balīyaṃ samās'aṃsate dharmeṇa yathā rājñaivaṃ. Yo vai sa dharmaḥ satyaṃ vai tat, tasmāt satyam vadantaṃ āhur dharmaṃ vadatīti, dharmaṃ va vadantaṃ satyaṃ vadatītyetahyevaitad ubhayaṃ bhavati.

[2] Anguttara iii, p. 147 f. : Idha rājā chakkavattī dhammiko dhammarājā dhammaññeva nissāya dhammaṃ sakkaronto dhammaṃ garukaronto dhammaṃ apachāyamāno dhammaddhajo dhammaketu dhammādhipateyyo dhammikaṃ rakkhāvaraṇaguttim saṃvidahati antojanasmim···khattiyesu anuyantesu balakāyasmim brāhmaṇagahapatikesu negama-jānapadesu samaṇa-brāhmaṇesu migapakkhīsu...saṃvidahitvā ...dhammeneva chakkaṃ pavatteti, taṃ hoti chakkaṃ appativattiyaṃ kenachi manussabhūtena pachchatthikena pāṇinā.

ideal of the Buddha, insisted on rearing up by the dharma, providing by the dharma, pleasing by the dharma, and guarding by the dharma (dhaṃmena pālanā, dhaṃmena vidhāne, dhaṃmena sukhiyanā, dhaṃmena goti, P. E. I). He, too, desired that the rulers should administer the dharma, standing firm in dharma and virtue (dhaṃmamhi sīlamhi tisṭaṃto dhaṃmaṃ anusāsisaṃti, R. E. IV).

In the early Upanishad phraseology, dharma was just another word for ṛita[1]. Dharma in the sense of Law was but the regulative principle of human conduct and compelling instrument in a socio-moral order, which was an actuality or truly existent fact (satya) and in consonance with the order of reality considered in its five contexts (pañchasu adhikaraṇeshu), viz., the physical order (adhilokam), the astronomical order (adhijyautisham), the procreational or biological order (adhiprajam), the cultural order (adhividyam), and the individuality of persons (adhyātmam)[2]. The dharma to be practised is the law of piety or duty in accordance with the past tradition or established usage[3].

As explained by Buddhaghosa, the dharma to be respected by a king overlord who was virtuous and a righteous monarch stood for the ten psycho-ethical principles of human conduct and character (dusa-kusala-dhammā) as also for the traditional path of virtue, the precedent (paveṇidhammaṃ).[4]

The dhamma spoken of by Aśoka was essentially the law of piety or duty. With him the tradition was the tradition of piety (dhaṃmānupaṭipati, P. E. VII) established by the former kings of India.

The Buddha, to be true to the ideal he had set forth, left behind him a constitution for the Brotherhood founded by him, which was to be worked out and maintained by the impersonal authority of the Dhamma in the sense of the collective body of the Doctrine and the Discipline promulgated by him. He declined to nominate his successor on the ground that he never thought that he was the leader of the Sangha or that the Fraternity waited for his lead[5]. The Doctrine embodying the principles and rules of conduct and character was to take his place in his absence.[6]

---

1 Taittirīya Up., I. 1. 1. ritaṃ vadishyāmi satyaṃ vadishyāmi.

2 Ibid, I. 3. 1.

3 Ibid, I. 11. 2.

4 Manoratha-pūraṇī to Rājavagga in Anguttara, iii, p. 147 ff.

5 Dīgha, ii, p.

6 Ibid, ii, p. : Yo vo mayā Dhammo cha Vinayo cha desito paññatto so vo mama achchayena satthā.

As for the power of the collective body of subjects or citizens of the Aśokan State, and, for the matter of that, of other monarchical states of Ancient India, it is not enough to say with the writer in the Cambridge History of India that the Indian king was no Sultan with the sole obligation of satisfying his personal caprice,[1] or with Mookerji that even apart from the living sense of his moral responsibility to his people, there was an important limitation upon his autocracy from the fact that he was not the source of Law.[2]

The agreed opinion in the matter is that there was no unchecked monarchical despotism in India. Raychaudhuri has convincingly sought to show that the power of the monarch was checked, in the first place, by the Brāhmans, or, as we might also say, the Brāhmaṇas and Śramaṇas who were the repositories, interpreters and disseminators of national culture. The second check came from the ministers and village headmen who aided in the consecration of the king and whom the king consulted regularly on important occasions. The third check (and we may say, the main check) was exercised by the general body of the people 'who were distinct from the ministers and Grāmaṇis, or Grāmikas, and who used to meet in an assembly styled Samiti or Parishad[3] in the Upanishads'.[4]

The late lamented Dr. Jayaswal was at pains to show that the Council of Ministers as a body politic evolved out of the Vedic popular assembly called Samiti or Parishad (Pali Parisā), and that as such, it retained its representative character. The Purohita (Royal Chaplain) who administered the oath to the monarch at the time of his installation and the Ministers or Councillors with whose consent and whole-hearted support he was to be installed on the throne were generally viewed as the trustees of popular interests. The presence and assent of the army, the important officers, the leading people of the community, and the collective body of the town and countryfolks was indispensable.

The Pali Mahāgovinda Suttanta, while narrating a story of the past stage of Indian monarchy, describes the Purohitas as 'king-makers' (rājakattāro, Sk. rajakṛits or rajakartris). The Śatapatha Brāhmaṇa, too, speaks of an earlier state of things when it represents the Sūta (Charioteer) and Grāmaṇi (Leader of the Host) as king-

[1] Vol. i, p. 491.

[2] Asoka, p. 47.

[3] Barua, Inscriptions, ii, p. 292 ff.

[4] Raychaudhuri, op. cit., p. 145 ff.

makers,[1] and makes them as well as other Ratnins (the chief members of the royal household and of the civil and military staffs) as recipients of the sacrificial honours at the time of the king's coronation[2]. Other Ratnins comprised the Chief Queen (Mahishī), the Royal Chaplain (Purohita), the Chamberlain (Kshattri), the Treasurer (Samgrāhitṛi), the Tax-Collector (Bhāgadugha), the Keeper of the Dice (Akshavāpa), the Companion in the Chase (Govikartana), the Courier (Palāgala), and, above all, the Commander-in-Chief (Senānī)[3].

The Pali Nikāyas including the Jātakas in verse amply testify to the importance of the Councillors and Officers (Amachchas, Pārisajjas) and Village Headmen (Gāmikas) in the body politic of a royal state. But the power behind them all was the will of the collective body of the people, the town and the country-folks (pora-jānapadā, raṭṭhika-negamā). When this went against the king, he had to go. When it went against the king and his Purohita and Ministers, they all had to go. The whole position may be realised from the following conversation between the king of Sivi and the people of Sivi in the Pali Vessantara Jātaka :

"The king was told :

The bidding of the Sivi folk if you refuse to do
The people then will act, methinks, against
your son and you.

The king replied :

Behold the people's will, and I that will do
not gainsay."[5]

The career of the king and his ministers was not interfered with so long as they were not found guilty of misrule and their conduct not reprehensible. When the citizens of Magadha became sick of the unworthy conduct of the successors of king Bimbisāra, all of whom happened, according to the Pali Chronicles, to be parricides, they rose up together against the last monarch of the line and replaced him by his minister. According to the Padakusala-mānavaka Jātaka, when a king and his Purohita were found guilty of theft,

---

[1], [2] S'atapatha Br , iii. 4. 1. 7, xiii. 2. 2. 18. In this connection Mookerji (Fundamental Unity of India, p. 88) observes that 'both official aud non-official or popular elements were represented in the function'.

[3] Aitareya Br., viii. 17.

[4] Cf. also Jaiminīya Up. Br., iii. 7. 6., Raychaudhuri, op. cit., p. 147.

[5] Raychaudhuri, op. cit., p. 146 ff.

the investigating officer brought the matter to the notice of the councillors and the citizens, and the latter got rid of both and elected a good man as king. In the case of Vessantara, the people of Sivi were enraged when the prince gave away the state-elephant whose presence in the kingdom was necessary for guarding against drought and food scarcity.

Thus it may be shown that the popular will ultimately prevailed in Ancient India and that it was expressed in extraordinary circumstances, no matter how. Rebellion or resort to physical force is everywhere the last weapon at the hands of the populace of a country. But we shall be far from the truth to think that in India of the Maurya age the people had not various civic institutions of their own,—societies, corporations, and trade-guilds and their respective leaders, to express their will in a constitutional or semi-constitutional form. The idea of natural leadership was generally prevalent. From the various 'set forms of speech' (kammavāchas) met with in the Gṛihya Sūtras, the Vinaya Texts and the Arthaśāstra, it is easy to infer that the parliamentary proceedings were not unknown.

4. **Government** : The government of a territory is, according to modern definition, the machinery through which the will of the State is expressed. It involves the consideration of two things, *viz.*, the constitution and its actual working, both of which are cemprehended by the system of administration.

The familiar Indian word for administration is râjya-śâsana or râjadaṇḍa-parichâlana. In the Buddha's phraseology, administration means āṇāchakka-pavattana, *i.e.*, setting the wheel of the sovereign command in motion. The same is implied in Khâravela's inscription by the expression, supavata-vijayachaka (supravartta-vijaya-chakra). The poetic imagery behind it goes to compare the running of a government to the driving of a royal chariot (râja-ratha). The Indian conception of government centred indeed round the imagery of a chariot, just as the modern conception does round that of a machinery. The Indian is distinctively an organic conception, the chariot being an organic combination of parts, brought into a working order :

Yathâ hi angasambhârâ hoti saddo ratho iti[1].

In the Upanishad poetry, the chariot stands for the living body or organism, soul for the lord of the chariot, intelligence for the chario-

[1] Saṃyutta., i, p. 134 f., Milindapañha, p. 28.

teer, mind for the rein-holder, the organs of sense and action for the horses yoked to the chariot, and the objects of sense and action for the field to be traversed by them :

> Ātmânaṃ rathīnaṃ viddhi, śarīraṃ ratham eva tu ।
> buddhi tu sārathiṃ viddhi, manaḥ pragraham eva cha ॥
> Indriyâṇi hayân āhur vishayâṃs teshu gocharân[1] ।

In the case of a government, the king (râjâ) is the lord of the chariot, the chief minister (amachcha) is the charioteer (sârathi, suta), the commissioner (rajjuka) is the rein-holder, the officers (yuktas) are the horses yoked to the chariot, the commander-in-chief (senâpati mahâmatta) is the door-keeper or guard.

In connection with the chariot procession came in the king's mother, chief queen, the crown prince, the chaplain, the banker, the master archer (or measurer of capacity), and the courtezan.

> Rājā mātā mahesī cha uparājā purohito ।
> rajjuko sārathi seṭṭhi doṇo dovāriko tathā ॥
> gaṇikā ekādasā janā Kurudhamme patiṭṭhitā[2] ।

From these, it may be realised that at the back of Aśoka's Rajjukas and Yuktas, maybe also behind his Prādeśikas, lingered the old poetic imagery of the royal state as a moving chariot.

5. **Constitution :** Aśoka's was a unitary form of government, inasmuch as all the powers of the State were centralised in the King and the Council of Ministers, and all the state-policy emanated from the capital, *i.e.*, from Pāṭaliputra (R. E. V.).

In the earlier part of Aśoka's reign, precisely as in that of the reign of his father, the central government was responsible for the administration of the empire, especially that of his domain proper. With the appointment of his Viceroys in the four of the outlying provinces, there took place the delegation of certain powers to them, although the policy, official directions and changes in the method of administration continued to be dictated from the centre (S. R. E. I, S. R. E. II). The four outlying provinces were the North-Western (Uttarāpatha), the Western (Avantī), the Eastern (Kalinga), and the Southern (Mahishamaṇḍala). Clearly in the case of the Eastern Province, we find that it had two administrative divisions, the major and the minor, each with its official headquarters, namely, Tosali and Samāpā (S.R.E. I, S.R.E. II). The Southern Province is also shown to have comprised two such administrative divisions, the major with

---

1 Kaṭha Up., i. 3. 3-4.

2 Jātaka, II, p. 367.

Suvarṇagiri and the minor with Ṛishila as their respective head-quarters (M.R.E., Bra.). Though such a clear case cannot be made out for the other two provinces, from the setting of the edicts, it may not be difficult to guess that the North-Western Province, too, consisted of two such divisions, the major with Takshaśilā and the minor most probably with Pushkarāvatī as their respective head-quarters, and that the Western Province was constituted of two divisions, the major with Ujjayinī and the minor probably with Vidiśā as their respective headquarters. The Mahāmātras placed in charge of the minor division of the province of Kalinga are represented as Imperial Commissioners (Lājavachanikā, S. R. E. I, S. R. E. II, J). It may be inferred from this, that prior to the appointment of the Kumāra Viceroys, the Mahāmātras in charge of the administration of the major division of the province also passed as Rājavachanikas. The same remark applies to the Mahāmātras entrusted with the administration of different divisions in other outlying provinces as well. As distinguished from the Mahāmātras in charge of the divisions in Home provinces, those placed in frontier provinces appear to have been designated Anta-Mahāmātras (Aṃta Mahamatā, P.E I), competent to deal with matters relating to frontiers (pachaṃtā) and frontagers (Aṃtā, Sāmaṃtā), in accordance, of course, with instructions from the capital (S.R.E. II).

Precisely how many were the Home provinces we cannot say. The inscriptions of Aśoka, hitherto known, enable us to state that Benares, Kauśāmbī, Virāṭanagara and S'rughna were official head-quarters of four divisions. One may include in the list of divisional headquarters such towns as Mathurā, Gayā, Sahasrām, and the town adjoining the rock at Rupnāth. The Mahāmātras of these divisions might also be regarded as Rājavachanikas, inasmuch as they were all entitled to receive directions from the capital and imperial agents in the provinces to carry out the imperial wishes (Schism Pillar Edict, Kauśāmbī and Sārnāth).

The occurrence of three versions of Aśoka's Rock Edicts at Girnār, which was the ancient capital of Surāshṭra, at Sopārā (Pali Suppāraka), which was the capital and main port of Sūnāparānta or Kukkurāparānta, and at Yerraguḍi in the modern district of Kārnul gives rise to an administrative problem which is not easy to solve.

As regards Surāshṭra, we learn from the Junāgarh Rock inscriptions of Rudradāman I that near Girinagara (Girnār) was excavated the Sudarśana Tank by Chandragupta Maurya's Vaiśya Rāshṭriya named Pushyagupta. Subsequently, after the reign of Aśoka

(Aśokasya Mauryasyaṃte[1]), the Yavanarājā Tushāspha built embankments and fitted the same with aqueducts (adhishṭhāya praṇālibhir alaṅkṛitaṃ). From the new reading aṃte in lieu of kṛite[2], it is evident that Tushāspha, probably a Perso-Greek from the North-Western region of India,[3] was a post-Aśokan chieftain or independent ruler of Surāshṭra as well as that the credit for the embankment of the tank and its aqueducts was due not to Aśoka but to Tushāspha.

If it be true, as supposed, that Rudradāman had a previous record to guide him regarding the origin of the tank and its embankment, etc., there is no escape from the conclusion that the Vaiśya Pushyagupta, the excavator of the tank, was a Rāshṭriya of Chandragupta Maurya. Here the whole political and administrative mystery lies in the word Rāshṭriya which, according to the Amarakosha, signifies the brother-in-law (wife's brother) of a king (rājaśyālas tu rāshṭriyaḥ).[4] Amarasiṃha is here guided by the sense in which the word was employed in the Sanskrit dramas. So the commentator Kshīrasvāmī is justified in pointing out that 'except in a play a Rāshṭriya is a Rāshṭrādhikṛitra, *i.e.*, an officer appointed to look after or supervise the affairs of a rāshṭra, state or province.'

With Kielhorn Pushyagupta, the Vaiśya Rāshṭriya of Chandragupta Maurya, was the provincial governor of Surāshṭra,[6] while with Raychaudhuri he was probably 'a sort of Imperial High Commissioner whose position was comparable to that of Lord Cromer in Egypt.' Raychaudhuri inclines to identify the Rāshṭriya with the Rāshṭrapāla[7] whose salary was, according to the Arthaśāstra, 'equal to that of a Kumāra or Prince.'[8]

Raychaudhuri's suggestion is evidently based upon the assumption

---

[1] Read Mauryasyāṃte, cf. kulasyānte, Andhraṇānte in Pargiter's Purāṇa Text, pp. 49, 59.

[2] Kielhorn is responsible for the completion of *te* after Mauryasya as kṛite. Bhau Daji was in favour of completing *te* as *tena*. But the anasvāra stroke over *sya* being certain, one must connect *te* with Mauryasyaṃ without unnecessarily presuming the omission by the scribe of *kri* before or of *na* after *te*.

[3] Tushāspha being a personal name, Vincent Smith was led to think that the Yavana-rājā bearing this name was a Persian, while the epithet Yavana-rājā indicates that he was a Greek.

[4] Amarakosha, V. 14. It is not altogether impossible that Pushyagupta was a s'yālaka of Chandragupta.

[5] Raychaudhuri, op. cit., p. 237.

[6] E. I., Vol. VIII, p. 46.

[7] Arthas'āstra, V. 3.

[8] Raychaudhuri, op. cit., p. 237.

'that Surāshṭra was probably an autonomous vassal state, or a confederation of vassal states, and not an imperial province.' The argument which leads him to this conclusion is worth quoting.

"The Kauṭilya Arthaśāstra refers to a number of Sanghas, *e.g.*, Kāmboja, Surāshṭra, etc. The Kāmbojas find prominent mention as a separate unit even in the Thirteenth Rock Edict of Aśoka. That Surāshṭra (Kāṭhiāwār) was antonomous in the time of Aśoka seems probable from the reference, in R.E.V, to various nations in the western border (aparātā) in addition to those named specifically, and from Rudradāman's inscription at Junāgaḍh which refers to the Rājā, the Yavana Tushāspha, the contemporary and vassal of Aśoka. The Yavanarājā was probably a Greek chief of the North-West who was appointed one of the Mukhyas or chiefs of the Surāshṭra Saṃgha by Aśoka, just as Rājā Man Singh of Ambar was appointed Subadar of Bengal by Akbar. His title of Rājā probably indicates that he enjoyed a certain amount of antonomy."

This observation, which is otherwise very weighty, is shaky for these two reasons[1] :

(i) That the verse in the Arthaśāstra (xi. 1) speaking of the Kāmbhojas, the Surāshṭras, and the like as the guilds (corporations) of warriors who lived by agriculture, trade and wielding weapons, as distinguished from others who bore the title of Rājā, may be taken to have referred to an earlier state of things, and

(ii) That the new reading Aśokasya Mauryasyaṃte renders the contemporaneity of Aśoka and Tushāspha highly problematical.

As for the official designation of Rāshṭriya, Buddhaghosa tells us in one context, that during a processional state-drive of king Ajātaśatru of Magadha the place assigned to the Rāshṭriyas (Raṭṭhiyaputta) among his retinue 'was just between the Mahāmatras who were nicely dressed and the fittingly dressed Brāhmans shouting the joy of victory. The Rāshṭriyas themselves 'are said to have been gorgeously dressed holding swords and the like in their hands (vividhālankāra-maṇḍitā nānāppakāra-āvudhahatthā).' In another context, he tells us that the king of the Kuru country came to see the Thera Raṭṭhapāla

[1] The Petavatthu, iv. 3, represents Pingala, king of Surāshṭra, as contemporary and adviser of a Maurya ruler of Pāṭaliputra. The commentary freely identifies this Maurya ruler with As'oka. C. D. Chatterjee has fully discussed the historical bearing of this in the Achārya Puṣpāñjali.

(Rāshṭrapāla) with a retinue consisting of the Mahāmātras, the Mahārāshṭrikas, and such like persons of higher and higher ranks[1] (Mahāmatta-Mahāraṭṭhikādīnaṃ vasena uggatuggatam eva parisaṃ gahetvā upasankami).[2]

Squaring up the two, we may understand that Rāshṭriya and Rashṭrika are one and the same designation. As for the connection of the Rāshṭriya or Rāshṭrika with Rāshṭrapāla, some light may be thrown from the Pali Raṭṭhapāla Sutta (Majjhima, iii) and Buddhaghosa's comment thereon. From the Sutta itself, it is clear that Rāshṭrapāla was the only son of a S'reshṭhī of Sthūlakoshṭhita, a fertile and prosperous place in the Kuru country of the Buddha's time. The S'reshṭhī who was a Vaiśya by caste lived in a right royal style. According to Buḍdhaghosa, the S'reshṭhin's was a Rāshṭrapāla family (Raṭṭhapāla-kula). By definition, a Rāshṭrapāla family was that of which the head was capable of maintaining and restoring the peace and order in a territory or any portion thereof in the event of party factions, capable of coping with or quelling any popular commotion or disturbance :

> Sarājikaṃ chatuvaṇṇaṃ posetuṃ yaṃ pahossati ।
> raṭṭhapālakulaṃ nāma ... ... ॥

In the prose portion of the Chulla Sutasoma Jātaka, the Commander-in-Chief (Senāpati) is placed at the head of the Amātyas (Councillors and Officers), the Chaplain (Purohita) at the head of the Brāhmans and the Rāshṭrika (Raṭṭhika) is placed foremost among the Naigamas (Negamā, i.e., the bankers, business magnates and rich landowners who functioned at the same time as Mayors, Sheriffs and Justices of the Peace).[3]

If such were the office and worldly position of a Rāshṭriya or Rāshṭrika, there is no wonder that Pushyagupta, a Rāshṭriya under Chandragupta Maurya, should be described as a Vaiśya in Rudradāman's inscription. But the question still is—Was he appointed by Chandragupta to function as the Governor or Imperial High Commissioner of Surāshṭra ?

From Rudradāman's inscription, it is evident, no doubt, that the Yavana-rājā Tushāspha became an independent chieftain or ruler of

---

[1] This shows that the Rāshṭrikas were higher in official as well as social status than the Mahāmātras.

[2] Barua, Inscriptions, ii., p. 264.

[3] Jātaka, V. p. 178 : Senāpati-pamukhāni asīti-amachcha-sahassāni Purohita-pamukhāni saṭṭhi-brāhmaṇa-sahassāni Raṭṭhika-negamādayo bahū pakkosāpetvā.

Surāshṭra, may be of Surāshṭra-Ānarta, i.e., the whole of Kāṭhiāwār, sometime after Aśoka. The ancient name of Junāgaṛh itself indicates that the city with the hill-fort was built by a Yavana ruler. Rudradāman himself appointed a Pahlava (Parthian or Persian), named Suviśāla, son of Kulaipa, as Amātya (Governor) for the whole of Surāshṭra and Ānarta. Can we say that this was in keeping with the Maurya tradition, particularly Aśokan ?

The Yerraguḍi copy of M.R.E. goes to show that the Imperial Agent or Commissioner at the place was a Rajjuka to whom the message to be proclaimed was despatched from the capital with the direction that he should, in his turn, commend it to the people (jānapadaṃ) as well as the Ṛāshṭrikas (Rāṭhikāni cha). If any inference is to be drawn from this, it is that in the janapada under this particular Rajjuka were the Rāshṭrikas besides the general populace.[1] Whether there were any Mahāmātras attached to this Rajjuka or not, this inscription has nothing to say. If the Rajjuka as Regent or Chief Commissioner virtually took the place of the Kumāras in the Home provinces, he, too, must have a body of Mahāmātras to assist him in deliberation as well as administration. That which was at the Yerraguḍi area was *ex hypothesi* in Surāshṭra (Girnār), Sūnāparānta (Sopārā), Mahārāshṭra (Kopbal), and Mūshaka (Maski).

Broadly speaking, as Regent or Chief Commissioner for a particular janapada (large administrative area, a Home province or Division), the Rajjuka was responsible to the king as the supreme administrative head of a particular imperial territory. He was to carry on the administration of the janapada placed in his charge with the aid of the Mahamatras and the Rāshṭrikas. He was the official medium through which the king's orders, directions and instructions were to be communicated to the Mahāmātras entrusted with the administration of towns or districts within his jurisdiction. The Purushas or Personal Secretaries of the king were the official agents to intimate to the Rājjukas the king's wishes, instructions and policy shaping the method of administration to be faithfully followed by them in order to please the king, to work to his satisfaction (P.E. IV).

---

[1] Cf. Vessantara Jātaka.
Samāgatā jānapahā negamā cha samāgatā.
Dīgha, iii, p. 61 : negama-jānapadā.

From this line of argument, it may be concluded that in the four outlying provinces the Rajjuka or his provincial substitute, namely, the Prādesika (R.E. III),[1] was replaced later by a Kumāra.

The janapada under a Rajjuka was divided into a certain number of āhāras (smaller administrative areas, say, districts defining the jurisdiction of different classes of Mahāmātras), with the koṭa-vishayas (fort-areas or fortified districts) here and there (Schism Pillar Edict, Sārnāth).

The capital of Aśoka was the seat of the Imperial Government. Here was his permanent residence, and within the palace area were located the Council Hall and the Secretariat. The subordinate officers in the Imperial Secretariat were known as Yuktas (R. E. III), and they were to work under instructions from the Purushas rather than from the Parishad or Council of Ministers which was a deliberative and advisory rather than an executive body. As clearly stated in P. E. IV, the Purushas or Personal Secretaries were intimately acquainted with the king's wishes (pulisāni me chhaṃdaṃnāni, P. E. IV).

The Purushas, as appears from R. E. VI, were probably also the Dāpakas and S'rāvāpakas to whom the king issued his oral orders concerning something to be communicated or publicly announced. They were the personal agents of the king to instruct the subordinate officers in the Imperial Secretariat as to how to codify the orders properly and effectively (hetuto cha vyaṃjanato cha, R.E. III). The Yuktas in this Secretariat must have been attached also to the various departments of the Mahāmātras, better Mantri Mahāmātras (Pali Mantino Mahāmattā), the Mantrins of the Arthaśāstra (I. 15), to whom the king entrusted all urgent matters (mahāmātresu achāyike āropitaṃ bhavati, R.E. VI). It was the main duty of the Mantri Mahāmātras as adepts in the science and art of royal polity to advise the ruler in all important and urgent matters and to take necessary diplomatic or administrative steps to save the state in times of emergency.[2]

The law-making organ of the Aśokan State was, as I sought to show, composed of the King and the Council of Ministers, the initiative and the right of final approval lying with the former. The enactments went by the name of Regulations carrying legal force.

---

1 See next Chapter for the official position of the Prādes'ikas.

2 Saṃyutta, i, p. 102: Santi.........imasmiṃ rājakule mantino mahāmattā ye pahonti āgate mantehi bhedayituṃ.

The king of India was the highest judiciary of a monarchical state. He represented the final court of appeal. P.E. IV goes to show that in the latter part of his reign, Aśoka delegated his own judicial authority to the Rajjukas and to corresponding state officials as regards provincial governments. In cities like Tosali and Samāpā, the administration, judicial or otherwise, was entrusted, as will be shown further on, to a body of City-judiciaries (Nagala-viyohālakā, Nagalakā, S.R.E. I) corresponding, more or less, with the Paura-vyavahārika or Nāgaraka of the Arthaśāstra (I. 12, III. 36, V. 3).

The supreme head of the Executive organ, too, was the king. All the orders, verbal or written, directions, instructions and policy shaping the method of administration and supervision, as well as the mode of carrying out the king's wishes emanated from the king and passed through the Council of Ministers before they took their final shape. These orders, directions, etc. were codified in the Secretariat by the Yuktas under instructions from the Purushas or the Parishad and officially despatched for execution to the Rajjukas, and in the case of the outlying provinces, to the Kumāra Viceroys since their appointment. who in their turn communicated them to the divisional or district heads. All despatches from the major division to a minor one in a province had to be sent on the joint authority of the Kumāra Viceroy and the Mahāmātras attached to him and with proper official courtesy observed.[1] The same courtesy was equally observed even when the king himself addressed anything to a religious fraternity like the Buddhist Sangha (Bhābru). It may be shown that this was in accordance with the convention established long before.[2] It may further be shown that the forms and style of Aśoka's inscriptions conformed to the prevalent rules that became systematised later in the prose treatise of the Arthaśāstra (II. 10). As for the promulgation of an ordinance or the proclamation of an imperial message, certain written copies were supplied from the capital to select centres from which other copies were to be made, circulated and suitably placed as far as went the jurisdiction of the officers concerned. These were to be also permanently incised on rocks and pillars (Schism Pillar Edict, Sārnāth, M.R.E., Rupnāth, Sahasrām). In communicating with the people of wild tracts (aṭaviyo), the officers commissioned

---

[1] M. R. E., Bra : Suvaṃṇagirite ayaputasa māhāmātānaṃ cha vachanena Isilasi māhāmātā arogiyaṃ eataviyā hevaṃ cha vataviyā. Cf. Nāsik Cave inscription of Gautamīputra Sātakarṇi : amacho samako aroga vatava.

[2] Barua, Inscriptions. ii,

to do the work were to verbally inform them (R.E. XIII). The communication with the Āntas or Sāmantas was maintained through the Dūtas (Envoys or Emissaries, R.E. XIII, S.RE. II).

The maintenance of law and order which is one of the essential duties of every state of stable character did not suffer in the least under the Aśokan regime. That the criminal laws were most rigorous in the country is reflected by Aśoka's inscriptions (R. E. V) as well as borne out by the collective literary evidence. The prisons (bandhana, R.E. V, P.E IV, S.R.E. I) existed, sudden arrest (akasmā bandhana) and coercion (parikilesa) ending in imprisonment (bandhanaṃtika) was not altogether out of the mischief of the law (S.R.E. I). The life behind the prison bars was a state of woe and it needed safeguards and humane consideration (R.E.V). The wild tribes and gangs of thieves (aṭaviyo) were a source of trouble to the State. But whenever they caused or tried to cause mischiefs within the territory, the miscreants were severely dealt with and warned (R E. XIII). Frontiers were zealously guarded and drastic measures, if necessary, were taken, to prevent the frontagers from planning encroachments on the home territory or creating any disturbance from outside (S.R.E. II). It was considered a bounden duty of the State to see that the people were not harassed or oppressed by any officer and were not driven into a state of rebellion by highhandedness on the part of government servants (S.R.E. I).

The Aśokan was not, however, a police type of government. It represented, on the other hand, a far advanced culturetype performing all the ministrant functions, e g., keeping itself fully informed of the actual condition of the people, whether it is prosperity and happiness or the opposite, identifying itself by an enlightened sympathy with them (P.E. IV), taking care of the poor, the needy, the aged, the children, the oppressed, the virtuous, and the persons engaged in disseminating culture, ensuring the reasonable and human treatment of slaves and servants (R.E. III, R.E. IV, R.E. V. etc.), promoting the cause of piety (dhamma-vaḍhi), doing works of public utility and humanitarian kind (R.E. II, Queen's Edict, P.E.V, P.E. VII), and, above all, educating the subjects to an excellence of moral and national character (R.E. III, R.E. IV, P.E. VII).

6. **Method and Policy :** Every State like that of Aśoka, which has a great mission set before it, has to ensure its own safety, increase its efficiency, and prove its effectiveness, and for that, the definition of its methods, principles and policy is a *desideratum*. This indeed

constituted the main task of Daṇḍanīti or the Science of Government which is presupposed by Aśoka's inscriptions (S. R. E. I : nīti). Aśoka himself as an enlightened ruler and political thinker has clearly defined them.

As for the theoretical purpose of the science, as well as those of other normative sciences of practical application to life, such as ethics, economics and medical science, it was set out, notably in the Buddha's thought-scheme, under four aspects, the first two of which may be characterised as negative and the second two as positive : to guard against the rise of the evil which has not arisen, to stop the evil which has not arisen, to pave the way for the rise of the good which has not arisen, and to increase the good which has arisen.[1] The same as to waste and income in the science of wealth, and disease and health in the science of medicine. The Arthaśāstra (I·4) while speaking of the purpose of the science of polity, expresses it thus : It is to be used as means to the attainment of that which has not been attained, the fostering of that which has been attained, the promotion of that which has been fostered, and the proper application of that which has been promoted.[2] The very same line of thinking is traceable in the words of Aśoka, e.g., when he said that the aim of all his efforts through government was not only that all the people were free from the innate proneness to sin (sakale apaparisrave asa, R. E. X), but also that they grew sufficiently with the growth in piety (anulupāyā dhammavaḍhiyā, vaḍheya, P. E. VII), or when he gave out that he had not only promoted the cause of piety (vaḍhitā, R. E. IV, P. E. VII) but would see that it went on being promoted immensely (vipulaṃ vaḍhisiti, M. R. E.).

The agreed opinion of the earlier teachers of polity was in favour of the strictest, severest or relentless method of administration (tīkshṇadaṇḍa). A ruler desirous of the progress of the world should always hold the sceptre raised (nityam udyatadaṇḍas syāt),[3] there being no better instrument than the sceptre to maintain peace and order. The diametrically opposite method was one of laxity

---

[1] anuppannānaṃ akusalānaṃ pāpakānaṃ dhammānaṃ anuppādāya,
uppannānaṃ akusalānaṃ dhammānaṃ pahānāya,
anuppannānaṃ kusalānaṃ pāpakānam dhammānaṃ uppādāya,
uppannānaṃ kusalānam dhammānaṃ bhiyyobhāvāya.

[2] alabdha-lābhārtha, labdha-parirakshaṇī,
rakshita-vivardhanī, vṛiddhasya tīrtheshu pratipādanī cha.

[3] This is also the method recommended in the Mahābhārata and Manu's Code.

and leniency (mṛidudaṇḍa), which was advocated by none of the teachers but was followed in practice by the sluggish or morally coward among the rulers themselves. According to Kauṭilya, both are wrong methods to follow, since the first makes the ruler repulsive to the people and the second contemptible. The wiser method consists in awarding punishment as deserved, with due consideration and full knowledge of the law and not under the influence of greed, wrath or ignorance (kāmakrodhābhyām ajñānāt). On the other hand, when the hand of justice is kept back, there prevails anarchy—the mâtsyanyāya (rule of might is right), as is popularly called. In the absence of a holder of the sceptre (daṇḍadhara) the stronger swallows up the weaker, while guarded by him, even the weak can overpower the strong.

Even the wiser method of Kauṭilya may be shown to have been rather in agreement with that which is described in the Pali Rājovāda Jātaka as the Kośalan way, falling short of the standard aimed at :

dalhaṃ dalhassa khipati, mudussa muduā muduṃ,

"matches violence with violence, mildness with mildness."

which tantamounts to the Mosaic principle of 'an eye for an eye', 'a tooth for a tooth'. Here neither the spirit of justice is enlivened with the quality of mercy, nor does forbearance (khaṃti) receive its due importance as moral strength.

The Buddha is historically known as the propounder of the wisdom of the *via media* (majjha, majjhimā paṭipadā) which was applicable alike to religious and secular life. The application of this as a method of government has been explicitly shown in the Jātakas. Aśoka enunciates as well as adopts the same as a definite method of administration.

Aśoka's definite instruction to his officers was to fulfil 'the mean' (majhaṃ, S.R.E. I), avoiding these two extremes, viz., acting under the influence of such immoral propensities as 'malignity, irascibility, cruelty and oppressiveness', on one side, and 'non-application, indolence and weariness for exertion', on the other.[2] Consistently with this, he defined kshānti (forbearance) as that kind of fortitude or moral strength which was to be displayed by the ruling authorities in dealing with miscreants and mischief-makers in taxing their

---

1 Arthas'āstra. I. 4.

2 See Ch. VII.

3 S.R.E. I ; Tata ichhitaviye : "majhaṃ paṭipādayemā" ti. Imehi cha jātehi no saṃpaṭipajati—isāya āsulopena niṭhuriyena tulanāya anāvutiyā ālasiyena kilamathena.

patience to its utmost limit, inwardly having the heart to forgive and and not to use the law of punishment beyond what is required.[1] Even in extreme cases, where a victory by arms was unavoidable, they should (with full preparedness) practise forbearance and prefer light action as far as practicable.[2]

Carefully scrutinised, however, Kauṭilya's opinion, minus its underlying spirit, tends to be identical with Aśoka's.

Two methods were to be adopted for the sufficient growth of the people with the growth in piety, viz., enactments in the form of imperial regulations (dhaṃma-niyama) and moral persuasion (nijhati, Pali nijjhatti),[3] the second being considered the more effective of the two.

The enactments included the special ordinance promulgated for the suppression of schisms in a religious community (Schism Pillar Edict). Moral persuasion consisted in—

1. the propounding and promulgation of the principles of piety or duty and the imparting of instructions in them (dhaṃmānusathini, R.E. IV, P.E. VII) ;
2. the periodical proclamations of piety (dhaṃma-sāvanāni, P.E. VII, M.R.E.) :
3. causing the principles and proclaimed messages to be incised permanently on rocks and pillars in order to keep them before the public eye,
4. the celebration of festivals and popular demonstration of rewards of pious life in heaven by the display of celestial mansions, celestial elephants, illuminations, and artistic representations of the fiery (sun, moon, stars, etc.) and other divine forms (divyāni rupāni dasayitpā janaṃ, R.E. IV),
5. the monumental acts of piety (dhaṃma-thaṃbhāni, P.E. VII) in the form of public and humanitarian works (R.E. II, P.E. VII, Queen's Edict) ;
6. the setting of personal examples (R.E. I, R.E. VIII, Lumbinī Pillar, Nigāli Sāgar) ; and
7. the maintenance of a tolerant, reverential and helping attitude towards all faiths and religious teachers (R.E. VII, R.E. XII, R.E. XIII, P.E. VII).

---

[1] R.E, XIII : yo pi cha apakarayati kshamitaviyamate va yaṃ sako kshamanaye. S.R.E. II : khamisati e chakiye khamitave.

[2] R.E. XIII : sarasake eva vijaye chhati cha (lahudaṃḍataṃ cha rochetu).

[3] P.E. VII.

The anusaṃyāna consisting in quinquennial and triennial tours of inspection on the part of the Rajjukas and Prādeśikas (R.E. III), or on that of the Rājavachanika Mahāmātras (S.R.E. I) was the method of official supervision introduced by Aśoka for the following purposes: (1) to collect a first-hand information about the actual condition of the people (sukhiyana-dukhiyanaṃ jānisaṃti, P.E. IV), (2) to bring good and happiness to town and country folks and do favour to them (janasa jānapadasa hitasukhaṃ upadahevu anugahinevu cha) by initiating various works of public utility (R.E. III, P.E. IV), (3) to educate them in the laws and ideals of piety (R.E. III, P.E. IV), and (4) to prevent the miscarriage of justice and breaches of duty (P.E. IV., S.R.E. I), in addition to their usual administrative duties (ahāpayitu atane kaṃmaṃ, S.R.E. I). As ordained at first, the anusaṃyāna was to be undertaken every five years, both in the Home and outlying provinces (R.E. III), which was modified later with the result that the five-year system was retained for the Home provinces, while the supervising officials in the outlying provinces were required to see that they had not exceeded three years (S.R.E. I). In introducing these tours Aśoka's intention obviously was to fully utilise the adhimāsa (additional month) which occurred at the end of every half-cycle or two additional months that were available at the end of a cycle of five years the working year consisting of 354 days and nights.[1]

The Aśokan age was pre-eminently dominated by the śraddhā or active form of faith. Accordingly the guiding principle of all human actions was apramāda of which uṭṭhāna (alertness), udyama (energetic effort), utsāha (ardour), and parākrama (strenuous exertion) were various synonyms or connotations. So there is no wonder that uṭṭhāna was regarded by Aśoka as by Kauṭilya and others before him as the principle of action in which lay the secret of success in administration (tasa cha esa mūle, R.E. VI). The prompt despatch of business (atha-saṃtīraṇā, R.E. VI) was, according to Aśoka, the real test of man's sense of duty borne by the energetic spirit within him. The sense of duty and great ardour in work on the part of the king, his ministers and officers are possible only where all of them are led by the spirit of service for a great cause, which, in the words of Aśoka, was the service to the country (desāvuti, S.R.E. I), and in the language of Aśoka and earlier political thought, doing good to the

---

[1] Arthas'āstra, II. 7: tris'atam chatuḥpañchās'aoh chāhorātrāṇāṃ karmasaṃvatsaraḥ.

whole world (sarva-loka-hita, R.E. VI), the promotion of the interests of all, both here and hereafter, immediate and remote.

Kauṭilya and other ancient political thinkers spoke of these three sources of state strength, namely, mantraśakti, prabhuśakti (i.e., prabhāva), and utsāha-śakti. The first is born of wise counsel, the second of state resources and fighting strength, and the third of energetic spirit[1]. Aśoka, too, laid stress not only on the very best kind of ardour (aga usāha, P.E. I, aga parākrama, R.E. X) but also on the other two. In warning the wild tribes and gangs of thieves against mischief-making, he desired that they should know his prabhāva (prabhave, R.E. XIII). Though the word mantra is not met with in Aśoka's inscriptions, it is not difficult to make out from his trend of thought that wise counsel is not possible where there is no unanimity in decision and no unity of purpose. This is why he laid so much stress on concord (samavāya, R.E. XII) in religious as well as secular life, on unity (saṃgha-samage, Schism Pillar) in a religious fraternity as in a body politic. Just as the Buddha was eager to see that there was always good understanding (nijjhatti) and no dissension in the Bhikkhu-parisā,[2] so also was Aśoka with regard to the Council of Ministers (Parisā, R.E. VI). He, too, gave the Council of Ministers the full liberty to discuss state-matters without the least interference from his side. The need of the same community of spirit and unity of purpose is felt in the Vedic conception of a Samiti or Parishad.[3] "United they meet, united they rise up, united they do their duties"[4]—this was laid down by the Buddha as one of the seven essential conditions of national as well as communal well-being.

Another condition laid down by the Buddha was that what is not in consonance with that which is established as a good usage (precedent, tradition) should not be introduced, nor should what is

---

[1] Ibid, VI. 2: S'aktis trividhāḥ: jñanabalaṃ mantras'aktiḥ, koṣadaṇḍa-balaṃ prabhu-s'aktiḥ, vikrama-balam utsāha-saktiḥ.

Amarakosha, Kshatriyavarga, 39:

s'aktayas tisraḥ prabhāvotsāha-mantrajāḥ.

[2] Anguttara-N., I, p. 66, Mahāvagga (Vinaya P. I, Ch, X; Sāmagāma Sutta (Dīgha, iii),

[3] Taittirīya Up., ii. 11: saha nāvavatu, saha nau bhunaktu, saha vīryaṃ karavāvahai.

[4] Mahāparinibbāna Suttanta, Ch. I. samaggā sannipatanti, samaggā vuṭṭha-hanti, samaggā karaṇīyani karonti.

established as a good usage be discarded.[1] Such was indeed the very method of Aśoka's government which was intended to uphold and strengthen the received tradition of righteousness, virtue and piety (porāṇā pakiti, M.R.E., Bra). Though the traditional or tried method of the former kings of India was not found adequate as means of furthering the cause of piety, it was supplemented but not discontinued (R.E. IV, P.E. VII).

The fifth condition insisted on holding the seniors in age and experience in high esteem and giving them the respect due to them. Association with the seniors (vṛiddha-saṃyoga) found its due importance in the Arthaśāstra (I.5) as well. There is no wonder then that Aśoka should be repeatedly insisting on the need of respectful attention to seniors and high personages in all walks of life (R. E. IX, R. E. XIII, etc.).

The seventh condition of the Buddha emphasized the need of providing all the existing institutions with necessary safeguards and lawful protection so that worthy persons visiting the country might find themselves comfortable and move about in safety. The Classical writers, such as Diodorus and Strabo, bear testimony to the fact that special care was taken of the foreigners by the Maurya government. There were officers appointed to see that they were not wronged. Arrangements were made for their treatment if they fell ill. When they died, their bodies were properly disposed of and their properties were handed over to their relatives. The judges, too, exercised greatest possible scruple in dealing with cases in which they were implicated.[2] Daṇḍin in his Daśakumāracharita (ii. 44), tells us that the Mauryas had granted this boon to the foreign merchants that 'if they were found to be in possession of stolen property, capital punishment should be excused in their cases',[3] an information, which may be shown to be in accord with the rules in the Arthaśāstra (II. 16).[4] The inscriptions of Aśoka do not throw any direct light on this point. But indirectly it may be inferred from them (R.E. II.

---

[1] Ibid, Ch. I ; apaññattaṃ na paññāpenti, paññattaṃ na samuchchhindanti.

[2] McCrindle, Ancient India, p. 42 ; Raychaudhuri, op. cit. p. 239.

[3] Maurya-datta esha varo vāṇijam, īdṛis'eshu aparādheshu nāsti ās'ubhih abhiyogah, cited by Rangaswami Aiyangar, op. cit., p. 136.

[4] *e.g.*, "Foreigners importing merchandise shall be exempted from being sued for debts unless they are (local) associations and partners." Cf. also Arthas'āstra, II. 28 : "Foreign merchants who have often been visiting the country as well as those who are well-known to local merchants shall be allowed to land in port towns."

R.E. V, R.E. XIII) that just as he himself was eager to see that his emissaries safely moved about in foreign territories and were allowed facilities for work and that the Brāhmaṇa and Śramaṇa teachers had their freedom of movement in the tribal States within his empire, so, on his part, he must have granted similar facilities to the emissaries and merchants from outside.

Now, as to the state policy of Aśoka. Vātavyādhi alone among the earlier political thinkers held that war and peace (sandhi-vigrahau) were the two real forms of the state-policy.[1] The agreed opinion of other teachers went to advocate the six forms of State-policy (shāḍguṇyam) and the fourfold diplomatic means (upāya-chatushṭayam). The six forms consisted in peace, war, observance of neutrality, marching, alliance, and making peace with one and waging war on another.[2] The fourfold means consisted in conciliation (sāma), creation of obligation (dāna), creation of division (bheda), and drastic action (daṇḍa). It is rightly pointed out in the Arthaśāstra (VII. 1) that the proper field of application of the state policy was the inter state circles (prakṛiti-maṇḍalam).

As defined in the Arthaśāstra (VII. 1), binding with pledges is peace. Offensive operation is war. Remaining indifferent is neutrality. Making war preparations is marching. Seeking the help of another is alliance. Double dealing is making peace with one and waging war on another.

Conciliation is to be effected by the promise of protection of villages, of those who live in wild tracts, of pasture lands and roads of traffic, as well as by the reinstatement of those who are banished or who have run away or done harm.

The creation of obligation is possible by the ceding of a territory, the gift of land, the offering of presents, entering into matrimonial alliances, or giving assurances of non-aggression (dānam abhayasya).

The creation of division is to be attempted by sowing the seeds of dissension.

Drastic action means the employment of threat or force against the enemy, open battle, or getting rid of the enemy by hook or crook.

Aśoka had adopted the most drastic measure (daṇḍa) against the Kalingas by wagaing an aggressive war on them and permanently

---

[1] Arthas'āstra, VII. I,

[2] *Ibid*, VII. 1, Amarakosha, Kshatriyavarga, 59 : sandhir vā vigraho yānam āsanaṃ dvaidham ās'rayah.

annexing their country to his imperial domain (R.E. XIII). In dealing with the wild tribes and gangs of thieves (aṭaviyo) who caused mischiefs within the territory, he severally punished them, and subsequently tried to conciliate them by an expression of regret (anutape), by entreating them and making them understand the iniquity of their action, by assuring them that the king would forgive them if they had not exceeded the limit of his patience and were sorry for their misconduct, as well as by reminding them of the king's might (pabhave): "Be judicious and do not get yourselves killed."[1] In other words, he made use of three out of the four strategic means, *viz.*, daṇḍa, sāma and dāna (R.E. XIII).

In connection with the Āntas or Sāmantas mentioned in R.E. II and R.E. XIII, he sought to follow the policy of dāna by carrying out certain works of public utility and philanthropic nature, as well as by conquering their hearts by the inculcation of the principles of piety in their territories. In the case of those Āntas who showed the least tendency to aggression, he while following the twofold means of sāma and dāna, though not without a veiled threat, desired these assurances on his part to reach them : (1) that they were as much entitled to his affection and care as his own subjects, (2) that they might remain unworried and consoled on his account, (3) that he meant them happiness and no misery, and (4) that he would tolerate them within the limit of his patience (S.R.E. II). Here we have the expression of the king's good will, of his desire to respect territorial integrity, as well as to render them benefit.

7. **Military strength and war policy** : We have no means other than Greek accounts of ascertaining the exact military strength of the last Nanda or that of the first Maurya king. Among the Classical writers, Curtius assesses the military strength of Agrammes, the last Nanda king, as consisting of 20,000 cavalry, 200,000 infantry, and 2,000 four-horsed chariots besides a most formidable force of 3,000 elephants, while Diodorus and Plutarch increase the number of elephants to 4,000 and 6,000 respectively.[2] "The Maurya (*i. e.*, Chandragupta) raised the number of the infantry to 600,000, and of the elephants to 9,000. But his cavalry is said to have mustered only 30,000."[3]

---

1 R.E. XIII : anuneti anunijhapeti anutape pi cha prabhave Devanampriyasa vuchati tesha kiti—avatrapeyu na cha hamñeyasu.

2,3 Raychaudhuri, op.cit., pp. 190,219. As Vincent Smith puts it (Oxford History of India, p. 82), "the force at the command of the last Nanda was formidable, being estimated at 80,000 horse, 200,000 foot, 8.000 chariots, and 6,000 fighting elephants."

We regard to Aśoka, the Pali Chronicles make it certain that his army, like that of other Indian monarchs, comprised all the four divisions called *haya-gaja-nara-radha* in Khāravela's inscription. In the inscriptions of Aśoka, we have mention in R.E. VI and M.R.E. (Ye), of the elephant-riders (hathiyāroha), the chariot-masters (yūgyāchariya), and the trained horses (vinīta). His military strength may only be guessed from the account he has given of his war with the Kalingas. Aśoka while speaking of the casualities suffered by the Kalingas, mentions 1,50,000 men made captives, 1,00,000 wounded (āhataṃ, R.E. XIII, G. ; slain, hata, other texts), and as many as that (*i e.*, 1,00,000) who died (mata). From his painful reminiscences, it would seem that he found the Kalinga army to be a formidable force. To overpower such a strong adversary, the Maurya army under him must have been by far the larger and stronger.

Certain it is that the territorial ambition impelled him to wage the aggressive war on the Kalingas. Profound reflections on after-effects of a war such as this, by which the cause of culture is bound to suffer most, brought about a great change in his life and career. Thenceforward he came to set the highest prize on dharma-vijaya or conquest by piety of which we shall see enough later on.

Here I am just to add that in so far as Professor Rangaswami Aiyangar observes that "this is a clear declaration by Aśoka of his preference of the method of extending his suzerainty or sphere of influence without recourse to arms as against the policy of force, and violence which succeeded in Kalinga,"[1] I have nothing to gainsay. But I do not see much reason why he should consider Hultzsch's translation of Aśoka's dhammavijaya by 'conquest by piety', as distinguished from "conquest by arms", 'a forced interpretation', when in the edict itself it has been contradistinguished from sarasaka (śaraśakya) or sāyaka vijaya.

Aiyangar's argument is vitiated in this as well as a few other instances by the wrong assumption on which it is based. We are not to say with Mr. Ramchandra Dikshitar that Aśoka made use of the 'well-known expressions popularised by Chandragupta's great Minister, Kauṭilya.'[2]

The prose treatise of the Arthaśāstra distinguishes between three kinds of conquerors, *viz.*, the righteous (dharma-vijayī), the avaricious

---

1 Rājadharma, p. 142.

2 Mauryan Polity, pp. 128 ff., 254 ff.

(lobha-vijayī), and the demoniac (asura-vijayī),[1] while the earlier distinction, as met with in the several Jātakas and Aśoka's R.E. XIII, and as implied in the words of Buddha, is between two kinds of conquest, *viz.*, dharma and asura, dhamma and adhamma, dhamma and sarasaka, dhammena (*i.e.*, adaṇḍena asatthena) abhivijaya and adhammena (*i.e.*, daṇḍena satthena). From this, it is clear as Professor Raychaudhuri, too, has sought to maintain, that behind Aśoka's nomenclature was the chakkavatti ideal of the Buddha.[2] The conception of three kinds of conquest, which must have developed out of the earlier two, takes us rather beyond the time of Aśoka.

Now, following up Aiyangar's trend of thought, we can say that the standpoints of Aśoka and the Arthaśāstra are diametrically opposite, the concern of the former being the noble way of a conqueror who is fully conscious of his superior strength and that of the latter the diplomatic way of a weaker ruler having to deal with powerful neighbours intent on invasion and conquest.

From the foregoing discussion of the general state policy of Aśoka, we may concede so far that however noble, lofty and idealistic Aśoka's Dhamma-vijaya might be, in actual practice and as circumstances needed, the Epic Dharma-vijaya as a diplomatic art from the point of view of a superior power could not altogether be dispensed with. It is this Epic idea of Dharma-vijaya that has been advocated under Rājadharma in the later Smṛiti works inculcating that "as far as possible recourse to arms should be avoided, and after victory in battle, if a battle becomes inevitable, no harassment of the conquered royal family or people should be permitted."[3] Aśoka kept in view this kind of Dharma-vijaya, which was really a conquest by arms, when he opined : "In a conquest possible indeed by the force of arms, let them (*i.e.*, his descendants) like to practise forbearance and light punishment,[4] and think of that conquest only which is the conquest by piety", he certainly made a distinction between the Dharma-vijaya as it was (with recourse to arms) and the Dharma-vijaya as ought to be (without recourse to arms).

8. **Sources of revenue :** The Arthaśāstra (II. 6) mentions forts (durga), country parts (rāshṭra), mines (khani), buildings and gardens

---

[1] Cf. Mbh. XII. 58-38 ; Harivaṃs'a, I. 14. 21.

[2] Barua, Inscriptions, ii, p. 320 ff.

[3] Aiyangar, op. cit., p. 142. Cf. Mahābhārata, S'āntiparva, 68. 25 : varjanīyaṃ sadā yuddhaṃ rājyakāmena dhīmatā.

[4] R.E. XIII : spakasi yo vijaya kshaṃti cha lahudaṃḍata cha rochetu,

(setu), forests (vana), herds of cattle (vraja), and roads of traffic (vaṇikpatha) as the body of income (āyaśarīram) meaning sources of state-revenue, and defines them clearly.

Though we have not mention of all of them in the inscriptions of Aśoka, it may be easily presumed that these were the various sources of income of the Aśokan State. In the Lumbinī Pillar inscription, we have mention of bhāga or the portion of land-produce payable to the government and bali or religious cess that are included in the second source of income called rāṣṭra. In the same may be included also fisheries (kevaṭabhogā) mentioned in P. E. V. The elephant forests (nāgavana) mentioned in P.E.V. come under the fifth source called vana. The traditional one-sixth portion of the land-produce was payable to the government. In the case of Lumbinī Aśoka reduced the land revenue to one-eighth portion of the produce (aṭhabhāgiye) and totally exempted the village from the payment of the religious cess (ubalike kaṭe). The foregoing of all taxes and duties constituted the main act of royal favour to the subjects.[1] It may be reasonably supposed that by the expression 'favour done to the town and country folks' (janasa jānapadasa anugahinevu, P. E. IV) was chiefly meant the remission or reduction of all forms of taxes, duties, bhāgas and balis.

[1] Cf. Hathigumphā inscription of Khāravela : sava-kara-vaṇa-anugaha-anekāni sata-sahasāni visajati pora-jānapadaṃ.

CHAPTER V

ADMINISTRATION

Administration is the functional or working feature of the constitution of a State. It implies both the act of management and the agent. Management means the systematic performance of various activities of the State channelled into different departments and under different authorities, such as imperial, provincial, divisional, district, urban and rural. The agent comprises the administrative and departmental heads and the officers under them besides some semi-official personages and leading citizens. The quality and success of an administration depends not only upon the efficiency of the ruling authority but also upon the loyalty and co operation of the ruled. In the light of these observations, we may proceed to adjudicate on and estimate the importance of the Aśokan system of administration.

1. **Imperial Administration :** The main function of the imperial administration of Aśoka was, as we saw, to unify the provincial governments for the realisation of a grand idea or ideal expressed through the organ voice of the emperor. As distinguished from them, the imperial government working apparently under the the dictatorial power and prerogative of Aśoka reserved to itself certain rights and privileges. The reservations included *inter alia* the power of legislation, the promulgation of special ordinances, the proclamation of imperial messages, the publication of edicts, the issue of general directions and instructions, the introduction of administrative changes, the initiation of state policy including fiscal, the framing of budget, foreign relations, war and peace, the exercise of general supervision, the appointment and dismissal of provincial heads and other imperial agents, and the creation of new departments. As regards the imperial seat of government, the appointment and dismissal of ministers, counciilors, the emperor's personal and household staffs, the departmental officers, the organization and maintenance of the imperial army and navy, the construction and maintenance of ports, road and water ways, irrigation, relief work, public health, and the like must have come also within the province of imperial administration.[1]

---

[1] Cf. Mookerji's Asoka, p. 54f.

The imperial administration of Aśoka, which is to say, that of Magadha, developed on a purely monarchical basis. Thus to understand its mechanism and actual working the light may be sought from the monarchical model in the Arthaśāstra. One may also utilise the information, however scanty, from the Classical sources fathered on Megasthenes, particularly that from Strabo, the inscriptions of Aśoka and the collective Indian literary evidence remaining as our main guide.

(*a*) **Sources of and charges on Imperial Revenue**: The important point needing clarification here is the source of income for the imperial exchequer, or, in other words, the financial obligation of the provincial governments to the parent or central body. The real cause of confusion arises from Aśoka's two positions, *viz*, as the king and administrative head of Magadha and as the emperor and paramount sovereign of Jambudvīpa.

The general economic principle to be followed by a state in India was the same as that prescribed for the Aryan household. As enunciated by the Buddha, in consonance, no doubt, with the accepted view of social economy, it consisted in collecting abundant wealth for strengthening the bond of friendship, just as the bees gather honey or the white ants build up their hill, and dividing it thereafter into four portions (chatudhā vibhaje). one for household management, two for investment and public works, and the remaining one for reservation against future contingencies.[1] This very domestic principle was at the back of the Arthaśāstra prescription laying down that one fourth of the total revenue (samudaya-pāda) should be spent for the payment of the staff, permanent or temporary, principal or subordinate, including occasional rewards and bonus.[2] This may enable us to say that after making due provision for these four needs in the provincial budget as approved by the imperial government, the surplus was to go to the imperial exchequer as contribution of each provincial government.

The highest office in a monarchical state was held by the king, just as in an imperial state it was held by the emperor. The Crown Prince (Yuvarājā) stood next to none but the King or the Emperor. Other high offices either in the royal household or in the king's civil

[1] Dīgha, III, p. 188.
ekena bhoge bhuñjeyya, dvīhi kammam payojaye ।
chatutthañ cha nidhāpeyya āpadāsu bhavissati ॥

[2] Arthaśāstra, V. 3.

and military services were held by Senānī (Commander-in-Chief), the Purohita (Royal Chaplain), the Mahishī (Chief Queen), the Sūta (Charioteer), the Grāmaṇī (Chief Citizen), the Kshatṛti (Chamberlain), the Saṃgrāhitṛi (Treasurer), the Bhāgadugha (Collector of the Royal Share), the Akshavāpa (the Dice keeper), the Govikartana (the Chase Companion), and the Pālāgala (Courier). As Raychaudhuri rightly suggests, the Kshatri of the Satapatha Brāhmaṇa was the precursor of the Antarvaṃśika of the Arthaśastra, the Saṃgrāhitri of the Sannidhatri, the Bhāgadugha of the Samāhartri, and the Pālāgala of the Dūta.[1]

The list of the high office-holders was somewhat differently made up in the Kurudhamma Jātaka, as will appear from the following enumeration : (1) Rājā (King), (2) Mātā (Queen Dowager) (3) Mahesī (Chief Queen), (4) Uparājā (Crown Prince), (5) Purohita (Royal Chaplain), (6) Rajjuka (Rein-holder), (7) Sārathi (Charioteer), (8) Seṭṭhi (Chief Citizen), (9) Doṇa (Measurer), (10) Dovārika (Door-keeper), and (11) Gaṇika (Courtezan).

According to the Commentary version of the birth-story, the King's younger brother was entitled to the office of the Crown Prince, the Purohita was the leading Brāhman in the king's service, the Rajjuka was the Land-surveyor (Rajjuggāho amachcho), the Sārathi, the Royal Charioteer, the Seṭṭhi, the Regulator of Equitable Transactions, the Doṇa, the Mahāmātra or the Measurer of things, the Dovārika, the Door-keeper, and the Gaṇikā, the Courtezan.

In the Arthaśastra (V. 3), the Crown Prince is called Yuvarājā instead of Uparājā, and there is no suggestion as to the office going ordinarily to the king's younger brother. It separates the office of the Purohita from those of the Ṛitvij (Sacrificial Priest) and the Āchārya (Royal Teacher). The Rajjuka would seem to be the forerunner of the Samāhartri (Collector General) of the Arthaśāstra just as the Doṇa that of the Sannidhātri. The Sārathi was no mere Chariot driver but allegorically either, perhaps, the Mantrin (Prime Minister) or the Gāṇanikyādhyaksha (Accountant General) of the Arthaśāstra. The Seṭṭhi probably stood for the Paura vyavahārika. Similarly the Dovārika was no mere the Door-keeper but the Commander-in-Chief (Senāpati), the Chief Constable (Nāyaka), and the like. The Gaṇikā may be taken to represent not only the leading dancing girl or songstress but also all professional artists employed to

---

[1] Raychaudhuri, op. cit., p. 141 f.

entertain the king. But the whole thing is so vague and veiled in poetic allegory that it is impossible to make all the points clear. Even the Arthaśāstra cannot be exonerated from this charge in spite of its methodical treatment of the subject. The confusion is apt to arise from the omission in the chapter on subsistences to Government servants of the officers mentioned in other books and chapters, as well as from the disparity of nomenclature detected in a few instances.

We can say, however, that the personal and household expenses of the King Emperor was a regular charge on the imperial revenue. Presumably these were included in the one-fourth share of the total revenue of the official year which usually commenced in the month of Āshāḍha (June-July). Other stipendiaries in the royal or imperial household were, according to the Arthaśāstra, the Queen Dowager, the Chief Queen, the new born prince (kumāra) and his nurse. The Sacrificial Priest, the Teacher, the Chief Minister (Mantrin), the Chaplain (Purohita) and the Commander-in-Chief (Senāpati) were entitled each to the emolument granted to the Queen Dowager, the Chief Queen or the Crown Prince, while the allowance to a young prince or his nurse equalled the subsistence allowed in the case of such high officers as the Nāyaka (Chief Constable), the Paura Vyavahārika (City Judiciary), the Karmāntika (Superintendent of Factories), the members of the Council of Ministers (Mantriparishad), the Daṇḍapāla (Commissary General), the Durgapāla (Fort-keeper), the Antapāla (Warden of the Marches), and the Aṭavīpāla (Warden of the Wild Tracts).[1]

In between them and those of the first grade (the Queen Dowager, the Chief Queen, etc.) are to be placed the Dauvārika (Door-keeper), the Antarvaṃśika (Superintendent of the Seraglio), the Praśāstṛi (Administrator General of Law),[2] the Samāhartṛi (Collector General of Revenue), and the Sannidhātṛi (the High Treasurer).

The Queen Dowager is altogether out of the picture in Aśoka's inscriptions. His Queens (Devī) and sons (dālakā) who were typical of the Princes of the Blood (Devikumālā) not only find respectful

---

[1] The designatory expression Rāshṭrāntapālāntapālas' cha (Arthas'āstra, V. 3) is rather misleading. I have made out the list from *ibid*, I. 12.

[2] Shama Sastri is not certain about the position of the Pras'āstṛi whom he represents in one place (Transl., p. 21) as 'the Magistrate', and in another, as 'the Commander' ib., p. 297). He appears to have been no other than the Akshadars'a (Milindapañha, p. 329) or Prāḍviveka (Amarakosha, Kshatriyav., 12).

mention in P.E. VII but are said to have been persons in the imperial household who, like the emperor himself, had their private funds to make charities on their own account. In the earlier edict, R.E. V, the households of his brothers, sisters, and other kinsmen are mentioned as rich enough to be capable of charities, while in the later edict, P.E. VII, his brothers and others are replaced by other princes of the blood royal in a similar connection. The Queen's Edict expressly speaks of the various donations made by his favourite second queen, Kāluvāki. In P.E. IV, Aśoka speaks by the way of a child being entrusted to the care of a clever nurse. The Buddhist legends tell us that Prince Tishya-Vītaśoka, the only uterine brother of Aśoka, was appointed as the Crown Prince, and that the office went abegging since he renounced the world. If by Āryaputra in M.R.E. (Bra) were meant one of the brothers of Aśoka, not to say, the only surviving brother, his position was not different from that of his sons, the Kumāras appointed to the office of Viceroys in three other outlying provinces, and as such, their case may better be considered in connection with provincial administration.

I should think that not only the Chief Queen but also other queens (not probably exceeding three at the same time),[1] not only the younger brother appointed to the office of a crown prince but also other brothers besides sisters, not only the king emperor's own sons but also nephews and nearest agnates were entitled to stipends in coin or kind.. The cost of bringing up the princes and princesses may also have been a charge on the state revenue.

Aśoka's household expenses consisted also in the maintenance of his family establishments, not to say, harems (orodhā, orodhanā, R.E. VI) at Pāṭaliputra and a few moffusil towns, in keeping the kitchen (mahānasa) going to daily feed sumptuously all the inmates of the palace and a thousand others from outside, in the maintenance of the royal pleasances (uyāna) and the upkeep of the equipages (vinīta, R.E. VI), for which provision had to be made in the budget even in accordance with the prescription in the Arthaśāstra (V. 3).

---

[1] "The monarch during the Brāhmaṇa period was usually allowed to have four queens, *viz.*, the Mahishī, the Parivṛikti, the Vāvātā, and the Pālāgalī. The Mahishī was the Chief wife, being the first one married, according to the S'atapatha Brāhmaṇa" (VI, 5.3.1). "The Parivṛikti was the neglected or discarded wife, probably one that had no son. The Vāvātā is the favourite, while the Pālāgalī was the daughter of the last of the court officials." Raychaudhuri, op.cit. p. 137. Here may be the common source of the Islamic Law restricting the number of wives to four.

Aśoka tells us that, prior to the promulgation of R.E. I, many hundred thousands of lives were being daily killed in the royal kitchen for purposes of curry, and Professor Bhandarkar relevantly cites the ancient instance of king Rantideva from the Great Epic, ii. 207. 8-10, of whom it is said that his queen caused to be daily killed in the royal kitchen two thousand cattle and that he acquired an unrivalled fame for having offered food with meat by daily killing two thousand cows, and that invariably during the period of chāturmāsya.

According to Pali tradition, as we noted, Bindusāra as a votary of the Brāhmans (Brāhmaṇa-bhatto) daily fed them including the Brahmanical ascetics and recluses other than Buddhists, and Aśoka was doing the same in the earlier part of his reign. From this, it may be inferred that the Ṛitvig (Brāhman sacrificial priest) and his assistants (purushāḥ) were in the service of Aśoka's imperial household, precisely as in that of his father and grandfather. Even since and after the promulgation of R.E. I one deer and two peafowls continued to be daily killed in his kitchen presumably for meat offerings to the family deity or idol (rājadevatā). Thus the office of the Ṛitvig must have continued along with those of the Brāhman teacher and the Purohita with their assistants.

The Physician (Chikitsaka) figured among the courtiers of an Indian king. Jīvaka, for instance, was the court physician of Bimbisāra and Ajātaśatru. Under him were employed certain medical experts including the veterinary surgeons, all with their assistants. Subsistences to them must also have created a charge on the imperial revenue. The employment of them may be inferred from the arrangements made by Aśoka for two kinds of medical treatment, one suitable for men and the other for animals (R R. II).

In connection with Aśoka's kitchen (mahānasa), eating (bhojana), life in the inner appartments of the palace (orodha), bedchamber (gabhāgāra), drives (vinīta), pleasances (uyāna)[1], and the like, his personal and household staffs creating charges on the imperial revenue may be said to have consisted of the officer in charge of the kitchen (Mahānasika)[2], the soup-maker (suda) and the cook (aralika) with their assistants, the bath-attendant (snāpaka), the shampooer (saṃvāhaka), the barber (kalpaka), the toilet-maker (prasādaka), the water-supplier (udaka-parichāraka), the troops of women (strīgaṇa), the

---

1 R.E.I., R.E.VI.

2 Arthasāstra, I. 21.

presenter of the coat (kañchukī), the presenter of the head-dress (ushṇishī), in short, the keeper of the ward-robe, the kubjas (hump-backed persons), dwarfs and pigmies, the artists such as actors, dancers, singers, players on musical instruments, buffoons, jestors, bards and the like (naṭa-nartaka gāyana-vādaka-vāgjīvana-kuśīlavāḥ).[1] Aśoka's personal staff included the Prativedakas or Reporters (R.E.VI).

It was in connection with the Queens and court-ladies, the maids-of honour and the maid-servants that there were appointed the Stryadhyaksha Mahāmatras (R.E.XII).

The Divyāvadāna speaks of the Bhāṇḍāgārika (i.e., Sannidhātri) of Aśoka, placed in charge of the imperial treasury and store-house (kosha-koshṭhāgāra), who was restrained by the emperor's grandson Samprati, then in the office of the Crown Prince, from lavishly supplying Aśoka's demands. This wise step against the depletion of the imperial treasury and store house was taken on the advice of the Ministers. The same authority introduces us also to Aśoka's Prime Minister Rādhagupta whom Jayaswal was inclined to regard as the descendant and successor of Kauṭilya Vishṇugupta without, however, any reliable evidence. The same alludes also to other imperial Ministers.

The Arthaśāstra, on the other hand, distinguishes between the functions and offices of the Samāhartṛi (Collector General of Revenue) the Sannidhātṛi (High Treasurer) and the Gāṇanikyādhyaksha (Accountant General), which is more to the point. Whatever were their actual designations, these three high officials must have been in the service of Aśoka.

(b) **Correspondence between the Amatyas of the Arthaśāstra and the Purushas of Aśoka**: Apart from and below the Mantrī or constant personal adviser to the king mainly in matters temporal or secular, the Chaplain or constant personal adviser mainly in matters religious or sacerdotal, and the Crown Prince holding the office of the deputy king, the Arthaśāstra speaks of the most important functionaries of the state. These functionaries, termed Sachivas,[2] are broadly distinguished as Mati-sachivas and Karma-sachivas in the Junāgarh inscription of Rudradāman I, both being endowed with ministerial qualities (amātya-guṇa-samudyuktaiḥ). The Mati-sachivas, otherwise called Dhī-sachivas, were those Amātyas who possessed the necessary qualifications to serve as Mantrins or Ministers to the king, either

[1] Ibid, I. 12, I. 21, V. 3. ; Cf. Dīgha, i, p. Jātaka, V, p. 506 ff.
[2] Ibid, I. 7.

jointly or individually, and the Karma-sachivas those who had the competence to serve as different ministerial officers, civil or military. This very functional distinction is sought to be made in the Arthaśāstra between the Mantrins and the general body of the Amātyas. It was evidently referring to the Amātyas that Megasthenes and with him other Classical writers spoke of the seventh caste or class of the Indian people as consisting of 'the councillors of state' in the language of Arrian, and of 'the councillors and assessors of the king' in that of Diodorus and Strabo. Arrian describes them as those 'who advise the king, or the magistrates of self-governed cities, in the management of public affairs.' In point of numbers, they were a small class, but they were distinguished by superior wisdom and justice, whence they enjoyed 'the prerogative of choosing governors, chiefs of provinces, deputy governors, superintendents of the treasury, generals of the army, admirals of the navy, controllers, and commissioners who superintend agriculture'.[1]

To Diodorus the Councillors and Assessors were those who deliberated on public affairs. Though numerically they were a small minority, they were the most respected, on account of their high character and wisdom, for from their ranks the advisers of the king were taken, and the treasurer of the state, and the arbiters who settled disputes. The generals of the army also and the chief magistrates usually belonged to them.[2]

These are but a faithful echo in foreign writings of what is stated in the Arthaśāstra (I. 9, I. 10) regarding qualifications of the Amātyas in general (amātya-sampat) and the appointment of the high state-functionaries out of them : "Native, born of high family, influential, well-trained in arts, possessed of foresight, wise, of strong memory, bold, eloquent, skilful, intelligent, possessed of enthusiasm, dignity and endurance, pure in character, affable, firm in loyal devotion (dridha-bhakti), endowed with excellent conduct, strength, health and bravery, free from procrastination and ficklemindedness, affectionate, and free from such qualities as excite hatred and enmity." According as they possess all, or one-half, or one-quarter of the above qualifications, they are to be broadly classified into three ranks : high, middle and low.

---

[1] McCrindle, Ancient India, p. 117 f.

[2] Ibid., p. 41 : Cf. Ibid., p. 85 f., where, to the same effect, Strabo says, "The seventh class consists of the Councillors and Assessors of the king. To them belong the highest posts of government, the tribunals of justice, and the general administration of public affairs."

Assisted by his Mantrī (Prime Minister) and his Chaplain, the king was to offer temptations to test the character and fitness of the Amātyas appointed at first to minor offices in government departments. Of those tried Amātyas, those tested under religious allurements were to be employed afterwards for the duties of the Judges (Dharmasthas) and Magistrates (Kaṇṭakasodhaneshu); those tested under monetary allurements, for those of the Revenue Collectors (Samahartṛis) and Treasurers (Sannidhātṛis); those under love allurements, for those of the superintendents of pleasure grounds (vihāra), internal and external; those by allurements under threat, for immediate service (āsanna-kāryesu); those by all allurements, for the duties of the various Ministers (Mantrinaḥ), while those found deficient under one or all of these allurements were to be employed in mines, manufactories, and timber and elephant forests.

The Amarakosha applies the designation of Mahāmātra or Pradhāna to the chief ministerial officers (Karma-sachivas). According to Buddhaghosa, too, the Mahāmātras were just the leading Amātyas (Mahāmattā ti Mahāmachchā). The Mahāmātra figures in the Great Epic as a warrior seated on the back of an elephant, i.e., as a Hastipakādhipa in the terminology of Dharaṇī. As Mookerji observes, "the Mahāmātra figures (in the Arthaśāstra as a minister (I. 10, 12, 13), and as the chief executive officer of a city under the title Nāgarikamahāmātra (IV. 5[1]), while his power and influence will be evident from the fact that the seditious Mahāmātra is a cause of much concern to the king."[2]

Here Mookerji is evidently guided by Shama Sastri's translation. But from the text of the Arthaśāstra, it is not clear that by the designation is anywhere meant a Mantrin. "Just as in the Arthaśāstra (II. 5), so in the Vinaya Piṭaka and the Amarakosha, the Mahāmātras are distinguished from the Judges (Dharmasthas, Akshadarśas). According to the Arthaśāstra (II. 5), the Dharmasthas and the Mahāmātras had their offices in buildings called Dharmasthīya and Mahāmātrīya respectively".[3] Buddhaghosa defines the Mahāmātras as great Amātyas holding different posts, placed in different charges (ṭhānantarappattā), and understands by the designation Magadhama-

---

[1] The designation, Nāgarika-mahāmātra, is not met with in the Arthas'āstra, IV. 5. It is evidently a coinage on the part of Mookerji. The Arthas'āstra designation in IV. 6. and elsewhere is Nāgaraka.

[2] As'oka, p. 107.

[3] Barua, Inscriptions, ii, p. 287.

hāmatta either the great functionary vested with a large measure of royal power (mahatiyā issariya-mattāya samannāgato) in Magadha or the highest officer of the Magadha king'. "In point of fact, Magadhamahāmatta is the epithet applied in Pali to Varshakāra who was a Brāhman chief minister of king Ajātaśatru of Magadha'.[1]

The Arthaśāstra designation of Amātya is nowhere employed in Aśoka's inscriptions. Aśoka speaks instead of the Purushas in P.E.I. and divides them broadly into three ranks, viz., the superior (ukasa), the intermediate (majhima) and the inferior (gevaya),[2] precisely in the manner in which the Amātyas are classified in the Arthaśāstra. Thus the correspondence being established between the Purushas of P.E. I and the Amātyas of the Arthaśāstra, one must discard Hultzsch's identification of Aśoka's Purushas with the Gūḍhapurushas in the Arthaśāstra representing as they do the secret agents or spies, and welcome Raychaudhuri's identification with the Rājapurushas or Royal Agents or officers in general.

The ministerial qualifications demanded by Aśoka of the officers deserving to be appointed to higher offices and entrusted with responsible duties are substantially those stated in detail in the Arthaśāstra and briefly in Classical writings. The Aśokan way of stating them agrees rather with those in the Great Epic and the Pali Nikāyas and Jātakas. The strength of character is to be judged by the power of self-control, the purity of sentiment, the feeling of gratitude and the firmness of devotion (R.E. VII). The baneful mental distempers to be avoided consist in wrath, conceit, malignity, irascibility, fierceness, cruelty and oppressiveness (S.R.E. I, P.E. III). Dealings with men to be effective must be enlivened by one's genial temperament avoiding rudeness and fierceness and expressing winsome cordiality (S.R.E. I). Little sin, much of good deeds, compassion, liberality, truthfulness, moral purity, gentleness and nobleness are the qualities that go to ennoble human character (P.E.II, P.E.VII). Moral and physical energy, ardour and enthusiasm, are to be applied to general good avoiding lethargy, inertia and weariness for exertion. The very best kind of longing for piety, self-examination, attentiveness, fear of public opinion and enthusiasm are needed for success in work. The instructions received are to be grasped in their letter and spirit and to be properly and fully carried out (R.E.III, S.R.E.I).

---

[1] Dīgha, II, p. 72 f.

[2] The nearest Sanskrit equivalent of *gevaya* is *gopyaka* meaning a menial.

The noble feeling to be cherished in rendering service is to think that one is just discharging his debt (S.R.E.I).

(c) **Mantri-mahamatras and Mantri-parishad :** The Arthaśāstra draws a distinction between the Mantrin, the Mantrins and the Mantriparishad. The Mantrin is placed in the same rank with the Chaplain, the Crown Prince, the Chief Queen and others entitled to the highest amount of subsistence. It is with the assistance of the Mantrin and the Chaplain that the king is advised to test capacity and fitness of the Amātyas or officers in general for the higher offices including that of the Mantrins whose salary is not mentioned. But the members of the Mantriparishad rank each with those entitled to one-fourth of the subsistence payable to the Mantrin par excellence. The king is advised to call both his Mantrins and the Mantriparishad when there is any 'work of emergency' to be done, to tell them of the same, and to follow the course of action suggested by the majority. It appears from the Arthaśāstra (I. 15) that the Ministers passed as Mantrins when they were consulted with individually and not all together, and that they formed the Mantri-parishad when they met together to deliberate upon the affairs of administration. If the Mantrins alone were empowered to meet for such deliberations, the Parishad was just a meeting of the cabinet. If the Mantrins as political advisers and the Karma-sachivas as high ministerial officers were summoned by the king to meet together for joint deliberations and advice in matters of urgency, the Parishad functioned as a 'Privy Council' having strict secrecy for its motto. With Mookerji one must treat the Mantri-parishad, as described in the Arthaśāstra, as a Privy Council rather than as a Cabinet. The school of Manu restricted the seats in the Mantri-parishad to twelve members, that of Bṛihaspati to sixteen, and that of Uśanas to twenty, while the Arthaśāstra makes the number depend on the needs of administration.[1]

Neither the inscriptions of Aśoka nor the Classical writings, throw any light on the nicer distinction between the Mantrin par excellence and other Mantrins. But Aśoka certainly speaks of the Parisā or Mantri-parishad in which his verbal orders and the urgent works entrusted to the Mahāmātras were discussed (R.E. VI). In his case, the members of the Parishad are left to themselves in the

---

[1] Mookerji (Asoka, p. 55) draws attention to the tradition stating that Bindusāra had a Privy Council of 500 members, which is palpably an exaggeration. The Arthaśāstra doubles the number while speaking of Indra's Privy Council.

matter of deliberations, and the king shows much concern to know immediately the course and final result of their deliberations from the Reporters (Prativedakas) who watched the proceedings on the king's behalf.[1] The records of Aśoka are, however, silent as to who the members of the Parishad were. Presumably the Mahāmātras to whom urgent works were entrusted were privileged to be present and to take part in the deliberations of the Parishad, at least to state and explain the matters. If so, these Mahāmātras might be identified with the high functionaries called Mantri mahāmātras in the Kosala-Saṃyutta, III. 5.[2] This class of Mahāmātras served as ministers as well as high ministerial officers. That such was the earlier office of the Mantri-mahāmātras is evident also from the fact that king Ajātaśatru of Magadha entrusted the responsible duty of fortifying the village of Pāṭaligāma to his two great ministers known as Magadha-mahāmattā.

(d) Other classes of Mahamatras : There were other classes of Mahāmātras. In Pali literature, for instance, we have mention of the Sabbatthaka-mahāmatta or Mahâmātra in charge of general affairs (*i. e.*, the Chief Minister),[3] the Vohārika-mahāmatta or Mahāmātra as administrator of justice, the Senānāyaka-mahāmatta or Mahāmātra as head of the army, the Gaṇaka-mahāmatta or Mahāmātra as accountant ; the Antepura-upachārakā mahāmattā or Mahāmātras in charge of the inner appartments of the royal palace, and the Vinicchaya-mahāmatta or Mahāmātra as judicial investigator of the cause of action, ranked below the Vohārika.[4] It may be shown that the Sabbatthaka-Mahāmatta stood for general administration and the Vohārika for the judicial, while the Senānāyaka-mahāmatta stood for military administration.

Aśoka defines the duties of the Dharma-mahāmātras (R.E.V, R E.XII, P.E.VII) and differentiates them as a class of high officials from other Mahāmātras, the sectarian Mahāmātras who were attached specifically to this or that religious sect. P.E.VII refers to the heads of various departments (bahukā mukhā) besides the Dharma and

---

[1] In the mediaeval development of the Council of Ministers, as Jayaswal has sought to show, the king was represented by his Deputy. Here it is definite that the ministers met in the absence of the king.

[2] As for the capacity and function of the Mantrimahāmātras, it is said : Santi rājakule mantino mahāmattā ye pahonti āgate paccatthike mantehi bhedayitum.

[3] Hitopades'a, ii. 39 : yaḥ sarvādhikāre niyuktaḥ pradhānamantrī sa(ḥ).

[4] Barua, Inscriptions, ii, p. 288 ; F. W. Thomas in J. R. A. S. 1914, p. 359 ; Raychaudhuri, op. cit., p. 168.

other Mahāmātras. Who were the other departmental heads besides them and did they bear the designation of Mahāmatra or not? The Arthaśāstra defines the duties of various Adhyakshas or Superintendents, but it nowhere indicates if they were entitled to the designation of Mahāmātra. Raychaudhuri aptly calls attention to the fact that at least in one case Aśoka applies the designation of Mahāmātra to a class of Adhyakshas, namely, the Stryadhyakshas (R.E.XII).

The sectarian Mahāmātras themselves were responsible officers of the State. The Pali Sāmaññaphala Sutta bears a clear testimony to the fact that among the councillors of a king some were admirers of one teacher and some of another.[1] The same may be inferred from tbe king's direction appended to the Schism Pillar Edict (Sārnāth) requiring a Mahāmātra to go by turn to attend the Buddhist fast-day service (ekike mahāmāte yāti posathāye) invariably on the eighth day of a lunar half-month. By implication there were Mahāmātras who went to attend the fast-day service of other religions in which they were believers.[2]

R.E.XII introduces us to the Vrachabhūmikas and other classes of officers along with the Dharma and Stryadhyaksha Mahāmātras.

In connexion with city-administration we are introduced to the Nagara-vyavahārika or Nagaraka Mahāmātras corresponding apparently with the Paura-vyavahārika or Nāgarika of the Arthaśāstra.

As regards the home provinces, we have mention of the Mahāmātras who were evidently placed in charge of the administration of such places as Benares, Kauśāmbī and Vidiśā. As for the outlying provinces or frontier districts, P.E.I mentions the Anta-mahāmātras corresponding to the Antapālas of the Arthaśāstra and the Pachchanta-vāsino mahāmattā of Buddhaghosa[3]. Though the Aṭavīpālas of the Arthaśāstra are nowhere mentioned in the edicts of Aśoka, their existence as a class of officers in the Aśokan regime is implied in R.E. XIII.

In S.R.E. I and S.R.E. II, the Mahāmātras of Samāpā are distinguished as Rājavachanikas from those of Tosali who were attached to the Viceroy of Kalinga presumably as Mantri-mahāmātras. It is

---

[1] Cf. Mahābodhi Jātaka, No. 528.

[2] The Pali Chronicles (Mahāvaṃsa, V. 236-240) do not, however, indicate the religious faith of the high officer (amachcha) deputed by the king to the local Asokārāma to cause its inmates to do the uposatha duty together settling the dispute.

[3] Atthasālinī, p. 245.

easy to infer that the Mahāmātras of Tosali, too, previously enjoyed the status of Rājavachanikas. The same remark holds true of the Mahāmātras of Suvaṃṇagirl, Ujeni and Takasilā who became attached afterwards as Mantri-mahāmātras to the Viceroys concerned, while the official position of the Mahāmātras of Isila was obviously on a par with that of the Rājavachanikas of Samāpā. It seems very likely that the Mahāmātras who were to be sent forth every five years by Aśoka on tours of official inspection and those to be sent forth every third year by the Viceroys concerned were all to be regarded as Rājavachanikas or Imperial Commissioners.

(e) **Other functionaries** : The functionaries required in R.E.III to go forth on tours of inspection every five years are broadly distinguished as Rajjukas and Prādesikas. Their connection with the Yuttas is still open to dispute. The statement concerning them and Rajjukas and Prādesikas differs in the available versions of R.E. III. There were Purushas or Personal Agents of Aśoka who served as intermediaries between him on the one hand and the Yuttas[1] and the Rajjukas[2] on the other. R.E. VI speaks of the Dāpaka and the Srāvāpaka who might be counted among officers entitled to receive orders from the emperor's mouth. Among the subordinate officers one must include the Lipikaras or Scribes who were not precisely the Lekhakas of the Arthaśāstra. The Dūtas as imperial emissaries to foreign countries and courts must have a very special significance of their own.[3]

(f) **Departments** : We have mention in P.E. VII of the Dharma-mahāmātras, the Mahāmātras in general, and many other departmental heads (bahukā mukhā), while the departments themselves are nowhere enumerated. It is certain that some of them were specifically imperial concerns, while the rest belonged to local administration. It may be readily conceded to Mookerji that the emperor's first duty consisted in formulating the fundamental principles upon which his government was to be based and run and the policy to be pursued by his administrators, issuing his notifications for them from time to time, and gazetting, on rocks or pillars of stone the Edicts announcing his policy, principles and the measures to be taken for their realisation. It may also be talen for granted that the subject of legislation was in certain matters imperialised, or that the subject of the public works of utility was also an imperial concern. There is no gainsaying 'the

---

[1] R. E. III. [2] P. E. IV. [3] R. E. XIII.

fact that the Department of Dharma, too, was under the imperial government of Asoka.' The weak point in Mookerji's otherwise weighty observations is that he seems to have mixed up Aśoka's personal concerns with those of his imperial administration.[1]

As for the newly created 'Department of Dharma', the Edicts contain a good deal of information. 'The public works of utility' were undoubtedly an imperial concern, but whether or not there was a separate department created for the purpose, and if so, how was it officered and operated are questions to which no definite answer can be given. The legislating authority was composed of the emperor and the Council of Ministers. The announcement of the imperial policy and the principles of government and the measures to be adopted, the engraving of the Edicts, the communication with the local administrators, etc. involve the question of the imperial secretariat. The subject of legislation has been fully dealt with in the previous chapter. Here we may conveniently discuss the remaining points concerning the 'Department of Dharma', the 'public works of utility', and the 'imperial secretariat'. The subject of foreign relations which, too, was a concern of Aśoka's imperial government may also be considered.

(g) **Department of Dharma** : This came into existence with the first appointment of the Dharma-mahāmātras by Aśoka in his thirteenth regnal year. The scope of its activity may be determined by the various duties assigned to the Dharma-mahāmātras who functioned at one and the same time as Moral Sponsors, Imperial Almoners, protectors and promoters of religious interests throughout the empire and outside, and may be also as religious advisers to the emperor. The office of the Dharma-mahāmātras developed evidently out of that of the Dharmasthas or Jurists who functioned either as judges or as interpreters of the Sacred Law in a civil court of justice.[2]

There is no evidence to warrant the surmise that the Dharma-mahāmātras interfered with the usual course of justice. "The question of treatment with mercy, sympathy or leniency of persons shut up behind the prison bars came indeed within their province. The only point of similarity between a Dharmastha and a Dharma-mahāmātra is that the former, too, had the authority to treat with

---

[1] Asoka, p. 54 f.

[2] Arthas'āstra, III. 1. The Dharmastha, as defined in the Dhammapada. verses 256-57, is generally taken to be the judge, while, in point of fact, his real business was to rightly guide the course of justice.

mercy a tīrthakara (founder of a school of thought), an ascetic (tapasvin), a diseased person, one who is wearied due to hunger and thirst or invalid due to old age···, one who has come from another country, one who has already suffered much from punishment, and one who is penniless, but that again only in the capacity of a Judge.[1] The Dharma-mahāmātras, on the contrary, figure prominently as royal almoners, dispensers of royal mercy, and, above all, as helpers of the cause of religion.[2]

The Dharma-mahāmātras were appointed to discharge the following duties :

"(1) In connection with all religious sects : (a) to establish the 'norm' effecting an increase in virtue and to work for the welfare and happiness of the virtuous amongst them ; [3] (b) to encourage the true spirit of tolerance enabling them to intelligently appreciate one another's faith and point of view and work together in harmony and concord for growth in the essence of the thing ; [4] and (c) to equitably distribute royal favour and do various other kinds of business as necessity arose ; [5]

(2) In connection with the royal family, including Aśoka's brothers, sisters and other kith and kin : (a) to distribute charity, (b) to found permanent institutions of piety ; (c) to satisfy their hankering for knowledge of the truth and the law of duty ; [6] and (d) to persuade them to honour and hold all sects of religion.[7]

(3) In connection with the inhabitants of Yona, Kāmboja, Gandhāra, Rishṭika, Petenika, and other western peoples, as well as the old and destitute, beggarly Brāhmans and ascetics, and slaves and servants : (a) to work for their good and happiness [8] and (b) to protect those who are devoted to religion against harassment and molestation ; [9] and

(4) In connection with the jail administration : (a) to provide one bound in chains with ransom, (b) to protect him against molestation, or (c) to grant him release in certain special and extraordinary circumstances."[10]

In the matter of ensuring the growth of all sects in the essence of the thing (sāravaḍhi), the Dharma-mahāmātras were variously

---

1 Ibid., III, 20.

2 Barua, Inscriptions, ii, p. 254.

3 R. E. V.

4 R. E. XII.

5 P.E. VII.

6 R.E. V ; P.E. VII.

7 R.E. XII.

8 R.E. V ; P.E. VII.

9 R.E. V.

10 R.E. V ; Ibid., ii, p. 253.

assisted by the Stryadhyaksha Mahāmātras, the Vrachabhūmikas, and many other classes of officers.[1] In the matter of welfare of the various sects including the Buddhists (Saṃghaṭas), they were variously assisted also by the Mahāmātras attached specifically to this or that particular sect.[2] In the matter of distribution of royal charities and of those of the queens and the princes of the blood, they were assisted by these Mahāmātras and many other departmental heads.[3] And in the matter of promulgation and propagation of the fundamental principles of piety, they were assisted within Aśoka's empire by the Purushas and such touring officers as the Rajjukas and the Prādeśikas,[4] and outside by the Dūtas or Emissaries.[5]

Stryadhyaksha Mahāmātras: They were undoubtedly the officers called Stryadhyakshas or Dārādhyakshas in the Mahābhārata[6]. The Arthaśāstra speaks of the Antarvaṃśikas[7] as well as the Gaṇikādhyakshas or Superintendents of Courtezans. They were, according to the Vinaya Piṭaka[8] and Buddhaghosa's Commentary on the Raṭṭhapāla Sutta,[9] the Mahāmātras placed in charge of the family establishment of a king (Antepure upachārakā mahāmattā, Orodhamahāmattā).

Mookerji[10] rightly observes: "Regarding women, perhaps it was necessary to preach the dharma of toleration to them as a class. That there were Mahāmātras attached to the royal harem is also indicated by Kauṭilya (I. 10); because they had to deal with ladies, their special qualification emphasized is sexual purity (kāmopadhāśuddhān), and they are to be placed in charge of the places of pleasure both in capital and outside···Again, in the Vinaya[11] there is a reference to the appointment of religious preachers for the royal harem (itthāgāraṃ dhammaṃ vāchehī ti)."

The Stryadhyakshas were, according to Raychaudhuri,the 'Guards of the Wives' or 'Superintendents of Women of the king's household'. As the Great Epic attests, 'they were to see to the safety of the queens and their female retinues whenever they were sent out under

---

1 R.E. XII. 2 P.E. VII. 3 P.E. VII. 4 R.E. III. 5 Ibid., XIII.

6 IX. 29. 68, 90; XV. 22. 20; 23. 12; referred to by Raychaudhuri.

7 Arthas'āstra, V. 3; Cf. Amarakosha, Kshatriyavarga, 16: Antaḥpure tvadhikṛitaḥ syād antarvaṃs'ikaḥ janaḥ.

8 Vinaya Chullavagga, vii.

9 Papañchaūdanī, II

10 Asoka, p. 161.

11 Vol. IV, p. 198.

their care.'[1] The Arthaśāstra (I. 20) insists on keeping away the queens 'from the society of ascetics with shaved head or braided hair, of buffoons, and of outside prostitutes (dāsī), and not allowing chances to 'women of high birth' other than appointed midwives, to see them'.

Though the word ithi (itthi, strī) generally means a wife or married woman, it stands also for the womenfolk as distinguished from men. If so, the duties of the Stryadhyakshas of Aśoka need not be confined to the queens and other women of the royal or imperial household. In other words, it is conceivable that, as suggested by Hultzsch, they might as well function as the Gaṇikādhyakshas of the Arthaśāstra.[2] It must have been their principal duty to guard the interests of women in general and of women in particular so as to keep them away from mischief. The women in general included the courtezans, prostitutes, actresses, and the like. It must have been also their duty to guard them so as not to corrupt social morality, particularly the morality of the Brāhmaṇas and the Śramaṇas belonging to different religious orders. But it was no less their duty under Aśoka's regime to arrange for their sound moral and religious education, or to persuade them to honour and support all religious teachers irrespective of sect or creed.[3]

Vrachabhūmikas: The Vrachabhūmikas whose business, like that of the Stryadhyakshas, it was to co-operate with the Dharmamahāmātras, to ensure the growth of different religious sects in the essential matters are not expressly described as Mahāmātras, though from the context of R. E. XII it might appear that they, too, formed a class of them. It is certain that their designation had something to do with vracha in R. E. VI. That the word vracha is the equivalent of vraja is evident from the Shahbazgarhi text of R. E. VI and R. E. XIII where the verbal forms vracheya and vrachaṃti occur, the root vraj meaning 'to go'. Even in the Dhauli version of R. E. V, we have Kaṃbocha for Kamboja. But Girnār, Kalsi and Mansehra afford no instances where j is represented by ch,

---

1 Cf. Mahābhārata, XV. 23 11—18 :

Arjunaś cha mahāteja rathenādityavarchasā ।
vaśī śvetair-hayair-yuktair-divyenānvagam nṛipaḥ ॥
Draupadī pramukhāś cha strīsangha śivikāyutāḥ ।
stryadhyakshaguptāh prayayur visṛijanto 'mitaṃ dhanaṃ ॥
samṛiddha-ratha-hastyaśvaṃ veṇu-vīnā-nināditaṃ ।

2 II. 27.

3 For other points, Cf. Barua, Inscriptions, ii, p. 315 f.

while in all the versions of R. E. VI the word is either vacha or vracha. The equation of vacha or vracha with the Sk varchas would be free from all objections, but unfortunately no sensible meaning can be made out of it. The choice lies at last between the two equations, namely, that with the Ardhamāgadhī vachcha and that with the Sk. vraja. In the Ardhamāgadhī dictum, muni ti vachche,[1] the word vachcha is Sanskritised in the commentary as vratya, a word, which does not occur in any Sanskrit lexicon. The word vrātya which might be proposed instead does not suit the context, its usual meaning being 'a man of the twice-born class who has not undergone the purificatory rite'. If the equation with the Jaina vachcha be allowed, the Aśokan word vachamhi, vachasi or vrachaspi (R. E. VI) must be taken to mean, 'while I am engaged in the religious practice, and the official designation Vrachabhūmika to mean 'the officers connected with the places where the religious rites or duties are performed.' In R. E. VI, the word vacha or vracha occurs just after gabhāgāra (bed-chamber), and it is enjoined in the Arthaśāstra (I. 19) that a king should enter the bed-chamber amid the sound of trumpets and enjoy sleep during the fourth and fifth parts of the night, and should recall to his mind the injunctions of sciences as well as the day's duties during the sixth part after being awakened by the sound of trumpets, while during the eighth division he should 'receive benedictions from sacrificial priests, teachers, and the high priest'. There must have been some such officers as to see that no living being whatsover was sacrificed in the name of religion or no convivial gathering with moral risks held (R. E. I). In the imperial household the Purohita, the sacrificial priest and the preceptor with their assistants were to be counted among the Vrachabhūmikas understood in the above sense of the term.

Various interpretations of vracha have so far been suggested on the strength of its equation with vraja.[2] I am inclined in the alternative to take the word to mean rathavraja, and the two words vracha and vinīta to stand together as the equivalent of the Pali rathavinīta, meaning 'the chariots drawn by well-trained horses'. Accordingly the Vrachabhūmikas may be taken to represent the officers, such as the elephant-riders, the chariot trainers, and the like (in a collective sense) to whom was assigned the duty of proclaiming the imperial messages to the people at large (M. R. E., Ye).

---

[1] Achāranga Sūtra, ed. by W. Schubring, i, p. 13.

[2] Barua, Inscriptions, ii, p. 316 f. Acc. to Amarakosha (Nānārtha, 95) vraja may mean goshtha (cow-pen), adhva (road) and nivaha (assemblage).

Dūtas : They were the imperial emissaries to the territories and courts of such independent 'frontagers' or 'borderers' as the five Greek potentates as the Cholas, the Pāṇḍyas, the Satiyaputras, the Keralaputras and the Tāmraparṇyas. The primary duty of the Dūtas was the faithful delivery of the imperial messages. According to the Arthaśāstra (I. 16), the duties of the envoys or emissaries consisted in 'transmission of messages, maintenance of treaties, issue of ultimatum (pratāpa), gaining of friends, intrigue, sowing (seeds of) dissension among friends, fetching secret force, carrying away by stealth relatives and gems, gathering information about the movements of spies, bravery, breaking of treaties of peace, winning the favour of the envoy and government officers of the enemy". The king is advised to receive a foreign envoy in the presence of the Council of Ministers.[1] The Dūtas are distinguished into three classes according as they possess the lesser and lesser of ministerial qualifications to be employed as Plenipotentiaries (nisṛishṭārthaḥ) or as *Charges d' affaires* (parimitārthaḥ), or as mere conveyers of royal writs (śāsanaharaḥ). Aśoka's Dūtas appear to have been at the most *Charges d' affaires* or 'agents entrusted with a definite mission', namely, that of good will (S. R. E. II). It was through them that Aśoka sought to achieve the conquest by piety in the territories outside his own (R. E. XIII). The Dūtas might herald religious missions, though as emissaries they were all imperial officers.[2] It is not inconceivable that some of the Dharma-mahāmātras were deputed as Dūtas by Aśoka.

(h) **Public Works of Utility** : These are comprehended by the Sanskrit term ishṭāpūrtam. In Aśoka's language, these are to be understood as 'monumental acts of piety' (dhammathaṃbhāni, P.E. VII). These are regarded as 'various means of causing happiness to the world' (vividhā sukhāyanā loke) and 'institutions of satisfaction' (tuṭhāyatanāni)[3]. In so far as they implied the construction of roads,

---

[1] Arthas'āstra, I. 20.

[2] Cf. Tevijja Sutta in Dīgha I where the leading Brāhman S'rotriyas figure as Dūtas.

[3] For other details, see Inscriptions, ii, p. 327 f. Dr. Hetti Aratchi inclines to equate As'oka's tuṭhāyatanāni preferably with Pali titthāyatanāni on these two grounds : (1) in Sinhalese, toṭa = tittha, Sk. tīrtha, and (2) in Pali, jīrṇi has changed into juṇṇi. I find it difficult to accept his valued suggestion for these three reasons : (1) the technical Pali meaning of titthāyatanāni (heretical views) does not suit the As'okan text (P.E.VII) ; (2) the Pali pārijuññaṃ or pārijuṇṇaṃ which is derived from parijīrṇi must be derived either from parijyāni (changing

the planting of shade-trees, the sinking of wells, the excavation of tanks, the laying out of fruit gardens, the erection of almshouses, the construction of religious mounds, the making of cave-dwellings, etc., they needed the service of the architects, the engineers and overseers. That some master architects (thapatayo, sthapatis) were in the service of Indian kings is evident from the Pali Dhammachetiya Sutta[1] as well as the later literary traditions and epigraphic records. From the inscriptions of Aśoka, however, no such information can be gathered. Though in these matters Aśoka had followed in the foot-steps of the former kings of India (P.E. VII), the edicts leave no room for doubt that he sought to accomplish them in a more systematic way.

If these works of utility be taken also to include the arrangements made by Aśoka for two kinds of medical treatment, one for men and the other for animals, both within his empire and outside (R.E. I), there must have been a regular medical department organised for the purpose with expert physicians and veterinary surgeons as imperial officers to advise him. For making such arrangements in the allied territories outside his empire, the agency of the Dūtas was needed. If so, the Dūtas had not only heralded religious mission but medical and humanitarian as well.

As for all these works of public utility within the empire, the edicts associate them with anusaṃyāna or quinquennial tours of inspection on the part of such high officials as the Rajjukas and the Prādeśikas (R.E. II, R.E. III). Buddhaghosa, too, connects them with anusaṃyāna on the part of a king.[2]

(i) **Imperial Secretariat** : This was the collective official agency, through which the imperial authority of Aśoka was exercised and the communication between the imperial and provincial governments was possible. It is not unlikely that the Arthaśāstra term Mahāmātrīya stood for the royal or imperial secretariat.

The imperial authority of Aśoka was issued in the form of śāsanas or orders. The Arthaśāstra (I. 10) applies the term śāsana exclusively

---

into parijvāni) or parijṛiṇi, and not from parijīrṇi, cf. jīryate, jṛiṇāti. Similarly the Sinhalese toṭe presupposes tṛirtha as a variant of tīrtha ; (3) there is no instance in Pali or Prakrit where tuṭṭha is a variant of tittha. As'oka's tuṭhāyatanāni is= tuṭṭhi + āyatanānī or tuṭṭhānaṃ āyatanāni.

[1] Majjhima, ii, p. 118 f., where we have mention of Isidatta and Purāṇa as two sthapatis in the service of king Pasenadi of Kosala.

[2] Barua, Inscriptions, ii, p. 248 f.

to the royal writs embodying and conveying the sovereign's command (rājājñā tu śāsanam). The śāsanas of Aśoka are met with in one of the following forms : (i) that of penal ordinances (Schism Pillar Edict) ; (ii) that of proclamations of piety (dhamma-sāvaṇa, M.R.E.) ; (iii) that of regulations of piety (dhamma-niyama, P.E. VII) ; (iv) that of instructions in piety (dhammānusathi) ; (v) that of official instructions and directions (Queen's Edict, Schism Pillar, Sārnāth) ; (vi) that of warning to the turbulent factors within the empire, such as the Aṭavis (R.E. XIII) ; (vii) that of the messages of good will to the 'frontagers' (S.R.E. II). The written form of a śāsana is called lipi or document (S.R.E. I, S.R.E. II, Schism Pillar, Sārnāth) ; When a śāsana was permanently incised on a rock or stone-pillar, it is said to have been caused to be written (lekhita, lekhāpita) in the sense of 'engraved' or 'incised'.[1] The Lipikara (M.R.E., Bra) was the scribe-engraver employed to incise a śāsana either on a rock or monolith. There must have been the Lipikaras also in the imperial secretariat to incise the śāsanas on portable materials for despatch to different destinations. Whether at this or the other end, the Lipikara of Aśoka did not fulfil the requirements of the Lekhaka of the Arthaśāstra. He was just a mechanical engraver of letters, while the latter was expected to be 'possessed of ministerial qualifications, acquainted with all kinds of customs, smart in composition, good in legible writing, and sharp in reading.[2] Chapaḍa the Lipikara employed at Isila to incise the three copies of M.R.E. was a person whose habitual script was Kharoshṭhī, and hence a dweller of Uttarāpatha. Thus the Lipikaras or mechanical scribe-engravers and copyists must have executed their work under the guidance of some officers in the imperial secretariat responsible for the codification of imperial orders or preparation of drafts and at the other end for editing them to suit local needs.

It appears from R.E. III that the Yuktas were the officers in the imperial secretariat expected to codify the orders under instructions from the Purushas (Secretaries) or the Council of Ministers (Parisā). These Purushas are represented in P.E. IV as those official agents who were intimately acquainted with Aśoka's real wishes as to how things should be done[3], and who were therefore required to intimate to the Rajjukas precisely the way in which they were to carry out duties to the king's satisfaction. They were, according to Hultzsch,

[1] Cf. Mookerji, Asoka, p. 55 ; also Pt. II, Ch. I.

[2] Arthaśāstra, II. 10.

[3] Chhaṃdaṃnāni, here the word chhanda meaning chikīrshā.

no other officers than the Gūḍhapurushas of the Arthaśāstra (1.10) denoting as they did the Secret Agents or Spies who were to be appointed by a king with the assistance of the Council of Ministers. They were, in other words, the Overseers of Megasthenes and other Classical writers to whom was assigned, precisely as to the Gūḍhapurushas, 'the duty of watching all that goes on, and making reports secretly to the king, some being 'entrusted with the inspection of the city, and others that of the army, the ablest and most trustworthy men being 'appointed to fill these offices.'[1] Such may have been the duty of Aśoka's Prativedakas (R.E. VI) and not necessarily that of the Purushas of R. E. III and P. E. IV. In P. E. VII, the Purushas are broadly distinguished from the Rajjukas as those who were placed over many people, while the latter are said to have been 'placed over many hundred thousands of beings'. It does not necessarily mean that the Purushas were the imperial officers under the Rajjukas. It would rather seem that as regards the imperial secretariat, the Purushas as Aśoka's Secretaries had many Yuktas to work under them.

The services of the Dūtas in the sense of Messengers or Conveyers of imperial orders must have been constantly in requisition to maintain the communication between the imperial and provincial governments. In the case of a proclamation of piety, some 256 copies of the imperial message were supplied to various administrative centres (M.R E.), which meant the employment of a messenger or missioner for the despatch of each copy thereof.

2. **Provincial Administration** : Certain amount of anomaly is apt to arise regarding the relation between the imperial and provincial governments from the fact that Aśoka was at the same time the administrative head of the province of Magadha and that of the empire of Jambudvīpa. It is, however, certain that the domain proper was divided into a number of provinces, divisions, districts and smaller administrative areas for the purpose of administration, each with its official headquarters. The term āhāra, as employed in Aśoka's inscriptions (Schism Pillar, Sārnāth), denoted the jurisdiction of a certain body of administrative heads. The village was un-

---

[1] McCrindle, Ancient India, p. 85. Arrian (*ibid.*, p. 217) calls them Superintendents, and says: "They spy out what goes on in country and town, and report everything to the king where the people have a king, and to the magistrates where the people are self-governed, and it is against use and wont, for these to give in a false report."

doubtedly the smallest unit of administration. In the inscriptions we have mention of just one village, namely, that of Lumbinī which was exempted from the payment of religious cess and granted the privilege of paying as revenue one-eighth of the total produce of land instead of one sixth.

(a) **General Administration** : To appreciate the Aśokan system of provincial administration, we may assume that like each province or division, even each district was placed in charge of a body of Mahāmātras. It is quite possible that in the case of the frontier provinces, divisions and districts, the Mahāmātras concerned were known as Anta-mahāmātras, and like the Antapālas of the Arthaśastra and the Pratyanta-Mahāmātras of the Atthasālinī, they were required to guard the frontiers and competent to deal with the 'frontagers' including the semi-independent tribal states. The Mahāmātras as administrative heads of the provinces or divisions passed as Rājavachanikas or Imperial Commissioners. Since the appointment and deputation of Viceroys as administrative heads of the four outlying provinces, the Imperial Commissioners at the provincial headquarters began to function as Mantri-mahāmātras.

We are not to think with Mookerji and others that the remoter provinces were placed under the Viceroys from the beginning. The Pali Chronicles definitely state that Aśoka was appointed the Viceroy of Avantī some eleven years before the death of Bindusāra, while the Divyāvadāna legends affirm that a prince was deputed to the province of Uttarāpatha only when an alarming report was received about the possibility of popular revolt against the government. The same fact is attested also by the inscriptions (S.R.E. I). The appointment of the Viceroys from among the sons of Aśoka and other princes of the blood must be assigned to the latter part of Aśoka's reign. It was when P.E. VII was promulgated in the 27th regnal year of Aśoka that his sons and other princes of the blood were grown up to make charities out of their own funds.

Bhandarkar (Aśoka, p. 54) puts the Viceroys of Aśoka in two categories : (1) those who wielded practically independent authority, and (2) those who wielded joint and limited authority subject to the control of the king himself. He argues his case thus :

"In the case of Ujjayinī and Takshaśilā, the Kumāras seem to have been regular viceroys with their power unfettered, but it was not so in the case of Tosali. Thus from Separate Kalinga Edicts it appears that although the Kumāras of Ujjayinī and Takshaśilā were to send on tour a Mahāmātra of their own every three years to make sure that there was no maladministration of justice, in the case of the Tosali Province, this Mahāmatra was to be deputed, not by the Tosali Kumāra, but by Aśoka himself. Secondly, in connection with the dispatch of such an officer, the Kumāras of Ujjayinī and Takshaśilā are mentioned by themselves and not associated with any state dignitaries, whereas in Separate Kalinga Edict II (Dh. version) where alone the Kumāra of Tosali is referred to; he is mentioned not by himself but associated with the Mahāmātras. Again, in regard to the latter Province we find that Aśoka issues admonitions or instructions to the Nagara-Vyavahārikas and others directly and not through the Kumāra-Mahāmātras."

This argument is apparently cogent and convincing. Its only weak point is that it proceeds on the questionable assumption that S.R.E.I was directly addressed to the City-judiciaries of Tosali and Samāpā when the Viceroy-in-Council remained in charge of the province of Kalinga. The evidence of S.R.E. I goes rather to prove that, previous to the appointment of the Viceroy for Kalinga, the province was under the direct rule of Aśoka himself. It states the circumstances under which Aśoka thought it expedient to depute a Rājavachanika Mahāmatra to the province for inspection and the prevention of the rule of tyranny and the miscarriage of justice. It must have been in the next stage that the province was placed in charge of a Viceroy-in-Council, while the administration of its southern division remained entrusted to the Rājavachanika Mahāmātras (S.R.E. II, J).

The argument that 'in connection with the dispatch of such an officer, the Kumāras of Ujjayinī and Takshaśilā are mentioned by themselves, and not associated with any state dignitaries' is not sufficient in itself to establish that they were practically independent rulers without the Mahāmātras attached to them. That would be against the general principle of the Aśokan[1] as well as the Maurya administration[2] which was against reposing the full trust in a single person and always thought it safe and wise to provide mutual checks. In incidental references to provincial affairs, such as those in S.R.E. I, the mention of the Viceroys concerned was enough without their association with the Mahāmātras. The argument would have been incontestable if it were based upon an independent

1 Barua, Inscriptions, ii, p. 288 f.

2 McCrindle, Ancient India, p. 86 f.; Arthaśāstra, III, 1; IV, 1.

document issued or forwarded on the sole authority of the Viceroy of Avantī or Uttarāpatha.

It is not acoordingly correct to say with Bhandarkar (op. cit., p. 55) that the Āryaputra and Mahāmātras stationed at Suvarṇagiri communicated 'certain orders of Aśoka to a Mahāmātra at Isila.' The preamble of the Mysore copies of M.R.E. definitely speaks of the Mahāmātras (in plural number) at Isila (Isilasi mahāmātā).

"Just as some provinces were ruled over by Kumāras, there must have been others which were governed by persons not related to the royal family." This poignant remark of Bhandarkar stands. The questionable part is its sequel where he observes : "It is true that no instance of such a provincial governor is known from Aśoka's inscriptions, but one such instance has been supplied by the celebrated Junāgaḍh inscription of Rudradāman. This epigraphic record tells us that the province of Surāshṭra or Kāṭhiāwār was governed by Vaiśya Pushyagupta in Chandragupta's time and by the Yavana king Tushāspha when Aśoka was king."[1]

The Rāshṭriya Pushyagupta, as I sought to show, was the mayor, business magnate and influential landlord of Girnār or Junāgaṛh, and Tushāspha came into power not when Aśoka was king but after the termination of his rule (Asokasya Mauryasyaṃte).

The Yuktas, the Rajjukas and the Prādeśikas were, according to R.E. III, the officers responsible for efficient administration in the provinces. I am inclined indeed to think that R.E. III's is a broad statement concerning the provincial administrators of Aśoka. To appreciate the Aśokan system of administration, it is necessary therefore to clear up the official position of these functionaries.

Yuktas : Figuratively they were 'the horses at work', the horses yoked to the royal chariot. Buddhaghosa defines the Rajayuttas or Rājāyuttas as 'royal officers carrying on the administrative duties in the districts'.[2] Mookerji treats Yukta as a general term for 'government employees' and cites the authority of the Arthaśāstra (II. 5) where the Yuktas, the Upayuktas, and their subordinates (tatpurushaḥ) are connected with all the department service (sarvādhikaraṇeshu).

---

[1] As'oka, p. 53.

[2] Manoratha-pūraṇī, Siamese Ed., II, p. 413 : Rājāyuttā ti rañño janapadesu kichchaṃ-saṃvidhāyakā āyuttaka-purisā. This definition applies well to the Ayukta purushas of the Gupta Age who figure, according to Raychaudhuri (op. cit., p. 265), 'as officers in charge of Vishayas or districts, and also as functionaries employed in restoring the wealth of conquered kings.'

Bhandarkar, on the contrary, observes (Aśoka, p. 57 f.) : "Kauṭilya speaks of both the Yuktas and their assistants the Upayuktas. Their duties, however, were of the same kind as described in two consecutive chapters, a careful reading of which leaves no (room for) doubt as to their being principally district treasury officers and had power to spend where expense was likely to lead to an increase of revenue. The verse quoted about the Yuktas by Dr. F. W. Thomas from the Mānava-dharmaśāstra confirms the Idea. For Manu says that lost property when recovered, should remain in charge of the Yuktas."

If the Yuktas of R.E. III be treated as all government employees, they become identical with Purushas of P.E. I, and Amātyas of the Arthaśāstra. But R.E. III does certainly accord to them a prominent official position, a fact which has led Mookerji to think that they probably represented the officers of gazetted ranks, although below those of the Rajjukas and the Prādeśikas. If we assume with Thomas and Bhandarkar that the Yuktas with their assistants principally figure in the Arthaśāstra (II. 5) as treasury-officers, the word 'treasury' must be taken in its much wider sense than that in which it is ordinarily understood ; it must be taken to mean the state funds and storehouses in the custody of all departments, income-earning or not. In R.E. III, they are connected with gaṇana or gaṇanā, a term, which Jayaswal took to be the Aśokan equivalent of Kauṭilya's gāṇanikya or Accounts department. But it has been found that the Aśokan words gaṇanā (R.E. III) and ganiyati (Queen's Edict) may be interpreted in the sense of 'codifying', 'recording', counting', 'labelling' or the like. The Yuktas may accordingly be connected with the Secretariat, whether imperial or provincial, as well as the district cutchery.

Rajjukas and Prādeśikas : The difficulty about the relative positions of the Yuktas, on the one hand, and the Rajjukas and Prādeśikas, on the other, arise from the fact that the statement concerning them varies in the available versions of R.E. III. According to the Girnār version, the Yuktas (Yutā, 1st case plural) are connected by the copulative conjunction *cha* ("and") with the Rajjukas and Prādeśikas (Rajuke Prādesike, 2nd case plural). With Mr. S. N. Mitra one may construe the Dhauli statement as meaning that the Rajjuka (Lajuke, 1st case sing.) and the Prādeśika (Prādesike, 1st case sing.) were just two main divisions of the Yuktas (1st case plural). Here the Rajjuka and the Prādeśika may also be treated as 2nd case singular. Except on the assumption that the Māgadhī form has occurred by mistake in the Girnār statement, Mookerji cannot take the Yuktas, the Rajjukas and the Prādeśikas to stand in an ascending order of official ranks. But the Rajjukas and Prādeśikas might also be counted among the Yuktas. In the Arthaśāstra (II. 6) rajju and chora-rajju are mentioned as two sources of revenue, and these imply two classes of subordinate officers, namely, the Rajjukas and the Chora-rajjukas, both under the Samāhartṛi or Collector General of Revenue. The Arthaśāstra (IV. 13) incidentally mentions one of the duties of the Chora-rajjuka,[1] which is analogous to that assigned by Manu to the Yukta. Figuratively the Rajjukas were the rein-holders of the royal chariot of administration, i.e., the Samāhartṛi of the Arthaśāstra, and the Prādeśikas were the watchers of enemies, or mischief-makers, i.e., the Pradeshṭṛis of Kauṭilya (Arthaśāstra, IV, 1). If so, the Yuktas as 'the horses at work' were to be controlled by the Rajjukas, and by implication, also by the Prādeśikas.

In the later prose version of the Kurudhamma Jātaka the Rajjuka is represented as a field-measurer or land-surveyor. This may naturally lead one to think that the rajju as a source of revenue was just the symbolical name for survey operations. But the Rajjukas as land-surveyors were officers under the Samāhartṛi of the Arthaśāstra. The Rajjukas do not appear in this capacity in the edicts of Aśoka. On the other hand, in P.E. VII, they are represented as the officials with ruling authority exercised over 'many hundred thousands of the populace.' The same statement occurs in a more elaborate form in P.E. IV. In it, Aśoka tells us that he had delegated his full royal authority to the Rajjukas and made them supreme heads of local administration. They are likened to expert nurses to whose sole care was entrusted the welfare of all the children, i.e., of subjects. In matters of the administration of justice and the maintenance of equitable transactions of human affairs they are made free agents so that they might initiate all necessary measures and proceedings on their own authority and responsibility with self-confidence and without any fear of interference. The Purushas intimately acquainted with Aśoka's desires as to how things should be done were the communicating agents between him and his Rajjukas. As regards criminal justice, they were the Supreme Judges in the sense that they were allowed to function as the final court of appeal, a position, which theretofore belonged

[1] The Chora-rajjuka is mentioned as an officer, who was 'to make good the loss by theft within his jurisdiction to traders who declared to him the value of their goods.'

to the emperor himself. Hence we may regard them as Governors or Imperial Commissioners directly responsible to the sovereign. Hence there is no cause of astonishment that communications from the capital were directly addressed to them with instructions for necessary action (M.R.E., Ye), or that, as suggested by Mr. S. N. Mitra, they were the same as the Rājavachanika Mahāmātras mentioned in S.R.E. I and S.R.E. II, The effective control of the collection and utilisation of revenue under various heads and through different departments which the Arthaśāstra relegates to the Samāhartṛi was the basic duty of the Rajjukas. It is interesting, therefore, to note that in the Dīpavaṃsa prince Priyadarśana as his father's Viceroy for Avantī is called karamolī, 'one charged to collect revenue.'

The Prādeśikas find mention only in R.E. III. Their designation must be derived from the word pradeśa, whatever its meaning. Taking it to mean a province, Mr. S. N. Mitra suggests that probably the Prādeśikas were the officials in the outlying provinces corresponding to the Rajjukas in the home provinces. But the word may mean a smaller administrative area under any jurisdiction. On the ground that the word pradeśa occurs in the Arthaśāstra in the sense of 'report', the Prādeśikas might be regarded as Reporters, but whether or not, on this ground they might be identified with the Pradeshṭṛis is still a disputed question. In the Amarakosha (X. 62), the word pradeśana is taken to mean 'presents (upahāra) due to the king.' Going by this, a Prādeśika might be regarded as an official who collected such presents, and this might be considered a connecting link between Aśoka's Prādeśika and Kauṭilya's Pradeshṭṛi. According to the Arthaśāstra (II. 35), "in those places which are under the jurisdiction of the gopa and sthānika, the commissioners (pradeshṭāraḥ) specially deputed by the collector general shall not only inspect the work done and means employed by the village and district officers, but also collect the special religious tax known as balī (balipragrahaṃ kuryuḥ)."

Thus indeed the connection may be established between the two, the Prādeśikas and the Pradeshṭṛis, the latter standing 'as intermediaries between the Samāhartṛi on the one hand and the Gopas, Sthānikas and Adhykshas[1] on the other". The main functions of

---

[1] Please note that in the Jātaka, III. p. 371, we have mention of itthāgārassa amachchā who were evidently the same functionaries as As'oka's ithijhakha-mahāmātā or Stryadhyakshas of the Great Epic. I am indebted to Mr. S. N. Mitra for this reference.

the Pradeshṭṛis 'consisted in the collection of taxes, administration of criminal justice, tracking of thieves, and controlling of the work of the superintendents and their subordinates' (adhyakshānam adhyaksha-purushānāṃ cha niyamanam). Accordingly the Prādeśikas may be regarded as subordinate functionaries under the Rajjukas, and the Yuktas controlled by them as the Adhyakshas with the Upayuktas and the rest as their subordinates.

In connection with the quinquennial anusaṃyāna or official tours of inspection to be undertaken by the Yuktas, the Rajjukas and the Prādeśikas, R E. III mentions certain pleasant duties to be done by them in addition to their usual administrative functions. These duties consisted in imparting instructions in the principles of piety and carrying out the public works of utility. By these extra-administrative duties they were to utilise the two additional months at the end of each yuga or period of five calendar years of the age, as well as to render assistance in the provinces to the Dharma-mahāmatras in the matter of furtherance of the duties specially assigned to them.

In S.R.E. I, the Rājavachanika Mahāmātras are required to undertake such tours every five years to prevent the miscarriage of justfce and high-handed actions along with their usual administrative duties and that in accordance with the emperor's instructions and under his command. Similar officials under the Viceroys of Uttarāpatha and Avantī are required to do the same at least every third year. Though one may not go so far with Mr. S. N. Mitra as to suggest that the Prādeśikas were the corresponding Rājavachanika Mahāmātras in the provinces under the Viceroys, it may be conceded that the Rajjukas were the Rājavachanikas.

The usual administrative duties assigned to the Rajjukas in P.E. IV and in the prose version of the Kurudhamma Jātaka cannot but remind us of the great officers of state (Agronomoi) who had the charge of the market. According to Strabo, they superintended the rivers, measured the land, as was done in Egypt, and inspected the sluices by which water was let out from the main canals into their branches so as to ensure an equal supply of it to all. They had the charge of the huntsmen and were entrusted with the power of rewarding or punishing them according to their deserts. They collected the taxes and superintended the occupation connected with land, as those of wood-cutters, the carpenters, the blacksmiths and the miners. They constructed roads and at every ten stadia[1] set up a pillar to indicate the by-roads and distances.[2]

Raychaudhuri (op. cit., p. 263) aptly observes that as far as the measurement of the land goes, these magistrates may be connected with the Rajjukas as represented in the Kurudhamma Jātaka, and that as regards the power of rewarding and punishing people, they have a point in common with the Rajjukas of Aśoka. If we look more closely into the matter, it cannot but appear that Strabo has simply sought to state the duties of various officers, the superintendents of various departments, as well as the Pradeshṭris which are detailed in the Arthaśāstra. The activities mentioned are all referable utlimately to the office of Kauṭilya's Samāhartṛi and *ex hypothesi*, to that of Aśoka's Rajjuka.

Thus indeed may be shown the executive side of all administrative affairs of a province for which either a Kumāra Viceroy or a Rajjuka as a Governor or Imperial Commissioner was held responsible to the Emperor.

(b) **Judicial Administration** : As for the administration of justice, a clear distinction is sought to be made in the Arthaśāstra between the cases to be tried by two kinds of tribunals : one for the trial of civil suits and certain quasi-criminal cases where fines only were to be imposed, and the other for the trial of criminal offences involving such severe punishments as arrest, imprisonment, mutilation of limbs, and death-sentence, and some quasi-civil cases. In the towns of the sangrahaṇa,[3] droṇamukha[4] and sthānīya[5] types and the places where the districts met, the first kind of tribunals was to be constituted of three Dharmasthas (jurists capable of interpreting the Sacred Law) and three Amātyas (judges capable of administering the king's Law, *i.e.*, the laws in force).[6] The second kind of tribunals was to be constituted of either three Pradeshṭṛis or three other Amātyas.[7] The Arthaśāstra does not, however, enlighten us clearly as to the

---

1 According to P.E. VII, at every half kos.

2 McCrindle, Ancient India, p. 86f.

3 The Sangrahaṇa type is defined in the Arthas'āstra (II, 1) as signifying a town with its jurisdiction over ten villages.

4 The Droṇamukha type is defined (Ibid, II. 1) as signifying a town in ihe midst of 400 villages.

5 The Sthānīya type signified a city in the midst of 800 villages.

6 Ibid., III. 1.

7 Ibid., IV. 2.

appellate jurisdiction of the first kind of tribunals over the second, and the proceedure to be followed in preferring and hearing appeals. It is simply by implication that the king represented the final court of appeal.[1]

The criminal offences mentioned in P.E. IV are those which involved arrest, imprisonment, and death-sentence as punishments,[2] and those which are relegated by Kauṭilya to the tribunals formed by three Pradeshṭris or three other competent Amātyas. It is, however, clearly stated in P.E. IV that in case of a death-sentence three days' respite was to be granted for having the judgement reviewed by the Raijukas as well as allowing the persons to die to be prepared for death in case the appeal failed. The Rajjukas became the final court of appeal since the delegation of the royal or imperial authority in this matter to them.

Going by Aśoka's statement, taken in its literal sense, we are to understand that the kinsmen (nātikā) of the convicts were the persons expected to make the judges reconsider their case for the sparing of life (jīvitāye tānaṃ). In Aśokan texts, the word nātikā may be taken not only to mean the relatives of a person, near or remote (P.E. IV, S.R.E. I) but also widely the kinsfolk, friends, associates, comrades and companions, even neighbours (R.E. III, R.E. IV, R.E. IX, R.E. XIII), in short, all persons who are interested in his welfare,—all active well-wishers. As a legal term, employed and interpreted in the Jātakas, the expression nijjhāpana means "convincing the judge of the innocence of the accused," and according to the gloss, "openly claiming one's innocence by producing witnesses and persuading the judge to believe it." But Mr. S. N. Mitra would cite three relevant texts from the Milinda to suggest that here, in Aśokan context, the term signifies not "revising the case, but interceding on behalf of the criminal not only with the king but also with the royal agents." He would go even further and contend for the interpretation of Aśoka's expression 'for the sparing of life' as implying rather 'the barest sparing af life and reduction of punishment than release." The main text quoted reads thus in its translation :—"Just as, O great king, a person powerful on the strength of his wealth, fame, prosperity and

---

[1] Cf. the Vajjian system of judicial administration as described by Buddhaghosa in his Sumangalavilāsinī, II, p. 519 ; Rhys Davids. Buddhist India, p. 22, B, C. Law, Some Kshatriya Tribes of Ancient India, p. 102f.

[2] Cf. R.E. V : McCrindle, Ancient India, p. 70.

people, causes a heavy punishment to be commuted on account of his (great) influence by way of intimate contacts in the case of a relative or friend who has received a heavy punishment from the king (*i.e.*, judge)." Whichever of the two be the more correct interpretation, the idea of interceding in its primary sense of 'pleading with a person for another' is there. In the Aśokan text, the nātikas were the typical persons expected to intercede or plead with the judges for a convict or convicts on whom the death sentence had been passed. Whether or not Aśoka actually thought of the bare or full sparing of life is more or less a matter of construction. Anyhow Aśoka's statement, as it is, does not preclude the idea of full sparing or total release. It is interesting to note that the Divyāvadāna legend preserves the tradition of Aśoka as abolishing capital punishment altogether, although it lacks corroboration from the edicts.[1]

As to the chance given to the unfortunate convicts to prepare for death and for better life in the next world, the interpretation of Aśoka's clause, niludhasi kālasi, signifying the time for observing the fast and giving gifts, has equally been open to dispute. "At the time of death," "when the time is over," "within the limited period," "when the time (of grace) has expired", "even in the time of their imprisonment," "in a closed dungeon," "when the time (of respite) has expired," and "though their hour of death is irrevocably fixed," are the various suggestions hitherto offered.[2] Although in Pali the word *niruddha* is also used in the sense of *mata* or dead, we may easily rule out the first of them, for here, as argued by Mr. S. N. Mitra, the clause stands for the time-which is *niruddha*, instead of the time of the *niruddha*. Fortunately, we now have two literary parallels to take us out of the wood. First we have the Pali idiom, *maggassa niruddhavelāyam*,[3] meaning "at the time when the road was closed to traffic."[3] Secondly, we have the Arthaśāstra idiom, niruddho deśakālābhyām,[4] to mean "when the payment of the subsidy is limited by place and time," "when it is made payable at the specified place and within the specified period of time." In both the instances we have the idea of a limited or fixed period of time.

Similarly, as to the interpretation of Aśoka's yote diṃne, here

---

1 Barua, Inscriptions, ii, p. 351 f.

2 Ibid, ii, p. 207.

3 Dhammapada-Commentary, III, p. 47.

4 Arthas'āstra, VII. 3.

taken to mean "respite given," there is no agreed opinion as yet. The proposed equation of Aśoka's yote with the Sk. yautuka, meaning legacy, is inappropriate. Mr. S. N. Mitra calls attention to the Sk. suhṛid-yuti (St. Petersburg Dict.) meaning "association or intercourse with friends". "This would have admirably suited the Aśokan context, but here *yuti* is a feminine word, while the Aśokan *yote* requires a neuter equivalent like the Pali yottaṃ, Sk. yoktram, meaning the rope", *i.e.*, a short limit ; 'the rope is given' is in accordance with the English idiom of 'giving one the rope', though here to save oneself.

In the same connection I am prepared to concede to Mr. S. N. Mitra that Aśoka's phrase, *ava ite* (Pali yāva ito), seen in the light of the Pali idiom yāva nābhito (up to the pivot, Jataka, IV, p. 149)' should be taken to mean 'up till now' instead of 'henceforth'.

The edicts of Aśoka do not enlighten us as to the actual forms in which the death sentence was executed. The Arthaśāstra broadly distinguishes between putting to death with torture (chitroghātaḥ, IV, II,) and putting to death without torture (vadhah, IV. 11). Beheading and drowning (apsu nimajjanam) may certainly and impaling doubtfully be mentioned as methods of execution without torture. The different forms of torture are listed in the Pali Nikāyas[1] and detailed in the Arthaśāstra. The offences that were punishable by death with or without torture have been carefully defined in the Arthaśāstra, and the reader may be referred to it for details.[2] The Pali texts mention robbery with violence as a typical offence which was punishable with different forms of death.[3] In R.E. XIII, Aśoka warns the aṭavis, meaning the predatory tribes or gangs of thieves with the forest as their hiding place,—warns with the words "Let them be judicious and not get killed" (avatrapeyu na haṃñeyasu), the extreme course of action taken in the Pali typical case.

(c) **Jail Administration :** The Arthaśāstra (IV. 9) not only speaks of the superintendent of jails as the officer placed in charge of prison but also prescribes certain specific rules for the guidance of jail administration. It distinguishes between the lock-up (chāraka) and the prison proper (bandhanāgāra). The rules prescribed provide that no obstruction should be caused to any prisoner in such of their daily avocations as sleeping, sitting, eating or easing nature. No person should be put in the lock-up without the declaration of the

---

1 Majjhima, I, p. 87 ; Anguttara, I, p. 47.

2 Arthas'āstra, IV. 11.

3 Dīgha, II, p. 82.

grounds of provocation. The prisoners should not be subjected to torture (parikleśa) or deprived of food and drink. They must not be beaten to death, unnecessarily harassed or molested. In the case of women, particular care must be taken to see that no rape was committed either in the lock-up or within the prison. The criminals condemned to death were put in the prison until execution.

Servitude, indebtedness and imprisonment were painted alike by Buddha as states of woe. A person would come out of them with a great sigh of relief. The philosophic opinion and the general law of the land were both in favour of granting relief to and releasiug persons suffering from them. The authoritative verses cited in the Arthaśāstra (II. 36) enjoin : "Once in a day, or once in five nights, jails may be emptied of prisoners in consideration of the work they have done or of whipping inflicted upon them, or of an adequate ransom paid by them in gold. Whenever a new country is conquered, when an heir-apparent is installed on the throne, or when a prince is born to the king, prisoners [should be] set free." The prose text of the Arthaśāstra (II. 36) enjoins : "On the days to which the birth-star of the king is assigned, as well as on full-moon days, such prisoners as are young, old, diseased or helpless (anātha), shall be let out from the jail (bandhanāgāra) : or those who are of charitable disposition or who have made any agreement with the prisoners may liberate them by paying an adequate ransom."

The Aśokan word for prison is simply bandhana. The triple purpose concerning the prisoners as stated in R.E.V is substantially the same as that behind the prescriptions and injunctions in the Arthaśāstra. Aśoka, too, shows much concern for making arrangements to provide the prisoners with money to pay the ransom, to protect them against coercion and oppression, and to see them released (paṭividhānāye, apalibodhāye, mokhāye cha), especially in the case of such prisoners as were minors or mere tools (ánubandhā)[1], or burdened with the maintanance of family (pajāva), or entitled to consideration by reason of their good conduct (kaṭābhikāle)[2], or aged (mahalake).

---

[1] This word stands in some versions separate from pajāva, and in others as the first member of the compound anubaṃdha-pajā, As a separate word, it stands for children as well as persons subservient to another person's will (mukhyānuyāyī, See Amarorkosha.

[2] If equated with kṛitābhichāraḥ, it must be taken to mean 'one who is bewitched'.

In S.R.E. I, Aśoka expresses his earnest desire that the city magistrates should always endeavour so that there may be no sudden restriction on man's liberty or sudden torture (akasmā palibodhe va akasmā palikilese va no siyā ti). "Well established is the rule", says he, "that if a single person suffers either arrest or torture, and there occurs on that account a sudden imprisonment (or death),[1] others, the blood relations and many people distantly related feel grieved." In P.E.V, Aśoka says that within the first twentyfive years of his reign he had effected twentyfive jail deliveries (baṃdhana-mokhāni kaṭāni), evidently once in one year. He does not tell us, however, on which particular occasion such jail deliveries were ordered. Obviously when he stated this fact, he kept a particular occasion in view, although we have no means of ascertaining what that occasion was. From the importance attached to the Tishya and Punarvasu days, the first, eighth, fourteenth and fifteenth days of the lunar half month, the first full-moon day in each of the three seasons, the first half month during the Indian Lent, as well as to other auspicious days in this edict, it may be inferred that the general rules which guided Aśoka's action were, more or less, the same as or similar to those met with in the Arthaśāstra. There is no reason to infer from either that ordinarily the whole prison or all prisons were emptied of all prisoners on any occasion.

3. **City Administration** : In R.E.V, Aśoka distinguishes his capital Pāṭaliputra from other towns that are described, according to their location, as outer (bāhira). Among these outer cities or towns, we have an incidental mention of Tosali and Samāpā situated in the province of Kalinga, Suvarṇagiri and Isila situated in the Southern province, Ujeni situated in the province of Avantī, Takasilā situated in the province of Uttarāpatha, and Kosambi situated in the home province of Vatsa. Pāṭaliputra served as the official headquarters of the imperial government, as also of the home province of Magadha. But nowhere in the inscriptions are the cities and towns classified according to their sizes and importance. The Arthaśāstra (II. 1)

---

1 The word baṃdhanaṃtika has exercised the brains of scholars. To Bhandarkar it means both imprisonment and death ; to Mookerji, death. One may prefer death ending the tie of the world, *i.e.*, *vadha* (cf. the literary trio—*bandhana, vadha, parikles'a*) but not renunciation, which is suggested by Mr. Manindra Mohan Basu and wide of the mark in the As'okan context. Hultzsch's interpretation "an order cancelling the imprisonment" does not explain why for that the relatives of the person should feel grieved.

classifies them broadly into four types called sthānīya, droṇamukha, kharvaṭika and sangrahaṇa.

The account given by Strabo of the city administration under the early Maurya regime is remarkable for perspicuity and clearness. It is not quite correct to say with Vincent Smith and others that this account differs materially from the Indian model of city administration as supplied in the Arthaśāstra (II. 36). Though the light shed on city administration by the Edicts of Aśoka is scanty, one cannot fail to observe that fundamentally it manifests the same traditional system to be in vogue.

According to Strabo, the officers, *i.e.*, City Magistrates, who had the charge of the city (evidently meaning the Maurya capital) were divided into six bodies or boards of five each. The first body looked after all things relating to industrial arts. The second body attended to the entertainment of foreigners. The third body kept records of births and deaths with a view not only to levying a tax but also in order that births and deaths, of both high and low, might not escape cognizance of government. The fourth body superintended trade and commerce with an eye to weights and measures so as to ensure that the products in their season were sold by public notice. The fifth body supervised manufactured articles which were sold by public notice. The sixth body used to collect the tenths of the prices of the articles sold. Such are the functions which these bodies separately discharged, while in their collective capacity they had charge both of their special departments and also of matters affecting the general interest, such as the keeping of public buildings in proper repair, the regulation of prices, the care of markets, harbours and temples.

Though the Arthaśāstra does not in such clear terms speak of the city administration being vested in six separate bodies or boards of five each functioning in their individual as well as collective capacity, it will be a misconstruction of the model given in the Arthaśāstra of the city administration to take it to mean that it was entrusted to a single officer called Nāgaraka. The Arthaśāstra envisages a system of city administration, which was modelled, upon the whole, on the administration of a distinct administrative unit (janapada) divided into four districts, each placed under a Sthānika with some Gopas under him. The Sthānikas with the Gopas as their subordinates were the four district officers under the Samāhartṛi or Collector general of Revenue. Thus in matters of revenue collection the Samāhartṛi may be said to have formed a Pañchāyat together with four Sthānikas. There must have been other Pañchāyats similarly constituted for the discharge of other administrative functions.

In the case of a city, which, too, was divided into four wards, there appear to have been four Sthānikas, each placed in charge of a ward,[1] with a number of Gopas as his assistants. In respect of the functions other than the collection of revenue, detailed in the Arthaśāstra as well as by Strabo, there were conceivably other officers to form different Pañchāyats with the Nāgaraka. Here one is to imagine that the city administrators were responsible for the proper discharge of their duties either to the king or to a Kumāra, or as the case might be, also to a Rajjuka. We have noticed that in the matter of judicial administration, the Arthaśāstra contemplates the existence of two kinds of tribunals, civil and criminal, one constituted of six judges, and the other of three magistrates. Let it not, however, be understood that I am holding brief for there being a complete agreement between the two accounts. Even as to there being a general agreement, the suggestion is merely a tentative one.

In S.R.E. I, Tosali and Samapā are spoken of as two cities, each of which was placed in charge of the City Magistrates called Nagara-vyavahārikas or Nāgaraka Mahāmātras. Thus the administration of neither was entrusted to a single officer. The city administrators were many, although from this edict it does not appear whether they had formed a single judiciary, a single body or board or more than one. In both the versions, the city administrators are addressed to in their collective capacity, no matter whether they had belonged to one body or to six.

The Arthaśāstra speaks of the Paura-vyavahārika and the Nāgaraka without connecting them. The emolument allowed (V. 3) to the Paura-vyavahārika is equal to that meant for a prince (kumāra). Shama Sastri treats Paura and Vyavahārika as two separate designations, and take the first to signify 'the officer in charge of the town' and the second to mean 'the superintendent of law or commerce'. This is not borne out by the text where Paura-vyavahārika is employed in a singular and not in a dual form. The Aśokan use of the designation Nāgaraka as a variant of Nagara-vyavahārika sets at rest all doubts as to Paura-vyavahārika being the same designation as

---

[1] From the extant text of the Arthas'āstra it rather appears as if one Sthānika was in charge of the four wards, which would be meaningless when judged from the general tenour of the Arthas'āstra scheme.

Nāgaraka. To be more precise, the Vyavahārika is a general designation, while the designation of Paura-vyavahārika is applicable only to a Nāgaraka in charge of the capital city.

In S.R.E. I, Aśoka reprimands the Nāgarakas for certain high-handed and rash actions on their part, sudden arrest, coercion and imprisonment, and takes steps to stop them. According to the Arthaśāstra (IV. 6), it was one of the main duties of a Nāgaraka to try to detect internal thieves inside a fortified town, while the duty of a Pradeshṭṛi consisted in detecting and bringing to book external thieves with the aid of the Sthānikas and Gopas. The designation of Vyavahārika does not necessarily imply that the duties of the Nāgaraka Mahāmātras were confined to those of Presidency and Police Magistrates; presumably the duties assigned to them embraced all administrative affairs of a city, including municipal. Thus they were not, except in their collective capacity, members of a single judiciary or magistracy.

6. **Frontier Administration** : The Arthaśāstra (II. 1) enjoins that forts should be constructed in the extremities of a territory and manned by the Antapālas or Wardens of the Marches whose main duty consisted in guarding the entrances into the kingdom, while the interior of the kingdom was to be watched by trap-keepers (vāgurika), archers (śabara), hunters (pulinda), chaṇḍālas and wild tribes (araṇyachara). The emolument allowed to an Antapāla (Ibid., V. 3) is equal to that of a prince, or to a member of the Council of Ministers, or a Paura-vyavahārika.

Aśoka in his P.E. I, speaks of the Anta-mahāmātras and insists on their following the general principles of administration as set out by him, namely, 'protection by piety, provision by piety, pleasing by piety, and guarding by piety'. The phrase 'so also the Anta-mahāmātras' (hemeva aṃta mahāmātā) indicates that they had their special jurisdiction over the frontier districts, and were the Wardens of the Marches like the Antapālas of the Arthaśāstra or the Pratyanta Mahāmātras of the Atthasālinī. It is also not unlikely that they represented alike those Mahāmātras who, like the Mahāmātras of Tosali and Samāpā, were competent to deal with the Antas or unconquered borderers.

7. **Forest Administration** : The Arthaśāstra (II. 2) broadly distinguishes between the reserve forests and the wild tracts (aṭavis). The former are again subdivided into game forests, elephant forests (hastivana), and forests for their own produce. The latter denote

such forest regions as are inhabited by predatory tribes or used as hiding places by thieves and plunderers. Of the game forests, some were to be specially reserved for the king's sports and others for people. The elephant forests were to be formed in out-of-the-way places and separated from the wild tracts. The Superintendent of elephant forests (Hastivanādhyaksha) was to maintain them with the assistance of forest guards, those who rear elephants, those who enchain the legs of elephants, those who guard the boundaries, and those who dwell in forests. The Arthaśāstra speaks also of the duties assignable to the Superintendent of forest produce (II. 17).

Evidently the main duty of the Aṭavīpālas (Pali Aṭavirakkhikas)[1] was to protect the royal territory against the depredations caused by the predatory tribes or gangs of thieves. According to the consensus of opinion, "robbers are ever bent on carrying off women at night, make assaults on persons, and take away hundreds and thousands of paṇas, whereas wild tribes, living under a leader and moving in the neighbouring forests, can be seen here and there causing destruction only to a part.' As Kauṭilya maintains (Arthaśāstra, VIII. 4), "robbers carry off the property of the careless, and can be put down as they are easily recognized, and caught hold of, whereas wild tribes have their own strongholds, being numerous and brave, ready to fight in broad day-light, and seizing and destroying countries like kings." The Mahājanaka Jātaka holds before us a vivid picture of the menace caused by the aṭaviyo to a kingdom, which is not well-guarded against them.[2]

The duties assigned to the Aṭavīpālas (Protectors of Wild tracts), the Śūnyapālas (Protectors of No man's lands), and the Vivītādhyakshas (Superintendents of barren tracts) were all allied, tending to implement the work of the Antapālas and Durgapālas. The nature of the task entrusted to an Aṭavīpāla may be realised from the following description in the Arthaśāstra (II. 34) of the duty of the Superintendent of a barren tract : "Hunters with their hounds shall reconnoitre forests. At the approach of thieves or enemies, they shall so hide themselves by ascending trees or mountains as to escape from the thieves, and blow conch-shells or beat drums......It shall be his main duty to protect timber and elephant forests, to keep roads in good repair, to arrest thieves, to secure the safety of mercantile traffic, to protect cows, and to conduct the transaction of the people."

---

1. Jātaka, VI, P. 335.
2. Ibid, VI, P. 55.

Aśoka in his R.E. VIII, speaks of hunting as a royal pastime, which presupposes the existence and maintenance of game-forests specially reserved for the purpose. Similarly we have mention in P.E. V of the elephant-forests (nāgavanā) which were used also as hunting grounds by the people. For their maintenance there must have been competent officers with their various assistants. The reference to the Aṭavis in R.E. XIII is a clear indication of the fact that they were a cause of mischief and trouble to Aśoka's dominions, and in the circumstances it is natural to suppose that there were competent officers appointed to effectively deal with them.

CHAPTER VI

PERSONAL LIFE AND PUBLIC LIFE

Aśoka the man is inseparable from Aśoka the king, and our discussion has now reached a point where we may conveniently examine how far one is consistent with the other. This certainly involves an inquiry into the precise bearing of Aśoka's personal life on his kingly career. From the etymological point of view, a rājā is either one who shines forth by his personal glory' (rājate) or 'one who pleases his subjects' (prajān rañjayati).[1] These very definitions of a rājā lead us to consider the two aspects of Aśoka's life, private and public.

1. **Aśoka the man :** In Aśoka's case the man is far greater than the king, and yet the greatness of the man depended largely on the greatness of his position as king. It was through the latter that the former got the scope for vigorous work, satisfactory development, full play and leaving an indelible impress on man's history and civilization. We know nothing of the man from the available records before he became the king. The information supplied by the extant legends about the earlier life of Aśoka the man is either insufficient or misleading. Our concern, therefore, is really with the king, either the king as a man or the king as a ruler.

The Arthaśāstra (VI. 1) mentions certain special qualities of the king as a man by which may be tested his fitness as a ruler. These are broadly classified under four heads as being the qualities of an attractive nature (ābhigamika-guṇā), as those of understanding (prajñā-guṇā), as those of enthusiasm (utsāha-guṇā), and as those of self-possession (ātmasampat).

Such qualities are in different ways emphasized also in the Rājadharma section of the Mahābhārata and throughout the Pali Jātakas and the two Sanskrit Epics. But for a systematic comprehension of the significance of Aśoka's personal as well as public life we may better proceed in the light of the Pali Cakkavatti-sīhanāda, Lakkhaṇa and Singālovāda Suttas, and in that of the Arthaśāstra. These authorities lead us to judge the fitness of Aśoka the man to occupy the enviable position of Aśoka the king by the application of such tests as those by the nobility of birth, physical form and

---

[1] Cf. pakatiyo raṃjayati in the Hātigumphā inscription of Khāravela.

personality, education and association, the refinement of manners and sense of dignity, intellectual faculties, the strength of will, idealism and human feelings, moral traits of character, and religious faith.

(a) **Nobility of birth** : The Arthaśāstra (VI. I) expects the king as a man to be 'born of a very high family' (mahākulīnaḥ). In the Pali Nikāyas all persons entitled to greatness are expected to be 'well-born on both sides, maternal and paternal' (ubhato sujāto, mātito cha pitito cha). In the Hāthigumphā inscription the court-panegyrist represents king Khāravela as the increaser of the fame of the Chedi royal House, and as 'one who issued from the family and line of royal sages'[1]. Thus the nobility of birth or family tradition is considered an indispensable condition of man's rise in life. That the high social status or noble lineage is an important contributory factor to man's easy recognition in society is undoubted. But whether or not this is an indispensable or necessary condition of man's rise into power or eminence is still a disputed question in history.

The inscriptions of Aśoka throw no light on his parentage and pedigree. It is the Junāgarh inscription of Rudradāman and literary traditions that connect him with the Maurya family and represent him as a descendant of Chandragupta Maurya. In the latter, he is represented also as the son and successor of Bindusāra. As for his mother, the Buddhist tradition in the Divyāvadāna speaks of her as being the daughter of a Brāhman of Champā, while that in the Mahāvaṃsa-ṭīkā, she is described as a khattiyā or princess. The only interesting fact the two traditions elicit alike is that she had for her religious preceptor an Ājīvika who solemnly predicted her son's succession to the throne of Magadha. The fact of dedication of four caves by Aśoka to the Ājīvikas may be taken to suggest that he had for some reason or other a soft corner for them. Aśoka, however, does not base his claims to greatness on the ground of birth or lineage ; he stands in this matter on his own rights.

His birth in the Maurya royal House was nevertheless a notable factor ; it enabled him to aspire for the throne of Magadha and to be the inheritor of the Maurya sovereignty and system of government. It was no mean privilege to him to have a grandfather like Chandragupta Maurya who by his prowess and strategy liberated the country from foreign thraldom, and who by his strong hand was able to found a stable form of government over an extensive empire with its distant political relations. The blood-connection of the Mauryas

---

1 Or, 'from the family of the royal seer Vasu'.

with the Nandas, their immediate predecessors, is shrouded in mystery. But whatever the actual origin of Chandragupta Maurya, none can doubt the true Kshatriya spirit of himself and of his line. At all events, Aśoka was a scion of the powerful Kshatriya family founded by Chandragupta, and through this connection he was able to feel that he had behind him the noble tradition of a long line of former kings. He was sincerely proud of this glorious lineage rather than his descent from the mere Maurya clan (P.E. VII). Such indeed is the way of thinking of all truly great men of history led by the spirit of progress, whether they be Buddhas or Tīrthankaras, Sages or Prophets, kings or emperors.

(b) **Physical form and personality** : The perfection of bodily form which goes into the make-up of kingly personality is regarded as another contributory factor. The ugly face with grim looks such as that of an owl is held as a positive disqualification.[1] The Brāhmans of India developed a popular science by the name of Mahāpurusha-lakshaṇam or 'Characteristic bodily marks of a great man', and the Jainas and Buddhists availed themselves of it in establishing the personal greatness of Mahāvīra[2] and Buddha[3] respectively. The Buddhist came to speak of the thirty-two major bodily marks and eighty minor characteristics. They were persuaded to believe along with the Brāhman interpreters of the signs that a person endowed with these marks and characteristics is destined to become a righteous king overlord, if he remains in the world, or in the alternative, a perfect type of Buddha, if he renounces the world.[4]

The inscriptions of Aśoka have, however, nothing to say about his complexion and other details of his bodily form. In the Divyāvadāna and other Sanskrit legends he is described as an ugly person with a repulsive appearance. This delineation was due, as I sought to show, to confusion made between Aśoka the Pious and Aśoka the Blackie. The brightness and majesty of bodily form may shed lustre on man's personality but is not to be wholly identified with it. Buddha truly said to his disciple Vakkali, "What's the use looking at this rotten body! He who sees the doctrine, sees me, and he who sees me, sees

---

1 Cf. Ulūka Jātaka, No. 270.
2 Aupapātika Sūtra, Sec. 16.
3 Lakkhaṇa Suttanta in Dīgha III.
4 Dīgha, III, p. 142,

the doctrine."[1] A great man is indeed a great mind, which conceives and cherishes a grand ideal. It is precisely in this light that one should evaluate the greatness of Aśoka the man as well as of Aśoka the king.

(c) **Education and association** : The Arthaśāstra (VI. 1) expects the aspirant for kingship to be 'endowed with intelligence (buddhisampannaḥ), possessed of intellect, talent, strong memory and keen mind (prajñā-pragalbha-smṛiti-mati), trained in all sciences and arts (kṛitaśilpaḥ), and waiting upon the wise men of great experience (vṛiddhadarśī). In the chapter on vṛiddha-saṃyoga (I. 5), the same text enjoins that a prince shall study the sciences and arts and strictly obey the discipline and rules imposed by them under the authority of his teacher. Having undergone the ceremony of tonsure, he shall learn the alphabet (lipī) and arithmetic (saṃkhyāna), and after investiture with sacred thread, he shall study Vedic system (Trayī), and speculative philosophies (Ānvīkshakī) under the teachers of acknowledged authority (śishṭebhyaḥ), the science of wealth (Vārtā) under the government superintendents (adhyakshebhyah), and the science of government (Daṇḍanīti) under the theoretical as well as practical politicians (vaktṛi-prayoktṛibhyah). To increase his efficiency in learning he shall ever keep up his contact with the experienced professors of sciences (vidyāvṛiddha-saṃyogah).

In the Lakkhaṇa Suttanta, a righteous king overlord is expected to be a man of great wisdom, unsurpassed by others in the matter of knowledge (mahāpañño, nāssa kochi paññāya sadiso), which is the ripe result of his waiting upon the eminent religious teachers with eagerness to learn from them the things that are conducive to human good. In the Singālovāda Suttanta, every man as a learner is required to serve well his teachers (āchariyā) by properly receiving the knowledge of the sciences and arts from them (sakkachchaṃ sippa-paṭiggahaṇena).

In the case of king Khāravela, it is claimed in the Hāthigumphā inscription that while a prince, he had learnt the rules of writing, currency, accountancy, and law (lekha-rūpa-gaṇanā-vavahāra-vidhi-visārada) and become a master of sciences and arts (savavijāvadāta).

We need not dwell here at length on the education of Indian

---

[1] Saṃyutta, III, p. 120 : Alaṃ Vakkali kin te iminā pūtikāyena diṭṭhena ? Yo kho Vakkali dhammaṃ passati so maṃ passati, yo maṃ passati so dhammaṃ passati.

princes, sufficient information about which may be gathered from the later praśastis and literary works of all schools of thought. It may suffice for our immediate purpose to observe that the inscriptions of Aśoka indirectly throw some lights on his education and association. That he was familiar with the two main alphabets then prevalent in India, namely, Brāhmī and Kharoshṭhī, is evident not only from the instructions issued as to the places where and the materials on which his inscriptions were to be incised, but also from the fact that he was aware of the errors committed by his scribes (R.E. XIV). His acquaintance with different local dialects and command over language is borne out by the inscriptions written obviously to his dictation. His long stay in Western India and occasional mission to North Western India must have enabled him to be acquainted with the dialects of those places. From the forms of his inscriptions, it may be easily inferred that he was an adept also in the rules of royal writs.

The inscriptions bear ample evidence to his sound knowledge of the principles of government. These bear a clear testimony also to his first-hand knowledge of the sacred texts and religious views of different sects (R.E. XII). R.E. XII goes to prove that he personally met from time to time the exponents of different faiths and discussed various problems with them. In P.E. VI, he has laid due stress on the importance of going personally to wait upon the representatives of all sects. Waiting upon men of experience and wisdom (thairanāṃ dasane, vudhānaṃ dasane) for instructions and discussions looms large in R.E. VIII. In R.E. XII, he figures as a great lover of learning, healthy discussions and helpful debates.

(d) **Refinement and dignity :** A person entitled to kingship is expected in the Arthaśāstra (VI. 1) to be 'possessed of dignity (hrīmān), making jokes with no loss of dignity or restraint, never brow-beating and casting haughty and stern looks' (saṃvṛitadīnābhi-hāsyajihma-bhrūkuṭīkshaṇah), capable of 'talking to others cheerfully with a smiling face' (śakya-smitodagrābhibhāshī), and observing the rules of behaviour as laid down by the learned (vṛiddhopadeśacharah). In Buddha's opinion, these are the qualities that go to make 'a man of graceful mien, felicitated by many' (piyadassano, bahunnam piyāyito), the reliever of the sorrow of many (bahunnaṃ sokanāsano)[1].

---

[1] Lakkhaṇa Suttanta, Digha, III, p. 168f.

Aśoka in his P.E. I, speaks of the very best kind of fear (aga bhaya), the fear of public opinion, while in R.E. XIII he insists on feeling ashamed of one's mischievous action (avatrapeyu). The open expression of regret or repentance (anutāpa, anusochanā) was certainly the outcome of a prick of conscience (R.E. XIII). The epithet Tīvala mātā applied to his second queen (Queen's Edict) is to be regarded as a respectful way of referring to one's wife after she has become a mother[1]. In addressing the Sangha (Bhābru), he is most careful to follow the established social convention. The observance of the same rule of courtesy on the part of his high officers is demanded in M.R.E. (Bra). He highly prized gentle speech, cool temper and winsome cordiality (S.R.E. I). The principle of toleration as propounded by him (R.E. XII), eloquently speaks of his refined manners, self-respect and respect for others' feelings. Seemly behaviour (samyapaṭipati) towards all was with him the guiding principle of dealings with men. It is in connexion with Aśoka the king that one may see better how well he deserved the two titles of Priyadarśin and Aśoka.

(e) **Intellectual faculties :** The Arthaśāstra (VI. 1) mentions intelligence, understanding, talent, sharp memory and keen mind as the typical intellectual faculties with which the king as a man may be expected to be endowed. The personal qualities that are helpful to the acquisition of knowledge (prajñā-guṇā) consist of respectful attention, hearing, grasping, retention in memory, knowing, reasoning, drawing the conclusion, and adherence to the truth arrived at (suśrūshā-śravaṇa-grahaṇa-dhāraṇa-vijñāna-uha-apoha-tattvābhiniveśāh).[2] The first of these implies four things in Buddha's language, namely, paying due respect to the teacher (uṭṭhāna), going to meet (pachchupagamana), regular waiting upon the teacher for lessons (upaṭṭhāna), and personal services (pārichariyā), while his term sussūsâ stands for attentive hearing (saddahita-savaṇaṃ). The rest of the approved modes are comprehended by Buddha's expression 'the proper way of learning the sciences and arts' (sakkachchaṃ sippa-paṭiggahaṇaṃ).[3] These ideas about the approved modes of learning are comprehended by the three words—sevā (waiting upon the learned men of experience), praṇipāta (homage), and paripṛichchhā (discussion). Buddha speaks of the three kinds of knowledge, namely, sutamayā

---

1 Cf. Pali Rāhula-mātā, Nakula-mātā.

2 Arthas'āstra, I. 5 ; VI, 1.

3 Singālovāda Suttanta, Dīgha, III, p. 189 ; Sumangalavilāsinī, III, p. 991.

paññā, chintāmayā paññā and bhāvanāmayā paññā,[1] that develop from the pursuit of the three modes which, in the language of the Upanishads, are śravaṇa (hearing), manana (thinking), and nididhyāsana (meditation). Knowing the true nature of things (pajānanā), preliminary inquiry (vichaya), thorough enquiry (pavicaya), investigation into the nature of truths (dhammavicaya), definition by general characteristics (sallakkhaṇā), definition by special characteristics (pachchupalakkhaṇā) thinking (chintā), and closer examination (upaparikkhā) are, according to Buddha, the various modes of understanding by which intellctual faculties may be exercised.

In many of his edicts Aśoka stresses the need of respectful attention to teachers, learned men of experience, elders and high personages (gurususrūshā, thaira-susrūsā, vudha-susrūsā, agabhuti-susrūshā (R. E. IV, R. E. XIII). He pleads for due reverence to the teachers (gurunaṃ apachiti, apachāyanā āchariyasa, R. E. IX, M. R. E., Ye). He equally lays emphasis on waiting on the wise men of experience for instruction and discussion (anusasṭi cha paripuchhā, R. E. VIII). In the Bhābru Edict he recommends the constant hearing (study) and remembrance of certain sacred texts with the comprehension of their meaning (abhikhinaṃ suneyu upadhāleyu). Here his expression abhikhinaṃ suneyu corresponds with abhikshṇya-śravaṇam in the Arthaśastra (I. 5). In P. E. I, he speaks of the very best kind of examination (agā palīkhā). He is argumentative throughout and his main method of convincing others is nijhati (Pali nijjhatti), i. e., appeal to reason (P. E. VII). His instruction to the Yuktas is to set forth the reason or argument in the document meant for publication (hetuto, R. E. III). The notable example of his argument may be cited from R. E. IX (K, Sh, M): "The rite of piety lies open to doubt —that the desired object may be fulfilled, but that may not be of any effect in this world. This is not (however) restricted to time. Even if the object be not fulfilled here, it produces unbounded merit hereafter. If the object be fulfilled here, then both the interests are secured—he (attains) the objects here and produces unbounded merit hereafter by the rite of piety." Preambles of R. E. XIII and P. E. V contain clear proofs of his power of reflection. In S. R. E. I and S. R. E. II his strong conviction in matter of human good is said to have been based on his own perception (aṃ kichhi dakhāmi).

---

[1] Dīgha, III, p. 219. Cf. Nettitpakaraṇa, p. 8.

(f) **Strength of will** : The Arthaśāstra (VI. 1) demands of a person qualified for kingship that he should be 'highly enthusiastic, not addicted to procrastination' (mahotsāhaḥ adīrghasūtrah) and 'of resolute mind' (dṛiḍhabuddhih). Valour (śauryam), readiness (amarshah), quickness (śīghratā) and dexterity (dākshyatā) are spoken of as the volitional factors that go to constitute enthusiasm (utsāha-guṇā). Buddha mentions energy (viriya), energetic action (viriyā-rambha), promptness (nikkama), strenuous exertion (parakkama), effort (uyyama), purposive activity (vāyāma), zeal (ussāha), enthusiasm (ussolhi), stamina (thāma), and endurance (dhiti) as the mental factors that represent the strength of the will[1].

These are the main personal qualities and principles of action on which Aśoka has harped in his edicts. The resoluteness of his mind has found its classical expression in the following statement : "I myself instructing you and making my wishes known until my fortitude and promise remain unshaken, will be a server of the land" (S.R.E. II). Parākrama (R E.II), pakama (M.R.E.) uyāma (R.E. XIII), usāha (P.E.I) and uṭhāna (R.E. VI) are the key-words of Aśoka's life as well as his government.

(g) **Idealism and human feelings** : The Arthaśāstra (VI. 1) demands, among other qualities, that the king as a man should have large aims' (sthūlalakshah). Large-heartedness goes together with man's true idealism, while human feelings and tender emotions are just the outcome of a large heart a man develops within himself. Admittedly the largest aim of man's life is 'doing good to the whole world' (sarva-loka-hita), and this was precisely the real aim of Aśoka's life (R.E. VI). The world, as we saw, was extended not only beyond the confines of his empire but also beyond those of the allied territories (R.E. XIII). It included also the animals as its denizens. He aspired by all possible means to be a servant of the land (desa-āyutike, S.R.E. II). All his earnest efforts were to be directed towards the elevation of man's nature and moral state (P.E. VII). These were to be equally directed towards the alleviation of human and animal sufferings (R.E. II, R.E.V, R.E. VIII, P.E. II, P.E.V, P.E. VII). He is just human when he expresses his natural affection for his wives and sons, brothers and sisters, other princes of the blood, other kith and kin, as also for his neighbours (R.E. V, Queen's Edict, P.E. VI, P.E. VII), or when he pleads for respectful attention to parents, teachers, elders and high personages, and seemly behaviour

---

[1] Dhammasangaṇi ; Atthasālinī, p. 146.

to slaves and servants, the aged and the helpless, the oppressed and the fallen.

(h) **Moral traits of character** : The Arthaśāstra (VI. 1) enjoins that the king as a man should be 'virtuous, truthful, not of a contradictory nature, grateful, and free from passion, anger, greed, obstinacy, fickleness, haste and backbiting habits'. In the Sarabhanga Jātaka (No. 522) and the Great Epic (XII. 65.39, 67.46, 67.57), he is expected to be grateful, wise, largehearted, of charitable disposition, and of firm devotion. Buddha lays stress, in the very language of the Arthaśāstra, on truthfulness and self consistency.[1]

Aśoka himself speaks of restraint, the purity of heart, gratefulness, and firm devotion as the four moral qualities that enhance the value of charity (R.E. VII). Pity, liberality, truthfulness, purity, gentleness and goodness are with him the fundamental principles of piety and human conduct (P.E. II, P.E. VII). Non-harming and friendly is his mental attitude towards the whole of life (R E. IV, P.E. II, P.E. V, M.R.E.). Sanity and sincerity characterise his thoughts, words and actions. Well-balanced is his mind. He shows throughout the courage of conviction and displays moral courage in stating his own ideas about persons and things.

(i) **Religious faith** : A man is known by the religion he professes. Aśoka's religion was Buddhism. Here Buddhism is taken to be a religion in the sense of a form of Doctrine and Discipline (Dhamma-Vinaya) which not only holds before us the higher ideals of life but also cherishes faith in their reality.

There is a substantial agreement, as we saw, between the Pali tradition and Aśoka's own statement regarding his conversion to Buddhism. It is not very material whether the Mysore copies of M.R.E. speak of a period of about three years and the remaining versions of that of four. Since he had become an upāsaka, meaning a lay worshipper inclined towards religion, he did not exert himself strenuously until he met the Sangha or the entire congregation of monks available at his capital (saṃghe upayāte). The evidence of the Dīpavaṃsa is decisive as to the meaning of the expression saṃghe upayāte. That he had not assumed monastic vows is certain from Aśoka's own statement, the account having been given of his life as an upāsaka (aṃ upāsake sumi). His conversion to the Buddhist faith is to be

[1] Digha, III, p. 171 : sachchapaṭiñño advejjha-vācho. Arthas'āstra, VI-I : satyavāg-avisaṃvādakaḥ.

dated from the time he approached or came in contact with the Sangha. I abandon my old position[1] that here Aśoka distinguishes between the two stages of his career as a Buddhist lay worshipper, the first when 'he had been only privately cultivating the company and receiving the instruction of an individual Buddhist teacher', and the second 'when he publicly declared himself to be a follower of the Sangha and entered upon a career of direct service to the Sangha.' As I now maintain, the intended distinction is between the earlier stage when he had adhered to other sects and the later stage when he began to follow the guidance of the Buddhist Sangha in matters of religious faith.

The bhikkhugatika theory started by Charan Das Chatterji has found its supporters in Bhandarkar and Mookerji. But Chatterji himself is not sure about it. Buddhaghosa understands by a bhikkhugatika "a person that dwells in the same vihāra with the bhikkhus". This does not necessarily mean that the condition of a Bhikkhugatika is intermediate between an Upāsaka and the Bhikkhu[2]. About the reading of the word, too, one cannot be sure, its variant in some of the manuscripts being *bhikkhussa bhatika* (one who is of service to a Bhikkhu), which is more appropriate to the Vinaya context.

Whether in the Bhābru, or in the Schism Pillar Edict, or in the Lumbinī Pillar Inscription, Aśoka figures as a king and a lay worshipper of Buddha. There is nowhere the slightest suggestion as to his withdrawal from the world[3].

The question is often raised if the Buddhist faith of Aśoka is conclusively proved by his inscriptions. I say, yes. Even apart from the evidence of M.R.E. where he distinctly refers to his coming in contact with the Sangha, we find that in the Bhābru Edict he addresses the Sangha in the most respectful terms, showing the usual courtesy due from a Buddhist upāsaka to the Sangha. In the Barābar Hill-cave inscriptions the Ājīvikas who were the donees of the caves are simply introduced as Ājīvikas, while in the Nāgārjunī Hill-cave inscriptions of Daśaratha, the epithet Bhadaṃta is prefixed to their name.

---

[1] This is upheld by Mookerji. See his Asoka, p. 24.

[2] Ibid, p. 23.

[3] If As'oka had turned a monk in his retired life, we are not concerned with that here.

In the same Bhābru Edict, like a devout Buddhist, he professes his profound faith in the Three Jewels and firmly believes that 'all that is said by the Blessed One is well said'. Here, moreover, he expresses his sincere solicitude for the long endurance of the Good Faith, and to that noble end in view he selects seven Buddhist texts and commends them confidently to the monks, nuns and laity for their constant study and remembrance.

He is not known to have gone on pilgrimage to places other than those sacred in the Buddhist eye, e.g., Bodhgayā (Saṃbodhi), the holy spot of Buddha's Enlightenment, Lumbinī, the place of Buddha's Nativity, and the Stūpa of Koṇāgamana, the shrine erected in honour of a former Buddha. Going to pay homage to the Sangha (Sangha-dassanaṃ, M.R.E.), the Bo-tree (Bodhidassanaṃ, R.E. VIII), and the Shrine (Chetiya-dassanaṃ, Nigāli Sāgar) on his part was the pious act of a Buddhist upāsaka for his growth in piety (dhammavuḍḍhi)[1].

In the Schism Pillar Edict he rejoices to state that he had made the Sangha united for all times to come.

The anuposatha (P.E. V, Sārnāth Pillar) as a special day set apart for the Buddhist laity to attend religious service at a local vihāra, taken in this technical sense, i.e., meaning the eighth day of a lunar half-month, is not a negligible proof of Aśoka's Buddhist faith. The quotation in R.E. IX (G. Dh) of a dictum[2] from the Sādhu Sutta[3] for comment is highly important as an additional proof.

Aśoka was not, however, an ordinary convert. As he expressly tells us in his R.E. XIII, he had the first religious vision of truth, good, and duty as a happy result of his own reflections on the after-effects of his aggressive war against Kalinga. If Buddhism made thereafter a deep appeal to him, it did so only for the reason that its teachings tallied with his own experience and personal conviction.

2. **Asoka the king :** In the political literature of India the king ranks first and foremost among the seven constituent factors on the strength or weakness of which depends the strength or weakness of the state. These are popularly known as the seven elements of sovereignty' (sapta rājyāngāni). Kauṭilya rightly emphasizes the relative importance of the first element : "It is verily the king who appoints the ministers, chaplains, and other servants including the

[1] Cf. Sumangala-vilasinī, I, p. 184. Indebted to S. N. Mitra for the reference.

[2] R.E. IX (G) : asti pi ti vutaṃ : sādhu dāna iti.

[3] Saṃyutta, I, p. 20.

superintendents of departments, applies remedies against the troubles of his subjects and of his kingdom, adopts progressive measures, and replaces his ministers and officers who fall into troubles by new ones. It is he who rewards the worthy and punishes the wicked. When he is well off, by his welfare and prosperity he pleases his subjects. The character of the king determines the character of the people ; for their progress or decline they depend on him. The king is, as it were, the peak of their lives."[1]

To the same effect the Rājovāda Jātaka (No. 334) teaches that the king is the acknowledged head and leader of men, precisely as the king of bulls is that of a herd of cattle. If he practises impiety and is given to vice, the rest of men forestall him in the same ; the whole kingdom prospers when the king is righteous.[2]

We have already discussed at length the extent of Aśoka's domain proper, empire and sphere of influence, the character of his state and his system of administration. Here we shall confine ourselves to certain relevant observations on Aśoka the king in respect of his personal enjoyments, statesmanship and ability for administration, and discharge of kingly duties.[3]

(a) **Personal enjoyments** : The Mahāsutasoma Jātaka speaks of the five kingly enjoyments. The first is eating (bhojana), the second, concupiscence (kilesa), the third, lying on the bed (sayana), the fourth, musical entertainment (nachcha-gīta-vādita), and the fifth, pleasance (uyyāna).[4]

As regards the first, the king of the Kurus particularly refers to the meat dishes nicely cooked and prepared by the cook with the flesh of edible quadrupeds and birds, and tasted with relish as it were the nectar eaten by Indra. The second is described as the pleasure of a king to be in the midst of the slim-bodied, beautifully adorned and most handsome wives as it were the enjoyment of Indra when he is in the midst of the heavenly maidens. The third is described as lying on a magnificent bed, which is capable of inducing sound sleep. The fourth is concerned with the most captivating of operas performed during the night by the female actresses. The charm

---

[1] Arthas'āstra, VIII, 1.

[2] Jātaka, III, p. 444.

[3] The traditional enumeration of these duties is to be found in the extant Rājavagga (Anguttara) and the Chakkavatti-sihanāda Suttanta (Dīgha, III, p. 64).

[4] Jātaka, V, p. 507.

of the fifth has reference to the royal pleasure-ground (uyyāna, migāchīrupetapura).

Aśoka specifically mentions a few occasions (R.E. VI) when he was not ordinarily supposed to have attended to the state-business, namely, (1) when he was taking his meal (bhuṃjamānasa), (2) when he was in the inner apartment of his palace (orodhanasi), (3) when he was in his bed-chamber (gabhāgārasi), (4) when he was engaged in vracha, (5) when he was out for a chariot-drive or ride (vachaṃhi va vinītamhi), and (6) when he was in a pleasance (uyāna).

In the Arthaśāstra (I. 16), eating (bhojana) is associated with bathing (snāna). The sumptuousness of royal dishes may be easily inferred from Aśoka's statement in R.E. I where many hundred thousands of creatures are said to have been previously killed every day and cooked in his kitchen. In the same edict he alludes to the performance of animal sacrifices followed by grand feasts and convivial gatherings (samājā) fraught with moral dangers.

Aśoka's orodhana is the same word as the Sanskrit avarodhana and the Pali orodha. In Buddhist literature, particularly the Jātakas, orodha is employed as a synonym of itthāgāra (stryāgāra) or female apartments set apart for the wives of various description with the maids of honour, nurses and maid-servants attached to them. In a royal or imperial household the married wives were generally entitled to the honour of queens (devis). The rest are known as nāṭakitthiyo or opera girls with all their pleasing arts who either permanently resided as concubines or lefthanded wives within the orodha or came in occasionally from without. According to the Arthaśāstra (I. 23), the inner chamber (antaḥpura) or female establishment of the palace was to be built on a best-suited and spacious site and it was to consist of many compartments, enclosed by a parapet and a ditch and provided with a door. These compartments included the bed-rooms of the queens as well as rooms for the residence of other women of the royal household.

Aśoka's gabhāgāra or bed-room was just one of the compartments in the king's own residence. According to the Arthaśāstra (I. 20, I. 21), the building was to consist of four compartments, one of which was to be used as bed-room, and another as wardrobe. The king was to enter the bed-chamber during the third division of the night amid the sound of trumpets, and sleep during the fourth or fifth division. Here on his rise from the bed he was to be received by the troops of amazons[1], while, according to Pali accounts, he was to be merrily entertained by the opera girls before sleep.

Aśoka's vracha may be confidently equated indeed with vachcha, Sk. vrātya (in the Jaina sense) meaning 'religious duty.' One might even think of a Sanskrit word like vṛitya as a possible variant of vṛitta (cf. nṛitya, nṛitta) meaning some sort of a central or circular hall serving as the upasthāna for receiving and entertaining visitors and guests (Arthaśāstra, I. 20, Mahābhārata, III. 46. 23-28.)

Aśoka's vinīta may be taken to correspond with the yāna and vāhana of the Arthaśāstra (I. 21) and with the Pali rathavinīta meaning the chariot drawn by horses that are well-trained and of good breed.[2] The Pali Dhammachetiya Sutta gives a description of king Pasenadi's chariot-drive to a forest at Nagaraka, the Bāhitiya Sutta of his going out of the city on the back of an elephant,[3] and the Sāmaññaphala Sutta[4] and its Commentary of a grand processional ride on elephants.[5] The grandeur and joy of a processional chariot drive to the king's pleasure-grove (vanantaṃ mohanaṃ) may be realised at once from the first stanza of the Achchharā verses : "resounded with the music of the troops of nymphs and guarded by the troops of armed women."[6] A similar account of the chariot-drive to the pleasance (uyyāna-bhūmi) outside the city is to be found in the Pali Nidāna-kathā.

Aśoka's uyāna is the same word as the Sanskrit udyāna and the Pali uyyāna. The royal pleasure-garden was enclosed by a wall provided with a gate. The garden house of a king was a fashionable building decorated with portraits and other paintings, such as Bimbisāra's chitrāgāra was[7]. It contained bathing tanks filled with transparent water and full of fish.[8] It was ranged by deer and gay with the carols of birds (migāchīrupeta).[9]

The king's pleasance was sometimes used as the hunting ground, and it is evident from R. E. VIII that going on hunting expedition was a favourite pursuit with the kings of India (abhirāmaka).[10] In fact, all pleasure-trips and pleasurable excursions (vihāra-yātrā) are typified in it by hunting (magavyā, mṛigayā).

---

[1] Strabo rightly observes that the care of the king's person was entrusted to women. McCrindle, Ancient India, p. 70.

[2] Majjhima, II, p. 118f.

[3] Majjhima, III.

[4] Dīgha, I. p. 49.

[5] Sumangala-vilāsinī, I, pp. 148-9.

[6] Barua & Mitra, Prakrit Dhammapada, p. 99 ; Barua, Inscriptions, ii, p. 302.

[7] Vinaya, IV, p. 289 ; Jātaka, VI, pp. 159, 223 ; Stella Kramrisch, The Vishṇudharmottara, Revised ed., p. 6.

[8], [9] Jātaka, V, p. 476.

[10] Barua, Inscriptions, ii, p. 299 f.

Here one may aptly cite the following observations of Strabo[1] :

"The king leaves his palace -- to go to the chase, for which he departs in Bacchanalian fashion. Crowds of women surround him, and outside of this circle spearmen are engaged. The road is marked off with ropes, and it is death, for men and women alike, to pass within the ropes.[2] Men with drums and gongs lead the procession. The king hunts in the enclosures and shoots from the back of an elephant. Of the women, some are in chariots, some on horses, and some even on elephants, and they are equipped with weapons of every kind, as if they were going on a campaign."[3]

(b) Statesmanship and ability for administration : Of the two main criteria for testing the statesmanship and administrative capacity of a ruler, the first is his proficiency in the science of government and the second his ability for timely and effective application of its principles for his own safety, the safety of his territory and subjects, the safety of other elements of sovereignty, and the furtherance of general good and happiness (Arthaśāstra I.5, VI. 1).

The inscriptions of Aśoka bear ample testimony to his position as an advanced political thinker and as a far-sighted and capable administrator. His knowledge of the science of government and the general philosophy of life was deep and profound. R.E.XIII, S.R.E. I and S.R.E. II attest not only his intimate acquaintance with the principles of politics but also his power of applying them as occasions demanded. The general principles of piety, duty and good conduct advocated by him in his edicts fall all within the scope of the most advanced rājadharma or political thought of India, and had all the regulations of piety (dhaṃmaniyamāni) typified by P. E. V been recorded and preserved, we might have a novel Arthaśāstra of Aśoka, which would do good to the political thought of the world. The ruler's capacity lies in devising and adopting means and measures and their adjustment to the laudable ends clearly kept in view. The administrative measures, changes and reforms adopted and effected by Aśoka sufficiently prove it. The institution of the quinquennial and triennial tours of official inspection (R. E. III,

---

[1] McCrindle, Ancient India, p. 70 f.

[2] Cf. Arthas'āstra, I. 20 : "On the occasion of going out of, and coming into (the capital), the king's road shall on both sides be well guarded by staff-bearers and freed from the presence of armed persons, ascetics, and the cripple."

[3] Cf. Sumangala-vilāsinī, i, pp. 148-9.

S.R.E. I), the appointment of the Dharmamahāmātras as a new class of officials with their duties clearly defined, the elaborate arrangements made for the education of the people, the improvement of the jail administration (R.E. V), the humanisation of the ruthless criminal laws (P. E. IV), the passing and enforcement of the various regulations of piety (P. E. V, P. E. VII), the promulgation of ordinances (Schism Pillar), and the like were all measures devised to implement the duties of the ideal state as conceived and cherished by him.

(c) **Discharge of duties :** Aśoka not only kept the Maurya empire intact but extended it by the annexation of Kalinga (R.E. XIII). He tried to consolidate his territory and carefully guarded it against internal troubles and foreign invasions. The internal troubles might arise either from the mischiefs caused by the aṭavis as well as from popular disaffection and revolt. He took proper measures to punish the offenders. The expression of regret and the declaration of might (pabhāva) on his part were intended to see that such mischiefs were not repeated. Behind the repentance was the drastic action which had to be taken, and behind the might was the consciousness of his financial resources and striking power (kośadaṇḍabalaṃ prabhuśaktiḥ),[1] while before them was the strong warning (R.E. XIII). He strongly warned the inimical or mischievous neighbours against encroachments into his territory along with assuring them of his good-will towards them and his sincere desire to respect the territorial integrity (S.R.E. II). In order to remove the cause of popular disaffection and revolt he took his officers to task and deputed higher officers to redress the wrongs done to the people as well as to prevent the miscarriage of justice (S.R.E. I).

Aśoka did his best to fulfil his obligations to his own people. In order evidently to prevent the hitch among his queens he had separate family establishments in his capital and outer towns (R.E. V, P. E. VII). He provided his wives and sons with funds to distribute charities on their own account. He appointed his own sons as well as other princes of the blood to responsible offices of the state when they became grown up and fit for work (P. E. VII, S. R. E. I). He took a keen personal interest also in the family affairs of his brothers, sisters and other kith and kin, and tried to assist them in all matters of piety and social importance (R.E. V).

---

[1] **Arthas'āstra, VI. 2.**

To his own officers Aśoka acted all along as a friend, philosopher and guide (P.E. I). He took them to task when they went wrong (S.R.E. I), and encouraged them when they were found diffident of of success (M. R. E.). He issued instructions to them as to how they should carry out his orders to his satisfaction (P. E. IV, Queen's Edict, Sārnāth Pillar). He did not forget to remind them of their importance as functionaries of the state (S.R.E. I, S.R.E. II).

Aśoka cherished the parental feeling towards his own subjects and expected that they should on their part cherish the filial feeling towards him (S.R.E. I, S.R.E. II). He aspired to be the servant of the country (desāvutike hosāmi, S. R. E. I). With him to love the people best was to serve them best ; he never felt tired of impressing this fact on the mind of his officers. The supreme task to which he directed all his efforts was the moral elevation of the people and their satisfactory growth in piety. To increase the good and happiness of the people was the normal duty of a good king. He did not apply to others any principle which he would not apply to himself. Thus he tried to stand as a living example of virtue to his own officers and subjects. Led by the altruistic idea of doing good to the whole world, he wanted to cherish similar feelings towards the people of the neighbouring territories.

Aśoka was fully aware of his duties to the needy, the distressed and the fallen[1]. The people in indigent circumstances, the aged, the destitute, the sick, the slaves and servants, and the imprisoned and those condemned to death by court sentence engaged his special attention (R. E. II, R.E. IV, R.E. V, P.E. IV, P.E. V). To provide the travellers with comforts he planted shade-trees on the roads and dug wells and tanks. The wells and tanks by the roadside must have served also to help the irrigation work.

His private faith did not stand in the way of his honouring the men of all sects with gifts and in various other ways of honouring them (R.E. XII). He desired all the Brāhmaṇas and the Śramaṇas to dwell everywhere in his empire and do their work without fear or molestation (R.E. VII, R.E. XII, R.E. XIII). He wished all of them well, and knew their great importance. The active form of tolerance advocated by him goes to make R.E. XII a unique document in the annals of the religious history of man.

---

[1] Cf. Mahābhārata, III. 2. 53-56 ; III. 28. 26-30.

The beasts and birds, the fishes and other animals equally engaged his attention[1]. Just as in the case of men, so in that of beasts, he arranged for medical treatment. The shade-trees and the wells and tanks were meant also for their enjoyment. He enacted the game-laws to minimise their slaughter (P.E. V), and prohibited the performance of animal sacrifices (R.E. I).

The keen sense of duty enlivens all his statements. At all times and in all places, even when and where he was supposed to have observed strict privacy, he attended to the business of the people (R.E. VI). There was no higher duty to him than doing good to all.

As a man of graceful mien and as one who viewed the world and all with loving eyes he justified the epithet of Priyadarśin. As a ruler devoted to the duty of relieving the sorrow and misery of all, he tried to deserve the name of Aśoka or Śoka-nāśana[2]. And as a righteous king emperor who was able to commingle the gods and men in an unprecedented world of piety, he well merited the epithet of Devānaṃpriya or 'Beloved of the gods.'

---

1 Ibid, III. 257. 6-12.

2 Ibid, III. 64. 107.

CHAPTER VII

DHARMA

If to appreciate a great man of history is to appreciate the doctrine or ideal with which he identified himself, it is meet that, after considering the position of Aśoka the man and king, we should take up his Dharma for discussion.

The inscriptions of Aśoka contain two sets of records : one relating to the Saddharma or Good Faith which he professed as his religion, and the other to the Dharma which he propounded and promulgated. If so, the question arises—how far is the Dharma which he propounded and promulgated consistent with the Saddharma professed by him ? Thus the consistency between the Saddharma or religion of Buddha Śākyamuni and the Dharma of Aśoka is the main problem which engages our attention here.

There are divergences of opinion on the real nature and character of Aśoka's Dharma. Three main views on the subject are that of Fleet, that of Vincent Smith, and that of D. R. Bhandarkar.

In Fleet's opinion Aśoka's Dharma is but a form of Rājadharma consisting in the politico-moral principles such as those embodied in the Great Epic. Fleet's opinion may be shown to have been based on the evidence supplied by Bühler.

Vincent Smith opines that the principles promulgated by Aśoka are common to all religions without being identical with those of any one of them. It is in agreement, more or less, with this view that Mookerji is inclined to appraise Aśoka's Dharma as something like a universal religion.

Both Senart and Hultzsch are inclined to interpret Aśoka's Dharma in the light of Buddha's Words. The most powerful advocate of this opinion is Bhandarkar with whom Aśoka's Dharma is nothing short of that aspect of primitive Buddhism which is meant for the upāsakas or lay worshippers of Buddha. Both Bhandarkar and Raychaudhuri rightly draw our attention to the ideal of the righteous chakravartin upheld by Buddha.

The position taken up by me is that Aśoka's Dharma is wholly consistent with the principles of secular Buddhism and not altogether inconsistent with those of other systems of faith and thought, and there is no reason as yet to give it up. Treat it as a form of Rājadharma, or as a form of Buddhist Upāsaka-dharma, or even as a form of Universal religion, this position remains unaltered. The acute observation of Rhys Davids that there is not a word about God or the soul in Aśoka's Dharma, not a word about Buddha or Buddhism,[1] makes no difference to it.

1. **As Rājadharma** : The Rājadharma in the narrowest sense of the term is based on the Science of Government (Daṇḍanīti)[2] of which the main problem is what is expedient or inexpedient (nayānayau), conducive or not conducive to the strength of the state (balābale).[3] Closely allied to this is the Science of Wealth (Vārtā) of which the main problem is what increases and does not increase material resources (arthānarthau).[4] Accordingly the Rājadharma was sought to be founded on both.[5] To be broadbased, the Rājadharma has to take cognizance of and uphold the approved social customs and usages and the general principles of law and equity,[6]—subjects that come within the scope of the Trayī or Vedic system of which the main problem is what is lawful and equitable and what is not (dharmādharmau).[7] To be full-fledged and unerring, the Rājadharma has always to seek guidance from speculative philosophy (Ānvīkshakī),[8] which came to be recognised as "light to all kinds of knowledge, easy means to accomplish all kinds of action and receptacle of all kinds of virtue."[9]

The extant prose treatise of the Arthaśāstra represents the final and most methodical form of the Rājadharma which developed in different Brahmanical schools of political or quasi-political thought. The Rājadharma section of the Mahābhārata and the Kārikā of 6,000 verses presupposed by the Arthaśāstra may be treated as two typical earlier Brahmanical treatises on Rājadharma. Though the Pali Jātakas have many maxims in common with the Great Epic and the Rāmāyaṇa, particularly the former, through them as well as the Rājavagga of the Anguttara Nikāya and the Aggañña, Chakkavatti-

---

1 Buddhist India, p. 297.

2 Such was the opinion of the school of the Aus'anasas. See Arthas'āstra, I. 1.

3 Arthas'āstra, I. 1.

4 Ibid, I. 1.

5 E.g., by the school of Bārhaspatyas. Ibid, I. 1.

6 This was the opinion of the school of the Manavas. Ibid, I. 1.

7 Ibid, I. 1.

8 This was the opinion of Kauṭilya. Ibid, I. 1.

9 Ibid, I. 1 : Pradīpas sarvavidyānām upāyas sarvakarmaṇām, ās'rayas sarvadharmāṇāṃ s'as'vad Anvīkshakī matā.

sīhanāda, Lakkhaṇa and Singālovāda Suttantas of the Dīgha Collection was advocated an ideal form of Rājadharma, which in its general tone and spirit and even in phraseology the same as that followed and upheld by Aśoka.

The first question is—What is Dharma from the point of view of Rājadharma ? To this, the Upanishad teacher returns the answer—Dharma is the king of kings (kshatrasya kshatraḥ).[1] To the question —What is the king of a king emperor ?[2] Buddha returns the self-same answer : Dharma is the king of a king emperor (dhammo rañño chakkavattissa rājā).[3] The former declares that there is nothing higher (more potent, mightier) than Dharma (dharmāt paraṃ nāsti), wherefore by Dharma the weaker person rivals the stronger, precisely as by the might of a king (yathā rājñā).[4] The latter, too, declares the paramountcy of Dharma among men (dhammo seṭṭho jane tasmiṃ), in the present life as well as the life to follow.[5] So far as the social order is concerned, both maintain the superiority of the warriors as rulers over other social grades, even over the worldly Brāhmans.[6]

According to the Upanishad teacher, to affirm Dharma is to affirm Satya or Ṛita, and *vice versa*. Thus to affirm any one of them is to affirm both. This may be interpreted in two different ways : (1) that Dharma in the sense of the socio-moral order which is an existing fact or actuality is a derivative (sat tyam) out of the cosmic life, which has either evolved by the Divine will out of or is founded on the world order ; (2) that Dharma in the sense of the moral or Divine law with its foundation in righteousness or piety is the guiding principle of the socio-moral order in which we find ourselves. From the point of view of Rājadharma, Dharma may be interpreted as law in the narrow legal sense of the term with its foundation in rājaśāsana or rājānuśāsana, i.e., the will of the sovereign authority of the state. Whether we treat it as the moral, sacred or Divine law or as the king-made or state-enforced law, it is a body of rules which carries with it the sanction from some unchallengeable sovereign authority,

---

1 Lit., the warrior of warriors.

2 Bṛihad Araṇyaka Up., I. 4. 14.

3 Rājavagga, Anguttara, III, p. 147.

4 Bṛihad Araṇyaka Up., I. 4. 14.

5 Aggañña Suttanta, Dīgha, III, p. 95.

6 Bṛihad Araṇyaka Up., I. 4. 11 : Kshatrāt paraṃ nāsti, tasmād brāhmaṇāḥ kshatriyaṃ adhasthāt upāste rājasūye ; rājā paramataṃ gacchfati.

whether it be the prevailing collective will and good sense of the society or community, or the express will of the king or state. The essence of both is justice, or, as one might say, both are only means to an end, which is justice. It is desired that to be used as a means of human good and happiness as well as of progress, the king-made or state enforced law must always be subservient to the moral Sacred or Divine law.

Buddha's view concurs with that of the Upanishad teacher in so far as he, too, maintains that the socio-moral order of men is the result of an evolutionary process of cosmic life.[1] The difference between the two lies in the fact that in Buddha's account of the process the notion of the operation of any arbitrary will, whether it be in the name of Brahman or God, is eliminated. With Buddha Dharma or moral law as the guiding principle of the socio-moral order is divine (brahmabhūta) only in so far as its end or underlying purpose is concerned. It is rather the collective experience, good sense and idea of expedience that guide and have guided the course of evolution of the socio moral order.[1] Buddha traces the origin of kingship or state in popular consent (mahājana-sammati)[2] which is behind all forms of social contract.

The common upshot of both the views, however, is that the Law is above the King, and not that the King is above the Law. The ideal of life or the ideal behaviour, conduct or action is, according to the Brahmanist view, one which is set forth by the best among the Brāhmans who are the leaders of thought and the accredited teachers of men.[3] According to the Buddhist view, the leaders of thought and the accredited teachers of men are the S'ramaṇas and the Brāhmaṇas or the Brāhmaṇas and the S'ramaṇas,[4] while the best or foremost of all,—the agra—is the Buddha.[5]

The perennial source of Dharma is either Brahmaveda as with the Brahmanist, or Dhammaveda or Atthaveda as with the Buddhist.[6] Dharma is characterised in the Jātakas as 'the good old rule'

---

1 Aggañña Suttanta, Dīgha, III.

2 Ibid, p. 93; mahājana-sammato ti Mahāsammato; Cf. Ulūka Jātaka, No. 270.

3 Taittirīya Up., I. 11. 3-4: ye kechāsmach chhreyāṃso brāhmaṇāḥ, ye tatra brāhmaṇāḥ saṃmarsinaḥ.

4 Dīgha, III, p. 95, 191: Jātaka, III, p. 312: brāhmaṇassa samaṇassa.

5 Sampasādaniya Suttanta, Dīgha, III, p. 98.

6 Majjhima, I, p, 37.

(charito purāṇo,[1] dhammo sanantano,[2] chirakālappavatto sabhāvo,[3] poraṇiyā pakati[4]), which is to say, the tradition of piety or duty, the traditional path of virtue. Thus Buddha speaks of the porāṇa-Vajjidhammā constituting the national tradition of the Vṛijis of Vaiśālī, the rules of life backed by noble precedents, customs and usages.[5] The Dharma enforced by rājaśāsana or the sovereign authority of the state is to promote the growth of men in such Dharma and not to hamper it. We can say that this is the common Indo-Aryan conception of Dharma from the point of view of Rājadharma with this difference, however, that in the Brāhmanist line the tradition is to be adhered to more in the letter, the departure being allowed to take place only through legal fiction or ingenious interpretation of the texts, and in the Buddhist line the tradition is to be followed more in the spirit, it meaning that the path of virtue or that body of rules which accords with both the supposed original state of the purity of man's nature, the instinctive prompting of unsophisticated human mind[6] and the ideal born of the supreme religious experience and profound meditation of the Enlightened Ones.[7]

With Aśoka, too, the Dharma from the point of view of Rāja-dharma is 'the good old rule' (porāṇā pakiti), 'that which is of long standing' (dīghāvuse, M.R.E., Bra, Ye). There exists even a verbal correspondence between the two ideas, Aśokan and Buddhist :

(a) esā poraṇā pakiti (M.R.E., Bra).
(b) esā te porāṇiyā pakati (Jātaka, VI, p. 151).

Though in R.E. III Aśoka lays equal stress on letter and spirit (hetuto cha vyaṃjanato cha), in S.R.E. I he takes his officers to task

---

1 Jātaka, V, p. 479 : satañ cha dhammo charito purāṇo.

2 Ibid, V, p. 488 : esa dhammo sanantano ; Cf. Dhammapada verse 5.

3 Ibid, III, p. 212 : porāṇo dhammo chirakālappavatto sabhāvo.

4 Ibid, VI, p. 151 : esā te porāṇiyā pakati.

5 Dīgha, II, p. 74. See Buddha's comment on porāṇa-Vajjidhammā in Sumangala-vilasinī, ii, p. 519.

6 Jātaka, IV, p. 101.

7 This is the whole trend of Buddha's argument which runs through the Aggañña Suttanta.

Dhammo have pātur ahosi pubbe ।
pachchhā adhammo udapādi loke ॥
jeṭṭho cha seṭṭho cha sanantano cha ।
Jeṭṭho 'ti pure nibbattabhāvena, seṭṭho 'ti porāṇako.

Cf. Book of Genesis in the Bible.

that they failed to catch the import of his instruction as far as it went (no cha pāpunātha avagamuke iyaṃ athe).

According to the Brahmanist and traditional definition, the rājā (king, ruler) is one who pleases his subjects (prajān rañjayati, pakatiyo raṃjayati). Buddha qualifies it by adding to it the saving clause—dhammena, meaning 'righteously', 'judiciously', 'in accordance with the law of piety or duty': Dhammena pare rañjetīti rājā,[1] the verb rañjeti being paraphrased by sukheti pīṇeti, 'makes happy, pleases.' The force of dhammena is sought to be augmented and emphasized by the explanatory clause: dhammen'eva, no adhammena, 'righteously indeed, not unrighteously', which is to say, discriminately, and not indiscriminately. Thus the exercise of discretion on the part of the king is explicit in Buddha's definition. Consistently with this, the righteous king emperor is expected to provide the lawful safety, cover and protection (dhammika rakkhāvaraṇa-gutti), depending on dharma, showing due respect to Dharma, venerating, reverencing and worshipping Dharma, honouring it in all humility, holding the banner of Dharma, raising the flag of Dharma, and acknowledging the authority of Dharma. Here safety (rakkhā) means the safety, of oneself and that of others, and four are the means of safety, viz, moral fortitude (khanti), non-harming mental attitude (avihiṃsā), friendly heart (mettachittatā), and compassion (anuddayā); cover (āvaraṇa) means the means of preventing discomforts; and guarding (gutti) means guarding against the action of thieves and other enemies of men and the country.[2]

Aśoka, too, lays down the same as the general principle of administration when he says (P.E. I): This is the rule, namely, that which is called rearing by Dharma, providing by Dharma, making happy by Dharma, guarding by Dharma" (dhaṃmena pālanā, dhaṃmena vidhāne, dhaṃmena sukhiyanā, dhaṃmena goti). He desired that his descendants and successors would administer the law of piety by taking each his stand on Dharma and virtue:

Dhaṃmamhi sīlamhi tisṭaṃto dhaṃmaṃ anusāsisaṃti (R.E. VI). This reminds us of Buddha's admonition in the Sutta-nipāta, verse 250: Dhamme ṭhito ajjave maddave sato.

"Standing on Dharma, being in moral rectitude and gentleness of spirit."

---

[1] Dīgha, III, p. 93. Cf. Mahābhārata, XIII. 142-30: pras'ādhi pṛithivīṃ rājan prajā dharmeṇa pālayan.

[2] Ṣumangala-vilāsinī, III, p. 850,

Anything approaching the above principle is the following maxim quoted in the Arthaśāstra (XIII. 5):

Charitram akṛitaṃ dharmyaṃ kṛitaṃ chānyaiḥ pravarttayet |
Pravartayen na chādharmyaṃ kṛitaṃ chānyair nivartayet ||

"(The king in a newly-acquired territory) should allow those customs in vogue among others to prevail, though these are not observed (in his own country). He should not allow any unrighteous custom to prevail, and should stop it, though it is observed by others."

The meaning of the saving clause 'by Dharma' is not far to seek. The performances of animal sacrifices followed by sumptuous feasts and convivial gatherings (samājā, R.E. I), the chariot-processions held in honour of the gods (R.E. IV), the royal chase (magavyā, R.E. VIII), and the like were the traditional means of entertaining the people. According to Aelian, "Aśoka's grandfather, Chandragupta, used to hold annually a great festival for animal fights. There were butting contests between rams, wild bulls, elephants, and even rhinoceroses, and also races between chariots drawn by two oxen with a horse between them." "It was by the twofold means, namely, the display of darpa (contests), nṛitya (dances), gīta (songs) and vādita (instrumental music), and the organization of utsava (festive occasions) and samāja (popular gatherings) that Khāravela sought to exhilarate the citizens of the Kalinga capital as the joy celebration of success in his first military campaign. Thus it is opined in the Rāmāyaṇa: utsavañ cha sāmājaś cha vardhane rashṭravardhanam. 'The festivity and popular gathering increase the popularity of the state". The Arthaśāstra (I. 21), too, recommends the organization of yātrā, samāja, utsava and pravahaṇa……Kauṭilya in one passage (ibid, II. 25) refers to utsava, samāja and yātrā, where the drinking of wine was unrestricted for four days, and in another passage (ibid, XIII. 5) points out the conqueror's duty of conciliating the conquered people by respecting their national devotion to their country, their religion (deśa-devatā), and their institutions, viz., their utsava, samāja and vihāra."[1]

The Great Epic (III. 207. 8-10) praises in no uncertain terms the pious deed and unrivalled fame of king Rantideva and his queen in daily killing in the royal kitchen two thousand cattle to feed the people with meat and that invariably during the period of chāturmāsya. It extols the vihārayātrā as sarvakāmapradā, "fulfilling all

---

[1] See note on samāja in Barua's Inscriptions, ii, p. 224 f.

desires for enjoyment" (XV. 1), and expressly declares going a hunting to be proper, fitting (mṛigayā uchitā, śobhanā, III. 238. 6).[1]

These traditional means of pleasing the people are deprecated by Buddha. The most unfortunate feature of the contemporary social life regretted by Buddha is that even certain classes of the S'ramaṇas and the Brāhmaṇas took delight in them.[2] The animal sacrifices are undervalued, and the release of helpless creatures brought to the sacrificial ground for slaughter by the monarchs in obedience to the dictates of good conscience awakened in them by the Bodhisats among the recluses is extolled.[3] The hunting expeditions of the monarchs are shown in several Jātakas to have ended in granting the boon of 'No fear' (abhaya) to all antelopes, to all quadrupeds, to all bipeds (birds), to all acquatic beings (fishes).[4]

Aśoka in his very first edict, holds that no sacrifices should be performed by immolating living beings and no convivial gatherings held as he found many faults in them. He did not, however, condemn the popular gatherings wholesale, without discrimination. He did not omit to mention that there were certain gatherings calculated as good by him. Even with regard to such gatherings as were approved by him, e g., popular religious demonstrations by the display of celestial mansions, celestial elephants, and the fiery and other divine forms, he was of opinion that these were by far the less effective as means of promoting the growth of the people in piety than the two novel methods introduced and tried by him, viz , imparting instructions in the law of piety or duty (dhaṃmānusathini) and issuing the proclamations of piety (dhaṃmasāvanāni).[5] The pleasure excursions (vihārayātā) typified by hunting expedition (magavyā) were replaced by the pilgrimage of piety (dhaṃmayātā (R.E. VIII). The rites of piety (dhaṃma-maṃgala) came to be preferred to the divers popular rites (uchāvacha-maṃgala (R.E. IX)[6] that found sanction in secular Brahmanism.[7]

---

1 Note on vihārayātā in ibid, ii, p. 301 f.

2 See the Sīla sections in the Brahmajāla Sutta, Dīgha, I, p. 4f.

3 Kūṭadanta Sutta, Dīgha, I.

4 e.g., Nigrodhamiga Jātaka (No. 445) and Ruru Jātaka (No. 482).

5 R.E. IV, P.E. VII, M.R.E.

6 "The rites or ceremonies were those performed or observed at the time of illness. at the marriage of sons and daughters, at the birth of sons (better, children), or for the advent of offspring, and in setting out on a journey to a distant place. Especially the womenfolk are said to have performed many and diverse rites that were minor and meaningless." Barua, Inscriptions, ii, p. 305. Cf. Jātaka, V, p. 380 :

> Akankhamānā puttaphalam devatāya namassati ।
> nakkhattāni cha puchchhati utusamvachchharāni cha ॥

7 G. P. Majumdar, Some Aspects of Indian Civilization, p. 297f.

As regards the general method of administration, Aśoka advocates one fulfilling the ideal of the mean between two extreme courses of action (majhaṃ paṭipādayema, S. R. E. I), namely, one in which is manifest the character of men determined by such immoral dispositions as malignity, irascibility, cruelty and oppressiveness (isyā, āsulopa, niṭhuliya, tulanā), and the other in which is manifest the character with non application, indolence and weariness for exertion (anāvuti, ālasiya, kilamatha) as its traits. This middle method grew out of a changed ideology. Extremism in thought as well as the mode of life was the order of the day when Buddha started his career as a teacher of gods and men. As against such extremisms, he propounded his doctrine of the Middle Path (majjha, majjhimā paṭipadā), which was not without its salutary effect on the course of the political thought of the country. In the case of a righteous ruler, the Jātakas recommend the middle method as the best method of government : anumajjhaṃ samāchare, "he should practise the *felt mean*." The argument advanced in its support is that if too mild a method is followed, the ruler becomes disregarded, and if too rigorous a method is followed, he is apt to provoke hostility.'

Paribhūto mudu hoti, atitikkho ti veravā,
etañ cha ubhayaṃ ñatvā anumajjhaṃ samāchare[1].

Though the term *madhya* is missed, Kauṭilya apparently advocates the same method and virtually in the same language in prose :

Tīkshṇadaṇḍo hi bhūtānāṃ udvejanīyaḥ. Mṛidudaṇḍaḥ paribhūyate. Yathārhadaṇḍaḥ pūjyaḥ[2].

"Whoever imposes severe punishment becomes repulsive to the people, while he who awards mild punishment becomes contemptiblc. But whoever imposes punishment as deserved becomes respectable."

The Arthaśastra (I. 4) rightly refers to the earlier agreed opinion that "whoever is desirous of the progress of the world shall ever hold the sceptre raised (udyatadaṇḍa)." This is the opinion which is advocated in the Great Epic by Kaṇika Bhāradvāja[3] and Manu's

---

[1] Jātaka, IV, p. 192.

[2] Arthas'āstra, I. 4 ; Mahābhārata, XII. 56. 40-41.

[3] Cf. Ibid XII. 140. 7-8 :

Nityam udyatadaṇḍaḥ syān nityaṃ vivṛitapaurushaḥ ।
achchhidras'chhidradars'ī cha pareshāṃ vivarānugaḥ ॥
nityam udyatadaṇḍasya bhṛis'am udvijate naraḥ ।
tasmāt sarvāṇi bhūtāni daṇḍenaiva pras'ādhayet ॥

Law-book. Though the acclaimed advanced political thinker of the eminence of Kauṭilya prefers a method which is verbally the same as that in the Jātakas and the edicts of Aśoka, its underlying spirit is different, it being that of 'paying in the same coin by way of awarding rewards or punishments' (upakārāpakārayor dṛishṭapratīkārī). Referring to the aṭavis, Aśoka, on the contrary, expresses himself thus : "Even he who today does mischief is considered pardonable by the Beloved of the gods, whom he can pardon" (R. E. XIII). In other words, Kauṭilya's method leans to the policy of Tit for Tat,[1] while Aśoka's middle method inclines more towards tolerating or forgiving the miscreants as long as their actions do not exceed the limits of patience (R.E. XIII, S.R.E. II).

The difference in the underlying spirit between the two middle methods is more manifest in the two forms of conquest by Dharma, one advocated in the Great Epic and the Arthaśāstra, and the other by Buddha and Aśoka.

The Great Epic (XI. 58. 38-39) distinguishes between Dharmavijaya and Asuravijaya, while the Arthaśāstra (XII. 1) distinguishes between the three types of conquerors, viz , Dharmavijayī (just conqueror), Lobhavijayī (greedy conqueror), and Asuravijayī (demon-like conqueror). "The first is satisfied with mere obeisance on the part of the weaker king who seeks his protection ; the second is satisfied with what he can safely gain in land or money ; and the third satisfies himself not merely by seizing the land, treasure, sons and wives of the conquered but by taking the life of the latter as well.' This is the very idea of Dharmavijaya which is behind Kālidāsa's account of Raghu's digvijaya (Raghuvaṃśa, IV). The Dharmavijaya on the part of Raghu consisted 'in depriving a defeated or weaker king of his glory but not of his territory' (śriyaṃ jahāra na tu medinīm). "This is well exemplified by Raghu's traditional treatment of his rival, the lord of the Mahendra Mountain, made captive and then released, the capture and liberation of the Deccan rulers by Samudragupta, and the subduing of the Raṭhikas and Bhojakas (of the Vidyādhara countries) and the Magadhan king Bahasatimita (Bṛihaspatimitra) by Khāravela. When some of the S'aka rulers and generals posed sometimes as Dharmavijayī (J. A. S. B., 1923,

[1] Cf. Rājovāda Jātaka, No. 151, where the method of the king of Kos'ala is stated to be : dalhaṃ dalhassa khipati, mudussa mudunā mudum, Cf. Mahābhārata, XV. 140. 65 : tīkshṇakāle bhavet tīkshṇaḥ, mṛidukāle mṛidur bhavet.

p. 343, Raychaudhuri, op. cit., p. 433), presumably they acted on this very principle of Dharmavijaya.[1]

I cannot but maintain, as against the opinion of Mr. T. N. Ramachandran, that this is different in its fundamental character from the Dharmavijaya of Buddha and Aśoka. The Epic or Kauṭilian Dharmavijaya is just the best form of what Aśoka calls Sarasaka or Sāyaka Vijaya, i.e., armed conquest, the necessity or possibility of which is not denied by him (R.E. XIII). The essential feature of the Epic Dharmavijaya is brought out by Aśoka himself when he says that even where it is a necessity, forbearance and light reprisal should be preferred (khaṃti cha lahudaṃḍatā cha lochetu).

With Buddha the Dharmavijaya is a fuller form of conquest by Dharma (abhivijaya) achieved over an extensive empire by a king overlord without the infliction of any punishment, without the use of any weapon (imaṃ paṭhaviṃ sāgara-pariyantaṃ adaṇḍena asatthena dhammena abhivijiya).[2] According to Buddhaghosa, here 'the infliction of punishment' may mean the imposition of fines, the issuing of orders for massacre, as well as the use of the armed forces, and 'weapon' means all weapons for torturing others. The Pali scholiast explains the phrase, dhammena abhivijiya, as meaning achieving a fuller form of conquest by making it a point not to take the life of a king who comes as desired by the rival king, and following such other principles of action.

It is evident from Buddha's account of the position of the Chakkavatti-monarch that he seeks to achieve such a fuller measure of the conquest by Dharma not out of the consciousness of his weakness but out of that of his irresistible strength in army, wealth and territorial solidarity[3]. Buddhaghosa has not fully brought out the significance of this form of conquest as described in the Chakkavatti-sīhanāda Suttanta. This may be realized from the Aśokan definition of Dharmavijaya according to which it consists negatively in not thinking of a new territorial conquest through a war of aggression entailing untold miseries and endangering the cause of culture (R.E. XIII), and positively in assuring the neighbouring states of the king emperor's good will and desire to respect the laws

---

[1] This agrees with the principle inculcated in the Dhamma Jātaka, No. 457 : khantibalo yuddhabalaṃ vijetvā.

[2] Dīgha, III, p. 59.

[3] Ibid, III, p. 59.

of territorial integrity (S.R.E. II) besides winning their affection and earning their gratitude through philanthropic and cultural missions[1] (R.E. II, R.E. XIII).

The ideal feeling relation between the ruler and the ruled is desired by Aśoka to be one that subsists between the loving parent and the loving children. The ruler is to inspire this confidence in the ruled that he is to them like a solicitous parent keenly interested in their welfare and eager to connect them with good and happiness. The ruled are to assure the ruler that they are to him like his children. Thus the parental feeling or attitude on one side is expected to be reciprocated by the filial feeling or attitude on the other (S.R.E. II). This is the best conceivable feeling relation which is expressible in terms of domestic relationship. The analogy is not, however, to be pressed too far, nor is it to be inferred from this that the Aśokan, and, for the matter of that, the ideal Indian government is a parental form of government, founded and run entirely on a domestic model.

In the Great Epic, the Arthaśāstra, the Buddhacharita, and other Indian works just the ruler's side is emphasized when it is enjoined that the king should look at, be solicitous about the welfare of, or do favour to his subjects precisely as he would do in the case of his own progeny.[2] Aśoka, too, lays stress on this side only when he states his own position in the words : "All men are like unto my progeny" : sava munisā pajā mamā (S.R.E. I). But he goes a step further when he claims that he cherished the same parental feeling also towards the people of the neighbouring states (S.R.E. II).

The scriptural authority for the idea of the mutual feeling relation between the ruler and the ruled is the Mahāsutasoma Jātaka. The verbal agreement between the two statements will at once indicate the fountain-head of Aśoka's ideal :

(a) Yathā pitā athavā pi mātā
anukampakā atthakāmā pajānaṃ,
evam eva no hotu ayañ cha rājā,
mayam pi hessāma tath'eva puttā.
(Jātaka, V, p. 504).

(b) Athā pitā hevaṃ ne lājā ti. Ath(ā) atānaṃ anukaṃpati hevaṃ apheni anukaṃpati. Athā pajā hevaṃ maye lājine (S.R.E. II).

---

[1] Ibid, III, p. 62 f.

[2] Mahābhārata, XII. 28. 51, XII. 68. 29 : Arthas'āstra, II. 1, IV. 3 ; Buddhacharita, ii. 85.

The supreme importance of the position of a king or king overlord in worldly life is recognized by all alike in India. In the authoritative verses cited in the Arthaśāstra, (III. 1), the king is represented as the founder and upholder of a socio-moral order (rājā dharmapravartakaḥ). According to Buddha, just as a Buddha is the founder of a religious order and propounder of a system of faith and thought, so a righteous universal monarch is the founder of a socio-moral order and propounder of a system of piety and duty.[1] In the Jaina Āgama, too, the Chakravartins are regarded as worldly counterparts of the Tīrthankaras.[2] The Nijjhatti and the Dhammaniyama may be shown to have occupied the same place in Aśoka's rājadharma as the Dhamma (Doctrine as in the Sutta Piṭaka) and the Vinaya (Discipline as in the Vinaya Piṭaka) in Buddha's śāsana or system of faith and thought. In the opinion of the Brahmanical thinkers, however, the king is expected to be the founder and upholder of only that kind of socio-moral order which is based upon the gradational system of varṇāśrama-dharma,—of four hereditary social grades and four stages of effort[3], while in Buddha's ideal scheme the hereditary basis of the four social grades[4] and the graduated system of self-training (kramaśikshā) except on the ground of expedience[5] are denied. Though the population is broadly divided into Brāhmans and Ibhyas (general body of householders) in Aśoka's rājadharma (R.E.V) as well as in Buddha's social scheme, there is nothing in the edicts to indicate that Aśoka intended to be the upholder of the Brahmanical system as such. In accordance with the ideal set up by Buddha the righteous king overlord is responsible not only for giving the people a good rule making for their welfare and happiness, both here and hereafter, but also for their sound moral and religious education. Thus his part as an anuśāsaka implies the double function of an efficient ruler and a sound educator of mankind, which Aśoka tried to discharge to the best of his capacity.

According to the Brahmanical thinkers, the tried policies of government consist in conciliating (sāma), bribing (dāna), creating

---

[1] Dīgha, III, p. 149 : vatteti chakkaṃ.

[2] Aupapātika Sūtra, Sec. 55 : arahantā>chakkavattī.

[3] Arthas'āstra, III. 1 :

Chaturvarṇās'ramasyāya lokasyāchārarakshaṇāt ।
nas'yatāṃ sarvadharmāṇāṃ rājā dharmapravartakaḥ ।

[4] Vāseṭṭha Sutta in the Sutta-nipāta, v. 1156.

[5] Gaṇaka-Moggallāna Sutta. Majjhima, III. 1.

dissension (bheda), and employing force (daṇḍa).[1] In Buddha's terminology, these go by the name of four sangahas or sangahavatthus and consist in offering presents and timely help (dāna), exchanging the greetings of courtesy (peyyavajjā), doing good (atthachariyā), and fellow-feeling (samānattatā). The wily art of creating dissension and division, and all forms of diplomacy and duplicity are condemned. In the former, there is the utter lack of sincerity ; in the latter, the tone is of sincerity. In the former, the four policies are vitiated by the diplomatic motive of self-aggrandisement[3] ; in the latter, the four sangrahas are intended to win the heart and to earn the gratitude of all. It is more the idea of four sangrahas which guided Aśoka whose ambition was to win the affection of all men (panayaṃ gachhema su munisānaṃ, S.R.E. I), not to care for any other glory or fame than that the people should be inclined to learn the ideal of piety or duty and to be trained therein (R.E.X), and to depute those officers to deal with the people who are not harsh in their language, not fierce in their nature but are of winsome cordiality (e akhakhase achaṃḍe sakhinālaṃbhe, S.R.E.I)[4].

With Aśoka pāsaṃḍa is not a term of contempt ; it denotes a religious order, sect or denomination. Its phonetic development out of the Sk. pārshada is traceable through its Shahbazgarhi variant prashaṃḍa. By the expression, save pāsaṃḍā, he referred to all religious orders, sects, denominations or schools of thought in India of his time. He broadly divided them into persons following the two modes of life, the pravrajitas and the gṛihasthas, the former renouncing the household life and the latter keeping to it (R.E. XII). The pravrajitas are broadly distinguished as the Brāhmaṇas and the Śramaṇas, or as the Śramaṇas and the Brāhmaṇas. The gṛihasthas figure in his edicts as the lay adherents and supporters of the different sects and schools (nikāyas) of the pravrajitas (R.E. XIII). Though *ipso facto* the gṛihasthas themselves were divided into different groups of devotees or worshippers of popular deities, the fact cannot be directly inferred from the edicts. Among the pravrajitas, the typical names mentioned are the Brāhmans, the Ājīvikas, the Nirgranthas (Jainas) and the Saṃghasthas (Buddhists). The Buddhists are distinguished as monks and nuns, and upāsakas and upāsikās

---

1 Dīgha, III, pp. 192, 292.

2 Ibid, III, p. 172 f,

3 Arthaśāstra, III, 9 ioll.

4 Cf. Jātaka, III, p. 262 : sangāhako sakhilo saṇhavācho.

(Bhābru). The same kind of distinction holds good also in the case of other orders of the pravrajitas. It is evident from this that women were till then allowed to renounce worldly life and to join the orders of the pravrajitas. The Brāhmans represented numerous orders of the pravrajitas as well as Brāhman householders in the service of the state and of the society at large (M.R.E., Ye ; R. E. V).

Aśoka desired that all the sects should dwell everywhere in his dominions (R.E. VII). He insisted on putting up seemly behaviour (saṃpaṭipati) and giving alms and making gifts (dānas) to the Brāhmaṇas and the S'ramaṇas, particularly on personally waiting upon them (atanā pachupagamane, P. E. VI). He knew them to be the persons in whom were well established the principles of piety or duty, such principles as respectful attention to high personages, respectful attention to parents, respectful attention to preceptors and teachers, and seemly behaviour to friends, associates, comrades and relations as well as to slaves and servants, besides strong devotion (daḍhabhatitā, R.E. XIII). He knew them to be the custodians of higher forms of culture and civilization as well as the disseminators of learning and culture in all parts of the country and outside (R.E. XIII). If they were affected and distressed, the cause of man's progress in culture and civilization would greatly suffer. Accordingly he completely changed his mind and launched upon a new career of cultural conquest throughout his empire and throughout the world with the Brāhmaṇas and S'ramaṇas as the brave soldiers of the Aryan faith, and appointed a special class of imperial officers, the Dharma-mahāmātras, to look after them while they were carrying on their noble missions (R. E. V). He liberally helped them with alms and gifts and honoured them in various ways. He tried to persuade them to co-operate with one another for their healthy growth in knowledge and matters essential so that they might be better equipped for the great work before them (R.E. XII). He dedicated four beautiful cave-dwellings to the Ājīvikas in the Khalatika hills. As regards the Buddhist Saṃgha, he sought to prevent division among its members, even by promulgating a penal ordinance (Schism Pillar). For the guidance of the Buddhists who were his co-religionists he selected seven texts out of the growing corpus of Buddha's Words and commended them for their constant study and meditation (Bhābru).

The information furnished by Megasthenes and other Classical writers about the philosophers or wise men of India of the 4th century B. C. is, in both detail and substance, the same as that which may be gathered from the inscriptions of Aśoka and the Pali Nikāyas and Jātakas. The philosophers are broadly distinguished as the Brachmanes (Brāhmaṇas) and the Sarmanes (Śramaṇaś), or as the Sarmanes and the Brachmanes. The Brachmanes are described as the wise men whose lives were regulated by the rules prescribed in the Gṛihya Sūtras, and as those persons who spent the first period of their lives as brahmachāris or resident pupils in the schools of different teachers and the second period as gṛihasthas or married householders. Their graduated system of training, ideal of simple living and high thinking, marrying many wives, reluctance to communicate their knowledge of philosophy even to their wives, and wrapping up their doctrines about immortality and future judgement, and kindred topics, in allegories, after the manner of Plato and the like are noticed. It is rightly observed by Megasthenes that their ideas about physical phenomena were very crude, for they were better in their actions than in their reasonings, inasmuch as their belief was in great measure based upon fables.[1]

The Sarmanes are distinguished as the Hylobioi who live in the woods, the Hylobioi who are the physicians, those who practise hard penances, and those who are diviners and sorcerers, adepts in funeral rites, and who go about begging both in villages and towns. Megasthenes mentions that there were religious women who pursued philosophy with some of the Hylobioi. Clemens likens the Hylobioi to the Enkratetai (Anchorites) among the Greeks, and distinguishes, as held by Colebrooke, the followers of Boutta (Buddha) from the general body of the Hylobioi[2].

Pseudo Origen speaks of a sect of philosophers among the Brachmanes par excellence who abstained from animal food and all victuals cooked by fire, went about naked, and lived on the banks of the river Tagabena (Tungabeṇā, Tungabhadrā). With them God was light, the Word (Logos), and the body the outermost covering of the soul. The leader of one such sect in Alexander's time was Mandanis (Maṇḍana ?), a Dandamis (Daṇḍin ?), one of whose unworthy disciples was Sphines (Aśvin ?) whom the Greeks called Kalanos probably for the reason that he greeted a person by uttering the auspicious word kalyāṇam.[1] This sect of the Gymnosophists, if not precisely a sect of the Ājīvikas, was at least a sect of the Achelakas or Avadhūtas closely allied to the Ājīvikas.

---

[1] McCrindle, Ancient India, p. 98 f.

[2] Ibid, p. 105.

Though the Nirgranthas or Jainas are not expressly mentioned, their inclusion among the Indian Hylobioi is evident from the reference to the ascetic practice of remaining 'for a whole day motionless in one fixed attitude',[1] say in the posture of one called ubbhaṭṭhika in Pali.[2]

Regarding the collective body of the philosophers in India Diodorus accurately observes that they were in point of number a minority, but in point of dignity predominant over all. They, being exempted from all public duties, were neither the masters nor the servants of others. They were, however, engaged by private persons to offer the sacrifices due in lifetime, and to celebrate the obsequies of the dead, for they were believed to be the most dear to the gods (Pali devatānampiyo), and to be the most conversant with matters relating to Hades (unseen world). In requital of such services they received valuable gifts and privileges, while to the people at large they rendered great service. When the people gathered together at the beginning of the year, they forewarned them about droughts and wet weather, propitious winds, health and disease, and other useful topics, so that they and their ruler might make adequate provision against a coming deficiency.[3]

Nowhere in a Brahmanical work, whether it be the Great Epic or the Rāmāyaṇa, the Arthaśāstra or any of the Law-books, is recognized a religieux other than one who is a Brāhman by birth and qualities and a Brahmanist by religious conviction and ideal of life, who, in spite of his being an anchorite or ascetic renouncing everything of the world (saṃnyāsin, parivrājaka, yati or bhikshu), is expected to be the upholder of the Vedic system sanctifying the socio-moral order based upon the scheme of four castes and four stages of effort (varṇāśrama-dharma). The attitude of the Arthaśāstra towards the Śākyas (Buddhists), the Ājīvakas, and such like 'runways' is naïvely hostile, and the language in which it introduces them, opprobrious. They are indiscriminately stigmatized as Vṛishala (S'ūdra) pravrajitas.[4] The rule it prescribes (II. 1) is to the effect that "when, without making provision for the maintenance of his wife and sons, any person embracing asceticism, he shall be punished with the first amercement ; likewise any person who converts a woman to asce-

[1] Ibid, p. 102.

[2] Majjhima, I, p. 92.

[3] McCrindle, Ancient India, p. 38 f.

[4] Arthas'āstra, III. 20. Cf. Bārhaspatya Sūtram, II. 5-35, III, 8-19, 31-50, 60-61.

ticism" may be taken also to go against their interests. In the Rāmāyaṇa, may be in an interpolated verse, Buddha is bluntly maligned as having been a thief and an atheist (choraḥ nāstikaḥ). The Brāhman Parivrājakas like Mārkaṇḍeya (Pali Māgaṇḍiya)[1] took Buddha to be a bhūnahā, bhūnahū (bhrūṇahan, foetus killer)[2] obviously for the reason that his opinion went against household life.[3] If at the time of a sacrifice any S'ramaṇa was sighted, the Brāhman performer of the sacrifice felt sore offended and tauntingly remarked, saying, "Here comes the shaveling, the S'ramaṇa, the Vṛishala !" In some of the Gṛihya Sūtras, the prejudice against the S'ramaṇas is sought to be made deep-rooted by giving a religious sanction to the superstitious belief that the sight of a S'ramaṇa in a dream portended evil.

John Caird is rudely shocked by the utter inconsistency between 'All is Brahman' doctrine of the Early Vedānta pantheism and the grossest monstrocities of the Brāhman-sanctioned polytheism. Here he was anticipated by Buddha, in one point at least, namely, that the boasting nature and fury of a Brāhman was wholly inconsistent with his acclaimed proficiency in Vedānta and advance in religious life. The only redeeming feature of the Arthaśāstra polity is that in Bk. III, Ch. 16, it ordains that the orthodox ascetics (āśraminaḥ) and the heretics (pāshaṇḍas) 'shall, without disturbing each other, reside in a large area' (mahatyavakāśe···vaseyuḥ), the new-comer being 'provided with the space occupied by an old resident', and that whether hermits of the Vānaprastha order, or the Yatis and Brahmachārins of the orthodox orders, or the heretics, may when found to be delinquents, in the name of the ruler, perform penances, offer oblations to gods, observe fasts, and the like in lieu of the payment of fines imposed, while in cases of defamation, theft, assault and

---

1 Majjhima, II, p. 501. I prefer this spelling in Siamese text to Māgandiya in P.T.S. text.

2 The word bhūna (Sk. bhrūṇa) always stands for foetus. If it means in some contexts for a learned Brāhman (Monier Williams, Sanskrit English Dict.) or a leading ṛishi (Jātaks, V, p. 266), it does so only figuratively, it primarily signifying Hiraṇyagarbha, an epithet of Brahmā or Brahman.

3 In the Majjhima context, the word bhūnahā or bhūnahū does not mean a learned Brāhman or leading Brahmarshi. See, for reasons for calling Buddha a bhūnahā, Malalasekera. Dict. of Pali Proper Names, ii, p. 595 ; E. J. Thomas, the Life of Buddha, p. 115. I take it to be the same word as ātmahan in Īs'a Up.

abduction of women they shall be compelled to undergo the usual punishment, the guiding principle for the ruler being that he shall forbid under penalty imposed by law the wilful or improper conduct among the runaways': pravrajyāsu yathācharan rājā daṇḍena vārayet.[1]

The authoritative maxim in the Arthaśastra (IV. 3) also desires that the king should honour the Siddhatāpasas, making them to dwell in his kingdom. But this is not to be mistaken for Aśoka's desire to see all sects dwell everywhere in his domain (rājā sarvata ichhati save pāsaṃḍā vaseyu, R.E. VII), in spite of their verbal agreement. The former keeps in view only those hermits or ascetics who are experts in magical arts and endowed with supernatural powers and may be employed to ward off providential visitations.

Totally different is the attitude of Buddha towards the S'ramaṇas and the Brāhmaṇas. In his terminology, the religieux who is a Brāhmaṇa is at the same time a S'ramaṇa, and *vice versa*.[2] As S'ramaṇa the bhikshu stills his nature by getting rid of sins (samitapāpo ti samaṇo), and as Brāhmaṇa he washes away his sins (vāhitapāpo ti brāhmaṇo). The religious status of a person is sought to be determined by the state of purity and all-round spiritual advancement, and not by birth or family or any outward sign (na jaṭāhi, na gottena, na jachchā).[3] The persons of all social grades are entitled alike to this status provided that they stand the test of saintship.[4] The Sangha or Gaṇa (the latter as in the case of the Jainas) is a common brotherhood or sisterhood of all persons who have come away from the world to live and work together in the pursuit of a common ideal of life irrespective of caste or family. Thus the value is set upon man as man, and not upon man in relation to any accidents of birth or social life.

A difference existed nevertheless between the S'ramaṇas and the Brāhmaṇas as such, and it is freely recognized in the early literature of the Jainas and Buddhists. Mahāvīra generally passed as Samaṇa

---

[1] Arthas'āstra, IV. 3:

Māyāyogavidas tasmād vishaye siddhtāpasāḥ |
vaseyuḥ pūjitā rājñā daivāpat-pratikāriṇaḥ ||

[2] Dhammapada, verse 142: so brāhmaṇo, so samaṇo, sa bhikkhu.

[3] Ibid, verse 393.

[4] Aggañña Suttanta, Dīgha, III, p. 95 f.

Mahāvīra, and Buddha as Samaṇa Gotama. The Wandering ascetics who were born in Brāhman families and belonged to the religious orders to which admission was restricted to persons of the Brāhman caste are bodily distinguished as Brāhmaṇa Parivrājakas[1] from the rest who are called S'ramaṇa pravrajitas.[2] According to the Sutta-nipāta Commentary, the Brāhmans stigmatized the S'ramaṇas as Vṛishalas, not because they were all Vṛishalas by caste but because they freely admitted even the Vṛishalas or S'ūdras into their orders and interdined with them.[3] Among the pravrajitas or 'runaways', the Tāpasas or hermits formed a class by themselves. All of them belonged to the Vānaprastha order, and were mostly twice-borns or persons of the three upper social grades, there having been rarely any Tāpasa from among the S'ūdras, touchable or untouchable.[4] In the early literature of the Jainas and Buddhists, precisely as in the inscriptions of Aśoka, the pravrajitas are broadly represented by the S'ramaṇas and the Brāhmaṇas. They were the objects of love as well as veneration to the people (manussānaṃ piyā ch' eva garukā).[5] They were the accredited teachers of religion and ethics (ovāda-dāyakā) to them. In a territory from which they were driven out, the people are shown to have become morally degraded and impious.[6] It is, therefore, repeatedly insisted that a righteous ruler aspiring to be a universal monarch owes a primary duty to them,[7] which consists not only in entertaining them with food and drink, clothing and shelter, but also in paying due homage to them, properly observing the rules of continence on the sabbath days, and waiting upon them for the cultivation of wisdom through instructions and discussions.[8]

---

1 Aupapātika Sūtra. Sec. 76 : attha māhaṇa-parivvāyā ; Dīgha, III, p. 180 : sambahulā brāhmaṇa-paribbājakā.

2 Ibid, Sec. 75 : pavvaiyā samaṇā ; Dīgha, III, p. 130 : samaṇā Sakyaputtiyā.

3 Paramatthajotikā, II, Vol. 1, p. 175.

4 For the distinction between the touchable and the untouchable among the S'ūdras, see Pāṇini, ii. 4. 10 ; B. C. Law, India As described, p. 141.

5 Jātaka, VI. p.

6 Ibid, III, p. 304 f. The reference is kindly supplied by S. N. Mitra.

7 Dīgha, III, p. 61.

8 Jātaka. VI, p. 296 :

Tappeyya annapānena sadā samaṇa-brāhmaṇe,
dhammakāmo sutadharo bhaveyya paripuchchhake
sakkachcha payirupāseyya sīlavante bahussute.

Cf. Dīgha, III, p. 191.

The legal authority of the king or state to inflict punishments on the priests and 'runaways' if they were found guilty of criminal offences of any kind or to take drastic measures against the recurrences of mischievous and irreligious actions on their part has nowhere been questioned either in the Arthaśāstra or in Buddhist literature. On the other hand, there are clear prescriptions[1] and positive evidences[2] to establish the existence of such an authority. The promulgation of a penal ordinance by Aśoka for the suppression of schisms in the Buddhist Order or even in a particular community of Buddhist monks and nuns may be shown to have its precedents in the past action of the kings of Northern India.[3] The measure adopted by Aśoka is preserved in the Theravāda tradition with a note of approval and without any adverse comment.[4] It was, moreover, in accordance with both the Vinaya rule[5] and the early Buddhist religious sentiment.[6] As the Pali legend suggests, the king exercised

---

[1] Arthas'āstra, IV. 8 :

Brāhmaṇaṃ pāpakarmāṇaṃ uddhusbyāṅkakṛitavraṇam
kuryān nirvishayaṃ rājā vāsayed ākareshu vā.

Ibid, III. 16 :

Pravrajyāsu yathāchārān rājā daṇḍena vārayet.

Cf. Divyāvadāna, p. 165 :

Yasyāyaṃ īdṛis'o dharmaḥ purastāl lambate das'ā
tasya vai s'ravaṇau rājā kshurapreṇāva kṛintatu.

[2] Jātaka, III, p, 804 : "Ime divā samaṇavesena charitvā rattim anāchāraṃ karontī" ti pabbajitānaṃ kujjhitvā......"mayhaṃ vijite sabbe pabbajitā palāyantu, diṭṭhadiṭṭhānaṃ n'eva rājānaṃ karissanti bheriṃ charāpesi.

[3] S. N. Mitra kindly draws my attention to the Dhammapada Commentary, III, p. 54, in which we are told that although Buddha was then alive, the bhikshus appealed successively to Anāthapiṇḍika and Vis'ākhā, and lastly to king Prasenajit to drive out a bhikshu associated with a woman from his kingdom (tumhākaṃ vijitā nīharatha), and the king coming to the vihāra, surrounded it with his men.

[4] Mahāvaṃsa, V. 270-281 ; Samantapāsādika, I, p. 61 : "Na ime bhikkhū, aññatitthiyā ime" ti ñatvā tesaṃ setakāni vatthāni datvā upapabbājesi. The Dīpavaṃsa word is nāsesi. Cf. Kathāvatthu Commentary, p. 8.

[5] The rule cited by Mookerji (Asoka, p. 198) from the Mahāvagga (I. 60. 67, 69) prescribes nāsana ("which is definitive and permanent expulsion from the Sangha") as the extreme penalty for the schism caused by a monk or nun :

Sanghabhedako anupasampanno na upasampādetabbo,
upasampanno nāsetabbo ti.

[6] Cf. Theragāthā, verse 973 :

odātakaṃ arahati, kāsāvam kiṃ karissati ?

Ibid, Verse 975 :

titthiyānaṃ dhajaṃ kechi dhāressanty-avadātakaṃ.

this authority with the consent of the leading men of the Sangha.[1] "The Buddhist law," as Mookerji observes (Asoka, p. 199), "has its counterpart in the Brahmanical law, according to which mischief-makers who tried to create or foment dissensions in the village communities and assemblies were punished by banishment."

Buddha enjoins it as a noble duty on the part of a righteous king-emperor (ariyaṃ chakkavatti-vattaṃ) and he should ask the virtuous S'ramaṇas and Brāhmaṇas, approaching them from time to time—what is wholesome, what is unwholesome, what is blameworthy, what is blameless, what is cultivable, what is not cultivable, what is that which being done, makes for harm and suffering for a long time, and what is that which being done, makes for good and happiness for a long time.[2]

Aśoka describes the S'ramaṇas and the Brāhmaṇas as suvihitā or 'well-established ones' (R.E. XIII), by which he meant the accredited religious teachers in whom the desired principles of piety or duty were established (yesu vihitā). The Hāthigumphā inscription speaks of 'the honoured recluses who are well-established' (sakata-samana-suvihitānaṃ), while the Theragāthā (verse 75) praises visiting the well-established saints as a meritorious deed (sādhu suvihitānaṃ dassanaṃ).

With Aśoka the supreme duty was doing good to the whole world, and there was no greater duty than it :

> Katavyamate hi me sarvalokahitaṃ ;
> nāsti hi kaṃmataraṃ sarvalokahitatpā. (R.E. VI).

To the same effect and virtually in the same language the Rāja-dharma Section of the Great Epic enjoins :

(a) hitārthaṃ sarvalokasya (Mbh., XII. 36. 26) ;
(b) sarvalokahite rataḥ (ibid, XII, 67. 5) ;
(c) sarvalokahitaṃ dharmaṃ kshatriyeshu pratishṭhitam (ibid, XII. 63. 5).

The authoritative dictum quoted in the Arthaśāstra, I. 2, respresents the ideal ruler as one who is devoted to the good of all beings : sarvabhūtahite rataḥ.

---

1 Barua, Inscriptions, ii, p. 382.
2 Dīgha, III, p. 61.

The Mahamora Jataka speaks of the righteous king-emperor as a ruler who grants the boon of 'No fear' to all beings : abhayaṃ cha yo sabbabhūtesu deti.[1]

It is said of Buddha, the religious counterpart of the righteous king-emperor, that he was brought forth by Māyā for the good of the many : bahūnaṃ vata atthāya.[2] Gotama the Recluse might be praised by the outsiders as the well-wisher of all living beings : sabbp-pāṇabhūta-hitānukampi.[3]

'The whole world' is rather a vague term. By this the Mahāmangala Jātaka understands the world of the devas, the pitṛis, the reptiles, and the rest of beings.[4] The beings may be conveniently distinguished as suprahuman, human and infrahuman. The suprahuman world is svarga (saga, svaga, M.R.E.)—heaven, the human world is prithivī (puthavi, R.E. V, Dh)—earth, and the infrahuman world is apāya (S.R.E.)—hell. The heaven is the grand world (vipule svage, M.R E.) in the sense that there one can obtain and enjoy grand results (mahāphale, S.R.E. I), or to use Buddha's phraseology, unbounded joy and happiness (vipulaṃ sukhaṃ).[1] The infernal world is a terrible state of woe (mahāpāye, S.R.E. I),—of apāya-duggati vinipāta in Buddha's words. In Buddha's terminology, the devas were either the gods by birth (upapatti-devā), such as Indra, Varuṇa, Agni, the Lokapālas, the sun, the moon, and the stars, or the gods by purity (visuddhi-devā), such as the S'ramaṇas and the Brāhmaṇas held in high esteem as the accredited religious teachers, or the gods by courtesy and popular consent (sammuti-devā), such as the kings and princes. The infrahuman world included also the whole of the animal kingdom (Pali tirachchhānagatā pāṇā),—the world of bipeds, quadrupeds, birds, fishes, and the rest (P.E. II, P.E. V). This is comprehended by Buddha's expression migapakkhī. The earth consists narrowly of the domain proper of a ruler, the vassal states, and the bordering territories of allies, enemies or strangers (R.E. II, R.E. V, R.E. XIII, S.R.E. II, M.R.E.). The Rajadharma of Aśoka, precisely like the Rājadharma of the Great Epic and the Arthaśastra and the Rāja-chakravarti-Dharma of the Nikāyas and the Jātakas, is intended to secure and promote

---

1 Jātaka, IV, p. 338 ; cf. Jātaka, IV, p. 76 : yo sabbalokassa nivātavutti.

2 Therīgāthā, verse 192.

3 Dīgha, I, p. 4.

4 Jātaka, IV, p. 75.

man's interests here in the present world and hereafter in the other world.

The expressiou 'doing good to the whole world' had a positive meaning for Aśoka. By this he meant that he should make all energetic efforts to see that 'all were free from the innate proneness to sins (sakale apaparisrave asa, R. E. X), that 'all men were actively joined with all good and happiness, both of this world and of the next' (savena hitasukhena hidalokika palalokikena yujevu ti, S.R.E. I), that 'the people might sufficiently grow with the growth in piety and sense of duty' (jane anulupāyā dhaṃmavaḍhiyā vaḍheya[1], P.E. VII), that, 'they might elevate themselves' (abhyuṃnamisati, P.E. VII). With Aśoka parisrava is just another word for apuña, meaning 'demerit.' In Mahāvīra's phraseology the two concepts of parissava (parisrava, spring of sin) and āsava (āsrava, influx of sin) and their opposites go together,[2] while in Buddha's terminology parissaya (pariśraya) stands for lurking danger, the internal spring of impiety and the unwholesome[3]. Aśoka employs the word vaḍhi (vṛiddhi, increase, growth, promotion) as the opposite of hini (hāni, decrease, decay)[4] the word dharmahāni occurring in the Bhagavadgītā[5]. Buddha employs antithetically two verbal forms, abbhunnāmeyyaṃ (should elevate, uplift) and na apanāmeyyaṃ (shouid not lower, degrade)[6].

The secret of success in this matter lies, according to Aśoka, in readiness to action and prompt dispatch of state business : tasa cha pana iyaṃ mūle uṭhāne cha aṭhasaṃtīlanā cha (R. E. VI). Aśoka says that he had no satiety (nāsti hi me toso) in respect of readiness to action and prompt dispatch of state business. Here the great Maurya emperor had just followed the wise adage of the age which is traceable almost in the same language in the Great Epic and the Arthaśāstra quotation of verses :

---

[1] Cf. imassa Sugatovādassa anurūpāyaṃ paṭipattiyaṃ ṭhatvā, Jātaka, III, p. 368.

[2] Achārāṅga Sūtra, p. 18 : ye āsavā te parissavā, ye pasissavā te āsavā, ye aṇāsavā te aparissavā, ye aparissavā te aṇāsavā.

[3] Anguttara, III, p. 388 ; Sutta-nipāta, verses 42, 45 ; Niddesa, I, p. 12, II, p. 420.

[4] R. E. IV.

[5] Cf. dharmahāni prajāyate.

[6] Dīgha, I, p. 124.

Mahabhārata, XII. 57.13 :
Utthānaṃ hi narendrāṇāṃ rājadharmasya yaṃ mūlam.

"Readiness to action on the part of the kings, which is the secret of success in royal administration."[1]

Arthaśāstra, I. 19 :

Rājño hi vratam utthānaṃ, yajñah kāryanuśāsanaṃ,
dakshiṇā vṛittisāmyaṃ cha dīkshā tasyābhisechanam.
Prajāsukhe sukhaṃ rājñah prajānāṃ cha hite hitaṃ,
nātmapriyaṃ hitaṃ rājñah prajānāṃ tu priyaṃ hitam.
Tasmān nityotthito rājā kuryād arthānuśāsanaṃ,
arthasya mūlam utthānaṃ, anarthasya viparyayah.
Anutthāne dhruvo nāśah prāptasyānāgatasya cha,
prāpyate phalam utthānāl labhate chārthasampadam.

"Of a king, the vow indeed is exertion, the performance of sacrifice the discharge of duties, the offer of fees the equal attention to all, and the baptizm the consecration.

In the happiness of the subjects lies the happiness of the king, and in their happiness his welfare. The (personal) welfare is not dear to the king, but the welfare of the subjects is dear (to him).

Hence the king should always be active and administer state-business. The root of advantage is readiness to action, of disadvantage it is the counteractive.

In the case of unreadiness to action surely perish that which is gained and that which is to be gained. He obtains the fruit (desired end) from the promptness in action, and gains in the wealth of advantage."

Of the two points stressed by Aśoka and the maxim in the Artha-śāstra, the first is ustāna, Pali uṭṭhāna and Sk. utthāna, and the second is athasaṃtiraṇā, Pali atthakaraṇa,[2], Sk. kāryanuśāsanam ; the first is the principle of action and the second its application. The idea of atha-saṃtīraṇa is traceable in the Jātaka expressions—vinichchhaye nisīditvā aṭṭe tīresi, "sitting in the court, tried cases", imaṃ potthakam olokentā aṭṭaṃ tīreyyātha, "Looking into this book of precedents, you should try a case."[3] As a Buddhist psychological term, santīraṇa means the preliminary investigation of the data of sense.

---

[1] Here mūlam might be translated also by 'the root or spring of action'.

[2] Kosala-Saṃyutta, I. 7 : atthakaraṇe nisinno.

[3] Jātaka, III, p. 292. The reference is kindly supplied by S. N. Mitra.

Though no Pali dictum showing verbal agreement with that of Aśoka is traced so far, it is incontestable that the whole emphasis of Buddha's teachings is on uṭṭhāna, which is but a synonym of appamāda (earnestness), daḷhaparakkama (strong power of action),[1] attakāra purisakāra (self-willed action), bala (strength of the will), viriya (mental energy), and the like. The Dhammapada inculcates that the glory of a person goes on increasing if he is ready for action, mindful, pure in deed, discreet in action, self-restrained, virtuous and earnest.[2] Just as in Aśoka's edicts the different aspects of the concept of uṭṭhāna are sought to be expressed by such terms as parākrama (power of action, R.E. X), pakama (strenuous exertion, M.R.E.), usāha (zeal, P.E. I), and uyāma (effort, R.E. XIII), dhiti (fortitude, S.R.E. II), and patiṃnā achalā (resolve unshaken), so in the Dhammasangaṇi, we have for the concept of sammā-vāyāma (right exercise of the will) such contributory terms as viriyārambha (energetic initiative), nikkama (strenuous exertion), parakkama (power of action), uyyama (effort), ussāha (zeal), ussoḷhi (ardour), thāma (stamina), dhiti (fortitude), asithila-parakkamatā (unabated powerful activity), anikkhittachhandatā (unabandoned will to act), anikkhitta-dhuratā (steadily keeping on to the path of action), and anikkhitta-sampaggāha (steadfast adherence to the path of action).

With Buddha appamāda is the single term by which the whole of his teaching might be summed up. In the Kosala Saṃyutta, II. 7-8, Buddha mentions appamāda to king Pasenadi of Kosala as the single principle of action which stands embracing both the interests, viz., that which appertains to the present existence and that which appertains to the future existence.[3] Here he advises the king to base on this very principle all his duties, private and public, as thereby he might keep him active, wakeful and guarded together with his family members and vassals, his subjects and officers, and his treasury and storehouse.

---

[1] Dhammapada, Ch. III.

[2] Ibid, verse, 24 :

> Uṭṭhānavato satimato
> suchikammassa nisammakārino,
> saññstassa cha dhammajīvino
> appamattassa yaso' bhivaḍḍhati.

[3] Appamādo kho mahārāja eko dhammo ubho atthe samadhiggayha tiṭṭhati-diṭṭhadhammikaṃ cheva atthaṃ samparāyikaṃ.

"Figuratively only utthāna means the active state of mind and body. The opposite state of usṭāna, according to S.R.E. I, is represented by anāvuti (non-application), ālasiya (indolence), and kilamatha (fatigue).

As observed elsewhere, "Aśoka's principle of utthāna or parākrama seeks its fulfilment through atthasantīraṇa, 'prompt dispatch of state business', and is directed to doing good to the whole world (sarvalokahita), to making all beings happy here and enabling all men to attain to heaven hereafter, particularly to promote other worldly interests (savaṃ pāratrikāya, R.E. X). It required all including him and his officers to apply themselves ceaselessly and eternally (sasvataṃ samayaṃ, S.R.E. I) to the noble cause espoused by way of faithfully and effectively discharging the duties assigned. In short, action, and action alone, was the underlying principle of Aśoka's Dhamma and system of administration."[1]

The two means by which Aśoka sought to promote the cause of piety and human duty in the world are appositely called nijhati and dhaṃmaniyama (P.E. VII), the first corresponding to the Pali nijjhatti,[2] and the second to saddhammaniyāma.[3] In Pali the term nijjhatti implies the sound method of reasoning, the appeal to reason and understanding, the way of convincing each other by fact and reason, as distinguished from ujjhatti or the obstinate way of suppressing reason by resorting to a kind of *argumentum ad verucundum*.[4] The niyāma is the order regulating the path of action (magga-niyāma)[5] which is inviolable (abhabbo okkamituṃ).[6] Aśoka sought to give effect to the means of nijjhatti or moral persuasion by the inculcation of the fundamental principles of piety or duty (dhaṃmānusathini), the proclamations of their usefulness (dhaṃmasāvanāni), and the tangible works of public utility (dhaṃmathaṃbhāni). The second of these is the duty assigned in Pali literature to the Dhammaghosakas.[7] The way of dhaṃma-niyama was sought to be given effect to by Aśoka through regulation or legislation.

---

1 Barua, Inscriptions, ii. p. 298.

2 Anguttara, IV, p. 223.

3 Ibid, III, p. 185. The reference is kindly supplied by S. N. Mitra.

4 Manorathapūraṇī, Siamese ed., III, p. 281.

5 Ibid, III, p. 64.

6 Anguttara, III, p. 174.

7 Jātaka, III, p. 161 ; Dhammapada Commentary, III, p. 81. I owe the Jātaka reference to S. N. Mitra.

Ministration to the whole world is possible through the discharge of certain essential duties that are traditionally known in Pali as dasa-rāja-dhammā or dasa-rājavaṭṭā. The number ten may be raised to twelve by following a slightly different mode of enumeration.[1] The categorisation of the duties is evidently based upon a certain statement of Buddha, which is just illustrative and not exhaustive. The essential duties of a ruler lie, according to the Arthaśāstra and other Brahmanical works on royal polity, to the seven elements of sovereignty, *viz.*, himself, the ministers and other officers, the territory and population, the defences, the financial resources, the army, and the allies.[2] These may be taken to consist, according to Buddha, of the obligations to the ruler himself (attani), to his own people (antojanasmiṃ), to his own territory (antojanapadasmiṃ),[3] to vassals (khattiyesu anuyuttesu),[4] to the friends and allies (mittāmachchesu), to the fighting units (balakāyesu), to the Brāhmans and other needy householders (brāhmaṇa-gahapatikesu), to the slaves and servants (dāsa-kammakaresu),[5] to the people of towns and districts (negamajānapadesu), to the Śramaṇas and the Brāhmaṇas (samaṇa-brāhmaṇesu), and to the beasts and birds and other animals (migapakkhīsu).[6]

As for the duty to himself, Aśoka's expression is 'just as he feels concern for himself' (athā atānaṃ anukaṃpati, S.R.E. II). The Pali idiom is precisely the same: attānaṃ anukampāmi, "just as I feel concern for myself."[7] The earlier Buddhalogy as developed in the Buddhavaṃsa, the Chariyā-piṭaka and Jātaka Nidāna-kathā speaks of a long course of preparation undergone by the Bodhisattva for serving these three great interests: doing good to oneself (attattha-chariyā), doing good to one's people (ñātattha-chariyā), and doing good to the world (lokattha-chariyā).[8] The first is individual, not to say egotistic; the second is national, not to say parochial; the third is universal, not to say altruistic. These are reduced to two in the Jātakas, viz., in the interest of oneself (attadatthaṃ) and in the

---

1 Sumangala-vilāsinī, III, p. 851.

2 Arthas'āstra, VI. 1: svāmyamātya-janapada-durga-kos'a-daṇḍamitrāṇi.

3 This is not included in the traditional list of ten but dealt with in many a text.

4 This, too is not included in the list of ten.

5 Variant, anuyantesu.

6 Dīgha, III, p. 61; Jātaka, IV, p. 421f.; V, p. 123, etc.

7 Jātaka, IV, p. 320.

8 Chariyā-piṭaka Commentary, p. 7. Here buddhattha-chariyā is really = attatthachariyā.

interest of others (paratthaṃ)[1]. The right application of oneself (attasammāpaṇidhi) is considered the best course of wisdom.[2] Before taking the responsibility of instructing others one should first establish oneself in what is proper.[3] To do so one must stand firm in piety and be endowed with moral rectitude and gentleness of nature (dhamme ṭhito ajjave maddave sato),[4] be well established in virtue (sīle patiṭṭhāya).[5] In words of Aśoka, standing firm in piety and virtue, they will be administering the form of conduct (dhaṃmamhi sīlamhi tisṭaṃto dhaṃmaṃ anusāsisaṃti, R.E. IV). The philosophic argument behind it is that the enlightened self-interest is *ne plus ultra.*[6] If one holds oneself dear to him, one should guard oneself well. The Arthaśāstra, I. 2, cites the word of wisdom according to which the king himself being well-disciplined in sciences, should devote himself to the task of regulating the conduct of his subjects.[7] The object is that he should be the pioneer in noble deeds,—the leader of the multitude, himself being firmly devoted to the practice of piety.[8] He is to be the ādikara or first-doer, an epithet applied in the Jaina Āgama to the founder of Jainism : āigare titthagare.[9] Aśoka says, "Doing a good deed is difficult. He who does it first, does a difficult thing (indeed). But many a good deed has been done by me" :

Kalāṇaṃ dukaraṃ. Yo ādikaro kalāṇasa so dukaraṃ karoti. Ta mayā bahu kalāṇaṃ kataṃ (R.E.V).

---

[1] Anabhirati Jātaka.

[2] Mangala Sutta.

[3] Dhammapada. verse 158 :

Attānam eva paṭhamaṃ paṭirūpe niveaye,
ath' aññam anusāseyya ... ...

[4] Sutta-pipāta, verse 250.

[5] Saṃyutta, I, p. 13.

No ve 'piyam me' ti janinda tādiso
attaṃ niraṃkatvā piyāni sevati.
attā va seyyo paramā va seyyo
labbhā piyā ochitattena pachchhā.

[6] Cf. Bṛihad Āraṇyaka Up., IV. 5. 6 : na vā are sarvasya kāmāya sarvaṃ priyaṃ bhavati, ātmanastu kāmāya sarvaṃ priyaṃ bhavati.

[7] Arthas'āstra, 1. 5 : Vidyā-vinīto rājā hi prajānāṃ vinaye rataḥ.

[8] Dīgha, III, p. 169 :

Pubbangamo sucharitesu dhammesu
dhammachariyābhirato anvāyiks bahujanassa.

[9] Aupapātika Sūtra, Secs. 16, 20 f.

This reminds us at once of the Jātaka dicta :

Yo pubbe katakalyāṇo akā lokesu dukkaraṃ.[1]

Katā me kalyāṇā anekarūpā.[2]

All the authorities agree in saying that the first duty of the king fit to rule is self-preparation through education, learning and training, and that the means thereof is constant contact with men of experience (vṛiddha-saṃyogāt). They also agree in insisting on his protecting himself as well as others against all possible harm. But Kauṭilya's king, like Machiavelli's prince, is advised to live always in a world of suspicion and dread, which is full of enemies, internal and external. He is to trust none, neither his wives nor his sons, neither his ministers nor his officers ; neither the food which is cooked nor the bed which is prepared for him, not even his friends, far less his enemies, not even himself.

Buddha's righteous king emperor is expected to live, on the other hand, in a world of trust and security where all are imbued with the same spirit of Dharma and all are devoted to the pursuit of the common ideal of life.[3] Aśoka's world is such a world of trust and security where all should be working for piety (savata vijitasi mama dhaṃmayutasi, R.E.V.)

By the expression 'own people' are narrowly meant one's family members consisting of wives and sons (children). Mother and father are to figure most prominently among them. One's own people may be taken also to include brothers and sisters and other kinsfolk (R.E.V). Aśoka speaks of parents, teachers (āchariyā), wives and sons, brothers and sisters, other kinsmen, other princes of the blood (R.E. III, R.E.IV, R E.V, R.E. IX, R.E. XI, R.E. XIII, P.E. VII). Along with kinsmen he mentions friends (mita), associates (saṃthuta), comrades (suhadaya) and companions (sahāya), all comprehended by Buddha's expression mittāmachchā or ñātisuhajjā. He does not omit to refer also to the neighbours (paṭivesiyā, R.E. IX). He distinguishes one's people as those who are closely (vage) and those who are distantly related (daviye, S.R.E. I), as those who stand near (paṭiyāsaṃnā) and those who stand afar (apakaṭhā, P.E. VI). With sons go

---

1 Jātaka, III, p. 12. S. N. Mitra refers to Milinda, p. 59, stating ādikammikassa dandhāyanā bhavati. For ādikaro, see Pāṇini, III. 2-21.

2 Ibid. V. p. 491.

3 Dīgha, III, p. 65 : Saṃvijjanti vijite amachchā pārisajjā gaṇaka-mahāmattā anīkaṭṭhā dovārikā mantass' ājīvino, mayañ ch'eva aññe cha ye mayaṃ ariyaṃ chakkavatti-vattaṃ dhārema.

grandsons, great-grandsons and the descendants after them (R.E.IV, R.E. V, R.E. XII). He speaks in the same breath of father, son, brother, master, friend, associate, even down to neighbour (R.E. XI). Though the individual words are met with in all literature of India, there is little doubt that Aśoka's language or manner of speaking is almost verbally the same as that in the Buddhavachana. Aśoka's word vijita for one's territory is typically a Pali word.

The Nikāyas mention the Śākyas as vassals (anuyātā, anuyuttā khattiyā) under the king of Kośala. Such vassals within Aśoka's empire were the Yonas, the Kāmbojas, and the rest (R.E.V, R.E. XIII). The idea of vassals is rather obscure in the Great Epic and the Arthaśāstra. Sāmantā in the sense of independent neighbours is as much a Pali or Sanskrit word as Aśokan (R.E. II), while the word Antā or Pratyantā in the same sense is peculiarly Aśokan. Aśoka's Baṃbhanibhā (R.E.V) is the very same expression as the Pali Brāhmaṇibbhā or Brāhmaṇa-gahapatikā[1] by which the needy people of the world are meant. Even the Brāhmaṇas and the S'ramaṇas (P.E. VII) in one aspect of their earthly existence, namely, mendicancy, may be taken to have been meant by the expression Brāhmaṇibbhā. In the Pali Nikāyas and Jātakas, precisely as in Aśoka's Edicts, the Brāhmaṇas and the Ibbhas, or the Brāhmaṇas and the S'ramaṇas are often associated with the four classes of beggars, viz. kapaṇā (kṛipaṇāh) meaning 'those in a pitiful condition, the poor people suffering from bodily infirmity', addhikā or street-beggars' (pathāvino), vaṇibbakā (vaṇīyakāh) or 'those beggars who induce the public to offer alms and make gifts by proclaiming the merit that accrues from alms-giving and gifts, and yāchakā or 'the beggars imploring the public to spare anything, however little or insignificant.[2] Aśoka's anāthas (orphans, destitutes), vudhas (age-worn persons), kapaṇa-valākā (the poor and the miserable)[3], and dāsa-bhatakā (slaves and servants) are rightly grouped with persons deserving of compassion (R.E.V, P.E. VII). One may take along with them also other persons in distress, such as those who are shut up in prison (baṃdhanabadhā)

---

[1] Jātaka, VI, p. 229.

[2] Barua, Inscriptions. ii, p. 271.

[3] Dīnāḥ kṛipaṇāḥ in the language of the Rāmāyaṇa. In Pali kapaṇa and varāka are often used as synonyms, Jātaka, IV, p. 285 ; Petavatthu Commentary, p. 120, cf. Samyutta, I. p. 231. By the word kapaṇā Buddhaghosa understands duggatā dalidda-manussā kāṇa-kuṇi-ādayo.

and those sentenced to death (patavadhā)[1]. The sick (vyādhitā) implied in R.E. II are to be counted also among the distressed.

The expression negama-jānapadā which is the same as pora-jānapadā applies to the people of towns and districts who are variously engaged in the transactions of life, particularly commercial.[2]

The expression samaṇa-brāhmaṇā as distinguished from brāhmaṇa-gahapatikā applies to the 'runaways' who are the accredited religious teachers of men.

And the expression miga-pakkhī (lit., beasts and birds) applies to all animals, whether bipeds or quadrupeds, terrestrial or aquatic.

The territory gained by a king is rightly said to be of three kinds: that which is newly acquired (navaḥ), that which is recovered (bhūtapūrvaḥ), and that which is ancestral (pitryah)[3]. In Aśoka's case the territory of the second kind is out of the question as he is not known to have lost any portion of his territory. The major portion of his territory is ancestral, Kalinga being the only territory newly acquired (adhunāladha, R.E. XIII). It is the agreed opinion of all Indian political thinkers that the primary duty of a king or king emperor is to see his territory consolidated (janapada thāvariya-ppatta),[4] or to guard it carefully if it is a newly conquered one (jitañ cha rakkhe anivesano siyā)[5].

In the ancestral territory the reigning king is advised in the Arthaśāstra (XIII. 5) to cover the faults of his father and to manifest his own virtues. The instance of king Siri Meghavaṇṇa who tried to make ample amends for certain tyrannical and revengeful acts of his father Mahāsena might here be cited from the history of Ceylon.

Aśoka in his edicts, does not think of his father or immediate predecessor but only of the former kings who had through several ages built up a noble tradition of piety. The works of public utility

---

[1] See Amarakosha, XI. 151, 152; Niḥsvas tu duvidho dīno daridro durgato pi saḥ | vaṇīyako yāchanako mārgaṇo yāchakārthiṇau ||

[2] Jātaka, V, p. 243:

Yo cha rājā janapadaṃ adhammena pasāsati |
sabbosadhībi so rājā viruddho hoti khattiyo ||
Tath eva negame hiṃsaṃ ye yuttā kayavikkaye |
ojadānabalikare sa kosena virujjhati ||

[3] Arthas'āstra, XIII. 5, Cf. pettikaṃ dāyajjam, Dīgha, III, p. 60.

[4] Dīgha, III, p. 59.

[5] Dhammapada, verse 40.

done by them was also being done by him just to keep up the tradition (dhaṃma-paṭīpati), though these in his opinion had but slight effect (lahuke esa paṭibhoge, P.E. VII). As for himself, he tried to fulfil their noble intention to see the people grow sufficiently with the growth in piety by adopting two novel methods (P.E. VII).

With regard to the newly acquired territory the king is advised in the Arthaśāstra (XIII. 5) to adopt, among others, the following means of pacification :

Trying to cover the faults of the fallen enemy with his virtues and excelling his virtues by doubling his own. Devotion to his own duties and works. The showing of favours (anugrahakarma), the offering of presents (parihārakarma), the giving of gifts (dānakarma), the bestowing of honours (mānakarma), and the doing of what is agreeable and good to the subjects (prakṛiti-priya-hitāni). The adoption of the same mode of life, the same dress, language and etiquette (samānaśīla-veśa-bhāshā-āchārata)[1] so as to avoid appearing as a stranger in the habits of life (prakṛiti-viruddhāchāra). The evincing of personal interest in their national, religious and social festivals and functions (deśa-daivata-samājotsavavihāreshu bhaktih). The honouring everywhere of religious orders (sarvatra āśrama-pūjanam). The offering of land, articles of use, and other gifts and presents to persons noted for their learning, eloquence and piety (vidyā-vākya-dharmaśūra-purushāṇāṃ bhūmidravya-dāna-parihāra). The release of all prisoners (sarva-bandhana-mokshaṇam) and the doing of favour to miserable, helpless and diseased persons (anugrahaṃ dīnānātha-vyādhitānām). The prohibiting of the slaughter of animals for half a lunar month during the period of chāturmāsya (chāturmāsyeshu ardhamāsikam aghātam), for four nights during the full moons (paurṇamāsīshu chāturātrikam), and for a night on the day of the birth-star of the conqueror king and on that of the national star (rāja-deśa-nakshatreshu ekarātrikam) ; the prohibiting as well of the slaughter of females and young ones and the castration of males (yoni-bāla-vadha-puṃstvopaghāta-pratishedhah).

One may observe that in this particular context the Arthaśāstra prescribes all the noble principles of rājadharma advocated by Aśoka through his edicts and that the prohibitions are precisely those embodied in his Regulation of Piety (P.E. V). But we lose all zest in the Arthaśāstra prescriptions and prohibitions as soon as we learn that

---

[1] This is precisely what is meant by Buddha's word samānattatā.

these are all meant to give the conqueror a good appearance before the people of a conquered territory. One is likely to wonder wherefrom the Arthaśāstra got the idea of these advantageous prohibitions when these are bodily against the rules of secular Brahmanism. Consider, for instance, Aśoka's prohibition of the branding of horses and cattle with marks on the Tishya, Punarvasu and chāturmāsī full-moon days, as well as for half a month during the period of chāturmāsya (Indian Lent). The Arthaśāstra has no prohibitory rules regarding the time of marking the cattle (II. 29). The most auspicious time for marking is the Kārtika full-moon or the star Revatī in the month of Āśvayuja, according to the Law-book of Vishṇu. The Āśvalāyana Grihya Sūtra adds the full-moon day of Vaiśākha, while the Sānkhāyana Grihya Sūtra prefers the new moon after the month Phālguna and the star Revatī after the full moon.

"Aśoka's Regulation was meant to restrain the people of India against the killing of she-goats, ewes, and sows, if they were found to be with young or in milk, as also against the killing of their offsprings, if they were within six months of age. Among the Smritikāras, Gautama alone, as pointed out by Bühler, forbids the meat of animals whose teeth have not fallen away.....In the Nigrodhamiga Jātaka, a doe desiring to put off her turn of going into the execution-block, pleads her case, saying, 'Sire, I am now with young (gabbhinī). There is not a word about the cow and her calf in the edict (P. E. V) in this particular connection. The oxen (gone) certainly find mention alongside of goats, rams and pigs in the context of the rule for branding. Following the custom of the Middle Country, Bodhāyana and Vasishṭha prohibited the meat of milch-cows and oxen. Kauṭilya penalises the killing of the calf, the bull, and the milch-cow (vatsa-vrisha dhenuś chaishām avadhyāh, Arthaśāstra, II. 26). The Buddha raised his strong voice against the killing of cows (Brāhmaṇa-dhammika Sutta, Sutta-nipāta), and succeeded in persuading some of the contemporary rulers and leading Brāhman teachers of the Middle Country to put a stop to the practice. The killing of milch-cows, oxen, and calves must have been out of the question in the Middle Country of Aśoka's time."[1]

The identity of Aśoka's saṃḍaka figuring in his list of inviolables (avadhyas) is still open to dispute. Bühler takes it to mean the bulls set at liberty that serve in India as stud bulls. If it really stands

[1] Barua, Inscriptions, ii, p. 366 f. For the branding of the cattle, cf. Mbh. III. 239. 4-6.

for such bulls, the reader might be referred to the Arthaśāstra (II. 29) prescribing rules to punish with the first amercement a person who causes the leading bull of a herd (yūthavrishah) to fight with another bull, and with the highest amercement when such a bull is injured thereby.

Though both the grounds and purposes of the game-laws in P.E. V and the Arthaśāstra (II. 26) are different, the birds, fishes, and quadrupeds declared as inviolables are for all practical purposes the same. "From the qualifying clause, 'that neither come into (men's) use nor are eaten' (P.E. V), Aśoka's purpose seems to have been to stop for good the unnecessary killing or torture of inoffensive creatures, not because they were *mangalyas* or sacrosancts (as in the Arthaśāstra, II 26). The abandonment of the practice of going on hunting expedition on his part must have been in accordance with the dictates of his new religious conscience. His intention of minimising the slaughter of and inflictions of cruelty on living beings which is clearly expressed in R.E. I is perceptible also behind all the restrictive measures contemplated in his Regulation."[1]

On the question of the king's or king emperor's obligations to the needy, the destitute, the minor, the aged, the diseased, the distressed and the fallen the Indian systems of rājadharma are hardly at variance.

To take, first of all, the case of the diseased among men and animals. With regard to them Aśoka tells us that he made throughout his dominions as well as in the territories of his friendly neighbours arrangements for two kinds of treatment (dve chikīchhā kata, R.E. II), one suitable for men and the other for animals (manusa-chikīchhā cha pasu-chikīchhā). To implement it he caused medicinal herbs and roots and fruits to be supplied and planted wherever these were not available (osuḍhāni cha mūlāni cha phalāni cha yatra yatra nāsti sarvata hārāpitāni cha ropāpitāni cha). The arrangements made by him may not strictly be taken to mean that he founded hospitals for men and cattle. Almost to the same effect and in the same language the Rājadharma section of the Great Epic (XII. 68. 64) enjoins :

> Aushadhāni cha sarvāṇi mūlāni cha phalāni cha
> chaturvidhāṃś cha vaidyān[2] vai saṃgṛihṇīyad viśeshataḥ.

[1] Ibid, ii, p. 365.

[2] Probably the physicians dealing with diseases of men, cattle, horses and elephants are meant.

"Medicinal herbs and roots and fruits and four classes of physicians should particularly be collected."

According to the Arthaśāstra (IV. 3), when pestilences (vyādhibhayam) and epidemics (marakāḥ) occur as a national calamity (upanipāta), the king should try to cope with them by such remedies (pratikāraih) as secret arts (upanishadikaiḥ), medicines (aushadhaih), and pacificatory and purificatory ceremonies. The medicines are to be applied by the physicians (chikitsakāh) and the pacificatory and purificatory ceremonies are to be performed by the siddhatāpasas. In the case of cattle diseases (paśuvyādhimarake), the king should perform the ceremony of nīrājana as well as the worship of the family deity. But elsewhere the Arthaśāstra (II. 29, II. 30, II. 31) speaks of the treatment of the diseases of cattle, horses and elephants by expert physicians.[1]

With regard to the helpless (anāthesu), the aged (vudhesu), the miserable and the distressed (kapana-valākesu), Aśoka ordained seemly behaviour (saṃpaṭīpati, P.E. VII) and appointed the Dharma-mahāmātras to work for their good and happiness (hitasukhāye, R.E. V). The religious mendicants are taken along with them. Among the prisoners, those burdened with the maintenance of family (anubadha-pajā)[2] and those advanced in years were made entitled to special consideration in the matter of ransom, leniency and release (paṭividhanāye apalibodhāye mokhāye, R.E. V).

The Nikāyas[3] and Jātakas[4] abound in admonitions to the kings persuading them to feed the mendicants of all description, to give them alms, and to liberally help them with gifts out of faith and without worried mind.

---

1 "Cowherds (gopālakāḥ) shall apply remedies to calves or aged cows or cows suffering from diseases."

"Veterinary surgeons (as'vānām chikitsakāḥ) shall apply remedies against undue growth or diminution in the body of horses, and also change the diet of horses."

"The superintendent of elephants...examines...the work of elephant doctors (chikitsakāḥ)."

2 In the Kalsi variant, anubaṃdhā pajāva, the first word may be taken independently to mean 'children.' See Amarakosha, Nānārthavarga, 309. According to Buddhaghosa, anubaddhā = anugatā, Sumangala-vilāsinī, I. p. 39.

3 Devaputta-Saṃyutta, III, 3 ; Kosala-Saṃyutta, III. 1.

4 Jātaka, IV, pp. 34, 53 foll. ; V, p. 492.

Regarding men and animals in old age, the general principle laid down in the Jātakas is :

Jiṇṇaṃ posaṃ gavassañ cha māssu yuñji yathā pure
parihārañ cha dajjāsi adhikārakato balī[1].

"The officers in their old age as well as the cows and horses should not be engaged in work as before, and they should be given due consideration on account of the good service rendered when they were in strength."

In keeping with the general spirit of the age the Arthaśāstra lays down the following rules to safeguard the interest of religion and the religieux, the infants and invalids, women and children, the poor and the helpless :

"The king shall personally attend to the business of the gods, of the Brahmanical ascetics, of the heretics, of the S'rotriyas, of cattle and sacred places, of minors, the aged, the afflicted and the helpless, and of women, either in the order of enumeration or according to the gravity or urgency of the duties."[2]

"The king shall provide the orphans, the aged, the diseased, the afflicted, and the helpless with maintenance. He shall also maintain (helpless) women when they are carrying and the children they give birth to."[3]

According to the Arthaśāstra (II. 36), on the days connected with the birth-star of the king and the full-moon days 'such prisoners

---

[1] Jātaka. VI, p. 251. Here the Pali expression jiṇṇaṃ posaṃ adhikārakato (same as katādhikāro, Jātaka, I. p. 56) exactly fits in with As'oka's katābhikāresu thairesu.

[2] Arthas'sāstra, I. 19 : devatās'rama.pāshaṇḍa-s'rotriyapas'upuṇyasthānāṃ bāla-vṛiddha-vyādhita-vyasanyanāthānāṃ strīṇāṃ cha krameṇa kāryān pas'yet kārya-gauravād ātyayikavas'ena vā.

[3] Ibid, II. 1 : bāla-vṛiddha-vyādhita-vyasanānāthānāṃs' cha rājā vibhṛiyāt strīyāṃ aprajātāṃ prajātāyas' cha putrān.

[4] The two stars whose importance is emphasized in the Arthas'āstra (XIII. 5) are the birth-star of the reigning king and the national star. The two stars to which the edicts attach special importance are the Tishya or Tishyā and Punarvasu, P.E. V. The prohibition of the castration and branding of animals under these two constellations is a point in common between the Arthasāstra injunction and As oka's Dhhaṃma-niyama. If on this ground the first be regarded as the birth star, the second may be regarded as the coronation-star of As'oka.

Barua, Inscriptions, ii, pp. 332, 372 f.

The pre-eminent position of the Tishya as the birth star may be inferred also from As'vaghosha's association of the Pushya (which is just another name for the Tishya) with the birth of prince Siddhārtha, Buddhacharita (Johnston's ed.) i, 9 ; Cowell's ed,, 1. 25 : tatah prasannas' cha Pushyah.

as are young, old, diseased or helpless (anātha) shall be let out from the jail (bandhanāgāra), or those who are of charitable disposition or those who have made any agreement with the prisioners[1] may liberate them by paying an adequate ransom'.

The authoritative maxims quoted in the Arthaśāstra (II. 36) mention the conquest of a new country, the installation of the heir-apparent, and the birth of a prince as the special occasions for jail delivery. "Once in a day," they say, "or once in five nights, jails may be emptied of prisoners in consideration of the work they have done,[2] or of whipping inflicted upon them, or of an adeqate ransom paid in gold."

As regards the prisoners on whom death sentence has been passed by the court, Aśoka says that he granted them three days' respite either to give a chance to their kinsmen to have their cases reviewed for the sparing of life,[3] or at least to observe religious fast and offer gifts within the specified time of death (niludhasi kālasi),[4] to prepare, in other words, for death. Nothing corresponding to this is to be found in the Arthrśāstra or elsewhere in Indian literature.

Servitude (dāsavya), indebtedness (iṇa), disease (roga), imprisonment (bandhanāgāra) and long journey, particularly one across a wildnerness (kantāraddhānamagga) are mentioned by Buddha as typical states of woe from which men seek release.[5] Servitude is described as the hard lot of slaves and hirelings (dāsakammakarā), of slaves and servants (bhaṭamayā, dāsa-bhatakā) in the words of Aśoka. Though indebtedness is not expressly mentioned in the edicts, it is included in the general problem of poverty and destitution dealt with by Aśoka and others. As a contributory cause of servitude and imprisonment, indebtedness may be regarded as a subhead of both.

Long journey, especially one across a wilderness, means the suffer-

---

1 Literally, 'those bound by an agreement' (samayānubaddhā).

2 karmaṇā, bringing out obviously the meaning of As'oka's katābhikāra and Pali katādhikāra.

3 For the bare sparing of life, acc. to S.N. Mitra.
Barua, Inscriptions, ii, p. 351 f.

4 Cf. Pali niruddha-velāyaṃ, Dhammapada Commentary, I, p. 297 ; niruddho des'a-kālābhyām in the Arthas'āstra (VII. 3). Barua. Inscriptions, ii, p. 207.

5 Ibid, ii, p. 308.

ing of the travellers including caravan merchants from fatigue as well as risks of life and fortune from the action of thieves and robbers. The construction and maintenance of roads, guarding them against inroads of thieves, highway robbers, wild tribes and animals, providing guides and escorts, shade-trees, inns and caravansaries, and the like are all meant for ensuring the safety and comfort of the travellers. The planting of shade-trees at every half *kos*, the sinking of wells and excavation of tanks, the construction of resting sheds and water-stations, the laying out of fruit gardens and retreats, the founding of almshouses, and similar other institutions of comfort were admittedly the time-honoured tradition of piety established by the former kings of India which was just kept up by Aśoka (P.E. VII). All of them come within the scope of ishṭāpūrtam praised in the Brahmanical Law-books as works of merit.[1] Similarly the Buddha praises the laying out of flower gardens and fruit gardens, the making of forest retreats, the construction of bridges, etc., the building of water-stations, and the digging of wells and tanks as meritorious works of public utility by which persons become entitled to go to heaven.[2] According to the Arthaśāstra, it was the duty of the superintendent of passports and the Antapālas and Aṭavīpālas to guard the frontiers, forest tracts and uninhabited tracts with a view to the safety of travellers and the control of travels and traffic, while the Pradeshṭṛis were specially charged with the duty of removing all thorns or internal troubles arising from the action of thieves, robbers, and the like. It recommends certain amount of leniency on the part of the judges in dealing with the cases of persons suffering from the fatigue of long journey. In Buddha's opinion it is one of the seven main conditions of national welfare that legal protection should be vouchsafed for worthy visitors so that they may be induced to visit the land and when they come they may find the place quite comfortable.[3] The Arthaśāstra (II. 36) refers to resthouses among the charitable institutions[4] in a town or

---

[1] Manu, IV. 226 : S'raddhayeshṭāñ cha pūrttāñ cha nityaṃ kuryād atandritaḥ ; Atri, verse 44: Vāpī-kūpa-taḍāgādi devāyatanāni cha । annapradām ārāmāḥ pūrttam ityabhidhīyate.

[2] Saṃyutta, I, p. 33.

[3] Mahāparinibbāna Suttanta, Ch. I: arahantesu dhammika-rakkhāvaraṇa-gutti susaṃvihitā kin ti te anāgatā cha arahanto vijitaṃ āgachchheyyuṃ, āgatā cha phāsuṃ vihareyyun ti.

[4] Dharmāvasatha, same as modern Dharmas'ālā.

city that were open to wandering ascetics and travellers.[1] The wayfarers going along a highroad are required to catch hold of any person whom they find to be suffering from a wound or ulcer, or possessed of destructive instruments, or tired of carrying a heavy load, or timidly avoiding the presence of others, or indulging in too much sleep, or fatigued from a long journey, or who appears to be a stranger to the place in the localities such as inside or outside the capital, temples of gods, places of pilgrimage, or burial grounds (ibid, II. 36). Among the Classical writers, Strabo refers to a board of town officers who attended to the entertainment of foreigners, assigning to them lodgings, keeping watch over their modes of life, escorting them on the way when they leave the country, taking care of them when they are sick, burying them if they die and forwarding their property to the relatives of the deceased.[2]

Slavery existed in different forms and degrees of servitude in India even when Megasthenes came as an ambassador to the court of Chandragupta Maurya, nay, it existed even in earlier times. The treatment of slaves was, nevertheless, so liberal and humane that slavery, even if it existed in the country, was nothing as compared with its Greek or Roman form. One of the remarkable facts, noted by Megasthenes about India was that all the Indians were free, and not one of them was a slave. Though the Lakedæmonians and the Indians agreed so far in this matter, the former held the Helots as slaves, but the latter did not even use aliens as slaves and much less a countryman of their own.[3] The statement of the Greek ambassador about the non-existence of slavery in India has rather been misconstrued by his modern critics. Diodorus truly represents the account of Megasthenes when he says, "Of several remarkable customs existing among the Indians, there is one drescribed by their ancient philosophers which one may regard as truly admirable; for the law ordains that no one among them shall, under any circumstances, be a slave, but that enjoying freedom, they shall respect the equal right to it which all possess."[4] Thus Megasthenes was concerned with

---

1 Dharmāvasathinaḥ pāshaṇḍi-pathikān āvedya vāsayeyuḥ.

"The managers of Dharmas'ālās should allow the heretics and travellers to reside after reporting their arrival to the city-officer concerned."

2 McCrindle, Ancient India, p. 87.

3 Ibid, p. 211 f.

4 Ibid, p. 38.

the ideal advocated by the philosophers and religious teachers and the underlying spirit of the law of the land, and not with the actual state of things. If we say that in England and Burma there is no harlot in the eye of law, we do not certainly mean that there is no harlot in fact ; all that we intend here is a distinction between *de jure* and *de facto*. Speaking of the philosophic and religious standpoint, he was careful to observe : "Those, they thought, who have learned neither to domineer over nor to cringe to others will attain the life best adapted for all vicissitudes of lot : for it is but fair and reasonable to institute laws which find all equally, but allow property to be unevenly distributed."[1]

The Arthaśāstra (III. 13) emphatically declares that servitude is not verily consistent with the condition of an Aryan (na tvevāryasya dāsabhāvaḥ), though it may not be improper among the unclean to sell or buy children for servitude (Mlechchhānāṃ adoshaḥ prajāṃ vikretum ādhātuṃ vā). The general tenour of the laws prescribed in this great work is to afford all possible chances to the slaves to regain their free state.

Buddha not only abstained himself from receiving slaves, male and female, as gifts but also restrained his disciples from it. He prohibited 'traffic in human beings' (satta-vaṇijjā, i.e., manussa-vaṇijjā) on the part of the laity.[2] In accordance with the Jātaka maxim, no person should offer himself to slavery.

Taking servitude to be an existing social institution, Aśoka pleaded for seemly behaviour (saṃpaṭipati, R E. IX, P.E. VII). Buddha defined in a concrete form the nature of such a behaviour, and the Arthaśāstra prescribed the laws for its regulation by the state.[3]

Going by Aśoka's statement that he had enacted many regulations of piety (bahukāni dhaṃma-niyamāni, P.E. VII), we cannot but understand that all of them were intended to give a practical effect to the principles of piety or duty enunciated in the edicts and promulgated through them. These regulations having not all been placed on record, to make an idea of what they might be we have no other alternative but taking our guidance from the theoretical scheme of the whole duty of a noble householder as advocated by

---

1 Ibid, p. 38.

2 Barua, Inscriptins, ii. p. 307 f.

3 Ibid, p. 308 f.

Buddha and to a great extent to infer from the state-enforceable laws of conduct as prescribed in the Arthaśāstra.

2. **As Upāsaka-dharma :** The term upāsaka is employed in the edicts to denote, precisely as in the Buddhist and Jaina works, the householders (gharastā, gahathā, R.E. XII, R.E. XIII) included in a religious community as lay adherents and supporters of a distinct body or sect (nikāya, R.E. XIII) of the S'ramaṇas or the Brāhmaṇas (Bhābru, R.E. XIII). The feeling of veneration and the cherishing of serene faith (gālave, pasāde) determined the devotional attitude of the upāsakas and upāsikās (Bhābru, R.E. XIII). Each sect or school of thought had its own doctrinal tradition (kalāṇāgama, R.E. XII), not to call it a scripture in the absence of writing being used for the purpose of recording and transmitting that tradition. The upāsakas attached to a particular sect were supposed to believe that all that was embodied in such a tradition was well said (subhāsite va, Bhābru). Apart from their adherence to this or that sect or school of accredited religious teachers, the upāsakas were mere householders belonging to different social grades and orders. As householders their lives were regulated by certain social customs and usages, certain rules of decorum and conduct, and certain laws of the land enforced by the state, while as upāsakas they were temperamentally disposed to cultivate certain special virtues and to shun certain vices emphasized by the ministers of the faith in which they were believers (tatra tatra prasaṃnā, R.E. XII).

Rājadharma being primarily concerned with secular affairs of men, it is ultimately reducible to Upāsaka or Gṛihastha Dharma. The difference between the two lies in the fact that there is state sanction behind the former, while the latter has nothing behind it but the force of customs and social approval or disapproval, not to call it social and religious sanction. The common aims of both are the attainment of good and happiness here and the attainment of heaven (svaga) hereafter ; the attainment of Nirvāṇa or Moksha is far beyond their scopes. The chief interests of both centre round the three topics of dāna (charity), sīla (virtue), and sagga (heaven), here dāna and sīla being just the two means to the attainment of heaven. The heaven in popular belief is a paradise of unbounded joy and happiness (vipule svage)— a higher world or state of existence where a pious man reaps the great fruit of his meritorious deeds on earth (bahu-kalāṇaṃ, sādhavāni, R.E. V, R.E. VII). The celestial mansions, celestial elephants, fiery and other celestial forms (divyāni rūpāni) symbolise the paradise of popular fancy which in the eye of the divines and philosophers is but a fools' paradise.[1] This paradise is either the heaven of of Indra, or that of the four Lokapālas, otherwise called Mahārājas, or at the best the divine world of Brahmā who is endowed with eternal youth and unsurpassed glory.[2] The commingling of the gods and men in Jambudvīpa is claimed by Aśoka as his most remarkable achievement through strenuous exertion (M.R.E). Aśoka's expression, misibhūtā (commingled), is explained in the Jātaka Commentary in a physical sense, meaning 'brought into close bodily eontact so that they might appear as clasping each other's hand'.[3] Thus here by commingling we are not to think of comradeship (sahavyatā) in heaven which is possible only after death but of coming together on earth in human form, e.g., in a mixed congregation (samāgama) of gods and men listening to an important religious discourse. To be a god, even one of an inferior rank (devo vā devaññataro vā), was the popular aspiration of a person practising a certain kind of virtue, conforming to a certain rule of conduct, keeping a certain religious vow (iminā sīlena, iminā ācharena, iminā vattasamādānena).[4] According to the Classical writers, the Brachmanes of India were regarded as 'dear to the gods.' This enviable position was contested by the Śramaṇas, and no less by a righteous king emperor like Aśoka bearing the title of Devānaṃpriya. The persons who became gods after death came down to the earth to express their gratefulness to the righteous universal monarch. To erect a ladder between heaven and earth was the ambition of the Devānaṃpriya as of other powerful monarchs and saints. The practice of virtue (sīla) came to be popularly extolled as the ladder for climbing up to heaven (saggārohaṇa-sopānaṃ).[5] The sculptural representātion of the ladder by which Buddha descended at Saṃkāśya in one of the Bharhut panels, with S'akra and Brahmā as umbrella-bearers, is too naively physical to retain the charm of the poetic metaphor behind the popular legend.

With regard to the position of Aśoka's Dharma as a form of Upāsaka Dharma, we may do no better than quoting below the

---

[1] Saṃyutta, I, p. 33 ; Ceylon Lectures, p. 221 f.

[2] Barua. Inscriptions, ii, p. 250.

[3] Jātaka, V, p. 86 : hatthena hatthaṃ gahetvā kāyamissibhāvam upagatā. Cf. Sāratthappakāsinī, I, p. 14.

[4] Saṃyutta, IV, p. 180. [5] Visuddhimagga, I, p. 10.

significant observation of Rhys Davids according to which "It was the Dhamma for layman, as generally held in India, but in the form, and with the modification, adopted by the Buddhists. The curious thing about this Dhamma, as a description of the whole duty of man, the good layman, is, especially when we consider its date—its extraordinary simplicity."[1]

Bhandarkar has ably discussed in this connection the importance of the Singālovāda Suttanta to which attention was drawn for the first time by me (J.R.A.S., 1915). This discourse of Buddha on the whole duty of a good householder was not unreasonably esteemed as Gihi-vinaya or 'Institute for the householders' The Mangala Sutta, with the Mahāmangala Jātaka in its background, is but a poetical summary of the Singālovāda Suttanta. The interest of the longer prose discourse lies in the fact that it sets out a scheme of the whole duty of a good householder, which is conceived on a reciprocal or relational basis and may as such serve as the doctrinal basis of a Law of Persons. The six typical relations of reciprocity are those between parents and son, teachers and pupil, husband and wife, kinsman and kinsman, friend and friend, master and slaves and hirelings, the S'ramaṇas and Brāhmaṇas and the lay supporter. There is nothing to prevent one from adding to these such other relations as those between king and subject, brother and brother, brother and sister, neighbour and neighbour, senior and junior, the rich and the poor, men and lower animals. The edicts of Aśoka presuppose all these relations, the systematic way of thinking in India in terms of such relations being pecularly Buddhistic. The stress is laid in the edicts on the most elementary duties probably under the thought that when these are fulfilled, the rest are bound to follow. Consistently with its limited scope a state can regulate the minimum of human good, leaving the maximum to be achieved by the collective effort of the nation or community. The elementary principles of piety or duty inculcated by Aśoka consist in the following :

(a) respectful attention[2] to parents (mātari pitari susrūsā, R.E. III, R.E. IV, R.E. XI, R.E. XIII, P.E. VII, M.R E., Bra, Ye) ;

(b) respectful attention to teachers and preceptors and honouring them in all humility (āchariye apachāyitaviye sususeta-

---

[1] Buddhist India, p. 294.

[2] I prefer this rendering to 'docility', 'obedience', or 'hearkening',

viye, M.R.E., Si, guru-susuṃsā, R.E. XIII, gurunaṃ apachiti, R.E. IX, also M.R.E., Ye, P.E. VII);

(*c*) respectful attention to high personages (agabhutisusūsā,[1] R.E. XIII);

(*d*) respectful attention to seniors or men of experience (thaira-susrūsa, vudha-sususā, R.E. IV), following their advice and waiting upon them (vayomahālakānaṃ anupaṭipati, P.E. VII, thairānṃ vudhānṃ dasane, R.E. VIII);

(*e*) seemly behaviour and liberality to the S'ramaṇas and the Brāhmaṇas (samaṇa-bābhaṇesu saṃpaṭipati, R.E. IV, P.E. VII, bamhaṇa samaṇānaṃ dānaṃ, R.E. III), as well as waiting on them (dasane cha, R.E. VIII);

(*f*) seemly behaviour and liberality to friends, associates, comrades and kinsmen (mita-shaṃthuta-shahāya-nātikeshu shamyāpaṭipati, R.E. XIII, dānaṃ, R.E. III, R.E. XI);

(*g*) seemly behaviour to slaves and servants (dāsabhatakamhi saṃyapaṭipati, R.E. IX, R.E. XI, P.E. VII);

(*h*) cherishing parental feeling towards the subjects and cherishing filial feeling towards the king (S.R.E. II);

(*i*) the non-slaughter of life and the non-harming attitude of mind towards living beings (anāraṃbho prāṇānaṃ avihisā bhūtānaṃ, R.E. IV).

The idea of mutual obligations in the discharge of duties by householders is clearly suggested in Aśoka's instruction—"This should be propounded by a father or a son or a brother or a husband (master ?)[2] or a friend, associate or relative, or even by neighbours: This is good, this should be done" (R.E. IX, R.E. XI).

The definitive modes of performing the duties stressed by Aśoka are catechetically enumerated as follows in the Singālovāda Suttanta :

(*a*) Five are the typical modes of discharging one's duty to one's mother and father, viz., maintaining them out of a

---

[1] Here the word agabhuti is to be equated with agrabhūti, cf. Subhūti, Bhavabhūti, and not with agrabhṛiti, meaning a person drawing higher salaries. The agrabhūtis or agras are really purisuttamas (purushottamas), such as Buddhas, Pratyeka Buddhas, Arhants, cf, varān in the Kaṭha Up. expression—prāpya varān.

[2] As'oka's word spamikena (svāmikena) which corresponds to pali sāmikena (Dīgha, III, p. 190 : sāmikena bhariyā pachchupaṭṭhātabbā) should be translated by 'by a husband'.

feeling of gratitude that he was reared up by them, doing their duties, keeping up the family tradition, deservedly inheriting their property, and performing funeral duties.

(*b*, *c*, *d*) Five are the typical modes of discharging one's duty to one's teachers and preceptors, viz., rising up from seat at their approach,[1] waiting upon them for instructions, attentively listening to their words, rendering personal services and preparing the lessons given.

(*e*) Five are the typical modes of discharging one's duty to the S'ramaṇas and the Brāhmaṇas, viz., friendly bodily action, friendly vocal action, friendly mental action, keeping the door of hospitality open to them, and supplying them with their temporal needs.

(*f*) Five are the typical modes of discharging one's duty to one's friends, associates, comrades and relations, viz., offering help and presents, pleasing with sweet words, doing good to them, expressing fellow-feeling, and keeping up amity among them.

(*g*) Five are the typical modes of discharging one's duty to one's slaves and hirelings, viz., employing them according to their capacity, giving them proper meals and wages, attending them in times of illness, sharing with them delicacies and special dishes, and occasionally granting them leave.

The Arthaśāstra prescribes the state enforceable laws relating to the slaves and hirelings (III. 13, III. 14), It prescribes similar laws to regulate man's duty to his parents, wife, children, brothers and sisters :

"When a capable person other than an apostate (patita) neglects to maintain his children and wife, mother and father, minor brothers and sisters, or widowed girls, he shall be punished with a fine of twelve paṇas.

When, without making provision for the maintenance of his wife and sons, any person embracss asceticism, he shall be punished with the first amercement."[2]

---

[1] Pali uṭṭhānena, which Buddhoghosa explains as meaning pachchuggamanaṃ katvā.

[2] Arthasāstra, II. 1.

3. **As universal religion**: The term 'universal religion' as applied to Aśoka's Dharma is sweetly vague in its connotation; it is just an empty word of praise until the meaning in which it is used is precisely defined. One can say that it is non-credal in fts stress and non-sectarian in its spirit,—non-credal in the sense that it eschews all matters of theology and speculative philosophy, and non-sectarian in the sense that it nowhere intends thrusting any man's views and beliefs upon another. As Rhys Davids puts it, "There is not a word about God or the soul, and not a word about Buddha or Buddhism." The Four Noble Truths, the Causal Genesis, Nirvāṇa, and other distinctive tenets of Buddhism find no place in it. The word Dharma which, according to Rhys Davids, corresponds with the Latin *forma*, means 'good form', and the two main points discussed in Aśoka's Dharma are what is proper for good men to do and what is improper for them not to do, or, as one might say, what are the things that lead to sin (āsinava-gāmini, P. E. III), to demerit and vice (apuña, pāpa, R.E. X, P.E. III) or innate proneness to sin (parisrava, R.E. X), in short, to the state of woe and the utter degradation of human nature (mahāpāya, S.R.E. I), and what are, on the other hand, the things that lead to much good (bahukayāna, P.E. III), to unbounded merit (anaṃtaṃ puñaṃ, R.E. IX), in short, to grand heaven (vipula svaga, M.R.E.) which is a state of unbounded joy and happiness and to the elevation of human nature (abhyuṃnamisati, P.E. VII). These are indeed the two main points with which religion is concerned, whether it be Buddhism or Jainism, Brahmanism or popular Hinduism, Christianity or Islam.

Aśoka's Dharma is broadbased upon the principle of tolerance. The Aśokan idea of toleration differs, however, from the general Indian idea in that it offers a scheme of active co operation (samavāya) among all sects for their growth in essential matters (sāravaḍhi asa savapāsaṃḍānaṃ, R.E. XII), and does not leave any sect to itself under the comfortable belief that all faiths lead ultimately to one and the same goal. It wants all sects and exponents to come together for frank and free interchanges of their thoughts and ideas in a mutually helping spirit. It urges that men of all sects should listen to and study each other's doctrines so that all may be well-informed (bahusrutā) and possessed of noble traditions (kalāṇāgama, R.E.XII). If there be any criticism in the course of discussions, it should be as light as possible and always to the point, but there must also be due appreciation of other sects in this or that point (tamhi tamhi prakaraṇe). One must not unduly extol one's own sect and condemn another sect because it is not one's own (ātpapāsaṃḍa-pūjā parapāsaṃḍa-garahā no bhave aprakaraṇamhi). He who does that, does so because of his devotion to his own sect and with the desire of glorifying it. In doing so, he not only does a great disservice to other sects but also digs the grave of his own sect. Concord (samavāya), therefore, is good, and at the root of it is self-restraint (sayama), particularly the guarding of the tongue (vachiguti).

Aśoka's samavāya is not precisely the modern Hindu idea of Dharma-samanvaya or harmony of all religious faiths. The basic idea of this harmony as advocated by Rāmakṛishṇa Paramahaṃsa is traced in the Ṛigveda dictum—"They designated one and the same Deity by many a name" (ekaṃ sadviprāḥ bahudhā vadanti). The Advaita axiom is upheld by Ṛishi Uddālaka when he declares the ultimate reality as one without a second (ekam evādvitīyam),[1] and by Buddha when he maintains that truth or reality is one (sachcham ekaṃ).[2] In the immediate background of Aśoka's tolerance is the exclusive mental attitude which finds its characteristic expression—"What I affirm is the only thing true and everything else is false" (idam eva sachchaṃ, mogham aññaṃ). In a tone of disapprobation Buddha observed : eke samaṇa-brāhmaṇā sakaṃ yeva vādaṃ dīpenti jotenti, paravādam pana khuṃsanti.[3] "Certain S'ramaṇas and Brāhmaṇas edify and glorify verily their own doctrine, but deprecate the doctrine of others." Here one may notice even a verbal correspondence with Aśoka's words : ātpapāsaṃḍa-pūjā parapāsaṃḍa-garahā,...ātpapāsaṃḍaṃ dīpayema iti. The Great Epic goes a step further when it cites the time honoured opinion of the exponents of piety according to which neither the condemning and honouring of oneself nor the condemning and extolling of others is the practice of the Aryans :

> atmanindātmapūjā cha paranindā parastavaḥ ।
> anācharitaṃ āryāṇām iti te Bhīshma naḥ śrutam ॥

---

1 Chhāndogya Up., VI. 2. 1.

2 Sutta-nipāta,

3 Anguttara, I, p. 88. Cf. Majjhima, I, p. : eke samaṇa-brāhmaṇā attānaṃ ukkaṃsanti paraṃ vambhenti (=garahanti nindanti).

4 Mahābhārata, II. 44. 24. As explained by the commentator Nīlakaṃṭha, the purport of the s'loka is that whether one praises and blames oneself or praises and blames others, he comes away from God to attach importance to men.

Now, to consider some of the behests of Aśoka's Upāsaka Dharma. The first of them is respectful attention to mother and father (mātari pitari susrūsā). This corresponds to Buddha's expression matā-pitu-upaṭṭhānaṃ. The valedictory address in the Taittirīya Upanishad (I. 11. 2) enjoins : mātṛidevo bhava, pitṛidevo bhava. "Honour thy father and thy mother" is one of the ten commandments in the Old Testament.

The second is respectful attention to teachers and preceptors (āchariya-susrūsā, guru-susrūsā). Respectful attention (susrūsā) is one of the five typical modes of fulfilling one's duty to teachers and preceptors (āchariyā, Dīgha, III, p. 189). The Taittirīya Upanishad (I.11.2) snjoins-āchāryadevo bhava. Covering the first two behests the Great Epic (XII. 54.17) lays down the following maxim of conduct :

> Mātāpitror hi śuśrūshā kartavyā sarvadasyubhiḥ,
> āchārya-guru-śuśrūshā tathaivāśramavāsinām[1].

These are covered also by the following stanza (332) from the Dhammapada :

> Sukhā matteyatā loke, atho petteyyatā sukhā,
> sukhā sāmaññatā loke, atho brahmaññatā sukhā[2].

The third is non-slaughter of life and non-harming mental attitude towards living beings (anārambho prāṇānaṃ, avihiṃsā bhūtānaṃ). That this is a common behest of Jainism and Buddhism goes without saying despite the fact that the expressions are more Buddhistic than Jaina. The Great Epic (XII. 109. 15) emphatically declares :

Ahiṃsārthāya bhūtānāṃ dharma-pravachanaṃ kṛitam.[3]
"Thou shalt not kill" is one of the ten Biblical commandments.

The universality of Aśoka's Dharma may be particularly appreciated with regard to its psycho-ethical concepts. In answer to the self-put question—Wherein does the Dharma consist ? Aśoka men-

---

[1] Cf. Saṃyutta, I, p. 178 :

> Mātari pitari vā pi atha jeṭṭhamhi bhātari ।
> āchariye chatutthamhi, tesu na mānaṃ kayirātha ॥
> tesu assa sagāravo, tyassa apachitā assu ॥

[2] S. N. Mitra draws attention to this Pali stanza which extols reverential attitude towards mother and father, the S'ramaṇas and the Brāhmaṇas. Cf. Dīgha, III, p. 169.

[3] Cf. Manu, II. 159 :

> ahiṃsāyaiva bhūtānāṃ kāryaṃ s'reyo'nus'āsanam,

tions the six principles of which the first two are apāsinave and bahukayāne. Here apāsinave corresponds in a sense to apaparisrava (R E. X) meaning 'little demerit', 'little sin', better 'little proneness to sin.' In the Jaina Āchārānga Sūtra, parissava and āsava are treated as synonyms. Evidently the two terms represent two sides of piety, namely, negative and positive: 'little evil' and 'much good.' The second term, bahukayāne or 'much good' as an abstract moral quality, finds its fulfilment in many good deeds (bahuni kayānāni, P.E. II). In R.E. IV, however, the expression bahukalānaṃ is employed in a concrete collective sense :

maya bahukalāṇaṃ kataṃ (R.E. IV).
me bahuni kayānāni kaṭāni (P.E. II).
katā me kalyāṇā anekarūpā, (J. V, p. 421).

The two directly antithetical terms are kayāne (kalyāṇaṃ) and pāpe (pāpaṃ) in which case āsinava must be treated as a resultant moral factor following from a sinful deed,—from an act of demerit (apuña, P. E. II, R. E. X). Corresponding to kayāna and pāpa in P.E. II, we have in R.E. V the use of the two antithetical terms sukataṃ and dukataṃ. It may be noted that in the religious literature of India, whether Buddhist, Jaina or Brahmanical, puṇya and pāpa, sukrita and dushkrita, sādhu and asādhu, and the like are frequently met with as antithetical pairs of terms. In the opinion of Bhandarkar āsinava corresponds more to the Jaina aṇhaya than to the Pali ādīnava, none of the Buddhist enumerations of the passions and acts with reference to ādīnava being suited to the Aśokan context. The Pali ādīnava is explained by Buddhaghosa in the sense of amadhurabhāva, upaddava and dosa. In the Nikāyas, ādinava in the sense of 'fault' (dosa) occurs as a synonym of okāra and saṃkilesa (staining of nature) due to which all passions become very painful and disappointing. In the phrase, ādinavo ettha bhiyyo, the term stands for trouble.[1] The Itivuttaka Commentary connects ādīnava also with such malevolent passions as kodha and māna.[2] In the Amarakosha, ādīnava, āsrava and kleśa signify three allied afflictions due to a disease, the first for the general weakening of the system, the second for the infuriating of the organs, and the third for the ailments. Referring to the Āchārānga Sūtra (P. T. S. Ed., p. 92), Bhandarkar observes: "Jainism specifies eighteen kinds of pāpa or sin and fortytwo kinds of āsravas. These

---

1 Saṃyutta, I, p. 9.

2 Itivuttaka Commentary, Siamese Ed., p. 60 : dose ādinave.

two lists have four malevolent affections in common, called kashāyas. Two of these are krodha and māna, exactly two of the passions named by Aśoka. The isyā of Aśoka, again, is to be found in the Jaina list of the pāpas, as īrshyā or dvesha ; chaṃḍiye and niṭhuliye are alone not traceable, though they are covered by the malaffection hiṃsā mentioned under āsrava. Thus the use of the term āsinava (aṇhaya), distinction between it and pāpa, and the inclusion of at least three passions of the Jaina lists are enough to convince anybody that in all likelihood, Aśoka has here adopted and assimilated same psychological concepts of Jainism."

Here the evidence of the Aupapātika Sūtra would seem more conclusive. In this Sūtra, the adjective aṇhaya-kare, meaning 'causing affliction', aṇhaya having to all intents and purposes the connotation of the term āsinava, is applied to a malevolent mind needing control. The other predicates of such a mind are chhedakare (swayed by the passion of cutting), bheyakare (swayed by the passion of piercing), paritāvanakare (causing distress), uddāvanakare (afflicting) and bhūopaghāie (hurting beings). This mind is characterised as sāvajje (impure), sakirie (offending), sakakkase (rough), kaḍue (paining), niṭṭhure (cruel), and pharuse (rude).

Aśoka's list of terms may be shown to have presupposed rather the Buddhist psycho-ethical concepts than the Jaina. In P.E. III, he mentions fierceness (chaṃḍiye), cruelty (niṭhuliye), anger (kodhe), vanity (māne), and isyā (malignity) as the malevolent passions that lead to evil (āsinava-gāminī). The list in S.R.E. I consists of such terms as malignity (isā), irascibility (āsulope), cruelty (niṭhuliye),[1] and oppressiveness (tulanā).[2] Almost all of these terms are grouped together in the Dhammadāyada Sutta (Majjhima, I) and the Purābheda Sutta as expounded in the Mahāniddesa. The two Pali lists, taken together, contain the following terms, among others : kodha, issā, māna, chaṇḍikka, and assuropa. The two adjectives, chaṇḍa and pharusa, are applied to one and the same people.[3] Aśoka's expressions akhakhase achaṃḍe sakhinālambhe or achaṃḍaṃ aphalusaṃ (S. R. E. I) have their Pali parallels in akakkasaṃ apharusaṃ (Jātaka, III, p. 282). Aśoka's sakhinālambhe exactly

---

[1] Pali niṭṭhuriyaṃ, Mahāniddesa Commentary to the Attadaṇḍa Sutta. Cf. niṭṭhuriyo in the text itself.

[2] For tulanā, Cf janapada-tudanā in Dīgha, III, p. 179.

[3] Majjhima. III, p. 268 : Sunāparantā manussā chaṇḍā pharusā. Cf. Amarakosha, I. 318, nishṭhuraṃ parushaṃ ; Bhagavad Gītā, XVI 4, krodhaḥ pārushyam.

corresponds to the Pali saṇhavācho[1] (Jātaka, IV, p. 110). Aśoka's list being illustrative rather than exhaustive, for the proper understanding of their significance the reference must be had to the Pali texts and their commentaries.

From the logical setting of the Buddhist psycho-ethical concepts it is easy to understand that the terms kodha and upanāha, issā and machchhera, māna and mada, chaṇḍikka and assuropa often go together as complements. The same may equally hold true of the two terms niṭṭhuriya and tudanā, Aśoka's niṭhuliya and tulanā.

The term kodha, here translated by the English 'anger', presupposes an agitated state of mind (kopa), implies an infuriated condition of the self, burning with wrath (amarsha rosha), and produces the disposition to strike, to hurt, to kill (pratigha).[2] The complementary term upanāha implies harbouring resentment, a brooding state of mind which follows as a sequel to anger.[3] Anger has fury for its distinctive feature, its functional tendency is to strike, and its resultant is an inimical action.[4]

The term isyā, isā (Pali issā, Sk. īrshā), here translated by 'malignity' in preference to 'envy' or 'jealousy', has either envy for other's prosperity or non-forgiveness for its distinctive feature, its functional tendency is to produce disgust, and its resultant is disappointing.[5] The opposite of issā in the sense of 'envy' or 'jealousy' is machchhera or meanness, niggardliness. It is in the other sense of non-forgiveness that isyā as a mental disposition is allied to kodha.

The term māna stands in Pali for both conceit and conceitedness, an unwholesome mental state which may arise both from a wilful overestimate and a wilful understimate of oneself.[6] It has vanity for its distinctive feature, its functional tendency is to produce pride and boasting, and its resultant is conceitedness.[7] The complemen-

---

1 Cf. Manu. II. 159 : vāk chaiva madhurā s'lakshṇyā prayojyā dharmamichchhatā.

2 Amarakosha, I, 417 ; Mahāniddesa, Purābheda Sutta.

3 Papañchasūdanī, I, p. 106 : pubbakāle kodho, aparakāle upanāho.

4 Ibid, I, p. 106 : kodho chaṇḍikka-lakkhaṇo, āghātana-raso, dussanapachchupaṭṭhāno.

5 Ibid, I, p. 106 ; parasampatti-khiyyana-lakkhaṇā issā, akkhamana-lakkhaṇā vā, anabhirati-rasā, vimukhabhāva-pachchupaṭṭhānā. Cf. Amarakosha, I. 412 : akshāntir īrshā.

6 Itivuttaka Commentary, Siamese Ed., p. 63.

7 Papañchasūdanī, I, p. 107 : unnati-lakkhaṇo māno, dhikkāro raso, uddhumātaka-bhāva-pachchupaṭṭhāno,

tary term mada signifies the pride of birth, the pride of wealth, position, learning, etc. The extolling of oneself and the condemning of others (attukkaṃsana paravambhana) are due to mada.[1] For the association of māna with the passion of kodha in Pali the reader may consider the following admonition of Buddha :

kodhaṃ jahe, vippajaheyya mānaṃ.

"Give up anger, conceit should be completely given up."

The Pali equivalents of Aśoka's chaṃḍiye and āsulope are chaṇḍikkaṃ and assuropa. The Pali scholiasts explain chaṇḍikka as meaning rigidity, which is the state of a rigid person (thaddha-purisa), while, as defined in the Amarakosha, the chaṇḍa is a person whose nature is fierce (atikopanaḥ). Thus Aśoka's chaṃḍiye may preferably be translated by fierceness. The Mahāniddesa Commentary defines assuropa as the distemper of mind (anattamanatā chittassa), while others take it to mean that violent passion in man which causes tears in others (assujananatthena, assuropanto).[2] The Pali word assuropa stops us from equating āsulope with āśulopa (quick loss of temper), just as Aśoka's āsulope prevents us accepting asurūpo as a variant ingeniously suggested in the Pali Commentary.

Niṭhuliye, here translated by cruelty, has niṭṭhuriyaṃ for its Pali equivalent. The adjective nishṭhura as applying to speech or words is paraphrased in the Amarakosha by kakkhaṭa, paurusha, krura, and the like, the first two having their equivalents in Aśoka's a-khakhase a-phalusaṃ.

The remaining term tulanā, here translated by oppressiveness, has been equated by some with tūrṇā which is not justifiable for the reason that tūrṇā is not used as a substantive. Its Pali equivalent is tudanā, meaning pīḍanaṃ, Cf. Pali janapada-tudanā or janapada-tudanaṃ.

The concepts belonging to the category of bahukayāne or 'much good' are dayā, dāne, sache, sochave, mādave and sādhave (P.E. II, P.E. VII). The four concepts of sayame (self-control), bhāvasudhitā (purity of motive), kataṃñatā (gratitude) and daḍhabhatitā (firm devotion) are connected with dāna (R.E. VII). These are reduced in the same edict to two, viz., sayame and bhāvasudhi. The concepts of savrabhutana(ṃ) akshati, saṃyama and samachariya are grouped

---

[1] Itivuttaka Commentary, op. cit., p. 63.

[2] Mahāniddesa Commentary, Siamese Ed., II, p. 11,

together with mādava in R.E. XIII. The two terms, anārambha and avihiṃsā, are mutually complementary. The guiding principle of Aśoka's Dharma, precisely as that of Buddhism and other early Indian systems of faith and thought, is the principle of action which is presented by such terms as usṭāna (readiness to action), parākrama (power of action), pakama (strenuous exertion), uyāma (effort), and usāha (zeal, ardour). The opposite states of mind and body are represented by anāvuti (non-application), ālasiya (indolence) and kilamatha (weariness for exertion). The whole activity is to proceed on the twofold basis of dhamma (piety) and sīla (virtue) which is the same as to say, through the practice of piety (dhamma-charaṇa, R.E. IV) and that of seemly behaviour (samachariyā, R.E. XIII), and it is to be directed towards feeling concern for oneself, feeling concern for one's own people, and doing good to the whole world.

The first pair of terms consists of dayā and dāna. Here dayā, translated by pity, has anuddayā for its Pali equivalent. According to Buddha, anuddayā presupposes fellow-feeling, sympathy (samānattatā) and a friendly heart (mettachittatā). From the set of synonyms given in the Amarakosha, it is evident that dayā presupposes compassion (kāruṇya) which is felt in the heart, and that it has two expressional forms, viz., anukampā (feeling concern) on the part of seniors and anukrośa (showing concern) by juniors. In Buddha's terminology avihiṃsā has the positive connotation of karuṇā, kāruñña or sakaruṇabhāva, i.e., the compassionate state of mind which finds its expression in feeling concern for the good of all beings (sabbabhūtahitānukampā). According to the Bhagavad Gītā (XVI. 2), dayā means feeling pity for all beings (dayā sarvabhūteshu). Pity as a noble feeling stands opposed to cruelty. Dāna, which may be translated by liberality, charity or charitable disposition, is a tangible expression of dayā. Dāna implies tyāga (Pali chāga, parichchāga), which is both the spirit and the act of self-sacrifice. Aśoka speaks of various forms and acts of dāna (R.E. II, R.E. XII, P.E. II, P.E. VII, Barābar). In P.E. II, he expressly refers to 'giving the eye' (chakkhudāne) and 'granting the boon of life to the lower creatures' (pāna-dākhināye). The monumental acts of piety (dhaṃmathaṃbhāni) mentioned in P. E. VII are all concrete instances of dāna. By the eye (chakkhu) is meant, of course, the eye of wisdom (paññāchakkhu, jñānanetra), and not the fleshy eye (maṃsachakkhu).[1] It is with reference to the

[1] Mahāniddesa, pp. 100, 354, Dīgha. III, p. 210, speaks of three chakkhus, maṃsachakkhu, dibbachakkhu (divine eye, clairvoyance) and paññāchakkhu.

eye of wisdom that Aśoka declared the gift of the doctrine (dhaṃma-dāna) to be the best of all gifts (R.E. IX, R.E. XI).

Dāna implies, according to Buddha and others. the visagga, e.g. dhaṃma-saṃvibhāga[1] (R.E, XI), dāna-saṃvibhāga[2] (P.E. IV), dāna-visaga[3] (P.E. VII). Dāna in itself is not a great thing in spite of the generally accepted maxim of the age that it is good (dānaṃ sādhu). Aśoka speaks of the four moral qualities that go to enhance the value of dāna, viz., sayame, bhāvasudhi or bhāvasudhitā, kataṃñatā and daḍhabhatitā of which the equivalents are met with in the Great Epic[4] and the Jātaka.[5] The very word bhāvaśuddhiḥ is met with in the Gɹeat Epic, XII. 167. 5 in the following ethical precept of Vidura :

> Bahuśrutyaṃ tapas tyāgaḥ śraddhā yajñakriyā kshamā |
> bhāvaśuddhir dayā satyaṃ saṃyamaś chātmasampadah ||

Nīlakaṇṭṭha paraphrases bhāvaśuddhi by nishkapaṭatvam, 'guilelessness, sincerity."

Here sayama (saṃyama) stands for restraint in body, speech and mind,[6] bhāvasudhitā for the purity of motive, for what is called akshudratā in the Great Epic ; kataṃñatā (kṛitajñatā, Pali kataññutā) for gratitude or gratefulness which consists not only in acknowledging the service rendered by the benefactor, not only in not harming the benefactor, but also in rendering the service in return (katavedita) ;[7] and daḍhabhatitā (dṛiḍhabhaktitva,[8] Pali dalhabhatti) for firm devotion (to the cause of piety), strong faith. The valedictory address in the Taittirīya Upanishad (I. 11) insists on giving out of faith (śraddhayā deyaṃ) aḥd not giving without faith (aśraddhayā adeyam), Buddha's

---

1 Pali dhamma-saṃvibhāga in Theragāthā, verse 9, supplied by S. N. Mitra,

2 Pali dāna-saṃvibhāga in Jātaka, III, p. 402. Cf. bhattasaṃvibhāga in Arthasāstra, IV. 8.

3 Pali dāna-visagga in Petavatthu, II, 9, supplied by S. N. Miira. Cf. deya-visarga in Arthasāstra, IX. 6.

4 Mahābhārata, XII. 65. 89, XII. 67. 46 ; XII. 67. 57. Cf. Dakkbiṇā-vibhanga Sutta in Majjhima, III, p. 258 f., and its commentary ; Sāratthappakāsinī, I, pp. Abhidharmakos'a, IV. 118-125 ; Manu, IV ; Bhagavad Gitā, XVII. 21-23. Anantalal Thakur, M.A., draws my attention to the word bhāvasaṃs'uddhi which occurs in the Bhagavad Gītā, XVII-16, as well as its synonyms, hṛits'uddhi and chittas'uddhi.

5 Jātaka, V, p. 146.

6 Jātaka, V, p. 146 ; Dhammapada, verses 360-362.

7 Ibid, V, p. 147 ; Barua, Inscriptions, ii, p. 300.

8 Arthas'āstra, I. 9.

word saddhādeyyaṃ (Dīgha, I. p. 5) conveying the same idea. Aśoka speaks of the restraint practised with regard to the whole of life (pāṇesu sayamo, R.E. IX, R.E. XIII), and the restraint in the form of guarding one's tongue (vachīguti, R E. XII). In the Pali list of terms,[1] saṃyama is sought to be distinguished from dama, the former meaning, according to Buddhaghosa, the restraint in accordance with the prescribed rules of conduct (sīla-saṃyamo) and the latter the control of the senses (dame ti indriya-damane).[2]

The next two categories of Aśoka's Dharma are sacha and sochaya, both of which are included in Buddha's list.[3] In Pali, however, the first is combined with dhamma (sachche cha dhamme cha), and the second with uposatha, which is conceived as the abode of virtue(sīlālayo, i.e., the proper occasion for taking and keeping the moral precepts). The combination of satya and dharma is as old as the older Upanishads.[4] In Aśokan context, precisely as in that of the Pali Lakkhaṇa Suttanta, the two terms, satya and dharma, are devoid of all metaphysical connotation. As Buddhaghosa rightly points out, here the first term stands for truthfulness in utterances (sachche ti vachīsachche), and the second for the system of piety relating to the ways of performing the ten wholesome acts (dhamme ti dasa-kusalakammapatha-dhamme).[5] That in Aśoka's terminology, too, the first term stands for truthfulness in utterances is evident from the insistence on speaking the truth (sachaṃ vataviyaṃ, M.R E. Bra). According to the general Indian notion, the truthful speech carries with it also the idea of a speech, which is pleasant, sweet, and appealing. So the adage goes to teach :

satyaṃ brūyāt priyaṃ brūyāt, mā brūyāt satyam apriyam.[6]

As Buddha puts it, "Abandoning lying speech, Gotama the Recluse who has completely abstained from it, is the speaker of truth, given

---

1 Dīgha, III, p. 147.

2 Sumangala-vilāsinī, III, p. 928.

3 Dīgha, III, p. 147.

4 Taittirīya Up. I. 11. 1.

5 Sumangala-vilāsinī, III, p. 928.

6 Dayānanda Sarasvati in his Satyārtha-prakās'a, modifies this maxim so as to suit his insistence on speaking the truth, whether it be pleasant or unpleasant : satyaṃ brūyāt, priyam apriyaṃ vā. Truth can never indeed be pleasant in the literal sense of the term ; by its very nature it is bound to be unyielding and uncompromising. All that is meant in the above maxim is that in speaking truth one should not offend the refined taste.

up to truth, truthful, utters words that are worthy of trust and not to be slightly doubted by the world. Abandoning harsh speech, Gotama the Recluse who has completely abstained from it, utters speech which is faultless, sweet to the ears, lovable, goes into the heart, agreeable to many, pleasing to many."[1] By the expression "that which is sweet to the ears" Buddhaghosa understands that which is sweetly worded (vyañjana-madhuratāya kaṇṇānaṃ sukhā), and by 'that which is lovable' he understands that which is sweet in meaning (atthamadhuratāya pemaniyā).[2] Aśoka, too, insists on uttering words that are not harsh, impetuous, rude and that are full of winsome cordiality (akhakhase achaṃḍe aphalusaṃ sakhinālaṃbhe, S.R.E. I).[3] The sweetness in meaning (athasa madhuratā) gets its due emphasis in R.E. XIV.

But the word sachcha conveys also the idea of sachchapaṭiññā implying as it does the resolve to keep the fealty to the oath taken, to keep the agreement entered into or word given, to keep the promise made under all circumstances, however trying.[5] The notion of such a resolve is comprehended by the term dhiti (dhṛiti, moral fortitude) which is met with in S.R.E. II. To be worth the name, both the dhiti and the paṭiṃnā must be of an unshaken character (ajalā, achalā, S.R.E. II). The four principles of sachcha in the above sense, dhamma (piety), dhiti (moral fortitude) and chāga (self-sacrifice) are grouped together in the moral of the Vānarinda Jātaka (No. 57). The term sochaye (Pali socheyya), here translated by purity, really implies the sense of purity or the consciousness of being oneself pure in body, speech and thought. This may be treated as the pre-requisite of a pious deed or an act of virtue, e.g., the observance of the sabbath.

The next pair of terms is composed of mādave and sādhave (P. E. VII). In the Pali lists maddava (Sk. mārdava) is invariably

---

[1] Dīgha, I, p. 4 ; Musāvadaṃ pahāya musāvādā paṭivirato samaṇo Gotamo sachchavādi sachchasandho theto pachchāyiko avisaṃvādako lokassa. Pharusavāchaṃ pahāya pharusa-vāchā paṭivirato samaṇo Gotamo yā sā vāchā neḷā kaṇṇasukhā pemaniyā hadayaṃgamā pori bahujanakantā bahujanamanāpā.

[2] Sumangala-vilāsinī, I, p. 75. Cf. Arthas'āstra, II. 10.

[3] Cf. Dīgha, III, p. 161 : sakhino.

[4] Cf. Dīgha, III, p. 171. Rāma is extolled in the Rāmāyaṇa as satyasandha.

[5] Cf. Jātaka, V, pp. 481, 488.

combined with the concept of ajjava (Sk. ārjava).[1] Corresponding to the grouping of tapas, dānaṃ, ārjavaṃ, ahiṃsā and satyavachanam in the Chhāndogya Upanishad (III. 17. 4.) we have in the Jātaka (V, p. 378) the categorisation of the following concepts :

Dānaṃ sīlaṃ parichchāgaṃ ajjavaṃ maddavaṃ tapaṃ
akkodhaṃ avihiṃsaṃ cha khantiñ cha avirodhanaṃ.

The word ajjava signifies moral rectitude or uprightness, which lies behind Aśoka's principles of uniformity in procedure and uniformity in justice (viyohāla samatā daṃḍa-samatā, P. E. IV). By maddava is meant gentleness, mildness, which is the opposite of intrepidity (sahasā) accounting for all rash acts of violence, detention and coercion (vadho baṃdhanaṃ palikilesaṃ).

In sādhava we have the concept of nobleness which underlies all noble deeds (sādhavāni, P.E. VII). The noble deeds are all good deeds (kalāṇaṃ, kayānāni, R.E. V, P.E. II). The kalyāṇas or good deeds emphasized in the Jātaka (V, p. 492) are precisely those repeatedly mentioned in the edicts.[2]

The concept of khaṃti (kshānti) is combined with that of lahudaṃḍatā (light punishment) in R.E. XIII. In the Mahahaṃsa Jātaka, we have the succession of the four concepts of akkodha, avihiṃsā, khanti and avirodhana. According to the scholiast, friendliness (mettā) is at the back of the first, compassion (karuṇā) is at the back of the second, the third implies the notion of toleration or forbearance (adhivāsana), and the fourth means non-hostility.[3] Though khanti and titikkhā are often used as synonyms, the former is taken to mean the toleration of a person who is physically stronger by one who is physically weaker and the second to mean the toleration of a weaker person by a stronger man. The Buddhist khanti is far more than the Christian idea of forbearance in that in the practice of this moral quality the oppressed are expected not only to patiently bear the pain of oppression caused but also to think well of the oppressor. In the Bhagavad Gītā (XVI. 43), kshamā (i.e., kshānti) is succeeded by dhṛiti or moral fortitude.

---

[1] Sutta-nipāta, verse 250 ; Cf. Manu, VI. 92, enumerating the ten principles of dhṛiti, kshamā, dama, asteya, s'aucha, indriya-nigraha, dhī, vidyā, satya and akrodha. The Jaina list of ten principles consists of kshamā, mārdava, ārjava, satya, s'aucha, saṃyama, tapa, tyāga, ākiṃchanya and brahmacharya.

[2] Barua, Inscriptions, ii, p. 253.

[3] Jātaka, V, p. 379.

CHAPTER VIII

DHARMA-VIJAYA

With Aśoka, precisely as with Buddha and other Indian thinkers, Dharma was not only a way of life or means of elevation of human nature but also a weapon for the conquest of men's hearts, a royal means of bringing about a permanent cultural understanding between the countries and peoples and building a new nation or imperialism on that very foundation. It remains yet to be seen how the Dharma-vijaya of Aśoka served to place India between the cultures, to create, in other words, a Greater India with universalism as its ideal for the furtherance of the common cause of humanity.

Aśoka's Dharma-vijaya was just one of the four great cultural conquests made by the Indo-Aryans in pre-Muslim India, the other three being the Digvijaya of Agni, the Dharma-vijaya of the Great Epic, and the Trailokya-vijaya of the Kāraṇḍavyūha.

1. **Definition of Dharma-vijaya :** Conquest is the dominant thought of a heroic age, a warrior king, a war-like people, a virile race, a militant faith. It presupposes in all cases consciousness of strength, a sense of certainty about the rightness of the cause espoused, a strong conviction about the success to be attained, a vision of the future to follow, an intrepid will to act, an unabated zeal to proceed, a great power of endurance to withstand the obstacles on the way, a sense of preparedness, a capacity to adjust means to ends, an uncommon energy for incessant action, and a well-disciplined army to carry out the orders. Its motive factors or springs of action may be either greed, malevolence and folly or magnanimity, amity and wisdom. It is possible by some kind of weapon. If it is possible by the sword, it goes by the name of Śaraśakya or Sāyaka-vijaya, and if by piety, it deserves the name of Dharma-vijaya (R.E. XIII). The weapons other than those implied by Dharma are taken to be comprehended by the antithetical term Adharma.[1] The sword symbolises the violent method with all its strategic skills and accessories resorted to on the failure of the diplomatic means of conciliating, bribing and causing dissension. Dharma stands for the peaceful method with all its friendly acts of give and take. Where greed is found to be the motive factor, the

---

[1] Jātaka, IV, p. 102.

conquest is to be classed as Lobha-vijaya,[1] and where malevolence is the motive factor, it is to be called Asura-vijaya.[2] With these two forms of conquest is to be contrasted what is called Dharma-vijaya or conquest by Dharma.[3] As a moral concept, the Dharma-vijaya implies some amount of human consideration and mental discipline to conform to the laws of approved human conduct.

As defined in the Arthaśāstra (XIII. 1), the Lobhavijaya aims at what may be safely gained in land or money and the Asura-vijaya aims not merely at seizing the land, treasure, sons and wives and all of the conquered but also at taking his life, while the aim of Dharma-vijaya is fulfilled with mere obeisance or surrender (abhyavapatti) on the part of the conquered. In the words of Kālidāsa, the Dharma-vijaya consists in robbing the conquered king of his glory but not of his territory.[4] Aśoka's Dharma-vijaya consists, on the other hand, in the expression of good will and the assurance of territorial integrity (S.R.E. II), the friendly acts of public utility (R. E. II), and the advancement of the cause of humanity through piety (R.E. XIII).

Professor Nilkanta Sastri poignantly observes : "Whatever the relative ages of our texts, the classification of conquests and conquerors in Hindu political theory is logically complete, and has the ring of antiquity, and we may take it that the expression Dharmavijaya was first carried in contrast to lobha-or-artha and asuravijaya" (Calcutta Review, 1943, Feb., p. 121). The Jātaka distinction between Dhamma and Adhamma-vijaya (IV, p. 102) and Aśoka's distinction between the Dhaṃma and the Śaraśaka (R.E. XIII) presupposes the idea of just two kinds of vijaya, one the Dharma and the other Artha or Āsura.

The idea of Dharma-vijaya developed in the Brahmanical as well as the Buddhistic line of thinking. The common point between the two conceptions is that both are free from the thought about territorial aggrandisements.[5] The mere acknowledgement of supremacy

---

1 Same as Arthavijaya in Mahābhārata, XII. 58. 33.

2 Same as Asuravijaya in ibid, XII. 58. 38.

3 Arthas'āstra, XIII, 1 ; Mahābhārata, XII. 58. 38 ; Harivaṃs'a, I. 14. 21.

4 Raghuvams'a, IV. 4.

5 Cf. Dīgha, III, p. 62f. : yathābhuttaṃ cha bhuñjatha, "Enjoy your territories as heretofore."

Nilkanta Sastri's paper—"Dharmavijaya and Dhaṃmavijaya" in the Calcutta Review, 1943, Feb., 115 ff. for an illuminating comment on the three kinds of vijaya,

by the weaker powers was sufficient, according to the Arthaśāstra, to satisfy the demand of Dharma-vijaya. It appears from the Great Epic account of the Digvijaya of the Pāṇḍavas that the offering of presents,[1] or of revenues, or of both was to be the tangible expression of obeisance or submission on the part of the conquered.

Though mere ultimatum or negotiation through the envoys sometimes sufficed to effect it, the Brahmanical Dharma-vijaya was undeniably a conquest by the sword. Aśoka rightly characterised it as a milder method of conquest where forbearance (kshānti) and light punishment (laghudaṇḍatā) were to be practised and preferred (R.E. XIII). The Buddhistic Dharma-vijaya was to be achieved, on the other hand, without the employment of the sword or armed force (adaṇḍena asatthena) but certainly by means of the doctrine meaning the superior ideal of humanity (dhammena abhivijiya).[2]

In neither case, the Dharma-vijaya implied the idea of disbanding the army or lessening the military equipment;[3] it presupposed, on the other hand, the sufficient strength and preparedness of the army and the full military equipment backed by adequate state resources and other elements of sovereignty. As Buddha emphatically puts it, invincible shall be the position of the righteous king overlord, not shaken by any human rival or enemy, internal or external, and the territory under his benign sway and protection shall be undisturbed, free from all signs of aggression and oppression, thornless, populous, prosperous, secure, tranquil and unulcerated.[4]

There is not the slightest hint in the edicts and legends of Aśoka that he either disbanded the army or was not fully prepared to cope

---

[1] Cf. Hāthigumphā Inscription in which the king of Pāṇḍya is said to have sent valuable presents to Khāravela.

[2] Dīgha, III, p. 59.

[3] The story of Viḍuḍabha in the Dhammapada Commentary, I, p. 346f., goes to show that the vow of non-violence on the part of the S'ākyas sadly failed to stay the cruel hand of the invader who carried out a plan of ruthless massacre in their territory. The overcoming of the brute force by virtue or soul-force, as advocated in the Mahāsīlava Jātaka, is a Utopian idea.

[4] Dīgha, III, pp. 59, 146. contains the following description of the stately position of the righteous king overlord :

chāturanto vijitāvi janapada-thāvariyappatto satta-ratana-samannāgato...... Paro sahassaṃ kho pan assa puttā bhavanti sūrā vīrangarūpā parasena-pamaddanā. So imaṃ paṭhaviṃ sāgarapariyantaṃ akhilaṃ akaṇṭakaṃ iddhaṃ phītaṃ khemaṃ sivaṃ nirabbudaṃ adaṇḍena asatthena abhivijiya ajjhāvasati. Avikkambhiyo hoti (abbhantarena vā bāhirena vā) manussabhūtena pachchattikena pachchāmittena, See also Sumangalavilāsinī, III. p. 922.

with the menace to the security of life and property of the citizens arising from the mischievous action of the Aṭavis (R.E. XIII) or to his territory arising from the inimical action of the independent neighbours (S.R.E. II).

Arrian's remark that 'a sense of justice prevented any Indian king from attempting conquest beyond the limits of India' must not be taken to mean that any Indian king was lacking in the ambition of gaining the coveted position of a chāturanta or conqueror of the earth extending as far as the four seas, i.e., of a supreme lord of Jambudvīpa. Brahmanism went to encourage the predatory instinct in man by according a popular religious sanction to the periodical hunting and military expeditions (mrigayā, digvijaya) on the part of a warrior king and a war-like people. It tended to foster the idea of conquest, no matter whether it was actuated by an avaricious, demoniac or righteous motive. The worldly motive was thereby kept in the forefront and the cultural motive in the background. In the Brahmanical tradition the Digvijaya of Agni was shown to have proceeded side by side with the Digvijaya of the warriors, the latter reaching its consummation in the performance of either the horse-sacrifice (Aśvamedha-yajña) or the still grander sacrifice called Rājasūya, each containing in its programme the holding of a Sabhā or Coronation Durbar.

With Buddha the Dharma-vijaya achieved without the employment of the sword or armed force implied the welcoming by the rival monarchs or powers of the cause of piety espoused by the righteous king emperor or superior power,[1] and this was precisely the underlying thought of the Dharma-vijaya of Aśoka. As the great Maurya emperor himself puts it, "This, of course, is considered the

---

[1] Dīgha, III, p. 62f. : Ehi kho mahārāja, sāgataṃ
mahārāja, sāgataṃ te mahārāja, anusāsa mahārājā ti.
Rājā chakkavatti evam āha : pāṇo na hantabbo, adinnaṃ
nādātabbaṃ,.........yathābhuttañ cha bhuñjathā ti.

Nilakanta Sastri acutely observes :

"In this conquest by Dhaṃma, the stress falls on the justice and virtue of the king who builds up for himself by long practice of Dhamma a high moral superiority symbolized by the presence of wheel ; and this superiority secures for him the voluntary obedience of all rival kings on the face of the earth. The army is indeed present with the king, but it is simply an ornamental adjunct, there being no fighting or any employment of force. But the conquest and empire are real, though the imperialism is mild and benevolent in its nature." The Calcutta Review, 1943, Vol. LXXXVI, p. 118.

chief conquest by the Beloved of the gods, namely, the conquest by piety. This has been achieved by the Beloved of the gods here as well as among all the borderers, even over a distance of six hundred leagues, (where the rulers are) the Greek king named Antiochus and four other (Greek) kings beyond the said Antiochus, namely, Ptolemy, Antigonas, Magas (and) Alexander, and constantly (the ruling peoples are) the Cholas, and Pāṇḍyas, even the Tāmraparṇyas. So also here, in the king's territory, among the Yaunas and Kāmbojas, the Nābhakas and Nābhapaṃktis, the (parent) Bhojas and their offshoots,[1] the Andhras and Pārinda-Pāradas,—everywhere (the people) follow the moral instruction of the Beloved of the gods. Even where the envoys of the Beloved of the gods do not go, even (there) they hearing of the system of piety and moral instruction of the Beloved of the gods, abide by and will abide by the Law of Piety" (R.E. XIII). The essence of Aśoka's Dharma-vijaya may be shown to have been recorded in the Gupta coin-legends: sucharitair svargaṃ jayati. "He conquers even the heavens by virtues."

2. **Dharma-vijaya of the Great Epic**: We have in the Sabhāparva of the Great Epic a graphic account of the digvijaya or military campaigns undertaken by the four Pāṇḍava brothers and of its sequel—the Rājasūya sacrifice performed by king Yudhishṭhira, all under the guidance of Krishṇa Vāsudeva. Its main narrative is concerned, however, with the great battle of Kurukshetra valiantly fought and won by the Pāṇḍavas under the same guidance of the Superman and God incarnate and with the laudable object of founding a dharmarājya. The victory at the battle of Kurukshetra, too, was consummated by the performance of a horse-sacrifice by the Pāṇḍavas and the convening of a Coronation Durbar. The Bhagavad Gītā contains a philosophic explanation of the battle of Kurukshetra, while the Sanatsujātīya Gītā presents an elaborate explanation of the doctrine of apramāda or principle of action which characterized Aśoka's Dharma and guided all his noble undertakings and efforts, and which, as a matter of fact, was the distinctive tenet of all the heroic Indo-Aryan faiths of the past rooted in śraddhā.

The digvijaya of the Jaina king Khāravela as described in the Hāthigumphā inscription, the digvijaya of the great Hindu king Samudragupta as described in his Allahabad Stone-pillar inscription and the digvijaya of Raghu as described by Kālidāsa in his Raghu-

[1] This discards the previous translation by 'the Bhojas and the hereditary Bhojas.'

vaṃśa partake all of the nature of the digvijaya of the Pāṇḍavas as described in the Great Epic and fall, therefore, within its scope.

The idea of this digvijaya occurred to Arjuna after the killing of Jarāsandha, the most powerful monarch of the Bṛihadratha dynasty of Magadha and a renowned scion of the Chedi race of warriors who were hostile to the aspirations of the Andhaka-Vṛishṇis or Yādavas of Western India. Kṛishṇa Vāsudeva himself belonged to the Sātvata or Andhaka Vṛishṇi family of Dvārakā which was matrimonially connected with the Pāṇḍavas as well as the Chedis of the Chedi country. The express motive behind this digvijaya is stated to be the increase of the liquid reserve and financial strength of the rising state by the collection of booties consisting in revenues and valuable presents.[1] This motive is praised as warrior-like in spite of its being predatory and earthly.

Four brothers started in four directions, each in one direction on an auspicious day, at an auspicious moment and under an auspicious asterism. Arjuna who proceeded to the north conquered the whole northern division of Jambudvīpa comprising the upper half of the Punjab proper, the whole of the state of Kāshmīr and Jammu, the Himalayan region extending as far east as the Upper Assam Valley, Maṇipur and Chin Hills, and the trans-Himalayan hill-tracts and countries extending as far north as the southern boundary of Uttarakuru. The list of the conquered included monarchs, ruling classes, hill tribes and savages. All of them were reduced to the position of karadas. Bhīma who proceeded to the east conquered the countries east of Kuru including Bengal and the Lower Assam Valley. Sahadeva who proceeded to the south conquered the conntries that lay to the south of Kuru and whole of the southern division of Jambudvīpa extending as far down as Pāṇḍya and Drāviḍa, Choṇḍra-Kerala and Siṃhala. The western countries that lay to the west of Kuru extended as far west as the Lower Indus Valley and even included the territories of the Pahlavas, the Barbaras, the Yavanas and the S'akas. The Rājasūya sacrifice was performed thereafter at Hastināpura. A grand feast was given. A sabhā was held to establish the paramount sovereignty of Yudhishṭhira and the divinity or supreme personality of Kṛishṇa (Yudhishṭhirābhishekañ cha

1 Mahābhārata, II. 25, 3 : Arjuna said—

Tatra kṛityam ahaṃ manye koshasya parivardhanaṃ
karam āharayishyāmi rājñaḥ sarvān nṛipottama.

Vasudevasya charhaṇam).[1] The military campaigns involved all the three forms of conquest.

Such a wide geographical vision of Jambudvīpa together with an intimate knowledge of the individual countries and peoples as we obtain from the Great Epic account of the digvijaya is inconceivable previous to the reign of the Nandas and Mauryas of Magadha. The inclusion of the name of the S'akas, Yavanas and Pahlavas in the list of conquered peoples and territories means that the account in the Santī Paurāṇikī version of the Great Epic is Gupta or pre-Gupta but definitely post-Aśokan, post-S'unga and post-Kushāṇa. Whether such an account of the digvijaya appeared or not in the earlier Vaiśampāyana or pre-Pāṇinian version of the Great Epic[2] is still a disputed question. The geographical references of Pāṇini[3] may be shown to be on a par with those in the pre-Aśokan Pali Canonical texts which confine our vision to Jambudvīpa. These allusions lead us to think of the countries and peoples in the Uttarāpatha or Punjab proper, comprising the Upper and Lower Indus Valleys, the Himalayan region, the Middle Country to the west of modern Bengal, the Western India and the Central India. These hardly take us further south than the river Godāvarī.[4] In such post-Aśokan Pali Canonical works as the Mahāniddesa, Buddhavaṃsa and Apadāna we have mention of India's trade-relations, internal and external. Even such a distant country as China (Chīna) finds mention in the Buddhavaṃsa and Apadāna. The Mahāniddesa list includes the name of Suvarṇabhūmi, Tāmraparṇī and Yava (Java). The Bāveru Jātaka refers to India's sea-borne trade with Bāveru (Babylon). The

[1] Mahābhārata, II. 89. 15. In this very epic, III. 253, we are given a similar account of the military expedition of Karṇa who went north, south, east and west. Here we have mention of the Haimavatika kings (Haimavatikān jitvā), a term by which are meant the rulers who hold their territories on the whole eastern extension of the Himalayan range from Rādhi (modern Rādhia in the Champāran district) to Assam. Here Nepāl is distinctly mentioned as a Haimavatika country with many principalities (Nepālavishaye ye cha rājānaḥ) and Anga, Vanga, Kalinga, Suṇḍikā, Mithilā, Magadha and Karkakhaṇḍa are placed in the Eastern division below the Himalayas. This campaign, too, was followed by a Rājasūya sacrifice and Durbar.

[2] Pāṇini, IV. 3. 104 ; VI. 2. 36.

[3] Ibid, IV. 1. 18. IV. 1. 19 ; IV. 1. 48 ; IV. 1. 84 ; IV. 1. 111 ; IV. 1. 114 ; IV. 1. 148 ; IV. 1. 153 ; IV. 1. 155 ; IV. 1. 157 ; IV. 1. 160 ; IV. 1. 169 ; IV. 1. 170 ; IV. 1. 172-178 ; IV. 2. 74-77 ; IV. 2. 109-110 ; IV. 2. 117-119 ; IV. 2. 122-129 ; IV. 2. 131 ; IV. 2. 133 ; IV. 2. 135 ; IV. 3. 91 ; IV. 3. 93-94 ; IV. 3. 128 ; V. 1. 41 ; VI. 2. 99-101 ; VII. 3. 14.

[4] B. C. Law *India As Described*, Ch. I.

geographical vision of India's trade-routes and trade-relations which these works give us agrees in many respects with that in the prose-treatise of the Arthaśāstra which in its extant form can hardly be treated as a pre-Christian work. Sylvain Lévi has successfully tried with the help of the Brihatkathā to locate many of the places mentioned in the Mahāniddesa along the eastern sea-coast extending from India to China and Java. But these places, *e. g*., Ajapatha Meṇḍapatha (two together = Ajamīḍa, Ājmīr), Mūsikapatha (= Mousika of the Greek writers), Takkola (near Ājmīr), Angaloka, Tangaṇa, Yona, Paramayona, Alasanda, may all again be connected with the North-Western trade-route[1] and located in the Punjab proper or near about. Referring to the Rāmāyaṇa, too, one may observe that the Pali story of Daśaratha locates the place of Rāma's exile in the Himalayan region, and that the earlier version of the Rāma story did not push Rāma's wanderings with Sītā and Lakshmaṇa beyond the banks of the Godāvarī. The realistic account of the land-route by which Rāma reached Pāṇḍyakapāṭa and the region of the Tāmraparṇī river to have a view of the Pārasamudra or Ceylon from the Indian shore and other incidental geographical references that appear in Vālmīki's epic are post-Aśokan but not, perhaps, post-Christian.

The account of Khāravela's military campaigns goes to show that he had by-passed the main territory of his contemporary S'ātakarṇi in carrying his conquest up to the town of Asika (Ṛishika) on the Krishṇveṇvā (Krishṇā), humbled the Rāshṭrikas and Bhojakas of the Vidyādhara countries (along the Vindhya range of hills), compelled the king of Pāṇḍya in the extreme south to send him presents, subdued Brihaspatimitra, the contemporary ruler of Anga-Magadha, drove back a contemporary Yavana (Greek) king to Mathurā, and defeated the rulers of Uttarāpatha.

Behind Kālidāsa's imaginary description of Raghu's India-wide digvijaya was the digvijaya of the Pāṇḍavas as well as that of Samudragupta. The account of Samudragupta's digvijaya holds undoubtedly before us the picture of an India-wide sovereignty resulting from the following forms of conquest: (1) the Dharma-vijaya (grahaṇa-moksha) bringing great fortunes (mahābhāgya) effected in the case of all the rulers of South India (Dakshiṇāpatha); (2) the Prasabha-uddharaṇa, a form of Asura-vijaya serving to greatly

[1] Pāṇini, V. 1. 77 : Uttarāpathenāhṛitam.

strengthen his treasury and army[1] (prabhāva-mahat) effected in the case of several rulers of Northern India (Āryāvarta); (3) the Asura-vijaya (parichārakī-karaṇa) effected in the case of all Āṭavika rulers; (4) the Lobhavijaya (karadānājñākaraṇa praṇāmāgamana) effected in the case of the frontier powers and war-like republican tribes; and (5) that by the virtue of granting a charter of liberty (garutmadanka) after the weaker power had made a voluntary self-surrender, or sought for a matrimonial allowance, or offered presents (ātmanivedana-kanyopāyana-dāna), a form of Dharma-vijaya effected in the case of Śakamuruṇḍas, the Sinhalese nation and the inhabitants of all other adjacent islands.

It is easily understandable even to common sense that the Rajasūya sacrifice was availed of as a socio-political and semi religious device for proclaiming and establishing the paramount sovereignty of Yudhishṭhira. What is bewildering to common sense is the question—was it the proper occasion for proclaiming Krishṇa Vāsudeva as the Superman and Supreme Being and establishing his divinity. The bewildering and overwhelming of common sense instead of organizing and enlightening it is, as we shall see anon, the main trend of the Great Epic thought which is vitiated throughout by its diplomatic undercurrent. Let us for the present examine the arguments put forward in the Great Epic in favour of the proposal for the unanimous acceptance of Krishṇa as the divinity, the supreme human personality, the highest object of popular adoration and the worthiest recipient of the homage of the sacrifice.

When among the invited, S'iśupāla of the Chedi royal house raised a dissentient voice, expressed resentment and openly challanged the propriety of the proposal, Yudhishṭhira gently besought him to agree to the proposal and tried to pacify him by advancing an *argumentum ad hominem* as well as an *argumentum ad verucundum.*[2]

Of the three arguments advanced by Bhīshma, the first is worldly, the second rational, and the third theological i.e., questionable. The first argument is based on the maxim :

> Kshatriyaḥ kshatriyaṃ jitvā raṇe raṇakritāṃvaraḥ,
> yo muñchati vaśe kritvā gurur bhavati tasya saḥ.

"A warrior becomes a victor in war by conquering another warrior. He who releases the conquered king after bringing him into subjection becomes a guru (superior) to the latter."

---

[1] Arthas'āstra, VI. 2 : kos'a-daṇḍa-balaṃ prabhus'aktiḥ.

[2] Mahābhārata, II. 38. 7-10.

At the Rājasūya Durbar there was not a single monarch present who was not conquered by the Pāṇḍavas through the power of Krishṇa. Many powerful kings were conquered by Krishṇa in battles. So he became a guru to all of them. The whole world became established in him in the sense, no doubt, that he came to hold then the balance of power in India.

The second argument proceeds on the axiom that he who excels the wise in moral and personal qualities is to be deemed most worthy of the homage :

Guṇair vriddhān atikramya Hariḥ archyatamo mataḥ.

Krishṇa excelled even the wisest among the Brāhmans in his knowledge of the Vedas and Vedāngas and the mightest among the Kshatriyas in his fighting strength (balādhikya). The moral and personal qualities with which Krishṇa was endowed consisted of liberality, skill, learning, heroism, judiciousness, fame, superior intelligence, lineage, luck, endurance, contentment and prosperity :

Dānaṃ dākshyaṃ śrutaṃ śauryaṃ hrīḥ
kīrtir buddhiruttamā,
santatih śrīr dhritis tushṭih pushṭiś cha
niyatāchyute.[1]

On this ground alone Krishṇa might be claimed to have been the teacher, the father and the guru, entitled to the homage by the consensus of opinion :

Tam enaṃ lokasampannaṃ āchāryaṃ pitaraṃ guruṃ
arghyam architam archārhaṃ sarve saṃkshantum arhatha.[2]

The third argument which is extraordinary rests on the popular veneration of Krishṇa as Divinity or God incarnate, the highest personality in all the worlds of life and existence :

Ūrddhvaṃ tiryag adhaś chaiva yāvati jagato gatih,
sadevakeshu lokeshu Bhagavān Keśavo mukham.

It passes common human comprehension how a human being, however mighty and perfect and great in soul-power, might be eulogized as the inexhaustible first cause and the final cause of the world :

Krishṇa eva hi lokānām utpattir api chāvyayah,
Krishṇasya hi krite viśvam idaṃ bhūtaṃ charācharam.[3]

---

[1] Ibid, II. 38. 17-20.
[2] Ibid. II. 38.21.
[3] Ibid, II. 38.23-29.

The Great Epic has not, however, concealed from view the other side of the picture. It has put into the mouth of S'iśupāla what might be the bold criticism of the whole affair of this Rājasūya sacrifice. Krishṇa's motive is construed to be self-establishment by taking full advantage of an earthly situation :

> Ayuktam ātmanaḥ pūjāṃ tvaṃ punar bahu manyashe,
> havishaḥ prāpya nishyandaṃ praāśita śveva nirjane.[1]

The things came ultimately to such a pass that there was no other alternative left but to stop the arrogance of S'iśupāla by a furious method, to silence the critic and to crush the rising party by killing its leader and spokesman. Krishṇa took upon himself the opprobrium of beheading S'iśupāla with his chakrāyudha. Before this drastic step had been taken S'iśupāla's mother interceded on his behalf and Krishṇa promised in the presence of all to forgive him. But to common sense the act of beheading is irreconcilable with the solemn promise of forgiving. The argument of the strong prevailed. Such is the rule of the majority which is guided by a mob psychology and is not infrequently arbitrary and tyrannical. This is not again the only instance recorded in the Great Epic where the critic having the moral courage of expressing his honest opinion was hooted out of the court. When at the victorious conclusion of the battle of Kurukshetra all the Brāhmans led by the greed of gifts and favours came in to pronounce their blessings on Yudhishṭhira, one of them had the audacity to condemn his action saying that he had gained this earthly sovereignty at the cost of many of his own people. The rest of the interested Brāhmans uttered *hum* and decried the fellow, saying in one voice that he was not a Brāhman but a chārvāka or goblin in disguise. Such has been the way of the madding crowd, the thoughtless world. When a person succeeds by hook or crook in establishing Rob Roy's simple rule of might is right, the priests with their blessings, the Pandits with their learned interpretations, the sycophants with their flatteries and the followers with their devotional sentiments change it into a divine rule of right is might.

Now let us see if the position at all improves by the philosophic explanation of the battle of Kurukshetra offered in the Bhagavad Gīta which is the most authoritative Book of the Hindus. According as we take this battle to be a historical event or an internal affair of oneself, a battle against one's internal enemies, the Bhagavad Gīta teaches either a war philosophy or a religious method of self-realiza-

[1] Ibid, II. 37.27.

tion through self-conquest. Whether the one or the other, the foundation of a dharmarājya is its avowed aim. In one respect, this dharmarājya means a Holy Empire of India without, and in another, a kingdom of righteousness within.

The Holy Empire of India is sought to be founded by an internecine and global war in the sub-continent which resulted in the destruction of all great warriors, the destruction of the Kurus, the descendants of the Pāṇḍavas, the annihilation of the Yādavas and the Brihadrathas ; and the general emasculation of humanity. The Great Epic goes to show that the New World sought to be created through the battle of Kurukshetra was a world of desolation and despair, the inhabitants whereof began to utter in their helplessness the pitiful cry of Hā Krishṇa, Hā Krishṇa ! The thrilling narrative of Rāma's exploits in Vālmīki's epic ends similarly in the most catastrophic tragedy of the destruction of the most prosperous city of Ayodhyā in the north and that of the equally prosperous city of Svarṇalankā in the south. Both the religion of the strong justifying all diplomatic artifices, violent methods, valiant feats, nefarious acts and self-aggrandisements in the name of God, Divine purpose, Holy Empire and New World, and the religion of the infirm seeking consolation in the Lord's name and through the thoughtless fatalism of some kind are equally reprehensible. The war philosophy, developed in the Great Epic in general and the Bhagavad Gītā in particular, seeks to establish the following beliefs : (a) that all beings are the creatures of time of which the decree is unavoidable ; (b) that the Divine Will works through and ultimately prevails in all the dramas of life in heaven and on earth ; (c) that the world-order and the astronomical universe are far far greater than a man, however powerful and mighty he may be ; (d) that the race-instinct is the real goading factor in man's life than the momentary prick of conscience or reflective mood ; and (e) that there is a mightier power than all earthly lords, led by the demoniac spirit of arrogance, self-conceit, atheism and defiance of all divine laws, to act as the arbiter of their fate.

So far as the war philosophy of the Bhagavad Gītā is concerned, its arguments are irrelevant, incongruous and unconvincing as answers to the points raised by Arjuna from the common sense point of view. When brought into the battle-field, Arjuna felt sad to think that to commence the battle was to fight against his own kith and kin, teachers and elders and other persons for whose good and happiness he would desire victory, sovereignty and fame ; if they were all killed, for whose sake he would attain it, what was the use of attaining it ? An internecine war is likely to result in the destruction of one's own people which in its turn results in the loss of the chastity of women.[1] The promiscuity of sex-relations leads to the loss of the purity of the blood and fusion of races which in its turn leads to the loss of the family tradition and race heritage. When the high tradition is lost, the whole human race is overtaken by corruption, impiety and sin.[2]

When Aśoka reflected upon the scene of carnage and bloodshed and after-effects of the aggressive war waged on Kalinga, it occurred to him : "In conquering indeed an unconquered country, the slaying or dying or deporting which occurs there is considered an extremely painful and serious matter by the Beloved of the gods. Even more serious than that is this, that those who dwell there, whether the Brāhmaṇas or the S'ramaṇas or other sects of householders in whom are established this respectful attention to high personages,..... , to them occurs hurt or death or deportation of beloved ones, or that even (as regards) those well-controlled ones whose affection has not diminished, if those who are their friends, associates, comrades and relatives encounter disaster, on that account that, too, becomes a cause of hurt to them. This is a common reaction to all men and a serious matter in the opinion of the Beloved of the gods." (R.E. XIII).

Instead of considering the points raised by Arjuna, Vāsudeva simply accuses him of cowardice (klaivya), insinuating that inwardly he was afraid of risking the fame of a great warrior earned by him, and proceeds with his grandiloquent discourses that are incoherent, and ultimately reveals his omniform to overawe the earthly hero, wanting Arjuna to do his behest.

The Dharmarājya in the sense of a kingdom of rightousness within is sought to be founded in the Bhagavad Gītā also on a set of beliefs indispensable to its syncretic philosophy of life and action. Looked at from the point of view of the literary history of India, the Gītā literature started by way of a deflection from the Upanishad. But for the synthetic religious setting of jñānayoga, karmayoga and bhaktiyoga, the docetic Sātvata cult of Purushottama, and the shifting of emphasis from jñāna and karma to bhakti (devotional sentiment) the Bhagavad Gītā has hardly any originality of its own as regards its ideas, principles and practices that are mostly drawn from different

---

1 Nripen Basu's book—Cupid joins the war. One may read with profit.

2 Bhagavad Gītā, I. 26-44.

sources. The catalogue of ethical concepts which gets prominence through the perorations of the poetical discourse was the fullest development, as we sought to show, from its humbler beginning in the instruction of the Upanishad teacher Ghora Āngirasa who is respresented as the guru of Krishṇa. The interested reader of the Upanishads is likely to be amazed at Kṛishṇa's being in the role of a Teacher himself of all the wisdom of the past and the future,—the pupil of whom it is said that at the time of his death, he took refuge in the Deity applying to Him the three attributes of being the undecaying, immutable and living one : akshitam asi, achyutam asi, prāṇasaṁśitam asi. It is further said that he ceased to thirst for things worldly on hearing Āngirasa's instruction (apipāsa eva sa babhūva). No part of a teacher is assigned to him even by mistake.[1] It is nevertheless important to watch how the idea of a grand edifice of religious thought came to be developed out of such crude materials. In the Gītā, Krishṇa Vāsudeva, the friend, philosopher and guide, is represented as saying to Arjuna, a typical warrior of fame and worldly man with strong common sense and goodness of nature :

(i) Believe that thy real self is the soul in a bodily garb, which is cast away when it is worn out and replaced by a new one in the process of metempsychosis ;

(ii) Believe that the soul which is thy true self is the entity that outlasts all apparent changes, it being by its essential nature unborn, undying, unchanging, immutable, imperishable and untouchable by all thy actions ;

(iii) Believe that the soul within thee and the soul within the universe are identical in their nature ;

(iv) Believe that thy first duty is to look into thyself and find out thy true self and the true self of the rest of things and beings by lifting the veil which hides the true nature and identity of the two ;

(v) Believe that thy folly lies in coming away from God and coming into thyself, being deluded by the thought that thou art different from Him ;

(vi) Believe that with the true vision of reality thou wilt see thee in the all and the all in thee, and ultimately nothing and none but God ;

---

1 Chhāndogya Up., III, 17.

(vii) Believe that placed that thou art in life, the utmost thou canst do is to purify thy motive ;

(viii) Believe that the right way to work in life is to surrender thy will to the Divine and to feel always that thou art not the agent but only an instrument to His will fulfilling itself ;

(ix) Believe that the possession of the godly estate far outweighs in value that of the demoniac ;

(x) Believe that God is the alpha and the omega of the universe, the almighty and the infinite, the incomparable, the imperishable, the inexhaustible, the immanent, the transcendent, the greatest of the great and the smallest of the small ;

(xi) Believe that all the modes of knowing, all the methods of action, and all the forms of worship are the manifold mode of approach towards Godhead, and hence meant ultimately for Him ; and

(xii) Believe that all the social grades and all the human institutions are to be respected and utilized and not to be interfered with, these being created by the Divine will.

Thus indeed was laid the stable and spacious philosophic foundation of the Hindu faith (śraddhā) enlivened with devotional sentiment (bhakti), the faith consisting of a set of beliefs, laying down certain principles of human conduct, commending certain rules of life, and emphasizing certain religious practices. A grand order of harmony, full of life, meaning, truth, good and beauty, is conceived to enable us to realize and appreciate the unity as truth behind the puzzling diversity or multiplicity of existences, forms, motives, expressions, thoughts, tendencies and actions. This order had behind it the Vedic and Upanishadic conception of the organic unity of the visible universe of the world, of life, of the society, as well as of the state, with a division of labour among the component elements or constituents of each. Herbert Spencer is the modern advocate of such an organic theory carrying too far the analogies between a living organism on the one hand and the material universe, the world of life, the society and the state on the other. Unfortunately for India the fanciful organic idea was sanctified in Hinduism into a captivating religious faith. The popular poetical imagery seeking to represent the alternate appearances and disappearances of the cosmic system in a fixed rotatory order in the analogy of a wheel turning round and round on its eternally fixed axle stood against the idea of a forward movement. In the cumbersome scheme of harmony where the diverse races of men with their distinctive traits, the different social grades and trade-guilds with their special caste privileges and handicaps and exclusive occupations on a hereditary basis, etc., were sought to be accommodated and the scope of their existence, competition, education and environment had to be narrowed down and curtailed. The rigidity of the restrictive rules as to *connubium* and *commensality* compelled them to live, move and have their being within hidebound compartments of an insular and unalterable socio-political and religio-economic organization. In bringing the social organization of men into harmony with the world order of life, it began to work no better than the social organization of the ants or wasps or honeybees, on the commodious principle of a division of labour, each class or section of men functioning as a cog fitted only for a special work of life. The social scheme thus sanctified in the name of the Divine order and dispensation went to present an aggregate of human beings permanently placed in divers groups, functioning as different limbs and organs of a living body, each being intended for a specific duty and all contributing to the well-being of the whole which is a unity with the diversity of functions. But the irremovable artificial barriers placed between one group or class and another served to make them all 'dependent on a common care-taker, divine or human'. The scheme of religious toleration proposed with non-intervention as the best policy went similarly to present congeries of faiths, all kinds of belief, all modes of approach, all forms of worship under the convenient axiom 'whatever is, is right in its own place'. Thus the multitudinous popular cults, even those rooted in the grossest kind of superstition, were justified and allowed chances to exist and thrive side by side with higher philosophic thoughts and religious ideals. The Hindu needed, as a modern saint points out, their supreme Deity, whether He be Śiva, Vishṇu, S'akti, Rāma, Kṛishṇa or Kalki, to be one who can hold the balance of power or maintain the harmony of the turbulent world by his unsurpassed might, illumine the minds of all by his unsurpassed knowledge, who can create, preserve as well as destroy,—who is omniform, omnipresent, omnipotent and omniscient, overwhelming, overpowering and all-conquering. The India-wide digvijaya and pilgrimage (tīrthayātrā) on the part of the Pāṇḍavas and Karṇa, as described in the extant Sautī version of the Great Epic, and finally the great battle of Kurukshetra fought and won by the former resulted in the founding of such a grand Holy Hindu Empire of a feudal type. On this very model was built the powerful Gupta empire under the aegis of which we reach the Augustan age of Sanskrit language and literature, Indian arts and crafts, religions and philosophies, dramas and kāvyas, opulence and enjoyment. All the earlier currents and cross-currents of linguistic development met at last to make Sanskrit the *lingua franca* of the cultured laity. The praśastis or royal panegyrics composed either by the court poets or Pandits in terms of hyperboles, mythological fancies and allegorical equivoques came to extol the later digvijayas as unprecedented achievements of far-reaching consequence in the annals of human history and culture. These are conspicuously lacking in the homely Prakrit diction and simplicity, the direct appeal and sincerity of the edicts of Aśoka. The analytical method of the earlier systems of science and thought, the formulation of ideas, the epitomizing of thoughts in aphorisms, etc. were followed by elaborations, scholastic niceties and logical discussions. The heroic spirit of the earlier age which was sought to be enlivened in the Bhagavad Gītā with the devotional sentiment of popular religions yielded place to the erotic and tended to find its satisfaction in the grandeur and aesthetic grace of arts and crafts. The clever art of diplomacy was degenerating into a degraded form of sychopancy in the sphere of religion and of life. Slavery not only continued to exist but tended also to become more numerous in its form[1] and to assume a feudal character. As the S'ukranīti indicates, the Council of Ministers was gaining more and more in power to deprive ultimately the king of his right of vetoing, which meant gaining in more power by the Brāhman Peshwās for creating feuds and divisions.

3. **Trailokya-vijaya of the Karaṇḍvyūha :** The Sātvata cult of Purushottama as advocated in the Bhagavad Gītā, was not without its lasting effect on other faiths in India, Buddhism included. In this cult Kṛishṇa was claimed to be the soul in the heart of all, the creator, preserver and destroyer of all living beings. He is the Vishṇu among the Ādityas, the sun among the luminaries, the Marīchi among the winds, the moon among the stars, the Sāma among the Vedas, the Vāsava among the gods, the mind among the organs of sense, so on and so forth.[2]

---

[1] As Atindranath Bose has shown, the list of different kinds of slaves is found to be the longest in the Law Book of Nārada, while the list in the Arthas'āstra stands midway between that given by Manu and that by Nārada.

[2] Bhagavad Gītā, X. 20-37.

These were evidently tbe current Hindu ideas in the immediate background of the Trailokya-vijaya of later Buddhism. This vijaya is defined in the Kāraṇḍavyūha and other later Mahāyāna works as a form of religious and cultural conquest to be achieved by offering Brahmatva *par excellence* to the worshippers of Brahmā, Vishṇutva *par excellence* to the worshippers of Vishṇu, S'ivatva *par excellence* to the worshippers of S'iva, Yakshatva *par excellence* to the worshippers of the Yakshas, Rakshatva *par excellence* to the worshippers of the Rakshas, Piśāchatva *par excellence* to the worshippers of the Piśāchas, and the like.[1]

Trailokya-vijaya as a distinctive epithet of Buddha is met with as early as the 7th century A.D. in the inscriptions of the Chandra kings of East Bengal. But the Trailokya-vijaya career of Buddhism must be associated with the Pālas of Eastern India headed by Dharmapāla Vikramaśīla during whose peaceful and prosperous reign several new Buddhist Universities were founded in Bengal and Behār, notably the Somapura Mahāvihāra at Behār Sarif and the Vikramaśīla Mahāvihārā probably at Sakri Gali,[2] South Behār and the earlier world-famous University of Nālandā was quickened into a most vigorous life. These Buddhist seats of learning of various sizes and degrees of importance and the newer ones that were subsequently ushered into existence were all in a flourishing state under the liberal patronage of the Pāla rulers.

The Mahābodhi Saṅghārāma which was caused to be erected at Bodhgayā by king Kitti-Siri-Meghavaṇṇa during the reign of Samudragupta for the accommodation of the monks from Ceylon was in a thriving condition when Hwen Thsang visited the place during

---

[1] Cf. Ekallavīra-Chaṇḍa-mahāroshaṇa-tantra quoted in Haraprasad Shastri's Descriptive Catalogue of Sanskrit Manuscripts in the Government collection, Vol. I, p. 124.

Sarvo' haṃ sarvavyāpī cha sarvakṛit sarvanās'akaḥ,
sarvarūpadharo buddhaḥ hartā kartā prabhuḥ sukhī.
Yena yenaiva rūpeṇa sattvā yānti vineyatāṃ
tena tenaivo rūpeṇa sthito'haṃ lokahetave.
kvachit Buddhaḥ kvachit siddhaḥ kvachit dharmo'tha saṃghakaḥ
kvachit Pretaḥ kvachit Tiryak kvachit Nārakarūpakah.

[2] Sultanganj, Pātthargħāṭā and Siloa are the places hitherto suggested for identification with the site of Vikramas'īla University. I am inclined to think that Sakrigali affords an extensive site going up west over a mile along the lower bank of the Ganges and with the breadth of about the quarter of a mile can alone meet all the requirements for correct identification.

the reign of king Harshavardhana of Kanauj in the middle of the 7th century A.D. The same continued to flourish even thereafter under the Pala rule.[1]

The new stream of the Chinese pilgrims headed by I-tsing began to flow into India to bear a glowing testimony to the greatness of India, the sacred land which had produced the world religion of Śākyamuni and was the cradle of a mighty Aryan civilization.[2] One among the late mediaeval pilgrims from China, namely, Chiang Hsia-pias (A.D. 1021), did not omit in his hymn composed in honour of the Bodhgayā Temple to pay his best compliment to Aśoka as the righteous emperor who lived in the right perception of the truth of the religion of Buddha and as the great builder of Buddhist shrines in India whose noble fame travelled far and wide.[3]

The trade-relations of India with Suvarṇabhūmi (Burma and Further India), Suvarṇadvīpa (Java), Sumātrā and Borneo not only facilitated inter-communication between India and those countries and islands and led to the foundation of Indian colonies in the Pacific islands but resulted also in the spread of Buddhism and Hinduism. So far as Suvarṇabhūmi is concerned, the substituion of the name of Suvarṇabhūmi for Suvarṇagiri in the tradition of the Buddhist mission under Soṇa and Uttara went to associate the name of Aśoka also with the history of introduction of Buddhism into Burma. Though the successive waves of Buddhist mission had reached the shores of Burma, first probably from South India and finally from Ceylon, from the time of the Chandras of Bengal and during the reign of the Pālas, the districts of Tippera and Chittagong served as the connecting link between the Buddhist art tradition of Bengal and Behār, while the Hindu art tradition which has left its impress on the Buddhist religious monuments of Pagan in Upper Burma was evidently carried by the architects and craftsmen brought over from Orissa. The legacies of the Buddhist art-tradition from the Deccan and the island of Ceylon came to be prominent in the frescoes inseveral Pagodas of Pagan. The S'ailendras of Suvarṇa-dvīpa (Java) under whose patronage and with whose munificence the shrine of Borobudur was built were contemporaries of the Pālas.

---

[1] Beal, Buddhist Records, II, p. 133f. ; Cunningham, Mahābodhi, p. 43 ; Barua, Gayā and Buddhagayā, II, p. 33f.

[2] Barua, Gayā And Buddhagayā, I, p. 214.

[3] Cunningham, Mahābodhi, p. 70.

The earlier Buddhist mission to Bhoṭa or Tibet is known to have been led by Padmasambhava during the reign of Srong-tsan Gampo, 'the most renowned of Tibetan kings', who introduced Buddhism into his kingdom under the influence of his Buddhist consorts from China. Nepāl was then subject to Tibet and Tīrhut too became subject to it. From the latter half of the 7th Century onwards the Lochāvas or Pandits from the Land of Snow came in larger and larger numbers to different Buddhist seats of learning for the study of Buddhist and Indian works during the reign of the Pālas. It was during this very reign that the later and more successful Buddhist mission to Tibet was led by Atiśa (Dīpankara-śrījñāna) in the first half of the eleventh century.[1]

Between the Guptas and the Pālas was the powerful and prosperous reign of Harshavardhana of the Pushpabhūti family who succeeded in founding a fairly large empire in Northern India extending from Valabhi in the extreme west to Assam in the extreme east. His reign is noted for the visit of the great Chinese pilgrim Hwen Thsang who left behind him a detailed account of India of his time as well as of the countries in Central Asia through which he passed on his way to and back from India. Harsha's system of administration, though less rigorous, was structurally the same as that of the Guptas. 'The provinces were governed in detail by tributary Rājās'. The only redeeming feature of it, and one connecting it with the tradition of the Maurya administration under Aśoka was the 'incessant personal supervision......which he (Harsha) effected by constantly moving about'. The large-hearted practice of religious toleration is another notable point of historical connexion of Harsha with the tradition of Aśoka. Nālandā was up till then the only great centre of Buddhist learning which had attained to the eminence of a University.

Be that as may, the secular side of Indian life was being regulated, as we shall see enough of it under the Digvijaya of Agni, by the law-books of the Brāhman jurists and the rituals of the Brāhman priests and dominated by Hinduism in matters of religious belief and forms of worship.

---

1 A. H. Francke, Antiquities of Indian Tibet, Calcutta, 1914, p. 52; Vincent Smith, Oxford History of India, p. 174f.

4. Digvijaya of Agni: The Digvijaya of Agni[1] which is presupposed by the Dharma-vijaya of Buddha and Aśoka signified the spread of Vedic religion and culture and the establishment of supremacy of the Brāhmans as a social grade and a privileged class of priests, teachers, law-givers, mystics and philosophers. Agni was regarded as the first and most important god of the Vedic Indians both as the purifier of all impurities, external and internal, and as the carrier of oblations to different gods. Agni whose essence is heat is fire on the earth, lightning in the firmament and sun in the sky. Agni manifests itself in various forms, terrestrial and celestial. As fire, Agni is the lord of every home, whether worldly or religious, whether in the common habitat of men or in the forest home. One can say indeed that it was by the genial warmth of fire that all the seeds of culture sprouted in India and Iran, nay, in all the ancient cradles of civilization. So far as India is concerned, Agni as sacrificial fire symbolized the Vedic cult of yajña in the widest possible sense of the term, which is to say, the whole of Vedic religion and culture as handed down, interpreted, elaborated, disseminated and utilised by the different schools of Brāhmans and Brāhman teachers.

To understand the real historical significance of the Digvijaya of Agni, it is necessary to differentiate broadly the two successive stages in the development and expansion of the Indo-Aryan culture and civilization, the earlier stage represented by Vedism and the later stage by Brahmanism. By the former we are to understand the one phase of the Indo-Aryan culture and civilization into which we can have glimpses through the windows of the collection of inspired hymns in the Ṛigveda and the Atharva-Angiras collection of charms, spells, incantations, imprecations and vrātya hymns in the Atharvaveda. The corridors to the first were formed by the Sāma collection of the Vedic psalms and the Yajur collection of the Vedic rituals, while that to the latter was formed by the Gṛihya hymns from the Ṛigveda adapted to the needs of domestic and social rites. It is through these corridors that one can pass from Vedism into Brahmanism.

The Vedic civilization which is characterized by race virility and indomitable spirit of man to resist and overcome the dreaded and inhospitable natural forces, the pestilences due to drought and the

---

[1] The idea of this may be formed from the S'atapatha Brāhmaṇa (I. 4. 1 ff.) account of the march of Agni Vais'vānara burning along this earth from the river Sarasvatī eastwards to the Sadānīrā.

prevalence of epidemics, the rivalry of the hostile powers and the mischiefs caused by the savages was primarily the civilization of the Saptasindhu, *i.e*, of the Uttarāpatha or Punjab proper watered by the Indus system of rivers. As may be easily inferred from the list of fourteen rivers mentioned by name in the Nadī-stuti hymn, the Aryandom became widened during the closing period of the Ṛigveda so as to include in it even the region between the Ganges and the Yamunā. Two easternmost rivers of the older Aryandom were the Sarasvatī and the Aśmanvatī (to be identified with the Dṛishadvatī). The remaining ten rivers, including the Kubhā (*i.e.*, Kābul) belonged all to the Indus group.[1] The Digvijaya of Agni implied in secular life the victorious career of the five confederate septs or clans (pañchajanāh) of a war-like people representing the Vedic Aryans. The same implied in religious life the establishment of the cultural tradition of the seven Ṛishis. The traditional number of the leading Ṛishi families increased with time, it being known in Buddha's time as ten. The Vedic civilization presupposes the powerful and materially advanced civilization of the Indus Valley of which the highly interesting but imperfectly understood remains have been unearthed at Mohenjo-daro and Harappa. The historical tradition in the Ṛigveda speaks eloquently of the victory of king Sudās over ten kings and of his extensive power and munificence.[2] The Dīgha Nikāya preserves the tradition of a magnificent old buried city, which was once the prosperous capital of a righteous king overlord called Sudarśana the Great. The site of this city is misplaced.[3] The name Sudarśana[4] which is also an epithet of the sun may be suggestive of the fact that its bearer was a warrior of the solar race. Nothing would be more astonishing to think than that Vedic Aryandom had extended further east than the river S'atadru, or that in the Vedas there is mention of any people or country outside the Uttarāpatha. The Gandhāris who are incidentally mentioned in the Ṛigveda (I. 126. 7) and the Atharva (V. 22 14) 'apparently as a despised

---

1 B. C. Law, Rivers of India, p. 9.

2 Ṛigveda, VII. 18 foll.; Aitareya Br., VII. 34-9. Sānkhāyana S'rauta Sūtra, XVI. 11-14; Vedic Index, ii, Sub vedic Sudās. "At one time Vis'vāmitra was his Purohita, and accompanied him in his victorious raids over the Vipās' (Beas) and S'utudrī (Sutlej)."

3 Dīgha, II, pp. 169-99; Saṃyutta, III, p. 144; Jātaka, I, p. 45.

4 It is not improbalde to think that the Vedic name Sudās was just a Prakrit form of Sudars'a = Sudars'ana, cf. Pali Piyadāso = Priyadars'a, Priyadars'ana.

people', in the latter, along with the Mujavats, Angas and Magadhas, were a people of Uttarāpatha. We may be certain about the Angas having been a people of Uttarāpatha, inasmuch as even in historical times there was a distinct tribal tract by the name of Angaloka or Angaṇa, which existed side by side with Tangaṇa.

The pre-historic sites hitherto discovered in South India and Ceylon abound in dolmens, cists, stone implements and other remains of a rude state of civilization attained by man in the palæolithic and neolithic ages. None of them has so far yielded any evidence of man's progress reaching up to the chalcolithic stage. The latter stage was abundantly reached in Sumer or Shinar in Mesopotamia and in the two ancient buried cities of Harappa and Mahenjo daro, *i.e.*, in the pre historic civilization of the Indus Valley.[1] The Pali tradition of the old forgotten buried city preserves the name of Kuśavatī reminding us of the earlier Sumerian city of Kush (Kish), the glory of which was eclipsed by the rise of Bāveru (Babylon) to importance, while the name of Sumer with its Biblical variant Shinar cannot but remind us of Mt. Sumeru with Sineru as the Pali variant of its name. The marked advance in civilization was made by human races in Egypt in the valley of the river Nile (Aigyptos), in Sumeria and Asia Minor in the valleys of the Euphrates and the Tigris, and in the Punjab proper in the valley of the Indus. A similar advance was made in China in the valley of the Yangtse. In the history of Babylonia, Assyria and Chaldea we get nothing but an account of the subsequent development of the Sumerian civilization. In the rise of the Hittites in Asia Minor as a powerful rival of both the Egyptians and the Mesopotamians one can trace not only the historical process of amalgamation of the two earlier forms of civilization but also a new type of civilization, which is more European than Indo-European in its essential features. From the Egyptian, the Babylonian and the Hittite stages, it is easy to watch the rise of the Phœnicians, the Israels, the Achæmenians, the Greeks and the Romans as civilizers of mankind on the Mediterranean shores.

The traditions of India refer all to the region of Mt. Sumeru or Sineru, say the table-land of Pāmir, as the centre of the then known

[1] For the uniqueness and high antiquity of the Indus civilization, read the views of Gadd, Sidney Smith and Langdon in the Mohenjo-daro and the Indus Civilization, Vol. II and Barua's Presidential address, Indian History Congress, Eighth Session, 1945 and article on Indus Script and Tantric Code in Dr. B. C. Law Volume, Part II.

earth extending as far as to the four seas and dividing the four subcontinents. This very region was remembered to have been the scene of contests between the Devas and the Asuras for supremacy with varying results. There is also a tradition, though a late one, that the higher and more powerful races of men came to India from the Western, Northern and Eastern subcontinents.[1] The Uttarāpatha or Punjab proper within the belt of the Western Himalayan range was indeed the portion of Northern India which became the most ancient of higher civilization and culture. It is here that one must trace the early settlements of divers races and scenes of conflict amongst them in prehistoric and historic times. It lay exposed to powerful invasions from outside and had to bear the brunt of first attacks and onslaughts of hostile and invading forces.

The worship of idols or concrete representations of various divinities was widely prevalent in all the ancient cradles of civilization and centres of culture. The first move in the direction of progress was aniconic, meaning as it did a struggle of the higher mind to get away from the concrete to find heart's delight in the realm of the abstract. With the open condemnation of idolatry and the monotheistic conception of Jehovah as the wrathful and Almighty God of the Hebrews commenced the history of Judaism as a higher religion in the eastern Mediterranean countries and later on that of Islam with its cenception of Allah as the All-merciful and Almighty God. With the conception of the gods and goddesses as finalities of beauty commenced the history of Greek religion. With the birth of a higher religious poetry in the Ṛiks tending to transform the concrete into the abstract and to endow the gods and goddesses with divine attributes of an ethical and aesthetic kind commenced the history of Vedism in the Saptasindhu.

Superseding the Egyptian Book of the Dead, Sumerian Psalms and Hittite state-treaties and religious texts by their dignified utterances, elevated moral tone, broadness of outlook, religious fervour, self-consciousness, imaginativeness and philosophic insight, the Ṛigvedic hymns came to represent a great upheaval of human

---

[1] This tradition recorded by Buddhaghosa runs cunter to the legend known to Diodorus saying that 'India, being of enormous size when taken as a whole, is peopled by races both numerous and diverse, of which not even one was originally of foreign descent', and that 'India neither received colony from abroad, nor sent out a colony to any other nation." McCrindle, Ancient India, pp. 34, 109.

mind and to raise the level of culture and standard of civilization. The Ṛigveda supplied to Brahmanism the sacred texts to be chanted as psalms, the mantras or charming ritual formulas of mystic potency, the notion of purifying agency in Agni, that of the source of light and heat in Sūrya, that of severeignty in Indra, that of an orderly universe in Varuṇa, that of organic individuality of the universe and of human society in Purusha or Nārāyaṇa, that of a divine architect in Viśvakarman, that of vitality in Anila, that of a scientific attitude towards the problem of creation in the Nāsadīya hymn, that of Brahmā or Brahman in Hiraṇyagarbha, and that of the Four Indian Graces in āśā, śraddhā, hrī and śrī.[1] The commercial spirit of the earlier civilization was at the back, nevertheless, of the business-like relationship between the deity invoked and the invoking priest promising the offer of oblations in return of the services to be rendered.

The historical tradition in the Manu-saṃhitā places the beginning of the history of Brahmanism in a narrow strip of land between the Sarasvatī and the Dṛishadvatī, honouring the region as Brahmāvarta or Brahmaland. The customs and usages of all the castes and mixed castes in that land, as handed down from generation to generation, were acknowledged as good (sadāchāra). The subsequent development of Brahmanism through interpretation and instruction as a system of religious thought is located in the countries of Kurukshetra, Matsya, Pañchāla and Śūrasena, all together constituting the land of pride hallowed by the advent of the renowned Brāhmans. Whatever its southern limit, the Pāriyātra mountain',[2] the Vindhya range, the river Narmadā or the Godāvarī, the name of Āryāvarta was restricted to the northern half of India proper, while the peninsular south was given the distinctive name of Dakshiṇāpatha or Dākshiṇātya.

Referring evidently to his empire, Aśoka says that there was no locality other than the solitary Yona territory where the distinct bodies of the Brāhmaṇas and the S'ramaṇas were not, and where the people had not sincere faith in one or another of them, which means that already before the promulgation of R. E. XIII in his 13th or 14th regnal year the whole of his empire with the single exception of the Yona country was Aryanised. In the face of this clear statement

[1] Barua & Sinha, Barhut Inscriptions, under Sirimā devatā.

[2] Cf. Bodhāyana Dharmasūtra, ii. 10 ; Patañjali's Mahābhāshya to Pāṇini, ii. 4. 10.

the question is apt to arise—when and by whom was the Indo-Aryan civilization and culture spread over the whole of South India and Ceylon, and ultimately over the whole of Jambudvīpa in the Buddhistic as well as the Great Epic sense of the term ?

I have so far sought to maintain that South India proper and the island of Tāmraparṇī had not loomed large in the geographical vision of Jambudvīpa or Bhāratavarsha before the Mauryas and Nandas. In support of this one may confidently cite the testimony of Megasthenes and later Classical writers from Arrian to Pliny, all of whom broadly divide Northern India into two portions, the north-western portion, i.e., the Punjab proper, watered by the Indus system of rivers, and the eastern portion covering the whole of the Buddhist Midland and the Lower Bengal watered by the Ganges system. They give us but a rough topographical outline of India proper in the manner of the Pali Mahāgovinda Suttanta. The account given of the trans-Himalayan countries and races is similar to those embodied in the Great Epic, the Purāṇas, the Jātakas and the Jaina Jambu-dvīpa-prajñapti. They offer us a fair account of Kalinga and a bare indication of India's sea-coast trade from the mouth of the Ganges to that of the Indus ; even the traditional distances from the mouth of the Ganges to Cape Calingaon and the town of Dantagula (Dantapura) to Tropina (Tripontari or Tirupantara opposite Cochin), to the cape of Perimula (a projecting point of the modern island of Salsette near Bombay), and to Patala (Prasthala at the Lower Indus Valley) are mentioned. The geographical account of Taprobane (Tāmraparṇī, Ceylon) and its trade-relations with South India and the kingdom of Kalinga is fairly accurate. A true picture of the political conditions of Northern India is held before us when the Punjab proper situated to the west of the Yamunā is stated to have been held by the Macedonian army under Alexander and the eastern portion called Gangaridae by such a powerful rival as Agrammes, the last Nanda king. It is also a correct statement of the fact that Sandrokottos (Chandragupta Maurya) grew powerful by the unification of the fighting peoples and states of the Punjab proper under his leadership and widened the growing Magadha empire by the annexation of the Punjab proper, as well as the four trans-Sulaiman territories ceded by Seleukos Nikator. Though the Purāṇas refer to Mahāpadma, the founder of the Nanda dynasty, as an exterminator of all Kshatriyas, as a monarch who brought all under his sole sway, the inclusion of Kalinga in the Magadha empire and a considerable portion of the Deccan below the Godāvarī remains still to be proved. though its probability cannot altogether be ruled out.[1] Among the Classical writers, Plutarch and Justin definitely speak of Chandragupta Maurya as a monarch in possession of India by overrunning and subduing the whole of the country 'with an army of 600,000 men.' In the Mudrārākshasa (III. 19), too, the supremacy of the first Maurya is said to have extended from the Himalayas to the shores of the southern ocean (dakshiṇārṇava). This, as Raychaudhuri suggests, may have been just a conventional description of the position of a chakravartin.[2] The Tamil traditions make 'frequent allusions to the Mauryas in the past having penetrated with a great army as far as the Podiyil Hill in the Tinnevelly district." The opinion differs as to who the Maurya leader was, Chandragupta or his son Bindusāra. Seeing that they are stigmatized as Vamba Moriyar or 'Maurya upstarts',[3] Raychaudhuri inclines to identify him with the first Maurya. On the strength, on the other hand, of Tāranātha's specific statement that sixteen kingdoms were overthrown by Bindusāra Mr. Sathianathaier of the Jayaswal school of historians[4] thinks that overwhelming is the evidence in favour of the second Maurya being the conqueror of Toṇḍamandalam if it was within Aśoka's empire.[5] In the edicts, however, Aśoka gives the credit to none but himself for the Dharma-vijaya achieved in the independent territories of the Cholas, the Pāṇḍyas, the Satiyaputras, the Keralaputras and the Tāmraparṇyas, as well as in the semi-independent states of the parent Rāshṭrikas and Bhojas and their offshoots and the Andhras and Pārinda-Pāradas.

Manu's first Brahmaland (Brahmāvarta), which is located between the Sarasvatī and the Dṛishadvatī, excludes the earlier Vedic Aryandom between the river Kabul and the Sutlej. The Mārkaṇḍeya Purāṇa speaks of two Brāhman settlements in Uttarāpatha, viz., those of the Ātreyas and the Bhāradvājas,—the Brāhmans whom Arrian connects with the country of the Mūshikas (Mūshikapatha of the Mahāniddesa)

---

[1] Cf. Raychaudhuri, op. cit., p. 189.

[2] Cf. Barnett's comment in Cambridge History of India, I, p. 596.

[3] Raychaudhuri, op. cit., p. 219.

[4] Jayaswal (An Imperial History of India, p. 17) notes : "Tāranātha attributes large conquests between the Eastern and Western seas, etc., (of the Deccan) in the reign of Bindusāra to this great Minister's (Chāṇakya's) regime." What reliance can be placed on the evidence of so late a chronicler as Tāranātha, and where do we get the allusion to the Deccan or Peninsular India ?

[5] Studies in the Ancient History of Toṇḍamaṇḍalam, p. 10.

[6] Chirnock, Arrian, p. 319.

in the region of Sindh. Pliny takes the Brachmanes of this region "to be, not what they actually were, the leading caste of the population, but a powerful race composed of many tribes."[1]

The compilation of the Vedic hymns in the form of four different Saṃhitās, which took place, according to tradition, in the land of the Kurus, the acceptance of them as the greatest book of wisdom of unquestionable authority, the preparation of different redactions of them, adherence to any one of them in preference to the rest in respect of their ritual values, the necessity felt for committing them to memory by methodical chanting instead of to writing, etc. gave rise to various schools of Brāhman hymn-chanters, priests and teachers. In the historical process of Brahmanism one may trace the course of origin and development of an enormous literature, sacred and profane, technical and popular, philosophic and scientific. There was no sphere of man's existence and activity, individual or domestic, socio-moral or politico-economic, religious or philosophic, where the usefulness and indispensability of the Brāhmans as a class was not acutely felt.

As shown by Dr. B. C. Law, the early Jaina and Buddhist books place the Brāhmans either in the usual social environment or in the hermitages. "In the first connection, they are introduced either as those who were in the service of the king (rājakammikā) or as those who had followed different professions of their own. In the second connection, they are introduced as those who went out of the social environments and lived the life of tāpasas or isis in forest homes called assamas with or without families and resident pupils. Of those in service of the king, the most important were the amachchas and mahāmattas (councillors and ministers). The yāchakas (sacrificers) and others were no better than assistants in the office of the Purohita. Partly in connection with the king, they held the position of mahāsālas or heads of Vedic institutions. They came to represent the sotthiya class of Brāhmans who were occasionally employed as dūtas (ambassadors). The Brāhmans also filled the office of senāpatis (generals) and issatthas or yodhājīvas (soldiers), chariot-drivers, trainers of elephants, legal experts and judges. To the people in general they rendered services as Purohitas and priests, as physicians and druggists, as astronomers and architects, as ballad-singers and matchmakers."[2]

---

1 McCrindle, Ancient India, p. 133f.

2 B. C. Law, India As Described, p. 15f.

This wonderfully agrees with the account of the Brāhmans by the Classical writers.

In dealing with the Digvijaya of Agni we are primarily concerned with the S'rotriyas, Purohitas and Ministers, all of whom were Brāhmans, and the Tāpasas, called Hylobioi by the Greek writers, who lived in the woods, where they subsisted on leaves of trees and wild fruits, and wore garments from the bark of trees.[1] They represented the various orders of Indian hermits practising hard penances, developing supernormal faculties and holding communion with God or gods and the different schools of Ṛishis or hermit teachers. Among the Tāpasas were men of all the three twice-born classes, and hardly any from among the S'ūdras and untouchables. The householder Brāhmans and the Tāpasas were equally the performers of sacrifices, believers in the practice of penances and upholders of the doctrine of purity, bodily or otherwise.

Going by Aśoka's statement, we have to say that the main agents for the Aryanisation of India or Greater India up till the 13th year of his reign were the various orders of 'runaways' and schools of thought represented by the Brāhmaṇas and the S'ramaṇas (R.E.XII, R. E. XIII). Among them, the Brāhmaṇas alone were popularly venerated in largest number as teachers of religion and philosophy, morality and piety in the three later stages of effort. As 'runaways', they mostly figured as Tāpasas and Parivrājakas (Wanderers). Even among the S ramaṇas who had not either strictly adhered to the Vedic rules of life or openly challenged them, the majority were Brāhmans.[2] The only powerful rivals of the Brāhmans in the matter of higher knowledge and social importance were the Kshatriyas. Leaving out of account the case of Viśvāmitra among the leading Vedic Ṛishis, we find in Pravāhaṇa Jaivalī, the Kshatriya leader of the oligarchy of the Pañchālas,[3] Pratardana, the son of Divodāsa,[4] and Ajātaśatru, the king of Kāśī[5], the three distinguished Upanishad teachers who were approached even by the Brāhman seekers of truth for the sake of higher knowledge. The Jātakas glorify the Kuru tradition of righteous rule established by king Arjuna, and the

---

[1] McCrindle, Ancient India, p. 102.

[2] Among the elder contemporaries of Buddha and the leading S'ramaṇa thinkers and teachers Pūraṇa Kās'yapa, Maskarin Kaus'alya (Pali Makkhali Gosāla), Kakuda Kātyāyana and Ajita Kes'akambala were Brāhmans. Even Sañjaya, the founder of the school of Sceptics, was a Brāhman, according to the Apadāna, see Sāriputta Apadāna.

[3] Chhandogya Up., V. 3. 1.

[4] Kaushitaki Up., III. 1.

[5] Ibid, IV. 1.

tradition of righteousness and renunciation established by the Janakas of Videha, the Brahmadattas of Kāśī and the S'ivis of Uttarāpatha. In the Hāthigumphā inscription, the Jaina king Khāravela is described as a worthy descendant of a long line of Rājarshis among the Chedi princes. Pārśva who was the founder of an order of S'ramaṇas in Eastern India with ahiṃsā as its main principle was a prince from the royal House of Kāśī. Though Mahāvīra and Buddha who were respectively the founders of the two most powerful orders of S'ramaṇas and Kshatriya schools of thought, the most eminent and distinguished among their disciples and later followers were all persons from Brāhman families. Thus the Brāhmans made all the noble heritages in Indo-Aryan religion and culture ultimately their own. But to appreciate the Digvijaya of Agni we must leave the S'ramanite Brāhmans[1] out of consideration, particularly the S'ākyaputrīyas or Buddhists, Aśoka's Saṃghasthas.

The history of the Brāhmans as priests and their usefulness and influence shows parallel to that of the Babylonian priests and their wide influence in Western Asia among the Assyrians, the Chaldeans, the Hittites, the Mittanies and others with this difference, however, that they have an unbroken history up till now. The tradition of the Brāhmans as law-givers and framers of the rules of life and conduct shows a parallel to that of the Jewish Prophets and Patriarchs. The Brāhmans, too, cherished the tradition of the successive advent of the Manus or Patriarchs. The legend of a great Flood during the dispensation of Manu Vaivasvata, as narrated in the Śatapatha Brāhmaṇa, cannot but remind one of the Biblical legend of the Flood at Babylon in the time of the Patriarch and Prophet Noah. Although the maximum span of man's life as one hundred years was recognised in the Vedic hymns, it is represented as 120 years in the Aitareya Āraṇyaka, which, too, is a point of agreement with the Jewish tradition of the time of Noah.

The Brāhmans of India, like the Jewish Patriarchs in Syria, were guided by the idea of purity and impurity, the clean and the unclean, in the matter of framing rules regarding eatables and non-eatables, and the rules prescribed by both were in many respects similar. The earlier Brahmanical rules that held ground, particullarly in the Midland, are clearly presupposed by Aśoka's argument, "that are not eaten" (no cha khādiyati), behind his list of birds, fishes and

---

1 Book of Genesis, vi. 3 : "And the Lord said, (man's) days shall be an hundred and twenty years."

quadrupeds made inviolables under the law (P.E.V).[1] The Mosaic code of prescriptions and prohibitions having many points in common with Manu's, had behind it the belief in the Divine sanction as communicated to Noah, enjoining that "every moving thing that liveth" was meant by the Creator to serve as "meat" for even as the green herb had he given him all things (Book of Genesis, ix. 3). The Divine sanction as stated in the Chhāndogya Upanishad (V.2.1) and Manu's Code (V. 28) is even verbally the same :

> Prāṇasyānnamidaṃ sarvaṃ Prajāpatir akalpayat ।
> sthāvaraṃ jangamaṃ chaiva sarvaṃ prāṇasya bhojanam ॥

"The Creator had meant all these as food for life ; all that is stationery and all that moveth were to serve as food to life."

The earlier dictum in the Upanishad reads : Prāṇa said : Kim me'nnaṃ bhavishyatī ti ? Yat kiṃchid idam aśvabhy ā-sakuṇebhya iti.

"What will be my food ? Whatsoever is the living thing, even the horses and vultures (birds ?)."

The earlier sanction allowing to man "every herb bearing seed, which is upon the face of all the earth, and every tree, in which is the fruit of a tree yielding seed" to be for meat (Book of Genesis, i. 29) had to be modified under the exigency of terrible circumstances, such as the cataclysmic Flood. This is missed in the Brahmanical tradition.[2]

The Patriarch Noah is credited in the Biblical tradition with the building of an altar for making burnt offerings unto the Lord of every clean beast and of every clean fowl, the sweet savour whereof was appreciated by Him. This is another remarkable point of agreement between Brahmanism and Judaism in that both insist on not eating the meat of any beast or fowl that has not been sacrificed on the altar built unto God.

In the opinion of Megasthenes, all that had been said regarding nature by the ancients was asserted also by philosophers out of Greece, on the one part in India by the Brachmanes, and on the other in Syria by the people called Jews. Clemens boldly maintained that

---

[1] Barua, Inscriptions, ii, p. 316f.

[2] The account given in the Pali Aggañña Suttanta of man's first food consisting in protoplasmic substance, a fungus-like herb, etc. before the development of the art of cooking is conceived in a totally different spirit. Dīgha, III, p. 85f.

40

the Jewish philosophy had preceded the philosophy of the Greeks.[1] As regards the story of creation, the main point of agreement between Brahmanism and Judaism is that, according to both, in the beginning was God (Prajāpati or Brahmā of the Brāhmans), and God alone, and it was by His will that the heaven and the earth, the beings and the things, the man and the woman were created, the usual language in both for the expression of the creative will of God and its product being "Let there be and there was."[2]

It is rather sad that the Gentile and Brahmanical traditions are full of curses (abhiśāpa), the pronouncement of which is a proof of one's moral weakness and morbid state of mind. Viewing in the light of both, we are to witness the dramas of life of which the plots are laid in effective curses and counter-curses, the prospect of blessedness being far off from the view.

In both, the position of woman is lowered and made subordinate to that of man. In the eye of the Brahmanical law the woman needs protection in all the three stages of her life and does not deserve to be free. As known to Megasthenes, the Brāhmans did not communicate a knowledge of philosophy to their wives, "lest they should divulge any of the forbidden mysteries to the profane if they became depraved, or lest they should desert them if they became good philosophers."[3]

With the householder Brāhman teachers and ministers suspicion or distrust was as much the guiding factor in conjugal life as in the system of royal polity, particularly that which was embodied in the Arthaśāstra ascribed to Kauṭilya. Pāṇini spoke indeed of devotion to one's country or nation,[4] and the Arthaśāstra of the importance to be attached to the national star (deśa-nakshatra), but the Brahmanical rājadharma having been concerned about one man's show, was far from arousing national sentiment or making the people conscious of their nationhood.

The Brāhmans as priests made the age-old popular superstitions deep-rooted in man's mind instead of eradicating them by having used them as the basis of mangalas or auspicious domestic rituals

---

[1] McCrindle, Ancient, India, p. 103.

[2] Book of Genesis, Ch. I ; Bṛihad Ar. Up., I. 4. 1 ; I. 4. 11f.

[3] McCrindle, Ancient India, p. 100.

[4] Pāṇini. iv. 3. 96, 100 ; ā-chittād ā-des'a-kālāt ṭhak ; janapadinānāṃ janapadavat sarvam.

and ceremonies, arranged stage by stage.[1] They allied themselves with the masses who were worshippers of various tribal gods and goddesses, of divers benevolent and malevolent spirits, and were mostly animists. They utterly failed to develop a congregational life in their religion. Even in such common matters as eating, there were no fixed hours when meals were to be taken in common, but each one ate when he felt inclined, the contrary of which would be, in the opinion of Megasthenes, 'better for the ends of social and civil life.'[2]

The great stumbling block in the way of the development of a healthy and strong national life in India was the caste system creating irremovable barriers between men and men, class and class, occupation and occupation. The most unfortunate feature of it was that it was founded on an apparently captivating organic idea of the universe, the society and the state, the scientific and philosophic drawback of which has not as yet been fully considered and understood. Though the Purusha Sūkta presenting this fond idea found its place in the Ṛigveda, the idea itself may be shown to have been more Brahmanical than Vedic. The subsequent history of Brahmanism shows nothing but a process of gradual hardening of the castes, creation of differences even in the heights of sepulchres after death, and that of social divisions within divisions, all causing social and civic injustice. As known to Megasthenes, the body-politic was so divided in India in the 4th century B. C. that no one was allowed to marry out of his own caste, or to exercise any calling or art except his own, for instance, a soldier could not become a husbandman, or an artizan a philosopher.[3]

The S'rotriyas as founders and heads of residential Vedic schools and colleges (none of which developed into a university) were recipients of brahmadānas or royal fiefs enabling them to maintain

---

1 G. P. Majumdar, Some Aspects of Indian Civilization; p. 293 f.

2 McCrindle, Ancient India, p. 69.

3 McCrindle, op. cit., p. 41. This social organization is biologically comparable to that of the bees where the kings are always kings and the drones are drones, or to that of the ants where the labourers are always labourers, the fighters are always fighters, and the messengers are always messengers, The Brahmanical rule of life allowing sexual union only for the purpose of begetting children of desired types was biologically unsound as it ignored the fact that human male and female were no mere animal pair mating only at breeding season for the purpose of procreation. So this rule was obeyed more in its flagrant breaches than in its observance.

those institutions independently of state control. Through the Digvijaya of Agni and with the wider and wider extension of Aryandom there came to be a net-work of those institutions seeking to convert India into a free gift for the spread and establishment of Vedic culture and Brahmanical socio-religious order, the varṇa-śrama dharma. It was among these great Brāhman teachers that there arose men with lofty vision and keen insight and true seekers of philosophic truth and propounders of higher religious ideals. The early Upanishad teachers were mostly Brāhmans of this class.

The S'rotriyas as S'rotriyas were not, however, the persons to be credited with the expedition in the annals of the Digvijaya of Agni. They were rather the consolidators of new territorial gains. The daring explorers of uninhabited and at first inaccessible forest tracts or woodlands in the mountain ranges or along the different rivers, the builders of peaceful and sombre religious homes with sylvan surroundings having a divine aroma about them, gay with the life of fauna and flora, lively with the movement of spirits, and endowed with idyllic beauty and charm were the Tāpasas or Hermits of various orders among whom flourished the great ṛishis (sages and teachers) endowed with psychic powers, spiritual visions and personality. They were attracted by the natural beauty of the woodlands (araṇyāni) and through them developed the āraṇyaka or vānaprastha life, the science of medicine and astronomy, and the schools of Sāṃkhya-Yoga or adhyātma-vidyā. In the solitude of woodlands they practised hard penances, cultivated friendly feelings towards all, lived on the bounties of nature, and bravely went to meet death instead of allowing death to come to them[1]. It is in their line that one must trace the continuity of the tradition of Vedic poets, sages and seers. With the spread of hermitages over the whole of India extended the range of kṛishṇasāra, (black antelope) and of sacrificial fire, which is to say, of the Digvijaya of Agni. Their mission was to sanctify the earth with sacrificial fire, to convert it, in other words, into a holy land (yajñīya deśa, devabhūmi).[2] The rivers, lakes and springs where they performed ablutions for the purpose of self-purification, the places where they built their hermitages, performed sacrifices and laid to rest their bones became

---

[1] Ibid, p. 106.

[2] Manu, II. 23. Cf. Bodhāyana, ii. 18 quoting a verse ascribed to the Bhāllavis :

Pas'chāt sindhur visaraṇī sūryasyodayanaṃ puraḥ ।
Yāvat Kṛishṇo vidhāvati tāvaddhi Brahmavarchasam ॥

tīrthas or places of pilgrimage to the Hindus. The gradual advance of the sacrificial fire in all the four directions and increase in the number of tīrthas are traceable through literary references and inscriptions, the list of tīrthas given in the Sautī version of the Great Epic having been unthinkable in pre-Aśokan and pre-Christian times. The typical list of seven tīrthas we have from the Buddha confines our geographical vision to the Midland between the Sarasvatī and the Phalgu.[1] Even as known to Megasthenes, the course of advance had not gone in the south beyond the river Tagabena (Tungabhadrā).[2] Tradition associates the first expedition to the extreme south with Agastya. That which was at first a mere foot-track to walk from one hermitage to another became afterwards a high road, notably the Southern Road connecting Rājagṛiha with Paiṭhān on the Godāvarī.[3] 'The neighbourhood of the hermitages became sites afterwards of many important cities.'[4] The hermitages that were surrounded by non-Aryan and aboriginal settlements needed from time to time the help of warrior kings and Kshatriya princes to secure them from the inimical action of the rude natives, the savages including cannibals. Thus the building of hermitages and that of the new Kshatriya states proceeded almost *pari passu*.

If the Hermits were, as Bhandarkar rightly thinks, the passive evangelists of Vedic religion and Indo-Aryan culture, there arose in Northern India and not long before the rise of Buddhism powerful bodies of active propagators of the same. They were the Wanderers and Recluses, the Brāhmaṇa Parivrājakas and the S'ramaṇas of various orders and schools of thought. The new order emerged at first out of and as a further step from the order of Hermits, and resulted later also from direct renunciation of worldly life. They indeed became known to Megasthenes and other Classical writers as two classes of Indian philosophers, viz., the Brachmanes and the Sarmanes. Theoretically they were all homeless in the sense that they themselves did not build abodes for them but sought for temporary shelters in abodes built for them by others, the royal pleasances, called ārāmas or vihāras having been originally the places where they used to halt for a night in course of their wanderings. Even when the permanent abodes were built for them, they came to be known by those names. The Brāhmaṇas and the S'ramaṇas differed from

---

1 Majjhima, I, p. 39.

2 McCrindle, Ancient India, p. 120.

3 Jātaka, V, p. 132 : *ekapadimagga*.

4 B. C. Law, India as described, p. 218.

each other not only in their outward signs, but also in their thoughts and ideals and general attitude towards the social and political institutions based on Vedic tradition and caste distinction. The general effect of the new movement was the undervaluation of the civic life and social rites under the control of secular Brahmanism. The Ājīvikas among the Brahmanite S'ramaṇas and the Nirgranthas (Jainas) among the S'ramaṇite Brāhmans appeared as heterodox in the eye of the orthodox Brahmanist. Though some were S'aivite, some Vaishṇavite, and others Jaina, all of them were believers in the practice of hard penances and profound meditations, and all were in different ways confirmed believers in the existence of souls as abiding entities in individuals that are not subject to the laws of change. None but the Nirgranthas amongst them openly challenged the Brahmanist position and developed a religious and cultural tradition, which is in some important respects similar to that of the S'ākyaputrīyas or Buddhists. When Aśoka spoke of the Aryanisation of almost the whole of India by the different denominations of the Brāhmaṇas and the S'ramaṇas other than the Saṃghasthas or Buddhists, he had precisely kept in view the evangelical activities of the Hermits, the Brāhman Wanderers and such typical S'ramaṇas as the Ājīvikas and Nirgranthas (P.E. VII).

5. **Dharmavijaya of Aśoka** : As propounders and propagators of Indo-Aryanism tending steadily and invariably to set higher value on the religious and cultural side of man's life and civilization, the Hermits, Brāhman Wanderers, Ājīvikas and Nirgranthas were the precursors of the S'ākyaputrīyas. This fact is stated in no uncertain terms by Aśoka in his R. E. XIII. The same is borne out by the evidence of the Pali Nikāyas and corroborated by the testimony of Megasthenes and other Classical writers. The Chronicles of Ceylon not only lead us to infer that the worship of the Nāgas and Yakshas, of Vishṇu Utpalavarṇa and the ascetic god S'iva was prevalent among the primitive dwellers of the island[1] but also clearly state that king Paṇḍukābhaya, the brother and immediate successor of Vijaya, caused hermitages to be built for the Hermits, retreats for the Brāhman Parivrājakas, and suitable abodes for the Ājīvikas and Nirgranthas.[2] They had held the ground before the arrival of the Buddhist mission under Mahendra in the 3rd century B. C. Even

[1] The point has been discussed in detail in my Ceylon lecture—A Bird's Eye View and Problems of the Ancient History of Ceylon,

[2] Mahāvaṃsa, X. 96-102.

referring to the time of king Vaṭṭagāmaṇi (1st century B. C.), the Chronicles tell us that they had had their rights and privileges left intact through twenty-one reigns since Paṇḍukābhaya.[1]

According to Jaina tradition, the Nirgranthas under their accredited leader Bhadrabāhu went to South India during the reign of Chandragupta Maurya. That the Jinakalpika or Digambara Jainas got a strong foothold in South India as far back as the 4th century B. C. may be taken for granted, and the Deccan proper, particularly the Canarese country, is still one of the strongholds of Jainism. That the Ājīvikas, too, got an early foothold there and maintained their identity as a distinct religious sect up till the 13th or 14th century A. D. may be seen from the ancient Tamil works as well as a number of South Indian inscriptions.

The pronounced cumulative effect of the pre-Buddhistic Brāhmaṇa-Sramaṇa movement was felt and acknowledged by Alexander, the great Macedonian conqueror, in going to deal with Dandamis (Daṇḍin), the leader of a Brahmanical sect of Gymnosophists (naked ascetics), evidently of S'aivite persuasion and closely allied to the Ājīvikas, who established themselves somewhere in the Punjab. The Ionians were the first among the Greeks noted for their commercial enterprise and came to the near east to be Persianised and to found a colony round the city of Nysa on the river Kophen or Kābul during the reign of the Achaemenian kings of Persia, better Iran. They became in the matter of their social organization and religious beliefs allied with the Kambojas, the Gandhāras and other autonomous tribes of the Upper Indus Valley as early as Buddha's time and remained so even till the reign of Aśoka and to a still later period. There is nothing to be disbelieved or thought improbable when Megasthenes says that the Macedonians under Alexander came across at the threshhold of India beyond the river Kābul a people whose manners and customs were akin to those of the Greeks. The Bhūridatta Jātaka contemptuously refers to the Kāmbojas as a people with the barbarous habit of killing the insects, moths, snakes and frogs (obviously for the purpose of eating) and believing in killing them as a meritorious act. As known to Megasthenes, the Oxydrakai (Kshudrakas) of Uttarāpatha were the orgic worshippers of a Bacchanalian god, or of yoni and phallus, who were presumably

[1] Ibid, XXXIII, 44. See foot note in Geiger's Edition.

scoffed at in the Ṛigveda as S'iśnadevas,[1] and the Sibae (S'ivis)[2] who 'carried clubs', and branded the mark of a cudgel on their oxen and mules, were the worshippers of Heracles (apparently S'iva)[3] like whom they wore skins[4].

According to Arrian, the regions beyond the Indus on the west were inhabited up to the river Kophen (Kābul) by two Indian tribes, the Astakenai (Ārshṭakas, Ṛishṭikas) and the Assakenos (Aśvakas) who were in old times subject to the Assyrians and submitted subsequently to the Persians, paying the tribute to the Achaemenian king Kyros, son of Kambyses[5]. Darius III Codomannus was the Achaemenian king when Alexander the Great conquered Persia.

Schwanbeck rightly observed : "The Aryan Indians were from the remotest period surrounded on all sides by indigenous tribes in a state of barbarism, from whom they differed both in mind and disposition. They were most acutely sensible of this difference, and gave it a very pointed expression. Other races, and these even Indian, since they had originated in an intermixture of tribes, or since they did not sufficiently follow Indian manners, and especially the system of caste, so roused the common hatred of the Indians that they were reckoned with the barbarians, and represented as equally hideous of aspect".

The Greek knowledge of India was imperfect prior to Alexander's invasion. The stories then current in Greece went nevertheless to dipict her 'as a land of righteous folks, of strange beasts and plants, of surpassing wealth in gold and gems.'[6] Although the Greeks came to India forming foreign elements in her population, ruling or otherwise, first as Ionians, next as Macedonians, and afterwards as Bactrians, they continued to be known by the name of Yona or Yauna,

---

1 The S'is'nadevas are generally taken to be worshippers of the phallus. M.M. Vidhusekhara Sastri treats s'is'nadeva as a word like mātṛideva, pitṛideva, and inclines to think that here s'is'na may be taken to signify sensual pleasures.

2 McCrindle, Ancient India, p. 112. According to Strabo, Heracles was worshipped by the philosophers who lived on the plains (ibid, p. 97), while Arrian (ibid, 203) informs us that he was held in especial honour by the Sūrasenas of Mathurā.

3 Haracles is to be identified with S'iva only when he became deified after his death and not when he had lived on the earth.

4 'Lion's skin', according to Diodorus.

5 McCrindle, Ancient India, p. 21.

6 Bury, History of Greece, p. 422.

the Indian and Achæmenian equivalent of Ionian.[1] "Although", as poignantly observed by Vincent Smith, "the direct effects of Alexander's expedition on India appear to have been small, his proceedings had an appreciable influence on the history of the country. They broke down the wall of separation between west and east, and opened up four distinct lines of communication, three by land and one by sea. The immediate formation of Greek kingdom in Western Asia ensured from the first a certain amount of exchange of ideas between India and Europe. The establishment of the Greco-Bactrian monarchy in the middle of the third century B. C. brought about the actual subjugation of certain Indian districts by Greek kings."[2]

Alexander's military expedition directed to Asia and Africa was designed undeniably also to spread the Greek civilization among the Barbarians, and accordingly his troops were accompanied by many men of letters, including the Sceptic philosopher Pyrrho of Elis and a follower of Democritus named Anaxarchus. But his pride as the son of the mighty god Zeus and the conqueror of many nations was humbled by two persons he met, one a robber who tried to convince him of the fact that he by his actions and intention was only a greater robber, and the other a famous leader of the Indian Gymnosophists who tried to convince him of the fact that there was even a far greater conqueror than he by having nothing to call his own.

Onesikrates was deputed to fetch Dandamis the great Indian ascetic leader in Uttarāpatha. "The emperor Alexander, the son of the great Jupiter, who is lord of the human race, has ordered that you should hasten to him, for if you come, he will give you many gifts, but if you refuse, he will behead you as a punishment for your contempt." When this message was thus delivered to him, "he rose not from his leaves whereon he lay, but reclining and smiling he replied in this way: The greatest God can do injury to no one, but restores again the light of life to those who have departed. Accordingly he forbids murder and excites no wars. But Alexander is no God, for he himself will have to die. How, then, can he be the lord of all, who has not yet crossed the river Tyberoboas, nor has

[1] One may read with profit Otto Stein's informative article—Yavanas in Early Indian Inscriptions (Indian Culture, Vol. I, p. 343f.).

[2] Oxford History of India, p. 66f. For the Greek influence on Indian art and other aspects of Indian culture, the reader may be referred to Gouranga Nath Banerjea's Hellenism in Ancient India.

made the whole world his abode, nor crossed the Zone of Gades, nor has beheld the course of the sun in the centre of the world? Therefore many nations do not even know his name...Let Alexander threaten with this them that desire riches or fear death, both of which I despise. For Brachmanes neither love gold nor death. Go, therefore, and tell Alexander this—Dandamis seeks nothing of yours, but if you think you need something of his, disdain not to go to him."

"When Alexander heard these words through the interpreter, he wished the more to see such a man, since he, who had subdued many nations, was overcome by an old naked man."[1]

Whilst the earlier evangelists of Indo-Aryanism were spread upon the face of India and Ceylon, Buddhism, the religion of S'ākyamuni, remained confined till the earlier part of Aśoka's reign to the territorial limits of the Middle Country.[2] The two countries in Western India outside the Buddhist Midland were S'ūrasena and Avantī where two important centres of Buddhism were founded in Buddha's lifetime, and just a sporadic attempt was made by a disciple of Buddha to preach the new Gospel of righteousness and piety to the rude and fierce people of Sūnāparānta. There were several semi-independent tribal states within Aśoka's empire but outside his domain proper where the Indo-Aryan culture and social organization resting on caste basis were not well established. Since Aśoka had declared the Dharma-vijaya or Conquest by Piety to be a state policy, the religious and cultural movements within the definition of Indo-Aryanism assumed a new aspect of self-consciousness on the part of the Brāhmaṇas and the S'ramaṇas of various orders and schools of thought. The appointment of the Dharma-mahāmātras as a class of imperial officers was purposed *inter alia* to ensure the personal safety of these active preachers and passive evangelists of Indo-Aryanism in those tribal areas as well as of those of the local people who became their adherents. Aśoka did not, however, mean to restrict the range of his noble cultural conquest to his domain proper or to his empire. He was out for a world conquest through it, and for this India needed a religion like Buddhism.

In Buddhism was found a religion with vigorous missionary zeal. It had behind it the stupendous dynamic personality of the Buddha and the highest ethical perfection of man. Although on its philo-

1 McCrindle, Ancient India, p. 128f.; Cf. ibid, pp. 106f., 116f. 123f.

2 Kathāvatthu, I. 3.

sophic and spiritual side it showed in many respects the continuity of the philosophy of the Upanishads, and on its secular and popular side it showed in many respects the continuity of the socio-religious and politico-moral system of the pre-Pāṇinian Mahābhārata, it differed fundamentally from both. The Brahmaveda of the Upanishads came to be replaced, supplemented and superseded by the Dharmaveda of Buddhism. The basic concepts of both had behind them two different kinds of intuition or mystical experience as to the nature of reality, one in which the static nature and the other in which the dynamic nature presented itself. While ātman remained the underlying notion of the Upanishad doctrine, anātman became the prevailing idea of Buddhism. The difference between the fundamenal axioms of both was analogous to that between the Parmanidean and Heraclitean axioms in Greek philosophy.

The main points of difference between secular Brahmanism on the one hand and Buddhism on the other were that one was sacerdotal, the other rational in form; one clannish, the other universal in spirit; the commitment of one was to forms and procedures, that of the other to the inner essence of the thing; that one sought to base domestic and social relations on caste basis, the other on that of morality and piety. Thus no other form of government than monarchical found favour in Brahmanical rājadharma, while in Buddha's view the form, whether monarchical, oligarchical or democratic, was immaterial, if the state in any form had fulfilled all its main obligations. The same as to the forms of marriage, the forms of manifold duties. However lofty the purpose set before the state or earthly sovereignty, the Brahmanical rājadharma could never abandon, in no stage of its development, the Tit for Tat policy.

Jainism, which has acted throughout its history as a half-way house between Brahmanism and Buddhism, nay between all isms that were come across its path, was, at least so far as its doctrine of ahiṃsā, non-harming mental attitude towards all beings and things, moral rectitude, idea of moral responsibility, denial of God, rejection of caste barriers, and the like are concerned, a definite move towards Buddhism. And yet its ascetic predilections, religious vows, penitent heart, such categories of its thought as bandha, saṃvara, nirjarā and moksha go to indicate that its main mental obsession was one of the bondage of sin, and its struggle was to release the soul therefrom. The task was left to Buddhism to shift the emphasis from thraldom to freedom, abstinence from killing to the cultivation of friendliness and compassion, from the prevention and cure of diseases to the generation and development of healthy states, from the arrest of the course and possibility of degradation and deterioration of human nature to the progressive paths (pāripūri) of the life.[1] Buddhism was the only religion of India which vigorously espoused the educational and cultural cause of humanity and did not go to form a new society among its lay followers by the enforcement of a social code of its own in spite of its giving a clear direction to the path of progress, and rational and refined human behaviour. There was no other religion before Christianity which had boldly proclaimed that hatred does not cease by hatred, and that it ceases only by amity and love. Its doctrine of the 'mean' (madhya) between any two extreme courses of thought and of action did not fail to exercise its potent influence on the later political thought of India.

Aśoka's scheme of the toleration of faiths based upon Buddha's (and partly also upon Mahavira's) doctrine of samyak (all-round consideration, comprehensiveness) stood for frequent cultural contacts, healthy discussions, helpful criticisms and hearty interchanges of thoughts and ideas, and had not cherished the non-intervention policy of the Bhagavad Gītā.

How long could an administration be efficiently run if it were based on suspicion and mutual distrust? How long could a state be at peace with the neighbouring peoples and powers if its foreign relations were always guided by the fourfold diplomatic means of conciliating, bribing, causing dissension and waging wars, as contemplated in Brahmanical rājadharma? The sordid art of diplomacy was sought to be superseded by the nobler policy of Dharmavijaya, both within and without, without the least thought about impairing the strength of the state and its military efficiency. The imperial envoys were despatched to convey the good wishes from this side to foreign courts and peoples, to carry on works of public utility and to promulgate the most elementary but fundamental principles of piety or duty in which lay the real happiness of men and the elevation of humanity.

Buddha was at pains to indicate the baneful reactions of drastic and vindictive measures adopted by a state on the life of the people.[2] Going by his trend of thought, the supreme duty of a state

---

[1] Barua, Pratītya-samutpāda as basic concept of Buddhism, Dr. B. C. Law Volume I; Ceylon Lectures, p. 198 f.

[2] Aggañña Suttanta in Dīgha, III.

that stands for the ideal of righteousness should be to educate the people to live better life and to help them by all means in their struggles for existence and in leading a decent and happy and comfortable life. Aśoka's scheme of Dharma-vijaya fully recognizes the wisdom in this line of thinking.

Buddhism was not made a state religion by Aśoka. It was Aśoka's personal religion, and he publicly stated that it was so. But the principles of the Dharma that he had advocated were neither propounded nor promulgated in the name of the Good Faith or any other religion. Buddhist missions were despatched to different places in India by the then head of the Buddhist Church, the most Venerable Moggaliputta Tissa, who was held in high esteem by him. The places to which they are said to have been sent in the Chronicles of Ceylon are all now found to be indicated by the find-spots of the Kalsi, Mansehra, Shahbazgarhi, Girnār and Sopārā versions of his Rock Edicts, the Hyderabad and Northern Mysore copies of his Minor Rock Edict. Suvarṇabhūmi and Tāmraparṇī are the two places that are not explicable by the find-spots of the hitherto discovered inscriptions. Once we assume that Suvarṇagiri[1] was the earlier name on the list replaced later on by Suvarṇabhūmi, the case of both the places can be met by the inscriptions in which they find mention, one as the official headquarters of the most southern province, and the other as the most southern of the independent countries in South India.

The historical foundation of the tradition regarding Moggaliputta Tissa and the personnel of the mission to the Himalayan region is evident from the Sāñchī relic-casket inscriptions.[2] The development of such later Buddhist sects and schools[3] as the Haimavatas (Central Himalayan), the Uttarāpathakas (North-west Indian), the Vājrīyas (Extreme north-west Indian), the Pūrvaśailas, Aparaśailas, Rājagiriyas and Siddhārthakas (all Andhrakas)[4] presupposes earlier missionary activities in these places. According to the tradition recorded by Hwen Thsang, the Buddhist mission under Mahendra was directed first to the country of Malayakūṭa, situated below Drāviḍa,—the Tāmraparṇī of the Great Epic—from which country

---

[1], This may be same as suvarṇavatī, which finds mention in the Hitopades'a, II. 1, as a city in South India : asti Dakshiṇāpathe Suvarṇavatī nāma nagarī.

[2] Geiger, Mahāvaṃsa, English Transl., introd.,

[3] Mahāvaṃsa, V. 12-13 ; Kathāvatthu Commentary, p. 3.

[4] Kathāvatthu Commentary, 1. 9 ; B. C. Law, Debates Commentary, p. vi.

he must have gone across to Siṃhala, i. e., the island of Tāmraparṇī. The contemporaneity of Devānampriya Aśoka of India and Devānampiya Tissa of Ceylon and the political and cultural relationship between the two countries in their time may now be established beyond all doubt by the evidence of the most ancient of the Brāhmī inscriptions of the island so far found carrying us back to the time of Uttiya, the brother and immediate successor of Tissa. There seems to be much force in the argument seeking to locate the site of Aśoka's Suvarṇagiri in the proximity of the Yerraguḍi rock.

The Dūtas or Emissaries were the imperial agents of Aśoka through whom the mission of his Dharma-vijaya was sought to be fulfilled in the territories of five Greek contemporaries forming then the five Mediterranean States, as well as in the five independent territories of the Cholas, the pāṇḍyas, the Satiyaputras, the Keralaputras and the Tāmraparṇyas representing then the five most powerful Dravidian nations of South India. The semi-independent tribal states of such Northern North-western ruling peoples as the Yonas, the Kāmbojas, the Gāndhāras, the Nābhakas and the Nābha-lines, and of such Southern and South-western ruling peoples as the parent Ṛishṭikas and Bhojas and their offshoots, the Andhras and Pārinda-Pāradas are also expressly included within the range of his embassies. So far as the latter were concerned, the Dharma-mahāmātras appointed in his 13th regnal year were charged with the duty of looking after the safety of the Indo-Aryan preachers and their local supporters. Were they officials who were employed also as Aśoka's Dūtas ? That they were not Buddhist missionaries is evident from the Chronicles of Ceylon that expressly state that the Dūtas forming the embassy despatched by Aśoka with coronation presents and happy wishes to his Ceylon contemporary Tissa consisted of Aśoka's nephew Mahāriṭṭha, his Brāhman Chaplain or Councillor, and a Vaiśya Treasurer[1] and they were the precursors of the Buddhist mission led by Mahendra. The only means by which Aśoka paved the way for the Buddhist mission which followed was to disclose the fact of his embracing the Buddhist faith in the personal message conveyed to his distant friend and ally, thereby persuading him to do the same.[2] Even if Aśoka had done so, it is difficult to say what actual

[1] Mahāvaṃsa, XI. 20-26.

[2] Ibid, XI. 34-35. The epistles addressed by the Apostles, especially by St. Paul, and short letters that are known to have been addressed by the Prophet Muhammad were to the same purpose in the history of the propagation of Christianity and Islam respectively.

effect it had produced as an earlier step. The account of Mahendra's mission goes, however, to show that its success in the island of Ceylon rested at first entirely on his personality and powerful preaching.

The veracity of Aśoka's statement concerning the despatch of embassies to the five Greek territories and the claim to the great success attained there through his new plan of Dharma-vijaya has been challenged—a bit rudely by Rhys Davids.[1] The cogent arguments by which this may be set at rest are as follows :

(i) "The restricting of the list to five names, faithfully Indianised, cannot but speak of sincerity and accuracy on the part of Aśoka.

(ii) The orderly manner of introducing them, keeping evidently in view the contiguity of the five Greek territories...was rendered possible only by a correct information about the relative geographical positions of the territories concerned.

(iii) The reality of the Dūtas (envoys) despatched by Aśoka to the Antas, including the five Greek 'frontagers', cannot be disbelieved. Aśoka needed the employment of these agents not only to initiate or encourage various works of piety and public utility (R.E. II), not only to inculcate the principles of piety (R.E. XIII), not only to proclaim Aśoka's happy messages of piety, year after year (M.R.E., Ye), but also to assure the 'frontagers' of his sincere desire to respect their territorial integrity and of his solicitude and good wish (S.R.E. II).

(iv) The treaty with Seleukos of about 302 B.C. was followed by the despatch to the court of Aśoka's grandfather of the famous envoy, Megasthenes, an officer of Arachosia, while Aśoka's father Bindusāra received at his court the homage of the next envoy, Deimachos, from Antiochus Soter. A third envoy named Dionysios was sent to the court of Pāṭaliputra by Aśoka's contemporary, Ptolemy Philadelphos of Egypt...either in his time, or in that of his father.' These facts are recorded by the Greek writers and ignored in Indian literature. Similarly Aśoka records the fact of

---

[1] Buddhist India, p. 298f. : "It is difficult to say how much of this is mere royal rodomontade. It is quite likely that the Greek kings are only thrown in by way of make-weight as it were and that no emissary had actually been sent there at all.'

> despatch of envoys by him to the courts and territories of his five Greek 'frontagers', and the Greek writers ignore it. The exchange of envoys by way of reciprocation of courtesy on either side was only too natural under the circumstances to be disbelieved. The Besnagar Garuḍa Pillar inscription records the name of Heliodoros as a Bactrian Greek ambassador (Yonadūta) from Mahārāja Antialkidas to the court of king Kāśīputra Bhāgabhadra."[1]

To these might be added also the argument : "Evidently the five Greek potentates were the direct descendants and successors of Alexander the Great's generals and supporters and their territories were but once component parts of the Greek empire left behind by the great Macedonian conqueror. It was indeed between the two empires, namely, the Mauryan and the Macedonian, that friendly intercourse and exchange of embassies remained possible until the reign of Aśoka."[2]

Although, as seems probable, Aśoka got the idea of promulgating the edicts from the Achæmenid kings of Irān, his epithet, Devānaṃpriya or Beloved of the gods, was Indian in origin, and the toleration of other faiths was a marked feature of his Dharma. These two features characterise the famous Rosetta stone inscription of the 2nd century B. C. caused to be written by Ptolemaios, king of Egypt.[3]

Two immediate and lasting effects of Aśoka's Dharma-vijaya were : (1) that it gave impetus and offered chances to Buddhism to become a great force in Asiatic and world civilizalion, and (2) that it placed India between the cultures.

In the opinion of Dr. Otto Stein "that position of India between the cultures cannot be better circumscribed than by a word of one of the noblest rulers in the history of mankind : dhammavijaya. India's relation towards West and East was never defiled by waging wars for material gain and only self-defence forced the weapons in her hands. Thus she won her victory in accordance with the command of Dharma, be it religion, be it morality, call it culture or humanity. That is the importance of India's role in the history in which a place hardly shared by any other country belongs to her, from the remote past upto this day, that is her unique and noble position between the cultures."[4]

---

1 Barua, Inscriptions, ii, p. 325.
2 Ibid, ii, p. 324.
3 C.L.T. Griffith, the Story of Letters and Numbers, p. 12.
4 Indian Culture, Vol. IV, p. 299.

CHAPTER IX

PLACE IN HISTORY

The success achieved by Aśoka through his noble and novel plan of Dharma-vijaya determined as much the position of India as placed between the cultures of the West and East as his own place in the history of mankind. On the all-important question of Aśoka's place in history the well-considered verdict of Mr. H. G. Wells stands as pronounced in his Outline of History. The subject has been so thoroughly discussed thereafter by Dr. Bhandarkar in his Carmichael Lectures on Aśoka that there remains hardly anything to add save and except by way of certain general observations on the points raised by him and other historians and scholars. The nature of the subject is such that it cannot but involve certain historical comparisons that are generally odious, and yet this unpleasant task has been well acquitted by Wells and Bhandarkar, to whose writings the reader may be referred for their findings.

The points that need special consideration here are : (1) Aśoka's services to Buddhism, (2) his role as nation-builder and (3) the political reaction of his Dharma-vijaya.

1. **Services to Buddhism :** Aśoka figured as the ideal universal monarch or righteous king emperor of Buddha in whose role the propounder of the ideal could not be as he had renounced the world. The Maurya emperor welcomed the lofty teachings of Buddha and openly accepted the Saddharma as his religion as a matter of choice, out of his profound conviction as to its intrinsic merit, rather because its underlying principles and spirit were found accidentally to be in harmony with his own perception as to the nature of human good and his own original vision as to the nature and course of human progress. This perception or vision came to him, as he tells us, when he had been seriously pondering over the immediate and after effects of an aggressive war waged on the country of the Kalingas. It was not so much the death and destruction and maiming of limbs or their deportation and captivity that caused so much pain to Aśoka as the injury caused to culture and the set-back to the course of human progress. Aśoka did for the religion of Buddha what Darius the Great or Xerxes had done for that of the Avesta and St. Paul did for

that of Christ.[1] He indeed raised Buddhism from the position of a local faith to the status of a world religion. The point of difference between the Achæmenid kings and Aśoka is that the former spoke of the greatness of Ahuramazda as the creator of the earth and the sky as well as of man,[2] and believed that whatever they had achieved in life was achieved by His grace, while Aśoka made selections out of the then known corpus of Buddha's words and presented the principles of Dharma on his own authority. In other words, he assumed the role of the founder of a socio-moral order with piety as its basis and the attainment of the grand heaven hereafter as its *summum bonum*. The elevation of humanity, the increase of the happiness of man in his present existence and the possession of heavenly joy hereafter were the common aims of the religions advocated by them.[3] The righteous king's position as a dharma-pravartaka or founder of such a socio-moral order was freely admitted in India by all schools of political thought, Brahmanical, Jaina or Buddhist. Whatever good thing Aśoka had learnt from the exponents of Buddhism and other men of religion he made it his own.

It is nevertheless true that just as the establishment of the Achæmenian suzerainty over a vast empire in Western Asia[4] implied the expansion of the inhabited area upon which the civilizing influence of the Avestan religion was exercised, so the extension of the sphere of Aśoka's political and moral influence implied the widening of the range of the civilizing influence of Buddhism beyond the territorial limits of India proper.

The Macedonian expedition under Alexander the Great ended in the foundation of the Greek suzerainty almost over the whole

---

1 Bhandarkar, As'oka, pp. 249-50.

2 Cf. Naqshi-i-Rustam inscription of Darius: Baga vazrka Ahurmazdā hya imām būmim adā avam asmānam adā hya martiyam adā hya shiyātim adā martihyahyā.

3 Cf. Persepolis inscription of Xerxes: utā jīva shiyāta bhavatiy utā mrta artāvā bavatiy.

4 This empire is claimed in the inscriptions to have comprised Media, Susiana, Arakhesia (Sarasvatī), Armenia, Drangiana, Parthia (?), Aria, Bactria, Sogdiana, Khorasmia, Babylonia (Bābru), Assyria, Sattagydia, Sparda, Egypt (Mudrā), the Greek (Yauna) colonies on the eastern Mediterranean coast and states on the northern coast, Maxyes, Arabia, Gandaria (Gadara, Gandhāra), the Indus region (Hidush, Sindhu), Kappadokia, Dahae, two divisions of Skythia, Skudria (the land of the Kshudrakas), Akaufaka, Puntia, Karkia, and Kushiya.

of the Achaemenid or Persian empire, and the establishment of the Maurya empire by Chandragupta came to mean the rescue of the Punjab proper, Beluchistan and Eastern Afghanistan from the grip of the Seleukidan rulers. So far as the history of the spread of Buddhism in the Punjab proper and the countries around beyond the Sulaiman range and the river Kābul from the latter half of the reign of Aśoka is concerned, it is interesting to watch how far Buddhism profited by assimilating the elements of the Pagan religion of the Greeks and succeeded in weaning the peoples and races from the fold of Zoroastrianism, primitive S'aivism, the worship of the Sun and Moon gods, the worship of Vaiśravaṇa Kubera, and sundry nature worship. Eastern Turkestan, the Himalayan regions and the eastern sub continent, Pūrvavideha, inhabited by the Mongolian races, including the Chinese, were destined to come under the civilizing influence of Buddhism. The itineraries of the earlier Chinese pilgrims record the traces of that great influence that might be found on their ways through Central Asia and Eastern Afghanistan. Whether or no, Zoroastrianism, which became the national religion of the Persians, was able to produce any appreciable changes in the Egyptian religion and the then religion of the Jewish races of Asia Minor is still a disputed question. The Greek power waned in the countries of Asia Minor when these came to be included in the Roman empire. The rise of Christianity in this very region a little more than two centuries after Aśoka by way of a forceful protest against the priest-ridden Judaism, the religion of the Pharisees and Scribes, showed the emergence of an emotional faith with an elevated moral tone and noble ideas of self-surrender to the Divine will, self-dedication and self-sacrifice. Although no satisfactory direct evidence is yet available, and the main historical background of Christianity lies in the religion of the Old Testament, the ethical purity of the religion of Zoroaster, the legends of the Sātvata cult of Purushottama, and the lofty messages of Buddha cannot but appear to have been somehow or other at the back of the religion of Christ and filled the hiatus between the Jewish tradition and the new tradition of Jesus of Nazareth. Anyhow, one cannot but be struck by many points of parallelism between Buddhism and Christianity. The modern historians tend all to agree to trace the influence of Buddhism in the development of the Jewish sects of the Therapeutæ and Essenes and that of the Gnostic and Nestorian forms of Christianity on the Eastern Mediterranean shores. The religion of Christ became destined to spread in Europe and America and subsequently in the countries in the Near East and Far East by the vigorous missionary work of the Christian Churches and under the influence of the Christian nations from the West.

A little more than six centuries after Christ there arose another powerful religion under the name of Islam in the northern portion of Arabia and practically within the same cradle of ancient civilization in Western Asia to try its strength with Judaism in Palestine, Syria, and Asia Minor and with Christianity in Southern Europe, being destined to become the ultra democratic monotheistic faith of the peoples and races in the extensive Persian empire of Darius the Great and Xerxes, weaning several nations that were once in the fold of Zoroastrianism, Buddhism and S'aivism. Since the rise and spread of the religion of the Quoran we have three world religions, each with its regional and national pre-dominance, viz., Buddhism, Christianity and Islam, while the rest of the earlier and later religions of the world have either become or are going to be clannish. It is in India proper between the Himalayas and the Indian Ocean that Hinduism exists and thrives with Vaishṇavism, S'aivism and S'āktism as its main forms, with Buddhism, Jainism and Zoroastrianism as the lingering sister faiths, with Islam and Christianity as the two rival faiths, and with S'ikhism, Neo-Vaishṇavism, Brahmoism, Ārya Samāj, Rāmkṛishṇa Mission and a few similar modern developments as the counteracting forces.

So far as India is concerned, one distinct service rendered by Aśoka to the cause of Buddhism was the heightening of the importance of the memorable spots associated with the life and career of the Buddha, then venerated as a Divine Master (Bhagavān), and the tradition of his noted Disciples. Buddha is said to have attached special importance to the visiting of the four places by the faithful, viz, those where took place his advent, enlightenment, first sermon and great decease. The Divyāvadāna preserves, correctly more or less, the tradition of Aśoka's pilgrimage to several places[1], and points out that the laudable object of this was the marking off of the sacred sites with tangible signs for the benefit of posterity, the future visitors. The monolithic pillars and stūpas (dharmarājikās) are mentioned in his inscriptions as, and are now found to be the architectural and artistic cognizances of the Buddhist holy places personally visited by him. His first visit to Sambodhi or Bodhgayā (R. E. VIII) signalling

[1] Divyāvadāna, p. 389f.

his conversion to Buddhism must have served to bring the Bo-tree Aśvattha itself into much prominence, and this is well attested by the subsequent history of Buddhism. The reverence shown to the stūpa of Koṇāgamana went alike to strengthen the tradition of the previous Buddhas among all the Buddhists.

In going to adapt his official language to various local dialects, Aśoka raised the language of the then known words of Buddha to the status of a *lingua franca* of India. Such adaptations must have given an impetus to the development of the language of the early Canonical texts of the different Buddhist sects and schools of thought.

Lastly, Aśoka sought to render another distinct service to the Saddharma by ensuring the unity and solidarity of the Sangha (Schism Pillar Edict). In this connection Bhandarkar has raised the important issue as to whether or no, any actual schisms had accurred then in the Buddhist community, giving rise to the earlier sects and schools of thought, traditionally known as eighteen in all.[1] His own finding on it is that Aśoka's statement, the Sangha has been made whole and entire, "no doubt shows that the Buddhist Church was then divided, but certainly not to such a serious extent as is implied by the Sinhalese tradition connected with the Council of Pāṭaliputra. The differences were unquestionably of small importance, such as they were when the council of Vesāli was convened. It seems that these differences were made up, that the whole Church was again united by Aśoka and that it continued to be so till at least the 27th year of Aśoka's reign."[2]

The weight of this opinion can by no means be minimised. Though the word Sangha is applicable to the whole of a particular Buddhist sect and to its sections and smaller divisions, its employment in the edicts creates nowhere the impression of there being any more than one Buddhist community in the mental purview of Aśoka; the employment of the word Saṃghaṭa (Saṃghastha, those belonging to the Buddhist Order) in its locative singular form, Saṃghaṭasi (P. E. VII), goes definitely to show that here Aśoka was thinking of the Buddhist Brotherhood as a single body. The evidence of the Schism Pillar Edict is indeed decisive as to a disturbed state of things, which was, after all, a temporary affair. According to the

[1] Mahāvaṃsa, V. 10; Beal, Buddhist Records, i, p. 177; Vasumitra's work, Nanjio, No. 1284.

[2] As'oka, p. 100.

Pali Chronicles, this disturbed state was but a local incident, which affected the internal life of the Aśokārāma. The uposatha and other ecclesiastical duties remained suspended for a period of nine years, the bonafide members of the Sangha being reluctant to perform them with other inmates who were all really outsiders. The undesirable elements are represented as men of other religious orders and other persuasions who managed stealthily to enter the monastery in the garb of Buddhist mendicants. The grievance of the former against the latter was that they were upholding the views according to their old ideas and beliefs. When the matter came to a head, king Aśoka arranged to get them examined, batch by batch, in his presence by Moggaliputta Tissa, the leading Thera of the time, and expelled those of them whose views were found incompatible with what was traditionally known as the real doctrine of the Buddha—the Vibhājyavāda *alias* Theravāda. Thus the disturbing factors were got rid of and the normal life of the local monastery was restored. We have got to see if this was precisely meant when Aśoka had stated that he succeeded in placing the unity and integrity of the Sangha on a stable footing for all times to come.

The Pali Canonical tradition speaks of a serious occasion when in the Buddha's life-time the unity of the Sangha was threatened with a division by the partisan spirit of the Bhikshus residing in Kauśāmbī, but this could be averted by the concerted action of the local laity.[1] It is aware of a schism, which was caused to be made in the Sangha by Devadatta and his co-adjutants. Though the Vinaya account tells us that many among the seceders were brought back to the Sangha and the whole movement died out with the death of its arrogant leader,[2] the itineraries of both Fa Hien and Hwen Thsang go to prove that the sect formed by him survived in Northern India till the seventh century of the Christian era, if not later still.[3] The Chullavagga account of the second Buddhist Council held at Vaiśālī, is silent on the action of the Vṛijiputra monks after the judicial committee, gave a unanimous verdict against them on all the ten points at issue arising from deviations from certain minor and lesser rules of conduct.[4] The Pali Chronicles supplement this account with

1 Vinaya Mahāvagga, Ch. X.

2 Chullavagga, Ch. VII.

3 Beal, Buddhist Records, I,P. xlviii ; II, P. 201.

4 Chullavagga, Ch. XII.

a narrative of what the Vṛijiputras did thereafter and to what effect. We are told that they staged a walk-out from the conference and subsequently held a council of their own, which was of a more representative character[1] and that this reaction on their part led to the rise of the first sect of schismatics, and within a century therefrom further divisions took place, five in the line of the Mahāsanghikas and eleven in that of the Sthaviras, the total number of sects and schools being eighteen before Aśoka's reign.

This later Pali tradition about the rise of the seventeen sects and schools of schismatics previous to the reign of Aśoka cannot be harmonized with other facts connected with them. The Dīpavaṃsa tells us, for instance, that each sect or school of schismatics (bhinnavādā) destroyed, when it arose, the original collection of the Canonical texts and made a new one in its place, made permutations and combinations of texts after taking them out of their contexts, distorted the doctrine and its meaning as they stood in the five Nikāyas. They put a meaning of their own into something said to convey quite another meaning. They destroyed the sense in many an instance in going to establish a mere verbal interpretation. Discarding some portions of the Sutta texts and Vinaya books, they prepared the new texts and books in their place. Dispensing with the Parivāra, Abhidhamma treatises, Paṭisambhidāmagga, Niddesas and some of the Jātakas, they made new ones instead. They changed the name, outward garb, requisites and approved rules of conduct to suit their own purpose, abandoning the normal mode of old[2].

Thus the oldest known Pali Chronicle of Ceylon speaks of a state of things, which did not exist in pre-Christian times. The Prakritic Sanskrit or Sanskritic Prakrit diction of the oldest known texts of the schismatics, as exemplified by the gāthās in the Mahāvastu and the Lalitavistara, bears a close affinity to the official language of India in its transitional stage during the reign of the S'aka and Kushāṇa rulers. This observation is supported also by the fact that the Indian inscriptions in which the different Buddhist sects and schools find mention are mostly post-Christian and pre-Gupta in point of chronology.

Vasumitra while writing an account of the early Buddhist sects

---

[1] It means that they allowed all monks, Arhats or not, to take part in the proceedings of the Council.

[2] Dīpavaṃsa, Ch. VI.

and schools in Kaṇishka's time traces the history of the rise of them from the reign of Aśoka which is wrongly placed 'a hundred and odd years' after the Buddha's demise. Following the Sarvāstivāda tradition, he confounds the celebrated Aśoka with Kālāśoka. If by Aśoka he had meant Kālāśoka, his account of the rise of the Mahāsanghikas and their earlier offshoots tallies with that in the Pali chronicles; it differs from the latter in so far as it places the rise of the seceders from the Sthaviras in the third and fourth centuries of the Buddha Era[1]. If by Aśoka he had meant, on the other hand, Dharmāśoka, to set right his dates we must allow a clear interval of a century, which is ignored by him. In that case we are not to think of the rise of the schismatics before the time of Aśoka.

Turning at last to the evidence of the Kathāvatthu, a Book of Buddhist controversies, which is traditionally known as a compilation of Aśoka's time, one may notice that it came to be included in the Abhidhamma Piṭaka on a very flimsy ground against the objection of some of the ancient Buddhist teachers.[2] The Milindapañha composed, according to tradition, five centuries after the Buddha's demise[3], say, in the first or second century A. D., in the prose style, more or less, of the Hāthigumphā inscription of Khāravela expressly presupposes the Kathāvatthu.[4] According to Pali tradition, the various points at issue discussed and criticised in the Kathāvatthu from the Theravāda point of view, though often unconvincingly and now and then foolishly, were the propositions representing the *laddhis* or cherished views of the outsiders of other religious persuasions. They are not described as the Buddhist Schismatics. The Kathāvatthu itself does not refer the views to any of them. They are brought in only in the commentary as partisans of those views, but Buddhaghosa is careful and cautious enough to refer to them as his contemporaries and to say while introducing them :

"Does everything exist ?—this question was asked by the Sakavādin in order to break down an opinion, 'held, for instance, *at present* (seyyathā pi etarahi) by the Sabbatthivādins'."[5]

"Some, for instance, *at present* the Mahiṃsāsakas and the Andhakas, held the view."

---

1 J. Masuda, Early Indian Buddhist Schools, Journal of the Department of Letters (C. U.), Vol. I, p. 5ff.

2 Atthasālinī, p. 3.

3, 4 Milinda, p. 3.

5 B. C. Law, Debates Commentary to Kathāvatthu, I. 6 and II. 9.

The only reasonable conclusion to be drawn from all these is that the opinions discussed and criticised in the Kathāvatthu of Aśoka's time were the opinions of certain leading individuals and their supporters within the Sangha. They were as good Buddhists as others, inasmuch as they all cited the Words of the Buddha as authorities, although their opinions appeared incompatible, and so alien, in the eye of the orthodox. The archaic prose style of the Kathāvatthu debates has its parallel indeed in at least three versions of R. E. IX (K, Sh, M).[1] It is also true that some of the debates refer to a time when Buddhism remained confined to the territorial limits of the Middle Country. But it will be historically sounder to maintain with Mrs. Rhys Davids that the Kathāvatthu in its earlier redaction did not probably contain all the debates that came to be included in it.

Looking a little closely into the matter, one can detect this difference between the tenour of Aśoka's Schism ordinance and that of the Pali schism tradition, that the former meant to expel from the Sangha a monk or nun who would cause schisms in it in future (bhākhati), while the latter purports to say that the propounders of alien views were disrobed and expelled. If it were only a difference of opinion or interpretation, which had then existed among certain leading individuals within the Sangha, and not a difference in any matter of discipline, it would be going against Aśoka's own principle of tolerance to penalise any person for holding an honest opinion about Buddha's doctrine. What Aśoka could possibly do, and probably actually did, being within his rights as king and well-wisher from the lay point of view, was to make all of them conform to the rules of uposatha and other established conventions of the institution tolerating the honest differences of opinion in matters of the doctrine.

2. **Role as nation builder** : The difference between modern definitions of a nation and a nationality is well-known. If a state needs an association of people in a particular territory and under an independent government, a nation needs, over and above these, two other factors, viz., common customs and traditions. A nationality differs from a nation by having for its requisite a common race instead of a particular territory with a separate political

---

[1] The same archaic style is met with also in the Vibhanga, the second book of the Abhidhamma Piṭaka.

organization or sovereign authority of its own. As regards the indispensability of these factors, the considered opinion is that any one or all of them may serve to constitute a nationality or a nation, but none is absolutely necessary. Nationality is largely a matter of sentiment in so far as the group of people belonging to it is expected to identify itself with a racial or cultural heritage, and a nation, too, is largely a matter of feeling in so far as an association of people is expected to identify itself with the vital interests of a country. From the cases thus made out, it follows that there may exist a nationality without going so far as to make a nation.

No other form of government than absolute monarchy was in harmony, as we sought to show, with the Upanishadic notion of soul as the paramount sovereign (samrāṭ) in a body politic coming into existence and functioning only for its sake. Thus there is no wonder that the Brahmanical schools of political thought cherished just the monarchical form of government as the ideal, and only that form of imperialism which is of a feudal and not of a federated type, monarchy remaining all the same as its mainstay. Kingship and the social order were believed to have originated from the Divine will and necessity. The king, queens, princes and princesses of the royal house were held in popular esteem as a class of devas. The majesty and happiness of the king were sought to be impressed on popular mind by the grandeur of dress and equipage, by pageantry and pomp. The religion through which the people were sought to be taught to appreciate and to aspire for such happy states of man on earth and in heaven was one which abounded in the grand performance of animal sacrifices, accompanied by sumptuous feasts, pompous processions, mirth and merry making, and the display of mansion-shaped celestial cars, celestial elephants, other celestial conveyances, illuminations and other conceivable celestial forms (R. E. I, R. E. IV). The Council of Ministers was to be used by the reigning monarch as a Privy Council at his sweet will. No one in the body-politic was to be trusted ; the whole machinery of government was to be efficiently worked with the art of diplomacy, operated by the engine of physical force, and keenly watched with the eye of suspicion and dread. The subjects were not to be given any opportunity to know the aims of the government or its principles and operative laws or to be conscious of their civic rights and duties.

Under such a system of royal polity as advocated in the Arthaśāstra of Kauṭilya and other Brahmanical treatises on the science of political advantage the only best thing to be expected, so long as a strong machinery of government could be kept in working order under the direction of a powerful king, was a state and not a nation. And if one can historically show that other factors that go to constitute a nation or nationality were developing nevertheless in the country, even then the fact remains that the processes were unconscious or subconscious ones and, as such, they were lacking in self-consciousness and co ordination.

As shown by Rhys Davids, although the knowledge of writing was known in India in earlier times, it was not used for recording literature and traditions until comparatively a late period in Indian history.

The employment by Aśoka of the Kharoshṭhī (Camel's lip) alphabet in the two sets of his edicts promulgate in the Punjab proper and that of the Brāhmī alphabet in the edicts and inscriptions caused to be engraved in the remaining part of his domain proper within India were fruitful in ways more than one : that, in the first place, the wise step taken by him gave a general incentive to the development of various local and national scripts and, secondly, that it showed and suggested the way of recording official documents and literary works and traditions on durable and handy materials. The first-named alphabet, written from right to left, which developed out of the Aramaic or Aramean in the Gandhāra region by way of an adaptation to the needs of Indo-Iranian languages remained as the local script of the Punjab proper and the Gandhāra extension within Eastern Turkestan until it was replaced by the Brāhmī and local scripts. The Brāhmī alphabet, written from left to right, became the parent script out of which developed the various local and national scripts in India as well as the Sinhalese, Siamese. Burmese and Tibetan alphabets. In the present world the contest for supremacy is going on among the four scripts, viz., the Roman, the Arabic, the Brāhmī meaning all its later variations, and the Chinese. Thus through the right effort of Aśoka India got a common script in Brāhmī to develop her national life as well as a Greater Indian nationality.

Besides a common script India needed a common language, a *lingua franca* or Esperanto to develop her national life. Rhys Davids was the first to clearly indicate how the Indian 'runaways', the Brāhmaṇas and the S'ramaṇas of various denominations wandering about in the country, carrying on a vigorous sophistic movement at the time about the rise of Buddhism and holding debates and discussions on subjects of religion, ethics, philosophy and nature-lore in a language intelligible to the people at large were helping to develop in the Middle Country a *lingua franca* or language of the cultured laity.[1] It is easily conceivable that when with the progress of time these powerful bodies of preachers of Indo-Aryanism spread over the face of India and Ceylon, as appears from the account of Megasthenes and Aśoka's clear statement in R.E. XIII, they were able to create a cultural atmosphere throughout for the appreciation of different forms of the Indo-Aryan speech. The Indian merchants speaking different local dialects and the Kshatriya princes and tribes who migrated to and founded territories in different parts of the country were no less instrumental in gradually widening the domain of the dialects or conversational forms of the Indo-Aryan speech. If by commercial relations, tribal migrations and settlements and Kshatriya territories one can account for the development of different provincial dialects, there must have arisen in this very process af Aryanisation the need of a common language to facilitate the communication as between the peoples and peoples, the provinces and provinces. By adapting the language of his edicts and inscriptions to different provincial dialects and their texts and phrases and idioms mostly to those of the then known Buddha's Words Aśoka served not only to accord state recognition to the common language closely allied to Pali but also to give a great impetus to the development of various local and national languages. As Bhandarkar acutely observes, 'The whole of the country had become Aryanised. But the different provinces had their different dialects. Owing, however to the stupendous efforts put forth by him (Aśoka) for the diffusion of his faith, the communication between one province and another became more frequent and brisk, and the universal desire of having a common language was felt—a language which would be studied and understood in all provinces and become the medium of thought not only in secular but also religious matters. This led to the acceptance of Pali or monumental Prakrit as the *lingua franca* of India."[2] The subsequent processes of linguistic, literary and political development combined by the time of the Guptas to raise Classical Sanskrit to the status of the *lingua franca* of India as well as of the countries around that came under the civilizing influence of Buddhism and

1 Buddhist India, Ch. VIII.

2 As'oka, p. 251.

Hinduism, and Sanskrit or Sanskritised Pali was in its turn replaced by the different provincial or national languages.

Just as India stood in need of a common religion to build up her national life on a solid foundation of human heart and virtue, so did the world to build up a nationality of mankind. But where was such a foundation to be found ? It was certainly in the 'universal character of Buddhism' as propounded by Buddha to all lay people,—the aspect of the religion of S'ākyamuni which Aśoka 'clearly perceived and emphasized.' The lofty message of the Dharma which he sought to convey to all the people within his vast empire through his edicts and to the whole of mankind through his Dūtas laid stress on what Bhandarkar calls 'the dynamic of conduct[1] ; and did not involve any question of theology or any subtle and cantankerous point of metaphysic. The scheme of toleration offered insisted on frequent meetings of the exponents of different faiths for a frank and free discussion and interchange of thoughts and ideas and aimed at the growth of all men of religion in the essence thereof.

As towards the development of the national art and architecture of India, Aśoka's efforts proved equally fruitful. The handicrafts of stone-cutters, wood-carvers, bricklayers, metal-and-ivory-workers, doll makers and painters were well-known in the country in earlier times. The four kubhās or rock-cut cave-dwellings caused to be made by Aśoka for the Ājīvikas in 'the hard and refractory syenitic granite' of the Khalatika (Barābar) hills with a vaulted or hemispherical domed roof, an oblong, rectangular or circular outer chamber, and bearing the distinctive 'characteristic of a bright polish shining from their walls as roofs'[2] marked indeed a glorious beginning of the cave architecture in India which followed such different lines of development as those of vihāra, chaitya, prāsāda (palace), harmya (mansion), ardhayoga, and guhā (natural cave. cavern, rock-slope, grotto), in combination gradually with sculptures and frescoes (lepyachitras). Prior to these, the guhās, ḍaris, kandaras and prāgbhāras were all mere mountain caves, crevices, grottoes and slopes altogether untouched or only rudely touched by human hand. The pre-historic cave-dwellings of men of which the vestiges are now traceable here and

---

[1] Ibid, p. 250.

Rajwade in his Grammar of Jñaneshwari also shows that Pali was the first Prakrit.

[2] See, for the latest account of these caves, Mookerji's Asoka, p. 89.

there in South India and Ceylon do not come up to that high level of artmanship which might entitle them to the name of architecture.[1]

The śilā-stambhas or monolithic pillars of Aśoka of which an up-to-date description and discussion are to be fonnd in Mookerji's Asoka (p. 89f.) marked similarly a proud beginning of the history of later Indian pillars of victory or ensigns of worship. According to Mookerji, "The raising of religious symbols for common reverence is a time-honoured Indian practice. Hindu temples have always before them their banner-torch or light-pillar, which are often adorned with the special symbol of the god, a wheel, or a trident. Vedic literature itself, by its descriptions of the banner of Indra, and of sacrificial posts, points to far distant origins of these pillars. The Aśokan pillar is the descendant of those royal or tribal ensigns or standards which were set up to mark off the sacrificial areas for ancient Vedic ceremonies" (Asoka, p. 99). The idea of setting up pillars on public roads (saṃsaraṇas) might have been suggested by the indrakīla (Pali indakhīla)[2] which, according to the Pali scholiast, was a city-gate pillar made of durable wood, to set up which in such a manner that it might remain unshaken by winds from four quarters a pit had to be dug to a depth of from eight to ten cubits.[3] The art of fashioning them with the ornamentation at the top, the capital and the abacus must have been the prevalent art of constructing the pillars of a pillared verandah or hall of a royal palace. "Gigantic shafts of hard sandstone, thirty or forty feet in length, were dressed and proportioned with the utmost nicety, receiving a polish which no modern mason knows how to impart to the material."[4] The polish giving to an unwary observer the impression that the monolith is 'brazen' or made of 'cast metal'[5] was a wonderful effect of the high polish done on stone of which the secret remained concealed with the artist or artists employed by Aśoka and could not

---

[1] Panchanan Mitra in Journal of the department Letters, of C. U., Vol. 1, pp. 151—2.

[2] Ratana Sutta: yathindakhīlo paṭhaviṃ sito sityā, chatubbhi vātebhi asampakampiyo.

[3] Indakhīlo 'ti nagaradvāra-samvaraṇatthaṃ vivaraṇatthaṃ ummārabbhantare aṭṭha vā dasa vā hatthe paṭhaviṃ khaṇitvā ākoṭitassa sāradārumayatthambhass' etaṃ adhivachanaṃ. In Sanskrit literature, Indrakīla is just another name for the Mandara mountain.

[4] Mookerji, Asoka, p. 91f.

[5] Vincent Smith, Oxford *History*, p. 113.

be reproduced in later ages, particularly in the imitation pillars of the Sunga Art. The lustre of the polish was such that Hwen Thsang was compelled to describe the monolith seen standing in front of a stūpa on the western side of the river Varaṇā as "bright and shining as a mirror" with its surface "glistening and smooth as ice" and on which the figure of Buddha could be "constantly seen as a shadow."[1] It would have been more appropriate, perhaps, on the part of the Chinese pilgrim to say that the finely polished surface of the monolith truly mirrored the serene heart of Aśoka.

The historical problem which arises in connection with the monoliths of Aśoka is pithily stated thus by Mookerji (op. cit , p. 98) : The best examples of art, "the Aśokan Pillars, are trace to foreign influence. While some of their element are traced to Greece, others are traced to Persia. Their so-called bell-shaped capitals, their smooth unfluted shafts, their polish, and even their inscriptions are traced to Persia."[2]

I am entirely at one with Havell to think that the full-blown-lotus capital of the Aśokan monoliths is mistaken for the Persepolitan bell. The circular abacus is to all appearance the pericarp of the lotus. Codrington's findings on the difference and distinction between the Persepolitan and Aśokan pillars and their capitals āre sound and thoroughgoing.[3] Mookerji rightly argues his case when he points out that "While (the pillars) at Persepolis and elsewhere are structural, the Aśokan ones are purely monumental."[4] There is no cause for astonishment that in both subject and inspiration, the treatment of the bull and the elephant, the Sārnāth abacus is entirely Indian. The excellence seen in the naturalistic treatment of animals and plants in spirited bas-reliefs need not be attributed to any inspiration from Greek Art 'which alone in that epoch of world's history distinguished itself in the modelling of living forms.' India developed the tradition of such an animated naturalistic art in the numerous seals from Harappa and Mohenjo-daro. One may claim that the modelling of the haṃsa or Brahmani duck in one of the Mohenjo-daro seals (Marshall, pl. CVI. 93) is superb. Here two important questions may arise—What might be the more prabable

---

1 Beal, Buddhist Records, ii, p. 45-

2 Asoka, p. 98.

3 Ancient India, pp. 18-19.

4 Asoka, p. 99.

reason for confining the crowning animal figures to the lion, the elephant, the horse, and the bull, and how far, if at all, could they be regarded as Buddhistic symbols ?

According to Kern, Senart and Bühler, the figure of an elephant stood on the Girnār rock, precisely as on the rocks at Dhauli and Kalsi, as the symbol of Buddha, which would now seem open to dispute The elephant at Dhauli is labelled as Seto (White), that at Kalsi as Gajatame (The superlative or best elephant), and that at Girnār as Sarvasveto hasti sarvalokasukhāharo nāma (The procurer of happiness for all the world). These elephants were obviously meant to serve as pointer meaning a sculptural device to draw attention to the spot where the set of edicts was. Nothing but the popular notion of *mangala* (victory, safety, prosperity, auspiciousness) was associated with them. In the Anguttara Nikāya (III, p. 345) one of the best royal elephants of Kośala is named Seta, and in the Dhammapada Commentary (II, p. 1) the same royal elephant is called Puṇḍarīka (White lotus). In the Jātakas, an elephant of noble breed, endowed with personality, is generally described as sabbaseta (all-white).[1] and occasionally as añjanavaṇṇa (collyrium-coloured)[2] or kālapasāṇa-kūṭavaṇṇa (blackstone-coloured .[3] In the Vimānavatthu stories the all white and best elephant (sabbaseto gajuttamo) figures as a vehicle of the gods. The Jātaka description, sabbaseto mangala-hatthi,[4] of the state-elephant of Vessantara corresponds with the Girnār label, while in the matter of phraseology there is the closest correspondence between sarvaloka sukhāharo and the Pali sabbakāmarasāharo.[5] The sight of an all white bull, and for the matter of that, also of a horse of the noble breed and a chariot drawn by such horses was auspicious in popular eye.[6] This is not all. According to the Pali account of the Anotatta Lake, the Lion outlet, the Elephant outlet, the Horse outlet and the Bull outlet stood for the four quarters,[7] which has its confirmation in the Chetiya Jātaka in which the all-while elephant

---

1 Jātaka, IV, p. 90 ; V. p. 45 : sabbaseto puṇḍarīkatacangi.

2 *Ibid*, II p. 365f.

3 *Ibid*, IV, p. 137.

4 *Ibid*, VI, p. 487.

5 *Ibid*, III, pp. 169-7. : sabbakāmarasāharo = aabbakāmarasāvaho, sukhasankhātam rasam āharitum samattho.

6 *Ibid*, IV, p. 72.

7 Paramattha-jotikā, II, pp. 437-39. The quarters indicated here are the eastern, the weatern, the southern and the northern respectively.

MAP OF ACHAEMENIAN EMPIRE

TIME DARIUS - XERXES

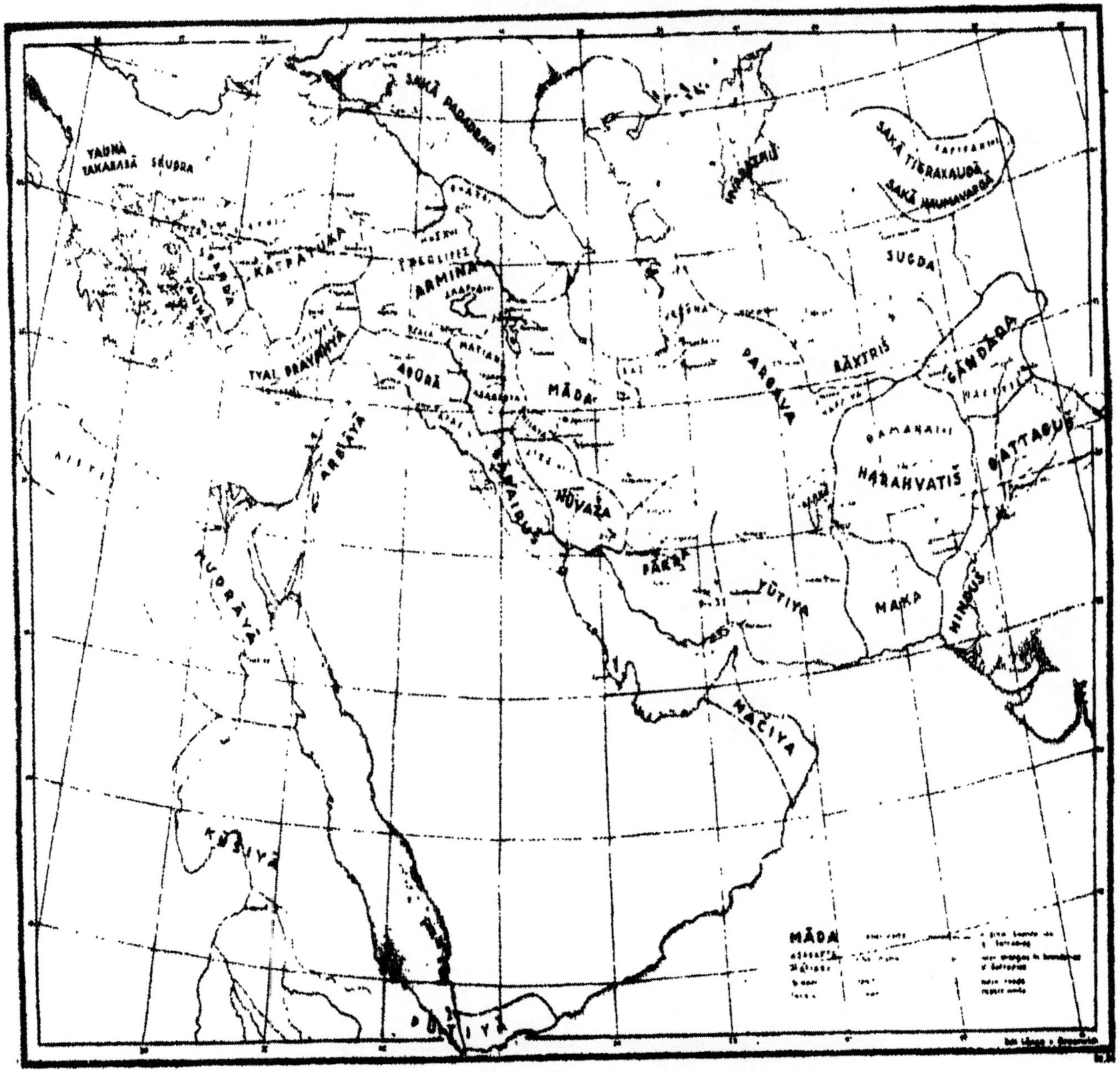

is associated with the eastern city-gate, the all-white horse with the southern, the lion-king with the western, and the all gem-studded wheel structure with the northern,[1] the fourth being really the gate with which the all-white bull was to be associated.[2] The Sarnath pillar of Aśoka bears the four wheel symbols of sovereignty, all placed between these very four animal figures.

Hwen Thsang noticed a horse as the crowning animal figure on Aśoka's monolith at Lumbinī. If Aśoka's bhīchā be equated with the Pali bhinkā having bhengā and bhiñjā for its variants, it may be taken, according to the Vinaya Piṭaka (II, p. 201), to mean 'young elephants' and to suggest that the figures of young elephants were caused to be carved in stone. But the more reasonable and philologically and historically sound interpretation of silā-vigaḍa-bhīchā will be to break it up into three words, silā, vigaḍabhī and chā[3] and to equate the second word with Sk. vigatabhī[4], meaning 'free from fear'. Accordingly the whole statement regarding the monolith may be rendered : "the stone was caused to be rendered free from fear and the stone-pillar to be erected." The equation of the Māgadhī vigaḍa with vikṛita is sanctioned by Vararuchi's rule, according to which kṛita becomes kaḍa and gata, gaḍa.[5] It is evident from the Mānasāra and other Indian treatises on architecture and kindred arts that before wood (dāru) or stone (śilā) was used as material for pillars (stambhas) and the like, it was required to be rendered faultless, meaning secure against evil effects arising, for instance, from the annoyance caused to the indwelling spirits. The twofold means thereto consisted in the performance of a prescribed ritual and the feeding of the Brāhmans. The Mānasāra, XV. 166-67, for instance, prescribes :

---

[1] Jātaka, III, p. 460. My attention to this text is drawn by S. N. Mitra.

[2] The Jātaka indication of the four quarters differs from that in the Paramatthajotikā, II, in that here the elephant is placed on the east and the lion on the west.

[3] Prof. Suniti Kumar Chatterji's objection to treating chā instead of cha as a copulative conjunction in the dialect of Lumbinī is not, after all, a very strong one. Cf. P.E. I (Delhi-Topra) for the random use of cha and chā in one and the same sentence.

[4] Bhagavad Gītā, VI. 14.

[5] Prākṛita Prakās'a, xi. 15 : Kṛin mṛin gamāṃ ktasya ḍaḥ.

Sarvadoshaṃ samuddiśya śāntiṃ kuryād vichakshaṇaḥ ।
paśuprahārahomaṃ cha brāhmaṇānān bhojayet tataḥ ॥
evaṃ śāntau kṛitāyāṃ tu doshaṃ naśyati, nānyathā ।[1]

If any Brahmanical ritual and the feeding of the Brāhmans were out of the question as means, the chanting of the Paritta Suttas by the Buddhist monks and the feeding of them might have been good substitutes in Aśoka's case. That some kind of propitiatory rite had preceded all works of the building art is evident also from the Great Epic, I. 207-29, II. 1. 18-20. The Great Epic description, sabhā śuśubhe vigataklamā (II. 11. 59-60) stands very near to Aśoka's statement, silā vigaḍabhī kālāpita.

I have nothing more to add to the relevant comment of Mookerji on the contribution of Aśoka to the development of palace-architecture in India.

There cannot be a nation, as we saw, without a true national feeling aroused and a national character formed. Similarly there cannot be a nationality where the group of people belonging to it does not consciously espouse a common cause of humanity, such as the elevation of human nature or the education of men to certain excellences of character (P.E. VII).

From Aśoka we have an open declaration that he aspired in his heart of hearts to be a servant of the land (desāvutike hosāmi, S.R.E. I), and that he tried his level best to infuse this very idea into the mind of all his ministers, officers, personal agents and subjects.

In the absence of newspapers and other modern means the inscriptions and proclamations were used by Aśoka as means of keeping the people informed of how his government was being run and to what ends in view.

As for nationality, the idea that we all belong to one and the same order of law and righteousness was shaping in India through the Vedic conception of Varuṇa. The same was strengthened when by the Upanishad teacher Dharma was declared to be the king of kings, and later on by Buddha, to be the king of king overlords. Although the aim and function of every true and great religion is to make the state and all other human institutions subservient to the cultural or spiritual cause, and to make all men believe that they are

---

[1] Cf. Vishṇudharmottara, Bk. III, Ch. 19 ; J. N. Banerjea's Development of Hindu Iconography, p. 237.

not servants of any man-made order but only those of a universal order of Dharma or Piety, the articles of faith that it introduces, the forms of worship and the practices that it enforces in order to develop and maintain its institutional character are bound to make it ultimately sectarian, rigid and dictatorial. While the forms get stereotyped, life moves on with new energies released from time to time. Aśoka clearly foresaw this danger. He therefore looked to the growth in the essence of all religions irrespective of their forms, and enunciated and promulgated only the fundamental principles of piety and conduct without introducing into them any theological or metaphysical questions.

3. **Political reaction of Dharma-vijaya :** While discussing the gain or loss the Dharma-vijaya career of Aśoka 'conferred or inflicted' on India, and without denying that indirectly the country gained considerably, Bhandarkar poignantly observes : "The effects of this change of policy, of the replacement of vijaya by Dharmavijaya, were politically disastrous though spiritually glorious. Love of peace and hankering after spiritual progress were no doubt engendered, and have now been ingrained in the Indian character. The Hindu mind, which was spiritual, became infinitely more spiritual. But that must have created some apathy to militarism, political greatness, and material well-being. This must have been the reason why after Kauṭilya we find the progress of the political theory and practice suddenly impeded and stunted,—especially at a time when the Magadha State was expected to create the feeling of nationality and raise India to a higher political plane. Aśoka's new angle of vision, however, sounded a death-knell to the Indian aspiration of a centralised national state and world-wide empire. The effects of his policy were manifest soon after his death. Dark clouds began to gather in the north-western horizon, and hardly a quarter of a century had elapsed since his demise when the Bactrian Greeks crossed the Hindukush which formed the north-western boundary of the Mauryan dominions, and began to cause the decay of what was once a mighty empire. We know how very afraid the Greeks were of the Magadha army, even when they were led by Alexander. What is worse is that the Greek inroads, soon after the demise of Aśoka, for which his change of foreign policy appears to be responsible, opened a passage into India to the various wild hordes, such as the Śakas, Pahlavas, Kushāṇas, Hūnas, Gurjaras and so forth, whom we now find pouring unceasingly into the country till the sixth century A. D. and eclipsing the sovereignty of the

indigenous rulers, with such few exceptions only as the Śungas and Guptas. Though, on account of the missionary activity of Aśoka, India, it appears, has been lost to nationalism and political greatness, she has doubtless gained in cosmopolitanism and humanitarianism which are the basic principles of Hindu society".[1]

Thus with an eloquence matching the speeches of Burke, Bhandakar has brought his bill of indictment against Aśoka who is known as the greatest emperor the world has ever seen. But we must faithfully reproduce the similar pronouncements and arguments from the powerful pen of Jayaswal and Raychaudhuri before we dispassionately consider the issue raised by them and impartially adjudicate on the facts and authorities relied upon. "The accident of the presence", says Jayaswal, "on the throne, at a particular juncture in history, of a man who was designed by nature to fill the chair of an abbot, put back events not by centuries but by milleniums."[2] And Raychaudhuri, proceeding in the same strain, adds : "The Magadhan successors of Aśoka had neither the strength nor perhaps the will to arrest the process of disruption. The martial ardour of imperial Magadha had vanished with the last cries of agony uttered in the battlefield of Kalinga. Aśoka had given up the aggressive militarism of his forefathers and had evolved a policy of Dhamma-vijaya which must have seriously impaired the military efficiency of his empire. He had called upon his sons and even great-grandsons to eschew new conquests, avoid the shedding of blood and take pleasure in patience and gentleness. These latter had heard more of Dhamma-ghosha than of Bherī ghosha. It is, therefore, not at all surprising that the *rois faineants* who succeeded to the imperial throne of Pāṭaliputra proved unequal to the task of maintaining the integrity of the mighty fabric reared by the genius of Chandragupta and Chāṇakya."[3] And, furthermore, in the footnote, "The royal hunt and jousts of arms in Samājas were abolished. The army seems to have been practically inactive during the last 29 years of the reign as the emperor himself declares with a feeling of exultation that the sound of the bherī had become the sound of the True Law, Dharma. The Chinese Hou Hanshu quoted by S. Konow, CII, Vol. II, p. lxvii, testifies to the fact that the people of India 'practise the religion of the Buddha ; it has become a habit with them not to kill and not to

---

1 As'oka, p. 258 f.

2 J. B. O. R. S., Vol. II, p. 83.

3 Political History of Ancient India, p. 304.

fight'. The ease with which general Pushyamitra overthrew his king in the very sight of the army shows that unlike the earlier kings of the dynasty who took the field in person, the last of the Mauryas lost touch with his fighting forces and ceased to command their affection. The largesses of gold lavished on the religieux must also have crippled the financial resources of the empire. The system of autonomous Rajukas instituted by Aśoka must have let loose centrifugal forces that his successors were unable to check."

It will be seen that in all the three pronouncements cited above Aśoka, like Adam of the Garden of Eden, is held responsible for the trials and tribulations and the decadence and downfall of his descendants and successors, in short, of the whole of Indian posterity, on account of the first sin committed through his disobedience to the behests of the political wisdom of Kauṭilya-Chāṇakya and departure from the traditional state-policy of Magadha. At the back of all is the grand assumption that the Arthaśāstra which in its extant form is ascribed to Kauṭilya-Vishṇugupta was a finished product of the time of Chandragupta Maurya, as well as that all that it prescribes and advocates as the science of political advantage spells the highest political wisdom which is good for the Indian state and the Indian nation.

Jayaswal and Raychaudhuri place their reliance on the doubtful evidence of a legend of Udadhī (Udāyin) and S'āliśūka from the Yuga-purāṇa section of the Garga or Gārgī Saṃhitā, as also on the legend of Aśoka from the Divyāvadāna stating that he had exhausted the financial resources of his state by the largesses of gold lavished on the religieux. The latter even seriously quotes the pious opinion of the Chinese Buddhist Hou Hanshu that following the behests of the religion of the Buddha, the people of India became accustomed not to kill and not to fight. Bhandarkar goes a step further and indulges in the reverie :- "And if the vision of the Chakravartī Dhārmika Dharmarājā had not haunted his mind and thus completely metamorphosed him, the irresistible martial spirit and the marvellous statecraft of Magadha would have found a further vent by invading and subjugating Tamil States and Tāmraparṇī towards the southern extremity of India and would probably not have remained satisfied except by going beyond the confines of Bhāratavarsha and establishing an empire like that of Rome." How difficult it is to undo the mischief once made, to create a clear atmosphere for viewing the matter in its proper perspective when it has been vitiated once for all by these apparently convincing arguments moving all in a vicious circle.

Bhandarkar's reverie has many parallels in history, and so it is not the first but rather the latest brand of it. "Alexander indeed came and overthrew in war all whom he attacked," says Arrian, "and would even have conquered the whole world had his army been willing to follow him,"[1] whereas the fact is that Alexander the Macedonian "abandoned as hopeless an invasion of the Gangaridai when he learned that they possessed four thousand elephants well-trained and equipped for war."[2] The Greek physicist Archimedes might say that if he could get a place to stand on and a fulcrum to work the lever, he might have moved the earth from its orbit, but this was not to be. It is so easy to say that with the mighty strength of elephants of the Maurya army, the heroism of Chandragupta and the political shrewdness of Chāṇakya, Aśoka might have, if he had not changed his foreign policy, to annex the Tamil States and Ceylon, to conquer the Greek territories beyond Afghanistan, and to enlarge the Maurya empire into the size of the empire of Rome. But in going to conquer and annex the country of the Kalingas alone, Aśoka found it a most difficult job to accomplish. I should think that the march through the desert of Persia and Western Asia with the elephants and heavy chariots would have been a mad project then as even now. This is no part of the historian's business to speculate on what might or might not have happened but to give his verdict only on what actually happened.

As for the legend of Udadhī and S'āliśūka from the Yugapurāṇa, the readers of the Calcutta Review (1943, Feb., April) are well aware of the controversy which took place over it between Professor Nilkanta Sastri and Dr. D. C. Sircar. The following nine ślokas were cited by Kern from a single manuscript of the Garga-saṃhitā in the introduction to his edition of the Bṛihat saṃhitā (p. 30) :—

Tataḥ Kaliyuge rājā S'iśunāgākhyājā balī
Udadhīr n(ā)ma dharmātmā pṛithivyāṃ prathito guṇaih.
Gangātīre sa rājarshir dakshiṇe samānānācharo
sthāpayen nagaraṃ ramyaṃ pushpārāmajanākulaṃ.
Te 'tha Pushpapure ramye nagare Pāṭalīsute
pañcha-varsha-sahasrāṇi sthāsyante hi na saṃśayah.
Varshāṇāṃ cha śatapañchaṃ pañcha-saṃvatsarāṃs tathā
māsapañcham ahorātram muhūrtān paṃcha eva cha.

---

[1] McCrindle, Ancient India, p. 209.

[2] Ibid, p. 32.

Tasmin Pushpapure ramyajanaśajāśatākale
ribhukshā (Kern ritukshā) karmasūtah S'āliśūko bhavishyati.
Sa rājā karmasūto dushṭātmā priyavigrahah
svarāshṭra mardate ghoraṃ dharmavādī adhārmikah.
sa jyeshṭha-bhrātaraṃ sādhuṃ ketīti prathitaṃ guṇaih
sthāpayishyati mohātmā vijayaṃ nāma dhārmikam.
Tatah Sāketam ākramya Pañchālaṃ Mathurāṃs tathā
Yavanā dushṭavikrāntā prāpshyanti Kusumadhvajam.
Tatah Pushpapure prāpte kardame prathite hite
ākulā vishayāh sarve bhavishyanti na saṃśayah.

Diwan Bahadur K. N. Dhurva's feat of ingenuity performed in emending the ślokas[1] is unwarranted from the scholarly point of view. There is nothing to change in the first four ślokas save Udadhī into Udāyī. In the first line of the fifth śloka, the only correction needed is that of ramyajanaśajāśatākale into ramye janaśataśatākule (cf. 2nd śloka, 1st line). In the second line, the word ṛitukshā should be amended and read as ribhukshā. All that is needed to do in the first line of the next śloka is to supply the expletive *hi* after *sa*, and in the second line of the seventh śloka, to read Vijaya as a personal name. Thus one can easily render the ślokas intelligible to any Sanskritist, the 5th, 6th and 7th ślokas reading as :

Tasmin Pushpapure ramye janaśataśatākule
ribhukshā (tu)karmasūtah dushṭātmā priyavigrahah.
Sa (hi) rājā karmasūtah dushṭātmā priyavigrahah
svarāshṭra(m) mardate ghoraṃ dharmavādī adhārmikah.
Sa jyeshṭha-bhrātaraṃ sādhuṃ ketīti[2] prathitaṃ guṇaih
sthāpayishyati mohātmā Vijayaṃ nāma dhārmikam.

"In that delightful city of Pushpapura teeming with hundreds and hundreds of men Ribhukshā (Indra) will be reborn as S'āliśūka, springing from his karma. He will (indeed) be the king as a result of his past deed, a wicked soul in an attractive bodily form. (He will) terribly oppress his own territory,—a vicious man, though outwardly swearing by the name of piety. He, the deluded man, will establish (in the throne) his good and virtuous elder brother, Vijaya by name,[3]

---

[1] J. B. O. R. S., 1930, p. 18ff.

[2] Kern wrongly took it to be a mistake for hatvā vi.

[3] Kern was led from the proposed change of ketiti into hatvā vi to treat Vijaya as the name of S'ālisūka's younger brother.

who was popularly known as ketī (kritī, the Illustrious One) for his qualities."

Nilkanta Sastri's objection stands that in the prophecy there is nothing concerning Aśoka, the propounder of the ideal of Dharma-vijaya, it being all about S'āliśūka. It is in the Vāyu Purāṇa list that we have mention of S'āliśūka among the successors of Aśoka, as the son of Samprati and the grandson of Daśaratha, who was succeeded in the throne by his son Devadharman or Devavarman. All that the ślokas want to say about Sāliśūka is that he had to abdicate the throne in favour of his elder brother in consequence of the terrible oppression caused by him to his subjects.

The Yuga-purāṇa tradition refers indeed to the inroads of the powerful Yavana invaders into Sāketa, Pañchāla, Mathurā, and ultimately into the city of Pāṭaliputra after the reign of Sāliśūka's immediate successor. This has in a sense its confirmation from the Junāgarh inscription of Rudradāman I (A.D.150) where it is stated that one Yavana king Tushāspa caused the embankment of the Sudarśana Lake in Surāshṭra to be repaired after (not necessarily immediately after) the reign of Aśoka (Aśokasyaṃte).

What historical conclusion can be built, I ask, on the hearsay evidence of the Chinese Hou Hanshu who never came to India and was piously dreaming from distance that here in India, the promised land, all men became lotus-eaters, coming under the influence of the religion of S'ākyamuni ? So an Indian without ever going to England may fondly believe as if all Englishmen there are above want and do not feel the pinch of poverty. Thus distance lends enchantment to the view.

We have already examined the historical weight of the Divyāvadāna legend concerning the depletion of the imperial treasury by Aśoka in erecting the Buddhist vihāras[1] and stūpas and lavishly giving gifts to the Sangha, nay, giving away the great earth (vast empire) in favour of the Buddhist Church (*ante* p. 61). In causing the four caves to be excavated in the Khalatika hills within a period of eight years, the stūpa of Buddha Koṇāgamana to be enlarged, a few other stūpas to be built, and a number of monoliths to be

---

1 Dhammapāla, the second great Pali commentator, refers (Colophon to Netti Aṭṭhakathā) a monastery at Negāputam in South India, which was known as Dhammāsoka-mahārāja-vihāra. This was evidently a much later Buddhist foundation named after As'oka.

erected, a huge sum of money was not necessary. If he had caused a new Maurya palace to be built, that, too, was just customary with all Indian kings and emperors. R. E. I corroborates the truth in the Pali legend that following the tradition of his father, Aśoka continued to daily feed thousands of persons from the imperial kitchen. He stopped this costly waste and adopted a five-year scheme of works of public utility. There is not the slightest indication in the edicts that extravagance in any respects proved ruinous to the financial resources of the state.

With regard to the successors of Aśoka, the only fact known of them from the inscriptions is that Daśaratha was a lay supporter of the Ājīvikas to whom he dedicated three caves in the Nāgārjunī group of hills. The Yuga-purāṇa tradition of S'āliśūka expressly says that he terribly oppressed his subjects, so much so that he was compelled at last to vacate the throne in favour of his elder brother. If so, he was far from following the behests of Aśoka. It is no argument to say with Bhandarkar that the descendants of Aśoka gave up wars and the idea of territorial gains, all acting up to his wish as expressed in his R.E. XIII. The Jaina tradition claims that among Aśoka's successors, Samprati (Sampadi of the Divyāvadāna), was, like Chandragupta the founder of the dynasty, a staunch supporter of Jainism, and the inscriptions go to prove that Daśaratha followed the guidance of the Ājīvikas. Who were the Ājīvikas ? Whatever else they might have been, as for the royal court, they functioned as a body of astrologers, diviners from signs and makers of prophecies, and as such, they were exactly the people whose predictions and advice decided in history the fate of many an Indian monarch and state. And what was Jainism ? Whatever else it might have been, so far as the political theory or royal polity is concerned, the one favoured by it is in all essentials the same as the anti-national-Brahmanical doctrine.

It is no sound reason to make Aśoka pay the penalty for the weakness of his successors in the line, nor is it a fact that Aśoka's missionary zeal made the Hindu people who were already spiritual infinitely more spiritual. This is not common human nature. If one possesses strength and means to fight, one will fight and resist. Although Buddhism became the national religion of Ceylon, its kings who emulated the fame of Aśoka, did not cease to kill or fight. The same remark holds true of other Buddhist countries. According to the Jewish religious tradition, even God Almighty himself failed to prevent the downfall of the best of His creation,—of the first parents placed in the Garden of Eden, not to speak of poor Aśoka with all his pious wishes for, and best behests to, his descendants. The Hindu people *qua* people had no concern whatever in the rises and falls of kingdoms and empires ; they were just passive spectators and fatalistic speculators. On the course of dynastic history we have this forceful pronouncement of Ibn Khāldūn[1] who saw in history "an endless cycle of progress and retrogression," that it passes through the same three phases of birth, maturity and death as the life of an individual. "Kingdoms are born, attain maturity and die within a definite period, which rarely exceeds three generations, *i.e.*, one hundred and twenty years." "During this time they pass through five stages of development and decay." He called the fifth man *al hadem* or the worst man.

When a building collapses, its main pillar of strength may contribute most to its fall, and there is no building or compounded thing which does not break down some day or other. There is no empire or civilization which has lasted for ever, through eternity. There were rises and falls of several states and dynasties even in India before the rise of Magadha, and it is rather most astonishing a fact that from the Brihadrathas down to the Guptas the political history of India was determined by the course of the history of Magadha with its ups and downs and several dynastic changes.

Raychaudhuri pities Aśoka that his army remained idle for three decades since the conclusion of the war against Kalinga. If it were a mere statement of fact, there would be nothing to gainsay, but as an argument, it carries no force. The Great Epic maxim (XII. 68.25), that a conqueror hankering for territorial gains should always avoid going into wars if he can[2]. This is a wise piece of advice, inasmuch as wars are costly risks.

It is not a fact that the zeal for military campaigns or the love of political conquests abated in the least in the country owing to the pacifism preached by Aśoka. Khāravela, the greatest known king of Kalinga, who was otherwise a pious Jaina, suffered from a great war-fever ; in every alternate year he would undertake a military campaign, now to the west, now to the north-west, and to keep his subjects, the people of Kalinga, constantly in the excitement of the joy of victory. But to what end ? The reply from history is—to be

---

1 Muqaddima, Beyrout ed., p. 179f. ; De Stane's Transl., Vol. I, p. 347f. ; summarised by Nicholson in his Literary History of the Arabs, p. 440.

2 Varjanīyaṃ sadā yuddhaṃ rājyakāmena dhīmatā.

nowhere from after the 13th or 14th year of his reign, and the Mahāmeghavāhana dynasty to cease to be, placing on record the bare name of a single king and a single prince among Khāravela's descendants. The Asia-wide Mongol invasion under the great Qublai Khan who was a Buddhist by his religious faith is notorious in history. No less sensational was the invasion led by his successor Chinghiz Khan. All these had but a cyclonic effect destructive of civilization. Nilkanta Sastri has aptly cited the instance of Aurangzeb and asked—Did he "who spent a whole lifetime in war leave the Mughal empire stronger and render the task of his successors easier ?"[1]

Aśoka got just two decades to work since the conclusion of the Kalinga war and had to spend one-third part of his reign in preparing himself for the great task he set himself, and during this short period at his disposal he carved out a permanent place for India in the comity of nations. The patriotic historians of India may find fault with him that he honestly tried to found his government on trust, that he gave opportunities to his ministers to meet together independently for deliberations over state-affairs, that he delegated certain judicial powers to the Rajjukas and aimed at the establishment of the uniformity of justice and procedure, or that he sought to strengthen the bond of internationalism through a cultural understanding without either disturbing the form of the Maurya administration or impairing the military efficiency of the state. And yet if his mission be deemed a failure, one can say with Nilkanta Sastri, "It seems pardonable to feel that his failure was worth more to humanity than the success of many others."

There is no worry about the decline of political thought after the Arthaśāstra ascribed to Kauṭilya. The treatise as we now have it embodies the development of the Brahmanical science of political advantage up to a late period,[2] and one may go even further and say that its statecraft has guided and is still guiding the administration in the large majority of the Indian States. But, again, to what end ?

---

[1] Calcutta Review, 1943, Feb., p. 123.

[2] Barua, The Arthas'āstra—a blend of things earlier and later, a paper contributed to Radhakumud Mookerji Volume, I.

APPENDIX TO CHAPTER IX

Asoka and His Dhamma-culture

By Dr. Ishwar Topa, Professor of History,
Osmania University, Hyderabad*

The political conditions and struggles of the times determined the Mauryan State. In it the political evolution of India reached its high water-mark. It also helped to institutionalise kingship. Even the Kauṭilyan Arthaśāstra bears testimony to the political ideal and practice of the Mauryan period. The cardinal principle of the Arthaśāstra was the universalisation of political principles and the intensification of political activities for safeguarding the interests as well as promoting the ends of the Mauryan State. Kauṭilya, the great Mauryan minister, visualised the importance of political factors and mobilized all his powers to bring about the solidarity of the Mauryan State and kingship on the firm foundation of the laws of politics and statecraft. The laws that governed the Mauryan State were political in nature and scope. He attempted the unification of all the diverse elements in the life of the Mauryan State with a view to strengthening and enlivening the institution of kingship and the state. The whole spirit of the Arthaśāstra is surcharged with politicisation of the whole machinery of government. In other words, the Mauryan political organisation throve on the totalitarian principles of statecraft and politics.[1]

Aśoka the Great was brought up in the Mauryan political traditions. The Mauryan spirit possessed him and his political outlook was stamped with it. He carried in his person the Mauryan heritage. This Mauryan aspect of Aśoka continued to affect all the phases of his personality till he fought the most 'bloody' war of Kalinga in order to actualise the Mauryan dream of political suzerainty. 'Chaṇḍāśoka' of the Buddhist tradition might have been the typical Maurya who idealised in him the Mauryan political ideal and practice. To the Buddhist world, the Mauryan ideology was, to all intents and purposes, base, useless and harmful. The ideal of the

---

* Paper read in Section I of the Indian History Congress held at Annamalai Nagar, in December, 1945.

[1] See for detailed reference author's The Minister as a King-maker, Allahabad.

Buddhists was to culturalise the lives of the people, while the Mauryans were after their politisation at the expense of socio-cultural values of life. Both represented ideals antagonistic to each other. The Mauryan ideal stood for the regimen of life on the basis of political principles. The Buddhist ideal also claimed the superiority of a regimen of life on the realisation of cultural values. This clash of ideals, Mauryan and Buddhist, seems to disclose the mystery of 'Chaṇḍāśoka' and his metamorphosis into a 'Dharmāśoka'. Although the Thirteenth Rock-Edict brings out in bold relief the character of 'Chaṇḍāśoka' as a true specimen of the Mauryan world, yet it shows the far-reaching change that had set in the personality of Aśoka.

The edicts of Aśoka stand out pre-eminent as a challenge to the laws of politics and proclaim a new message of understanding, co-operation and integration for human welfare. The complete culturalisation of politics, government and the state was the avowed aim of Aśoka who made it known through his edicts. He destroyed with his own hands the creation of the Maurya without any remorse or compunction. The existence of the Mauryan political state was set at naught and in its place arose the Aśokan 'State' as the upholder and promoter of cultural values.

Aśoka found solace in the law of the Buddha after his disillusionment. The undercurrents of the Buddhist thought must have been effecting imperceptible changes in the evolution of the personality of Aśoka. As the war of Kalinga shook him thoroughly, he realised the importance of Buddhism as a philosophy of activism. He did not give up the world and turn a recluse in search of Nirvāṇa in the world of non-activity and struggleless living. The message of the Buddha was an inspiration to him in the struggle of life. It is this aspect of Buddhism that touched his innermost chord. Aśoka was a man of action. To lay down weapons as a defeatist is the antithesis of Aśoka. Even his whole unhingement is a proof of his sterling qualities as a man of action. Turning his back to the world was impossible for the man in Aśoka. Buddhism gave more impetus in activising him. The philosophy of Buddhism in its practical bearing on life and its problems was a quick incentive to his complete identification with principles of individual and social welfare. Although Aśoka ultimately became a staunch Buddhist in the orthodox sense of the term, yet he was no orthodox or a bigot or a fanatic. He had none of the spirit of a persecutor or an inquisitor. His soul was saturated with humanism.

The edicts not only reveal his evolutionary stages from 'Upāsaka' to a 'Budha-śaka' (Buddha-upāsaka) but also his all-absorbing interest in the preservation of the Buddhist 'Triad' and the promotion of the Buddhist doctrines. Aśoka's all comprehensive genius worked itself out in interpreting the law of the Buddha in a way that had baffled the minds of men of all times and climes. For the Buddhist world, he was staunch among the staunchest and spared no pains in bringing about the unification of the diverse elements in the Buddhist world and the intensification of the Buddhist activity. He was responsible for the discipline of the Buddhist Order as well as for the encouragement of the Buddhist literature among the Buddhists of the esoteric orders. In this respect, his contribution was positive and permanent. The Buddhists extolled him for his true zeal in matters of welfare of the Buddhist world. Though Aśoka was a great power and a pillar of strength for the Buddhists, his dynamic personallity was still a greater power for the general development of the non-Buddhist people along cultural lines. Therein lay his real greatness. It was in the universalisation of the Buddhist ideology as well as culture in the lives of the people in general that made him supreme among the great kings of the world.

The promulgation of the Buddhist culture in the form of a humanised culture was Aśoka's mission of life. That it could be adopted by all peoples without the distinction of caste, creed and colour was his faith. For him the philosophy of Buddhism was neither labyrinthine thoughts nor intellectual acrobatism; it was a simple message of cultivation and development of life-forces inherent in human personality. Aśoka understood and imbibed the true spirit of the Buddha and popularised it through his edicts. The Buddhist message of Aśoka was clear, plain, simple and non-cryptic. He analysed and denuded Buddhism and out of it gleaned and garnered what he considered as its 'basic' nucleus and essence. The masses of people of different faiths could not relish the subtle, though simple, philosophy of Buddhism. The truth of the matter is that the Buddha propounded his philosophy of life as a philosophy of commonsense and rationalism, but the man in the street, with all his prejudices, ignorance and shortcomings due to his milieu, could not possibly appreciate its real significance. His difficulty in falling in line with the Buddhist thinking and activity was the world of his own creation. He even failed to tackle intellectually his own life-problems. To assess 'things' in the term of values, a disciplined mind of the Buddhist is needed. In the light of the Buddhist philosophy, man and the world are judged in the scale of ultimate values. No religion of the world except Buddhism stressed upon the importance of the application of psychological laws to the solution of the mystery of life.

To appreciate, understand and realise the true spirit of the law of the Buddha presupposes an actively cultured mind. The Buddhist way was straight but uphill. Only those who had trained themselves in the Buddhist way could have gone far on the road of Buddhism or even reached their destination. But the masses steeped in ignorance and superstition could not have dared to look at the uphill highway to salvation. Though the teachings of the Buddha had a profound influence on the lives of the people of his age as well as of succeeding ages, the real message was restricted to the Buddhist community only. But the culturalising forces in Buddhism had worked wonders in humanising man and society.

The Kalinga war opened Aśoka's eyes to inherent dangers in the supreme political organisation for the well-being of human life. Aśoka so intensely visualised the dreadful and soul-killing nature of the political state that his hatred for political principles, guiding and controlling the life of the state, set deep in his heart. To him the political state was an embodiment of grossest instincts, finding outlet and expression in the field of politics. It sheds human blood without remorse for realising its ends; it creates and fosters hatred and disunity; it asserts, moreover, its own feigned superiority over political powers by infusing awe, dread and fear in the lives of the people. As an ugly and crude instrument of political forces, it debases and de-humanises the personality of man.

After Aśoka had waded through human blood on the battle-field of Kalinga, it dawned upon him that the Mauryan State was rotten to the core and its further retention would mean the perpetuation of evil in an organised form. It was a demon-like power under the garb of parading virtues. The Thirteenth Rock-Edict about the Kalinga war is a living confession of the futility of political principles of the Mauryan sovereign. In the eyes of Aśoka, war not only creates morbidity and callousness in man but actually smothers all his humaneness also. Society, culture and civilization are destroyed by it. The laws of politics sow seeds of hostility between country and country. The spirit of politics thrives on war. Right or wrong, war does not decide. The victory of power politics is no conquest of right. The success of politics and the victory in war are considered as political wisdom, but in the scale of ethics victory thus scored is no real victory. The psychological result of such a victory is the perpetuity of war between the conqueror and the conquered, because the foundation of their relation is not laid on human values. The conqueror is and remains a conqueror, while the conquered is kept down as conquered. Between them no co-operation of purpose, no commonness of ideal or interest and no social integration can be possible. Thus war ends no war but perpetuates itself.

Having discredited the utility of gross political principles, Aśoka rebuilt the foundation of the state on humanising principle of common weal. He arrived at conclusions that man, society and the state could eventually prosper on cultural factors alone. That man and society are for the state and the well-being of the state is the welfare of man and society, as expounded by Kauṭilya, is disclaimed by Aśoka. To him, the *raison d'etre* of the state was rooted in the idea of the welfare of man and society. For no other purpose except human welfare did the state exist. This was the fundamental difference between the Mauryan and Aśokan States. As the all-comprehensive principle of the Aśokan 'State' was human welfare, it was for this reason alone that Aśoka gave clear indications in his edicts that every moment of his life would be dedicated to the welfare of all men. In this way, he bridged the gulf of discrimination between the state and the people and formed a family relationship of common interest and purpose. Aśoka brought home to the people through his edicts that he was their father, the people his children and the officials of the government their intelligent nurses (P.E. IV). By adopting such a method of government Aśoka made his point crystal clear that the forming of human relationship between the state and the people was not possible on the basis of fear and dread, exploitation and conquest. Thus stamping out tyranny, fear and dread, he established a father-children relationship on Ahiṃsā as a principle of humanism. The word 'father' conveyed to him a deep sense of responsibilities. He was too keen to discharge them as a father and the people as his children should feel obliged to him as their father (S.R.E. II). The Aśokan 'State' thus resolved into a great family which was governed by the law of the heart.

The paternal law of Aśoka was not only enacted for the people of the state, but he also acquainted the people of other states with the spirit of his paternal message through the principle of Ahiṃsā and assured them that they should not dread him as his behaviour towards them would be that of a father towards his children. He would regard their well-being and welfare as a father. Thus his adoption of a paternal principle towards them strikes at the root of political concept and pupose of the state, viz., the establishment of political supremacy, the existence of diplomatic service and of sixfold policy, the activties of espionage. the propaganda for political exploitation. Aśoka was desirous of bringing the whole country under the sway of a humanised culture with a view to deadening the universal law of politics and to developing the personality of man on the principle of humanism. This tendency of his was the signpost of a new culture for man.

The culturalising forces in Buddhism worked wonders in humanising man and society. Such Buddhist factors as a lever in the cultural upbuilding of the people were no unknown facts to Aśoka The resuscitation of Buddhism could be made possible, to a limited extent, through the Buddhist organisations, but Buddhism as a humanised culture, could universalise and become a common heritage for all peoples on the basis of its cultural forces inherent in the law of the Buddha. It is this aspect of Buddhism that had impressed Aśoka.

Aśoka's dedication to such a humanised culture was an indirect service to Buddhism. The Buddhist culture signified to him harmony and co-operation in human relationship. Through abiding peace among different peoples as a cardinal principle in the regulation of human affairs, the Buddhist culture could generate forces of social adjustment and understanding, co-operation and integration. In the realm of peace, Aśoka visualised the end of all disintegrating and corrosive elements in the lives of lhe people As the existence of the supreme political power and organisation depends upon war and its paraphernalia, bringing in its trail the war-mindedness of the people, so the principle of peace negates the spirit of political aggrandisement and establishes a new human relationship between people and people as well as a new social order for promoting human welfare on the basis of human persuasion, understanding, appreciation and toleration. This is what Aśoka tried to achieve through his cultural 'state'.

On the evidence of his edicts, it becomes clear that Aśoka differed from the ideal kings of the past in the method of promoting the cultural growth of their people. Not the 'sound of instruction' but the 'sound of festivity' was heard in their realms. If it suited their political scheme, they did do some sort of public good. But the political well-being of the state was the main consideration in the cultural propaganda and activity. The people as human material for further development and culturalisation did not form the basis of their political progress. Not the 'political' state but the people had to adjust and fit in the scheme of politics. The upbuilding of the state on the science of human relationship, understanding, cooperation and integration was beyond the comprehension of the kings of the past. Though the people as a chief factor in the life of the state are discussed in the ancient political literature on polity and government, they were not given their rightful place and status in the political organisation according to the Aśokan standpoint.

Aśoka was well aware of the fact that the kings of the past had taken no practical steps so that "the men might (be made to) progress by adequate promotion of morality". It was their wishful thinking or a pious desire that never materialised. The governments of the pre-Aśokan periods had no departments which could promote cultural activities. No 'Dharma-Mahamatras' existed then. The Fifth Rock-Edict shows that "these are occupied with all sects in establishing morality; they are occupied with servants and masters for the happiness of those who are devoted to morality, they are occupied everywhere." The Aśokan 'State' not only undertook to discharge the function of educating the people in Buddhist culture but also aligned itself with the ideas of public weal. It was the spirit of public welfare that permeated the whole activity of the Aśokan 'State'. The happiness of the people was the Aśokan aim. The Aśokan 'State' came into existence only for the welfare of the people. "In times past," Aśoka observes," neither the disposal of affairs nor submission of reports at any time did exist before. But I have made the following arrangement. Reporters are posted everywhere with instructions to report to me the affairs of the people at any time. For I am never content in exerting myself and in dispatching business; for I consider it my duty (to promote) the welfare of all men. The radical change that had been wrought by Aśoka in the spirit and form of the state was indicative of transvaluation of values. The Sixth Rock-Edict is a serious utterance of Aśoka. The affairs of the people were his affairs and their disposal was considered no easy task by him.

He was of the opinion that unless he dedicated his entire life to the selfless service of the people, the responsibility of public welfare could not be discharged. For him there was no halfway house and to do public work in a half-hearted manner would be futile. It was the ardent and burning desire of the man in Aśoka to identify himself completely with the affairs of the people, so that he could be able to do real service to them. He was also aware of the fact that without 'exertion' in the way of promoting the welfare of all men nothing could be achieved. To him this was the 'root' of all good work[9]. "For no duty is more important," observes Aśoka, "than promoting the welfare of all men and whatever effort I am making is made in order that I may discharge the debt which I owe to living beings that I may make them happy in this world and that they may attain heaven in the other (world)![10]

Being conscious of the 'debt' of service to all living beings and of his limitations in paying back the debt honourably, he had to discipline and drill his sense of life to the higher needs and aspirations of humanity or to the ideal of maximum good to all, because it was difficult to accomplish the ideal without great zeal.[11] The materialisation of the Aśoka's mission rested upon his intense love and affection for the people, his unflagging exertion in attaining *summum bonum* for all, his undying zeal in promoting the welfare of all and his indomitable will in giving concrete shape to his ideal.

The Aśokan ideal, the welfare of all men, arose out of the social philosophy of Buddhism. Aśoka expounded it with a view to popularising Buddhist culture for all men without the distinction of race, country and religion. It was not the drastic way of a rabid fanatic that he adopted for the actualisation of his socio-cultural ideal, but sought it in unity and harmony among the diversified phases of family life and society. Unless the principle of humanism were applied to family and society, no co-operation and fellow-feeling among the members of family as well as of society could be possible. Their mutual behaviour and relationship was determined and regulated by their sense of co-operation, self-control, regard and reverence. In this way the family, a community in miniature, could adjust itself to a greater society of human beings.

For cultivating cultural values the family members including elders and youngers, friends and acquaintances, servants and slaves should become conscious of their mutual obligations towards one another. Aśoka laid importance on obedience to elders and parents; on liberality to relatives, friends and acquaintances: on courtesy to Brāhmaṇas and Śramaṇas and on kindness to servants and slaves. Thus the members of family, while keeping the principle of humanism in tact, would succeed in cementing human relationship with the spirit of co-operation, unity and harmony. What Aśoka meant to convey was that even the smallest, though important units of a greater society, should be a living model of human concord and happiness, but such small units could function alone on principles of social co-operation, unity and toleration.

In the multiplicity of social phenomenon, Aśoka perceived the presence of the continuity of oneness of life and its culturalisation was his mission. That life in its myriad manifestations is exposed to dangers and exploitation was no unknown fact to Aśoka. The survival of all-pervading life depends upon the principle of the sanctity of life. It was the supreme duty of Asoka to preserve, develop and culturalise life-forces because the destruction of life implied the end of all activities, human and non-human. The sanctity of life, as a Buddhist idea, is the basis for the development of human personality. In the higher struggle of life, it plays a great role in accomplishing its end in view, the salvation of life. Any attempt at its destruction is to let the work of the life-mission remain unfinished and incomplete. Only in its preservation can life unfold its hidden potentialities for its own good and well-being. The whole human personality is at the mercy of the concept of the sanctity of life. Killing or destruction is unhuman, inhumane and non-human. Such were the Buddhist ideas regarding the sanctity and preservation of life which Aśoka laconically explained in his Girnar Rock Edict.

The non-destruction of life creates in man new values, a new standard of morality and a new approach to human behaviourism. It humanises instincts, ideas and actions and tends to sublimate them. The underlying idea in the Aśokan philosophy was to elevate the life of the people to a higher plane of thinking and living on the basic principle of the sanctity of life. As living is an art, not an erratic flow of life-force in its crude form, so Aśoka brought home the Buddhist view to all the people that right living requires certain conditions for its development and survival. He calls it "an ancient rule", whereby he takes the Buddhist 'sting' out of it so that the principle of living may be acceptable to all without any bias or hindrance. This "anciant rule" comprised four cardinal principles on which life could flourish and prosper in accordance wlth the Aśokan way. Obedience, liberality, abstention and moderation were considered meritorious by Aśoka. Under these active principles the socialisation or culturalisation of human instincts and behaviour could be made more effective, dynamic and creative. These would help in the development of the sense of social discipline and control, of social concord, of social commonsense in the preservation of life forces and of social freedom from coercion and exploitation.

The upbringing of an individual on lines of social education and culture, as chalked out by Aśoka, would also lead to the 'promotion of morality.' 'Nearly all the Aśokan edicts are replete with ideas and feelings of morality. It is the word, Dhamma, that has been used for morality in the edicts. Thus in the textual meaning Dhamma assumes a moral or humanising principle, as a guide to the general development of man in his individual as well as social capacities. Dhamma is not a creed of a particular sect. It is neither a negative assertion nor a 'No' to expressions of life. Dhamma is assertive, positive and a big 'Yea' to life. It squares with the basic principle in all the religions of the world which claims the remaking of man on lines that promote his human aspects and faculties. It was the unifying and unified spirit of Dhamma that Aśoka made his own: It was the idea of universality and commoness in Dhamma with other religions that had a hold on him. Out of the basic concept of Dhamma, Aśoka evolved and promulgated his own philosophy, to be appreciated by all as their common philosophy of life. In his own 'microcosm' of religion, he visualised a macrocosm of universal religion. In his own person the world reflected ; in his own mind the minds lived and experienced the universality of Dhamma. It was with such fervour and zeal that he expounded through the edicts the eternal principle of human likeness, sameness and oneness in all the races of the world. Man was, to him, the same man all over the world ; his likes and dislikes attract and repel him to the world. All human beings are under the immutable law of cause and effect.

Through the promotion of Dhamma, Aśoka did not wish to create a society of utopians, or of cranky moralists, or of spiritual maniacs, but men of robust commonsense and sanguine instincts. As the ultimate aim of Dhamma was the happiness of all human beings in this as well as in the other world, so Aśoka made it plain to them that happiness could be achieved by all. The condition laid down was that it could not be attained "without great love, careful examination, great obedience, great fear (of sin) and great energy." This clearly shows that the people have to realise the importance of cultural forces in the scheme of human education for human progress and welfare. Aśoka was too well aware of the inherent weakness of man. That a "person devoid of good conduct" could not possibly come in line with the progressive attainments of those who have earned the credentials of Dhamma was Aśoka's belief. Human discipline bestowing meaning and content to life, is the necessary condition to 'good conduct.' What Aśoka meant to say was that man requires certain moral assests to neutralise the disintegrating forces in his own person. He made it too plain in his edicts "Sin is easily committed" and that "it is dfficult to perform virtuous deeds." The idea of 'sin' as conceived by Aśoka was different from that of religionist. "Passions" of "fierceness, cruelty, anger, pride, envy" tend to undermine, demean and de-culturalise the personality of man. Aśoka considered these 'sinful'. The Aśokan insight into the working of human mind reveals the fact that men "do not at all regard (*their*) *evil deeds* (*thinking*)." The committal of 'evil deeds' or 'sin' is the result of a non-thinking attitude of mind and the 'virtuous deeds' are done deliberatively and consciously. Aśoka looked at evil deed as a deculturalising process and virtuous deed as a process of culturalisation. In the culturalisation of man, "compassion, liberality, truthfulness, purity, gentleness and goodness are essential factors that go to bestow "the gift of spiritual insight." This is the message of Dhamma which Aśoka gave out to the people of the world. For the progress of Dhamma, Aśoka had adopted two ways : moral restriction and conversion. In the Aśokan scale of ultimate values, 'moral restriction' is of little consequence" as compared with 'conversion' that promotes Dhamma more considerably. The edicts of Aśoka give a vivid picture of Aśokan propaganda and activity in the promulgation of Dhamma either by moral-restriction or by conversion, but no evidence is forthcoming on the data of edicts that Aśoka only insisted on the conversion of the people. To him, conversion was a desideratum, an ideal to be pursued constantly and incessantly, but "there is no such gift as the gift of morality, or acquaintance through morality, or the distribution of morality, or kinship through morality."

In the realm of Aśoka, all classes and sects of people resided. Their conversion would have been an impossible task. The greatness of the Aśokan genius exhibited itself in promotion, infiltration, percolation and absorption of the basic principle of Dhamma into the deverse systems of different sects or religions. The forces in Buddhist culture were engendered to surcharge the whole atmosphere of the Aśokan 'State' with a view to Budhifying. The edicts bear the testimony to the fact that Buddhist culture progressed far and wide and set deep in the hearts of the people of that age. The Seventh and Twelfth Rock-Edicts are glaring and outstanding examples of the Aśokan principle of tolerance towards all sects residing in the kingdom of Aśoka. He gave them freedom to follow their religions, but made them realise the importance of "self-control and purity of mind" as enjoined on them by their religious principles, in consonnance with the basic ideas of Dhamma. Aśoka explained to them that humanising forces or effects of "great liberality" could be nullified, if "self-control, purity of mind, gratitude and firm devotion" were lacking in them. Indirectly, Aśoka encouraged Dhamma through the phraseology and ideology of the different living sects or religions of his time. He showed them their way according to their lights, but that way was the Buddhist way. the Twelfth Rock-Edict shows the working of the Aśokan mind in bringing about cultural transformation of all sects or religions on the amalgam of Dhamma.

Thus Aśoka established a true ideal for the man of religion as a Buddhist or non-Buddhist. It was the burning desire of Aśoka to attain either glory or fame in the socio-cultural domain of Dhamma and not in the political sphere of activity. "King does not think," reads the Tenth Rock Edict, "that either glory or fame conveys much advantage, except (on account of his aim that) in the present time, and in the distant (future), men may (be induced) by him to practise obedience to morality and that they may conform to the duties of morality. On this (account) king is desiring glory or fame. But whatever effort king is making, all that is for the sake of merit in the other world and in order that all men may run little danger." In the popularisation of Dhamma, Aśoka hoped to achieve glory or fame which meant that he would be an active instrument in bestowing the gift of morality' or the 'benefit of morality' on all men. So glory or fame signified to him the ultimate glory of Dhamma in the lives of the people.

The cultural activities of Aśoka were not confined to the people of his own kingdom. "The unconquered borderers" outside his kingdom were also addressed by him. His message to them reveals his hatred for the idea of political conquest, aggrandisement and exploitation. As a cosmopolitan Buddhist, his heart yearned to welcome the 'outsiders' into a common brotherhood of Dhamma. The Second Separate Rock-Edict levels upon the concept of a political state, of political suzerainty, of political domination. It is an open chapter written by Aśoka for all men to read with their own eyes the futility of political maxims and practices, of artifical barriers between country and country, between people and people, between state and state. The loftiness of the personality of Aśoka is the cosmopolitan way. As a real cultured man and not as a king-conqueror, he approached the 'unconquered borderers' with a heart full of sympathy, affection and humaneness. Here lies ths greatness of Aśoka's achievement in the field of humanism

It is an undeniable fact that Aśoka gave out his messages through the edicts in connection with the significance and beauty of the principle of Dhamma, but certain edicts are special messages to those who looked after the welfare of the people. These disclose the working of the Aśokan scheme of humanism. Steps that were taken by Aśoka to materialise the ideal of humanism were of practical nature. He himself was a zealous and untiring worker in the cause of Dhamma through his 'tours of morality.' In this way he came in direct touch with the people, "instructing them in morality and questioning them about morality" Aśoka was a personification of the spirit of Dhamma. He also instructed his Mahamatras in the spirit of Dhamma with view to achieving his ideal through their active agency. As these were the high officers of the Aśokan 'State' who were "occupied with many thousands of man, with the object of gaining the affection of men, they should remember in their dealings with the people that all men were the children of Aśoka and as on behalf of his own children, he desired that they should be provided with complete welfare and happiness in this world and in the other world, the same he desired also on behalf of all men The Mahāmātras must pay attention to such instructions in the discharge of their work. They should be ever ready to administer justice to all without any traces of impartiality. Aśoka was of the opinion that he who is fatigued in the administration of justice, will not rise, but one ought to move, to walk, and to advance. The failure of the Mahāmātras in the rightful observance of duties was not only "a great evil" in itself, but it would be a hindrance in the realisation of the Aśokan ideal. To other officers (Lājukas) of the Aśokan 'State', he brought home that the welfare and happiness of the country people was their prime duty and they were to look after them like intelligent nurses.

This is how Aśoka, not in his personal capacity alone hut also through his 'agents', discharged the debt of Dhamma honourably. In propagating and popularising Buddhist culture, the Aśokan edicts were the real sources of inspiration to the people of all times. During the time of Aśoka, the people were persuaded to penetrate deep into the meaning and significance of the edicts and to realise the part they had to play in achieving the Aśokan ideal. In creating a new 'State' for the well-being, welfare and happiness on socio-cultural foundation, Aśoka served tha cause of Dhamma by spreading Buddhist culture among all men.

INDEX TO PART I

Abbotabad, 64
abhayadāna, 161
ābhigamika-guṇā, 207
abhirāmaka, 220,
Abhisāra, 101, 103, 126
abhiśāpa 314
abhisheka, 5, 7f, 10, 13, 25, 31f, 36f, 52ff, 57ff, 61f, 131
aboriginal settlements, 317
Achæmenian, 305, 319f
empire, 331, influence, 100, inscription, 93n, 96, 98, suzerainty, 330
āchariya-susrūsā, 273
Achelakas, 240
Adhammavijaya, 284
adhimāsa, 131, 158
adhirāja, 91
Adhyȧksha, 178, 194
adhyātmavidyā, 316
ādīnava, 274
Administration, 166f, Magadhan system of, 123
Aelian, 67n, 231
agaparākrama, 159
Agastya, 315, 317
aga usāha, 159
aghātam ardhamāsikam, 257
Agni, 283, 286, 302f, 304, 307, 311f, 316
Agnibrahmā, 10, 35, 37, 52, 54
Agni Gṛhapati, 14, 16
Agni Vaiśvānara, 333n
Agrammes, 42, 47, 65f, 104, 162, 308
Agronomoi, 195
āhāra, 152, 188
ashiṁsā, 100, 282, 312, 323, 360
Ahura Mazda, 330
Aindra mahābhisheka, 13
Aiyangar, Rangaswami, 134ff, 139, 160, 163f, 164n
Aiyangar, S. K., 112, 116n
Ajamīda, 290
Ajantā, 106
Ajapatha, 290
Ajātaśatru, 15n, 17, 22, 24, 39f, 40n, 118f, 149, 171, 175, 177, 311
Ajitakeśakambala, 311n
Ājīvakas, 7f, 10, 25, 29, 37f, 44, 57, 65, 208, 216, 238ff, 318f, 341, 353
ajjava (ārjava), 282
Ākbar, 149
Ākrandasāra, 128
Akshadarśa, 169n
akshati sarvabhūtānaṁ, 277
Akshavāpa, 144, 168
akshudratā, 279
Alasanda, 96n, 290
ālasiya, 233, 251, 278
Alexander, 42, 45, 47, 51, 66, 69, 98, 101, 103f, 110, 129, 240, 287, 308, 319, 321, 322, 328, 330, 350, Invasion of, 42n, 96, 103, King of Epirus, 7, 128, 110, life of, 51n
Alexandria, 96, 96n

Alikasudara, 109f
Allitrochades, 46
Amachcha, 144, 146, 178, 274, 310
Amarasiṁha, 124, 148
Amarāvatī, 112
Amātya, 60f, 150f, 172ff, 176, 192, 196f
Āmbhi, 103
Āmbhīyas, 122f
Amitrachates, 46
Aṁtā, 147, mahāmātā, 147
Aṁtekini, 109f
Aṁtiyoka, 7, 109
anaṁtaṁ puñaṁ, 271
anārambho prāṇānaṁ, 139, 269, 273, 278
anātha, 255, 257, 260, 262
Anāthapiṇḍika, 245n
anāvuti, 233, 251, 278
Anaxarchus, 321
Andhraka, 81n, 89, 100, 325, 336
Andhra, 77ff, 84f, 89ff, 106, 110, 127, 129, 287, 309, 326, Pāradas, 83, Parindas, 83, patha, 90
Andhra people,- 89, pura, 89, race,
Anga, 35, 72f, 289n, 305
Angalaukikas, 102, 290, 305
Ang-Magadha, 40n, 58, 126, 290
aṇhaya, 275
Anotatta lake, 18, 82, 344
Antamahāmātras, 147, 178, 189, 204, —pālas, 117, 169, 178, 189, 204f, 263
Antarvaṁśika, 168f, 182
Antialkidas, 328
Antigonas Gonatas, 7, 110, 128f, 287
Antiochus, I, 110, 327, Theos, 7, 69, 109f, 128
anubadha - pajā, 260
anugraha, 257
anukampā, 278
anuposatha, 217
Anurādhapura, 110, 114
anusaṁyāna, 158, 186, 195
anuyātā khattiyā, 255
apalibodha, 260
apaparisrava, 274
Aparagoyāna, 71, 84, 89, 107, 107n, 109
Apara Matsya, 76, 91, Kuntibhoja, 76
Aparānta, 51, 71, 76f, 81ff, 88ff, 101f, 106, 116, 125
Apara-rājagiri, 81
Aparaseliya, 81n, 325
aparāṭā, 149
Āpastamba, 139
apāya, 247
aphalusam, 275
Appollodotus, 96
appamāda, 27, 158, 250, 287
apuña, 248, 271, 274
Arabia, 330n, 332
Arabic alphabet, 339
Arachosia, 69, 105, 327
Arhants, 25
Arachi, Hetti, 185n
Archimedes, 350
Ardhamāgadhī, 122f, 184
arhaṇa of Vāsudeva, 189
Ari, 127
Arimitra, 128
Arimitra-mitra, 128
Chakkavattivattam, 246
Arjuna, 82, 95, 288, 288n, 295ff, 311
Arkatos, 111

Armania, 330n
Aramaic, 339
Arrian, 69, 100, 120f, 173, 188n, 265, 286, 308, 309, 309n, 320, 320n, 350
Ārshṭaka, 85, 100, 320
Arthavijaya, 284, 284n
Aruppakottai, 115
Aryan civilization, 301
Aryandom, 304, 316
Aryanisation of India, 311
Āryaputra, 37, 57, 62, 170, 191
Āryasaṁgha, 60
Āryāvarta, 116, 307
Āsamudrā pṛithivī, 63
Āsandimitrā, 53, 54n, 60
Asia Minor, 94n, 96, 305, 331f
Asiatic civilization, 328
Asika, 86, 96, 296
āsinava, 275, gāmini, 271, 275
Aśmaka, 89, 91
Asokārāma, 11, 25, 178n, 334
Aśokavalla, 2
Aspacians, 103
āsramapūjanam, 257
āsrava, 248, 274f
Assaka, 89, 100
assama, 65, 68, 82, 101, 103f, 106, 116n, 118, 289n, 302, 310, 275ff
Assyrians, 100, 312, 320
āsulopa, 233, 275, 277
Asura Conquest, 164, 234, 284, 284n, 290
Aśvaghosha, 39, 124, 261n
Aśvaka, 70n, 87, 89, 91, 100, 320
aśvamedha, 15
Aṭavī, 83, 85, 91f, 116f, 117, 199, 204, 206, 286
Āṭavika, 83, 91f, 291
aṭaviya, 127, 130, 153, 162
Aṭavirakkhikas, 92, 205
Aṭavīpāla, 92, 117, 169, 178, 263
Āṭavyas, 127
aṭhabhāgiye, 165
atthakaraṇa, 249
athasaṁtīrana, 158, 239
Athenaios, 46
Athens, 98
Atiśa, 302
ātman, 323
ātmasampat, 207
Ātreya, 102, 309
atpapāsaṁḍapūjā, 272
attukkaṁsana, 277
Augrasainya, 42n
Augustan age, 299
Aurangzeb, 355
Auśanasas, 122, 226n
Avanti, 35, 51, 58, 64, 73f, 76, 78, 85ff, 89, 117, 146, 189, 191, two kingdoms of, 86
Vindhyan, 75n, 86
viceroy for, 194
Avadhūtas, 240
avadhyāḥ, 258
avarodhana, 219
Avestan religion, 330
avihiṁsā, 230, 269, 273, 278, 282
avijitas, 117
Ayomukha, 79
āyushmān, 131

Bairāṭ, 75
Babylon, 104, 305, 312, 330
Bactrians, 320, 347
Baghelkhand, 85
Bahasati Mita, 234
bahukalāṇam, 271, 274

bahuśrutā, 271
balādhikya, 292
Balkh-Badkshān, 95
Baltistan, 95
baṁbhanibhā, 255
Bāṇa, 41
bandhanam, 154, 200, 282
bandhanāgāra, 199f, 262,
mokshaṇam, 257
Bandhupālita, 55, 57
Bandyopadhyaya, N. C., 121
Banerjea, Gouranganath, 321
Banerjea, Jitendra Nath, 346
Barābar Hills, 278, 341,
cave inscriptions, 17, 126, 216
Barbaras, 100ff, 104, 129, 288
Barbarians, 321
Bārhadratha dynasty, 39
Bārhaspatya, 122, school of, 266n, system, 241n
Barua, 37n, 40n, 91f, 100ff
Basu, Manindra Mohan, 201n
Beal, Samuel, 24n, 26n, 49n, 65n, 66n, 70n, 103n, 107n, 111n, 115n, 301n, 334n, 343
Beluchistan, 69, 81, 100, 105, 331
Benares, 8, 106, 147, 168
Bengal, 65, 68f, 72f, 82, 106, 288f, 300f, 308
Berar, 74, 86
Berhut, 75n
Bhadaṁta, 216
Bhadrā, 40
Bhadrabāhu, 319
Bhadrāśvavarsha, 107, 109
Bhāgabhadra, Kāsīputra, 328
Bhakti, 257, 295, 297, Yoga, 297
Bhallavis, 316n
Bhāṇḍāgārika, 172
Bhandarkar, D. R., 4, 27, 31, 64, 75, 83, 85, 89, 91, 97f, 112, 117, 132f, 171, 189, 191f, 201n, 216, 225, 268, 274, 317, 329f, 333, 340, 347ff, 353
Bhandarkar, Sir R. G., 111
Bharadvāja, 102, 122, 122n, 309
Bhāratavarsha, 70f, 108, 128f, 308, 349
Bharhut, 50n, 267
Bhāsa, 129, 129n, 257
bhaṭamaya, 262
Bhattasali, Dr., 116n
Bhau Daji, 148n
Bhavabhūti, 15
bhāvaśuddhi, 279
bherighosha, 348
Bhikkhu-gatika, 28, parisā, 159
Bhikkhussa bhatika, 216
Bhīma, 288, military expedition of, 68
Bhīmaratha, 85
Bhīshma, 291
Bhogavardhana, 91
Bhojas, 72, 74, 83f, 88, 91, 127, 287, 287n, 309, 326
Bhojaka, 78, 83, 85f, 88, 91, 129, 234, 290
bhojana, 171, 218f
Bhojapitaras, 83ff, Pitinikas, 83
putras, 84, 85, rulers, 85
bhrūṇahan, 242
Bhuvaneswar, 8
bhūtatā, 136
Bhṛigukachchha, 76
Bimbisāra, 17, 24, 39, 144, 171, 220
Bindusāra, 3, 9, 24, 33ff, 46ff, 58f, 100, 176n, 189, 208f, 309n, 327

Bloch, Jules, 71
Black Forest (Kāḷakavana), 72
Brachmanes, 240, 310, 313, 317, 322
Brahmā, 267, 300, 307, 314
Brāhmaṇa, as lawgiver, 312, chaplain, 326, families, 111, 244, gahapatika, 252, 255f, parivrājakas, 242, 244, Śramaṇa movement, 319, Śramanite, 318, Śrotriyas, 185n, settlements, 309, teachers, 258, 303
Brahmanical ascetic, 171, 261, doctrine, 353, idea, 315, ritual, 346, school of political thought, 226, 330, 338
Brahmanism, 55, 136, 232, 258, 271, 286, 303, 307, 310, 313ff, secular, 318, 323
Brahmatva, 300
Brahmāvarta, 307, 309
Brahmaveda, 228, 323
Brāhmī, 2, 57
Brahmoism, 322
Bṛihadratha, 39, 288, 294, 354
Bṛihantas, 101
Bṛihaspati, 55, 176, Mitra, 234, 290
British constitution, 140
Bodhāyana, 72, 139, 258, 316n
Bodhgayā, 2, 4, 106, 217, 300, 332, Temple, 301
Bodhi-dassana, 217
borderers, 117, 185, 367
Borobudur, shrine of, 301
Bo-tree, 12, 32, 53, 60, 317, 333, destruction of, 12
Buddha, 122, 126ff, 142, 145, 155, 159, 164, 167ff
Buddhadatta, 110
Buddhaghosa, 2, 4f, 9n, 16f, 26, 53, 81n, 83f, 84n, 88f, 100f, 106, 106n, 110, 142, 149f, 174, 178, 182, 186, 191, 194, 216, 235, 255n, 260n, 270n, 274, 280f, 306n, 336
Buddha Koṇāgamana, 7f, 352, 357, 359
Buddha Śākyamuni, 225
Buddha's Sāsana, 10, 237, social scheme, 237, teachings, 250, words, 239
Buddhism, 113, 215, 217, 225f, 271, 273, 278, 299ff, 317, 322ff, 328ff, 337, 337n, 339, 340, 353, 359, 361, 363, conversion to, 33, philosophy of, 357f, rise of, 39
Buddhist brotherhood, 333, Canon, 31, Canonical texts, 137, church, 61, 325, 333, Community, 333, 359, Council at Vaiśālī, 334, countries, 353, symbol, 344, khanti, 282, laity, 216f, learning, 302, legend, 49, 82, 170, literature, 71, 107, 219, 245, 274, mendicant, 334, midland, 78, 80, 89n, 103, 308, 322, mission, 129, 301f, 318, 325f, monks, 245, nuns, 245, order, 52, 54, 245, 333, philosophy, 358, psychoethical concepts, 275f, psychological term, 249, religious sentiment, 245, Sangha, 153, 215, schismatics, 336, seats of learning, 302, sects, 325, 333, 335, shrines, 301, teachers, 215, 336

Buddha - śaka, 358
Bühler, 132, 225, 258, 344
Bunio Nanjio, 137n
Burmese alphabet, 339
Bury, 320n

Caird, John, 242
Calingae, 69, 77n
Canarese Countries, 319
Cambyses, 100
Cāruvākī, 52
Caste distinction, 318, privilege, 298
Central Asia, 108, 302, Himalayan region, 101, 129, kingdom, 102, India, 91, 289
Cerobothra, 112
Ceylon, 65, 108, 112ff, 208, 300f, 305, 308, 322, 326f, 335, 340, 342, 350, Buddhist mission to, 52, national religion of, 353
Chaitya, 26, 54, 341, dassanaṁ, 217
chakravāka, 293
Chaldea, 305
Chaldeans, 312
chaṁḍiye, 275, 277
Champā, 38, 39n, 48, 208
Champāran, 65, 82, 104, 289
Chāṇakya, 46, 48, 309n, 348, 350
Chaṇḍāśoka, 19, 22, 33, 356f
chaṇḍikka, 275ff
Chaṇḍagirika, 23
Chandragupta, 37, 44f, 48ff, 58, 69, 81, 88, 104, 119, 121, 147f, 148n, 150, 162f, 191, 208f, 231, 264, 308f, 331, 348, 353
Chandras of Bengal, 301
Chang Kien, 96
Chapaḍa, 187
Chaplain, 172, 176
Charaka, 199
charito purāṇo, 229
Charmakhaṇḍikaṣ, 102
Charpentier, 46
Charsadda, 93
Chatterjee, G. D., 2n, 6, 48, 159n, 216, 345n
Chāturanta, 130, 286
chāturmāsya, 171, 231, 257
Chedi, 39, 73, 88, 288, 291, 312, royal house, 208
Chinghiz Khan, 355
Chera, 112
Chiang Hsia-pias, 2f, 301
chikīchhā, 259
China, 80n, 289f, 301f, 305
Chīnapati, 105
Chinese alphabet, 339
Chin Hills, 82, 103, 288
Chirnock, 101n, 309n
Chitaldrug, 88, 111
Chola, 69, 77, 79, 90, 101, 106, 109ff, 111n, 113f, 117, 129, 185, 287, 309, 326
Choṇḍrakerala, 111n, 288
chora rajju, 193
Christ, 330, 332
Christian Churches, 332, Era, 334, idea of forbearance, 282, nations, 332
Christianity, 271, 324, 326n, 331f
Chulla Himavanta, 108
City Judiciaries, 59, 117, 153, 169, 190
civilization of the Saptasindhu, 304

Classical Sanskrit, 340, sources, 167, writers, 65, 103, 105, 109, 113, 118, 121, 126, 160, 162, 175, 188, 239f, 264, 267, 308f, 310n, 317f
Clemens, 240, 313
Codomanus, 101
Colebrooke, 240
Conjeeveram, 110
Cophes, 69
Codrington, 343
Coromondel, 110
Coronation Durbar, 286f
Council, 143, 335, 335n, Second, 41n
Council of ministers, 299
Crown prince, 172
Cultural Conquest, 283
Cunningham, 67n, 68, 73, 73n, 76, 94n
Curtius, 42, 47, 65f, 67n, 162
Cyrene, 110
Cyrus, 100, 105

daḍhabhatitā, 277, 279
Dakshiṇāpatha, 71, 74, 79, 83, 91, 290, 307
Dākshiṇātya, 67, 71, 74, 90
dālakā, 169
daḷhaparakkama, 250
daṁḍa-samatā, 282
Damilas, 110, 114
dāna, 161f, 237, 239, 257, 266, 269, 277ff, 282, karma, 257, sālā, 43, saṁvibhāga, 279
daṇḍa, 161, 238, dhara, 156
Daṇḍaka, 86f, 91
Dāṇḍakya Bhoja, 86
daṇḍa - nīti, 155, 210, 226
Dandamis, 240, 319, 321
Daṇḍapāla, 169
Dantapura, 77, 308
Dāpaka, 152, 179
Daradas, 94f, 101
Dārādhyaksha, 182
Daripatha, 94n
Darius, 2, 94n, I, 100, 329, 332, III, 101, 320
dasa rājadhammā, 252
Daśārṇas, 74, 76n, 85
Daśaratha, 1, 2, 56ff, 216, 290, 352f
dāsavya, 262
Dauvārika, 169
Ḍavāka, 68, 116
ḍayā, 278
dāyāda, 10
Deccan, 74, 90, 111, 301, 308, 319, people, 90, rulers, 234
Dehra Dun, 65, 80
Deimachos, 47, 327
Democracy of Europe, 140
Democritus, 321
deśāchāra, 135, devatā, 231, nakshatra, 314
Deva, 51, 267, 306
Devabhūmi, 316
Devadatta, 334
Devadharman, 352
Devānampriya, 16f, 124, 131, 224, 267, 326, 328
Devaprastha, 101
Devatānampiyo, 241
Deva, world, 247
Devī, 9f, 12, 24, 51, 169, 219
devīkumālā, 169
dhamma, 137, 142, 251, 268, 278, 286n, 365ff
dhaṁmacharaṇa, 278
dhamma-ghosha, 348, ghoshakas, 251, mangala, 232,

niyama, 138f, 157, 187, 221, 237, 251, 261n
dhammānupaṭipati, 142
dhammānusathini, 157, 187, 232, 251
Dhamma-thambhāni, 157, 185, 251, 278
Dhammavaḍhi, 154, vidhi, 138, vijaya, 125, 163, vinaya, 215, vuḍḍhi, 217
dhammena abhivijiya, 164
Dhammo Sanātano, 229
Dhanananda, 42f
Dhanushkoṭi, 70n
Dharaṇī, 174
Dharma, 37, 134ff, 141f, 225, 227ff, 230, 235, 237, 254, 257, 268, 271, 273, 278, 280, 283, 324n, 328, 346, Aśoka's, 267, 287, department of, 180
dharmahāni, 248
Dharmamahāmātras, 7, 35, 195, 222, 239, 260, 322, 326, 362
Dhamma-niyāmatā, 136
Dharmapāla, vikramaśīla, 300
dharma-samanvaya, 272
Dharmāśoka-Maharājavihāra, 352
Dharmapravartaka, 136, 330
Dharma, principles of, 330
Dharma samanvaya, 272
Dharmāśoka, 6n, 20, 22, 41, 49, 336, 257, mahārāja-vihāra, 352n
Dharmasthas, 174, 180, 180n, 196
Dharmasthīya, 174
dharmatā, 136
Dharma, universal order of, 346, Upanishad, idea of, 141
Dharmavardhana, 53
Dharmaveda, 228, 323
Dharmavijaya, 163f, 283f, 290, 309, 322, 324n, 327ff, 352
dharma-yātrā, 232
dhātu-chaityas, 26
Dhī-sachivas, 172
dhiti, 214, 250, 282
Dhuṇḍirāja, 48
Dhruva, K. N., 351
Digambara Jaina, 319
Dīgha Kārāyana, 122
Digvijaya, 285ff, 288f, 299, 311f, 316, of Agni, 283, 286, 302ff, of Khāravela, of Samudragupta, 287, of Pāṇḍavas, 95, Raghu's 287, 290
Dikshitar, Ramchandra, 163
Diodorus, 70, 160, 162, 173, 241, 264, 306, 320n, 327
Dionysos, 98
Dīpankara Śrījñāna, 302
Dirghāyus, 16, 131
Divine law, 227f, master, 332, order, 298, sanction, 313, will, 294, 297, 331, 338
doctrine, Buddha's, 142
Drangiana, 330n
Drāviḍa, 106, 110, 111n, 114f, 288, 325
Dravidian nations of South India, 89, 326
Dṛishadvatī, 80f, 304, 307, 903
Droṇamukha, 196, 196n, 202
Dudley Stamp, 109n
Durbar, 289n
Durga-pala, 169, 205
Dūtā, 63, 124, 127, 154, 168, 179, 185, 185n, 186, 188, 310, 326f, 341
Dvārakā, 95f, 96n, 288

Eastern Afganistan, 81, Himalayan region, 101, India, 80n, 300, 312, province, 146, range, 109, Subcontinent, 107, trade-route, 80n, Turkestan, 339
Egypt, 110, 148, 195, 305, 327f, 330n
Egyptian religion, 331
Elephant outlet, 344
England, limited monarchy of, 140
Enkratetai, 240
Enlightened Ones, 137, 229
Epirus, 128
Erannaboas, 120n
Erostosthenes, 70, 109
Esperanto, 339
Essenes, 331
European Civilisation, 305
Executive Council, 133

Fa-Hien, 1, 7, 9, 24, 56, 65, 102; 334
Far East, 332
Feudatory states, 122
Five Greek potentates, 185
Five Indies, 73
Fleet, J. F., 2n, 6, 46, 54n
Forest kingdoms, 85
Four Indian Graces, 307
Francke, A. H., 302n
Frontager, 63f, 117, 127, 185, 187, 189, 327
Frontier people, 100, province, 147
Further India, 80n

gabhāgāra, 171, 184, 219
Gadd, 305n
gajatame, 344
48
gāmagāmanika, 83
gaṇanā, 192
Gāṇanikyādhyaksha, 168, 172, 182f
Gandhamādana range, 81, 107
Gaunardas, 90
Gautama, 97n, 139, 258
Gavīmaṭh, 8, 78
Gayā, 106, 147
Gedrosia, 100, 105
Geiger, Wilhelm, 2n, 3, 6, 319, 325n
Gentile tradition, 314
gevaya, 175
gharastha, 266
Ghora Angirasa, 296
Ghoṭamukha, 122
Gihivinaya, 268
Girinagara, 126, 147
Girivraja, 39
Girnar, 75, 77, 112, 126, 157, 183, 191, 193, 325, 344, rock, 344
Gnostic form of Christianity, 331
Godāvarī 73f, 77n, 79, 85, 87, 89, 91, 289f, 307f, 317
Godhāpura, 74
Gokarṇa tīrtha, 115
Gonarda, 74
Good faith, 217, 325
Gopa, 194, 202ff
Govikartana, 144, 168
Govishāṇa, 106
Grahaṇa - moksha, 290
Grāmaṇis, 143, 168
Grammarians, 97
Greater India, 125, 283, 311
Great Vehicle, 24
Greek accounts, 3, 45, 162, ambassador, 264, 328, art,

343, chief, 149, city states, 140, civilization, 321, colonies, 330n, Colonists, 97, contemporary, 109, of Asoka, 326, Empire, 110, 328, frontager, 328, influence on Indian Art, 321n, kings, 287, 321, 327n, philosophy, 314, 323, potentates, 328, religion, 306, ruler, 109, satrapies, 69, 71, 81, suzerainty, 330, territories, 327, 350, writers, 51, 65ff, 89, 97, 108n, 113, 290, 311, 327f
Grierson, George, 99
Griffith C. L. T., 328n
Gṛihastha, 238, 240, dharma, 266
Gūḍhapurusha, 175, 188
Gujrāṭ, 76
Gupta, 289, 302, 340, 348, 354, age, 191n
Gurjaras, 347
guruṇaṁ apachiti, 269
Gutti, 230
Gymnosophists, 240, 319, 321
Haimavata, 109n, 289, 325, division, 81ff, 101, 104, state, 102, region, 92

Hārahūnas, 102
Harrappa, 2, 304f, 343
Harivarsha, 102
Harshavardhana, 301f, 302
Haryanka dynasty, 39, 41
hasti, 103
Hastināpura, 288
Hastipakādhipa, 174
hastivana, 204
Hastivanādhyaksha, 205
Hathiyārohā, 163
Havell, 343
Hebrew, 306
Hekaitos, 93
Heliodoros, 328
Hellenic world, 104
Helots, 264
Hemachandra, 47f, 50
Hemakūṭa range, 108
Hemodos Mt., 70, 109n
Heracles, 320, 320n
Heraclitean axiom, 323
Herāt, 69
Hermits, order of, 317
Herzfeld, E. I., 1, 97n
Hillebrandt, 121
Hill States, 81
Hilobioi, 311
Himālaya, 70ff, 102, 109n, 129f, 130n, 289n, 309, 332
Himalayan, Central States, 103
Himalayan Extension, Central, 82
Himālayan range, 69, 82, 103, 108, 109n, 289n, 306, region, 81, 288, 325, 289, 331, territories, 103, tribes, 105
Himavanta padesa, 72, 81
Hindu, art tradition, 301, authoritative Book of, 293, Holy Empire, 298
Hinduism, 271, 297, 301f, 332, 341
Hindukush, 105, 347
Hindu people, 353f, political theory, 284, society, 348, Temples, 342
Hiraṇmayavarsha, 108
hitasukha, 260

Hittites, 305
Holdich, 97
Home provinces, 147, 158
Hou Hanshu, 348f, 352
Horse outlet, 344, sacrifice, 287
Hultzsch, 27, 29, 78, 110n, 163, 175, 183, 187, 201n
Hūṇas, 347
Hwen Thsang, 1f 24, 26, 45, 49n, 65f, 67n, 68ff, 70n, 73, 73n, 76, 81, 93, 94n, 102n, 104, 110, 115, 119, 300, 302, 325, 343, 345
Hyderabad, 87f, 325

Ibbhas, 237, 255
Ibn Khāldūn, 354
Ilāvṛita varsha, 107f
Imperial Almoners, 180, commissioners 179, 189, 194, 196, secretariat, 133, 152
Independent frontager, 63, neighbours, 286
Indian aspiration,347, character, 347, coloniser, 114, culture, 54, 321n, 328n, hermits, 311, states, 335, systems of faith, 278, thinkers, 283
India's trade relations, 289, routes, 290
Indo - Aryan, 96, 99f, 229, 283, 340, civilization, 308, culture, 303, 317, 322, faith, 287
Indo - Aryanism, 312, 318, 322, 340
Indra, 176n, 218, 267, banner of, 342
Indragupta, a thera, 25
indrakīla, 342, 342n
Indrapālita, 55
Indus, 65, 69f, 81, 93ff, 96n, 100, 109, 308, 320, Civilisation, 305, Group, 80, 304, 308, lower, 102, region, 330n, Valley, 304, Upper, 319
internationalism, 355
Ionian, 93n, 94n, 319ff
Iran, 98, 303, 319
Iranian, 96, 98, words, 99
isṭāpūrtam, 185, 263
Isila, 37, 79, 179, 187, 191, 201
isyā, 233, 257f
Islam, 271, 306, 326, 326n, 332
Islamic Law, 170n
Israels, 140, 305
itthāgāra, 219,
Iyengar, Srinivas, 89

Jacobi, 121
Jaina, 29, 40, 108, 109n, 184, 209, 220, 238, 241, 243f, 275, 282, 287, 318, 354
Jainism, 253, 271, 273f, 319, 323, 332, 353, psychological concepts of, 275, school of political thought, 330, traditions, 58, 64, 319, 353
Jalalabad, 105,
Jālandhar, 116n
Jalauka, 61, 105
Jambudvipa, 10, 18f, 21f, 25, 42, 63f, 71, 81f, 84, 101, 104, 106ff, 126, 129, 132, 167, 267, 286, 288f, 308, empire of, 188
jana jānapada, 124
Janasāna, 37
Janapadas, 88, 116f, 125, 134, 151, 152, 202, 256

Jarāsandha, 39, 288
Jatinga Rāmeswara, 8, 79
Java, 90n, 290
Jayaswal, K. P., 40n, 43, 44n, 47, 47n, 55, 55n, 60, 61n, 83f, 94, 309n, 348f
Jinaprabha Sūri, 56f, 64n
Jīvaka, 39, 171
Jñāna yoga, 295
Jolly, 121
Judaism, 306, 313f, 331f
Justin, 49, 51, 104, 309

Kābul, 69, 69n, 81, 94, 96f, 100, 103, 105, 309, 319f, 331
Kāfiristan, 95
Kaikeyas, 97, 102
Kailāsa, 18
Kajangala, 66, 72f
Kālada, 90
Kālakūṭas, 103, 105
Kālatoyaka, 102
Kālamukha, 76
Kalaṇāgamā, 266, 271
Kalanos, 240
Kālāśoka 6, 24, 41, 41n, 336
Kalavinkā, 52
Kalhaṇa, 61, 95, 105
Kālidāsa, 234, 284, 287, 290
Kalinga, 2, 32, 64, 69, 77f, 85f, 86, 88, 106, 117, 146f, 161, 163, 190, 201, 217, 222, 231, 256, 289n, 295, 308, 329, 348, 350, 354, 356, army, 163, battlefield of, 359, conquest of, 7, 18, 62, Viceroy of, 178, war, 31f, 355, 357
Kalsi, 102, 183, 325, 344
Kāluvāki 52ff, 54n, 57, 170
Kāmandaka, 44
Kāmanďakīya, 125
Kāmarūpa, 65, 68, 103, 116
Kāmbojas, 81, 83, 90, 92, 94, 94n, 95ff, 104, 106, 127, 129, 149, 181, 183, 255; 287, 319, 321
Kambyses, 320
Kanakagiri, 78n
Kānārā, 87, 112n
Kanauj, 160, 301
Kāñchīpura, 110, 112n
Kaṇinka Bhāradvāja, 122, 122n, 233
Kankhal, 73
Kaṇṇapeṇṇā, 86n
Kanyopāyaṇa-dāna, 291
Kaṇishka, 336
Kapilavastu, 49, 74, 100, 103, 105, 106, 126
Kappadokia, 330n
Karadānājñākaraṇa, 291
karamolī, 194
Karmasachiva, 172f, 176, Yoga, 295
Karṇa, 289, 298
Karṇa-suvarṇa, 65, 106
Karṇāṭa, 76, 78, 87
Karnool, 79, 147
Karoura, 111f
Kartṛipura, 116
Karūshas, 75, 85
kāryāmuśāsanam, 249
Kasergode Taluk, 112n
Kāśī, 72f, 312
Kāśmīra, 61, 81, 93, 102, 104f, 288
katābhīkāra, 262n
kataṁñatā, 277, 279
Kāťhiāwar, 76f, 96n, 149, 151, 191
Kātyāyana, 97, 122f, 135, 311n

Kātyāyana, Kakuda, 90
Kauliya territories, 103
Kauṇapadanta, 122
Kauśāmbī, 8, 53, 74f, 80, 147, 178, 334
Kauṭilya, 44, 117, 121n, 121f, 158f, 163, 172, 182, 192ff, 196f, 205, 217, 226n, 231, 233f, 254, 258, 314, 338, 347, 349, 355f, 360, Vachana, 134
Kāverī—paṭṭana 110
Kenneti, 112
Kern, 344, 350, 351n
Kerala, 79, 90, 111n, 112
Keralaputra, 69, 77, 79, 109, 129, 185, 309, 326
Kevaṭabhoga, 130, 165
Khalalika Hill, 7f, 239, 341, 352
Khāravela, 2, 5, 131, 145, 207f, 210, 231, 234, 285n, 312, 336, 354f
Kharoshṭhī, 51, 187, 211, 339
Khaśas, 90, 100, 102
Kielhorn, 148, 148n
Kimpurusha, 101, Varsha, 108
Kirātas, 100ff, 129
Kirthar range, 105, 109
Kishkindhyas, 75, 85
Kitti—Siri—Meghavaṇṇa, 300
Kolapaṭṭana, 110
Koṭigāma, 118
Kokanadas, 101
Konganāḍu, 112n
Koṇāgamana, stūpa of, 217
Konkan, 76, 115
Konow, Sten, 348
Kopbal, 88, 151
Kophen, 97f, 100, 319f
Kośala, 40, 49, 72f, 250, Commander-in-chief of, 122
Kaosār people, 112n
Koṭa Vishayas, 152
Kṛishṇagiri, 92
Kṛitamālā, 113f
Krodha, 275
Kshatri, 168
Kshatriya, 50, 97, 100, 208f, 292, 308, 311f, leader, 311, princes, 317, states, 317
Kshayārsha, 100
Kshemendra, 48
Kshīra Svāmī, 148
Kshudrakas, 98, 101, 103, 319
Kubhā, 81, 97, 130, 304, 341
Kukkuras, 76n,
Kulindas 90, 103
Kumāra, 60ff, 148, 151f, 170, 189ff, 203, mahāmātras, 190, Viçeroys, 35, 147, 153, 196
Kuṇāla, 53ff, 59f, Dharmavardhana, 56, 62, Tīvala, 56, 61
Kurkuṭārāma, 21, 60
Kuru, 67, 72f, 218, 288, 294, 310, country, 150, king of, 149, kshetra, 287, 293f, 298, 307
Kuruvarsha, 108f
Kush, 305
Kushāṇa, 289, rulers, 335
Kusinārā, 74, 106
Kushiya, 330n
Kusumapura, 19, 118f

laghudaṇḍatā, 282, 285
lājā, 17
Lājavachanikā, 117, 147
Lakedaemonians, 264
lampāka, 85, 102, 105
Langdon, 305n

Langhan, 95, 105
Lānguliya, 77f
Lassen, 94n, 108n, 109n
Lauhitya, 103
Lauriyā Ararāj, 8, Nandangarh, 8
Law, B. C., 18n, 66n, 70n, 72n, 76n ; 99n, 107n, 113n, 197n, 244n, 99n, 107n, 113n, 107n, 244n, 289n, 304n, 310, 310n, 317, 325, 336n
Law, N. N., 121, 127n, 128n
Law of Piety, 142, 287, persons, 268, source of, 143, wheel of, 137
Lekhaka, 179, 187
Lévi, Sylvain, 96, 290, 299
Lion outlet, 344
lipi, 210
Lipikara, 179, 187
Lobhavijaya, 164, 234, 284, 291
Lohas, 94f, 101
Lokapāla, 267
Lower Assam Valley, 288, Indus Valley, 288f, 308
Lumbinī, 73, 82, 104, 189, 217, 345 ; pilgrimage to, 8, pillar, 157, Inscription, 126, 165, 216

Macedonia, 103, 110
Macedonian, 94, 98, 319f, army, 308, conqueror, 110, 328, expedition, 330
Macco Calingae, 67
Machiavelli, 254
mādava, 278
madhya, 324
Madhyadeśa, 71, 90
Madoura, 111, 113f
Madra, 72, 97
Madrakalingas, 78
Magadha, 6, 40, 51, 58, 65, 72ff ; 103 ; 119, 126, 132, 149, 167, 177, 188 ; 288f, 289n, 305, chancellor of, 121, citizen of, 144, empire, 308, kingdom of, 42, imperial, 348, province of, 210, rise of, 354, state, 347, state craft, 349, staṭe-policy, 349, throne of, 32, 36, 44, 208
Magadhan king, 126, 132, 234, Successor of Aśoka, 348
Magas, 7, 109f, 128f, 287
magavyā, 220, 231f
Mahābhojas, 88
Mahābodhi, 12, 32, Sanghā-rāma, 300
Mahāhimavanta, 108, 109n
Mahāhimātras, 37, 52f, 59, 117, 122, 133, 147, 149f, 150n, 151, 168, 174, 176ff, 182, 189ff, 204, 368, 177, 177n, 178f, 189, Nāgaraka, 178, Stryadhyaksha, 178, 182
Mahāmātrīya, 186
Mahāmaṫtā 146, 310, Antepura, upachārakā, 177, gaṇaka, 177, Magadha, 174f, 177, Pachchantavāsino, 178, Senānāyaka, 177, Vinichchhaya, 177, Vohārika, 177
Mahāmeghavāhana dynasty, 355
Mahānandi, 41, 47
mahānasa, 170f
Mahānasika, 171
Mahapadma, 43, 47, 308
mahāpaṭhavī, 63
mahāpāya, 247, 271
mahāphala, 247

Mahāpurusha Lakshaṇam, 209
Mahārājas, 267
Mahārāshṭra, 87, 151f
Mahārāshṭrikas, 150
Mahāraṭhis, 88
Mahāsāla, 39n, 66, 106, 310
Mahāsanghikas, 335f
Mahāsena, 256
Mahasenāpati, 88
Mahāvira, 40, 209, 243f, 248, 312, 324
Mahendra, 24, 52, 54, 61, 92, 111n, 116, 122n, 318, 325f, birth of, 9, ordained as monk, 10, mission, 327
Mahendra mountain, 234
Mahiṁsakaraṭṭha, 86f
Mahishamaṇḍala, 87
Mahishī, 144, 168, 170n
Mahishika, 85f, 90
Māhīshmatī, 88f
Majumdar, G. P., 232n, 315n, R. C., 80n
Malalasekera, G. P., 44n, 66n, 72n, 73n, 76n, 81n, 84n, 106n, 107n, 119n, 242n
Mālavas, 102f
Malaya, 42, 75n, 92
Malayakūṭa, 111n, 113f, 325
Mālyavat range, 107f
māna, 274ff
Mānas sarovar, 18, 82, 101, 109
Mānavas, 122f, 226n
mangala, 314, 344
mangalya, 259
Manipur, 82, 101, 103, 288
Mansehra, 126, 183, 325
mantra, 159, 307, śakti, 159
Mantrin, 168f, 172, 174, 176
Mantri Parishad, 132, 169, 171
Manu, Svāyambhuva, 122n, Vaivasvāta, 312
mārdava, 28
Marshall, Sir John, 343
Marco Polo, 94n
Mārkaṇḍeya 70, 242
Martin, M. de, St., 98
Marukachchha,75
Marukāntāra, 76, 80
Maskarin, Kauśalya, 311n
Maski, 29
Masuda, J., 336n
Mathurā, 80, 88, 147, 290, 320, 352
Matisachivas, 172
Maťsya, 73, 75, 85, 88,91, 307
mātsya nyāya, 156
Maurya administration, 121, 190, 302, 355, age, 145, army, 163, 350, clan, 209, Capital, 119, 202, constitution, 132, 140, dynasty, 55, emperor, 66, 148, 286, 329, empire, 66, 69, 105, 222, 331, 350, govt, 160, family, 208, high officials, 117, history, 54, king, 162, leader, 309, palace, 353, regime, 202, Royal House, 208, rulers, 33, state, 121, 128, 131, 140, 356, line, 66, 115, tradition, 151, upstarts, 309
Mauryan dominions, 347, empire, 328, heritage, 356, ideal, 357, political ideal, 356, organisation, 356, state, 359, polity, 163n, sovereign, 359
Max Müller, 99n
Mayūraputra, 46n
mayūrakhādakas, 50

mayūraposhakas, 49f
Mc Crindle, 42n, 46n, 51n, 66n, 67n, 68ff
Medhātithi, 139
Media, 330n
Mediterranean Countries, 109, 306, powers, 110, 326
Megasthenes, 3, 45, 49, 67, 67n 69f, 97, 109, 113f, 118, 120f, 167, 173, 188, 239f, 264, 308, 313ff, 317ff, 327, 340
Mekalas, 75, 85, 90
Meṇḍapatha, 290
Meru, 70, 97f
Mesopotamia, 305
Michelson, 83
Middle Country, 66, 69, 72f, 75, 80f, 102, 139, 258, 289, 312, 322, 337, 340
Middlepath, 233
Midland, 75, 80f, 102, 139, Buddhist, 117
Ministers, Council of 132f, 137, 143, 146, 152, 159, 180, 183, 185, 187, 188, 338
misibhūtā, 267
Mithilā,289n
Mitra,127
Mitra - mitra, 128
Mitra,Panchanan, 342n
Mitra, S. N., 192, 194, 194n, 195, 197, 198, 199, 217n, 244n, 245n, 249n, 251n, 254n, 262n 273n, 279n
mittāmachchā, 254
Mittanies, 312
Mlechchha, 265
Mohenjodaro, 2, 304f 343
moksha, 260, 266
monarchy, Greco - Bactrian, 321
Mongolian races, 331
monoliths of Aśoka, 332, 343
Monumental Prakrit, 340
Mookerji, R, K., 34, 36n, 48n, 54, 78, 121, 131, 133f, 134n 140, 143, 144n, 166n, 174, 176, 176n, 179, 182, 187, 189, 191ff, 201n, 216, 216n, 225, 245, 246, 341n, 342, 342n, 343, 346, 349
Moral Law, 228
Moral sponsors, 180
Moriya, 49f
Moses, 140
Mosaic Code, 313, law, 139, principle, 156
Motichandra, 82n, 95, 95n, 96n, 102n
mṛidudaṇḍa, 156
mṛigayā, 220, 232, 286
Mughal Empire, 355
Mujirikuḍu, 112
Mukhyas, 149
Muktāpīḍa, 95
Mūlaka, 87, 89
Mūlasarvāstivāda, 16
Murā, 48
Mūshikas, 67f, 90, 103f, 151, 290, 309
Mūsikapatha, 290, 309
Muṭasiva, 12
Muṭivas, 117
Mysore, 78f, 98, 111f

Nābhaka, 92, 101f, 103f, 129, 326
Nābhalines, 71, 92, 101f, 104f, 127, 129, 287, 326
Nagala-viyohālakā, 153
Nāgaraka, 202f, 220, mahāmātras, 178, 190, 203f

nāgavana, 206
Nahapāna, 86, 91
Naigamas, 150
Nālandā, 74, 106, 302
Nanda dynasty, 39, 44, 308, king, 162, 308, last, 192n
Nandānvayā, 46n, 48
Narmadā region, 86, 129
nātikā, 179, 198, 269
negama-jānapadā, 252, 256
Negāpaṭam, monastery of, 352n
Nepāla Vishaya, 289n
Nestorian form of Christianity, 331
New world, 294
Nīchas, 102
Nicholson, 354
Nigliva, Aśokan monolith at, 82
nijhati, 213, 237, 251
nijjhāpana, 97
nikkama, 214, 250
Nīlakaṇṭha, 272n, 279
Nirgranthas, 10, 25, 65, 238, 241, 318f
Nyagrodha, 20f, 25ff, 30ff, 33n, 49
Nysa, 70, 94, 97f, 319

Olbenberg, 24n
oligarchical tribes, 127
Onesikrates, 321
orodhā, 170f, 219
Orodha-mahāmattā, 182
Oxydrakoi, 98, 103, 309

pabhāva, 222
pachaṁtā 116, 147
Pachupagamana, 212
Padmasambhava, 302
Padmāvatī, 53f
pagan monuments of, 301, religion, 331
Paītrayanika,83ff, 91
pakama, 27, 214, 278
porānā pakiti, 229
Pakudha Kachchāyana, 90
Pālada, 90, 90n
Palaeolithic Age, 305
Panchālas, 72f, 307, 352, oligarchy of, 311
Paṇḍaranga paribbājakas, 10
Pāṇḍavas, 285, 287f, 292, 294, 298
Paṇḍukābhaya, 318f
Pāṇḍya, 69, 77, 79, 106, 109ff, 111n, 112f, 114f, 129, 185, 285, 287f, 309, 326
kapāṭa, 113, 115, 290
king of, 290
Pāṇini, 43, 45, 80, 97, 97n, 99, 131, 289n, 290n,244n,254n, 289, 307n, 314, 314n
pāpa, 271, 274
parākrama, 27,158, 214,250f,278
Paramakamboja, 94f, 101
Paramarshika, 96
Parama Tangaṇa, 102n
Parama Yona, 94, 96, 290
Paranavitana, 18n
parapāsaṁḍa-garahā, 272
Pārasakavaṇṇā, 100
Parāśara 122f, 136
Pargiter, 33n, 39n, 40n, 42n, 44n, 47, 47n, 56n, 90n
parichārakikaraṇa, 291
parihāra, 257, karma, 257
parimitārthāḥ, 185
Pāriṁda, 79, 90, 90n, 129, Pāradas, 77ff, 84, 85, 89ff, 127, 187, 309, 326
pariprichchhā, 212
Parisā, 132f, 143, 152f, 159, 176f, 187
pārshada, 238

parisrava, 248, 271
Parivrājakas, 24f, 311
Paropanisadai, 69, 96, 105, 108n
Pārshṇigrāha, 127f
Parvatāśrayī, 72, 102
Pārvatīya, 101
Pasenadi, 220, 250
Pāshaṇḍas, 238, 242
pasu-munisā, 124, vyādhi-maraka, 260
Pāṭaliputra, 8, 10f, 17, 19ff, 23, 25, 34ff, 40, 40n, 42, 42n, 43f, 49, 50, 52f, 56, 58, 61, 65, 74, 106, 118f, 126, 146, 201, 327, 348, 352, Council of, 333, Maury ruler of, 149n
Patañjali, 46, 87, 97, 119n, 131, 307n
paṭimnā achalā, 250
paṭivesiya, 254
Patiṭṭhāna, 83
paṭividhāna, 260
Patriarchs, 312
Paura-vyavahārika, 152, 168f, 178, 203f
paurṇamāsī, 257
Peacock palace, 50n
Persepolis, 2, 343, architecture of, 51
Persepolitan bell, 343
Persian Empire, 100, 105, 331f, influence, 100
Perso-Greeks, 97
Peshāwar, 64, 93, 105
Peshwās, 299
Peṭeṇikas, 83, 91
Pharisees, religion of, 331
Philosophers, 240f, 303
Phœnicians, 305
Pilgrimage, Asoka's, 332, places of, 317
Piyadasi, 18, lājā Māgadhe, 19, 63
Pingalavatsa, 38
Pilindavachchha, 107
Pipphalivana, 49, 49n, 50
Piśācha, 300
Piśachatva 300
Piśuna, 122
Piśunaputra 122
Piyadāsa, 17, 22
Pliny, 65, 68f, 77n, 78, 100, 177, 308, 310
Plutarch, 51, 162, 309
Poros, 96
prābhuśakti, 159, 222, 291
Prāchya, 67, 71, division, 82, 118
pradeśa 194
pradeśana, 194
Prādesikas, 146, 152, 152n, 158, 179, 182, 186, 191, 193ff
Pradeshtṛis, 193ff, 297, 204, 263
Pradhāna, 174
Prāḍvivāka, 169n
Prāgjyotishapura, 103
prakṛitayaḥ, 124, 161
prakṛiti-priyahitāni, 257, viruddhāchāra, 257
prajāḥ, 124
prajñāguṇā, 207, 212
prasabha-uddharaṇa, 290
Praśāstṛi, 169, 169n
Prasenajit, 40, 245n
Prasians, 120n
Prasii, 65, 67, 67n, 104, 126
Prasthalas, 102, 308
pratāpa, 185
Pratīchyas, 67, 71
pratikāra, 260
pratishedhah, 257
Pratishṭhāna, 74, 83, 87, 89, 120
Prativedakas, 133, 172, 177, 188
Pratyantas, 63, 116f, 124, 127, 255

Pratyanta Mahāmātra, 189, 204
pṛavrajita, 238, 241, 244
preacher—Indo Aryan, 326
Pre Alexandrian Ionian, 97,
 Greek settlement, 94
Pṛithivī, 63, 125, 247
Privy Council, 176, 176n, 338
Priyadarśana, 16ff, 22, 33, 35, 37, 132, 194
Priyadarśin, 11, 16f, 26, 28, 37, 212, 22[illegible]
Police type of state, 141
Political thinkers, 161
porāṇā pakiti, 229, porāṇā-vajji-dhammā, 229, 229n
Ptolemaios, 328
Ptolemy, 94, 96, 287
Ptolemy II Philadelphos, 7, 47, 110, 128, 287, 327
Pubbaseliya, 81n
Pulindas, 90, 90n, 91f, 100, 204
puṁstvopaghāta, 257
punarabhisheka, 13f, 18
Punarvasu, 132, 261n, day, 201
Puṇḍarīka, 344
Puṇḍra, 66, 79, 90, nagara, 66
Puṇḍravardhana, 65f, 66n, 72, 106
Pūraṇa Kāśyapa, 311n
Purandara, 122n
Pūrvadeśa, 71
Purohita, 143f, 150, 168, 169, 171, 184, 304n, 310f
Pūrvaśailas, 325
Pūrvavideha, 71, 107, 109, 331
Purushas, 151ff, 171, 175, 182, 187, 192, 257
purushapura, 93, 105
purushottama cult, 295, 299, 331
Pushkarāvati, 93n, 103, 120, 126, 147
Pushpabhūti, 302
Pushpapura, 18f, 49, 118f, 351
Pushya, 261n
Pushyagupta, 51, 147f, 148n, 150, 191
Pushyamitra, 55, 349
Pyrrho, 321

Qublai Khan, 355

Rādhagupta, 172
Rādhasvāmi, 24
Raghu's Digvijaya, 234
rājā, 15ff, 72, 131f, 149, 168, 207, 230, 157
rāja chakravartin, 138
Rājagiriya, 81n, 325
Rājagṛiha, 24, 39f, 74, 106, 119f, 317
rājakammikā, 310
rājakṛits, 15
Rājanakshatra, 132
rājānuśāsana, 227
rājaratha, 145
rājaśāsana, 134f, 140, 227
Rājaśekhara, 72f, 80
rājasūya, 13ff, 17, 186ff, 289n, 291ff
Rājavachanika, 147, 158, 178f, 189f, 195
rājavishaya, 63, 125
Rājayuttas, 191
rajju, 193
Rajjuka, 79, 88, 146, 151ff, 158, 168, 179, 182, 186, 188, 191ff (-197), 203, 349, 355
Rajwade, 341n
Rāmachandran, T. N., 235
Rāmagrāma, 106
Rāmaṭhas, 102
Rāmkrishna Mission, 332
Rantideva, 171, 231
Rāshṭrādhikṛita, 148

Rāshṭrapāla, 51, 148, 150,
Rāshṭrika, 78, 83, 85f, 91, 127, 129, 150f, 290, 309
Rāshṭriya, 51, 148f, 150, Vaiśya, 88
Ratnins, 144
Raṭhikas, 85, 88, 116, 234
Raṭṭhiyaputtā, 149
Ray Chaudhuri, H. C., 6,14,15n, 16n, 18, 18n, 39n, 41n, 42n, 43, 43n, 45, 45n, 46, 46n, 48n, 49n, 50, 50n, 51, 54n, 55, 56, 56n, 57n, 58n, 61n, 65, 65n, 67n, 72n, 73n, 77, 78n, 79n, 80n, 88n, 89, 89n, 90, 90n, 93, 93n, 96n, 100, 101n, 102f, 103n, 104n, 110, 110n, 112, 113n, 123n, 143, 143n, 144n, 148, 148n, 160n, 162n, 164 168, 170n, 175, 177n, 178, 182, 182n, 191n, 196, 225, 235, 309, 309n, 348f, 354
Regulation of Piety, 139
Reporters, 172
Republican form of Govt. 97, tribe, 102
Rhys Davids, T. W., 2, 3, 30, 36n, 74, 96, 137, 197n, 226, 268, 271, 327, 337, 339
Ṛishis, 304, 311, 316
Ṛishika, 87, 95, 101
Ṛishṭika, 290, 87f
Ṛishṭikas, 83f, 85, 88, 90f, 181, 320, 326
Ṛishṭika-Peteṇikas, 83ff (87)
Robber tribes, 95, 101
Roman Empire, 331, 349f
Rudradāman K, 1, 3, 75, 86f, 148ff, 150f, 172

Sabbatthaka-mahāmatta, 177
sacha, 112, 280,
Sachivas, 172
Sacred Law, 180, 796
Saddharma, 26, 225, 329, 333
sādhava, 282
sāḍguṇyam, 161
saggārohaṇa sopāna 267
sahāya, 269, 254
śailendras, 301
śaiśunāga Dynasty, 39, 39n, 41f, 47f
śaiśunāgī Kākavarṇa, 41
śaivism, 331f
śālisūka, 56, 56n, 57, 349ff
śaka, 90, 94n, 97, 99, 102, 288f, 347
śakamuruṇḍas, 291
śaka rulers, 335, 234
śāktism, 332
śākyamuni, 301, 322, 352
śākyaputrīyas, 312, 318
samachariyā; 277f
Samāhartṛi, 168, 172, 174, 193f, 196, 202
samāja, 219, 231, 348
Samaṇa, 31, 243, 269, 318, brāhmaṇā, 256, 272
Samāpā, 59, 117, 126, 146, 153, 178f, 190, 201, 203
Sāmanta, 127ff, 147, 154, 162, 255, maṇḍala, 127, territories, 131
Samataṭa, 65, 68, 106, 116, 116n
samavāya, 159, 271f
samayānubaddhā, 262n
Sambodhi, 7, 32, 217, 332
saṁḍaka, 258
Saṁgha-samage, 159
Saṁghaṭa, 182, 133
Saṁgrāhitṛi, 144, 168
Saṁkāśya, 8, 73, 267
Sāṁkhya-yoga, 85

Sampadi, 55f, 60, 353
saṁpaṭipati, 260, 265, 269
Samprati, 56ff, 64, 172, 352f
Samrāj, 16
Samrāṭ, 17, 72, 338
saṁsaraṇa, 342
saṁthuta, 269
saṁtīraṇa, 249
Samudra, 20f, 30
Samudragupta, 85, 92, 103n, 116, 234, 290, 300
saṁyama, 280
sandhi - vigraha, 161
Sandrokottos, 46, 49, 104, 308
Sangha, 11, 20f, 26ff, 30, 61, 142, 149, 212, 215, 216f, 238, 243, 245n, 246, 333f 337, 352, dassanam, 217
Sanghamitra, 9, 10, 12, 35, 52, 54
Sanghārāma, 104
Sanghasthas, 238, 312, 318
Sannidhātṛi, 168f, 172, 174
Saptagaṇas, 101, rājyāngāni, 217, Sindhu, 306
Sarasvatī, Dayānanda, 28n
Sarasaka-vijaya, 163f, 235, 283f
Sircar, D. C., 76, 90n
Satiyaputra, 77, 79, 109, 111ff, 129, 185, 309, 326
Satpute, 111
Sattagydia 330n
Sātvata, 288, 299, 331
Satyabhūmi, 112n
Saurāshṭra, 94
savamunisā, 124
svapāsamḍā, 124
Sāyaka—vijaya, 235, 283
Schwanbeck, 67, 320
Schism ordinance, 337
tradition, 337
Scribes, 331
Sea-coast trade of India, 308
seats of learning, Buddhist, 300
Secretariat, Imperial, 186
Seleukos Nikator, 38, 45, 51, 81, 104, 110, 308, 327
Senart, E, 2, 344
Senarveatne, 2n, 6
Secriyāputa, 111
Shastri, Ganapati, 121n
Sthaviras, 336
Siamese alphabet, 339
Sibae 320
Siddhatthika, 81n, 325
Sikhism, 332
śilāstambhas, 342
Simhapura, 101, 105
Sindhu, 97
Kulindakāh, 90
pulindakāh, 90
Sauvīra, 75, 80, 102
Sineru, 305
Sirimādevatā 307n,
śiśnadevas, 320, 320n,
Sisunāga dynasty, 39, 39n, 41
śiśupāla, 291, 293
śiva, 298, 300, 318, 320n,
śīvis, 102, 144f, 312
Skudras, 94n, 98
Skudria, 330n
Skythia, 70, 330
Smith, Sidney, 305n
Smith, Vincent A, 23, 34, 58, 89, 112, 119, 121, 148n, 162n, 202, 225, 302, 321, 342
sochaya, 280f
social grades, 298
Sogdiana, 330n
Somadeva, 48
Somapura, Mahāvihāra, 300
Somaśarman, 56
Soṇa, 301
Soṇadaṇḍa 39n

Sornāgas, 111
Sotṫhiya, Brāhmaṇas, 310
Southern division, 73
Province, 78, 201
Road, 75f, 84, 87ff, 91, 118, 120, 317
South-western Road, 79f, 80, 84
Sparda, 94n, 330n,
Spencer, Herbert, 297
Sphines, 240
śramaras, 255, 266ff, 270, 272, 273n, 295, 307, 311, 311n, 312, 317, 322, 339, 363
Brahmanite, 318
Pravrajiṫas, 244
Sramanite, Brāhmaṇas, 312
Srāvāpaka, 152, 179
śṛingavān range, 108
Srong—tsan gam-po, 302
śrotriya, 261, 311, 315f,
State—treaties, 306
Stein, Otto, 121n, 328
Sthānika, 194, 202f, 203n, 204
Sthānīya, 120, 196, 196n, 202
Sṫhapatis, 186
Sthavira 335
Sthūnā 73
St. paul, 326n, 329
Strabo, 46, 98, 101, 160, 167, 173, 173n, 195, 202f, 220n, 246, 320n
Stryadhyaksha, 178, 194n
mahāmātra, 172
Subhadrāngī, 37
Sudarśana Lake, 2, 147, 357
Sudarśana, a ring, 304
Sudās, 304, 304n,
suhadaya, 254
śukra, 122n, 134
Sumana, 32f, 33n, 35f, 52, 54
Susima, 36
Sumerian Civilization 305
Sumeru, 71, 81, 97,107f,129,305
Sūnāparānta, 64, 75f, 76n, 87, 147, 151, 322
śunga, 289, 348, Art, 343
Sunīdha, 118
Suppāraka, 111, 147
śūrasena, 41, 41n, 73, 307, 320n, 322
Susīma 32ff, 330n
Sushūsā, 9, agabhuti, 213
Sūta, 143, 146, 168,
Suvarṇabhūmī, 12, 129, 301, 325
Suvarṇagiri, 37, 57, 62, 64, 78f, 126, 147, 179, 191, 201, 325, 326
Suvarṇa parvata, 79n
Suzukī, D. T., 137n
Svarga, 247, 266
Svaśarāshṭra, 100, 117
śvetaparvata, 101, 108
Syria, 109, 312f, 332

Tagabena, 240
Takabharas, 94n, 98
Takakusu, 2n, 6
Takshaśilā, 34f, 44f, 51, 53, 56f, 60, 60f, 80, 93, 105, 117, 120, 126, 147, 179, 189, 190, 201
Takkola, 123
Tāmralipta, 65, 69, 77, 106
Tāmraparṇa, 71
Tāmraparṇī, 12, 112f, 289f, 308, 325, 326, 349
divipa, 114f
Tamraparṇika, 114
parṇya 69, 77, 79, 108f, 113, 115, 129, 185, 287, 309, 326
territory, 111
Tangaṇas, 102, 102n, 290, 305
Tāpasa, 244, 310f, 316

Taprobane, 113f, 308
Tāranātha, 36, 42n, 46n, 57, 61, 61n, 309, 309n
Thakur, Anantalal, 279n
thaira—susrusā, 213, 269
Thomas, E. J., 242n
Thomas, F. W., 53n, 123, 192, 277n
Tibetan alphabet, 339
tīkshṇadaṇḍa, 155
tīrthas, 317
Tīrthankaras, 181, 209, 237
tīrthayātrā, 298
Tishya, 33, 36,132,261,261n,275
Tishya, Asoka brother, 10
Tishya, Maudgalīputra, 11, 22f
Tishyarakshā, 12, 13, 53, 60
Tishya—Vītaśoka, 37, 54, 170
Tissa, Devānampiya, 12, 15n, 18, 18n, 113, 326
Tīvala, 52, 54, 57
Tīvalamātā, 212
Tīvarā, 52, 54, 54n
Topa, Ishwarlal 356f
Tosali, 35, 59, 61, 117, 126, 146, 153, 178f, 189f, 201, 203f
Trailokya, Vijaya, 283, 299f
tribal states, 64, 104, 189
Trans—Himalayan countries, 308
Tulamaya, 7, 109f
Tuluva country, 112n
Tushāspha, 148, 148n, 149f, 191, 352
tuṭhāyatanāni, 185

Uchāvachamangala, 232
Udāsīna, 128, 128n
Udaya, 24, 39f, 119
Udīchya, 71
—Uttarāpatha, 90
Ugrasenananda, 42, 42n
Ujeni, 34, 61, 179, 201
Ujjayini, 9, 51f, 74f, 89, 106, 126, 147, 189f
Upagupta, 22ff
Upāsaka, 20, 26f, 29, 215f, 225, 226
—dharma, 266f, 273, 280
Upayuktas, 191f
uposatha, 11, 170n, 280, 334
Uśanas, 122n, 176
Usavadāta, 74n, 75n
Uśīnaras, 67, 72f
Uttamabhadra, 74n
Uttamarṇas, 74, 85
Uttara, 301
Uttarakuru, 102, 107ff, 288
Uttarāpatha, 51, 59f, 64, 71, 79ff, 81n, 83, 88ff, 92f, 96f, 99ff, 117, 120, 129, 146, 187, 189, 191, 195, 201, 289f, 304ff, 309, 312, 319, 321
Uttarāpathaka, 325
Utthāna, 27, 212, 214, 249ff, 258
Uttiya, 326
uyāma, 27, 214, 218f, 278
uyāna, 220, 250
—bhūmi, 220

Vaidarbhas, 91
Vaidiśas, 90
Vaiśālī, 118, 229
Vānaprastha order, 242, 244
Vanavāsī, 87f, 111
Vanavāsikas 87f
Vanga, 289
Vanibbakā, 255
Varṇāśramadharma, 237, 241, 316
Vararuchi, 43, 345
Varuṇa, 14, 307, 346

Vasishṭha, 139, 258
Vāsudeva, 289, 295
Vasumitra, 335
Vātavyādhi, 122, 161
Vatsa, 73, 75, 258
    province of, 201
Vedic Aryan, 304
    Aryandom, 304, 309
    Civilization, 304
    Colleges, 39, 310
    cult, 303
    Culture, 316
Vedisā mahādevī, 51, 53
Vibhājyavāda, 11, 334
Vidyādhara countries, 234, 290
    settlements, 85, 91
    tracts, 86
Vidyalankāra, Jaya Chandra, 9
vigatabhī, 345
vihārayātrā, 220, 231f, 232n
Vikramaśīla mahāvihāra, 300
Vindhya
    division, 85
    forest, 65
    hills, 129
    mukhyas, 91
    pṛistha, 74
range, 72, 85, 92, 290, 307
    region, 83, 86, 88, 91f
vinīta, 163, 170, 171, 220
Vīrahotras, 86
Viśākhadatta, 44f, 48
Viśālāksha, 122, 122n
Vishṇu, 136, 139, 29ff
Vishṇugupta, 121, 123
Vītaśoka, 33, 36n
Viviṫādhyakshas, 205
Vogel, 115
Vrachabhūmikas, 178, 182ff
Vṛijiputras, 33f

Wells, H. G., 329
Westerners, 116
Western division of India, 84
    people, 181
    province, 147
    range, 109
    Sub Continent of Asia, 89
Wickremasinghe, 2n, 6
Williams, Monier, 240n
Wilson, 48
worship of idols 306

Xerxes, 94n, 100, 329

Yājñavalkya, 135n, 136, 139
yajñīyadesa, 316
yakshas, 300, 318
Yāska, 99
yātrā, 31
Yaunas, 81f, 92, 93n. 94, 94n, 97f, 98, 100f, 127, 129, 181, 255, 257, 287, 290, 307, 320, 326
Yavana, 90, 94, 97ff, 102, 191, 288ff
Yavanī, 97
Yavanāni, 97
Yonadūta, 328
    territory, 94n, 95
Yūgyāchariya, 163
Yukta, 133, 146, 152, 153, 187ff, 191ff, 195, 213
Yule, 77n, 94n

Zoroaster, 331
Zoroastrianism, 332

PART II

INSCRIPTIONS

CONTENTS

CHAPTER I — PAGES

INTRODUCTORY ... 1—28

1. Number and Classification of Inscriptions ... 1— 2
2. Discovery of other inscriptions anticipated ... 2— 3
3. Location ... ... 3— 8
4. Alphabets and orthography ... 9—10
5. Chronology ... ... 10—18
6. Forms, merits and defects ... 18—24
7. Problem of variants ... ... 24—26
8. Canon of interpretation ... 26—28

CHAPTER II

BEARINGS ON LITERATURE ... 29—46

CHAPTER III

BEARINGS ON DIALECTS ... 47—59

CHAPTER IV

PHRASEOLOGY AND STYLE ... 60—90

CHAPTER V

GRAMMAR AND PHONOLOGY ... 91—98

INDEX

ABBREVIATIONS

As to Rock and Separate Rock Edicts :

Dh = Dhauli ; G = Girnār ; J = Jaugaḍa ; K = Kalsi ; M = Mansehra ; Sh = Shahbazgarhi ; So = Sopārā ; Ye = Yerraguḍi.

As to Minor Rock Edicts :

Bai = Bairāṭ ; Bra = Brahmagiri ; Ga = Gavīmaṭh ; Ja = Jaṭinga — Rāmeswara ; Pa = Pālkiguṇḍu ; Ma = Maski ; Ru = Rūpanāth ; Sa = Sahasrām ; Si = Siddāpura ; Ye = Yerraguḍi.

As to texts :

Ang. = Anguttara Nikāya ; J = Jātaka ; Dhp = Dhammapada ; Dhp. A. = Dhammapada Aṭhakathā.

Inscr. = Inscriptions of Asoka by Barua, Part II.

A.S.I. = Archæological Survey of India.

The rest are self-evident.

CHAPTER I

INTRODUCTORY

1. Number and Classification of Inscriptions: The number of Aśoka's inscriptions discovered and deciphered so far has increased by seventeen within the last sixteen years. The present total stands at one hundred and fifty-four. These may be conveniently divided, according to the materials whereon and the manner in which they are engraved, under these seven heads: (1) Hill-cave, (2) Rock, (3) Seperate Rock, (4) Minor Rock, (5) Stone-block, (6) Pillar, and (7) Minor Pillar. Conformably to this classification, the proposed figure can be worked out as follows:

1. Hill-cave: Barābar Hill-cave Inscriptions, I-III — 3
2. Rock: (a) ten Rock Edicts, I-VII, IX, X and XIV, each in seven recensions: Girnār, Kalsi, Yerraguḍi, Shahbazgarhi, Mansehra, Dhauli and Jaugaḍa. 10 × 7 = 70
   (b) one Rock Edict, VIII, in eight recensions: Girnār, Sopārā, Kalsi, Yerraguḍi. Shahbazgarhi, Mansehra, Dhauli and Jaugaḍa 1 × 8 = 8
   (c) three Rock Edicts, XI-XIII, each in five recensions: Girnār, Kalsi, Yerraguḍi, Shahbazgarhi and Mansehra 3 × 5 = 15
3. Separate Rock: two Edicts, separately incised on the Dhauli and Jaugaḍa rocks, each in two recensions 2 × 2 = 4
4. Minor Rock: one Edict in ten recensions: Brahmagiri, Siddāpura, Jaṭiṅga-Rāmesvara, Maski, Gavī math, Pālkiguṇḍu, Yerraguḍi, Rūpnāth, Bairāṭ and Sahasrām 1 × 10 = 10
5. Stone-bolck: one Edict, the Bhābru or Calcutta-Bairāṭ, in one recension — 1

6. Pillar : (a) six Edicts, I-VI, each in six recensions : Delhi-Topra, Delhi-Mīrāṭh, Lauriya-Ararāj (Radhiah), Lauriya-Nandangarh (Mathiah), Rāmpūrva and Kauśāmbī (Allahabad-Kosām) $6 \times 6 = 36$.
   (b) one Edict, VII, in one recension 1.
7. Minor Pillar : (a) one Schism Pillar Edict in three recensions : Sārnāth, Kauśāmbī (Allahabad-Kosām), and Sāñchī $1 \times 3 = 3$
   (b) Queen's Edict in one recension 1
   (c) Two Votive or Commemorative Inscriptions, one incised on a pillar at Lumbinī (Rummindeī) and the other on a pillar found near Nigāli Sāgar in the village of Niglīva 2

Total—154

Presumably there was a complete set of Fourteen Rock Edicts at Sopārā, of which only one, namely, VIII, is taken here into consideration. The additional matters of the Brahmagiri, Siddāpura and Jaṭiṅga-Rāmesvara versions of M.R.E. are generally treated as those belonging to M.R.E. II. The additional matters of the Yerraguḍi copy, too, might be treated so. But here these are treated as contents of one and the same edict. The above figure excludes two missing inscriptions, one incised on the so-called Lāṭ Bhairo of Benares, smashed to pieces during a riot in 1809, and another on a pillar at Pāṭaliputra, numerous fragments of which were found by Purnachandra Mukherji (V.A. Smith's Asoka, 3rd Ed., p. 28, f.n. 1).

2. Discovery of other inscriptions anticipated : If the Yerraguḍi rock had not represented the Suvarṇagiri of the Northern Mysore (Isila) copies of M.R.E., and if the city of Suvarṇagiri which was the seat of the Southern Viceroyalty were situated somewhere in Southern Mysore, one can anticipate the discovery of a far southern set of Rock Edicts together with one or more copies of M.R.E. Similarly the discovery of an Isila set of Rock Edicts is not as yet beyond expectation. A few copies of M.R.E., engraved on pillars, instead of on rocks, ought to have been found out in Northern India. One copy of Rock Edicts, one copy of M.R.E., and one copy of the Schism Pillar Edict may have vanished with the inscribed Pāṭaliputra pillar which is reported to have been destroyed in our days. The same catastrophe may have befallen a copy of Rock Edicts and a copy of M. R. E., that were, perhaps, engraved on the inscribed

Benares pillar, smashed to pieces not long ago. The ancient site of Pāṭaliputra may yet keep concealed original drafts and inscribed copies of Aśoka's edicts. Some copies of P.E. VII, engraved on pillars as well as stone-slabs count still among new discoveries to be made. The stump of Aśoka's monolith which is being worshipped as a phallic emblem in the Bhāskareswar temple of Bhuvaneswar may still bear a copy of M. R. E., and Schism Pillar Edict together with a set of Pillar Edicts. A few copies of the Queen's Edict and some inscriptions recording the donations of the second queen Kāluvāki are still to be included in the list of future archæological finds.

3. Location : The rocks bearing the eight sets of Rock Edicts are so situated as to make the general outline of Aśoka's domain proper. A full set, first noticed by Mr. Forrest in 1860, remains engraved "on a huge boulder of quartz on the northern bank of the Jumna just above her junction with the Tons river and about 15 miles to the west of Mussorie (Mausurī). The rock is situated about a mile and a half of Kalsi in the Dehra Dun District, U. P." The place itself, as Professor Bhandarkar thinks, lay close to the ancient and most prosperous city of Śrughna. Presumably the rock stood on the northern boundary of the northern portion of the empire under Aśoka's direct rule and the southern boundary of the semi-independent territory of the Nābhakas and Nābhalines who were counted among the *aparāntas* or peoples who lived near about the terminus of the trade-route leading to Śrughna.

Two incomplete sets, each of eleven edicts, are to be seen engraved in the newly conquered country and newly created province of Kaliṅga. The northern set, discovered by Mr. Kittoe in 1837, is engraved "on a rock called Aswastama, situated close to village of Dhauli........, about seven miles to the south of Bhuvaneswara, in the Puri District, Orissa." Though it is much easier to derive the name of Dhauli from Dhavali (a cow of the Vaishṇava fame), the phonetic change of Tosali into Dhauli through the intermediate *Tohali, Dohali* is not an impossiblity. The southern set "(first copied by Sir Walter Elliot in 1850) is engraved on the face of a picturesque rock in a large old fort called Jaugaḍā (Lack Fort), near the bank of Rishikulya river, about 18 miles to the west-north-west of the town of Ganjam." The rock was evidently situated close to the town of Samāpā, the official headquarters of the southern division of the Province of Kaliṅga. The Dhauli and Jaugaḍa rocks bear each copy of two Separate Rock Edicts.

A full set, found out by Mr. A. Ghose in 1929, is engraved on a few boulders of a rock near the village of Yerraguḍi just below the Tuṅgabhadrā, "about 8 miles north by west from Gooty in the Karnul District, Madras Presidency." Obviously the rock formed the natural boundary of Aśoka's empire at a point where it adjoined on the independent territory of the Cholas, and was situated in the vicinity of the official headquarters of the Rajjuka mentioned in the Yerraguḍi version of M. R. E.

As the fragment of R. E. VIII, discovered by Pandit Bhagvanlal Indraji in 1882, goes to prove, one (presumably complete) set was engraved at Sopārā, which preserves the modern identity of Sūrpāraka (Pali Suppāraka, Periplus Suppara, Ptolemy Soupara), the capital and highly important port of the ancient country called Aparānta or Sūnāparānta. Modern Sopārā is situated in the Thāna District to the north of Bombay.

One full set, first noticed by Colonel Tod in 1822, is to be seen "on the north-eastern face of the large rock on the road to the Girnār hill, half a mile to the east of the city of Junāgaḍ in Kathiawar." Girnār is undoubtedly the modern name of Girinagara, which was once the capital of Surāshṭra. The same rock bears also the inscription of Rudradāman I and that of Skandagupta, both of which locate near it the Sudarśana Lake caused to be excavated by Chandragupta Maurya, grand-father of Aśoka.

Two other full sets are to be seen on two sides of the Indus. That on the eastern side is engraved on three boulders, the first two of which were discovered by Cunningham and the third was first noticed in 1889 by an Indian subordinate of the Punjab Archæological Survey. The rock itself is situated "at Mansehra in the Hazara District of the North-West Frontier Province, about 15 miles north of Abbotabad." Apparently it marked the boundary between the Province of Gandhāra under the direct rule of Aśoka's Viceroy and the semi-independent territory of the Kāmbojas. The set on the western side of the Indus, first drawn attention to by General Court of Raja Ranjit Singh's service in 1836, is engraved on two separate boulders of a hill "with its western face looking down towards the village of Shahbazgarhi." This place is situated on the Makam river, "9 miles from Mardan in the Yusufzai subdivision of the Peshawar District of N. W. F. P., and about 40 miles from north-east of the town of Peshawar." It is just two miles distant from Kapurdagarhi. Evidently it marked the natural boundary between the Province of Gandhāra under the direct rule of Aśoka's Viceroy and the semi-independent territory of the Gāndhāras.

The Separate Rock Edicts stand together with the Dhauli and Jaugaḍa sets of Rock Edicts on the same two rocks. Among the ten copies of the Minor Rock Edict, the one at Yerraguḍi goes together with a full set of Rock Edicts. Of the remaining nine copies that stand independently of Rock Edicts, three lie to the north of the Narmadā and the Godāvarī, three between the Kṛishṇā and the Tuṅgabhadrā, and four to the south of the latter. The three copies that lie to the north of the Narmadā and the Godāvarī, are engraved, one "on a rock in an artificial cave near the summit of the Chandanpīr hill to the east of Sahasrām (Shahbad district, Bihār"), one "on the Rūpnāth rock (Jabalpur District, Central Provinces), lying at the foot of the Kaimur range of hills", and one, discovered by Carlleyle in 1872-73, "on a huge isolated block standing at the foot of a hill called Hinsagir hill near the ancient city of Bairāṭ (Jaipur State, Rajputānā)." The Bhābru Edict remained, before its removal to the Indian Museum, Calcutta, engraved on a small block of stone, which stood near the block bearing the Minor Rock Edict of Bairāṭ.

The three copies between the Kṛishṇā and the Tuṅgabhadrā are all to be found within the State of Hyderabad, which is to say, within the southern part of the old Maharāshṭra area. The two northern versions belong to the town of Kopbal "situated on the left bank of the stream Hire Halla, an important tributary to the river Tuṅgabhadrā", its distance from Maski being 54 miles (as the crow flies) and from Hamphi 21 miles (Yazdani, Hyderabad Arch. Series, No : 10, p. 18). One of them, is engraved on the highest spur of a range of hills to the west of the town, called Palkiguṇḍu (Palanquin or Canopy Boulder, 76° 10 E), and the other on a spur to the east of the town, called Gavīmaṭh (15° 21 N), attention to both being drawn by Mr. Narayan Rao Sastri in 1931. The third copy, discovered by Mr. C. Beadon in January, 1915, lies engraved on a rock "in the neighbourhood of Maski (*masgi, Masigi, Mosaṅgi)* of the Chalukya inscr. of Jayadevamalla), a village in the Lingsugur Taluk of the Raichur District of the Nizam's dominions."

The three copies, discovered by Mr. B. Lewis Rice in 1892, lie below the Tuṅgabhadrā and are all to be found within the State of Mysore, probably within the ancient country of Vanavāsī (now identified with North Canara). They remain "incised in three localities, all close to one another, in the Chitaldrug District of Mysore, namely, Siddāpura, Jaṭiṅga-Rāmeswara and Brahmagiri, not far from the site of an ancient locality (probably Isila of the Edict)."

The range of Aśoka's Pillar Edicts and Inscriptions is confined to Northern India. Of the six monoliths bearing each a copy of the Pillar Edicts, three are to be seen *in situ* in the Champāran District of North Behār. The nearest of them from Aśoka's capital, Pāṭaliputra, is the pillar which is "situated close to the small hamlet of Lauriyā, at a distance of one mile to the south-west of the much frequented Hindu temple of Ararāj-Mahādev, two miles and a half to the east-south-east of the village of Rādhia and twenty miles to the north-west of the Kesaria Stūpa, on the way to Bettia."

The Lauriyā Nandangarh or Māthiah pillar stands next to the Lauriya-Ararāj or Rādhiah on the road towards Nepāl. "It stands near the large village of Lauriyā, 3 miles north of Māthiah and very close to the ancient site of Nandangarh." Bloch (A. S. I., Annual Report, 1906-7, p. 119f.) has taken this pillar to mark the sacred site of the 'Charcoal Stūpa' (Aṅgāra-thūpa) of Pippalivana.

The third Champāran pillar is situated in the hamlet of Rāmpurva, about 20 miles north-north-east of the large village of Lauriyā and more than a mile north-east of the village of Piparia.

Of the remaining three monoliths, the so-called Allahabad Pillar which "stands near Ellenborough Barrack in the Fort" and bears a copy of the first six Pillar Edicts besides the Queen's Edict and one copy of the Schism Pillar Edict, must have been set up originally in the ancient city of Kauśāmbī (modern Kosām) on the right bank of the Yamunā, "about 30 miles south of west of Allahabad." The so-called Delhi - Toprā or Delhi-Sivālik, popularly known as Firoz Shah's Lāṭ, was brought to Delhi in 1356 by Sultan Firoz Tughlak "from a place called Toprā, on the bank of the Jumna, which was at the foot of the mountains, ninety *kos* from Delhi, and was erected on the summit of Kothila on Firozabad".

The second of the Delhi pillars, called Delhi-Mīrāṭh was also brought, according to Shams-i-Sirāj by the same Sultan from Mīrāṭh and set up near his "Hunting Palace".

Of the three copies of the Schism Pillar Edict, one is inscribed on the Kauśāmbī (Allhabad-Kosām) pillar. The fullar version, discovered by Mr. Oertel in 1905, is engraved on a pillar at Sārnāth, about three miles and a half north of Benares. The stump of this pillar still stands immediately to the north of the Dharmarājikā built by Aśoka. The third copy remains engraved "on a fallen and broken pillar at the southern entrance to the Great Stūpa of Sāñchī in Bhopal State, Central India."

The Lumbinī Pilgrimage inscription, commonly known as the Rummindeī Pillar Inscription, is engraved on a pillar, which stands to this day "at the shrine of Rummindeī, about one mile north of Paḍeria and 2 miles north of Bhagawanpur in the Nepalese Tahsil of that name situated to the north of the British District of Basti."

The second commemorative Pillar Inscription is one discovered on the western bank of a large tank called Nigāli Sāgar, "near the village of Niglīva in the Nepalese Tarai to the north of the Basti District." This pillar lies 'at a distance of about 13 miles to the north-west of' Lumbinī.

The three Hill-cave Inscriptions are engraved each on the wall of the cave-dwelling dedicated by Aśoka to the Ājīvikas in the Khalatika group of hills, now identified with the Barābar group, "situated sixteen miles due north of Gayā, or nineteen miles by the road." Close by is the Nāgārjunī group containing three caves excavated by king Daśaratha for the same sect of ascetics. The modern name Barābar is derived from Pravaragiri, a name by which the group of hills concerned was denoted in a mediæval Sanskrit inscription, while its earlier name, met with in the Mahābhārata, the Hāthigumphā Inscription of Khāravela and two short inscribed labels, was Gorathagiri, Goradhagiri, its earliest name being, of course, Khalatika, meaning 'bald-headed'. The three caves inscribed with the first, the second and the third inscription are known now-a-days by the name of Karṇa Chaupar, Sudāmā, and Viśvajhopri (Viśvāmitra) respectively, while the fourth bearing no inscription of Aśoka is named after Lomaśa Ṛishi. The last-mentioned cave is really the third in order. Aśoka designates the first cave as *Nigoha-Kubhā* (Banyan Cave).

(b) Clue to the placing of Aśoka's Rock inscriptions from the tradition of Buddhist missions : According to the Pali *Chronicles* and *Samanta-pāsādikā*, Thera Majjhantika was sent to Kasmīra-Gandhāra. In this region we have the Mansehra version of Aśoka's Rock Edicts. Thera Mahārakkhita was sent to the Yonaraṭṭha or Yonaloka. In this region we have the Shahbazgarhi version. Thera Majjhima was deputed to Himavanta or Himavantappadesa. Here we have the Kalsi version. Thera Mahādhammarakkhita was deputed to Mahāraṭṭha where we have the Kopbal copy of Aśoka's M. R. E. Thera Yonaka Dhammarakkhita went to Aparantaka where we have the Sopārā set of Aśoka's Rock Edicts. Thera Rakkhita was sent to Vanavāsa or Vanavāsī where we have the Isila copies of Aśoka's Minor Rock Edicts. Thera Mahādeva was sent to Mahisamaṇḍala or Mahisarattha where probably lies the Suvarṇgiri copy of M. R. E. The tradition of the Buddhist mission under the leadership of Soṇa and Uttara despatched to Suvannabhūmi, identified generally with Burma, is still open to dispute. According to the *Samanta-pāsādikā* and *Mahāvaṃsa*, Suvaṇṇabhūmi was a country which bordered on a sea and which was under the sway of a ferocious *rakkhasī*, who was evidently its presiding female deity. The text of the *Dipāvaṃsa*, as appears in Oldenberg's edition or in the *Samanta-pāsādikā*, preserves the earlier tradition which does not connect Suvaṇṇabhūmi with any sea or ocean and represents it as a place inhabited by the Piśāchas[1]. None need be surprised, therefore, if Suvaṇṇagiri were the intended name instead of Suvaṇṇabhūmi.

---

1. As quoted in the *Samanta-pāsādīkā*, the verse reads :
Suvaṇṇabhūmiṁ gantvāna Soṇuttarā mahiddhikā ।
Pisāçhe maddayitvāna Brahmajālaṁ adesisuṁ ॥

4. Alphabets and orthography : Aśoka's inscriptions are found engraved in two different scripts or alphabets, viz., Brāhmī and Kharoshṭhī. All but the two sets of his Rock Edicts at Shahbazgarhi and Mansehra are written in Brāhmī, which is written from left to right and rightly regarded as the Parent Script of which the various local scripts of India as well as the Sinhalese, Siamese, Burmese and Tibetan alphabets are later offshoots or variations. The Kharoshṭhī script, written from right to left like the cuneiform or wedge-shaped script of the Achæmenian inscriptions of Ancient Iran, was confined to the Gandhāra region in the extreme north-western part of Northern India and to that part of Khotān which lay contiguous to Aśoka's province of Gandhāra. The right half of an Aramaic inscription, discovered at Taxila, is assigned by Dr. Herzfeld to the reign of Aśoka. Evidently many of the scribes *(lipikaras)*, employed by Aśoka to engrave his records, were persons who hailed from Uttarāpatha and with whom the habitual form of writing was Kharoshṭhī. The Mysore scribe at least, who has signed his name in Kharoshṭhī as *Chapaḍa*, was such a person. The scribe engaged for 'Yerraguḍi, must have been another such person to whose Kharoshṭhi proclivity we owe the abra cadabra of a piece of record with one line written left to right and another from right to left, I mean, written boustrophedon. The Girnār scribe, too, appears to have endorsed his signature, but unfortunately the portion of the rock containing his name is peeled off irrevocably. The scribe of Sahasrām, the initial of whose name is *Hi*, must also have been a habitual Kharoshṭhī writer, otherwise we would not have three letters, *ti le ke*, written from right to left.

I cannot agree with Buhler and Professor Bhandarkar in thinking that the inversion of certain letters, noticed here and there in some of Aśoka's inscriptions, lends weight to the theory of development of the Brāhmī characters from the Aramaic or some such Semitic script, written from right to left. The inverted letters in Aśokan records seem due to the old habit of the Kharoshṭhī scribes to write from right to left. The letters resembling some in Brāhmī are traceable in the numerous inscribed seals of the Indus Valley. We are not as yet aware of their orthographic values. The Lalita-vistara list of 64 scripts mentions Brāhmī, Kharoshṭhī and Pushkarasārī as three parent scripts of India. None need wonder if by the third name was meant the script of Mohen jo-daro and Harappa.

As to orthography : All long vowels, including the two diphthongs, are of no use to the dialects of Sh and M. For the orthography of Dh, J, Barābar, Lumbinī, Nigāli Sāgar and Pillar Edicts, *ṛi*, *ḷi*, two diphthongs and *ḥ (visarga)* among the vowels, and *ṅ*, *ś*, *sh*, and *ksh* among the Sanskrit consonants are unnecessary. The orthography of P.E.V. shows the use of both *ḍ* and *ḷ* in *duḍi* (A) *duḷi*, while the orthography of all the copies of Rock Edicts makes use of *ḍh in vāḍhaṃ* (R.E. VII). The Ardhamāgadhī orthography is lacking in the use of *ḷ*, which is a Vedic and Dravidian consonant, and the Pali orthography employs *ḍ* and *ḍh* only in combinations, e.g., *niḍḍaṃ (nīḍam)* and *vuḍḍhi (vṛiddhi)*, but nowhere alone. The orthography of G employs *ri* and *ai* as vowel adjuncts, e.g., *risṭika* (R.E.V), *nisrito* (R.E.V), *thaira* (R.E.IV) and *traidasa* (R.E.V). Sh and M, too, make use of *ri* as a vowel adjunct in *driḍhabhatitā* (R.E.VII). The use of the diphthong *ai* as a vowel adjunct is met with in M.R.E. (Bra)—*mai (me)*, and also that of *ra* as a stop in *drahyitavyam*. All the three sibilants have their place in the orthography of K, Sh and M. The orthography of G provides for the use of *r* as a flag and of *ra* as a stop. The orthography of Sh and M has no need for *r* as a flag. Both *r* as a flag and *ra* as a stop are not found in the orthography of Ardhamāgadhī, but the Pāli orthography needs *ra* as a stop, e.g., for such words as *yatra, tatra, brahmā, brāhmaṇa, gadrabha, udriyati*. The orthography of G provides for such conjoint consonants as *mh, st, by, tp, db, sṭ, st* and *sv*. Pali orthography, too, makes provisions for *mh, ky, vy, by vh, st,* and *sm*. The Sh and M orthography makes room for a few more Sanskritic conjoint consonants.

5. Chronology : There still exists a sharp passage of arms over the vexed question of chronology of Aśoka's records. As regards the dated records, the pivot on which the dispute hinges is the question whether the recorded date is the date of engraving or it is the date of its codification or drafting. And as regards the undated records, the question of chronology rests entirely on the internal evidence of a record or a set of records, correctly ascertained and carefully weighed. An interval of time, however short, must be allowed between the date of codification of a record and that of its engraving on a rock, or a slab, or a pillar. But the question still

is—what should be our actual concern, the date of codification or that of engraving? The conventional phraseology of Aśoka is that something is 'caused to be written' (*likhapitā, lekhāpitā*) in a particular year of *abhisheka*, something is caused to be erected (*usapāpite*), or something is 'dedicated' (*dinā*). Did Aśoka mean by 'written' engraved or merely codified? Professor Bhandarkar opines that wherever a record is said to have been written with a view to its permanency, there the expression 'caused to be written' must be taken to mean, 'caused to be engraved.' I have sought to show that wherever a *Dhaṁmalipī* is said to have been written there are phrases to indicate Aśoka's motive to see it long endure (*Inscr.*, ii, p. 223). Behind the very idea of causing something to be engraved in stone was the certainty of its durability (cf. Aṅguttara I; p. 283: *pāsāṇe lekhā chiraṭṭhitikā*). When Aśoka by way of an apology said (R. E. XIV) that it was not possible to cause *Dhaṁmalipis* to be 'written' all over his empire owing to its vastness, he must have meant by 'wtitten' engraved, promulgated.

This settled, we may easily proceed to put the dated records in their following chronological order:

1. (a) Barābar Hill-cave Inscriptions, I-II .. 12th year.
   (b) Rock Edicts, I-IV .. .. ,,
2. Barābar Hill-cave Inscription, III .. .. 19th year.
3. (a) Lumbinī Pillar Inscription .. .. 20th year.
   (b) Nigāli Sāgar Pillar Inscription .. .. ,,
4. Pillar Edicts, I-IV .. .. 26th year.
5. Pillar Edict VII .. .. 27th year.

Here we have a clear-cut chronological scheme, workable in three stages of progress. In the first stage Aśoka started engraving his records in the 12th year of his *abhisheka*, in the second, in the 19th year, and in the third, in the 26th. In his P. E. VI, Aśoka tells us that he caused the *Dhaṁmalipī* to be engraved for the first time in the 12th year of his *abhisheka*. The data of chronology pertaining to the second and third stages go to show that the work of engraving was continued through a period of two years at least. The internal evidence of R. E. V. namely, the mention of the fact of the first appointment of the *Dharmamahāmātras* in the 13th year, is sufficient to prove that this and remaining records of the Rock series were not engraved in the 12th year, and that they must have been promulgated sometime after that, either in course of the 13th year, or later still. Thus we definitely know the *terminus ad quo* of each period of activity but not its *terminus ad quem*. As for the *terminus ad quem* or lower limit, we may take guidance from Aśoka's quinquennial system (R. E. III, S. R. E. I), which is borne out also by the Sarvāstivāda tradition in the Divyāvadāna (p. 45). Allowing an interval of 5 years between two successive stages or periods, the 14th year is found to be the *terminus ad quem* of the first period and the 21st year that of the second, while, in default of a dated record, referable to the fourth stage, the *terminus ad quem* of the third period must be left open. The presumed *terminus ad quem* of the first period is confirmed by the recorded date (14th year) of enlargement of the Stūpa of Buddha Koṇāgamana (Nigāli Sāgar).

The first four Rock Edicts appear to have been despatched in two batches for engraving successively in the 12th year, the remaining edicts of this series were sent out in as many as five despatches from the capital, R. E. V. alone in one despatch, R. E. VI, VII and VIII in another, R. E. IX and X in a third, R.E. XI, XII and XIII in a fourth, and R.E. XIV alone, last of all. R.E.V may be definitely referred to the 13th year and R. E. XIV to the 14th (*Inscr.* ii, p. 47). Over and above the introductory clause : *Devānaṁpiye Piyadasi lājā hevaṁ āha* in R.E. XI, the reason for putting R.E. XI, XII and XIII in one despatch is clear from the fact of exclusion of them all at Dhauli and Jaugaḍa. R. E. XIII alone deserved on account of its allusion to the conquest of Kaliṅga to be withheld from promulgation in all parts of Kaliṅga, but neither R. E. XI nor R. E. XII. Their omission was undoubtedly due to their being in a bad company. Obviously R. E. XII merited wide publication everywhere.

The Rock Edicts speak nowhere of the stone-pillars (*silāthaṁbhā*). The fact of their erection is recorded in the two commemorative inscriptions, one engraved on the Lumbinī pillar and the other on the Nigāli Sāgar, while their existence is presupposed by P. E. VII and M. R. E. (Ru, Sa). Both the commemorative Pillar inscriptions, dated in the 20th year of *abhisheka*, record the fact of Aśokā's pilgrimage, while of the two pillars, one was erected on the site of the village of Lumbinī because it was known as the sacred place of nativity of

Buddha Sākyamuni, and the other on the site of the enlarged Stūpa of Buddha Koṇāgamana. The three Champāran pillars, inscribed each with a set of the first six Pillar Edicts dated in the 26th year of *abhisheka*, stand, as pointed out by Vincent Smith, on the road towards Nepāl, which is to say, towards Lumbinī and Niglīva, in short, towards Kapilavastu. In Bloch's opinion, one of them, namely, the Lauryia-Nandangarh pillar, stands on the ancient site of the 'Charcoal Stūpa' of Pippalivana. Thus the erection of these pillars may be associated with the course of Aśoka's pilgrimage to the Buddhist sacred places undertaken, according to the Divyāvadāna legend, under the guidance of his religious preceptor Upagupta. The king said to Upagupta : *Ayaṁ me manoratho ye Bhagavatā Buddhena pradeśā adhyushitās tān archeyaṁ, chihṇāni cha kuryaṁ paśchimasyāṁ janatāyām anugrahārtham.* "This is my mental resolve that the places hallowed by the presence of Buddha, the Blessed One, I should worship and mark them out with tangible signs for the benefit of (lit., as a matter of favour to) posterity."

One may take it that the tangible signs put up to mark the sacred sites were the monolithic pillars erected by Aśoka on the various sacred sites of the Buddhists at the second stage of his vigorous action which commenced in the 19th year of *abhisheka*. It is to this period of Aśoka's reign that the Pali traditions refers the episode of fresh troubles in the Buddhist Saṅgha threatening it with schism and heresy and necessitating the adoption of a drastic measure by the king. The erection of commemorative pillars at Sārnāth, Kauśāmbī and Sāñchī (and, may be, also at Pāṭaliputra) must have preceded the engraving thereon of the Schism Pillar Edict, a copy on each pillar. In other words, the engraving or promulgation of Aśoka's special ordinance in the Schism Pillar Edict is to be dated shortly after Aśoka's piety-tour, probably undertaken in the 19th and completed in the 20th year of *abhisheka,* despite the fact that it is referable to the same period of activity. The edict in question was promulgated either towards the close of the 20th or in the 21st year. The relative position of the so-called Queen's Edict, engraved on the very same Kauśambī pillar, which is inscribed with a copy of the Schism Pillar Edict, seems to suggest that its engraving took place either at the time of Aśoka's visit to Kauśāmbī, anyhow earlier than the promulgation of the schism ordinance. The placing of the date of the Queen's Edict in between that of the Rock and that of the Pillar Edicts is justifiable also on the following three grounds :

(1) That the erection of Aśoka's monoliths is unthinkable previous to the second stage of activity, particularly Aśoka's systematic pilgrimage ;

(2) That for the first time the Queen's Edict introduces us to the young prince Tīvala (apparently, a pet name), son of Aśoka by the second Queen Kāluvāki, while the whole set of Rcck Edicts is reticent on Aśoka's sons ; and

(3) That the existence of Aśoka's pillars, the donations made by his queens, and the charities on the part of his sons are all presupposed by P.E. VII, engraved in the 27th year.

All that now remains for me to do is to settle the date of engraving of the Minor Rock and two Separate Rock Edicts.

As regards the Minor Rock Edict, the opinion of scholars has swayed so far to two extremes, either that it is the earliest, or that it is the latest record of Aśoka. Hultzsch inclines even to connect it with a stage, which commenced with Aśoka's pilgrimage to Saṁbodhi, undertaken in the 10th year of *abhisheka* and preceded the engraving of the *Dhaṁmalipis* in the 12th year. He suggests further that by the clause, *athi saṁkhitena* in R.E. XIV Aśoka must have meant the text of M.R.E. But as shown (*Inscr.* ii, p. 329), all the distinguishing clauses in R.E. XIV are applicable only to the set of Rock Edicts, previously published. There are, moreover, texts in the Rock series that are even smaller than M.R.E.

Professor Mookerji employs a much subtler argument to prove an early date of M.R.E., namely, that when it was promulgated, the engraving of a record on a rock or a stone-pillar was just an idea, and not a *fait accompli*. But this is falsified by the fact that the direction as to engraving on rock or pillar,occurring at the end of M.R.E. (Ru, Sa) is in language and effect the same as that at the end of P. E. VII, as will appear from the following citations :

1. M.R.E. Rūpnāth : *Iya cha aṭhe pavatisu lekhāpetavālata, hadha cha athi silāthabhe silāthaṁbhasi lākhāpetavāyata.*
2. M.R.E. Sahasrām : *Ima cha aṭhaṁ pavatesu likhāpayātha, ya* (*ta*) *vā athi silāthaṁbhā tata pi likhāpayātha.*
3. P.E. VII : *Iyaṁ dhaṁmalibi ata athi silāthaṁbhāni vā silāphalakāni vā tata kaṭaviyā yena chilaṭhitike siyā.*

Comparing them, none can fail to notice that the direction appended to M.R.E. presupposes the existence of rocks and stone-pillars, while that appended to P.E. VII presupposes the existence of stone-pillars and stone-slabs as engraving materials The direction in M. R. E. does not suggest the use of stone-slabs as engraving material, but that in P. E. VII does, and the reason undoubtedly is that already prior to the engraving of P. E. VII these were used as material for the engraving of the Bhābru Edict. Thus whatever the actual date of the *dhaṁma- sāvaṇa*, the date of its engraving is posterior to the erection of pillars by Aśoka, which, as I tried to show, is unthinkable before the second stage of activity. R. E. VI speaks indeed of giving verbal orders for announcement or proclamation (*s›āvāpakaṁ*), but not necessarily of the particular proclamation contained in M.R.E. The preamble of P E VII, on the other hand, reveals the process of thinking which led Aśoka to inculcate the principles of piety and to proclaim the messages of piety. The proclamations of piety were, however, many, precisely like the formulations of the doctrine of piety—*dhaṁma-sāvanāni sāvāpitāni*, in which case the extant Minor Rock Edict records just one of the many. Fortunately, apart from a general statement concerning the proclamations, P.E. VII contains a specific statement regarding a particular proclamation made (*dhaṁma-sāvane kaṭe*), and the principles of piety emphasized in M.R.E. are obviously repeated in P.E. VII.

R.E.IV, promulgated in the 12th year, speaks of the wonderful result in the matter of promotion of the cause of piety by means of *dhaṁmānusathi*, and it was left to M.R.E. to proclaim the wonderful result in the same matter achieved by means of *parākrama*. R.E. VI and R.E. X tell us how and why Aśoka was exerting himself vigorously and with what ends in view his officer should be energetic, while the achievement of the desired result left to be boldly proclaimed in M.R.E.

In Professor Bhandarkar's opinion, the statements in M.R.E. conclusively prove that the proclamation is concerned just with the short period of one year or more when Aśoka stayed with the Saṅgha. The use of the present tense in the statement; *sumi upāsake*, "when I am a lay worshipper", unmistakably suggests the fact of the case.

I am unable to accept this finding for this reason at least that in the Chariyā Piṭaka thre are narrations, where *homi*, a Pali equivalent of *sumi* of the edict, is used as historical present, cp. Sachchatāpasa-chariya, (Chariyā Piṭaka,III. 8) :

Punāparaṃ yadā homi tāpaso sachchasavhayo ।
sachchena lokaṁ pālesiṁ, samaggaṁ janam akās ahaṃ ॥

Note that in the above stanza *homi* (present tense) occurs in the first line, and *pālesiṁ* (aorist past) in the second.

Without wrangling about the force of the expression, *iminā kālena* (by this time), or of its variants, *imāyaṁ velāyaṁ* (at this hour) and *etena aṁtalena* (at this interval of time) which may refer as well to the short period of one year or more when Aśoka was exerting himself strenuously, as to the *interim* period between the commencement of strenuous effort and the formal promulgation of the edict, I may point out that the relative positions of R.E. and M.R.E. on the face of the same rock suggests at once a later date of engraving of the latter. It is quite possible that although the proclamation was made earlier, it was caused to be engraved later,—later even than the engraving of the Minor Pillar Edicts and Inscriptions and the first six Pillar Edicts, which is to say, in course of the 26th or 27th year.

The attention of all is focussed on the enigmatic phrase, *vyuṭhena, vivuthena*, 256. Happily with the elimination of the word *lati* from the Sahasrām text (*Inscr.*, ii, p. 107) the nightmare of night theory is gone off for ever. The contest at last remains between the correctness of equating Aśoka's *vyutha, vyuṭha, vivutha* with Kauṭilya's *vyushṭa*, a technical term meaning dating in terms of the regnal year, month, fortnight and day, and that of equating it with *vyavasita, vyushita, vyushṭa* meaning 'something issued, sent out, despatched' or simply 'despatch', and having connection with Kauṭilya's *vyavasyanti (Arthaśāstra*, II. 10) : *vividhaṁ taṁ vyvasyanti*. To accept the first equation is to interpret *vyuthena* 256 as 'by date 256', 256 B.E., 256 years from the Buddha's demise. And to accept the second equation is to interpret the same as 'by despatch of 256 (missioners or copies)'. The date interpretation does not stand in the face of the explanatory clause—*256 sata vivāsāta* (Ru), *duve-sapaṁnā sata vivuthā ti*, "two hundred and fifty six (missioners or copies the message, preferably the latter) were dispatched."

The two Separate Rock Edicts are undated like the

Minor Rock Edict. Although one of them is addressed to the City-judiciaries and the other to his personal and official representatives at Tosali and Samāpā, the general tenor of the two records is the same. As a matter of fact, they form two cognate records, despatched at the same time and intended for the same places. From the manner of their engraving on the face of the same two rocks bearing the Rock Edicts, it is evident that they were engraved later than the latter set of records. The Rock Edicts speak of households of Aśoka and of those of his brothers, sisters and other kinsfolk raṅking with him in family relationship but nowhere of his sons or children. The Queen's Edict alone among the Minor Pillar Inscriptions introduces his second queen as the mother of Tīvala, certainly then quite a young prince. In the Mysore copies of M.R.E. a brother or son of his figures as his Viceroy in the southern frontier provinc. For the first time in P.E. VII, engraved in the 27th year of *abisheka*, we read of the charities of his sons who typified the princes of the blood *(devikumālas)*. The Separate Rock Edicts, on the other hand, represent three of the *Kumāras* as his Viceroys, stationed at Tosali, Takasilā and Ujeni. Presumably these Kumāra Viceroys were appionted from among his grown up sons.

The Separate Rock Edicts must be dated later than the Rock also on the palpable ground of modification of the general fiive-year rule of official tours of inspection in the case of the three frontier provinces of Kalinga, Gandhāra and Avantī, with a view to the checking of miscarriage of justice and pacification of popular feelings, which must then have run very high against official tyranny. Professor Mookerji's argument other way about is untenable (*Inscr*, ii p. 244 f). These also indicate signs of frontier troubles arising from the action of the independent 'frontagers' *(aṁtānaṁ avijitānaṁ)*. The Divyāvadāna legend refers the rise of frontier troubles to the closing period of his reign. So far as the Rock and Minor Rock Edicts are concerned, they speak only of cordial relationship and peaceful intercommunication with all the important 'frontagers'. The only internal trouble to be dealt with then was that which arose from the mischievous action of the Āṭavikas.

These considerations cannot but lead us to the conclusion that the two Separate Rock Edicts were promulgated even later than P.E.VII. There is, however, no means as yet to ascertain the exact date of their engraving.

6. Forms, Merits and Defects : Kauṭilya (Arthaśāstra, II. 10) distinguishes between the following seven forms of royal writs śāsanāni : (1) *prajñāpana-lekha*, public notification, 'writ of information'; (2) *ājñālekha*,'writ of command', orders, official instructions; (3) *paridāna-lekha* 'writ of remission'; (4) *nisṛishṭi-lekha*, 'writ of licence' ; (5) *prāvṛittika-lekha*, 'writ of guidance' ; (6) *pratilekha*, 'writ of reply' ; (7) *sarvatraga-lekha*, 'writ for wide circulation'.

The 'writ of information' is defined as an epistolary form of writing by which the person or persons concerned are informed of the contents of a message to be faithfully delivered with the words—"Thus saith the king" (*anena vijñāpitaṁ 'Evam āha'*).

The 'writ of command' is a form, which contains the king's orders, either for rewards or punishments, particularly meant for the officers (*bhartur ājñā bhavet yatra nigrahānugrahau prati, viśeshena tu bhṛityeshu*).

The third is meant for 'the bestowal of honour for deserving merit', either in the manner of a specific relief or as gifts.

The fourth denotes a form to be adopted in announcing to the classes of people or to the localities concerned certain special privilege (*anugraha*) by way of remission, granted in obedience to the king's orders (*anugraho yo nṛipater nirdeśāt*).

This denotes rather a form meant for granting licence or permission by word or deed, which deserves therefore to be treated rather as a verbal order (*vāchika-lekha*).

The fifth is a form meant for timely giving guidance as to how to provide against or ward off possible and impending calamities.

The sixth is to be adopted in sending a suitable reply to a letter in accordance with the king's orders.

The seventh represents a form to be adopted in issuing general directions to all official agents concerned in matters of general welfare and public safety.

Going by Kauṭilya's classification and definition of the different forms of royal writs, the three Barābar Hill-cave Inscriptions must be put in the category of *paridāna-lekha*, and the second half of the Lumbinī Pillar Inscription in that of *parihāra-lekha*. The concluding portion of P.E. IV granting as it does three days' respite to criminals condemned to death by court sentence deserves the name of *paridāna* and *parihāra* as well as of *nisṛishṭi*. R.E. VIII and Lumbinī Pillar and Nigāli Sāgar Inscriptions that are, on the whole, mere records of the king's pious tours and works carry no other force than that of writs of public 'information, even without the words "Thus saith the king."

The Schism Pillar Edict is typically an *ājñālekha* or writ of command, in so far as the Buddhist schismatics go, and a *sarvatraga-lekha* as regards the general directions issued to the *Mahāmātraṣ* concerned. Similarly, though the Queen's Edict, when judged by its content, is just a *paridāna-lekha,* according to its technical form, it is just an example of *sarvatraga.*

The First Separate Rock Edict which is addressed to the city-judiciaries of Tosali and Samāpā is an *ājñālekha* beyond any doubt. As for S.R.E. II, it contains certain directions to his official representatives as to the general policy to be followed in dealing with the frontier peoples and 'frontagers', whence it deserves the name of Kauṭilya's *sarvatraga.*

The text embodied in the Minor Rock Edict is by Aśoka's own nomenclature *dhammasāvana* or proclamation of piety. R.E. II, R.E. XIV, P.E. VI and P.E. VII deserve the same appellation by their contents. They are *sarvatraga* in the literal sense of the term, though not according to Kauṭilya's definition.

According to Aśoka, P.E. V stands as a typical instance of his *dhaṁma-niyama* or regulation of piety. A regulation is in its substance an *ājñālekha* as well as a *sarvatraga* under Kauṭilya's definition. R.E. I, R.E. III, R.E. V, R.E. VI, R.E. VII, R.E. XII, R.E. XIII, P.E. IV and Bhābru Edict partake all of the character of a *dhaṁma-niyama.* R.E. IV, R.E. IX, R.E. X, P.E. I, P.E. II and P.E. III just inculcate Aśokā's *dhaṁmānusathini* or principles of piety.

But all as engraved are *prajñāpana-lekha*, writs of information, or what Jayaswal would call 'public notification.'

Viewing Aśoka's records in the light of Kauṭilya's forms of royal writs, Jayaswal has reasonably doubted the propriety of the name of 'Edicts' applied by European scholars to them. Judged by Kauṭilya's prescriptions, they are either of these two descriptions, public notifications and proclamations, but not edicts.

By definition an edict is an order proclaimed by authority. Strictly adhered to this definition, the name of edict is not applicable to the bulk of Aśoka's records. But liberally construed, most of the records are edicts in the sense that whether apparently moral instructions or public proclamations, they tacitly carry with them the will and authority of the sovereign to enforce obedience to the principles of piety as inculcated, emphasized and enforced by Aśoka.

Aśoka's edicts fulfil almost all the thirteen purposes *(arthāḥ)* of the royal writs mentioned by Kauṭilya, viz., *nindā* (condemnation), *praśaṁsā* (commendation), *pṛichchhā* (interrogation), *ākhyānaṁ* (narration), *arthanā* (beseeching), *pratyākhyānam* (refusal), *upālambha* (censure), *pratishedha* (prohibition), *chodanā* (urging), *sāntvam* (conciliation), *abhyavapatti* (promise of help), *bhartsanam* (threat), and *anunaya* (persuasion). These may be illustrated as follows :

1. Condemnation : R.E. IX—"Womenfolk perform many, diverse, minor and meaningless rites."

   S.R.E. I—"Some one gets indeed at this, (but) he, too, does a part, not the whole of it".

2. Commendation : R.E. I—"There are, however, certain festive gatherings approved of as good."

   R.E. III—"Good is respectful attention to mother and father."

3. Interrogation : P.E. II—*Kiyaṁ chu dhaṁme_ti ?* "What is piety ?"

4. Narration : R.E. III—*Hevaṁ āha*, "Thus saith."

5. Beseeching : S.R.E. I—"You better see to this."

6. Refusal : S.R.E. I—"These propensities may not be mine."

7. Censure : P.E. III—"These are the things that lead to evil."

   S.R.E. I—"You do not get as far as this matter goes."

8. Prohibition : R.E. I—"Here no sacrifice shall be performed by immolating a living thing whatsoever, and no festive gathering held."

9. Urging : R.E. VI—"This is to be reported to me in all places, at all times."

10. Conciliation : S.R.E. I—"To me all men are like my progeny."
11. Promise of help : P.E. VII—"These and many other chief officers are occupied with the dispensing of charities."
12. Threat : R.E. XIII—"They shall be ashamed of their conduct and not get killed."
13. Persuasion : R.E. XIII—*ta pi anuneti anunijhāpeti*, "them, too, he entreats and persuades to think."

According to Kauṭilya, the qualities of composition of a writ *(lekhasampat)* consist in proper arrangement of subject-matters *(arthakrama)*, relevancy *(sambandha)*, completeness *(paripūrṇatā)*, sweetness *(mādhuryam)*, dignity *(audāryam)*, and lucidity or clearness *(spashṭatvam)*, and its faults or drawbacks *(lekhadoshāḥ)* lie in ugliness *(akāntiḥ)*, contradiction *(vyāghātaḥ)*, repetition *(punaruktam)*, bad grammar *(apaśabdaḥ)*, and mis-arrangement *(samplava)*.

The first quality, called *arthakrama*, is no other than what is held out as the essential feature of a discourse of the Buddha having a good beginning, a good middle, and a good end *(ādi, kalyāṇaṁ, majjhe kalyāṇaṁ, pariyosāne kalyāṇaṁ)*. Such texts of Aśoka as R.E. I, R.E. IV, R.E. V, R.E. VI, R.E. IX, R.E. XII, S.R.E. I, P.E. IV, P.E. V, and P.E. VII are conspicuous with this quality of presentation.

The second quality of *sambandha* is what the Buddha insisted on as *pubbāparānusandhi*, consistency or harmonious linking of that which precedes with that which follows. Both relevancy of statements and consistency of thoughts are possessed in abundance by the texts of Aśoka. Sometimes a chain of argument on a particular question runs through consecutive texts, e.g., R.E. IX, R.E. X and R.E. XI.

The third quality of *paripūrṇatā* or completeness is just the opposite of what Aśoka regrets as being *asamati (asamāpti)*, *i.e.*, incompleteness (R.E. XIV). Kauṭilya's definition of completeness is fully brought out in the Pali Canonical description of the Buddha's mode of presentation of a text of Discourse : *satthaṁ savyañjanaṁ kevala-paripuṇṇaṁ parisuddhaṁ brahma-chariyam pakāseti*—claiming that "It expresess an idea of unalloyed holy life through a statement, complete in all respects, replete with sense and well-articulated sounds." The ten tests of well-articulated sounds, mentioned by Buddhaghosa, are :

> *sithila-dhanitañ cha dīgha-rassaṁ,*
> *lahuka-garukañ cha niggahītaṁ,*
> *sambandhaṁ va vavatthitaṁ vimuttaṁ,*
> *dasadhā vyañjanabuddhiyā pabhedo ti.*

"There is maintained the tenfold distiction between high and low accents, long and short syllables, heavy and light measures, nasals, combined, properly placed and free sounds."

The remaining three qualities of sweetness, dignity and lucidity are fully covered by those by which the Buddha sought to characterise a noble form of speech (Brahmajāla Sutta) : *Pharusa-vāchaṁ pahāya . . yā sā vāchā neḷā kaṇṇa-sukhā pemanīyā hadayaṅgamā porī bahujana-kantā bahujana-manāpā.* "Avoiding harshness, that form of speech which is faultless, pleasant to the ears, captivating, appealing to the heart, urban, agreeable to many, charming to many."

In this connexion Buddhaghosa points out the distinction between *kaṇṇasukhā* and *pemanīyā* by the sweetness of expression (*vyañjana-madhuratā*) and the sweetness of sense (*atthamadhuratā*). Aśoka himself claims the sweetness of sense (*athasa madhuratā*, R.E. XIV) as a distinctive quality of his edicts.

As for the sweetness of expression and winning force, Aśoka records thus his preference for a person endowed with these qualities : *e akhakhase (aphalusaṁ) achaṁḍe sakhinālaṁbhe...hosati* (S.R.E. I), "he who will be found to be not of harsh speech and fierce nature, but possessed of winsome cordiality."

Kauṭilya's *agrāmya* corresponds to the Buddha's *porī*, meaning that which is urban, polite, dignified, chaste. Shama Sastri thinks that by *agrāmya* Kauṭilya banned 'colloquial words', which is far from the case. All that he meant was a language avoiding that which is uncouth, ugly, vulgar, unpolished, slang. Aśoka's texts abound with colloquialisms or current popular idioms glowing with lucidity and dignity.

As for the use of colloquial words, the followers of the Buddha had a clear mandate from the Master in whose judgement it was sheer dogmatism to ban a local word or expression because it is not in vogue in another locality. There are various words, for instance, current in different localities for one and the same thing, say, "bowl" : *pāti*, *patta*, *vittha*, *sarāva*, *dhāropa*, *poṇa*, and *pisila*. Each man thinks that his word is the only correct form of expression, whereas each local word is as good as another, provided that it denotes to a person precisely the thing for which it is meant. In this connexion, as pointed out by Winternitz (History of Indian Lit. II, p. 603) and myself (Old Brāhmī Inscriptions in the Udayagiri and Khaṇḍagiri Caves), the Buddha's direction is "not to insist unduly on his own provincial dialect (*janapadanirutti*) and at the same time not to deviate from general linguistic usage" (Araṇavibhaṅga Sutta, Majjhima III, p. 234 f.). Consistently with this the Buddha disapproves the ideā of putting his words in the *Chhandas* or Vedic Sanskrit, governed by the law of Metre and Rhythm, and enjoins that these should be studied by each follower "in his own dialect" (*sakāya niruttiyā*), "each in his own language" (Winternitz, *op. cit.* p. 603 ; Oldenberg and Rhys Davids, S.B.E. XX, p. 150 f.). Buddhaghosa understands by *saka-nirutti*, 'Māgadhī, the language spoken by the Buddha', as distinguished from 101 spoken dialects of the time. If the expression were *sakāya sakāya*, there would have been no ground of dispute over the interpretation of the Buddha's injunction. But from the context, it is clear that the Buddhist brethren who were recruits from different nationalities, different communities, different castes, and different families, were apt to corrupt the Buddha's words by going to reproduce or represent them each in his own dialect (*sakāya niruttiyā Buddhavachanaṁ dūsenti*, Chullavagga, V. 33).

The intelligibility, lucidity and dignity of Aśoka's language need no comment. He was certainly aware of repetition (*punarukti*) as a defect of composition. As for grammatical irregularities (*apaśabda*), we need not rigidly apply the canon of Pāṇini or the standard of Pali in adjudicating upon the composition of Aśokan texts which follows its own grammar and idiom.

As for drawbacks, Aśoka in his R.E. XIV, has offered explanations for three of them, noticed in the previously published Rock Edicts. These are : (1) the impossibility of their promulgation all over his empire on account of its vastness ; (2) the repetition of the same thing over and over again, justifiable only on the ground of sweetness of its meaning; and (3) the incompleteness of the records to be accounted for either by the comprehension of local circumstances, or by the consideration of other reasons, or by the fault of the *Lipikara*. R.E. XIII was precluded, for instance, from promulgation at Tosali and Samāpā owing to its unsuitability to Kaliṅga. But the preclusion of R.E. XI and R.E. XII, was certainly due to an error of judgement on the part of the *Lipikara* in Pāṭaliputra and his instructor.

The consideration of other reasons as an explanation of incompleteness is unintelligible otherwise than on the supposition that the engraving of the Rock Edicts was thought unnecessary in those parts of his empire where he had not to reckon with ruling peoples, alien and hostile to the Indo-Aryan religion and social system.

The errors due to the fault of the *Lipikara* consist generally in omissions of a few words, clauses, or sentences, or in mis-spellings. The omissions in one copy may now be easily supplied from another, which is fuller. The spelling mistakes may be rectified by means of a comparative study of the phonetic system and orthography of the language of a particular set. The usual Girnār word for *iha is idha*, but accidentally we have *iloka* for *idhaloka* in R.E. XI. Here *iloka* is palpably a mis-spelling. In the case of Shahbazgarhi, the word is *hida* (R.E. I) or *iha* (R.E. XIII), but in several edicts we get *ia*, which is undoubtedly a mis-spelling of *iha*. In discussing the phonetic distinction and orthography of each set, the philologist must beware of these minor errors due to the scribe-engraver's faults.

7. Problem of Variants: The problem of variants arises in connection with the edicts that are found in copies more than one, such as Rock, Separate Rock, Minor Rock and Schism Pillar. As regards the first six Pillar Edicts, barring the omissions and commissions committed by the king's agents responsible for drafting, editing and engraving, the variations in spellings are confined to the lengthening of the final vowel *a* in the Delhi-Toprā, Delhi-Mīrāṭh and Allahabad-Kosam copies, *e.g.*, *chā*, *chevā*, *ahā*, *yevā*, *agāyā*, *asvasā*, *goṇasā*, which is a marked tendency of the Kalsi version of the Rock Edicts, and to the shortening of the final vowel *a* in the remaining three copies, *e.g.*, *lāja*, *likhāpita*, *vaḍhita*, which is a marked

tendency of the Lumbinī and Nigāli Sāgar Pillar Inscriptions. The variations suggest only a slight phonetic difference in one and the same Prakrit dialect as it prevailed in the western and eastern halves of the Buddhist Middle Country. It is imaginable that two separate drafts had to be made, one for the western half and the other for the eastern; two additional copies for each half were left to be made from each draft. The *Yukta* entrusted with the duty of drafting for any half was competent to draft the text of P.E. VII (DT) despite its greater resemblance with the first six edicts of the western half.

As regards the Rock Edicts, the Dhauli and Jaugaḍa versions were either one a copy from the other or both copies from one and the same original draft. The clause containing the name of the rock on which one of the two versions was inscribed (R.E. I) must have been inserted by the local editor. The few variants, *drakhati* (R.E. I), *Piyadrasine* (R.E. I), *savatra* (R.E. II). and *drasayitu* (R.E. IV), that occur in J, were apparently due to the unconscious influence of the Shahbazgarhi copy on the *Yukta* who prepared the copy for Jaugaḍa. Here one is to imagine that one and the same *Yukta* did the copying from drafts for both the places. From the instance of *drakhati* (J), *dakhati* (Sh), it is evident that the *Yukta* concerned made a confusion between the two places.

The Kalsi and Yerraguḍi texts so closely resemble each other that they may be regarded almost as based upon two copies from one and the same draft intended originally for Kalsi.

In one or two places, a grammatical form which befits M, occurs in Sh, and a form which befits Sh, occurs in M, such as *dhramanisite* (R.E. V, Sh), *dhramanisito* (M); in one or two places the Sh form occurs also in M, *e.g.*, *mukhato* (R.E. VI); and in one or two places the M form occurs also in Sh, *e.g.*, *mokshaye* (R.E. V), and even the same Māgadhī form, *apalibodhaye*, in both. These may be accounted for by the fact that one *Yukta* prepared both the drafts with habitual or unconscious predilection for the Eastern dialect.

The Girnār texts agree generally with the Dhauli and Jaugaḍa, and occasionally with Yerraguḍi, and yet, on the whole, they appear to have an originality or distinct individuality of their own.

It is difficult to say anything definitely regarding the

Sopārā texts. The small fragment of R.E. VIII, which now survives, goes to show that they were just local phonetic adaptations from Yerragudi. The Dhauli and Jaugada versions of Separate Rock Edicts exhibit some variations here and there, which cannot be accounted for otherwise than by the fact that they were based on two slightly different drafts, and not simply copies from one and the same draft.

With regard to the Minor Rock Edict, one may observe that the three Mysore texts were based on three copies from one and the same draft. The same remark holds true of the two Hyderabad versions found at Gavīmaṭh and Pālkiguṇḍu. The Maski text has a distinct form of its own. The same remark applies equally to the Yerraguḍi text which in the wealth of its contents compares favourably with the Mysore copies. The Rūpnāth, Bairāṭ and Sahasrām texts appear to have been based upon similar but not identical drafts.

The variations in the three texts of the Schism Pillar Edict, too, presuppose three similar but not identical drafts.

It will be somewhat bold to think with Professor Mookerji that just one draft in the official language of Pāṭaliputra was prepared in the Imperial Secretariat, from which translations were made in preparing copies suiting different provinces or localities in India.

R.E. III goes to show that the *Yuktas* of the Imperial Secretariat codified the king's orders or messages under the instruction from the *Parishad* or *Purushas* acquainted, according to P.E. IV, with the king's desires (*chaṁdaṁnāni*). And it is clear from R.E. VI, that these orders and messages were issued verbally at first by the king. The drafts prepared on the basis of the king's verbal orders and dictations by the different personal agents were bound to vary. We are, moreover, to presume that among the *Yuktas,* some were considered competent to prepare the draft for Shahbazgarhi, some for Mansehra, some for Dhauli, some for Kalsi, some for Yerraguḍi. In the case of the Minor Rock and Schism Pillar Edicts, the king's instruction was to have copies made from those supplied from the capital for wide circulation.

8. Canon of interpretation : The scientific approach to a subject implies a dispassionate attitude of mind towards all things that concern it. Such a mental attitude is not in itself a great thing unless it results from a readiness of the self

to leave no stone unturned in exploring all avenues of information and truth, a courage to view facts as they are, an intellectual equipment for discriminating facts in reference to their proper contexts, the preparedness of reason to consider all suggestions and all view-points with an open mind, and no less the capacity of the scholar or investigator for pronouncing sound judgements and arriving at a rational conclusion. There is no hide and seek policy, no concealment of facts, all cards, all available materials being laid on the table for inspection, consideration and adjudication. The question is not so much whether Chandragupta Maurya or Aśoka is the greater hero, the question is not so much whether Aśoka was a Buddhist or Jaina by his religious faith as how far the progressive trend of Indian and world thought found a tangible expression through his records and various actions, how far he succeeded in fulfilling the cherished ideals of political administration, or how far and in what ways he was able to direct the course and advance the cause of Indian and world civilization.

His own records being the first-hand and most trustworthy source of information, a canon of their interpretation in their true historical and linguistic bearings is a *desideratum*. The best method of interpretation is to make one record explain the other, which means an interpretation of any single word, term or statement in the light of a concordance of all available records. In case the records themselves suffice to establish a definite interpretation, it may be strengthened by the exact literary parallels from the texts bearing upon the age. In case these in themselves are insufficient for the purpose, the aid may be sought from either contemporary literature or works that stand near about the age, as well as from the available traditions of Aśoka or the Mauryas in general, the subsequent inscriptions of India and the Greek writings and other foreign accounts. But in all circumstances the first and main reliance must be placed on the records themselves.

It will be seen that Aśoka himself has suggested some keys to the understanding of his records. He tells us that all that he did was to promote the cause of piety or duty amongst all within his empire, outside his empire, nay, all the world over, if possible. Two were the means whereby he sought to achieve this end, namely, the regulations (*dhaṁmaniyamāni*) and moral persuasion (*nijhati*). The inculcation of the principles of piety *(dhaṁmānusathis)*, the proclamations of piety *(dhaṁmasāvanāni)*, and the monumental acts of piety (*dhaṁmathaṁbhāni*) were the three distinct modes of moral persuasion (P.E. VII). Thus in the light of the main purpose and the two chief means and their modes we are to view and evaluate his records. Secondly, it will be noticed that he has adopted throughout the conventional literary *uddesa-niddesa* method of the age of presenting first a thesis and then elaborating or elucidating it. Thus there runs a chain of argument through his records, which may be more easily followed up and better appreciated by setting them in their chronological order. That is to say, one must understand the textual connection of R.E. II, which reads like a proclamation, with R.E. III, that of R.E. IV with R.E. III, the chain of argument through R.E. VII, R.E. IX and R.E. XI, R.E. V, R.E. VII, R.E. XII, R.E. XIII and P.E. VII, through R.E. X, P.E. I and M.R.E., so on and so forth. Thirdly, his records, containing as they do certain general statements, are not meant to be exhaustive. The general statements go on typifying things and ideas and the definition is suggested in terms of its illustrative instances. Thus there is no wonder that the banyan trees (*nigohāni*, P.E. VII) typify all shade-trees (*vrachhā, lukhānī*, R.E. II) ; the wells (*kūpā, udupānāni*), all artificial reservoirs of water, tanks, ponds, and the rest ; the antelopes (*magā*, R.E. I), all eatable quadrupeds ; the peafowls (*morā*, R. E. I), all eatable birds ; the mango-groves (*aṃbavaḍikā*, Queen's Edicts), all orchards ; while the celestial mansions, elephants and clusters of luminaries, typify all celestial forms *(divyāni rūpāni*, R.E. IV) ; the *Dhrmamahāmatras* typify all high officials entrusted with the duty of distribution of royal charities (R.E. V, P.E. VII) ; P.E. V and M.R.E. typify respectively all Regulations and Proclamations of Piety (P.E. VII).

Lastly, the sentences and clauses in Aśoka's statements must be properly punctuated so as to avoid all possibilities of misinterpretation. The difficulty of punctuation confronts us particularly in R.E. III, R.E. IV, R.E. V, R.E. VIII, S.R.E. I, M.R.E, and P.E. VII.

CHAPTER II

BEARINGS ON LITERATURE

The inscriptions of Aśoka have their bearings on Indian literature in general and on Buddhist literature in particular. As regards their bearings on the latter, the seven *Pariyāyas* or Pieces selected from a then known corpus of *Buddhavachana* and strongly recommended in the Bhābru Edict for constant study and comprehension by the monks, nuns and laity loom large in our view. As a devout Buddhist, Aśoka upheld the traditional belief : "All that is said by the Master is well said". His pronouncement on this point is nothing but a verbatim reproduction of a dictum now traceable in the Aṅguttara Nikāya (IV, p. 164).

His own word for the doctrinal tradition of each sect is *āgama* (R.E. XII : *kalyāṇāgamā*), while *āgatāgamā* ("masters of the received tradition") is an oft-recurring Pali epithet applied to early *Theras*. Thus the Buddhist doctrinal tradition was nothing then but a growing corpus of *Subhāshitas* or *Pravachanas* of the Buddha (cf. Mahāparinibbāna suttanta, vi : *Satthu-pāvachanakaṁ*). But *Pravachanam* is the name by which the whole of Vedic tradition was being honoured in the earlier Upanishads (cf. Taittirīya, I. 11.1. : *svādhyāya-pravachanābhyām* ; Kaṭha, I. 2.22 : *nāyam ātmā pravachanena labhyaḥ*). The words of Mahāvīra, too, passed as *pavāyaṇaṁ (Pravachanam)*.

The name *Pariyāya* was suggested by the Buddha himself for a connected discourse or reasoned statement on a point of his Doctrine or Discipline. This has been replaced in the extant Pali Canon by *sutta*, which matches with *sūkta* ('well-said something') as well as *sūtra* ('threaded or aphoristic something'). In the Sarvāstivāda Canon we have *paryāya-sūtra* instead of a mere *paryāya* or a mere *sūtra*, which, to say the least, is an overdoing of things. A *Pariyāya* with its methodical setting of propositions and logical sequence of thoughts bears out the true textual significance of the term Pāli.

To see the Good Faith long endure *(hevaṁ sadhaṁme chilaṭhitike hosatī ti)* is the pronounced Buddhist motive which actuated Aśoka to suggest seven texts as the best of all, according to his own idea, from his own point of view. Whatever a Budddhist did, it was in the interest of his religion, the stability or stabilisation of the Good Faith *(Sadhammaṭṭhiti)* was invariably his main motive, and whatever the Master himself set out or laid down for the guidance of his disciples or followers was inspired by the same motive.

The selections from the then known corpus of *Buddhavachana* proposed by Aśoka served as models for similar selections recommended by the Pali commentators. The Bharhut sculptures of the 2nd century B.C., with or without labels, presuppose selections from the traditional texts, made from the point of view of Buddha's biography. Similarly selections are listed in the Milindapañha and Mahāvaṁsa. A selective process was at work in Buddhist literature, even from earlier times, and it tended to attach a ritual value in chanting to a single *Sutta* or a group of select texts from the corpus of *Buddhavachana*. The Pali Aṭṭhaka and Pārāyana groups of sixteen poems were hot favourites with the immediate disciples of the Buddha. Later on the Munigāthā was combined with the former and the Khaggavisāṇa Sutta with the latter. The Buddhist missions reported to have been despatched to different countries and localities in Aśoka's time found it expedient to base their first discourse on a select text or a group of texts, and put together, all the texts used by them go to make a handy book of selections (Mahāvāṁsa, xii, xiv. 22, 58, 63). Similar selections are mentioned by name in the Milindapañha (p. 349 f.) and the Mahāvaṁsa (xxx. 82, 83, etc.). Attention might here be drawn to a smaller list of six in the Sutta-nipāta Commentary (Paramatthā-jotikā, II). But much seems to have been made of Buddhaghosa's list of four passages in the Visuddhimagga, Kammaṭṭhānagahaṇa-niddesa, viewed as one having common texts with Aśoka's list (Bhandarkar, *op. cit.*, p 89f.; Kosambi, I.A., XL, p. 40). The passages are catalogued as Rathavinītapaṭipadaṁ (identified with Aśoka's Upatisapasine), Nāḷaka-paṭipadaṁ (identified with Aśoka's Moneya-Sute), Tuvaṭaka-paṭipadaṁ (sought to be identified with Aśoka's Vinaya-samukase), and Mahā-ariyavaṁsa-paṭipadaṁ (indentified with Aśoka's Aliyavasāni).

The same selective process is in fact much earlier, and it is clearly traceable through the Gṛihya Sūtras. There, too, it has served to set ritual values on certain select hymns, the list varying with authorities in spite of a basic agreement. The list swelled up with the addition of such later works as the Bhārata of Jaiminī and the Mahābhārata of Vaiśampāyana.

The ritual side is absent in Aśoka's selections. He conceived them on a rational consideration of their use or utility in terms of stability of the Good Faith. The first piece is called Vinaya-samukase, "The Vinaya Exalted", "The Vinaya Extolled." With Oldenberg and Rhys Davids (S.B.E., XIII, p. xxvi f.) we may take the title to mean "Abstract of Vinaya." In P.E.I, *ukasa* is used in the sense of "the exalted;" the Buddha's teaching of the Four Noble Truths is praised in Pali as *sāmukkaṁsikā dhaṁmadesanā* (Vinaya Mahāvagga, I. 7. 6 ; Udāna, V. 3), meaning "the most excellent sermon" (Winternitz) or "the essential teaching". But the Pali scholiasts explain *sāmukkaṁsika* as "self-seized", "self-discovered" *(attanā va uddharitvā gahītā)*, which is far-fetched. To the ancients, as Buddhaghosa points out, the Anumāna Sutta (Majjhima—N. I.) was known as Bhikkhu-vinaya, and the Siṅgālovāda Sutta (Dīgha—N. III.) as Gihi-vinaya. Whether Aśoka's piece is "The Vinaya Exalted" or "The Vinaya Outlined", with Mr. Sailendranath Mitra I agree in thinking that its Pali counterpart is no other than the Vinaya passage in the Aṅguttara Nikāya, I, p. 98f., inasmuch as this is the only Canonical tract in which the Vinaya is both exalted or extolled in terms of its purposes and outlined or crystallized as regards its topics. One of the main purposes in terms of which the Vinaya is extolled is the stabilisation of the Good Faith.

The Second piece is Aliyavasāni. Rhys Davids identifies this with the passage dealing with Dasa-ariyavāsā, ("The ten abodes of the elect"), and Dharmananda Kosambi, with the passage dealing with *Chattāro Ariyavaṁsā* ("The fourfold heritage of the elect"). Presumably Aśoka's passage does not refer to a bare enumeration of the four *Ariyavaṁsas* but to a regular Discourse on the subject which is found embodied in the Aṅguttara Nikāya and to which Buddhaghosa applies the name of Mahā-ariyavaṁsa Suttanta. The text is described by Buddhaghosa as one which is edificatory of the practice of contentment as to the four requisites of a *bhikshu* and delight in meditation. The Pali title, as explained by Buddhaghosa, signifies the uninterrupted, long-continued tradition of the elect (*Ariyatanti, Ariyappaveṇi*). But Aśoka's title presupposes a neuter word *vasaṁ*, meaning 'control', 'habitual practice.' Accordingly the Pali equivalent of Aśoka's title is *Ariyavasā* or *Ariyavasāni*, which is more appropriate to the subject-matter of the Mahā-ariyavaṁsa Suttanta.

As to *ariyavasaṃ* being the word presupposed by the Aśokan title, one may cite here the corroborative evidence from the Tonigala inscription of Ceylon of Meghavaṇṇa's time (E.Z., III, p. 182) in which the word *Ariyavasa* occurs twice—*Ariyavasa vaṭavi, Ariyavasa karaṇa*. In Aśokan dialects the neuter : plural suffix *āni* is nowhere used in the declension of masculine stems but in accusative plural or nominative plural when the voice is a passive one. Dr. Paranavitana himself is not sure of the equation of the inscriptional *vasa* with *vaṃsa* or *vassa*. For "the significance of Ariyavaṃsa," the reader is referred to Rev. Rahula's informative article in the University of Ceylon Review for April, 1943, p. 59ff.

The third piece called Anāgatabhayāni is found to be a conglomeration of four cognate Discourses, each enumerating the five future dangers of the Good Faith. The first two of them categorise the five dangers keeping which in view a *bhikshu* should immediately start a life of energetic effort for the attainment of that which has not yet been attained, and the last two enumerate them in such a manner that the right-thinking *bhikshus* should strive to avoid after apprehending them. The future dangers anticipate the prevalence of food-scarcity or famine, and of fear of life and property due to internecine feuds, the split in the *Saṅgha*, the moral, intellectual and spiritual degradation, deterioration or degeneration of the *bhikshus*, the wilful neglect of the study of the Buddha's profound Discourses and preference for the study of the skilfully composed poetical works of other schools of thought, the lack of earnestness in the right cause, the growth of ease-lovingness and of fondness for personal requisites, and constant association of the *bhikshus* with the *bhikshuṇis* and women learners or with the resident householders waiting for ordination.

The stress laid on a life of exertion, wakefulness, watchfulness or alertness, the fear of schism in the *Saṅgha*, the emphasis laid on a life of moderation, patience and forbearance, etc., are all in keeping with Aśoka's edicts.

The fourth piece is entitled Munigāthā, precisely as in the Divyāvadāna (pp. 20,35) which is a Mūlasarvāstivāda work in Sanskrit. The Pali poem in the Sutta-nipāta bears the name of Munisutta. Like the Khaggavisāṇa, the Munisutta stands out prominently as an early type of didactic Buddhist ballad poetry, couched in easy-flowing but vigorous language, characterised by the sublimity of thought, filled with genuine religious sentiment, singing of the glory of the life of lonely meditation, free from worldly cares and anxieties, and contrasting the same with the care-worn life of a householder. The recommendation of such a piece as this even to the laity for constant study and comprehension goes direct as an evidence against the theory that Aśoka was opposed to the idea of turning a monk, severing connexion with the world.

The next piece, called Moneyasute, has been identified by Rhys Davids with a short Sutta on *moneyyas* in the Itivuttaka, and by Kosambi with the Nāḷaka Sutta in the Sutta-nipāta. The Itivuttaka Sutta giving as it does a bare enumeration of the three *moneyyas* (modes of quietude), does not match well with Aśoka's intended passage. It is obviously a larger Discourse such as one presented in the Nāḷaka Sutta of which the Lokottaravāda version is cited in the Mahāvastu. Aśoka's title leads us, no doubt, to think that the Discourse in its earlier stage was called Moneyya, and that at that stage it stood without the first stanza introducing Nāḷaka as interlocutor. The elimination of this stanza does not impair the wholeness of the Discourse.

The consensus of opinion is in favour of identifying the sixth piece, called Upatisa-pasine ("The Questions of Upatishya"), with the Rathavinīta Sutta in the Majjhima Nikāya. This Sutta might indeed go by the name of Upatisa-pasine, inasmuch as the questions answered in it were all put by Śāriputra who, according to his own declaration, was generally known by the name of Upatishya. His questions anticipating the replies received from the interlocutor set out the seven successive modes of purity, all ultimately leading up to *Nirvāṇa*. Thus the Sutta contains the *mātikā* or ground plan of such later exegetical works as the Abhidhammāvatāra, the Vimuttimagga and the Visuddhimagga. But the choice lies yet between this and the Sāriputta Sutta (Suttanipāta, iv. 16), the latter, too, being a Discourse in reply to a question of Sāriputta. The Milinda list of select texts includes the name of the Sāriputta Sutta (ib., p. 349), and by the Therapañha Sutta the Mahāvaṁsa (XXX. 82) probably meant this very Discourse.

The seventh piece, called Lāghulovāde, is accurately identified by Senart with the Ambalaṭṭhika Rāhulovāda Sutta (Majjhima- N., II). Aśoka specifies it as that particular text of Rāhulovāda which contains the Buddha's admonition on falsehood, addressed to Rāhula *(musāvādaṁ adhigichya bhagavatā budhena bhāsite)*. Obviously his intention is to distinguish this particular admonition from other texts bearing the same title. As placed in the Majjhima Nikāya, the three texts of Rāhulovāda are distinguished from one another as Mahā (Greater), Chūla (Lesser), and Ambalaṭṭhika (with reference to the place). The Mahā-Rāhulovāda was one of the popular Discourses, as evidenced by the Milindapañha (p. 349) and the Mahāvaṁsa (XXX. 83). Thus from the way in which Aśoka refers to the particular Rāhulovāda, we can easily infer that he was acquainted with a corpus of *Buddhavachana*, which contained more than one Rāhulovāda.

These are not all. Aśoka in his R. E. IX (G, Dh, J), has quoted a dictum (*asti cha pi vutaṁ : sādhu dana iti, dāne ti*), which is traceable in the Sādhu Sutta (Saṁyutta-N. I, p. 20). Not only that. Another dictum *(pāṇesu sayamo sādhu)*, which occurs in the same edict, is traceable to the same source. Aśoka's pronouncement on the superior value of *dhaṁmadāna* (the gift of the Doctrine), which occurs in R.E. IX and is repeated in R.E. XI, is to be found in the same Sutta, as also in a verse of the Dhammapada (verse 354 : *sabbadānaṁ dhammadānaṃ jināti)*. A similar adage can indeed be traced in Manu, iv. 233, but here the word is *brahmadānaṁ*. The protocol of the Bhābru Edict cannot but remind us of similar conventional expressions in the Suttas of the Dīgha and Majjhima Nikāyas.

The words, *athā pitā* etc. (S.R.E. II), expressing the desired mutual relationship between the ruler and the ruled, have their exact counterpart in a *gāthā* of the Mahāsutasoma Jātaka. The parallels cited from the Arthaśāstra,

Mahābhārata and Buddhacharita (II. 97) are one-sided, wherefore these do not fully fit in with Aśoka's statement.

Anuposathaṁ in P.E. V and Schism Pillar Edict (Sārnāth) is a Buddhist technical term, which is met with in the Vinaya Mahāvagga, II. *Anāvāsasi āvāsayiye, vāsāpetaviye* (Schism Pillar Edict) is also found to be a Vinaya technical phrase. As a matter of fact, the whole text of the ordinance in the Schism Pillar Edict has behind it a Vinaya injunction in the Mahāvagga, which reads : *Saṅghabhedako upasampanno nāsetabbo,* and the precise nature of the measure adopted by Aśoka is faithfully described in the Samantapāsādikā and Pali Chronicles (Inscr. ii, p. 154).

Pilgrimages to Lumbinī and Sambodhi (Bodhgayā) were undertaken by Aśoka in accordance with the Buddha's express opinion (Mahāparinibbāna Suttanta, Dīgha-N.II, p. 140), and the expression, *hida Budhe jāte,* or *hida bhagavaṁ jāte ti* (Here the Blessed One was born), which occurs in the Lumbinī Pillar Inscription with reference to the village of Lumbinī, has *idha Tathāgato jāto ti* (Mahāparinibbāna Suttanta) for its Pali parallel.

Aśoka's claim, *mayā bahukalāṇaṁ kataṁ* (R.E.V), *me bahuni kayānāni kaṭāni* (P. E. II), is just an echo of the Bodhisattva's declaration, *katā me kalyāṇā anekarūpā* (Mahāsutasoma Jātaka, No : 437).

The purposes of *anusaṁyāna*, as stated in R.E. III (read with reference to R.E. II) and in S.R.E. I, correspond to those mentioned by Buddhaghosa (Inscr. ii, p. 12). The public works, mentioned in R.E. II, P.E. II, P.E. VII and Queen's Edict, may be supposed to have been inspired by the Ārāmaropa Sutta (Inscr. ii, p. 157). The duties of a pious householder stressed by Aśoka throughout his edicts fall all within the scheme of the Siṅgālovāda Suttanta (Dīgha-N. III). The phrase, *porāṇā pakiti,* is met with only in the Pali Jātakas (Inscr. ii, p. 113), Aśoka's *āsulope* (S.R.E. I) is peculiarly Buddhistic (ib., p. 90). The same holds true of (*saṁvaṭa-kapā* (R.E. IV, V), *sukaṭaṃ dukaṭaṃ* (R.E. V), *svage* (R.E. VI, IX, M.R.E.) and *apāye* (S.R.E. I). For the popular significance of the *vimānas, hastins, agniskandhas,* and other celestial forms, mentioned in R.E. IV, one must in the first instance look into the Vimāna stories in the Vimānavatthu and those interspersed in the Jātakas.

Even behind Aśoka's idea of causing his edicts to be permanently engraved on *pavata* (a rock), *silāthaṁbha,* (a stone-pillar), or a *silāphalaka* (a stone slab) was the Buddha's opinion that a writing in stone is not easily delible, that it endures long (Aṅguttara N. I. p. 283 : *pāsāṇe lekhā na khippaṁ lujjati . . chiraṭṭhitikā hoti).*

The instances need not be multiplied. The Bhābru Edict distinctly presupposes a traditional corpus of *Buddha-vachana,* constituted of Discourses in prose as well as those in verse. Out of the seven recommended texts, four are found to be prose Discourses, two to be poems or poetical Discourses, and one to be a Discourses in prose or verse. The Rāhulovāda on *musāvāda* suggests the existence of other Rāhulovādas. These texts are embodied in the Majjhima Nikāya (the Sarvāstivāda Madhyamāgama), the Aṅguttara Nikāya (the Sarvāstivāda Ekottarāgama), and the Sutta-nipāta. The Sādhu Sutta, presupposed by R.E. IX, is contained in the Saṁyutta Nikāya (the Sarvāstivāda Saṁyuktāgama). The idea of Saṁvaṭṭa-kappa, the protocol of the Bhābru Edict, and the undertaking of pilgrimages to the places of importance to the Buddhists presuppose some *Suttas* in the Dīgha Nikāya (the Sarvāstivāda Dīrghāgama). Several parallel dicta and idioms lead us back to the Jātaka gāthās. The main text and appendix of the Schism Pillar Edict (Sārnāth) cannot but have in its background the Vinaya Mahāvagga and Chullavagga which in their turn presuppose the existence of the two books of the Vinaya Suttavibhaṅga. The serial Discourse on Anāgata-bhayāni refers to Abhidhamma-kathā and Vedalla kathā. The latter is embodied in the two *Suttas* of the Majjhima Nikāya, called Mahāvedalla and Chūḷavedalla. By the former, too, we shall not perhaps be justified in thinking of the books of the Abhidhamma Piṭaka ; it probably denoted certain special *Suttas* like those canonised by the Sarvāstivāda sect as Abhidharma treatises, standing as these do half way between the *Suttas* proper and the Pali Abhidhamma books. The Vinaya Mahāvagga and Chullavagga, taken together, outline the Buddhist ecclesiastical history from Buddhahood to the Second Buuddist council, held in 100 B.E., and present a systematic account of the origin and development of the Vinaya rules and conventions. All accounts but those of the First and Second Councils fall within the life-time of the

Buddha, while the two Councils enclose between them just a century, which elapsed after the Buddha's demise. The account of the First Council speaks of the canonisation of the two books of the Vinaya Sutta-vibhaṅga, and the five Nikāyas without, however, the enumeration of the books of the then known Khuddaka Nikāya. The Vinaya passages cited in the account of the Second Council are mostly from the Suttavibhaṅga; while two of them are now to be found in the Mahāvagga. Of the two passages, the first is cited as a *saṁyutta* and the second as a *vatthu* instead of as Khandhakas. The naming of the first as Uposatha-saṁyutta is important as indicating that it originally formed an integral part of the Saṁyuttāgama. Besides the account of the Second Council assigned to 100 B.E., the Serissaka story in the Vimānavatthu claims to have been a composition of the same time *(vide* B. C. Law's History of Pali Literature, I).

Aśoka uses the word *nikāyā* to denote either the bodies or classes of officers (R.E. XII, cf. Arthaśāstra, II. 4. *śreṇipravahaṇīnikāya),* or religious bodies or sects (R.E. XIII), or species of living beings (jīvanikāyānī, P.E. V), but nowhere applies it to mean separate collections of texts. As noted, his word for the literary tradition of a sect is *āgama*. The Theravāda is the only Buddhist sect which replaced *āgama* by *nikāya* in the case of the Sutta collections. The Dīpavaṁsa which is the oldest among the Pali Chronicles designates the Sutta Piṭaka as Āgama Piṭaka. But once used, *Nikāya* continued to be used as a textual title by the Theriyas, and *Pañchanekāyika* (one who knows the five Nikāyas by heart) is even met with as a personal epithet in some of the donative inscriptions at Bharhut (more accurately Berhut[1] from Vīrahotra) and Sāñchī (2nd century B.C.). The Mūla Sarvāstivāda sect, on the other hand, retained the name *Āgama*. But in connection with the Pali expression, *āgatāgamā*, Buddhaghosa points out : *eko Nikāyo eko Āgamo,...pañcha Nikāyā pañcha Āgamā nāma.*

The growing corpus of *Buddhavachana*, precisely like Vedic literature, was being handed down as an oral tradition from teacher to teacher until its commitment to writing, and there were regular Institutions of *Bhāṇakas* or Reciters of the Sacred Texts, charged with the twofold duty of preservation and transmission by methodical and periodical chanting (Barua and Sinha, Barhut Inscriptions, *sub voce* bhānaka). The Sutta and Vinaya texts were being regularly chanted at different places by the *bhikshus* even while the Buddha was alive and facilities were given for the purpose (Mahāvagga, iv. 15.4; Chullavagga, iv 4.4.). As regards the Theravāda tradition, the corpus underwent some six redactions prior to its commitment to writing, three in India and three in Ceylon, and at least two books were added to it after that. The Pali Canon, as is now preserved in Sinhalese, Burmese and Siamese MSS., is wanting in certain passages and stories cited in the later exegetical works and commentaries or otherwise preserved in the scriptures of other sects. The history of its development, as far as we can envisage it, shows the processes of reshuffling or permutation and combination, amplification, annotation, adaptation, and affiliation.

As regards other Buddhist doctrinal traditions, the Dīpavaṃsa rightly points out that each sect or school with its rise appreciably modified the Theravāda corpus by the reshuffling as well as elimination of texts, by additions and alterations, by textual distortions and novel interpretations, and no less by changes in nomenclatures, phraseologies, phonetics, and grammar. The Sarvāstivāda is the main sect whose Canon closely resembles the Theravāda minus some texts and portions of the Abhidhamma Piṭaka. But judged text by text by the evidence of the edicts of Aśoka and other Indian inscriptions, the extant Canons of other Buddhist sects are chronologically later than the Theravāda.

As for bearings on Indian literature in general, there are certain things in the inscriptions of Aśoka that cannot be wholly accounted for by the Canon of Theravāda and Sarvāstivāda. For instance, the three words, *parisrave*, *aparisrave*, and *āsinave (=aṇhaya)*, of which the first two occur in R.E. X and the third occurs in P.E. II, III, are peculiarly Jaina. The citation from the Āchārāṅga Sūtra : *je āsavā te parissavā, je parissavā, je aṇāsavā te aparissavā*, is a traditioal Jaina dictum, which may easily be supposed to have been at the back of Aśoka's opinion : *eshe tu parisrave yaṁ apuñaṁ*.

Aśoka's interesting list of birds, fishes and quadrupeds in P.E. V, in short, of creatures as *abhakshyas* is on a par with those in the Law-books of Bodhāyana and Vasishṭha which in their turn presuppose the works of Gautama and Vṛiddha

Manu. In the background of the lunar days and half months specified by Aśoka in the same edict as those to be strictly observed for abstinence from certain acts of cruelty to animals are the injunctions in the Vinaya Mahāvagga as well as the prescriptions in the Gṛihya Sūtras. But as regard his list of creatures as *avadhyas* (P.E. V), its substantial agreement is with that in the Arthaśāstra (Inscr. ii, p, 360 ff.).

The popular maxim, *evaṃ samavāyaḥ kartavyaḥ* (Pañchatantra, I. 15), is echoed by Aśoka's dictum : *samavāyo eva śādhu* (R.E. XII), which does not, however, prove the greater antiquity of the sanskrit text Pañchatantra wherein the maxim is embodied. It suggests only the priority of the fable conveying the maxim with its Pali counterpart in the Sammodamāna Jātaka illustrated in the Bharhut sculpture (Barua, Barhut, Bk. III, Pl. LXXII. 93).

Among the ancient grammatical works, Kātyāyana's Vārttika notices the word *Devānāṁpriya* (Pali *Devatānaṃpiyo)*, and Patañjali's Mahābhāshya discloses its significance as a personal epithet or mode of address. The Mahābhāshya makes also mention of the *Khalatika parvata* which figures in two of Aśoka's Barābar Hill-cave inscriptions. Pāṇini's *ādikaraḥ* (Jaina *āigare)*, *lipikaraḥ*, *livikaraḥ* (III. 2.21) are presupposed by Aśoka's *ādikaro*, *ādikare* (R.E. V) and *lipikāra* (R.E. XIV).

As regards the Smṛiti literature, lists of non-eatable or forbidden animals, birds, beasts and fishes (*abhakshyas*), contained in the older Law-books, are certainly in the literary background of Aśoka's list of *avadhyas* (P.E. V). In this respect the Dharmasūtras of Bodhāyana and Vasishṭha deserve special notice, particularly for the reason that both the works prohibit the eating of the flesh of rhinoceros and allow the eating of the meat of peafowls. Furthermore, Vasishṭha's *pāṇḍukapota* is the same species of birds as the *setakapota* in Aśoka's list. It is again in the treatises of Bodhāyana and Vasishṭha that we come across the phrase *kāmaṁ* or *kāmaṁ tu* corresponding to Aśoka's *kāmaṃ chu* (S.R.E. II). Manu's text, which in its extant form is later than Aśoka's time, has a distinct saying in verse corresponding to a dictum in Pali and in *Aśokavachana*.

Aśoka's insistence on the middle course (*majha*, S.R.E.I) is quite in keeping with Kauṭilya's wisdom (Arthaśāstra, I.4).

Without sidelights from the Arthaśāstra we are helpless in accounting for the importance attached by Aśoka to the two asterisms of Tishya and Punarvasu (S.R.E. I, II, P.E. V.). The human treatment of slaves and servants, the grounds of release of prisoners before they have served out the full term of court sentence, the king's obligations to the aged, the destitute, the orphans, etc., and the consultation of the Council of Ministers, in connection with urgent matters are common, more or less to the edicts and the Arthaśāstra. Both emphasize the need of practice of *utthāna* (exertion) as secret of success in administration.

But the prose treatise of the Arthaśāstra, as we now have it, is not only post-Aśokan but post-Śuṅga in date. Its mode of dating a record in terms of the regnal year, month, half-month and day *(rājavarshaḥ māsaḥ pakshaḥ divasaḥ)* tallies with that in the Kushāṇa, Ikshvāku and other later Indian inscriptions and differs appreciably from that in the inscriptions of Aśoka.

Its list of about ten kinds of slaves stands, as pointed out by Dr. Atindranath Bose, midway between that of Manu and that of Nārada.

It counts the seasons as six and defines each of them (II. 20), while Aśoka's phrase *tīsu chātuṁmāsīsu* (P.E. V.) clearly suggests the adherence of his inscriptions to the tradition of three seasons. The tradition of six seasons may be shown, however, to be a pre-Buddhistic one.

The *Lekhaka* of the Arthaśāstra is not the same functionary as the *Lipikara* of Aśoka. The leaves *(patra)* are the writing material contemplated by the Arthaśāstra (II. 10) and writing meant the employment of some sort of an ink, while with Aśoka the writing material was a hard substance like stone, and writing meant engraving of letters on such a material. The Arthaśāstra suggests the wisdom on the part of the king of consulting sometimes his ministers by sending letters (*patra-preshaṇena*, I. 15), a procedure which is inconceivable much before the birth of Christ. The Arthaśāstra classification and rules of royal writs (II. 10) may be made applicable to the inscriptions of Aśoka, but the records of Aśoka fall far below the standard of perfection in epistolary correspondence as set up in the Arthaśāstra.

The difference in spite of general agreement between the

two list of *avadhyas*, one offered in Aśoka's P.E. V and the other in the Artharśāstra (II. 16) is remarkable. Whilst Aśoka's list is prepared on the twofold ground that the creatures included in it are those which were neither eaten by men nor came into men's use, the Arthaśāstra list is based on the consideration that the creatures included in it were sacrosancts in the people's eye (*maṅgalyāḥ*).

Some of Aśoka's *Mahāmātras* (R.E. XIII) were indeed like the *Adhyakshas* of the Arthaśāstra, but on this ground it cannot be held that all the *Adhyakshas* (Superintendents) of the Arthaśāstra were Aśoka's *Mahāmātras*. It is only by *suggestio falsi* that one may seek to identify wholly Aśoka's *Stryadhyaksha Mahāmātras* with the *Gaṇikādhyaksha* of the Arthaśāstra.

The Rajjukas and Prādeśikas who were the highly important but not newly appointed officers of Aśoka are rather missed in the Arthaśāstra. Even the Maurya capital Pāṭaliputra is not mentioned in it. It has moreover nothing to say about the Greek contemporaries of the Mauryas. Its hostile attitude towards the Śākyas (Buddhists), Ājīvakas, and other so-called *vṛishala pravrajitas* suggests its partiality to the Brāhmans and Brahmanical ascetics, and its predilections for the *rājasūya* and horse sacrifices suggest its connection with a post-Mauryan age of Brahmanical reaction against Buddhism, Jainism, and Ājīvikism. The Pali tradition represents, no doubt, Bindusāra, father and predecessor of Aśoka, as a votary of the Brahmanist and a lay supporter of the Brāhmans and Brahmanical ascetics. But there are at the same time traditions in Pali and Sanskrit to show that the Ājīvikas at least among the Indian ascetics, banned in the Arthaśāstra, had some amount of influence in the court and household of Bindusāra.

The *Dharmasthas* of the Arthaśāstra correspond neither to the *Rajjukas* nor to the *Dharmamahāmātras* of Aśoka, although it may be shown that their duties coincided in some respects with those assigned to the *Rajjukas* and in some respects with those assigned to the *Dharmamahāmātras*.

The connexion or difference between the *Amātyas* and *Mahāmātras* is not quite clear from the Arthaśāstra. They do not find mention in the list of Government servants receiving subsistence (V.3). Although distinguished from the *Mantrins*, it would seem that some of the *Amātyas* were members of the

Mantriparishad. In Chapter 6 of Bk. V, *Amātya* and *Mahāmātra* seem to have been employed as one and the same designation. In adopting *Mahāmātra* as a common designation of the members of the *Parisā* (R.E. VI) and all high officers of the State, Aśoka appears to have followed the tradition of Magadha and Kośala as represented in the older stratum of the Pali Canon, whereas the prose treatise of the Arthaśāstra appears to have been the compilation of a time when the designation *Mahāmātra* tended to pass out of use. Like *Sachiva*[1], *Amātya* was evidently a general designation for all classes of officers.

The prose treatise of the Arthaśāstra is compiled in strict conformity to a textual and exegetical methodology *(Tantrayukti)* defined in its concluding chapter (XV. 1). This methodology with its 32 terms is presented in the same language and in the same manner as in the concluding chapter of the Suśrutasaṁhita, whereas the textual form and *uddeśa-nirdeśa* method of the edicts of Aśoka are on a par with that in the Pali Suttas.

The extant prose treatise of the Arthaśāstra presupposes an anthology of 6,000 ślokas, which is ascribed to Kauṭilya, and the *ślokas* in this earlier *kārikā*, as may be judged by those still preserved in the prose treatise, were mostly, if not wholly, verses in the *Śloka* or *Anushṭubh* metre. The anthology was *ex hypothesi* in the nature of a *Nīti* work, a treatise containing moral maxims on the conduct and duties of the king, his ministers, councillors and officers as well as on the art of administration,—in short, a work on *Daṇḍanīti* or *Rājadharma*. Aśoka's first Separate Rock Edict, too, presupposes such *nītis* or moral maxims. The Canonical Jātaka Book and the Mahābhārata abound in such *Nīti* anthologies that are traditionally ascribed to different teachers and sages noted for their wisdom. Thus the extensive anthology which had formed the literary basis of the prose treatise of the Arthaśāstra was just one of the many such treatises. None need therefore be surprised that counterparts of or parallels to some of these maxims are traceable as much in the edicts of Aśoka as in the *gāthās* of the Jātaka and the *ślokas* of the Mahābhārata.

---

1. Arthaśāstra, 1.7. Amarakosha, IX. 89.

Even apart from the occurrence of certain common maxims and phrases and idioms, we cannot, without keeping some of the earlier Arthaśāstra verses in the immediate historical background of Aśoka's edicts, account for the reason behind Aśoka's insistence on the quinquennial tour of official inspection (R. E. III, S. R. E. I) and the inspection tour to be undertaken within the third year (S. R. E. I). According to one of the earlier Arthaśāstra verses (II. 20), an additional month (*adhimāsa*) occurs periodically in the middle of every third year and at the end of the fifth, and in instituting the quinquennial and triennial tours Aśoka's plan was to fully utilise the additional months so that the usual administrative duties of the officers concerned would not be unduly interfered with. The Arthaśāstra verse reads :

Evam ardha-tṛitīyānām abdānām adhimāsakam /
grīshme janayataḥ pūrvaṁ, pañchabdānte cha paśchimaṁ //..

Similarly behind Aśoka's ordinance compelling a monk or nun found guilty of the offence of dividing the saṅgha to live in a non-monastic residence is the prescription in the following Arthaśāstra verse (IV. 8) for either banishing from the country or compelling a Brāhman offender to reside in a non-residence like a mine :

Brāhmaṇaṁ pāpakarmāṇaṁ udghushāṅ kukṛitavarṇam /
kuryān nirvishayaṁ rājā vāsayed ākareshu vā //

Similarly the verses may be cited from the Arthaśāstra (II. 36) to show what was the customary practice of earlier times as regards jail-deliveries :

Divase pañcharātre vā bandhanasthān viśodhayet /
karmaṇā kāyadaṇḍena hiraṇyānugraheṇa vā //
Apūrvadeśābhigame yuvarājābhishechane /
putrajanmani vā moksho bandhanasya vidhīyate[1] *//*

The anthology presupposed by the prose treatise of the

---

1. For a detailed consideration of the chronological position of the Arthaśāstra in Indian literature, the reader is referred to Dr. Shama Sastri's Preface to third edition of his translation of the Arthaśāstra.

Arthaśāstra and ascribed to Kauṭilya is just one of the many such anthologies, large or small, that dealt with the subject of *nīti, daṇḍanīti or rājadharma*. The Pali Jātakas contain several examples of them associated with the name of different teachers noted for their worldly wisdom. Even other books of the Pali Nikāyas are not wanting in such words of wisdom in verse. Here attention might be particularly drawn to the verses in the Siṅgālovāda Sutta, the Lakkhaṇa Suttanta, the Kurudhamma Jātaka, the Dasa-rājadhamma Jātaka, the Mahāhaṃsa Jātaka, the Mahāsutasoma Jātaka, the Mahābodhi Jataka, and the Vidhurapaṇḍita Jātaka. But the great storehouse of Nīti anthologies was the Mahābhārata ascribed to Vaiśampāyana in some of the Grihya Sūtras[1] and referred to by Pāṇini (VI. 2. 38). This pre-Pāṇinian Great Epic is equally presupposed by the Pali Jātakas, the Rāmāyaṇa ascribed to Vālmīki, the edicts of Aśoka and no less by the Arthaśāstra as a whole.[2] The Rājadharma section of the Śāntiparva offers us an extensive anthology on royal polity, which contains many striking parallels to the principles inclucated by Aśoka and emphasized in the Arthaśāstra. The phrases, idioms and adages, cited

---

1. Āśvalāvana Gṛīhya-Sūtra, III. 4.4. where we have mention of both Jaimini and Vaiśampāyana, and of the Bhārata and the Mahābhārata.

2. For the date of compilation of the Arthaśāstra, see my article—*The Arthaśāstra—a blend of old and new* published in the *Bhārata-Kaumudi*, 1, pp. 84—119. Here I must rectify three mistakes that appear in this article and which I had not the opportunity of correcting : P. 109 : Read "though the prose treatise of the Arthaśāstra does not depart from the earlier literary tradition when it counts the seasons as six" for "the prose treatise of the Arthaśāstra departs from......"

P. 118 : Read "takes no notice of *dināras* that find mention in the Nāgārjunīkoṇḍa inscriptions" for "takes no notice of *dināras* that find mention in the Junāgaṛh inscription of Rudradāman I". P. 118 : Read "*Sachivas*, distinguished into two classes, *Mati* and *Karma*,—a distinction which is met with in some passages of the Mahābhārata but not in the Arthaśāstra (cf. I. 7)" for "*Sachivas*, distinguished into two classes, *Mati* and *Karma*, but this is conspicuous by its absence in the Arthaśāstra".

from the Brahmanical works other than the Mahābhārāta as parallels to those occurring in Aśoka's edicts are inadequate to indicate the literary and linguistic development of India prior to Aśokavachana.

It is in the Mahābhārata (XII. 207. 43) alone that we have the Sanskrit name *Yauna* corresponding to the Pali and Aśokan Yona. It is again here that the *Yaunas, Kāmbojas* and *Gāndhāras* are grouped together as socially and politically allied peoples precisely as in Pali and Aśokavachana (R. E. V). The word *anusaṁyāna*, too, is met with in the Great Epic (1. 2. 123) *punyatīrthānusaṁyānam*, though not in the technical sense of Aśoka. The *Mahāmātras* mentioned in it are no other than those called *Senāpati Mahāmātras* in Pali. The Mahābhārata (Bhīshmaparva, 6. 13) locates the four Great Continents, Jambudvīpa included, precisely in the same way as in Pali.

In point of chronology Vālmīki's Rāmāyaṇa is later than the bulk of the Pali Jātakas and the pre-Pāṇinian Mahābhārata. Professor Raychaudhuri seems inclined to treat it as a Maurya epic, which like the edicts of Aśoka is characterised by the remarkable simplicity of diction and the loftiness of the moral ideal. In both we notice the upsetting of the human mind at the sight of cruelty. But, in spite of the fact that the Sanskrit name *Ṛishṭika* corresponding to Aśoka's *Risṭika* (R.E.V,G) is met with in the Rāmāyaṇa (IV. 41. 8-11), or that certain parallels to the moral maxims and principles of Aśoka may be cited from it, chronologically it is rather post-Aśokan than pre-Aśokan.

Aśoka in his S.R.E.I, propounds certain maxims of conduct for the guidance of government servants (*suvihitā nitiyaṁ, nītiyaṁ*), certain principles of judicial administration, of *daṇḍanīti*, as held by Hultzsch. This he must have done either by way of an improvement on the pre-existent and current maxims. If, on the other hand, we take him at his word, he himself had made and enforced several regulations of piety (*bahukāni dhaṁmaniyamāni yāni me kaṭāni*, P. E. VII), as typified by that embodied in P. E. V. If all of them were preserved, no wonder that we would have before us a highly important and instructive treatise on politics by Aśoka. Even the solitary example preserved to us is sufficient to indicate the line of advance attempted to be made in the method and ideal of administration and the fulfilment of the king's obligations to men and animals. Thus it remains still to be seen how far the advanced ideas of governmental duties as found embodied in the subsequent Indian literature on law, polity and general morality were influenced by Aśoka's principles.

CHAPTER III

BEARINGS ON DIALECTS

The official language of Aśoka presents five main dialectical varieties, namely, those at Girnār, Shahbazgarhi, Kalsi, Brahmagiri, and Dhauli. The Dilectical peculiarities of the language of the remaining inscriptions of Aśoka tend to belong to this or that among these five types.

The Dhauli and Jaugaḍa versions of the Rock Edicts, for instance, represent one identical type except for a few irregular spellings in J, e.g., *drakhati* (R.E. I), *savatra* (R.E. II) standing midway between *savata* in Dh and *savratra* in M, and *drasayitu* (R.E. IV) standing midway between *dasayitu* in Dh and *drasayitu* in Sh. In respect of dialectical peculiarities, the Dhauli and Jaugaḍa versions of the two Seperate Rock Edicts belong to the same Dhauli type, and as for themselves, only three phonetic discrepancies are detectable, viz., *saṁpatipāda, vipaṭipāda* (Dh). *saṁpaṭipāta, vipaṭipāta* (J) ; *desāvutike* (Dh), *desa-āyutike* (J) ; *hidaloka-palalokaṁ* (Dh), *hidalogaṁ palalogaṁ* (J), although in one instance, apparently by mistake somewhere, we get *hidalogika-pālalokikāye* in J.

Despite certain omissions, certain minor variations, and some phonetic differences the Kalsi and the Yerraguḍi may justly be treated as the northern and the southern version respectively of one and the same text of the Rock Edicts. The phonetic differences between the two versions lie in the marked tendency of K to lengthen the final vowel *a, e.,g., chā* for *cha* ; to spell *ke* as *kye, e.g., nātikye* (R.E. V) ; and to change semetimes the intervocal *k* into *g*, and *t* into *d, e.g., Aṁtiyogasa* (R.E. II, K), *pasopagani* (R.E. II, K), *hidasukhāye* (R.E. V, K). K, however, retains the intervocal *t* unchanged in *savalokahitena* (R.E. VI). In some instances we have *g* for *k, e.g., Aṁtiyogasa* (R.E. II). In R.E. X, K has *palitiditu for palitijitu,* cf. Pali *Pasenadi,* Bharhut *Pasenaji, naji* Sk. *Prasenajit*.

If we ignore, as we should, the few phonetic irregularities due to the influence of K, the dialect of Ye is the same as that of Dh and J. The same holds true even of the dialect of K barring its distinctive phonetic peculiarities. The phonetic distinction of K becomes increasingly manifest from the latter half of R. E. IX in its tendency to replace *s* by *ś* or *sh*,—a characteristic which connects its dialect with Sh and M, and lingers also in *Devānaṁpīyashā* of the Queen's Edict on the Kauśāmbī pillar.

It will, however, be a mistake to suppose that the Rock Edicts fully represent the phonetic distinction of the dialect of Ye. On looking into the Yerraguḍi text of M. R. E., we find that it differs entirely in one respect from those of the Rock Edicts, namely, that it nowhere substitutes *l* for *r*. So far as the use of *r* goes, *e.g.*, in *savacharaṁ*, *ārādhetave*, it fully agrees with all the copies of M.R.E. but those at Bairāṭ and Sahasrām. It agrees also with the Sopārā version of the Rock Edicts. In *mahātpaneva* (Ye) we have an important link between the Yerraguḍi and three Mysore texts of M. R. E., while the change of *m* of *tm* into *p* is a phonetic peculiarity of the dialect of Shahbazgarhi and Mansehra. In one point the three Mysore and Hyderabad texts (Ga, Pa) differ from those of Ye and Ru, namely, that these cerebralise the dental nasal in the word *pakamaniṇena*; Ga and Pa cerebralise the dental nasal even in such words as *māṇusehi* and *dāṇi*. Ignoring these few phonetic variations, the dialect of the Sopārā version of the Rock Edicts and the Mysore, Hyderabad, and Yerraguḍi versions of the Minor Rock Edict may be shown to be in agreement with that of Dhauli and Jaugaḍa. Strictly speaking, the dialect in question stands, in respect of its phonetic peculiarities, midway between the Girnār and Dhauli types.

The dialect of the Sahasrām text of M.R.E., as also that of the Bairāṭ copy, belongs entirely to the Dhauli type. The remark may apply equally to the dialect of the Bhābru or Calcutta-Bairāṭ Edict in spite of the trace of r in *Priyadasi*, *prasāde*, *sarve*, and doubtful *abhipretaṁ*.

The Dhauli type covers the entire field of the dialect of the Pillar, Minor Pillar and Barābar Hill-cave inscriptions may be totally ignored. The word *vigaḍa* for *vikaṭa*, *vikṛita* in the Lumbinī Pillar Inscription[1] is traceable in Ardhamāgadhī, and

---

1. It is more probable that Aśoka's *vigaḍabhī* is the Old Māgadhi equivalent of Sk. *vigatabhī* meaning 'free from fear', 'free of danger'.

so also *chiṭhitu* for G *tisṭaṁto,* which occurs in R. E. IV (K, M, Dh).

The Shahbazgarhi and Mansehra texts of the Rock Edicts show some common phonetic peculiarities, the most striking of which is the absence of the long vowels, *ā, ī,* and *ū,* in their orthography. All the three sibilants occur, precisely in the words that tend to keep to Sanskrit spellings. The palatal sibilant *ś* is generally substituted for *sh, e.g., arabhiśaṁti, manuśa, hapeśati, hepeśadi.* In an exceptional case *sh* is retained, *e. g., kashaṁti=karishyanti* (R.E.V). The Sanskrit letter *ksh* is retained in such words as *kshanāti* (*R.E.* XII, Sh), *kshamanaye, kshamitaviyamate* (R.E. XII, Sh), *vrakshaṁti* (R.E.V, Sh), while in the Mansehra dialect it is represented by *chh, e. g., ruchhani* (R.E. II), *chhanati* (R. E. XII), *chhamitave* (R.E. XIII), the exception being *mokshaye* (R.E. V).

Turning to conjoint consonants, we notice that unless there are lapses into the Dhauli *si* (which are frequent), the seventh case-ending *smi* changes into *spi* in both Sh and M, *e.g., samayaspi* (R.E.I, Sh), *vrachaspi vinitaspi uyanaspi* (R.E. VI, Sh, M) ; that the initial *sva,* too, changes into *spa,* e.g., spasana (R.E.V, Sh), *spasuna* (M), *spafra* for *svarga* (R.E. VI, Sh, M), *spamikena* for *svāmikena* (R.E. IX, Sh, M); that *st,śr.,* and *sr* remain unchanged ; that *shṭh* is assimilated and reduced to *ṭh,* rarely to *th.* The consonant *r,* whether employed alone or in combination with another consonant, remains unchanged. The *r* as the flag of a consonant changes into a stop, *e.g., athraye. savratra,* or is shifted back to be conjoined as a stop with the preceding consonant, *e.g., draśi* for *darśī, dhrama* for *dharma,* while the vowel *ṛī* is either changed into *ri* or *ru* or shifted on to be conjoined as *ra* with the succeeding consonant, or represented by *a, i,* or *u* as in the Dharuli type, *e.g., mrugo* (Sh), *mrige* (M) for *mṛigaḥ* (R.E.I) ; *kiṭraṁ* for *kṛtaṁ* (R.E.V, Sh); *viyapuṭa* for *vyāpṛita.*

All the distinctive phonetic characteristics of *Sh* but the tendency to dispense with the long vowels, *ā, ī,* and *ū,* are scant in M, which latter shows constant learnings to the Dhauli type. In rare instances where there are vestiges of the Dhauli dialect, *e.g.,* in R. E. V, we detect at once that the draft for M was despatched to Sh and that for Sh to M. And in instances where the two texts read alike, we are to understand that one and the same draft was prepared by mistake for both the places.

Ignoring these irregularities, we may safely premise that without losing its integrity as a dialect type Sh has a greater affinity to the dialect of Girnār, and M to that of Dhauli.

There is no gainsaying the fact that the Sanskrit phonetic system has a greater hold on the dialect of Shahbazgarhi and Mansehra than on that of Girnār. But on this ground alone one sould not maintain with Mookerji that "the dialect of the Shahbazgarhi and Mansehra redactions is much nearer to Sanskrit than the dialects of the other versions of the fourteen edicts." The phonetics must not be mistaken for the whole of a language. In the opinion of Michelson this dialect cannot be regarded "as a mere lineal descendant of Sanskrit, inasmuch as it presents certain forms that go to establish its affinity to Avestan rather than Sanskrit". The Avestan legacy extends as far as Girnār, and it is detectable in the hardening of *v* into *p*. Michelson offers for comparison G *susrūsā*, *susrūsaṭāṁ* with Avestan *Susrusemmo*, and G *sruṇāru*, *Sh* and M *śruṇeyu* with Avestan *surunaoiti*.

The Girnār type effects at first sight a happy compromise between the Shahbazgarhi and the Brahmagiri. It systematically retains the consonant r, and optionally *r* as a stop, *e. g.*, *priyena*, *priyadasi*, *prajūhi*, *dhruvo*, *sarvatra*, *vrachhā*, *prādesike*, *srāvāpakaṁ*, *mahāmātresu*, *brāhmaṇa-sramaṇa* as well as *r* as a flag *e. g.*, *sarvatra*, *sarve*, *dasavarsābhisito*. Even the Shahbazgarhi tendency to change *r* as a flag into *r* as a stop and to conjoin it with the preceding consonant is traceable in G *bhutapruvaṁ* (R. E. V, VI). Although in agreement with the Dhauli and Brahmagiri types it does away with the palatal and cerebral sibilants *ś* and *sh*, in its orthography, the vestige of *sh* lingers in the conjoint consonant *sṭ*, *e. g.*, *tisṭaṃto* (R.E.IV), *sesṭe* (R.E.IV), *usṭānaṁ* (R.E.VI). The Shahbazgarhi tendency to harden *v* and *m* into p, undoubtedly through the intermediate *b*, is detectable in K *tpa* for *tva* and *tma* for *tpa e.g.*, *ārabhitpā* (R.E.I),*dasayitpā* (R. E. IV), *dbādasa* (R. E. IV), *ātpapāsaṁḍa* (R.E.XII). The uses of the dental and cerebral nasals are governed by the rules of Sanskrit spellings. It differs entirely from the Shahbazgarhi type as regards the tendency of the latter to dispense with the long vowels, *ā*, *ī*, and *ū*.

The language of the inscriptions of Aśoka is Prakrit, the phonetic variations of which may be broadly distinguished in terms of the following local areas ; (1) Gāndhāra or

North-Western, typified by Shahbazgarhi ; (2) Saurāshṭra or Western, typified by Girnār ; (3) Mahārāshṭra, typified by Brahmagiri ; (4) Haimavata Madhyadeśa or Northern Central, typified by Kalsi ; and (5) Kālinga or Eastern, typified by Dhauli.

From the grammatical point of view, however, the Eastern area extends as far north as Dehra Dun and Nepāl Terai, as far north-west as the eastern side of the Indus, as far west as Rājputānā, as far south-west as Sopārā, as far south as Northern Mysore, and as far east and south-east as Orissa. Thus viewed, such phonetic areas as the North-western to the east of the Indus, the Western, the South-Western, the Northern Central, and the Eastern may justly be regarded as so many sub areas of the grammatical eastern area. From the phonetic point of view the Gāndhāra or North-Western area is co-extensive with the region where Kharoshṭhī was the prevalent form of alphabet. From this point of view, just as the region to the east of the Indus was the eastern extension, so Khotan was the Central Asian extension of the same area, particularly that part of Khotan where was founded a colony of the people from Gāndhāra. Here indeed, in this part of Khotan and in the midst of the ruins of the Gośṛiṅga Vihāra, was discovered a Kharoshṭhī MS. of a recension of the Dhammapada in the Gāndhāra Prakrit influenced to certain extent by the Iranian dialects. The language of this version of the Dhammapada bears all the fundamental traits of the dialect of Shahbazgarhi despite its being three or four centuries later in age. It shows, however, a great option for interchanges between *i* and *e*, *u* and *o*, *j* and *y* to meet the exigency of metre. In it, as to some extent also in the dialect of Shahbazgarhi, one may trace certain elements of what is termed Paiśāchī or Apabhraṁśa Prakrit by Hemachandra.

The phonetic affinity between the dialects of Shahbazgarhi and Mansehra is conceivably the closest. But as one steps eastward, the further the area reached, the less marked is the vestige of the phonetic influence of Shahbazgarhi. The same linguistic phenomenon is bound to strike a person when he travels further and further south from Shahbazgarhi to Girnār and from there to Sopārā, Maski, Yerraguḍi, and Brahmagiri. Whilst thus the phonetic influence of Shahbazgarhi may be shown to have extended as far east and south-east as Kalsi and

Kauśāmbī, the grammatical preponderance of the Eastern Prakrit goes up to Mansehra. Similarly the dialect of Shahbazgarhi may be shown to have followed the grammatical system of Girnār in the matter of declension, the few instances of irregularity having been due to confusion with the Mansehra forms.

The phonetic influence of the dialect of Girnār extends over the whole of the Mahārāshṭra area, bounded on the north by Sāñchī and Rūpnāth, on the south by Yerraguḍi, Brahmagiri and Gavīmaṭh, on the west by Sopārā, and having in its centre Maski, while the dialect of the latter area follows the grammatical system of Dhauli in the matter of declension. On the eastern side Bairāṭ stands as the meeting place of the phonetic systems of Girnār and Dhauli with the predominance of that of the latter place.

Thus through the portals of the inscriptions of Aśoka one may have just a peep into the geographical distribution of the dialectical peculiarities of Aśokan prakrit as well as into the interesting picture of the fluidity of the linguistic situation in which one area encroached on or partly overlapped another either in respect of the predominance of its grammatical system or in that of its phonetic influence. And it may be legitimately asked—is the nomenclature of the classified Prakrits of the Prakrit grammarians applicable to the dialectical varieties of Aśokan Prakrit ?

The linguistic data afforded by the inscriptions of Aśoka are not sufficient for the identification of any of the dialectical varieties of Aśokan Prakrit with any of the classified Prakrits of the later age.

The nominative singular case-ending *e* of all masculine and neuter stems or bases of *a* declension is the most striking grammatical characteristic of Māgadhī. Judged by this characteristic alone, all the dialectical varieties of Aśokan Prakrit but those at Shahbazgarhi and Girnār might be termed Māgadhī. The domain of Māgadhī is apt to become narrower or more limited in area as soon as we apply its fundamental phonetic characteristic, namely, the substitution of *l* for *r*, which is missed in the dialects of Mansehra, Rūpnāth, Yerraguḍi(M.R.E.), Brahmagiri, Maski, Gavīmaṭh, Pālkiguṇḍu, and Sopārā. Similarly the substitution of *ś* for *s* which is another important phonetic characteristic of Māgadhī is wanting in all the inscriptions of

Aśoka but those at Kalsi, Shahbazgarhi, Mansehra, Bairāṭ and Maski, where, too, it is rather an exception than a rule, *e.g.*, *śe*=*se* (K. R. E., XI), *śiyā* (K. R. E. XII), *pāśaḍa*=*pāsaṁḍa* (K. R. E. XII) ; *manuśanaṁ* (Sh, R. E. II), *muniśanaṁ* (M. R. E. II); *anapeśaṁti* (Sh, R.E. III), *anapayiśati* (M. R.E. III), *anuśasiśaṁti* (Sh. M. R. E. IV) ; *śvage*, = *svage*, = *svargaḥ* (*Bai*, M. R. E.) ; *budhaśake* = *budha-*(*upā*)*śake* (Maski, M. R. E.). I say rather an exception, because from the latter half of R. E. IX the prevailing tendency of Kalsi is to cerebralise the dental and palatal sibilants, the general tendency of Shahbazgarhi and Mansehra being to employ all the three sibilants precisely as in Sanskrit, the instance cited from Maski is doubtful, and that from Bairāṭ solitary.

In Māgadhī *dy* and *dhy* invariably become *yy* and *yyh* respectively. As for the change of *dy* into *yy*, it nowhere occurs in the dialect types of Aśokan Prakrit but in words where *dy* happens to be preceded by *u*, *e,g.*, *uyānesu* (G, R.E, VI), *uyānasi* (Dh, J. K. Ye), *uyanaspi* (Sh. M.) and *uyāma* = *udyama* (K. R. E. XIII). But, as a rule, *dy* and *dhy* become *j* (jj) and *jh* (jjh) respectively in Aśokan Prakrit *e.g.*, *aja* = *adya* (R. E. I, R. E. IV), *majhaṁ* = *madhyam* (S. R. E. I), *majhamena*, *majhimena* = *madhyamena* (R.E. XIV).

In Māgadhī *ry* and *rj* invariably become *yy*. In Aśokan Prakrit the change of *rj* into *yy* is exemplified by *ayaputasa* = *āryaputrasya* (M.R.E., Bra, Si, Ja), which is however, a solitary instance. The Aśokan texts are wanting in words indicating the phonetic change of *rj*.

In Māgadhī the initial *y* remains and replaces *j*. The Aśokan Prakrit affords no instance where the initial *j* is replaced by *y*. *Y* is represented by *e* invariably at Sahasrām and Sārnāth and optionally at Dhauli, Jaugaḍa, Kalsi, Yerraguḍi, Bairāt, Delhi, Mīrāṭh, Kauśāmbī, Lauriya Ararāj, Lauriya Nandangarh, Rāmpūrva, and Mansehra, *e.g.*, *aṁ* = *yaṁ* (M.R.E., Sa), *ya*, *aṁ* = *yam* (Bai), *e* = *yaḥ* (Sārnāth), *adā* = *yadā* (R.E.I, Dh, J,), *e* = *yaḥ* (R.E. II, Dh, J), *aṁ* = *yaṁ* (R.E. IV, K, M), etc. In the solitary instance of *āva* = *yāvat*, the initial *ya* is represented by *a* or *ā* in all the versions of the Rock Edicts.

In Māgadhi *ṇy*, *ny*, *jñ*, and *ñj* become *ññ*. The change of *jñ* into *ñ* (*ññ*) is a distinctive feature of the dialects of Girnār and Brahmagiri, and occasionally of those of Shahbazgarhi and Mansehra, *e.g.*, *rāñā*=*rājñā* (R.E. I, G) *raño*=*rājnah* (R.E. I, Sh), *ñātika*, *ñatika*=*jñātikaḥ* (R.E. V, G, Sh), *ñatika*=*jnātikaḥ* (R.E. V, M), *ñātikesu* (M.R.E., Bra), *kataṁñatā*=*kṛitajñatā* (R.E. VII, G), *kiṭrañata* (*Sh*), *kiṭañata* (M).

Girnār and Shahbazgarhi invariably change *ny*, and *ex hypothesi* also *ṇy*, into *ñ* (*ññ*) ; Mansehra does so mostly.

In Māgadhī *shṭa, shṭh* become *śṭa or sṭa*. These Māgadhī characteristics are paralleled nowhere in Aśokan Prakrit but at Girnār, *e.g.*, *Risṭika* (R.E. V) for *Ṛishṭika* and *nisṭānāya* (R.E. IX) for *nishṭhānāya, tisṭaṁto* for *tishṭhantaḥ* (R.E. IV).

In Māgadhī, precisely as in Sanskrit and all other classified Prakrits but Ardhamāgadhī, the only infinitive suffix is *tum* or its Prakrit equivalent, while it is invariably *tave* in Aśokan Prakrit.

In Māgadhī *rth* becomes *śt* or *st*, which is nowhere the case with Aśokan Prakrit.

The predominant tendency of Māgadhī is to cerebralise the dental nasal, while just the opposite is the tendency of Aśokan Prakrit at all places with the exception of Girnār, Shahbazgarhi, Mansehra, Mysore and Hyderabad. The general tendency of Girnār, Shahbazgarhi, Mansehra, Hyderabad and Mysore is to use the cerebral nasal *ṇ* in the right place precisely as in Sanskrit. The only exception to be noted at Girnār is *darsaṇā, dasaṇe* for *darśana* (R.E. IV). A similar exception is met with in the Mysore and Hyderabad copies of M. R. E., and that in the word *pakamamiṇena, pakamamīnena*.

The Māgadhī locative singular suffix is *ssiṁ*, while the Aśokan Prakrit makes use of *mhi* at Girnār, of *spi* at Shahbazgarhi and Mansehra, and *si* at all other places.

The instances cited above may suffice to establish that none of the Aśokan dialects is wholly identical with the Māgadhī of the Prakrit grammarians.

Ardhamāgadhī of the verse portions of the Śvetāmbara Jaina Canon agrees fully with the dialect of Girnār and mostly with that of Shahbazgarhi in the nominative singular in *o*, while that of the prose portions of the same Canon agrees with the rest of Aśokan dialects in the nominative singular in *e*.

On the whole, Ardhamāgadhī agrees with the Aśokan dialects at Girnār, Shahbazgarhi, Mansehra, Sopārā, Brahmagiri, Maski, Gavīmaṭh, Rūpnāth, and Yerragūḍi (M.R.E.) in the retention of *r*. It is, however, wanting in the use of *r* as a flag and *r* as a stop.

The gerund *tūna* or *ūna* which is frequently used in the Ardhamāgadhī verses is paralleled only in the word *abhivādetūnaṁ* of Aśoka's Bhābru Edict found at Bairāṭ.

The Ardhamāgadhī use of *ttu* or *ṭṭu* as a gerund is a common characteristic of all the Aśokan dialects but that at Garnār, *e.g.*, *kaṭu*=*kṛitvā* (S.R.E.I, Dh), *palitijitu*=*parityaktvā* (R.E. X, Dh, J, Ye), Ardhamāgadhī prefers *ttae to uṁ (tuṁ)* as an infinitive suffix, while *tave* is the only suffix for the infinitive in Aśokan Prakrit. Both *ttae* and *tave* correspond undoubtedly to the Vedic suffix *tave*, *taveñ* or *taven* (Pāṇini, III. 4.9.).

The Ardhamāgadhī locative singular suffiix *ṁsi* is missed in Aśokan Prakrit. The *si* of Aśokan Prakrit corresponds better to *ssi* of Śauraseni *ssiṁ* of Māgadhī.

The Ardhamāgadhī dative in *āe (āye)* is abundantly used in all the Aśokan dialects but those at Girnār, Mysore and Hyderabad.

Ardhamāgadhī does not sometimes retain the initial *y*, *e.g.*, *ahā*=*yathā*. But its predominant tendency is to replace the initial *y* by *j*, *e.g.*, *jahā*=*yathā*, *jāva*=*yāvat*. It also changes *yy* into *jj*, *e.g.*, *sejja*=*sayya*, Pali *seyya*.

Ardhamāgadhī not only retains the dental sibilant *s* but replaces by it the palatal and cerebral sibilants, precisely as in Pali. This is paralleled in all the Aśokan dialects but those at Shahbazgarhi and Mansehra; certain exceptions to the rule are to be noticed also at Kalsi and Kauśāmbī, *e.g.*, *Devānaṁpiyashā* (R.E. XIII, K, Queen's Edict), *shuneyu*, *shamavāye* (R.E. XII, K), *śiyā*=*syāt* (R.E. XII, K).

Aśoka's *chiṭhitu* (R.E. IV, Dh, J, K, M) corresponds to the Ardhamāgadhī *chiṭṭhittā*. The Ardhamāgadhī *daṃsaṇa* for *darśana* has its parallel in the Girnār *darśaṇā*, *dasaṇā* (R.E. IV).

The Ardhamāgadhī retention of *r* is a common characteristic of the Aśokan dialects at Girnār, Sopārā, Mysore, Hyderabad, Rūpnāth, Shahbazgarhi, and Mansehra, as also in the dialect of the Yerraguḍi copy of M.R.E. But Ardhamāgadhī dispenses with *r* as a flag and *r* as a stop.

The dominant tendency of Ardhamāgadhī to cerebralise the dental nasal is lacking in all the Aśokan dialects but those at Girnār, Mysore and Hyderabad, even at the last mentioned three places, the cerebralisation of *n* is rather an exception than a rule.

Aśokan Prakrit agrees with Ardhamāgadhī in so far as the latter language retains *v* in all case of assimilation, *e.g.*, *save*=*savve*, Pali, *sabbe* (R.E. VII, G, K, Dh, J).

Like Ardhamāgadhī and Pali, Aśokan Prakrit, employs *śiya*, siya (Sh, M), *shiyā*, *siyā* for *syāt*.

Ardhamāgadhī has its future form in *hiti* for *syati*, and in *hisi* for *syasi*. These two as archaic forms occur in Pali *gāthās*, *e.g.*, in *hohiti*, *hohisi*. The future form *siti* for *syati* is met with in the Mysore, Hyderabad, Rūpnāth and Yerrāguḍi dialects of M.R.E., *e.g.*, *vaḍhisiti*=*vaḍhisati* (Sa, Bai).

The instances cited above are enough, I think, to establish that the phonetic and grammatical characteristics of any of the Aśokan dialects are not wholly identical with those of Ardhamāgadhī.

Turning to Śauraseni, we may note that it agrees with Ardhamāgadhī of the verse portions of the Jaina Canon in its retention of *r*, in having the nominative singular in *o*, in the use of the single sibilant *s*, in the cerebralisation of even the initial *n*, and in the replacement of the initial *y* by *j*. So far as these characterstics go, the reader is referred to the observations made in connexion with Ardhamāgadhī.

The Śauraśenī and Māgadhī *idha* for *iha* is a phonetic peculiarity of the dialect of Girnār.

The Śaurasenī tendency to change the intervocal hard mute *t* into *d* is accidentally met with in the dialects of Kalsi, Shahbazgarhi and Mansehra in the word *hidasukhāye*, *hidasukhaye* (R.E. V). Elsewhere, even these three dialects have *hita* for *hita*.

The locative singular in *si* which occurs in all the Aśokan dialects but those of Girnār and Shahbazgarhi is identical with the alternative Śaurasenī suffix *ssi*.

In Śaurasenī *vāvuḍa* stands for SK. *vyāpṛita*, a characteristic which is missed in Aśokan Prakrit, cf. *vyāpaṭa* (R.E.V, G), *viyapuṭa* (R.E. V, Sh), *viyāpaṭa* (R.E. V, K, Dh; P.E. VII, DT).

The Śaurasenī change of *stha* into *chiṭṭha*, is paralleled by the Aśokan *chiṭhitu* (R.E. IV, K, Dh). But nowhere in Aśokan dialects *eva* changes into *jjevva*.

The instances need not be multiplied. Those cited

above are enough to indicate that none of the Aśokan dialects is wholly identifiable with Śaurasenī.

In Pāiśāchī *jñ* and *ny* become *ññ*, *e.g.*, *viññāna*=*vijñāna*, *kaññā*=*kanyā*. These two special characteristics of Paiśāchī are traceable in the Aśokan dialects of Girnār and Shahbazgarhi. The change of *ch* into *j*, such as in *rāchā* for *rājā*, may be illustrated by the Aśokan *Kaṁbocha* for *Kaṁboja* (R.E. V, Dh). Similarly *tūna* as a substitute for the gerund *ktvā* has its Aśokan parallel in *abhivādetuñaṁ* for *abhivādetvā* (Bhābru). But nowhere in Aśokan dialects *iva* becomes *piva* or *rjh* (as in *nirjhara)* becomes *chchh*.

Just as in Maharāshṭrī, so in the Aśokan dialects of the Mahārāshṭra, Girnār and Shahbazgarhi areas *l* is not substituted for *r*. The first case in *o* of *a*—declension is the usual form of declension at Girnār, Sopārā and Shahbazgarhi. The Mahārāshṭrī tendency to use *ṇ* in the right place as in Sanskrit is also the characteristic of the Aśokan dialects of the above areas. But there is no instance in Aśokan Prakrit where the intial *n* is cerebralised as in Mahārāshṭrī. Similarly there are several other characteristics of Mahārāshṭrī that are missed.

The historical position thus made out of Aśokan dialects in relation to later Prakrits is in no way new. It has been elaborately discussed by Senart and clearly outlined by Woolner. The new point stressed in the foregoing discussion is the broad demarcation of five phonetic subdivisions within two main grammatical divisions.

It will be seen that the typical Aśokan Prakrit as an official language is standardised in the diction of the Seven Pillar Edicts. This Prakrit diction was developed evidently within that portion of Northern India which is known to the Buddhists as the Middle Country. Call it Eastern Dialect or Prakrit if you please. It cannot be wholly identified with the Māgadhī of the Prakrit grammarians, and yet one cannot help thinking that it is a form of Old Māgadhī, which is presupposed by the Pali Canonical texts, I mean, that form which the Pali Canon preserves while reproducing certain philosophical doctrines, particularly those ascribed to the six Titthiyas or Tīrthaṅkaras including Mahāvīra[1]. Ardhamāgadhī,

1. Barua, *The Ājīvikas*, Journal of the Department of Letters, C.U., Vol. II. pp. 46—49.

the language of the Śvetāmbara Canon, shows a grammatical as well as a phonetic blending of the standard Aśokan Prakrit and the Aśokan dialect of the Mahārāshṭra area as defined above. Whether or no there ever existed a Buddhist Canon in that Old Māgadhī is still problematical. No inference should be definitely drawn as to the existence of such a Canon from the titles of seven texts (Bhābru Edict), though they are accidentally all in Old Māgadhī. As the Vinaya Chullavagga attests, the *Buddhavachana* was being studied, preserved and orally handed down at different centres, even in the life-time of the Buddha, by his followers recruited from different localities, races, social grades and families. There was reason for apprehension that the *Buddhavachana* might become distorted unless it was put in Vedic language (to *Chhandas*, Lit., language of the Vedic hymns). From a significant statement of the Buddha occurring in the Araṇavibhaṅga Sutta (Majjhima-N., III), it is clear that different provincial words were used, such *patta, vittha, poṇa, dhāropa, sarāva,* to denote one and the same thing or object, such as a pot or bowl. Affiliated into a single language, they would serve as synonyms. The local variants in Aśokan Prakrit, such as *mahiḍāyo* (R.E.IX, G), *ithi* (Dh), *striyaka* (Sh), *abakajanika* (M), *abakajaniyo* (K), suggest not only the local currencey of a certain word but also the local phonetic variation of one and the same word.

Thus, in spite of the received common traditional formulations of the Buddhavachana, it is most probable that there existed several local recensions of texts showing variations in matter, diction, grammar and phonetics. In the matter of codification and antiquity the Pali Canon is certainly entitled to highest respect. The language of this authoritative recension has not only the Vedic Sanskrit in its background but also presupposes a definite dialectical basis. One may hold without much fear of contradiction that a clear idea of the main dialectical basis of Pali may be formed from the diction of the Girnār version of Aśoka's Rock Edicts. I am not prepared to call that basis either Śaurasenī[1],

1. Professor S. K. Chatterji inclines to think that in respect of morphology and phonology there is a good deal of similarity between Pali and Śaurasenī. *Origin and Development of the Bengali Language.* P. 54.

Paiśāchī[1] or Mahārāshṭrī, for to do so would be to put the cart before the horse. In order to get a true insight into what was in the background one must not argue back but forward : given such a dialectical basis, we can account for the possibility of the development of Pali, and subsequently of the development of Śaurasenī, Paiśāchī and Mahārāshṭrī.

1. Dr. N. Dutt argues in favour of Paiśāchī. *Early History of the Spread of Buddhism*, P. 256ff.

CHAPTER IV

PHRASEOLOGY AND STYLE

The records of Aśoka are remarkable for their homely diction in prose. It follows a law of rhythm and cadence of its own and combines the sincerity of purpose with the dignity of expression. It is enlivened throughout by the noblest sentiment of a well-meaning heart, and vivid with the grandest vision of a righteous world of ceaseless activity promoting the cause of piety and promising the attainment of the desired object here and of a grand heaven hereafter. It conveys the lofty message of an enlightened seer of eternal good and happiness, and serves as a fitting vehicle of sparkling thoughts of a highly sensitive and practical mind. Its pathos is well-suited to its theme, and its appeal goes direct into the heart. The epigraphs read as so many antobiographical sketches of Aśoka. In going through them one is apt to feel that they were written either to his dictation or, at any rate, under his direction. Thus they are intended to reproduce and preserve the very words of the Maurya emperor. So far as their phraseology and style go, they are very closely related to the Pali Discourses of the Buddha. There is no other recorded literary tradition which so wonderfully fits in with them. And this alone may suffice to indicate that none was, perhaps, more steeped in the knowledge of the *Buddhavachana* than Aśoka, that none drank deeper at that fountain of inspiration.

The first point of similarity between the Buddha's Pali Discourses and Aśoka's Prakṛit Epigraphs is the race between the statement in first person and that in third. The redactor's or editor's part in both is to substitute third person for first for converting a direct narration into an indirect one. The first person remains intact in both where the received words of mouth are sought to be faithfully reproduced or preserved. In both, the stress is laid on the authoritative *vachana*, *sāsana*, and *anusathi* (Pali *anusatthi*, *anusiṭṭhi*) :

Buddhavachana	*Aśokavachana*
mama vachanena te bhikkhū āmantehi (Majjhima, I, pp. 258. 321)	*Devānaṁpiyashā vachanena savata mahāmātā vataviyā* (Queen's Edict)
Tathāgato āha, Bhagavā etad avocha (Dīgha, III, p. 181)	*Devānaṁpriyo . . . . hevaṁ āha, etaṁ*
	Devānaṁpiye hevaṁ āha. (R.E. III, P.E. VII).
Bhagavato arahato sammāsambuddhassa.	*iyaṁ sāsane* (Schism Pillar, Sārnāth)
	Devānaṁpriyasa priyadasino rāño (R. E. I).

The protocol of the Bhābru Edict literally conforms to the conventional form of courtesy met with in Pali :

Rājā Māgadho Ajātasattu Vedehiputto Bhagavantaṁ abhivadetvā. Bhikkusaṅghassa añjaliṁ paṇāmetvā appābādhaṁ ...phāsuvihāraṁ puchchati, also *appābādhataṁ* (Kakachupama Sutta, Majjhima I).	*Piyadasi lājā Māgadhe Saṁghaṁ abhivādetūnaṁ āha apābādhataṁ cha phāsuvihālataṁ cha* (Bhābru).

In M. R. E. (Bra), Aśoka directs the Viceroy-in-Council to observe the conventional courtesy in officially forwarding a copy of his proclamation to the *Mahāmātras* of Isila. Here the form is implied in the order : *ārogyaṁ vataviyā*, "health is to be inquired of, health is to be wished." The inquiry of health and comfort and welfare was made, as a matter of course, in all greetings of civility exchanged between two persons of distinct social rank or religious status. The oft-recurring Pali description is : *sammodaniyaṁ kathaṁ sārānīyaṁ vītisāretvā*, "having exchanged the greetings of civility." This corresponds to the Sanskrit *kuśalapraśnam uktvā* (Rāmāyaṇa, Araṇya, XII. 26). Buddhaghosa explains the word *sammodi* (greeted) as meaning such personal inquiries as *kachchi bhoto . . . . appābādhaṁ . . . . phāsuvihāro ti.* But exactly corresponding to Aśoka's *ārogyaṁ vataviyā*, we have in Buddhaghosa's Papañchasūdanī : *mama vachanena punappunaṁ ārogyaṁ puchchhitvā 'rājā tumhehi saddhiṁ mittabhāvaṁ ichchhatī 'ti vadatha.*

One must note that *arogiyo preseti, arogya pariprochati* is the usual conventional form of courtesy with the Kharoshṭhī documents of Khotan. Strangely enough, Kauṭilya's śāsanādhikāra prescribes no such convention.

The *Buddhavachana* and *Aśokavachana* show a very close correspondence as regards the construction of sentences, so much so that one cannot help regarding the former as the literary basis of the latter :

BV	AV
'Idha Tathāgato jāto' ti saddhassa kulaputtassa dassanīyaṁ ṭhānaṁ (Dīgha, II, p. 140).	*'Hida Budhe jāte Sakyamunī' ti silā vigaḍabhī chā kālāpita.*
Asmin pradeśe Bhagavañ jātaḥ (Divyā., p 390).	*'Hida Bhagavaṁ jāte' ti.* (Lumbinī Pillar).
Tassa mayhaṁ etad ahosi : Kin nu kho aham aññadatthu bhayapāṭikankhī viharāmi . . . . tathābhūto va bhayabheravaṁ paṭivineyyan ti (Majjhima, I, Bhayabherava Sutta).	*Esa me huthā : . . . . se kinasu jane anupaṭipajeyā, kinasu jane anulupāyā dhaṁmavaḍhiyā vaḍheyā ti.* (P.E. VII).

The influence of the Pali *gāthās* on the diction of *Aśokavachana* is traceable in the mannerism of the latter in inculcating the principles of piety. The Sādhu Sutta, quoted in R. E. IX, is undoubtedly the main Canonical authority. But the mannerism is not restricted to the stanzas of this Sutta, as will appear from the following citation from the Dhammapada :

BV	AV
kāyena saṁvaro sādhu *sādhu vāchāya soṁvaro* (Dhp. 361).	*sādhu mātrai cha pitari cha susrūsā, b(r)āmhaṇa-s(r)amaṇānaṁ sādhu dānaṁ,*
dhammaladdhassa pi sādhu dānaṁ (Saṁyutta, I, p. 21).	*prāṇānaṁ sādhu anārāṁbhọ,* *apavyayatā apabhaṁḍatā sādhu*

The Pali prose discourses typified by the Kinti Sutta (R. E. III, Majjhima-N. III) may be shown to have influenced the mannerism of *Aśokavachana* in stating the purpose of an action by *kiṁti* (SK, *kimiti*), 'what for', put in the middle of a sentence:

BV	AV
Yam pi Tathāgato . . . . *pubbe manussabhūto* *samāno bahuno* *janassa atthakāmo* *ahosi hitakāmo* *. . . . kinti me saddhāya* *vaḍḍheyyuṁ. dhammena* *vaḍḍheyyuṁ* (Dīgha, III, P. 164)	*Ya cha kiṁchi* *parākramāmi ahaṁ* *kiṁti bhūtānaṁ* *ānaṁṇaṁ gachheyaṁ,* *idha cha nāni* *sukhāpayāmi paratra* *cha svagaṁ* *ārādhayaṁtu* (R. E. VI).

The *Aśokavachana* employs several technical terms that are characteristically Buddhist and were evidently drawn from the *Buddhavachana* :

BV	AV
saṁvaṭṭa-kappā (Dīgha, I, p. 81)	*saṁvaṭa-kapā* (R. E., IV, V)
sukaṭa-dukkaṭa (Dīgha, I, p. 55)	*sukataṁ dukataṁ* (R. E. V)
apalibodha	*apalibodha* (R. E. V)
vītagedho, agiddho	*aparigodha* (R. E. V)
dhammādhiṭṭhānaṁ (Netti)	*dhaṁmādhiṭhāne* (R. E. V)
sambodhi (J. IV, p. 236)	*saṁbodhi* (R. E. VIII)
dhammadānaṁ (Dhp. 354)	*dhaṁmadānaṁ* (R. E. IX, XI)
dhammānuggaho (Ang. I, p. 78)	*dhaṁmānugaho* (R. E. XI)
samachariyā (Ang., I, P. 55)	*samachaliyaṁ* (R. E. XIII)
dhammena abhivijiya (Dīgha, III, P. 51)	*dhaṁmavijayo* (R. E. XIII)
suvihitānaṁ (Thera., P. 75)	*suvihitānoṁ* (R. E. XIII)
majjhena, *majjhimā paṭipadā*	*majhaṁ paṭipādayema* (S. R. E. I)
assuropa (Vibhanga, P. 357)	*āsulope* (S. R. E. I)
kilamatho	*kilamathe* (S. R. E. I)
saṁghaṁ saraṇaṁgato	*saṁghe upayīte* (M. R.E.)

saṁghaṁ upayantu (Dīpava VI. 58)	
porāṇiyā pakati (J. VI, P. 151)	*porāṇā pakiti* (M. R. E., ye)
yoggāchariyo (Majjhima, I p. 124)	*yūgyāchariyāni* (M. R. E., Ye)
Satthu-gāravatā *Dhamma-gāravatā* *Saṁgha-gāravatā* (Ang., IV, P. 28)	*Budhasi Dhaṁmasi Saṁghasi* *gālāve chaṁ pasāde cha* (Bhābru)
Buddhe Dhamme *Saṁghe avechchappasādo* (Ang., I, P. 222)	
saddhammo chiraṭṭhitiko hoti (Ang., III, P. 247)	*sadhaṁme chilaṭhitike hosati* (Bhābru)
dhamma-pariyāyo	*dhaṁmapaliyāyāni* (Pl.) (Bhābru)
Vinaya (Ang., I, P. 98f.)	*Vinaya-samukase* (Bhābru)
Ariyavaṁsā (Dīgha, III, P. 224)	*Aliyavasāni* (Bhābru)
Anāgata-bhayāni (Ang., III, p. 103ff.)	*Anāgata-bhayāni* (Bhābru)
bhikkhu bhikkūṇi	*bhikhu bhikhuni* (Bhābru, - Schism Pillar)
upāsaka upāsikā	*upāsaka upāsikā* (Bhābru)
dhammaniyāmatā	*dhaṁmaniyame* (P. E. VII)
anuposathe (Vinaya Mahāvagga, II., 4. 36)	*anuposathaṁ* (P. E. V, Schism Pillar, Sārnāth)
pachchuggamanaṁ (J. IV, p. 321)	*pachupagamanaṁ* (P. E. VII)
saddhāpadāna (Ang., V,P. 337)	*dhaṁmāpadāna* (P.E. VII)
saṁghaṁ samaggaṁ karoti (Ang., V, P. 74)	*saṁghe samage kaṭe* (Schism Pillar)
saṁghaṁ bhindati (Vinaya, II, p. 198)	*saṁghaṁ bhākhati* (Schism Pillar)

In many instances Aśoka's sentence or clause just puts in prose order a Pali saying in verse :

BV	AV
devatānaṁ piyo ahuṁ (Apadāna, Pilindavachcha)	*Devānaṁpiyo* (R. E. III)

<table>
<tr><td>Dhamme ṭhito ajjave
maddave sato (Sutta-nipāta, 250)</td><td>Dhammamhi sīlamhi
tisṭamto (R. E. V).</td></tr>
<tr><td>Yo pubbe katakalyiāṇo akā
lokesu dukkaraṁ (j. III, P. 12)
pubbangamo sucharitesu
(Dīgha, iii, P. 169)
Ta mayā bahukalāṇaṁ
kataṁ ; me</td><td>Yo ādikaro kalāṇasa so
dukaraṁ karoti (R. E. V).</td></tr>
<tr><td>Katā me kalyāṇā
anekarūpā (J. V. p. 491)</td><td>bahuni kayānāni kaṭāni
(R.E. V, P.E. II).</td></tr>
<tr><td>pāpaṁ pāpena sukaraṁ
sādhuṁ pāpena dukkaraṁ
Chullavagga, vii)</td><td>Sukaraṁ hi pāpam,
Papaṁ hi sukaraṁ (R.E.V).
Kalāṇaṁ dukaraṁ (R.E.V.)</td></tr>
<tr><td>saddhāya pi sādhu
dānaṁ (Saṁyutta, I, p. 21)</td><td>sadhu d(ā)na iti, dāne sādhū
ti (R.E. IX).</td></tr>
<tr><td>Dhammaladdhassa pi
sādhu dānaṁ (Saṁyutta, I. p. 21)</td><td>B (r)āmhaṇānaṁ
sādhu dānaṁ (R.E. III).</td></tr>
<tr><td>Pāṇesu sādhu saṁyamo
(Saṁyutta. I, p. 21)</td><td>Pāṇesu sayamo sādhu (R.E. IX).</td></tr>
<tr><td>Sabbadānaṁ dhammadānaṁ
jināti (Dhp. 354)</td><td>Na tu etārisaṁ asti dānaṁ
yārisaṁ dhammadānaṁ (R.E.IX)</td></tr>
<tr><td>(Na hi mangale kiñcanaṁ)
atthi saccaṁ (J. V. p. 78)</td><td>nirathaṁ maṁgālaṁ (R.E. IX)</td></tr>
<tr><td>Yasmiṁ kataññutā natthi
(Javasakuṇa J.)</td><td>Yasa nāsti......kataṁñatā
(R.E. VII).</td></tr>
<tr><td>Yathā pitā athavā pi mātā
anukampakā atthakāmā pajānaṁ
Evameva no hotu ayañ cha rājā,
mayam pi hessāma tatheva putta
(J, V. p 504)</td><td>Athā pit (ā) hevaṁ ne lājā
ti, atha atānaṁ
anukaṁpati hevaṁ apheni
anukaṁpati; athā pajā
hevaṁ maye lājine
(S.R.E. II).</td></tr>
<tr><td>Nattano samakaṁ kiñchi
atirekañ cha maññisaṁ
(Theragā., 424)</td><td>Duāhale imasa kaṁmasa same,
kute
mane atileke (S. R. E. I, J).</td></tr>
</table>

Esā te porāṇiyā pakati (J. VI, *p*. 151)	*Esā porāṇā pakiti* (M.R.E.Ja, Ye)
Yaṁ kiñchi subhāsitaṁ sabbaṁ taṁ (pan) assa Bhagavato vachanaṁ sammā-sambuddhassa|| (Ang., IV, p. 164)	*E kechi Bhagavatā Budhena bhāsite sarve se subhāsite va* (Bhābru)
Tañ cha arahāmi vattave (J. III, p. 309)	*Alahāmi hakaṁ taṁ vātave* (Bhābru).
vaḍḍhat'eva suve suve (J. V, p. 507)	*suve suve vaḍhitā* (P. E., I)
Sachche cha dhamme cha dame cha saṁyame| *socheyya-sīlālayuposathesu cha*|| *Dānaṁ sīlaṁ parichchāgaṁ ajjavaṁ maddavaṁ tapaṁ* (Dīgha, III, p. 147)	*Dāya dāne sache sochave mādave sādhave* (P. E., VII)
sussūsā cha garūnaṁ (Thera-gāthā, verse 369)	*guruna suśrusha* (R. E., XIII).

The legacy of the older Pali gāthās is palpable in the diction of *Aśokavachana*. First, the use of *re* as an *ātmanepada* verbal suffix (3rd person, plural) is one of the archaisms met with in the Pali gāthās. This occurs as a regular form in the dialect of Girnār :

PG	GD
dissare, vijjare, jāyare, miyyare bhavissare, vinibujjhare	*ārabhare, ārabhisare* (R.E.I.); *anuvatare* (R.E., XIII), *anuvatisare* (R.E., V).

The Vedic infinitive *tave* which is met with here and there in the ancient Pali gāthās is found to be a regular form in Aśokan Prakrit. This suffix is totally discarded in Pali prose and in all later Prakrits. The correspondence in this respect between the *Buddhavachana* in verse and the *Aśokavachana* in prose may be illustrated as follows :

BV	AV
vattave, netave, dātave, pahātave	*vātave* (Bhābru), *bhetave* (Schism Pillar), *nijhapayitave* (P.E. IV), *chhamitave, khamitave* (R.E. XIII).

The two archaic forms of expression are met with alike in the old Pali gāthās and the *Aśokavachana* :

kenassu nivuto loko (Sutta-nipāta, verse 1032)	*kinasu jane (su = svid)* (P. E., VII).
kiṁchchhando kimadhippāyo (J.V, p. 3)	*kiṁchhaṁde, kīchhaṁde* (S. R. E., II).
samūhatāse (Sutta-nipāta, verse 4)	*viyāpaṭāse* (P. E. VII).

Certain archaic future forms of the verbs *kṛi* (to do), *hu* (to be), and *dā* (to give) are features of both the old Pali gāthās and the *Aśokavachana* :

(1) √kṛi (to do)

kāhati, kāhanti, kāhasi, kāhatha, kāhāmi, kāhāma	*kāsati* (R. E., V), *kachati* (P. E., II), *kachhaṁti* (R.E.,V), *kachhāmi, kashami* (R. E., IX).

(2) hu (to be)

hessati (hohiti), hessanti (hohinti), hessasi (hohisi), hessatha (hohitha), hessāmi (hohimi), hessāma (hohima)	*hosati* (Bhābru), *hosāmi* (S. R. E., II), *hohaṁti* (P. E., VII).
hessaṁ (Theragāthā, verse 1100)	*husaṁ* (M. R. E.)

(2) √dā (to give)

padāhisi (Theragāthā, verse 303)	*dāhaṁṭi* (P.E., IV)

As for the correspondence in phrases and idioms, the following instances may be cited for comparison :

BV	AV
chha kho ādīnavā samajjābhicharaṇe (Dīgha, III, P. 18[illegible])	*bahukaṁ hi dosaṁ samājamhi* (R. E., I).
ekachcho samaṇo vā brāhmaṇo vā (Brahmajāla Sutta)	*ekachā samājā* (R. E., I.)
sādhusammato bahujanassa (Dīgha, I, P. 49)	*sādhumatā Devānaṁpriyasa* (R. E., I)
mago vā moro vā; (Majjhima, I, P. 20)	*dvo morā eko mago* (R. E., I)
so nichcho dhuvo	*so pi mago na dhruvo* (R. E., I)
vijite (J., I, P. 262)	*vijite* (R. E., II)
Brahmadatto nāma Kāsīrājā (Vinaya Mahāvagga, Ch .X)	*Aṁtiyoko nāma Yonalājā* (R. E., II).
osadhā (Sutta-nipāta, verse 296)	*osadhāni* (R. E., II)
Rajjuko (J., II. P. 367)	*Rajuke* (R. E., III, P. E., IV, P. E., VII. M. R. E., Ye).
anusaññāyamāna, anusaññātuṁ (Ang. I, P. 68)	*anusaṁyānaṁ* (R. E., III)
babubhaṇḍa (Vinaya, III, P. 138)	*apabhaṁḍatā* (R. E., III)
atthato cha byanjanato cha	*hetuto cha vyaṁjanato cha* (R.E. III)
tīṇi saṁvachchharāni atikkantāni (J., II, P. 128)	*atikātaṁ aṁtaraṁ* (R.E. IV)
dīgham antaraṁ (Petav., I. 10)	
bījagāma-bhūtagāmasamārambha pasūnaṁ cha samārambho (Dīgha, I,P.5)	*prāṇāraṁbho* (R.E. IV)
pasūnaṁ samārambhā (Sutta-nipāta, 311)	
gihino vā pabbajitassā vā sammāpaṭipatti (Saṁyutta, XLIV, 24)	*ñātinaṁ saṁpaṭipati br(ā)mhaṇasamaṇānaṁ saṁpaṭipati* (R.E. IV)
vihiṁsā, avihiṁsā (Dīgha, III, P. 215; Vibhanga, 86, 363)	*vihiṁsā, avihiṁsā* (R.E. IV)
ahiṁsā sabbabhūtesu	*avihiṁsā bhūtānaṁ* (R.E. IV)
vimānadassi (sutta-nipāta, 887)	
visūka-dassana (Digha-N.I)	*vimāna-darsaṇa* (R.E. IV)
dhammaghosako (Dhp. A., III, p. 81)	*dhaṁmaghoso* (R.E. IV)
dhammabherī (Milinda, P. 21)	*bherighoso* (R. E. IV)

aggikkhandha (Vinaya, I, P. 26)	*agikhaṁdhāni* (R. E. IV)
dibbāni rūpāni (Dīgha, I, P. 153)	*divyāni rūpāni* (R. E. IV,
dussīlassa (Dīgha, III, P. 235)	*asīlasa* (R. E., IV)
kāmesu yuñjatha (Theragāthā, 346)	*vadhi yujaṁtu* (R. E.. IV)
hāni (Ang., I, P. 434)	*hini* (R. E., IV)
mā saṅghabhedo ruchchittha (Bhikkhu Pātimokkha)	*hini cha mā alochayisu* (R. E., IV)
moneyyaṁ dukkaraṁ (Suttanipāta, 701,	*kalāṇaṁ dukaraṁ* (R. E., V)
ādikammiko, pubbakārī, pubbaṅgamo sucharitesu (Vinaya, III, p. 116)	*ādikaro kalāṇasa* (R. E., V)
sīlālayuposathesu (Dīgha, III, p. 147)	*pāpe hi nāma supadālaye* (R. E., V)
Yona-Kambojesu (Majjhima, II, p. 149)	*Yana-Kaṁboja-Gaṁdhārānaṁ* (R. E., V) *Yona-Kāṁbojesu* (R. E., XIII)
raṭṭhikassa pettanikassa	*Raṭhikānaṁ Pitinikānaṁ* (R. E., V)
Yona-Kambojesu aññesu cha pachchantimesu janapadesu (Majjhima, II, p. 149)	*Yona-Kaṁbocha-Gaṁdhālesu . . e vā pi aṁne apalaṁtā* (R. E., V)
brāhmaṇibbhesu (J. VI, p. 229)	*bramaṇibheshu* (R. E. V)
hitāya sukhāya	*hitasukhāye* (R. E. V)
katādhikāro (J. I, p. 56, VI, p. 251)	*kaṭābhīkale, kiṭabhikaro* (R. E. V)
theresu, mahallako	*thairesu mahalake* (R. E. V)
ratha-vinīta (Majjhima., I, p 149)	*vinīta* (R. E. VI)
atthakaraṇaṁ (Digha, II, p. 20)	*athakaṁme, aṭhakaṁme* (R. E. VI)
rājino paṭivedayi, rañño paṭivedesi	*me paṭivedetha* (R. E. VI)
achchāyikaṁ karaṇīyaṁ (Majjhima, I, p. 149)	*achāyike, atiyāyike* (R. E. VI)
bhuñjamāne (Theragāthā)	*bhuṁjamānasa* (R. E. VI)
vādo te āropito (Dīgha, I, p. 81), *rajjaṁ amachchesu āropetvā* (Petavatthu—A., p. 154)	*mahāmātresu achāyike (ā) ropitaṁ* (R. E. VI)
kalaho viggaho vivādo, yassaṁ	*vivādo vā nijhati v (ā)*

parisāyaṁ . . . . . . saññattiṁ upagachchhanti . . . nijjhattiṁ upagachchanti (Ang., I, p. 66)	*saṁto parisāyaṁ* (R. E. VI)
ānantarikaṁ (Vinaya, I p. 32)	*ānaṁtaliyaṁ* (R. E. VI)
idañ cha mūlaṁ kusalābhivuḍḍhiyā (Saṁyutta—N. I)	*tasa cha esa mūle* (R. E. VI) *bhūtānaṁ ānaṁṇaṁ* (R.E. VI)
anaṇo ñatinaṁ (J. VI, p. 36)	*chilaṭhitikā hotu* (R. E. VI)
pāsāna-lekhā chiraṭṭhittkā hoti	*añatra agena parākramena* (R. E. VI) ;
(Ang., *aññatra bhikkhu-sammutiyā, aññatra tiriyantaranāya*	*añatra. . agāya palīkhāya agena bhayena* (P.E. I)
āhārasuddhi, saṁsārasuddhi	*bhāvasudhi* (R.E. VII)
(Maj-*daḷha-parakkamo, daḷha-dhammo, daḷhabhattikā* (Dīpavaṁsa, XI. 25)	*daḍhabhatitā* (R.E. VII)
migavam nikkhamitvā (Samanta-pā., I, p. 55).	*nikhamisu heta migaviyā* (R.E. VIII)
tena taṁ madhuraṁ	*tena sā dhaṁmayātā* (R.E. VIII)
samaṇānaṁ cha dassanaṁ (Mangala Sutta)	*thairānaṁ dasane cha* (R.E. VIII)
bhiyyo no arati siyā. sukhā uppajjati bhiyyo somanassaṁ	*tadopayā esā bhuya rati bhavati* (R.E. VIII)
aññabhāgiyam (Bhikkhu Pātimokkha)	*bhāge aṁñe* (R.E. VIII)
uchāvachā paṭipadā (Sutta-nipāta, 714)	*uchāvachaṁ maṁgalaṁ* (R.E. IX)
mangalaṁ karoti (Dhp-A, I. p. 184)	*maṁgalam karoti* (R.E. IX)
ābādhesu	*ābādhesu* (R.E. IX)
āvāha-vivāhesu	*āvāha-vīvāhesu* (R.E. IX)
itthi, mahilā, mahiḷā	*ithī, mahiḍā,*
ambakā janikā (Vinaya, I, p. 232; Samanta-pā, I. p. 385)	*abak (a)janik(ā)* (R.E. IX)
mātari pitari	*mātari pitari* (R.E. III)
na cha khuddaṁ,	*chhudaṁ (khudaṁ) cha*
nirattham va	*nirathaṁ cha* (R.E. IX)
appaphalaṁ mahapphalaṁ taridaṁ	*apaphalaṁ mahāphale* (R.E. IX) *tateta (ṁ)* (R.E. IX)
etāriso satthā	*etārisaṁ dhaṁmamaṁgalaṁ* (R.E. IX)
mittasanthavaṁ, santhutena	*mita-saṁthutena,* (R.E. IX)

itivuttaṁ, vuttaṁ h' etaṁ Bhagavatā (Itivuttaka)	*asti iti vutaṁ,* *athi hevaṁ vute* (R.E IX)
ñāti-mitta-sakhā, mitto suhado, mitto sahāyo (Singālovāda Sutta)	*mitrena va suhadayena vā ñātikena va sahāyena va* (R.E. IX)
ovaditabbā	*ovāditavyaṁ* (R.E. IX)
dhammo akāliko (Dīgha, II, p. 93)	*dhaṁmamaṁgale akālike* (R.E. IX)
sukhaṁ nibbatteyya (Milinda. 276)	*athaṁ nivaṭeti* (R.E. IX)
bahuṁ puññaṁ pasavati (Saṁyutta, I, P. 182)	*anaṁtaṁ puñaṁ prasavati* (R.E. IX, XI)
āyatiṁ, āyatike	*āyatiye* (R.E. X)
yaso kitti cha (Sutta-nipāta, 817)	*yaso va kiti va* (R.E. X)
ussaṭāya (Majjhima, II, P. 15)	*usaṭena* (R.E. X)
etaṁ dukkaraṁ	*dukaraṁ tu kho etaṁ* (R.E. X)
paṭipatti, sammāpaṭipanno	*saṁmapaṭipati* (R.E. XI)
sabba-pāsaṇḍa-gaṇa (Milinda P., J. 359)	*sava-pāsaṁḍāni* (R.E. XII)
etasmiṁ nidāne etasmiṁ pakaraṇe dhammiṁ kathaṁ katvā (Vinaya Mahāvagga, VI)	*atpapāsaṁḍa-pūjā . . lahukā vā asa tamhi tamhi prakaraṇe* (R. E. XII)
attānam khaṇati (Majjhima, I, p. 132)	*atpapāsa(ṁ)ḍaṁ chhaṇati, ataprashaṁḍaṁ kshaṇati* (R.E. XII)
vachiguti	*vachiguti* (R.E. XII)
eke samaṇa-brāhmaṇā sakaṁ yeva vādaṁ dīpenti jotenti paravādaṁ pana khuṁsanti (Ang., I, P. 88)	*yo hi kochi atpapāsaṁḍaṁ pūjayati parapāsaṁḍaṁ va garahati. kiṁti atpapāsaṁḍaṁ dīpayema iti* (R.E. XII)
upahaññati	*upahanati* (R.E. XII)
bahussutā āgatāgamā samavāyo (Saṁyutta, IV, P. 68)	*bahusrutā cha kalāṇāgamā samavāyo* (R.E. XII)
tatra-tatrābhinandinī, pasannā Buddha-sāsane	*ye tatra-tat(r)a prasaṁnā* (R.E. XII)
huveyya (Majjhima, I, P. 171)	*huveyu* (R.E. XII)
khattiyassa muddhabhisittassa	*aṭhavasābhisitasa* (R.E. XIII)
dhammakāmo	*dhaṁmakāmatā* (R.E. XIII)

tibbaṁ chhandaṁ cha pemañ cha (Sāriputta theragāthā)	*tīvo dhaṁmavāyo dhaṁmakāmatā* (R.E. XIII)
samaṇa-brāhmaṇa-sabba-pāsaṇḍagaṇa (Milinda, p. 359)	*bābhanā va samanā va aṁne pāsaṁḍā* (R.E. XIII)
paṭibhāgo (Majjhima, I, p. 304)	*paṭibhāgo* (R.E. XIII)
sahassabhāgo te maraṇaṁ	*(saha)srabhāgo va garumato* (R.E. XIII)
aṭaviyo samuppannā raṭṭhaṁ viddhaṁsayanti te.	*yā cha pi aṭaviyo Devānaṁpiyasa pijite (ho)ti* (R. E. XIII)
tass'eva anuvidhiyyati (=*anusikkhati*, J. No. 48)	*dhramaṁ anuvidhiyaṁti* (R.E. XIII)
aparādhaṁ khamati	*khamitave* (R. E. XIII)
vajanti dhīrā (Dhammapada)	*dūtā na vrachaṁti* (R.E. XIII)
ghaṭissaṁ (Theragāthā)	*ghaṭitaṁ* (R. E. XIV)
ghatitaṁ (Bodhicharyāvatāra, V)	
saṁkhittena bhāsitassa vitthārena atthaṁ (Theragāthā, verse, 570)	*asti eva saṁkhitena . . asti vistat(e)na* (R.E. XIV)
mahallakaṁ vihāraṁ (Bhikkhu Pātimokkha)	*mahālake hi vijitaṁ* (R.E. XIV)
ayaṁ mahāpaṭhavī dīghā āyatā . . . . visālā vitthiṇṇā vipulā mahantā (Milinda, p. 311)	*mahaṁte hi vijaye* (R. E. XIV)
atthamadhuratāya pemaṇīyā (Sumangala vilā., I, p. 75)	*athasa madhuratāya* (R.E XIV)
punappunaṁ	*punapuna-vutaṁ* (R. E. XIV)
saṅkhāya	*sachhāya, saṁkhāya* (R.E. XIV)
ekato ghaṭitaṁ	*na sarvaṁ sarvata ghaṭitaṁ* (R. E. XIV)
āchariyupajjhāyānaṁ anusatthi (Milinda—P., p. 397)	*aṁ tuphesu anusathi* (S.R.E.I)
atthassa dvārā pamukhā (J. I, p. 366)	*esa me mokhyamata-duvālaṁ* (S.R.E.I)
samachariyā daḷhā dhiti (J. VI)	*dhiti paṭiṁnā achalā* (S.R.E.I)
akakkasaṁ apharusaṁ (j. III, p. 282)	*akhakhase achaṁḍe, achaṁḍaṁ aphalusaṁ* (S.R.E.I)
vadho cha bandho cha parikkileso (Petavatthu)	*baṁdhanaṁ vā palikilesaṁ vā* (S.R.E.I)
dakkhanti, dakkhiṁ	*dekhatha, dekhata* (S.R.E.I)
khaṇe khaṇe (Dhp., 239)	*khaṇasi khaṇasi* (S.R.E.I)
etadantika, maraṇantikaṁ	*ba(ṁ)dhanaṁtika* (S.R.E.I)

imaṁ tesaṁ pāpuṇātū ti (Milinda, p. 294)	*aṁtesu pāpunevu te iti* (S. R. E. II)
sassatisamaṁ, sassatī samā	*sasvatam samaṁ, sasvataṁ, samayaṁ* (S. R. E. I, II)
antarā cha Rājagahaṁ	*aṁtalāpi Tisena* (S. R. E. II)
asaṁbhīto anubbiggo (Milinda, p. 340)	*anuvigina* (S. R. E. II)
attānaṁ anukampāmi (J. IV, p. 320)	*atānaṁ anukaṁpati* (S.R.E. II)
aḍḍhatiyāni yojanasatāni	*aḍhatiyāni vasāni* (M. R. E.)
hessaṁ (J. I, p. 49)	*husaṁ* (M. R. E.)
Jambudīpe	*Jaṁbudīpasi* (M. R. E.)
missam bālehi paṇḍitaṁ (J. V, p. 599)	*munisā misā devehi* (M. R. E.)
missībhūtā missībhāvaṁ gato (J. V, p. 86, Dīgha, II, p. 267)	*misibhūtā* (M. R. E.)
tassa suchiṇṇassa ayaṁ vipāko (Serissaka-vimānavatthu)	*pakamasa hi iyaṁ phale* (M. R. E.)
katam pūññaphalaṁ mayhaṁ (Buddhāpadāna)	
vipulaṁ sukhaṁ (Dhp., 27)	*vipule svage* (M. R. E.)
evameva kho kusalaṁ bhiyyo bhiyyo	*iyam cha athe vaḍhisati*
pavaḍḍhati (Milinda., p. 297)	*vipulaṁ pi cha vaḍhisati* (M. R. E.)
diyaḍḍhaṁ	*diyaḍhiyaṁ* (M. R. E.)
yāvatako assa kāyo	*yāvataka tupaka ahāle* (M. R. E.)
sachaṁ bhaṇe nālīkaṁ	*sachaṁ vataviyaṁ* (M. R. E.)
dhammaguṇā (J. IV, p. 321)	*dhaṁmaguṇā* (M. R. E.)
jeṭṭhāpachāyana (J. V, p. 326)	*apachāyanāya* (M. R. E.)
chakkaṁ pavattemi	*dhammaguṇā pavatitaviyā* (M. R. E.)
so dāni (Theragāthā, 291)	*se dāni* (M. R. E., Ye)
yoggāchariyo (Majjhima, I, p. 124)	*yūgyāchariyāni* (M. R. E.)
abhiṇhaṁ, abhikkhaṇaṁ	*abhikhinaṁ* (Bhābru)
hina-m-ukkaṭṭha-majjhimā (Vinaya, IV, p. 7)	*ukasā gevayā majhimā* (P.E.I.)
omakā majjhimā ukkaṭṭhā (J. III, p. 218)	

alaṁ gilānaṁ upaṭṭhātuṁ (Ang. III, p. 142)	*alaṁ cha palaṁ samādapayitave* (P. E. I)
paraṁ cha samādapeti (Ang., II, p. 253)	
pachchantavāsino mahāmattā (Atthasā., p. 245)	*aṁta-mahāmāta* (P. E. I)
dhammena gutto (J. V, P. 222)	*dhaṁmena goti* (P. E. I)
ālokadā chakkhudadā (Theragā., 3)	*chakhudāne* (P. E. II)
attano pana (*vajjaṁ*) *duddasam* (Dhp., 176)	*dupaṭivekhe chu kho esa* (P.E.I)
uddhagāminī, adhogāminī, dukkhanirodha-gāminī	*imāni āsinavagāmini* (P. E. III)
bodhiyā yeva kāraṇā (Chariyā-Piṭaka) ; *yena kāraṇena* (Milinda, p. 255)	*isyā kālanena va* (P. E. III)
issā mānena vañchito (Theragāthā, 375)	*māne isyā kālanena* (P. E. III)
mā akkosatha paribhāsatha rosetha vihesatha (Māratajjanīya Sutta, Majjhima I)	*hakaṁ mā palibhāsayisaṁ* (P. E. III)
abhihāro	*abhihāle* (P. E. IV)
na kareyya parapattiyaṁ (Petava., II. 1. 32)	*atapatiye kaṭe* (P. E. IV)
paṇdito byatto medhāvī paṭibalo	*viyatā* (R. E. IV)
sukha-parihaṭo (Majjhima, II, p. 60)	*sukhaṁ parihaṭave* (P. E. IV)
dhātusamatā Milinda, (p. 351)	*daṁḍasamatā* (P. E. IV)
sattame divase	*tiṁni divasāni*
kālaṁ dammi (Mūlapariyāya Jātaka)	*yote diṁne* (P. E. IV)
dāna-saṁvibhāga-rata (Saṁyutta, I, Sakka-Saṁ, II.,)	*dāna-saṁvibhāge* (P. E. IV)
seyyathā	*seyathā* (P. E. V)
suka-sāḷi, suva-sālikā	*suke sālika* (P. E. V)
chakkavākā haṁsā	*chakavāke haṁse* (P. E. V)
ambaka-maddari, ambaka-pachchari	*aṁbā kapilikā* (P. E. V)
anaṭṭhikālaṁ	
ukkapiṇḍakā (*pl.*)	*anaṭhika-machhe* (P. E. V)
palasatā (*pl.*)	*okapiṁḍe* (P. E. V)

paribhogaṁ, paṭivātaṁ eti,	*palasate* (P. E. V)
enti Māravasaṁ (Saṁyutta-N. I)	*paṭibhogaṁ no eti* (P. E. V)
ajeḷakā sūkarā	*ajakā eḷakā sukalī* (P. E. V)
anatthāya	*anaṭhāye* (P. E. V)
chātuddasī pañchadasī	*chāvudasaṁ paṁchada (saṁ)*
aṭṭhamī cha pakkhassa(Majjhima I, Bhayabherava Sutta)	*aṭhamipakhāye* (P. E. V)
sattanikāyā (Majjhima, I, P. 49)	*jīvanikāyāni* (P. E. V)
pāṭīhāriyapakkhassa	*chātuṁmāsi-pakkhāye* (P. E. V)
bandhanamokkhaṁ (Dīgha, I, p. 73)	*baṁdhanamokhāni* (P. E. V)
sukkhaṁ āvahati (Saṁyutta I, Yakkha, 12)	*sukhaṁ āvahāmi* (P. E. VI)
pachchuggamanaṁ(J.IV, p. 321)	*pachupagamane* (P. E. VI)
abbhunnameyyṁ (Dīgha, I, P. 126)	*abhyuṁnāmayehaṁ* (P. E. VII)
dhammānusatthiṁ	*dhaṁmānusathini*
anusāsiyati (Milinda, p. 186)	*anusāsāmi* (P. E. VII)
bahuna janassa (Dīgha, III, p. 167)	*bahune janasi* (P. E. VII)
kataññutaṁ pekkhamāno (J. III, p. 109)	*etam eva anuvekhamāne* (P. E. VII)
lahukā esī (Chariyā-piṭaka, I. 9)	*lahuke cha esa* (P. E. VII)
etadatthā (Vinaya, V, P. 164)	*etadathā* (P. E. VII)
gahaṭṭha-pabbajitānaṁ	*pavajitānaṁ cheva gihithānaṁ* (P. E. VII)
Ājīvikesu, Nigaṇṭhesu	*Ājīvikesu. Nigaṁṭhesu* (P. E. VII)
vayomahallākānam	*vayomahālakānaṁ* (P. E. VII)
kapaṇa-varākesu	*kapaṇa-valākesu* (P. E. VII)
saṁghaṁ samaggaṁ karoti (Vinaya, I, p. 355)	*saṁghe samage kaṭe* (Schism Pillar)
saṁsaraṇam (Vinaya, III,)	*saṁsalanasi* (Schism Pillar)
andhakāre nikkhitto (Ang., III, p. 233)	*saṁsalanasi nikhitā* (Schism Pillar)
aññaṁ viññāpeyya (Bhikkhūṇi-pāti, Nissaggiya, 4)	*viṁnapayitaviye* (Schism Pillar)
bhikkhūnaṁ bhikkunīnañcha (Theragāthā, 125)	*bhikhūnaṁ cha bhikhunīnaṁ cha* (Schism Pillar)

posathaṁ (J. IV, p. 332)	*posathāye* (Schism Pillar)
byañjanena	*viyaṁjanena* (Schism Pillar)
mahita, mahāhitvāna (Majjhima, II, p. 110. J. W, p. 236)	*mahiyite* (Lumbinī Pillar)
dhajam ussāpesi	*silāthabhe usapāpite* (Lumbinī P.)
suvaṇṇatthambhaṁ ussāpesi (J. IV, p. 236)	
Lumbinī	*Luṁmini* (Lumbinī Pillar)
aṭṭhabhāgika, atthabhāgiya	aṭhabhāgiye (Lumbinī Pillar)
Indasālaguhā (Dīgha, II, p. 263)	*Nigoha-kubhā* (Barabar I)
jalūkā (Milinda, p. 405)	*Jalūghā* (Barabar III)
sabbaseto maṅgala-hatthi (J. VI, p. 487)	*sarvasveto hasti, seto, gajatame* (Misc. III.)
sabbaseto gajuttamo (Vimānavatthu)	
Seto (Ang., III, p. 345)	

MR. S. N. MITRA'S LIST OF PARALLELS

sūpavyañjanatthāya mige māressāmi (J. III, p. 438)	*prāṇa-sata-sahasrāni ārabhisu sūpathāya* (R. E. I)
pupphupago phalupago rukkho (Dhp. A. p. 189)	*osaḍhāni munisopagāni pasu —opagāni* (R. E. II)
anusaṁyāyitvā (Majjhima. III, p. 174) = *anupariyāyitvā, anuyāyato* (Milinda, p. 391)	*anusaṁyānaṁ niyātu* (R. E. III)
Rājā dhammaghosakaṁ alankata-hatthipiṭṭhiṁ āropetvā ghosanaṁ kāreti (J. IV, p. 264)	*dhaṁmaghoso* (R. E. IV)
dhammaghosakā hutvā gāmāgāmaṁ nagarānagaraṁ vicharissāma (paramatthajotikā, II, p. 216)	
aho dhammasavaṇaṁ. (Sumangalavilā., I, p. 214)	*aho dhaṁmaghoso* (R. E. IV)
vimānaṁ disvā (J. V, p. 165) *ākāsa-vimānāni dassetvā* (J. VI, p. 124)	*vimāna-darsaṇā. . . . .dasayitpā* (R. E. IV)

anīka-dassanaṁ =*(hatth)ānīkassa dassanaṁ*	*hasti-dasanā* (R. E. IV)
dibbāni pi rūpāni passato Sumangala-vilā; I, p. 215)	*divyāni rupāni dasayitpā* (R.E. IV)
atthāpāye (J. III, p. 387).—the opposite of	*athasa vaḍhi* (R.E. IV)
parihīne (J. III, p. 387)	*hini* (R.E. IV)
desaṁ (Saṁyutta, II, p. 15)	*desaṁ* (R.E. V) = a part, a portion
pāpaṁ pāpena sukaraṁ (Udāna, v. 8)	*sukaraṁ hi pāpaṁ, papaṁ hi sukaraṁ* (R.E. V)
padvāra (J. V, p. 433, J. VI. p. 627)	*supadarave* (R.E. V)—*supadvāraṁ* (well-entranced)
anubaddhā (Sumangala-vilā. I. p. 39) = *anugatā*	*anubadhā pajāva* (R.E. V)
dukkaraṁ karoto (Ang., IV, p. 37)	*dukaraṁ karoti* (R.E. V)
vinichchhaye nisīditvā aṭṭe tīresi (J. III, p. 292)	*aṭha-saṁtiranā* (R.E. VI)
bahu aṭṭaṁ me tīritaṁ (J. III, p. 334)	
atthaṁ karissaṁ (J. III, p. 394)	*athe karomi* (R.E. VI)
kāyena vāchā cha yo saññato,	*sayame bhāvasuhitā va kataṁñatā va*
Yo ve kataññū katavedī dhīro kalyāṇamitto daḷhabhatti cha hoti, dukkhitassa sakkachcha karoti kichchaṁ (J. V, p. 146)	*daḍhabhatitā* (R.E. VII)
tassa ayañ ch'eva loko āraddho	*ubhe ladhe hoti* (R.E. IX, cf. R.E. VI)
hoti paro cha loko (Digha, III. p. 181)	*hidata-pālate āladhe hoti* (R.E. VII)
uchchāvache yaññe (Theragāthā, verse 34)	*uchāvache maṁgale* (R.E. IX)
sāhu dānan ti (Ang., IV, p. 43)	*sādhu dāna iti* (R̄.E.IX)
devamangalikā (J. III, p. 145). *chattamangalaṁ, vivāha-mangalaṁ* (J. III, p. 407) *kotūhala-mangaliko* (Sumangalavilā., I, p. 226)	*uchāvachaṁ maṁgalaṁ āvāha-vivāhesu* (R.E. IX)

etadaggaṁ bhiyyo dānam yadidam dhammadānaṁ (Ang. IV, p. 364)	*na tu etārisaṁ asti dānaṁ yārisaṁ dhaṁmadānaṁ* (R.E. IX)
yaso kitti cha (J.III, p. 106)	*yaso va kiti va* (R.E. X)
mahatthiyaṁ (J.III, p. 376)	*mahāthāvahā* (R.E. X)
dhamma-saṁvibhāgo (Theragātha, V. 9)	*dhaṁma-saṁvibhāgo* (R.E. X)
itthāgārassa amachchhā (J. III, p. 371)	*ithijhaka-mahāmātā* (R.E. XII)
anuvidhiyeyyaṁ (Saṁyutta, IV, p. 131)	*anuvidhiyare* (R.E. XIII)
tumhākaṁ khamitabbaṁ tāva khamāmi (Dhp. A., I, p. 405)	*khamisati e sakiye khamitave* (S.R.E. II)
	khamitaviyamate yaṁ sakiye khamitave (R.E. XIII)
na cha sakkā āghātamānena (Theragāthā, V. 513)	*na cha sarvatra ghaṭitaṁ* (R.E. XIV)
kammadvāra (J. IV, P. 14)	*kaṁmanā . . . duvālaṁ*
dinna-naya-dvāre (J. IV, p. 341)	*aṁ tuphesu anusathi* (S.R.E. I)
nāttano samakaṁ kiñchi atirekañ cha maññisaṁ (Theragāthā V. 424)	*duāhale etasa kaṁmasa same kute mane atileke* (S.R.E. I, J)
kuto pana kāyena (Ang. IV, p. 66)	
anumajjhaṁ samāchare (J. IV p. 192)	*majhaṁ paṭipādayema* (S.R. E. I)
vippaṭipajjitvā (J. III, p. 116)	*vipaṭipajamine* (S.R.E. I)
raññо chittaṁ arādhenti (J. III,)	*lājaladhi* (S.R.E. I)
rājānaṁ ārādhetuṁ asakkonto (Milinda, p. 6)	*yena maṁ lajukā chaghaṁti ālādhayitave* (P.E. IV)
apāye (J. III, p. 387) *apāye*=*apagamane, parithīne*	*maha-apāye* (S.R.E. I)
atthaṁ aññāya dhammānudhammapaṭipanno (Ang;IV,p.296)	*athaṁ jānitu tathā kalaṁṭi athā anusathi* (S.R.E. I)
assuropo (Itivūttaka, VI, 122) =*anattamanatā chittassa* (Comy.), "mental distemper"	*āsulope* (S.R.E. I)
kammaṁ . . . karontassa kāye kilamissati (Anguttara, IV, p. 332)	*kilaṁte siyā* (S.R.E. I)

ekaṁ saṁvachchharaṁ (J. III, p. 440)	*ekaṁ savachharaṁ* (M.R. E.)
missībhūtā (J. V, p.86)	*misibhūtā* (M.R. E.)
hatthena hatthaṁ gahetvā kāyamissībhāvaṁ upagatā	*amisā devā samānā te dāni misibhūtā* (M. R. E)
pakkamate bhusaṁ (Saṁyutta, I, p. 69)	*pakaṁte husaṁ* (M. R. E.) *husaṁ = bhṛiśam* (?)
daḷham enaṁ parakkame (Dhp. 313)	*bāḍhaṁ me pakaṁte* (M. R. E.)
mahantāni khudakāni (Dhp. A., I, p. 282)	*khudakā cha mahatpā* (M.R.E.)
kāmaṁ (J. III, p. 368) = *ekaṁsena*, 'verily'	*kāmaṁ tu kho* (M. R. E.)
na sukaraṁ akkhānena pāpuṇitum (Majjhima, III, p. 167)	*na hīyaṁ sakye mahātpeneva pāpotave* (M. R. E.)
dhamma-pariyāyo (Ang, IV, p. 166)	*dhaṁma-paliyāyāni* (Bhābru)
paraṁ cha samādapeti (Ang., II, II, p. 253 f)	*palaṁ samādapayitave* (P.E.I)
yāva nābhito (J. IV, p. 149) up to the pivot.	*ava ite* (P. E. IV) meaning not 'henceforth' but 'up till now.'
na kareyya parapattiyaṁ (Petavatthu, II. I. 32)	*atapatiye kate* (P. E. IV), *atapatiye* opp. of *parapatiye*
dhāti pariharena	*dhāti . . . palihaṭave* (P. E. IV)
abhihāraṁ (J. V, p. 58) = *pūjaṁ*	*abhihāle* (P. E. IV)
te (purisā) parichārayissaṁti (Saṁyutta, I, p. 79)	*pulisāṁ paṭichalisaṁti* (P.E.IV)
janapadassa hitasukhāya (J. V, p. 116)	*Janapadasa hitasukhāye* (P. E. IV)
(aṅke) nisīdāpetva (Dīgha, II, p. 20)	*nisijitu* (P. E. IV)
pattadaṇḍa (Theragāthā. V. 449)	*tilitadaṁḍānaṁ patavadhānaṁ*
niruddha-velāyaṁ (Dhp. A. I, p. 207)	*niludhasi kālasi* (P. E. IV)
niruddho = mato (J. IV. p. 109)	
dāna-saṁvibhāgassa (J.III.p.409)	*dāna-saṁvibhāge* (P. E. IV)
nilachchhesi (Therigā, 437)	*nilakhiyati* (P. E. V)
pachchuggamanaṁ (J. III, pp. 330, 388)	*pachupagamanaṁ* (P. E. VI)

bandhanamokkhaṁ kātuṁ (J. III, p. 429)	*baṁdhana-mokhāni kaṭāni* (P. E. V)
dhammayuttaṁ kathaṁ (J. III. p. 365)	*viyovadisaṁti janaṁ dhaṁmayutaṁ* (P. E. VII)
ovādaṁ dentena yutta-janass' eva dātabbo, na ayuttajanassa (J. III, p. 231)	
dānavisagge (Petavatthu, II. 7) = *dānagge, parichchāgaṭṭhāne*	*dānavisagasi* (P. E. VII)
daṭṭhu (Sutta-nipāta, verse 424) = *disvā*	*sutu* (P. E. VII)
paṭipādayāmi (J. IV, p. 19) = *dadāmi*	*paṭi* (*pādayaṁti*) P. E. VII.
saddhamma-niyama (Ang., III. p. 185)	*dhaṁma-niyamāni* (P. E. VII)
dhamma-niyāmatā (Ang., I. p. 286)	
anurūpāyaṁ paṭipattiyaṁ (J, III, p. 368)	*anulupāyā dhaṁmavaḍhiyā* (P. E. VII)
avāsesi (J. V, p, 33)	*āvāsayiye* (Schism Pillar)
kammāyatanāni (J. III, p. 542) = *kammāni*	
tushṭadānam (Arthaśāstra, I. 11)	*tuṭhayatanāni* (P. E. VII)
rājā (*mātiposikassa hatthissa*) *samānarūpaṁ*	*silāvigaḍa-bhīchā kālāpita* (Lumbinī)
sīlā-paṭimaṁ kāretvā (J. IV. p. 95)	
anāvāsa (Vinaya, II, 22, 33, J. II, p. 77)	*anāvāsasi* (Schism Pillar)
ussāpento dhammayūpaṁ (Milinda. p. 21)	*silāthabhe usapāpite* (Lumbinī)
thūpaṁ vaḍḍhāpesi (Mahāvaṁsa, 35. 32)	*Konākamanasa thube dutiyaṁ vaḍhite* (Nigāli Sāgar)
dutiyam pi balaṁ vaḍḍhāpesi (J. III, p. 9)	
dutiyaṁ meaning 'for the second time'	
Koṇāgamana-buddhassa maṇḍapo (Theragāthā A.,p.6)	

khalita (Petavathu, p. 46)	*khalatika* (Barābar)
sabbasetaṁ hatthiratanaṁ (J. III, p.460)	*Seto, gajatame, sarvasveto hasti* (Dhauli, Kalsi, Girnār Rocks).
sabbaseto sīlavā hatthirājā (J. IV, p. 91)	

Ṛigveda	INSCRIPTIONS
piteva sūpāyano (I. 1)	*pāpe hi nāma supadālaye* (R.E.V)

Rāmāyaṇa	INSCRIPTIONS
saptarātroshitaḥ (II, 73. 16)	*duve sapaṁna-lāti-sata vivāsāta* (M. R. E., Sa)
paura-jānapadaṁ janaṁ (II, 43. 13)	*janaṁ jānapadaṁ* (P. E. IV)
anunīta (II, 61. 28. 30)= *anuśishṭa*	*anuneti* (R. E.XIII)
kiṁ syāt priyaṁ janasyāsya	*kimaṁ kāni sukhaṁ āvahāmī ti* (P.E. VI)
kāṅkshitaṁ kiṁ sukhāvaham | iti chintayitā tena jano'yaṁ paripālitaḥ (II, 57. 14)	*esa me huthā—se kinasu jane . . . anulupāyā dhaṁmavaḍhiyā vaḍheyā ti, kinasu kāni abhyuṁnāmayehaṁ dhaṁmavaḍhiyā ti ?* (P. E. VII) *idha cha nāni sukhāpayāmi* R.E. VI)
etad aupayikam (II. 53. 37)	*tadopayā* (R. E. VII)
yajñabhāgaḥ (II, 46. 15)	*bhāge aṁne* (R. E. VII).

The *Buddhavachana* alone can satisfactorily account for some of the most striking and interesting variants in the *Aśokavachana*. R. E. IX offers *mahiḍā, abakajanika, abakajaniyo* and *striyak(a)* as variants of Dh *ithī*. Corresponding to them we have in Pali *itthī*, *mahiḷā (mahilā)*, *ambakā* and *itthiyikā* (Buddha ghosa). In lieu of J *alam*, Dh offers us *paṭibalā* (S.R.E. II), and these very words are employed as synonyms in the Aṅguttara Nikāya. Pañchaka-nipāta, Gilāna-vagga : *alaṁ gilānaṁ upaṭṭhātuṁ, paṭibalo hoti bhesajjaṁ saṁvidhātuṁ*. Corresponding to the two variants, *mahālake* and *mahaṁte* in R.E. XIV; we have in Pali *mahallakaṁ* and *mahantaṁ*.

The specimen of dialectical style offered by the four versions of R.E. IX (K, Sh, M) closely resembles those which may be gathered from all sections of the Kathāvatthu :

Kathāvatthu IV (I. 1)

Hañchi puggalo upalabbhati sachchhikaṭṭha-paramaṭṭhena, tena vata re vattabbe yo sachchikaṭṭho paramaṭṭho tato so puggalo upalabbhati sachchhikaṭṭha-paramaṭṭhenā ti. Yaṁ tattha vadesi vattabbe kho puggalo upalabbhati . . sachchhikaṭṭha-paramaṭṭhenā ti michchhā.

R. E. IX

Haṁche pi taṁ aṭhaṁ no nivaṭeti hida, aṭhaṁ palata anaṁtaṁ punā pasavati. Haṁche puna taṁ aṭhaṁ nivateti hidā tata ubhaye saṁladhe hoti-hida chā se aṭhe palatā cha anaṁtaṁ punā pasavati tena dhaṁmamaṁgalenā.

The *Aśokavachana* contains but a very few traces of what may be called the distinctive Jaina phraseology, now preserved in the Ardhamāgadhī Canon of the Śvetāmbaras. The *Nirgranthapravachana or Jinavachana*, too, employs such technical terms as *samaṇa māhaṇa*, *bhikkhu*, *bhikkhuṇī*, *uvāsaga*, *uvāsigā*, *samaṇovāsagā*, *gihatthānaṁ*, *pavvaiyānaṁ*, *Nigganthā*, *Ājīviya*, *posahaṁ (posathaṁ)*, *(posatha-upavāso)*, *puṇṇa (puṇya)*, *pāva (pāpa)*, *kallāṇa*, *sukaḍe dukkaḍe*, *parakkame*, *vihiṁsā*, *avihiṁsā*, *vahabandha-parikilesā*, *bandha-mokkha*, *saṁkhāya*, *koha (kodha)*, . . *māṇa (māna)*, *dayā*, *dāṇa*, *sachcha*, *soya (śaucha)*, *bhaya*, *ajjava*, *maddava*, *chauddas*, — *aṭṭham'-uddiṭṭha-puṁṇamāsinīsu*, *ihaloga-paraloga*, *dūya (dūta)* and *parisā* (Āchārāṅga and Aupapātika Sūtras).

Besides the technical terms listed above, the *Jinavachana* makes use of the following idioms corresponding to those in BV and AV :

JV	BV	AV
hiyāe sukhāe	*hitāya sukhāya*	*hitasukhāye* (R. E. V, P.E. IV),
jārisa tārisa	*yārisa tārisa, yādisa tādisa*	*yārise tārise ādise tādise* (R.E. IV)
puno puno (Āchārāṅga)	*punappunaṁ*	*puna-puna* (R.E. XIV)
chaṇaṁ chaṇaṁ (ib)	*khaṇe khaṇe*	*khanasi khanasi* (S. R. E. I)
puḍhavi-nissiya (*ib*)	*dhamma-nissita*	*dhaṁma-nisita* (R.E.V)
amma-piu sussūsaga (Aup. 71)	*mātā-pitu-upaṭṭhānaṁ, āchariya pachchupaṭṭhātabbā sussūsāya*	*mātā-pitu-susūsā, mātā-pitusu sususā. mātari cha pitari cha susrūsā* (R. E. III)
nālaṁ tāṇāe (Āchārāṅga)	*alaṁ dārābharaṇāya*	*alaṁ asvāsanāye* (S. R. E. II)
atihi-saṁvibhāgo (Aup. 57)	*dāna-saṁvibhāgo*	*dāna-saṁvibhāge* (P. E. IV)
posahovavāso (Ib. 57)		*pālatikaṁ upavāsaṁ* (P. E. IV)
chiraṭṭhitiyā (Ib. 56)	*chiraṭṭhitikā*	*chiraṭhitikā* (M. R. E.)
dhamme daḍhā paiṇṇā patiññā (Ib. 105)		*paṭiṁnā achalā* (S. R. E. II)
gevejja-vimāna (Ib. 163)		*pulisā gevayā* (P. E. I)
Bhagavaṁ (ib. 21)	*Bhagavā*	*Bhagavaṁ* (Lumbinī Pillar)
āigare (ib. 38)	*ādikammiko*	*ādikale, ādikaro* (R.E.V)
dupayam chauppayaṁ	*dipadānaṁ chatuppadānaṁ*	*dupada-chatupadesu* (P. E. I)
tivva-dhammānurāga (Aupa. Sec. 54)	*tibbo gāravo*	*tīvo dhaṁmavāyo* (R. E. XIII)

JV

je ya maṇe sāvajje sakirie
sakakkase kaḍue (kaṭuke)
niṭṭhure pharuse aṇhayakare
chedakare bhedakare
(Aupapātika Sūtra, Sec. 30)
je āsavā te parissavā
je parissavā te āsavā ;
je aṇāsavā te aparissavā,
je aparissavā te aṇāsavā
(Āchāraṅga)

AV

imāni āsinava-gāmini nāma
ath(ā) chaṁḍiye niṭhūliye
kodhe māne isyā (P. E. III)

sakale apaparisrave siyāti
eshe tu parisrave yaṁ apuñaṁ
(R. E. X)

In the *Jinavachana*, too, *koha* and *māṇa*, *sachcha* and *soya* (*śaucha*), *ajjava* and *maddava* are grouped together.

Certain phrases and idioms in *Aśokavachana* agree almost *verbatim* with those in the Rājadharma Section of the Śānti-parva of the Mahābhārata. As the following instances will increasingly show, the statements of Aśoka were nothing but a faithful reproduction in prose of the *Rājadharmapravachana* in verse :

MBH	AV
Aushadhāni cha sarvāṇi *mūlāni cha phalāni cha/* *chaturvidhāṁś cha vaidyān* *vai saṁgṛihṇīyād viśeshataḥ||* (XII. 68. 64)	*osadhāni cha . . . mūlāni cha . .* *phalāni savata ata ata* *nathi hālāpitā cha lopāpitā* cha (P. E. II)
ahiṁsārthāya bhūtānāṁ *dharmapravachanaṁ kṛitam* (XII. 109. 15)	*nijhatiyā . . . dhaṁmavaḍhi* *vaḍhitā avihiṁsāye bhūtānaṁ* (P. E. VII)
Yauna-Kāmboja-Gāndhārāḥ (XII. 207. 43)	*Yona-Kaṁboja-Gaṁdhāränaṁ* (R. E. V)
mātāpitror hi śusrūshā *kartavyā sarvadasyubhiḥ/* *āchārya-guru-śusrūshā* *taithaivāśramavāsinām ?* (XII. 64. 17)	*brāhmaṇa s(r)amaṇānaṁ* *saṁpaṭipati, mātari pitari* *susrusā thaira-susrusā* (R.E.IV) *agabhuti-susūsā,* *mātā-pitu-susūsā,* *gulu-susūsā* (R. E. XIII)
uṭṭhānaṁ hi narendrāṇāṁ	*tasa esa mūle usṭānaṁ cha*

rājadharmasya yan mūlam (XII. 57.13)	*athasaṁtīraṇā cha* (R.E. VI)
hitārthaṁ sarvalokasya (XII. 36.26)	*anuvataraṁ sa(r)valokahitāya* (R.E. VI)
sarvalokahitaṁ dharmaṁ (XII. 63.5)	
ānṛiṇyaṁ yāti dharmasya (XII. 13.14)	*bhūtānaṁ ānaṁnaṁ gachheyaṁ* (R.E. VI)
ārādhayet svargaṁ imaṁ cha lokam (XII. 27.57)	*idha cha nāni sukhāpayāmi paratra cha svagaṁ ārādhayaṁtu* (R.E. VI)
kṛitajño dṛiḍhabhaktiḥ syāt saṁvibhāgī jitendriyaḥ (XII. 65.39) *bhāvaśuddhir dayā satyaṁ saṁyamaś chātmasampadaḥ* (XV. 167.5)	*sayame bhāvasudhitā va kataṁñatā va daḍhabhatitā* (R.E. VII)
viharayātrāsu (XII. 1. 18)	*vihārayātāṁ* (R.E. VII)
uchchāvachāni vittāni (XII.96.23)	*uchāvachaṁ maṁgalaṁ* (R.E. IX)
dānam eke praśaṁsanti (XII. 21.9)	*dāne sādhū ti* (R.E. IX)
dharmayuktaṁ prasastam āyatyāñ cha tadātve cha (XII.16.6)	*dhaṁmayutaṁ anuvidhiyatu tadatvāye āyatiyaṁ cha* (R.E.X)
kshamā kartuṁ samartho (XII. 72.1)	*sakiye khamitave* (R.E. XIII)
varjanīyaṁ sadā yuddham (XII. 68.25)	*(na)vaṁ vijayaṅ mā vijetavyaṁ maṁñā* (R.E. XIII)
kshudra-pipīlikāḥ as abhakshyas (XII. 50.21)	*aṁbākapilikā* (P.E. V)
Yathā putrās tathā paurā drashṭavyāḥ (XII. 68.29) *yo'nvakampatu vai nityaṁ prajā putrān ivaurasān* (XII. 28.51)	*athā pit(ā) hevaṁ ne lājā ti, ath(ā) atānaṁ anukaṁpati hevaṁ apheni anukaṁpati* (S.R.E. I)
vadha-bandhaparikleśo (XII. 68.19)	*baṁdhanaṁ vā parikilesaṁ vā* (S.R.E. I)
dharmāpekshī (XII. 55. 29)	*dhaṁmāpekhā* (R.E. XIII)
dharmakāṅkshatā (XII. 67. 48)	*dhaṁmakāmatā cha* (P.E. I)
samyābhīhāraṁ kurvīta (XII. 68.39)	*abhihāle* (P.E. IV)

sattvaiḥ sattvā hi jīvanti (XII. 115.20)	*jīvena jīve no pusitaviye* (P.E.V)
dhārmikaṁ dharmayuktam (XII. 19. 11)	*janaṁ dhaṁmayutaṁ* (P.E.VII)
dhārmika-janaḥ (XII. 19.5)	
puṇyatīrthānusaṁyānam (I. 2.123)	*anusaṁyānaṁ* (R.E. III, S.R.E. I)
vigatabhī (Bhag. G. VII.)	*vigaḍabhi* (Lumbinī)
dharma-saṁsthāpanārthāya (Bhagavadgītā, IV. 8)	*dhaṁmādhiṭhānāye* (R.E. V)
sarvadharmān parityajya (Bhagavadgītā, XVIII. 66)	*savaṁ parichajitpā* (R.E. X)

It is in the Mahābhārata (XII. 20.7.43) alone that we have the Sanskrit name *Yauna* corresponding to *Yona*. It is again here that the Yaunas, Kāmbojas and Gāndhāras are grouped together, precisely as in Pali and *Aśokavachana*. The word *anusaṁyāna*, too, is met with in the Great Epic (I.2.123) *puṇyatīrthānusaṁyānam*, though not in the technical sense of Aśoka. The *Mahā*-mātras mentioned in it are no other than the *Senāpati Mahāmātras* in the *Buddhavachana*. The location of the four Great continents including Jambudvīpa (*ibid*, Bhīshmaparva 6. 13) is almost on a par with that in Pali.

As regards the Smṛiti literature, the lists of non-eatable or forbidden animals, birds, beasts and fishes, contained in the older Dharma Sūtras and Śāstras are certainly in the immediate literary background of Aśoka's list *of avadhyas* (P. E. V). In this respect the Dharmasūtras of Bodhāyana and Vasishṭha deserve special notice, particularly because both prohibit the flesh of rhinoceros and allow the meat of peafowls. Further, Vasisṭha's *pāṇḍukapota* is the same species of birds as the *seta-kapota of* Aśoka.

Legal, Popular and Grammatical Works.	AV
kāmaṁ, kāmaṁ tu (Bodhāyana, (Vasisṭha)	*kāmaṁ tu kho* (M. R. E., Bra.)
pāṇḍukapota (Vasishṭha)	*setakapote* (P. E. V)
pārāvata (Vasishṭha) = *grāmavāsī kapotaḥ* (Kulluka)	*gāmakapota* (P. E. V)
abhakshyāḥ (Bodhāyana, Vasishṭha)	*ye na cha khādiyati* (P. E. V)
Sarveshāmeva dānānāṁ brahmadānaṁ viśishyate (Manu, IV. 233)	*nāsti etārisaṁ dānaṁ yārisaṁ dhaṁmadānaṁ* (R.E. IX. XI)
evaṁ samavāyaḥ kartavyaḥ (Pañchatantra, I. 15)	*samavāyo eva sādhu* (R. E. XII)
ādikaraḥ (Pāṇini, III. 2. 21)	*ādikaro* (R. E. V)
lipikaraḥ, livikaraḥ (Pāṇini, III. 2. 21)	*lipikara* (R. E. XIV) *lipikareṇa* (M. R. E., Ja)
avarārdhāt (Pāṇini, V. 4.4.57)	*avaradhiyā* (M. R. E., Bra.)
putrapautram (Pāṇini, V.2.10)	*putāpapotike* (P. E. VII)
Tishya-Punarvasvoḥ (Pāṇini, I. 2.63)	*Tisāya Punāvasune* (P. E. V)
tad gachchhati pathidūtayoḥ Pāṇini, V. 3.85)	*yata pi dutā no yaṁti* (R.E.XIII)
Devānāṁpriya (Kātyāyana)	*Devānaṁpriyo, Devānaṁpiyo* (R. E. III)
khalatikasya parvatasya (Patañjali)	*Khalatika-pavatasi* (Barābar, II)

The highly important Sanskrit text which is still left for comparison in this connexion is the Arthaśāstra containing Kauṭilyavachana. In accordance with its two forms, earlier and later, we must consider it both as a Kārikā of verses in *śloka* metre and as a treatise of the Sūtra-Bhāshya type. The earlier form will be referred to simply as Kārikā, and the later one as Prose Treatise.

The following instances may indicate the nature of correspondences between the *Kauṭilyavachana* in the Kārikā on the one hand and the *Aśokavachana* on the other, as regards their phrases and idioms :

KV (Kārikā)	AV
putrapautrānuvartinaḥ (VII. 16)	*putāpapotike* (P. E. VII, Schism Pillar Edict, Sanchi)
anyatrāpadā (I. 17), *anyatra guptisthānebhyaḥ* (II. 26)	*añatra Yonesu* (R. E. XIII) *aṁnata agāya dhaṁmakāmatāya* (P. E. I)
praṇayād rakshyate (VII. 9)	*panayaṁ gachema*
praṇayena (VIII. 5)	*su munisānaṁ* (S. R. E. I)
āṭavīshu (VII. 6)	*aṭaviyo* (R. E. XIII)
pratyante (VII. 6)	*prachaṁtesu* (R. E. II)
sāmantāṁ(VII. 6)	*sāmaṁtā lājāno* (R. E. II)
niruddho deśakālābhyām (VII. 3)	*niludhasi kālasi* (P. E. IV)
ekadeśaṁ (V. 4)	*ekadesaṁ* (R. E. VII)
āyatyāṁ cha tadātve cha (V. I)	*tadatvāye āyatiye cha* (R. E. X)
uchchhulkan (II. 21)	*ubalike* (Lumbinī Pillar)
abhirāmaṁ (II. 13)	*abhilāmāni* (R. E. VIII)
ātyayikaṁ kāryam (I, 12)	*atiyāyike* (R. E. VI)
arthasya mūlam utthānam, rājño hi vrataṁ utthānaṁ, yajñāḥ kāryānuśāsanaṁ (I. 12)	*tasa esa mule usṭānaṁ cha athasaṁtirana cha* (R. E. VI).
anuśaya (in a different sense).. ..	*anusaye* (R. E. XIII, in the Amarakosha sense of *anuśochanā, anutāpa*)

Though the prose treatise of the Arthaśāstra is a post-Aśokan compilation, it employs or preserves several phrases and idioms showing correspondence with those in Aśokavachana, as will appear from the following tables :

Arthaśāstra (PT)	AV
anyatra mātuḥ (II. 1), *anyatra vyapadeśena* (II, 25). *anyatra pratishedhāt* (IV. 13), etc.	*añatra Yonesu* (R. E. XIII), *aṁnata agāya dhaṁmakāmatāya agena bhayena.* etc. (P. E. I)
anyaṁ pratipādayishyāmaḥ (I. 10)	*majhaṁ paṭipādayema* (S.R.E.I)
mahānase (II. 27)	*mahānasamhi* (R. E. I)

rājñaḥ prabhāvaḥ	*pabhave Devānaṁpiyasa* (R. E. XIII)
dvipada-chatushpadānām (III.15)	*dupada-chatupadesu* (P. E. II)
putradāraṁ ātmānaṁ	*atānaṁ* (S. R. E. II)
pratyāsannam (III. 20)	*paṭiyāsaṁnesu* (P. E. VI)
anarthyāḥ (V. 4)	*anaṭhāye* (P. E. V)
hastivanabhogaḥ (VIII. 11)	*kevaṭabhogasi* (P. E. V)
nāgavana (II. 2)	*nāgavanasi*
shāṇmāsikīm (II. 29)	*ā-saṁmāsike* (P. E. V)
sukaro hi mitreṇa sandhiḥ (VII. 13)	*sukaraṁ hi pāpaṁ* (R. E. V)
viśvāsayet (VII. 14)	*visvaṁsayitave* (Sarnath)
Pushyena (XIV. 3)	*Tisena* (S. R. E. I)
kṛishṇa-chaturdaśyāṁ	*chāvudasāye paṁnadasāye*
paurṇamāsyāṁ Pushyayoginyām (XIV. 3)	*Tisāye, Tisāyaṁ puṁnamāsiyaṁ* (P. E. V)
chāturmāsyeshvardha-māsikam	*chātuṁmāsiye pakhāye*
aghātam (XIII. 5)	*lakhane no kaṭaviye* (P. E. V)
anugrahaṁ dīnānātha-	*anāthesu vuḍhesu*
vyādhitānām (XIII. 5)	*hitasukhāye* (R. E. V)
śāsanamuktaṁ	*yaṁ kiṁchi mukhato*
mukhājñaptam (II. 6)	*āñapayāmi dāpakaṁ vā*
dāpaka (IV. 6)	*srāvāpakaṁ vā* (R. E. VI)
mahāntaṁ saṅghaṁ (IV. 4)	*mahaṁte vijaye* (R. E. XIV)
yātrāvihāragato (V. 1)	*viharayātāṁ ñayāsu* (R. E. VIII)
ātyāyike kārye (1. 15)	*atiyāyike* (R. E. VI)
āvasayeyuḥ, āvaseyuḥ (II. 4)	*āvāsayiye, vāsāpetāviye*
vāsayeyuḥ (II. 36)	(Schism Pillar)
ayaṁ parihāpayati (II. 8)	*desaṁ hāpayisati* (R. E. V)
mādhuryam (II. 10)	*madhuratāya* (R. E. XIV)
punaruktam (II. 10)	*puna-puna-vutaṁ* (R. E. XIV)
uchchhulkam (II. 21)	*ubalike* (Lumbinī Pillar)
prāptavyavahārānām (III. 5)	*patavadhānaṁ* (P. E. IV)
apravṛittavadhānām (II. 26)	
yogyāchāryāḥ (II. 30)	*yugyāchariyāni* (M. R. E.)
āsannebhyaḥ parebhyaś cha (L. 17)	*paṭiyāsaṁnesu hevaṁ apakaṭhesu* (P. E. VI)
deyavisargo (IX. 6)	*dānavisagasi* (P. E. VIII)
abhikshṇam upajapet (IX. 6)	*abhikhinaṁ upadhāleyu* (Bhābru)
yathārham (IX. 9)	*yathārahaṁ* (M. R. E.)

alpavyayaḥ (IX. 4)	*apavyayatā* (R. E. III)
mahābhāṇḍena (II. 28)	*apabhaṁḍatā* (R. E. III)
sāmantāṭavikān (IX. 3)	*sāmaṁta-lājāne* (R. E. II)
pratividhānam (VII. 16)	*paṭividhāne* (R. E. VIII)
mittravargaḥ (VIII. 15)	*vage bahujane* (S. R. E. I)
utsāhayukta (VIII. 4)	*usāhena* (P. E. I)
kumāra (V. 3)	*kumāle* (S. R. E. I)
devīkumārāṇām (VII. 15)	*devikumālānaṁ* (P. E. VII)
pauravyavahārika (V. 3)	*nagalaviyohālaka* (S. R. E. I)
rāshṭrāntapāla, antapāla (V.3)	*aṁta-mahāmātā* (P. E. I)
mṛiga-paśu-pakshi-byāla-maṭsyārambhān (IV. 3)	*prāṇāraṁbho* (P. E. IV)
paribhoga (IV. 6)	*paṭibhogaṁ* (P. E. V)
apavāhayanti (IV. 9)	*apavuḍhe* (R. E. XIII)
mahāmātrāḥ (II. 9)	*mahāmātā* (Queen's Edict)
bhakta-saṁvibhāgam (IV. 3)	*dāna-saṁvibhāge* (P. E. IV)
paribhāshaṇam (IV. 11)	*palibhāsayisaṁ* (P. E. III)
pāshaṇḍā (III. 16)	*save pāsaṁḍā* (R. E. VII)
parichareyuḥ (I. 21)	*paṭichalisaṁti* (P. E. IV)
dharmadānam (III. 16)	*dhaṁmadānaṁ* (R. E. IX, XI)
samavāyaḥ (III. 12)	*samavāyo* (R. E. VII)
asaṁpratipattau (III. 11)	*asaṁpratipati* (R. E. IV)
ghaṭetu (VI. 2)	*ghaṭitaṁ* (R. E. XIV)
hiraṇyadānam (III. 10)	*hiraṁnapaṭividhāno* (R. E. VIII
hiraṇyānugraham (II. 36)	
dṛiḍhabhaktitvam (I. 9)	*daḍhabhatitā* (R. E. VII)
avadhyāḥ (II. 26)	*avadhiyāni* (P. E. V, VII)
ashṭabhāgikam (II. 12)	*aṭhabhāgiye* (Lumbini Pillar)
dharmavijayī (XII. 1)	*dhaṁmavijayo* (R. E. XII)
dūtā (I. 16)	*dūtā* (R. E. XIII)
abhīkshṇya-śravaṇam (I. 5)	*abhikhinaṁ suneyu* (Bhābru)

CHAPTER V

GRAMMAR AND PHONOLOGY

We have seen that the style or diction of *Aśokavachana* in Prakrit is closely akin to that of Buddhavachana in Pali. The phrases and idioms were mostly prose adaptations from *gāthās* and *ślokas,* in short, traditional verses, such as those preserved in the Pali Nikāyas including the Jātakas, the Rājadharma Section of the Śāntiparva of the Mahābhārata, and the Kārikā presupposed by the extant prose treatise of the Arthaśāstra. The prose texts of *Buddhavachana* in Pali and those of *Jinavachana* in Ardhamāgadhī, too, supply parallels to many a phrase and idiom in *Aśokavachana.* If similar phrases and idioms as well as technical terms occur also in the prose treatise of the Arthaśāstra, we are not to infer from it that *Aśokavachana* derived them directly from it. It is equally true that the extant Pali Canon and Jaina Āgama, too, presuppose an earlier stage of development when their linguistic affinities with *Aśokavachana* were still closer. Even the Sanskrit diction of that stage of literary and linguistic development bore many traits in common.[1]

Minute analysis of the grammatical forms and phonetic peculiarities of *Aśokavachana,* offered by Hultzsch, edict by edict and inscription by inscription, and subsequently by Professor Turner in respect of the Gavīmaṭh and Pālkiguṇḍu versions of M.R.E., has made easy the path of "A Comparative Grammar of Asokan Inscriptions" by Mr. M.A. Mahendale, the phonology part of which is already published in the Bulletin of the Deccan College Research Institute, Vol. III. In the face of these important publications, full of objective data of scientific research, there is hardly anything to add except by way of certain correctives. The unscientific feature of the scientific procedure adopted by Hultzsch and Mahendale is that in citing instances from any particular inscription or set

1. Burua in *Proceedings and Transactions of the Tenth All-India Oriental Conference,* p. 209f.

of records they have not taken into their consideration the errors due to Aśoka's Lipikaras' oversight, carelessness, incapacity or idiosyncrasy, in short, omissions and commissions. A few instances may make the point clear.

DT (P.E.) reads āhā or ahā instead of ahā of LA, LN and R. A, too, reads *āhā*. K (R.E.) invariably reads *āhā*, and we meet with the same reading also in Ye, Dh and J. One may justify this reading for K, DT, DM and A by the general tendency of the dialect of that area to lengthen the final *a*. But what about Ye, Dh and J ? Here the presumption must be that the intended reading was *āhā ti*, and this is corroborated by Sh (R.E. XI) *haha ti*. DT *ahā* is the scribe's mistake for *āhā*. The omission of *ti (iti)* after *āhā* may easily be treated as a case of oversight. In P. E. III all the versions read *nāmā ti*. When DT reads *pavatayevū* and remaining versions *pavatayevū ti*, the inference should be that the omission of *ti* in DT is due to the scribe's error.

The G equivalent of *iha* is *idha*. But in R.E. XI one has *iloka* instead of *idhaloka* and in R.E. XIII *ilokika* for *idhalokika*. Here the scribe is responsible for the dropping of *dh*. The Sh and M equivalents of *iha* are *hida* and *ia*, the first occurring more frequently in M and the second in Sh. And yet it is improbable that *ia* was precisely the Sh spelling of *iha* ; had it been the case, we would have *aa* instead of *aha*. The reading *iha*, met with in R.E. XIII, confirms the suspicion about the scribe's error in *ia*.

In R.E. VII, all the six versions read *sayame* for *saṁyamaḥ*. In R.E. XII the Sh spelling is *sayamo*, while in R.E. XIII Sh reads *saṁyamaṃ* (Acc.). Similarly in R.E. IX, K reads *saṁyame* and Sh *saṁyamo*. From these data, the inference is irresistible that the omission of *ṁ (anusvāra)* is just an instance of the scribe's oversight.

G has *rājūke* and *prādesike* for *rājūko* and *prādesiko* in R.E. III, *sayame* for *saṁyamo* in R.E. VIII, *athakaṁme* for *athakaṁmaṁ* in R.E. VI, and *mūle* for *mūlaṁ* in R.E. VI. These, as we know, are not the *bonafide* grammatical forms of the dialect of Girnār.

Such instances need not be multiplied. Those cited above are sufficient, I think, to convince us of the reasonableness of fixing the grammatical and phonological standard of each dialect by typical forms only, and not by any and every form on record.

In connection with orthography and phonology, the question is apt to arise—were all the words pronounced as written ? An extremist like the late Dr. Fleet will maintain that they were not pronounced as written. Take, for instance, the word *dukkaraṃ*, *dukkare* or *dukkale* which is written as *dukaraṁ* (G), *dukara* (Sh), dukare (M), *dukale* (K, Dh, J, R.E. V). The debatable point is whether the word was meant to be pronounced as *dukkaraṁ*, *dukkare*. *dukkale* or as *dukaraṁ*, *dukare*, *dukale*. Though nothing can be said dogmatically on this point, the reader may have his guidance in forming his opinion from the fact that the Prakrit dialects of Aśoka do nowhere show the tendency to what is called phonetic decay. Guided by the Law of Mora (Metre), they retain in tact the phonetic values of all words. We are not to think of any loss of sound without some compensation provided against it. In default of the compensation in spellings on record, the presumption ought to be that something is wrong somewhere. Consider, for instance, the case of Dh *kichhaṁde*, J *kiṁchhāṁde* (S. R. E. II) for the Pali *kiṁchhando*. In J, *ā* in *chhaṃde* is redundant. In Dh, *ki* ought to have been spelt as *kī*. In default of the compensating feature, the presumption must be that the spelling *ki* with the omission of *ṁ* after it or without the lengthening of *i* is due to the scribe's ignorance or oversight.

As to R. E. III, G offers *vāsesu*, and K, Dh and J *vasesu* for the Pali *vassesu*. In the former, there is a compensating feature in the lengthening of *a* in *va* ; in the latter, there is no such feature. In metrical measure *vāsesu* and *vassesu* are of an equal phonetic value, and *vasesu* and *vassesu* are not so. So in the case of *vasesu*, the presumption should be that it was meant to be pronounced as va(s)sesu.

There are a few special cases, where compensation is sought to be effected by the shifting of emphasis. Take, for instance, the Sh and M *Priyadraśi* for Sk. *Priyadarśī*, Pali *Piyadassi*, *dhramaṁ* for G *dhaṁmaṁ*, Sk. *dharmaṁ*, and G *bhūtapruvaṁ* for Sk *bhūtapūrvaṁ*. Here the emphasis is shifted, in the case of *Priyadraśi*, from the fifth to the second syllable ; in the case of *bhūtapruvaṁ*, from the third to the second. In Pali, for instance, one may choose to adopt the spelling *vīriyaṁ* or *viriyaṁ* for Sk. *vīryam*. In adopting *vīriyaṁ*, he will be putting the emphasis on the first syllable, while in adopting *viriyaṁ*, he will be shifting the emphasis on to the third syllable.

One may go indeed so far as to premise that there is no instance of phonetic decay in any dialect or language, which is not accompanied by a compensating feature. Let us consider, for instance, the language of the Prakrit Dhammapada having all the main important features in common with the Sh Prakrit of Aśoka. It shows a good deal of phonetic decay, as will appear from the comparison of the following stanza with its Pali counterpart :

Prakrit :—.*ujuo namo so magu, abhaya namu sa diśa* |
radho akuyano namu dhamatrakehi sahato ||

Pali :—.*ujuko nāma so maggo, abhayā nāma sā disā* |
ratho akūjano nāma dhammachakkehi saṁyuto ||

It is easy to guess that the manner of chanting behind the Prakrit verse is different from that behind the Pali gāthā,—that, in other words, the phonetic decay took place in the Prakrit Dhammapada of Khotan so as to adapt its verses to local and racial needs. One has got to chant the Prakrit stanza, quoted above, in the manner of the Tibeto-Chinese people, by swaying one's head to and fro. Here the compensation is effected by means of gesticulation and intonation.

In many an instance the system of spelling and grammatical forms have been determined by the Law of Rhythm and Cadence or the Law of Euphony governing the construction of sentences :

R.E.X. : *Etakāya Devānaṁpiyo Piyadasi rājā yaso vā kiti vā ichhati*, *yaso* for *yasaṁ*, *kiti* for *kitiṁ*.

S.R.E.I. : *Save munise pajā mamā, mamā for mama.*

P.E.I. (LA) *Devānaṁpiye Piyadasi lāja hevaṁ āha : saḍavīsati-vasābhisitena me iyaṁ dhaṁmalipi likhāpita, Piyadasi* for *Piyadasī*, *lāja* for *lājā*, *lipi* for *lipī*, *likhāpita* for *likhāpitā*.

Provided that the rhythm is maintained, the cadences are all right, the sounds are sweet and appropriate in rhyming, and the cæsuras come spontaneously, it is immaterial whether certain rules of number and gender are obeyed or infringed :

M.R.E. (Bra, Si) : *Pakamasa hi iyaṁ phale, no hīyaṁ sakye mahātpeneva pāpotave kāmaṁ tu kho khudakena pi pakamamiṇeṇa vipule svage sakye ārādhetave. Etāyaṭhāya iyaṁ sāvane sāvāpiteyathā khudakā hca mahātpā cha imaṁ pakameyu ti, aṁtā cha mai jāneyu, chiraṭhitike cha iyaṁ pakame hot (u). Iyaṁ cha aṭhe vaḍhisiti vipulaṁ pi cha vaḍhisiti avaradhiyā diyaḍhiyaṁ vaḍhisiti.*

Thus the text of Aśokavachana is skilfully composed so as to be suitable not so much for reading as for chanting, and in this respect we cannot fail to notice a striking similarity between the Pali and Aśokan texts. Though the words of the Buddha are in prose, they follow a law of rhythm and cadence, if not exactly that of metre, and the sentences spontaneously come to their natural stops in course of chanting :

Evam me sutaṁ : Ekaṁ samayaṁ Bhagavā viharati jetavane Anāthapiṇḍikassa ārāme. Atha kho aññatarā devatā kevalakappaṁ Jetavanaṁ obhāsetvā yena Bhagavā tenupasaṅkami ; upasaṅkamitvā Bhagavantaṁ abhivādetvā ekam antaṁ aṭṭhāsi. Ekamantaṁ ṭhitā kho sā devatā Bhagavantaṁ gāthāya ajjhabhāsi.

The old *Gāthā* tradition or Vedic mode of chanting lingers even in the texts of *Jinavachana* in Ardhamāgadhī. But these texts often lack the spontaneity and vigour of *Buddhavachana* in Pali. Even the verses in such old *Āgama* texts as the *Āchārāṅga* seem to be on a par with some in the extant treatise of the *Arthaśāstra* :

Āchārāṅga Uvahāṇa-suyaṁ, ix. 2-3 :

Āvesaṇa-sabhā-pavāsu paṇiya-sālāsu egayā vāso
adu vā paliyaṭṭhānesu palālapuñjesu egayā vāso
Āgantare ārāmāgāre nagare vi egayā vāso.
susāṇe suṇṇāgāre vā rukkhamūle vi egayā vāso.

Arthaśāstra, III. 19.

Kalahe dravyam apaharato daśapaṇo daṇḍaḥ
kshudraka-dravya-hiṁsāyām tachcha tāvachcha daṇḍaḥ
sthūlaka-dravya-hiṁsāyāṁ tachcha dviguṇaś cha daṇḍaḥ.

Among the Buddhist brethren, those who were master reciters of *Buddhavachana* are claimed in the Milindapañha (p. 344) to be adepts in the discrimination of high and low accents, long and short syllables, heavy and light measures of letters : *(bahussutā āgatāgamā dhammadharā . . . sithila-dhanita-dīgha-rassa-garuka-lahukakkhara-parichchheda-kusalā)*. It is in respect of this discrimination of accents, etc., that Buddhaghosa has sharply distinguished the language of *Buddhavachana* from Tamil and other non-Aryan speeches of Ancient India (Sumaṅgala-vilāsinī, I, p. 276). The texts of all other Buddhist sects but the Theravāda are found lacking in the distinctive characteristics of the language of the Pali Canon. Their so-called "Gāthā dialects", saturated with Prakrit elements, show resemblances to the Sanskritic Prakrits of the Śaka, Kushāṇa, Kshaharāta, Śātavāhana and Ikshvāku inscriptions. Their prose texts betray only imperfect Sanskritisations from those in some earlier language, allied to Pali. So far as the rhythm, cadences and cæsuras are concerned, the records of Aśoka fully maintain the literary and linguistic tradition of Pali. In Aśokavachana, too, the syntax of words in a sentence is governed by the law of rhythm and cadence :

R. E. III : *sādhu mātari cha pitari cha susrūsā,*
mitra-saṁstuta-ñātinaṁ bāmhaṇa-
samaṇānaṃ sādhu dānaṁ, prāṇānaṁ
sādhu anāraṁbho, apavyayatā
apabhaṃḍatā sādhu.

Here the word *sādhu* is put first in one clause, in a penultimate position in the second clause, in the middle of the third clause, and last in the fourth clause.

Barābar Hill-Cave I :

Lājinā Piyadasinā duvādasa-vasābhisitenā
iyaṁ kubhā dinā Ājīvikehī, instead of
Ājīvikehi dinā.

To do full justice to a comparative grammar of *Aśoka-vachana* from the historical point of view a distinguished from the merely analytical or scientific standpoint, one has got to return a definite answer to the question as to which of the three languages, Old Classical Sanskrit, Old Pali and Old Ardhamāgadhī, has the greatest share in the phonetic peculiarities and grammatical froms of *Aśokavachana*. The real tug of war lies between the claims of Old Pali and Old Ardhamāgadhī, the languages that in their maturity kept clear of the eighteen *Mlechchhabhāshās* or *Deśibhāshās* (Aupapātika Sūtra, Sec. 109). Tamil, Telugu, and the rest. By the consensus of expert opinion the Ardhamāgadhī of the extant Śvetāmbara Canon is junior in age to the Pali of the extant Buddhist Canon, preserved in Ceylon, Siam and Burma (Preface to Jacobi's edition of the Āyāraṁga. P.T.S). According to the Aupapātika Sūtra, Sec. 56, Mahāvīra loudly, distinctly and forcibly chanted his doctrine in Ardhamāgadhi, a language, which is claimed as the super-excellent language comprising in its wide scope all idioms (*savva bhāsāṇugāmiṇie . . . sareṇaṃ Addhamāgadhae bhāsāe bhāsai*). The examples of formulations cited in illustration, *atthi loe, atthi aloe, evaṁ bandhe mokkhe*, etc., we see that *e* stands as the first sing, case-ending for the *a* - declension, precisely as in Māgadhī of the Prakrit grammarians.

The Ardhamāgadhī of the Jaina Canon presupposes the Māgadhika or bardic songs, ballads and moral verses (*Māgahiyaṁ gāhaṁ gītiyaṁ silogaṁ*, Aupapātika Sūtra, Sec. 107).

In such texts as the Āchārāṅga Sūtra there is throughout a hopeless blending of Māgadhī and Ardhamāgadhī elements : it is difficult in places to discriminate which is which. Pali shows a conscious tendency to get rid of Māgadhism and to keep it distinct from it. The Philosophical views of some of the elder contemporaries of the Buddha are represented in Old Māgadhī as well as in Pali. By comparison of the two ways of representation, we can understand the difference between Pali and Old Māgadhī formulations of Indian thought, *e.g.*, *n'atthi attakāre, n'atthi parakāre, n'atthi purisakāre* ; *sukhe dukkhe jīvasattame* (Sāmañña-phala Sutta). In the Ariyapariyesana Sutta (Majjhima-N. I) and the Mahāvagga, I, the very word of Upaka, the Ājīvika, is faithfully reproduced : *hupeyya āvuso'*, '*huveyya āvuso'*. This Old Māgadhī verbal form is met with in *Aśokavachana* ; *huvevūti, hveyū* (S.R.E. II). The Vedic *tave* which occurs as a regular infinitive suffix in *Aśokavachana* is occasionally met with in Pali *gāthās*. But for the Aśokan Gerund *tu* for *tvā* (Dh, J, etc.), one must refer to the Māgadhi *gāthās* in the Jaina Canon ; *viṇaittu soyaṁ* (Āchārāṅga, Logasāra), *jānitta dukkhaṁ (ib.* Loga-vijao). Just as in Aśokan Eastern dialects, so in Ardhamāgadhī, *dupada* is the equivalent of Sk *dvipada*. The *āye* as the Dative sing. case-ending has its counterpart in *āe* : *viosaraṇāe*. The Girnār *darsaṇa* (R.E. IV) corresponds to the Ardhamāgadhi *daṁsaṇa*. But the phonetic peculiarities and grammatical forms, particularly those of Girnār, correspond mostly to those in Pali.

= Śubham astu =

INDEX TO PART II

abhakshyas, 41f
abhisheka, 11f, 18
abhyavapatti, 21
adhimāsa, 45
Adhyakshas, 43
āgama, 31, 39f
āgatāgamā, 31
agrāmya, 24
Ājīvikas, 7, 44
ājñā-lekha, 18, 20
akāntiḥ, 22
ākhyānam, 21
Aliyavasāni, 33
Allahabad - Kosam pillar, 6f
Amātyas, 44
Ambalaṭṭhika - Rāhulovāda Sutta, 36
Anāgatabhayāni, 34, 39
Antā avijitā, 18
anugraha, 19
Anumāna Sutta, 33
anunaya, 21
anuposathaṁ, 37
anusaṁyāna, 47
Apabhraṁśa Prakrit, 53
aparāntas, 3f, 8
apaśabda, 25
Aramav inscription, 9
Ardhamāgadhī, 51, 56f, orthography, 10
arthāḥ, 21
arthakrama, 22
arthana, 21
asamati, asamāpti, 23
Aśokan Prakrit, 55f, 59f
Āṭavrkas, 18
arthamadhuratā, 23
audāryam, 22
avadhyas, 41f
Avanti, 18

Baīrāṭ, 5, 27, 50, 54f
Barābar Hill-cave inscriptions, 11, 19, 42, 50
Barua, 40f, 47n, 60, 89n
Basti, a district, 7
Beadon, C., 6
Bethia, 6
Bhābru Edict, 5, 20, 31, 37f., 57, 60, 63
Bhandarkar, D.R., 3, 9, 11, 16, 32, 40
bhartsana, 21
Bhikkhu Pātimokkha, 70
Vinaya, 33
Bindusāra, 44
Bloch, 6, 13
Bodhāyana, 37, 41f, 88
Bose, Atindra Nath, 43
Brahmagiri, 6, 49, 52f
Brāhmaṇas, 44, 46
Brāhmī, 9f
Buddha Koṇāgamana, Stupa of, 12f
Buddha Sākyamuni, place of the nativity of 13,
Buddhavachana, 31f, 38, 40, 60f, 65, 68f, 93
Buddhism, Brahmanical reaction against, 44
Buddhist ballad poetry, 28, 31, 35, 38, 60
Council, 39, literature 31f, Middle Country, 26, Mis-

sions, 32, sacred places, 13, Sangha, 13, Schismatics, 20, sects, 40, tradition, 31, 40
Bühler, Hofräth, 9
Burmese alphabet, 9

Carlleyle, 5
Champāran, a district, 6, pillars, 13
Chandragupta Maurya, 4, 28
Chapaḍa, a scribe, 9
Chatterji, S. K., 61n
Chhandas, Vedic language, 24, 60
Cholas, 4
Cuneiform script, 9
Cunningham, 4

daṇḍanītī, 45f
Daśaratha, 7
Delhi, 7, 56, Mīrāṭh copy, 26 - Sīvalik, 7, - Topra, 7
Devānampriya, 41
dhamma, - anusathi, 16, 20, 29, - dāna, 37, - lipi, 11f, 14, - nīyama, - sāvana, 15f, 20, - thambhānī, 29
Dharmasthas, 44
dharmarājīkas, 7
Dhauli, 1, 3f 12, 16f, 27f, 49f, 51f, 56
Dutt, N. 61n

Eastern dialect, 27, Prakrit, 54
Elliot, Walter, 3

Firoz Shah Lāṭ, 7
Forrest, 3
Frontagers, 18, 20

Goradhagiri, 2, 8
Gośṛingavīhāra, 53

Haīmavata Madhyadeśa, 53
Harappa, 10
Hemchandra, 53
Herzfeld, 9
Hultzsch, 14, 48

Indraji, Bhagawanlal, 4
Indus, 4, 53, - Valley, 7
Inscriptions, Achaemenian, 9, Barābar Hill-cave, Commemorative, 13, Hill Cave, 1, Minor Pillar, 1, Pillar 1, Rock 1, Separate Rock, 1, Stone-block, 1
Iranīan dialect, 53
Isila, 6, copies of M. R. E., 8, Mahāmātras, 63

Jainini 47a, Bhārata of, 33
Jaīna, 28, 41, Canon, 57f, dictum,41
Jainism, 44
Jambudvīpa, 47
Jaṭinga - Rāmeswara, 6
Jaugaḍa, 1, 4, 12, 26f, 49f
Jayaswal, K. P., 20

Kalīnga, 3f, 12, 18, 25, 53
Kalsi, 1, 3, 8, 27f, 49, 53f, 59
Kāluvāki, 3, 14
Kamboja, 4f, 47
kaṇṇasukhā, 23
Kapilavastu, 13
Kapurdagarhi, 5
Karṇa Chaupar, 8
Karnul, 4
Kasmīra - Gandhāra, 8
Kauśāmbī, 2, 6, 14, 54, 56, pillar, 7, 14, 50
Kauṭīlya, 17f, 21, 23f, 45f, - Vachana

Khalatika Hills, 7f, 42
Kharoshṭhī alphabet, 9f, documents, 64, Ms, 53, scribes, 9
Kittoe, 3
Kopbal, 5
Kośala, 44
Kosambi, Dharmananda, 33
Kumāras, 18
Kushāṇa, 42

Lāghulovāda, 36
Lāṭ Bhaīro, 2
Lauriya, Ararāj, 56
Nandangarh, 26, 56
Law, B. C., 39
Lekhaka, 43
lekhadoshāḥ, 22
Lekhasampat, 22
Lipikara, 9, 25, 42f
Lokottaravāda, a Buddhist seet, 35
Lomaśa Rishi cave, 8
Lumbinī, 7, 13, 26, 37, pillar, 13, 64, inscription, 11, 19f, 37, 50f

mādhuryam, 22
Maga, 30
Magadha, 44
Māgadhī, 24, 27, 54f, 58, 60
Mahā-Ariyavaṁsa Suttanta, 34
Mahādeva, a thera, 8
Mahādhammarakkhita, a thera, 8
Mahā-Rāhulovāda, 36
Mahārakkhita, a thera, 8
Mahārāshṭra, 5, 8. 53f, 59f
Mahārāshṭrī, 59f
Mahendale, M.A., 93
Mahisamaṇḍala, 8
Majjhantika, a thera, 8
Majjhima, a thera, 8
Mansehra, 1, 4, 28, 50, 54f, 58, dialect, 51f.
Mitra, Sailendra Nath, 33
Mohenjo-daro, 10
monolith, Aśoka's 3, 13f
Mookerji, R. K., 15, 18,28, 52
Mukherji, Purnachandra, 2
Mūlasarvāstivāda, 35, 40
Munigāthā, 32, 35
Mysore, 6, 53, 56f

Nābhakas, 3
Nābha-lines, 3
Nāgārjunī caves, 7
Nāḷaka Sutta, 35
Nigāli Sāgar, Inscription, 7, 10, 11f, 20, 26
Niglīva, 2, 7, 13
nijhati, 29
nindā, 21
nisṛishṭi-lekha, 18f
Nīti anthologies, 47

Oertel, 7
Oldenberg, 8, 24, 33

Paiśāchī, 53, 59, 61
Pālkiguṇḍu, 5, 27, 55
Pali canon 31, 40, 44, 61, chronicles, 8, 37, 40, commentators, 32, gāthās, 64, Jātakas, 37, 47f orthography, 10, prose discourses, 64, scholiasts, 33, Suttas, 45
Pañchanekāyikas, 40
Pāṇini, 25, 42, 47
parākrama, 16
Paranavitana, Dr., 34

paridāna-lekha, 18f
parihāra-lekha, 19f
paripūrṇatā, 22f
Parishad, 28
Pariyāya, 31f
Parent Script of India, 10
Pāṭaliputra, 3, 6, 14, 25, 28, 44, pillar, 2, 3
Patañjali, 41f
paṭipadaṁ, Mahā-ariyavaṁsa, Nāḷaka, Rathavinīta, Tuvaṭaka, 33
pemanīyā, 33
Periplus, 40
Pilindavachchha, 66
Pillar Edicts, 2, 3, 6f, 14, 17f, 20, 27f, 50, 63, 68
Piśāchas, 8
porī, 24
projñāpana-lekha, 18, 20
Prādesikas, 43
Prakrit, 26, 53f, 56, 60, Aśokan, 60f, 68, grammarians, 54, 57, 60
praśaṁsā, 21
pratilekha, 18
pratishedha, 21
pratyākhyānam, 21
pravachanas, 31
Pravaragiri, 7
pravṛitti-lekha, 18
pṛichchā, 21
pubbāparānusandhi, 22
punaruktam, 22
punarvasu, 42
Purushas, 28
Pushkarasārī, 10

Queen's Edict, 2f, 6, 14, 18, 30, 38, 50, 58, 63

Radhia, 6
Rāhulavāda, 36, 38
Rahula, Rev., 34
Rajjukas, 4, 43f
Rājputānā, 5, 53
Rakkhita, a thera, 8
Rāmpūrwā, 2, 6, 56
Rathavinīta Sutta, 36
Raychaudhuri, H. C. 48,
Rhys Davids, T. W., 33, 35
Rice, B. Lewis, 6
Rock Edicts, 2f, 9f, 17f, 25f, 49f, 56f
Rudradāman I, inscription of, 4
Rummindei, 2, 7
Rūpnāth, 5, 27, 55, 57f

Sachiva, 44, 47n
saddhammaṭṭhiti, 32
Sādhu Sutta, 36, 38, 64
Sahasrām, 5, 9, 17, 27, 50, 56
sakāya niruttiyā, 24
Samāpā, 4, 17, 25, City Judiciaries of, 20
sambandha, 22
sambodhi, 14, 37
samplava, 22
Saṁvaṭṭakappa, 38
Sāñchī, 7, 14, 40
Sanskrit, 10, 35, 44, 52f, 55f
sāntvam, 21
Sāriputta Sutta, 36
Sārnāth, 7, 14, 37f, 56
Sarvāstivāda, 12, 38f, 41
sarvatragalekha, 18, 20
śāsanāni, 18
Sastri, Shama, 24, 46n
Śaurasenī, 58f, 61
Schism pillar, 15, 26
scripts of India, 9

Senart, E., 36, 60
Shahbazgarhi, I. 5, 8f, 25f. 28, 49f, 53f, dialect, 52
Shastri, Narayan Rao, 6
Siddāpura, 6
silāthambhā, 13
Singālovāda Sutta, 33, 38, 46, 72
Sinhalese alphabet. 9
Skandagupta, 4, 13
Smith. V. A., 2
Smṛiti literature, 42, 88
Soṇa, 8
Sopārā, 1f, 4, 8, 27, 53f, 57f
spashṭatvam, 22
Srāvāpakaṁ, 15
Stryadhyaksha mahāmātras, 43
Sudāmā cave, 8
Sudarśana Lake, 4
Śūnāparānta, 4
Sūrpāraka, 4
Suvarṇabhūmi, 8
Suvarṇagiri, 2, 8
Śvetāmbara canon, 60

Takasilā, 18
Tantrayukti, 45
theravāda, 39f
Tibetan alphabet, 9
Tīrthankaras, 60
Tishya, 42
Tīvala, 14, 18
Tod, Col., 4
Tosali, 3, 17f, 25

uddesa-niddesa method, 29, 45
udupānāni, 30
Ujeni, 18
Upagupta, 13
upālambha, 21
Upatisapasine, 36
Upatishya, 36
Uttara, 8

vāchikha-lekha, 19
Vaiśampāyana, 33, 47
Vālmīki, 47f
Vasishsṭha, 41f, 88
Vedic consonant, 10, hymns, 60, language 60f, literature 40, tradition 31
Vinaya-samukase, 33
Viśvajhopri cave, 8
Viśvāmitra, 8
Votive inscriptions, 2
Vṛiddha Manu, 41
vṛishala-pravrajitas, 44
vyāghātaḥ, 22
vyañjana-madhuratā, 23

Winternitz, 24, 33
Woolner, 60

Yerraguḍi, 1f, 4f, 27f, 49, 54f
Yona, 47
Yonaka Dhammarakkhita, 8
Yuktas, 28